MW01252868

TOGETHER AND LONELY

LONELINESS IN INTIMATE RELATIONSHIPS – CAUSES AND COPING

PSYCHOLOGY OF EMOTIONS, MOTIVATIONS AND ACTIONS

Additional books in this series can be found on Nova's website
under the Series tab.

Additional e-books in this series can be found on Nova's website
under the e-book tab.

PSYCHOLOGY OF EMOTIONS, MOTIVATIONS AND ACTIONS

TOGETHER AND LONELY

LONELINESS IN INTIMATE RELATIONSHIPS – CAUSES AND COPING

AMI ROKACH

AND

AMI SHA'KED

publishers

New York

Library of Congress Cataloging-in-Publication Data

Together and lonely : loneliness in intimate relationships : causes and coping / editors, Ami Rokach and and Ami Sha'ked (School of Psychology,The Centre for Academic Studies, Or Yehuda, Israel).
pages cm
Includes bibliographical references and index.
ISBN: 978-1-62417-201-4 (hbk.)
1. Loneliness. 2. Intimacy (Psychology) 3. Marriage. 4. Interpersonal relations. I. Rokach, Ami. II. Sha'ked, Ami, 1945-
BF575.L7T664 2013
158.2--dc23
2012046624

Published by Nova Science Publishers, Inc. † *New York*

Dedicated with Love to Pnina, Natalie & Benny Rokach.
And to Drora, Tal, Sharon, Eli, and Hagit Sha'ked & Aviad Erenrich

"The only individuals who crave
solitude are those who are not condemned to it."
(Mijuskovic, 2012, p. 152)

CONTENTS

GENERAL INTRODUCTION

With the exception of one chapter, this book is a coproduction of Ami & Ami. Sha'ked completed his doctoral studies in psychology at the University of Wisconsin, Madison in the United States and practiced as a couples and sex therapist in the United States and Israel. Rokach, an Israeli as well, did most of his studies in North America, and practiced as a clinical psychologist dealing with anxiety conditions, sex therapy, and relational issues, as well as palliative care. He conducted research in those areas in Canada. Israel afforded them the opportunity to meet and collaborate. Both teach in the same academic center, and as such, they had the opportunity to talk, get to know, and befriend each other.

During a discussion of our clinical experience and the challenges we face, we realized that while both of us are relatively well versed with the literature on loneliness, intimacy, and couples therapy, we faced a scarcity of research articles and books when searching for material on loneliness and intimate relations. We did find material on loneliness in general, loneliness after divorce or widowhood, and the loneliness of children who have to face life after losing their parents, but very little material was out there on experiencing loneliness in intimate relationships. Since we couldn't find it, we decided to produce it, and this book is the result. The following is a brief description of the chapters and the message each is trying to convey.

INTRODUCTION

Chapter 1 provides a general overview of loneliness in our lives how technological advances affect our lives and loneliness, changes in the family structure with its variety of forms and frequent mobility, and the realization that loneliness is nothing new. Although we pride ourselves as inventers (the Internet, computers, reaching the moon), we did not invent this one; loneliness was here way before any of us were, and consequently we can find it in the Bible, literature, art, and philosophy. As things appear now, it is here to stay.

WHAT EXACTLY IS LONELINESS?

Chapter 2 delineates the various attempts at understanding and describing loneliness. We also review Rokach's phenomenological research that explored what loneliness is and its emotional, cognitive, and behavioral components. Loneliness, a painful and powerful experience, has a huge effect, and sometimes a lasting one, on us. In this chapter we delineate the effects of loneliness on our health, and we then describe the lonely—who they are and how they behave. We also discuss loneliness anxiety and the difference between loneliness and depression. They may seem to go together, but they are actually quite different. When people think of loneliness, they commonly imagine being alone, but that is not necessarily so. Moreover, solitude, which entails being alone, can be a blessed and pleasant experience. We explain why this is so.

LONELINESS AND THE LIFE CYCLE

While loneliness is experienced throughout our lives, it is not experienced to the same extent, nor is it qualitatively similar. Based on both others' research and our own, in Chapter 3, we discuss loneliness from (almost) the cradle to the grave. Suffice it to say that contrary to expectations, the aged are *not* the loneliest segment of the population. We discuss who suffers the most from loneliness.

LONELINESS OF MARGINALIZED GROUPS

Our society is not homogeneous so when we speak of loneliness, we must recognize that some feel lonelier than others. People from different segments of society may all experience loneliness yet report quite different experiences. In Chapter 4, we survey the loneliness of the homeless, those with physical disabilities (who, in addition to suffering physically, may suffer social alienation and even rejection), and those with psychiatric problems, who feel like they are on—and often live in—the fringes of society. People of different sexual orientations and those with intellectual disabilities are two groups who experience loneliness the most frequently and most intensely.

LONELINESS IN ILLNESS AND DYING

Ben Rokach, a physician, wrote Chapter 5 about the segment of society that neither is healthy and functioning nor lives on the fringe of society. He addresses the ill, those hospitalized with acute and even life-threatening illnesses, as well as those disabled by chronic and debilitating illnesses. The dying depart this world and leave behind all they have known and acquired. Do they experience loneliness? What is that experience like, and how do they face it?

THE CAUSES OF LONELINESS

In Chapter 6, we begin with a search to find out *why* we are lonely. What makes us lonely at some times and not others? How are the causes viewed by the different theoretical approaches? Once we know why we feel lonely, we may be better at coping with loneliness.

OUR NEED TO BELONG

Now that we have addressed loneliness and explored its causes, in Chapter 7, we discuss the most basic social need that all humans have: the need to belong, to be part of a community, to feel connected. That need, in evolutionary terms, is what ensured our survival as a species, and it will help us face emotional, health, and social concerns and challenges.

COPING WITH LONELINESS

We believe that loneliness is an inescapable element of being human, just like death and taxes. While we may be prone to loneliness, however, we may have developed various ways of coping with it—learning to either avoid it or cope with it better—by lessening its pain. Chapter 8 examines the various ways we can successfully deal with loneliness.

ON LOVE AND LONELINESS

Can there be two more unconnected (and even contradictory) words than *love*—the feeling that is so fulfilling, binding, and wonderful—and *loneliness*—the wretched pain that is part of feeling alienated and alone? Apparently, there may be a variety of situations where people in love feel lonely despite their love—the one they give and the one they receive. In Chapter 9, we look at this puzzling phenomenon and attempt to explain it.

Marital education interventions with premarital and marital couples focus on instructing participants in promoting and enhancing relationship protective interactions. At the same time, efforts are made to identify relational risk factors and provide couples with knowledge and skills to reduce their negative impact.

MARITAL ENRICHMENT AND EDUCATION

Chapter 10 presents various modalities of marital prevention and enhancement education for both premarital and marital spouses. One of the most important evidence-based programs is PREP—the Prevention and Relationship Enhancement Program—which is covered in this chapter.

Other marriage education programs covered and discussed are Relationship Enhancement, the PREPARE/ENRICH Couple Program, the Couple Communication Program, Training in Marriage Enrichment (TIME), the Compassionate and Accepting

Relationship through Empathy (CARE), the Self-Regulated Positive Relationship Education Program (SELF-PREP), and the Association for Couples in Marriage Enrichment (ACME).

MARRIAGE AND THE FAMILY

Chapter 11 explores the various definitions and our understanding of and yearning for romantic relationships, as exemplified by marital unions. We take a closer look at one's family of origin and its influence on the individual and his ability to relate, connect, and interact with others.

MARITAL DEVELOPMENTAL STAGES

Chapter 12 views the formation and development of intimate marital relationships through developmental perspectives. The first section of the chapter examines the premarital stage and the factors that are predictive of marital success. During this stage, the unattached young adult is required to accept separation from his family of origin in order to present a well-differentiated self, capable of forming and investing in an intimate relational bond.

The second section of this chapter deals with the marital developmental stage of couple formation. This transition into the marital state, despite the joy and blissful nature of the union of two loving individuals, can cause stress and complexities. The cognitive, interactive, and interpersonal skills required for success during this stage are identified and discussed. Finally, the chapter explores and describes another important developmental stage: the transition to parenthood, and the expectations, requirements, and challenges it imposes on parents.

Establishing a long-lasting, intimate relationship has been recognized as a core human motivation that is essential to partners' physical and emotional well-being. We draw on theoretical models and extensive empirical research in addressing these topics.

THE DEVELOPMENT OF INTIMATE RELATIONSHIPS

Chapter 13 presents various components that relate to the development and promotion of intimate relationships. Several theoretical models relevant to this topic are presented and discussed. These include Reis and Shaver's model of the interpersonal process of intimacy, which identifies relational interactions that contribute to closeness and intimacy; Fredrickson's Broaden-and-Build model, which presents the intimacy-enhancing implications of partners expressing positive emotions; Mills and Clark's Communal Relationship model, which outlines the fundamental role of communal interactive behaviors in intimate relationships; Harvey and Omarzu's Minding Theory of intimate relationships, which emphasizes the central role of cognitive elements in forming and maintaining closeness and intimacy; and Aron's Self-Expansion Theory, which describes how intimate connectedness and ongoing interactions in close relationships contribute to the expansion of one's self through self-other inclusion. Also discussed in this chapter are the importance of accommodation, sacrifice, positive attribution, and trust to the formation, enhancement, and maintenance of relational intimacy and closeness.

Considerable theoretical and empirical research has been devoted in the marriage science literature to identifying the ingredients of successful marital unions.

INGREDIENTS OF A SUCCESSFUL MARRIAGE

Chapter 14 deals with the happy marriage, presenting the characteristics of well-functioning, high quality marriages and, in contrast, those factors that predict marital distress and dissolution. Empirical work conducted by Gottman and his associates is extensively presented. They identified the characteristics of successful and unsuccessful marriages, including some practical implications that potentially, if practiced, can enrich and enhance marital relationships.

Also discussed in this chapter are various theoretical models that conceptualize marital commitment and its importance for marital quality and satisfaction. One of these models is Rusbult's investment model of marital commitment and its role in the development of well-functioning and rewarding marital relationships. Additionally presented and discussed are individual traits and interpersonal, interactive characteristics associated with the positive marital outcomes of success and stability.

MARITAL SATISFACTION

Chapter 15 focuses on this construct that has been viewed as a summative, subjective evaluation of the fulfillment of needs and desires that partners receive from their marital relationship. More specifically, the chapter presents and discusses the various research-based psychological, interactional, and contextual factors that contribute to marital satisfaction. Some of these factors are cognitive, behavioral, and affective processes in close relationships, relational intimacy, partners' fulfillment of security and belongingness needs, marital commitment, partners' mutual support, schema-focused views of relational satisfaction, and other marital satisfaction related variables. Special attention has been given to the topic of sexual satisfaction and its impact on general marital satisfaction.

ESSENTIAL AND TRANSIENT LONELINESS

This book addresses two main areas in human relationships: loneliness and its causes and consequences, and romantic relations, which are commonly thought of as the antidote to loneliness. This chapter, 16, is a combination and interweaving of the two. Written from the point of view of two clinicians, we have addressed the two forms of loneliness as they are expressed in intimate relationships. The first one deals with essential loneliness, which is so primal that it becomes part of one's personality. By drawing on our experience with couples, we have shown how such loneliness may affect the intimate connection. We then address transient, reactive loneliness, which is usually triggered by the dynamics of the couple's interactions and, as such, can be coped with and ameliorated by changes and improvements to the very same interactions that may have initially caused it.

AS A SUMMARY

We tried to include the most recent and methodologically sound research in these pages. There is much that relates to, and is influenced by, our clinical experience and life lessons and struggles. We hope that whether you are a clinician, an academician, or a member of the public at large, this will add to your conceptualization, understanding, and coping with loneliness, especially those who are in relationships. We know there is much more to be explored, researched, and understood. You may be one of those who will take the lead and further our present understanding.

Special thanks goes to Marlene Almeida of York University in Toronto, for her tireless help with editing and preparation of the manuscript, and to Geri Venegas for her much appreciated assistance with typing of the book.

We also extend our thanks to Professor Bolek Goldman, President, and Mr. Gil Reshef, CEO, both of the Center for Academic Studies in Israel who wholeheartedly supported this project.

Enjoy your reading,
Ami R. & Ami S.

Chapter 1

INTRODUCTION

The whole conviction of my life now rests upon the belief that loneliness, far from being a rare and curious phenomenon, peculiar to myself and to a few other solitary men, is the central and inevitable fact of human existence.

—Thomas Wolfe

Chances are you would not hesitate to reveal a troubled family history, medical problems, or even depression, but you would not openly admit to being lonely. Susan Schultz (1976) poignantly wrote, "To be alone is to be different. To be different is to be alone, and to be in the interior of this fatal circle is to be lonely. To be lonely is to have failed" (p. 15). There is a stigma to being lonely. Society—meaning us—does not look kindly on people who complain about their ailments. In my (A.R.) classroom or when I give a lecture, I ask my audience if any of them have never experienced loneliness. Invariably, no hands go up. When I further inquire whether anyone is feeling lonely that very day, I usually get dead silence. In my 30 years of researching this topic, I have found no one who had the courage to publicly admit to feeling lonely. The sad and surprising fact is that there are many lonely people walking around us. Many years ago, a community college brochure advertised a workshop I was giving titled "Dealing with Loneliness." Only two people registered. Two years later, however, 25 people signed up for my workshop, "Helping Our Clients Cope with Loneliness." It was quite clear that while those who attended were "not lonely" and could not remember the last time they were, they were more than happy to learn how to help their clients who were willing to admit their loneliness.

Loneliness carries a significant social stigma because a lack of friendships and social ties is socially undesirable, and the social perceptions of lonely people are generally unfavorable. Lonely people often have very negative self-perceptions, and their inability to establish social ties suggests that they may have personal inadequacies or socially undesirable attributes as well (Lau and Gruen, 1992). Lau and Gruen (1992) said, "The extent of the stigma tends to range from personal deficiency to dislikableness...Lonely people are perceived as less psychologically adjusted, less achieving, and less intellectually competent in relating to others" (p. 187). Research has demonstrated that gender has a great deal to do with the seriousness of the social stigma of loneliness. Symptoms of loneliness—for example, depression—are regarded as unmasculine and consequently more undesirable for men (Lau,

1989). Furthermore, men may hesitate to admit that they are lonely because of those very same negative connotations (Borys and Perlman, 1985).

SOCIAL ISOLATION

Social isolation does not mean loneliness, and loneliness does not mean social isolation. Social isolation is commonly taken to mean the objective absence or reduction in one's social network. Scientific evidence has shown that not all socially isolated people experience loneliness (Dahlberg, 2007), and some people who are socially well connected still feel lonely (Routasalo and Pitkala, 2003).

Loneliness has become an almost permanent and all-too-familiar way of life for millions of Americans. Every day, the single, the divorced, adolescents, housewives, and scores of others call suicide prevention centers and hotlines. It is so widespread and pervasive that loneliness is now a billion-dollar industry (Meer, 1985; Rokach, 1988b). The loneliness business includes videotaping clubs, health spas, self help books, and online dating sites, and it is growing rapidly. It tempts the public with an array of relational possibilities, social skills upgrading, and semiforced group activities. Many lonely people join the ride in an attempt to cure their loneliness, and they frequently end up more hopeless than before they started. Online matchmaking and the explosive growth of Facebook are examples of attempts to create virtual communities that may someday completely replace flesh-and-blood companions.

Ours is the age of relationships. We tend to believe in the uniqueness, importance, and availability of relating to others, thinking that we know how to conquer the barriers against closeness that we erect. Whereas in the past, work was seen as the valued solution to self-fulfillment, today, relationships are considered the main, if not the only, source of self-esteem. A paradox is thus created, where on the one hand, we yearn for close, intimate relationships, but on the other hand, our present environment is not conducive to the development of human relationships. Our lifestyles in the dawn of the twenty-first century have both created isolation and made it more difficult to deal with it (Rokach, 2000). It seems that today many people are seeking companionship but are unable to find it. Good, close, intimate relationships have become scarce, and when scarcity occurs, there is usually somebody around to exploit it (Gordon, 1976; Meer, 1985).

"Mark," a 20-year-old single man, was one of my students. His description of loneliness relates to New Year's Eve when everyone is "supposed" to be with somebody to celebrate a happy, new beginning. For Mark, however, it was a time of struggling to understand his isolation from others:

> It occurred on New Year's Eve. I had broken up with my girlfriend three days earlier. Two of my closest friends and I spent New Year's Eve in a bar. At about 4 o'clock we went home to the apartment. My two friends passed out, and I was left alone thinking about what all my other friends were doing. I suddenly felt very alone, to the point where it felt that I did not understand why I was acting this way. I got scared that I might be going crazy, so I put on the TV and watched French TV (which I do not understand) until I passed out myself. My feelings were of sadness and isolation, to the point that I didn't really exist, and if I did, it didn't really matter to anyone. There was no one to turn to and no one who could understand.

Let's look more closely at how we live and how our lifestyles invite loneliness. A recent study about the prevalence of social isolation at the beginning of the twenty-first century revealed that Americans are far more isolated than they were previously. Our social circles now include fewer and fewer people: our family, our spouse, or even no one at all. Unfortunately, a growing number of people appear to have no one in whom they can confide, resulting in an increasingly fragmented society. Social ties that were such an integral part of daily life in past generations are shrinking or disappearing altogether (McPherson, Smith-Lovin, and Brashears, 2006).

Friedman (2007) said the following:

> Indeed, the social fabric of American life is rapidly changing in reaction to the collision of contemporary social forces, touching most of us in one way or another. Increased mobility and social isolation, the stress of a fast-paced and high-pressure lifestyle changes in the family unit, the impact of technology and the rise in consumerism are forces that disrupt our ability to create strong and lasting social connections. (p. 3)

In today's fast-paced, ever-changing world, when virtual reality sometimes replaces the real one, people have no time or energy for establishing a connection with anything beyond the narrow frame of their own hurried lives in a culture that gives little priority to human relationships and that rewards nothing but the individual acquisition of power and money (Carter, 1995). Putnam (2000) observed that during the first two-thirds of the twentieth century, Americans were involved in their communities through political, civic, and religious participation; volunteering; and connections that they formed in the workplace. The last third of that century, however, saw the tide drastically reversed resulting in a disconnection among Americans from those around them and their community. Those years saw a significant decrease in contact with friends and neighbors, in club meetings, and in church attendance (Freidman, 2007)—hence the term, *cocooning*.

During most of human history, people lived their entire lives and died in one city or town (Lewis et al., 2000). In contrast, today's society—especially in North America—is made up of people on the move: moving out of cities to find open space and less-polluted air; moving into cities to avoid long commutes; moving for reasons of employment, health, or financial status; or moving simply in search of a better life. Putnam (2000) found that nearly 20% of Americans relocate each year and up to 40% expect to move within the next five years. While the American culture is made up of immigrants who are accustomed to uprooting and setting up homes in new places, "for people as for plants," as Putnam so aptly observed, "frequent repotting disrupts root systems" (p. 204). It is true that mobility may lead to positive ties with the new community and the possibility of new opportunities, but it usually results in a breakdown of close-knit networks and increases marital tension as well as familial fragmentation (Anderson, 1982). As Josselson (1996) remarked, in today's mobile society, the community, the extended family, and the neighborhood have all weakened as pillars of human exchange.

In contrast to the past, it is now quite common to see many people living alone or spending extended periods of time without the comforting security that close and regular association with a community can bring. In a study of Generation Xers (those born between 1965 and 1980), Putnam (2000) found that this group experienced increased social isolation, reported more malaise and unhappiness, and had higher rates of depression and suicide than previous generations. These people were highly individualistic, inwardly focused, and materialistic. McPherson, Smith-Lovin, and Brashears (2006) found that during the last two decades, the number of those who had "no one to talk to" doubled. It appears that in every age group there is a large portion of the population that is lonely (Pilisuk and Hillier Parks, 1986) and despite Facebook, emails, cell phones, blogging, and text messaging, social isolation is at an all-time high (McPherson et al., 2006).

T. S. Elliot (cited in Putnam, 2000) declared many decades ago—wisely, I might add—when television had just been introduced that "it is a medium of entertainment which permits millions of people to listen to the same joke at the same time, yet remain lonesome" (p. 217). His words are truer than ever today. Workers can now work from home, and children may spend hours "connecting" with others online, thus eliminating the need for face-to-face interaction. Although Lewis et al. (2000) observed this about children, it is probably true of adults as well. "A child's electronic stewards (such as) televisions, videos, and computer games are the emotional equivalents of bran; they occupy attention and mental space without nourishing" (p. 198). People thus depend more and more on technology and less and less on one another. Many households have more than one television set, and often each family member has his or her own TV, so even watching TV with somebody else is rare. Many lonely, alienated people flick on the television set for "company," surfing from channel to channel. Putnam (2000) suggested that the correlation between channel surfing and social surfing (engaging in wider, occasional social relations) is more than just metaphorical. Television watching has become the escape of lonely, alienated, and socially disconnected individuals; they watch television without really paying attention to what's on. It is comforting to simply have the TV on and to have background noise to fill the void.

THE AMERICAN CONSUMER CULTURE

Consumerism is believed to have started in the post–World War II era, when Americans focused on personal growth and self-improvement to a degree unknown previously (Cushman, 1995). Those needs gave rise to such endeavors as the cosmetics, diet, and electronic entertainment industries. While psychology has not yet properly addressed the impact of materialism, consumerism, and commercialization on our culture, it is becoming clear that this insatiable quest for personal fulfillment borders on narcissism (Kanner and Gromes, 1995; Kasser and Kanner, 2003).

Friedman (2007) observed that right after purchasing a stream of consumer goods, emptiness sets in as the euphoria of spending and acquiring gives way to reexperiencing one's emptiness. For example, consider shopping malls—modern public meeting places designed to afford a convenient, climate-controlled, and pleasant shopping experience. The sad paradox is that despite its technologically advanced state and physical comforts, few (very few) people may feel connected to the hordes of strangers roaming around in search of new, improved, and exciting products. Buying via the Internet leads to even more social isolation as it has become "a culture of strangers surfing for goods and services, advice, and friendship—without eye contact and without nuance, searching for connection, yet isolated" (Friedman, 2007, p. 32).

We yearn to acquire, own, and consume as a way to heal our insecurities, subdue our fears of being alone, and avoid experiencing our inner void. Working harder and for longer hours to pursue riches and objects, however, inevitably exhausts the time, energy, and even financial resources that are needed to nurture family and community bonds (Cushman, 1995; Friedman, 2007).

Does all this mean that people have only recently (say, in the twentieth century) become acquainted with loneliness? Far from it. Loneliness has always been a devoted companion to both men and women. From my (A.R.) reading of the literature on loneliness, offering psychotherapy to many who experience loneliness, and researching this experience for the past 30 years, I now believe that loneliness is a complex and intricate experience that has been with us since time immemorial.

Loneliness and Technological Advances

Ours is the era of technology, leading a fast-paced life, and an explosive accumulation of knowledge. It is said to be the first time in human history where parents are taught by their children (when it comes to the computer, that is). While we would expect that the avalanche of iPhones, computers, and the Internet would bring people closer together, according to Clay (2000), "to the researchers' surprise, they discovered that greater use of the Internet resulted in a small, but statistically significant, increase in depression and loneliness, and decrease in social engagement." Intimate, supportive relations were thus replaced by the Internet and other gadgets that may assist us in "staying connected with the world." While attempting to stay connected, Internet users reported that their time online reduced the amount of time they spent interacting with family and friends. Other researchers, however, found that the Internet has provided a safe way for socially anxious people to interact and enhanced their expression of what they consider their "real selves" (Clay, 2000). Romantic relationships were helped by online contact and constant interaction.

Kraut et al. (1998) suggested that the effects of the Internet and TV on social relationships are mostly negative. Studies indicated that people report using TV to alleviate loneliness, and it was hypothesized that watching TV caused social disengagement and had a negative effect on one's cognitions and emotions. A longitudinal study of Internet use called the HomeNet study (Kraut et al., 1998) concluded that a positive correlation between Internet use and loneliness was associated with frequent interpersonal contact, deep feelings of affection, and broad content domain. At the dawn of the twenty-first century, it seems our Western culture is magnifying the alienation and separation that people feel, while at the same time they yearn to belong, to be needed, and to be loved.

The Internet has become an integral and important part of our lives. The vast majority of American children have access to the Internet (Jones, 2009). In other developed countries, the situation is quite similar (Margalit, 2010). Adolescents use technology even more than younger children do. They engage in social networks such as MySpace and Facebook, where they post new and detailed information for others to respond and react to. Most children and youth connect with others and find new friends on the Internet. Mark Zuckerberg, the creator of Facebook (said to be a "nation" of 500 million "inhabitants"), was voted *Time* magazine's Person of the Year in 2010. It is clear that virtual connections and friendships are growing in popularity and, in some instances, replacing real ones.

Cell phones have become an essential part of life in the Western Hemisphere. The cell phone has become a symbol of identity that supports its owner's independence both within and outside the home. Research found that adolescents felt that using a cell phone enabled them to widen and deepen friendship connections to the point that they preferred talking on cell phones to face-to-face conversations (Margalit, 2010). Interestingly, many lonely individuals prefer online social interactions because they consider them less threatening and more rewarding than meeting someone in person (Caplan, 2003, 2005). They felt that they could rely on their online friends and get their support at times of need (Subrahmanyam and Lin, 2007). During their childhoods, their parents frequently complained about them tying up the phone and not wanting to do things with the family. Now, as adults, they berate their children for being "glued" to the TV, the Internet, iPhones, and laptops.

Sleek (1998) suggested that technology, such as the Internet, was geared toward helping us establish relationships. As it happens, the same technology that has allowed people to strengthen their contact with distant family members and friends and to develop friendships with people around the world is actually replacing day-to-day human interactions. As easy as it may be to connect via the Internet with people who are thousands of miles away, Sleek says, "a computer monitor can't give you a hug or laugh at your jokes" (p. 1). In fact, Kraut et al. (1998) reported that increased use of the Internet leads to shrinking social support and happiness, and results in depression and increased loneliness. Ornish (1998) echoes those findings by observing that "at their best, email and chat rooms can be another way of staying in touch and keeping up with loved ones who may be thousands of miles away in real space but instantly available in cyberspace. All too often, however, technology provides a way of numbing loneliness without experiencing real intimacy" (pp. 100–101).

When asked about the effect of technology on people, Sherry Turkle, author of the book *Alone Together* (Price, 2011), poignantly observed, "People today are more connected to one another than ever before in human history, thanks to Internet-based social networking sites and text messaging. But they're also more lonely and distant from one another in their unplugged lives" (p. 26). Turkle found the most dramatic change in our communication and relationship patterns is our ability to be "elsewhere" at any point in time, to sidestep what is difficult and what would make personal interaction demanding, awkward, or just plain difficult. We escape to websites and Facebook, cell phones, and BlackBerrys. When asked whether social technology increases people's isolation, Turkle suggested that some people do use social networks to keep up with friends and to keep their friendships with "real" people lively and up to date. Others, however, "friend" people they do not even know or where the connection is unclear or even questionable. People may have many "friends" on Facebook, people they have never met, do not know, and can barely relate to. These "friends" may provide the illusion of companionship without the demands and expectations of friendship and without its intimacy. Another unfortunate change that technology has brought, according to Turkle, is that "we are tempted to give precedence to people we are not with over people we are with" (Price, 2011). It is as if real life and relationships are still important, but as soon as the cell phone rings, the email arrives, or the text message pops up on our phone, we give that our undivided attention. Turkle also reported that people dislike social networks because they don't represent us as we really are. Trying to be the person in the profile can be demanding. She observed that young people are nostalgic for something they may never have had: real friends, intimacy with their parents (who often themselves are obsessed with technology), and the ability to be and present themselves.

The Internet has brought with it a proliferation of cybersex and intimate relationships. Smith (2011) observed that Americans now spend equal amounts of time on the Internet and watching TV. While the time spent watching TV has remained constant for many years, surfing the web has increased dramatically recently. With increased Internet use, decreased social contact in everyday life, and the ease of communicating in cyberspace, cybersex is rapidly escalating. According to Smith, "while there is no universally accepted definition, an Internet affair involves intimate chat sessions and sexually stimulating conversations or cybersex, which may include (among other things) filming mutual masturbation with a web camera...With the Internet, we are moving away from just physical ideas about infidelity and acknowledging emotional infidelity" (p. 49).

Due to the usually secretive nature of cybersex and online affairs, it is difficult to get statistics on it, but a 2005 Swedish study reported that one-third of its participants admitted to having had cybersex and online affairs. A 2008 Australian study found that 10% of its participants had formed intimate online relationships, 8% had experienced cybersex, and 6% had met their Internet partners in person (Smith, 2011). While most personal relationships are hampered by such realities as housework, jobs, daily chores, paying the bills, and other responsibilities, online relationships make it possible for people to interact whenever they want and assume whatever identity they desire. The ability to type, delete, and paste may help them to create the kind of fantasy relationships they desire but do not know how to get. The drawbacks of that easily available, secretive, intimate, or sexual cyber relationship can be quite severe. The partner who has engaged in it may require therapy, and the other party may be unable to forgive the betrayal. People who concentrate on such relationships do not experience meeting someone, dating, and marrying. This can leave them yearning for intimacy while hampering their confidence in their ability to meet and impress a potential partner.

Given those facts, is loneliness caused by external situations, by our time and lifestyle, or by who we essentially are? I believe that loneliness is interwoven in our existence, just like joy, hunger, and self-actualization. Humans are born alone; they often experience the terror of loneliness in death, and they usually try desperately to avoid loneliness in between. To be human is to be part of, yet distinctively different from, the rest of the universe. As technological advances affect more and more areas of our daily lives, as humanity matures, and as we come to understand more about the magnificent universe that houses our tiny planet, we come to understand the extremely small stature and impact that each of us has upon life. Such a realization is instrumental in inducing anxiety and a sharp awareness of our limitations and mortality.

In our limitless and awesome universe, which humans have not yet fully grasped, and under harsh social conditions, feelings of self-alienation, emptiness, and meaninglessness are almost inevitable. Although an existential phenomenon—and one that everyone who ever walked on this earth has experienced—loneliness is usually experienced continuously, and people may not even be aware of it. In my view, loneliness is a "potential" aspect of humans, rather than an undifferentiated aspect of their existence. To put it more precisely, to be human is *to be able* to experience loneliness. Consequently, loneliness is like a recessive, nondominant trait that is fully experienced under the "right" conditions. These conditions almost always include dramatic changes in one's world, such as an unfulfilled need for love, belonging, or intimacy; estrangement from one's loved ones, country, or children; and a realization of the continuous and never-ending walk along the path that leads to death.

The Family and How It has Changed

In the past, "family" was a "fixed" unit that was often large, included two parents and their children, and was intertwined with an extended family that often lived close by. As such, the family unit was the main provider of social support from one's birth until death (Pillisuk and Hillier Parks, 1986).

Following the significant changes in the American social and economic structures, including the woman's liberation movement, mobility, and one-parent families, the family unit began to unravel. As the Industrial Revolution took work out of the home, it made the worker, according to Lewis et al. (2000), "a mass of undifferentiated equals, working in a factory or scattered between the factories, the mines, and the offices, bereft forever of the feeling that work was a family affair, done within the household" (p. 225). In the 1960s, women shed their narrowly defined roles as the "homemaker," and many times the hub of the family, in favor of work outside the home, personal development, self-sufficiency, and independence (Putnam, 2000).

The 1980s highlighted the strengthening of what was called the "me generation" as people sought to "do their own thing," look after their own needs and wishes—sometimes at the expense of others—and search for personal fulfillment. All of this led to an increasing number of people becoming what Cushman (1995) called "isolated, self-contained individual(s)" (p. 6). That resulted in an endless search for community, belonging, and human contact.

Since then, there has been a shift in the composition of family households, with the traditional nuclear family model becoming less common. Since the 1930s, the average household size has gone from 4.1 members to 2.8 in 1980 (Pilisuk and Hillier Parks, 1986). In 2004 it was further reduced to 2.4 (American Community Survey, 2004). As recent statistics indicate, more than half of first marriages end in divorce, and projections indicate that a whopping 67% of all recent first marriages may dissolve (Mills and Sprenkle, 1995). Family diversity is another component that significantly affects the familial landscape in America. This diversity more commonly includes gay and lesbian families, cohabiting families, and interracial families (Friedman, 2007). The multitude of familial changes surveyed above is believed to lead to a host of social problems. Paramount among them are social isolation and loneliness, and as Brehm (1987) observed, "In the face of extensive geographical mobility, smaller nuclear family size, and a 50% divorce rate, the modern American family is a fragile social organization" (p. 34). Such overwhelming social and familial changes inevitably lead people to search for ways to compensate for the loss of community support and for the emptiness they may feel.

Loneliness is darkness
A never-ending night.
Even though the black won't go away,
You'll never fall asleep.

Because loneliness sparks a fear
And unlike other nightmares
Awakening will not vanish it.

For the darkness is too strong
To allow any rest.

It makes memories into ghosts
And dreams into spirits.
Too vague to remember
Too important to forget.

Author unknown

LONELINESS IN ART, PHILOSOPHY, AND LITERATURE

The current zeitgeist is that of neuroscientific and psychopharmacological advances where increased attention is given to finding biological pathways to emotional states and experiences such as loneliness (Rosedale, 2007). The reductionistic nature of the current diagnostic process encourages clinicians to deconstruct suffering into a series of solvable problems. Wang, Snyder, and Kaas (2001) suggested that, as such, loneliness may be viewed as a symptom, clustered with associated presenting symptoms and seen as components of a mood or adjustment disorder, to be treated possibly with antidepressants (Hansen et al., 2007). The problem is thus identified, diagnosed, treated, and eliminated (Paul et al., 2006).

Until now, we addressed loneliness in our generation as it has been seen and examined through the eyes of the inhabitants of the twentieth and twenty-first centuries, meaning you—the reader—and us. As mentioned earlier, however, loneliness has always been part of being human. It has always been humankind's unwanted shadow, ready to become visible under the "right" conditions. If, indeed, loneliness has been here since the dawn of time, it stands to reason that we will find mentions of it in literature, philosophy, and the arts.

Greek Myths and Legends

Examining ancient Greek myths can put to rest some people's belief that loneliness is merely a modern-age phenomena or that it has at least significantly increased during the twenty-first century. Greek mythology repeatedly demonstrates people's attempts to escape a lonely and forlorn existence. The biblical figure of Job and the Greek character Oedipus are examples of enforced solitude.

Jung (1960) further proposed that there is a symbolic connection between the Prometheus myth and loneliness. He maintained that Prometheus's theft of fire represented a step toward greater consciousness and illumination. In doing so, Prometheus helped humanity, but he also raised himself above them, which resulted in his punishment by the gods. "The pain of his loneliness is the vengeance of the gods, for never again can he return to mankind. He is, as the myth says, chained to the lonely cliffs of the Caucasus, forsaken of God and man" (Jung, 1960, pp. 156–157). Just as Prometheus, the friend of man has no friend, Sisyphus similarly bears his punishment alone, having only himself and the boulders for company where the mechanistic and repetitive task that he is forced to endure provides his mind ample time to realize how alone he is. Odysseus's homelessness reminds us of the painful estrangement from home and friends and the resultant loneliness it produces.

In Hellenic literature and poetry, we can similarly find powerful illustrations of the intrinsic isolation of humankind. In Lucretius's *De Rerum Natura,* we find a description of a society where every human basically lives apart from others and looks after only himself, which creates what Hobbes later described as an individual who is "solitary, poor, nasty, brutish, and short" (in Mijuskovic 1979, p. 12). That kind of existence causes individuals to attempt to escape it via sexual relations that, again, result in a feeling of emptiness and desperate aloneness (see also Rokach, 1998).

The state of exile, to the Latin mind, may have symbolized loneliness and isolation, such as in the case of Ovid's *Tristia* or *Letters from Exile,* which were powerful expressions of the author's longing for family, friends, and country while he was in exile in Rome.

Medieval man posited a perfectly self-conscious being, absolutely eternal and all-knowing, and thus only slightly aware of loneliness and abandonment. Interestingly, while not overtly concerned with loneliness, the medieval individual was, above all, afraid of being estranged from God, afraid of being alienated from the all-receiving, accepting, and forgiving God. Even with this fear, in Old English literature, such as *The Wanderer, Seafarer, Women's Message,* and *Ruin,* the themes of exile and loneliness are quite clearly expressed. Dante's *Inferno* symbolizes how the author perceives an existence separated from himself and God as being one that is "lost in darkness, abandoned on a lonely slope in life" (Mijuskovic, 1979, p. 21).

Despite the passage of time from Oedipus's tragedy to Shakespeare's Richard II, King Lear, and Anthony, it is not too difficult to recognize that they are all bound by the struggle humankind has with solitary life. Their deep sadness comes from realizing they are alone in this world and, while being aware of their own uniqueness, they also experience much mental anguish, realizing their separate and distinct state of existence. Similarly, in *Death of a Salesman,* Willy Loman travels from town to town, staying with his suitcases full of merchandise in hotels while yearning for human companionship and affection. Even in his own home and in the company of his children, he is lonely. This man who always smiled and pretended to know everyone realizes in the end that he traveled the highways of America like an atom—alone, unseen, and suffering for what he cannot have: human closeness and love.

> Loneliness universally forges its powerful expression in (Philosophy) and all great literature, often in disguise, but in many instances, quite openly...and, indeed, our own contemporary art alternately whispers and shouts this identical sound of human loneliness.
>
> —Mijuskovic, 1979, p. 3

This loneliness, suggests Mijuskovic, can be recognized in the verses written by Emily Dickinson or T. S. Elliot, and even in Saint-Exupe'ry's *Little Prince*; loneliness has continually dominated the human consciousness. Art and philosophy attend to the constant, futile struggle where people battle against their isolated existence and attempt to escape it. Such is the story of George Elliot's Silas Marner, a hermit, who progressively withdraws into himself until the day he finds an abandoned child who "replaces" his purloined gold, at which point, Silas is forced outward. Prior to meeting that child, Silas was driven inside by loneliness and desperately attempted to give meaning to his life through the accumulation of gold. Only by caring for and attending to the child could Silas escape the confinement of the self-consciousness that became his prison. *Silas Marner*, contends Mijuskovic (1979), is successful in making clear two fundamental points:

1. Man is alone and lonely on this earth.
2. Man can escape that loneliness by utilizing his mind to focus not just on himself but on people, and relationships, in the world around him.

The famed Russian author Dostoyevsky believed that only God or society can protect the individual from disintegration. In his book *The Brothers Karamazov*, he wrote about the "intellectual disease" or insanity that loneliness may bring about. He seeks to transform man into a spiritual being who would recognize that his own salvation is intertwined with that of his fellow man.

> To transform the world, to recreate it afresh, men must turn into another path psychologically. Until you have become really, in actual fact, a brother to everyone, brotherhood will not come to pass...All mankind in our age have split up into unites, they all keep apart, each in his own groove; each one holds aloof, hides himself and hides what he has, from the rest, and he ends by being repelled by others and repelling them...For he is accustomed to rely upon himself alone and to cut himself off from the whole. Everywhere in these days men have, in their mockery, ceased understanding that the true security is to be found in social solidarity rather than in isolated individual effort.
> —*The Brothers Karamazov*, 11, vi, and ii in Mijuskovic, 1979, p. 6

Thus, Dostoyevsky does not deny the existence of loneliness but rather hopes that it can *occasionally* be alleviated.

In *Man's Fate*, Malraux describes men as never being able to truly know another man, as being unable to join or be joined by others, and as being fundamentally unique, different, and isolated. T. S. Elliot, in *The Waste Land,* powerfully describes our self-imprisonment:

> I have heard the key
> Turn the door once and turn once only
> We think of the key, each in his prison
> Thinking of the key, each confirms a prison
> (in Mijuskovic, 1979, p. 14)

Defoe's very famous *Robinson Crusoe* is the fable of a man who finds himself on an island, suffering from prolonged isolation and loneliness. His consciousness reveals to him the horror of being so isolated, which is how we may feel in our world. His existence may remind us of Dante's *Inferno*, where Hell is not the worst place because at least people can grieve with others. Mijuskovic (1979) suggests that being condemned for eternity to self-consciousness and the realization of our utter aloneness is the true hell.

In his book *The Hill of Dreams* (1923), Machen's main character progressively retreats inward, as if terrified of the surrounding world. In the introduction to his book, Machen clearly states the theme and purpose of this story:

> I asked myself why I should not write a *Robinson Crusoe* of the soul...I would take the theme of solitude, loneliness, separation from mankind, but, in place of a desert island and a bodily

separation, my hero should be isolated in London and find his chief loneliness in the midst of myriads of men. His should be a solitude of the spirit, and the ocean surrounding him and disassociating him from his kind should be a spiritual deep.

(in Mijuskovic, 1979, p. 30)

The American author Thomas Wolfe presents loneliness as the primary concern of humankind. He likens our lives to walking the streets of life alone and isolated. We see faces out there, but we may never see them again, so we become acutely aware that they are strangers to us just as we are to them. We are "all of us, separately, strangers on earth, intruders in the realm of material being, trespassers in this crude, unfeeling sphere of existence that has preceded us and will continue without us after we are gone" (Mijuskovic, 1979, p. 32). Wolfe sees loneliness as the primary concern of humans. He describes us as naked and lost in America, walking the streets of life alone. As such, Wolfe maintains that the fear of loneliness and the desire to avoid are the central themes in a human's life (Mijuskovic, 2012).

Olds and Schwartz (2009) reviewed some of the movies that presented the American Lonesome Hero, featuring characters that were often played by Gary Cooper, Clint Eastwood, and John Wayne, who singlehandedly fought the "bad guys" and bravely defended the community. Those movies included such classics as *Shane*, *Dirty Harry*, *Rio Bravo*, and *The Man Who Shot Liberty Valance*. According to Olds and Schwartz (2009), these movies "both reflected and reshaped the country's collective self-image. Through their cultural offspring, which are numerous, they continue to affect us today" (p. 37).

PHILOSOPHICAL VIEWS

Plato (428–347 BC) viewed loneliness as human motivation to avoid the social isolation that had the potential to profoundly influence a person's behavior and consciousness (Adler and Van Daren, 1972). Aristotle (384–322 BC), the Greek philosopher, agreed that no one would voluntarily choose a friendless existence and that once lonely, a person may "develop either into the God or the brute...reflecting the twin nature of loneliness" (in Rosedale, 2007, p. 203). Aristotle (2004) added that "he who is unable to mingle in society, or who requires nothing, by reason of sufficing for himself, is no part of the state, so that he is either a wild beast or a divinity" (p. 9). Kierkegaard, a Christian existentialist, described loneliness as a path of self-discovery, signifying humanity's fear of death. Once that fear was accepted and lived with peacefully, many could achieve freedom and discover threats about existence. Similarly, other existentialists saw loneliness as intertwined with the human condition, offering the ones who experience it a chance to reflect, search for freedom, discover truth, and find courage and meaning in despair (Heidegger, 1962; Sartre, 1957; Tillich, 1963).

Buber (1958), in contrast, saw loneliness as an unnatural part of the human condition and, thus, as a difficulty to overcome. He maintained that the unique nature of what being human means was expressed when an individual authentically related to another human being. The Dutch phenomenologist and psychiatrist Jan Van Den Berg (1972) suggested that loneliness is at the core of all illnesses. He saw loneliness as the nucleus of psychiatry.

Moustakas (1961) saw loneliness as a crucially significant experience, especially when some essential aspect of life is suddenly challenged and one enters the search for meaning. He maintained that the conditions that evoked loneliness included a personal tragedy, illness, or death and added that "loneliness was necessary to shatter old perceptions and ideas, to break new ground, and to become aware of new meaning so that one can live more fully" (p. 203).

In general, and despite their differing views and understanding of the experience of loneliness, these philosophers seem to agree on several tenets about loneliness:

1. It embodies the consciousness of a person's own isolation.
2. It is an essential element of the human condition.
3. It is a motivator for an individual to connect with others and pursue truth and meaning.
4. It is a vital element of critical life transitions.
5. It is potentially a bridge to new possibilities.

Chapter 2

WHAT EXACTLY IS LONELINESS?

Loneliness and the feeling of being unwanted—it is the most terrible poverty.
—Mother Teresa

Loneliness is a prevalent, common, and disconcerting social phenomenon (Cacioppo and Patrick, 2008). Recent estimates suggest that up to 32% of adults experience loneliness and up to 7% report feeling intense loneliness (see Hawkley and Cacioppo, 2010). When we discuss loneliness, it is clear that all of us wish to avoid it but what is this experience we dread so much? While some writers describe loneliness as a specific and unique pain, an undifferentiated stressor, others view loneliness as a response to various needs, circumstances, and situations, and as such they finely differentiate it into several types. Although doing so may be useful as an intellectual tool, these types are artificial. Such individuals conceive of loneliness as a unified experience and in so doing, they fail to capture the complexity of this experience.

Charles Darwin (1959, in Cacioppo et al., 2006a), in the now well-known thesis about the origin of the species, asserted that survival means competition, where only those who can secure resources will survive. In contrast to many animals, "humans are not particularly strong, fast, or stealthy relative to other species...It is the ability to think and use tools, to employ and detect deceit, and to communicate, work together, and form alliances that makes *Homo Sapiens* such a formidable species" (Cacioppo et al., 2006a).

Tonnies (1957) distinguished two forms of social organization: the organic community and the contractual or atomistic society. *The organic community* is one where "the whole defines the individual and the individual could not exist without it...The individual not only needs the group in order to live, but he needs their mutual support in order to be happy or virtuous" (Mijuskovic, 1992, p. 149). Aristotle referred to this kind of community when he observed that people are social animals, and their happiness lies in the Polis. In such a society, there is organic unity that offers a sense of belonging and identity, a sharing with others, and social duties that prevail over individual rights. That is why, for Hegel, organic vitality consists of communal self-consciousness and sharing a common language, institutions, religions, political ideals, and laws. Consequently, in the organic community, the good of the whole is valued above that of the individual; that sensibility is both the strength and the danger of this model.

The *atomistic society,* by contrast, is composed of individual parts rather than members. In their community the parts are regarded as equal, interchangeable, and replaceable, and each unit is sufficient unto itself. Relationships in the atomistic society are regarded as contractual, legalistic, and formalistic. Society, then, is the outcome of artificial agreement. Mijuskovic (1992) asserts that the Western countries—the United States, France, Germany, the United Kingdom, and others—are atomistic societies. He observes that in the organic model, people are less lonely due to the spirit of unity, mutual interdependence, and reciprocal support that this model offers. In the organic family, tribe, or community, however, when there is indeed loneliness, it tends to be extreme, since one may feel disconnected from the others who are connected and part of the communal life of the whole. The situation in the atomistic society is different, because the disconnected and alienated individual feels not unlike the rest of the individuals in that community and may therefore not feel lonely. The individual is simply like everyone else but in general, the atomistic society intrinsically enhances loneliness among its individuals.

> The contemporary American society is primarily and overwhelmingly organized along atomistic and contractual principles. Relations between husband and wife, employer and employee, student and teacher, landlord and tenant, bank and home buyer, doctor and patient, social worker and client are all fundamentally formalistic, legalistic, and rule-oriented.
>
> (Mijuskovic, 1992, p. 155)

Since loneliness is so painful, and since our society seems to enhance it, it follows that we can, in our Western societies, find a growing number of unhappy people suffering from a variety of emotional disorders. Mijuskovic (1992) contends that we have polluted our social environments and all share in the growing awareness of our separation. We naively rely on materialistic and individualistic criteria to gauge well-being, thus, doing well economically is a cherished state of being. Competition is encouraged and rewarded and the ethical salvation of families and society is the commitment of people to one another, because all else will breed alienation.

PSYCHOLOGICAL VIEWS OF LONELINESS

Rank (1929) maintained that the oneness a fetus once had with its mother ends with birth. As such, that separation creates a sense of fear, loss, and loneliness, but it also brings forth the capacity for individuals to be their unique selves, to accept their differences, and to know the power of their creative will.

Fromm (1941) saw birth as the beginning of the process of individualization. As the child proceeded along the course of individualization, he would grow stronger and become more independent, but he would also experience a great fear of loneliness. To avoid the feeling of being totally alone, which Fromm likened to starvation, he maintained that people seek relatedness with others by sharing ideas, beliefs, values, and meanings.

Sullivan (1953) viewed loneliness as a result of a child's unsuccessful attempts to engage an adult—attempts that were met with either indifference or punishment. Consequently, the child came to view himself as a failure and one who was unable to validate meaning and reality with another person. Sullivan, like Weiss (1973), also viewed loneliness as a response to repeated social and emotional crises.

Weiss (1973), who is most widely credited with stimulating empirical research on loneliness, believed there are two kinds of loneliness: emotional and social. *Emotional loneliness* is a consequence of the lack of an intimate partner and results in feelings of anxiety and isolation, while *social loneliness* results from an inadequate or unsatisfying social support network and enhanced feelings of boredom and aimlessness. Weiss saw loneliness, in evolutionary terms, as a proximity-promoting mechanism that may improve survival. Winnicott (1958) believed that our goal should be not overcoming loneliness but better tolerating it. He believed that the capacity to be alone and experience loneliness was a sign of emotional maturity.

Cognitive theorists saw loneliness as the result of a perceived difference between actual and desired satisfaction with one's social relationships (Peplau and Perlman, 1982). When such a feeling was attributed to a belief about oneself (i.e., personal inadequacy), it contributed to the resultant loneliness as "the absence, or perceived absence, of satisfying social relationships, accompanied by symptoms of psychological distress that are related to the actual or perceived absence" (pp. 171–172).

In general, the psychological views share several common tenets about loneliness, although they differ as to whether it is a one-dimensional or multidimensional experience:

1. Loneliness is an experience of separation.
2. It may arise at birth or in childhood and remain throughout one's life.
3. It is associated with the invalidation of meaning.
4. It is difficult to tolerate.
5. It motivates humans to seek meaning and connection.
6. It may have an evolutionary basis.
7. It signals the potential for growth and new possibilities.

Cacioppo et al. (2006b) suggest that loneliness is like physical pain in that while it is unpleasant, it has a protective function and serves as an alarm bell to guard against damage to the organism. Loneliness is a social pain that is triggered by disconnection from others, from the group to which the individual belongs, and that can assure us of food, protection, social connection, and support in the struggle to survive (see also Eisenberger, Lieberman, and Williams, 2003). Consequently, Cacioppo et al. (2006a) suggest viewing loneliness from an evolutionary perspective where one also ends up feeling unsafe, which activates a survival mechanism that heightens the person's sensitivity to threats and attacks. It is this fundamental threat to one's survival that may arouse a constellation of unpleasant and alarming emotions and experiences such as anxiety, anger, dysphoria, low self-esteem, faultfinding, and hostility (Berscheid and Reis, 1988, in Cacioppo et al., 2006b; Ernst and Cacioppo, 1999; Cacioppo and Hawkley, 2009).

In general, an over inclusive and somewhat simplistic definition is that loneliness results when we *perceive* that our social relations are not up to par with our expectations (see also Peplau and Perlman, 1982). Additionally, as Heinrich and Gullone (2006) concluded, lonely and nonlonely people do not differ in the amount of time they spend alone or in the daily activities they engage in. They maintained that loneliness is not the same as solitude, social isolation, or aloneness. Loneliness is a universal experience that does not respect the boundaries of age, gender, race, marital status, or socioeconomic status, and it may be either persistent and continuous or short lived (Neto and Barros, 2000; Heinrich and Gullone, 2006; McWhirter, 1990).

Based on the various theoretical sources, and my own research, I propose three distinguishing characteristics of all loneliness experiences:

1. Loneliness is a universal phenomenon that is fundamental to being human (see also Peplau and Perlman, 1982; Wood, 1986).
2. Although shared by all of us periodically, loneliness is in essence a subjective experience that is influenced by personal and situational variables (see also Rook, 1984a).
3. Loneliness, which is a complex and multifaceted experience, is always very painful, severely distressing, and individualistic (see also Moustakas, 1961; Rokach and Brock, 1997b).

Rolheiser (1979) eloquently captured those points by declaring that "no person has ever walked our earth and been free from the pain of loneliness. Rich or poor, wise and ignorant, faith-filled and agnostic, healthy and unhealthy, have all alike had to face and struggle with its potentially paralyzing grip. It has granted no immunities. To be human is to be lonely" (p. 9).

As was previously mentioned, over the years, there have been a variety of attempts to describe and define loneliness. Most of the earlier theorists (e.g., Bowlby, 1973; Moustakas, 1961, 1972; Parkes, 1973; Potthoff, 1976; and others) relied on general theoretical approaches, clinical experience, and personal journeys, which helped shape their understanding of loneliness (see Rokach, 1988b). As a consequence of being human, and being able to think about abstractions, some view loneliness as internally generated, while others see it mainly as situationally bound and brought about by external changes in one's world.

My research on loneliness, carried out over the last three decades, indicates that loneliness is a multidimensional experience that is composed of five factors, or dimensions. Not all of them may always be present when one experiences loneliness and each separately may indicate some specific psychological maladjustment but when our experience includes two or more of those elements, we invariably experience loneliness.

Emotional Distress

This is the most salient dimension of loneliness. It describes the agony, turmoil, feelings of anguish and internal upset, emptiness and hopelessness, and lack of control that one may feel when lonely. This element also captures the inner search for answers and insights, the desperation to understand and to see one's way through the maze of pain and agony. There is a feeling of lack of direction, fear, and anxiety.

One of my study participants, a 47-year-old woman who had recently separated from her husband, described it as follows:

I looked around the room; here was my own apartment at last. I have waited all the years of my life for it. I had gone from my father's house to my husband's house, and finally I had left there and taken off on my own. This is what I had wanted all along, but as I looked around at the faces of my friends, I felt lonelier than I ever had before. I quietly left the party room and went into the bedroom and sat on the bed. I wanted to identify my feelings. It was as if a void was slowly opening inside me, an almost physical sensation of stretching open and nothing there, blackness and sadness, and hopelessness. I was alone and completely unable to relate to another living soul. No one knew how I felt or cared, and I desperately wanted someone to care. I didn't know how to let them know I needed them, all those party people in the next room. The loneliness was like a heavy weight on my head and shoulders, it was a burning in my throat, a wall of unsheddable tears behind my eyes, a soundless scream of pain in a world bereft of compassion. It was darkness and coldness and dread of death and oblivion.

I myself had a similar experience, and that is what brought me to research loneliness. In 1981, I attended a psychological conference in Ottawa, Canada. At the time, I lived in Toronto and took a flight to the conference. The conference lasted from Thursday to Saturday afternoon, and during that time I was with my friends and professional acquaintances and had a very good time. Since I had booked a super-saver flight, I had to stay in Ottawa until Sunday, while most, if not all, of my colleagues returned home. I remember standing on the 15th floor of the hotel, knowing no one in Ottawa, looking through the thick glass window at the people and the cars on the street, but being unable to hear anything and realizing— possibly for the first time in my life—that this is how loneliness must feel. I felt sad, restless, and upset. Upon my return to Toronto, I started my search for resources on loneliness, and because what I found was quite limited and unsatisfactory for what I was looking for, I began my own research. The items in our loneliness questionnaire, which was developed over the years, and which addresses this dimension, include the following:

- I experienced feelings of intense hurt.
- I felt hollow inside, like an empty-shell.
- It felt like my heart was breaking.
- It felt as if I was crying inside.

Ornish (2007) indicated that physical as well as emotional pain is beneficial in that it motivates us to move and initiate change. Pain is our key to awareness. It gets our attention; it helps us direct ourselves to the cause of that pain, and thus it serves as the first step toward healing.

Social Inadequacy and Alienation

> No one would choose a friendless existence on condition of having all the other things in the world. —Aristotle

This dimension of loneliness addresses the perceived—and not necessarily actual—social isolation and sense of aloneness that almost invariably results, at least in the North American culture, from social comparison and the subsequent self-devaluation. The items that pertain to this dimension include the following:

- I felt that people wanted nothing to do with me.
- I felt I was boring and uninteresting.
- I felt inadequate when interacting with others.
- I felt ignored.

Loneliness invariably causes us to devalue ourselves. Ours is a couple culture—a culture of connection and community (although much of it today is virtual). When we experience loneliness, it is relatively easy for us to conclude that it is a result of others not wanting to connect with us, and thus we conclude that we must be unacceptable or undesirable; we may come to view ourselves as "damaged goods." The nearly inevitable result of perceived social ostracism and lowered self-esteem is an attempt to minimize further alienation and grief by way of self-generated social detachment. Imagine that you burned your arm. As the burn is healing, you undoubtedly will get into the habit of putting your other arm in front of your burned arm to protect it so other people or objects cannot harm or irritate it. This action is similar to what loneliness may cause us to do: reject others so that we do not end up getting close to people, trusting them, and ultimately being rejected and hurt.

Numerous studies have concluded that people without social contact—the lonely ones—are at the greatest risk of illness (Mate, 2003). Thus, feeling neglected or even abandoned may not only result in a deep feeling of loneliness, but our body may malfunction as well in an attempt to carry on without the fundamental necessity of human connection, closeness, and acceptance. Mate (2003) observed that people who deny their need for others end up feeling bitter and angry, and "behind our anger lies a deeply frustrated need for truly intimate contact" (p. 279).

Although this separation from others may minimize future rejections, it also prevents the formation of alliances and friendships that could alleviate loneliness. One study participant said the following:

> The most significant time of loneliness for me was when my second wife and I separated. I was a widower at the time of my second marriage. I hibernated myself in my home, not wanting anyone to know of my failure in marriage, as my first one was good. I wouldn't talk to anyone outside of my workplace. I was completely drawn within—not even wanting to have anything to do with anyone—even wanting to do away [commit suicide, A.R.] with myself. I did not care about anything—even my daughter. I was devastated. My thinking changed. I could not think. I wanted the world to stop so I could get off. I had to have help professionally. It took four years to complete this cycle.

Interpersonal Isolation

This is how most people would describe loneliness. Here we find the sense of utter aloneness associated with the perceived lack of social support and the painful feelings of rejection one feels in light of the realization that one does not connect with and cannot rely on others. The resultant feelings are often those of having been forgotten, unwanted, or ignored. In addition to those painful feelings, there is a yearning for the closeness that characterizes friendships or intimate romantic engagements that allow one to feel cherished and valued, cared for, and wanted. The following items compose this dimension:

- I felt I had no one to love or be loved by.
- I felt the absence of a meaningful romantic relationship.
- I felt I did not matter to those closest to me.
- I felt I had no one I could lean on in a time of need.

People can feel lonely in a marriage or in a crowd, but some situational factors make it even more painful and difficult to endure. These factors include low socioeconomic status, poor marital quality, infrequent contact with one's support network, lack of participation in voluntary organizations, and physical health problems. Another study participant related that:

It hurts. You want to reach out, but you don't know how or to whom. It's confusion with a feeling of a loss of words, or not being able to express them. It's being tongue-tied. It's hoping that when people see you at your outside value that they can see what's going on inside, hoping they'd understand. It's the feeling of other people's ignorance at your dilemma, which you're not able to control, and you are trying to reach an outstretched hand that someone somewhere is not being given or offered. You're crying inside and out, not knowing how to comprehend or see, or justify itself or yourself. You question yourself. Am I, should I, have I, and then, who am I really? Your world that you have presented to yourself seems now awkward, confused, unreal, unknown, disintegrated, and oblivious to yourself, lost a million miles away. It's hurting that no one hears your cry.

According to Olds and Schwartz (2009), "Man is a social animal. That commonplace observation is true at the most basic level. Our biological survival depends on our attachments, and our capacity for attachment is built into our biology. And not just our capacity for attachment but our longing for it" (p. 44). Three areas of investigation help us to understand the experience of being left out: evolutionary psychology, the neurobiology of attachment, and common sense. Humans survive only through their attachment to one another. Consequently, when these attachments are broken, the individual experiences both physiological and psychological stress. In times of loss, we are more vulnerable to illness and more at risk of dying. The evolutionary perspective on the experience of being left out starts with the fact that human beings are remarkably helpless at birth and remain dependent for a very long time. Secondly, even as adults, we need others if we are to survive in our dangerous and complicated world. Due to the fact that it is so essential for our survival, humans are endowed with both the capacity and the impulse to connect with others.

The neurobiology of attachment is expressed by the two neuropeptides oxytocin and vasopressin that are found only in mammals. They help manage stress and are crucially involved in social bonding. They reduce social anxiety and fear, leading humans to approach, rather than avoid, one another (Olds and Schwartz, 2009). Oxytocin in particular, is released during positive social interactions and has a calming effect on both behavior and physiology.

The common sense approach is highlighted by the basic requirement that when we have already joined a group, we monitor our standing within it, see how other members relate to us, and are alert and sensitive to small cues that we left out. That alertness is simple common sense.

Self-Alienation

> God made everything out of nothing, but the nothingness shows through.
> —Paul Valery

This dimension, which is commonly associated with serious mental disorders, captures the human reaction to unbearable pain, just as intense physical pain causes fainting, which provides relief. When the pain of loneliness is too much to bear, the response is self-detachment. Akin to depersonalization, it involves estrangement from one's self, feeling that one's mind and body are separate—a true attempt to distance one's self from the pain of alienation. Along with it, we also find denial. It may not be as extreme as depersonalization, but for the short run, denial may work just as well. Denial expresses the need one may have to distance one's self from the profound pain associated with loneliness. The items in our questionnaire that described this dimension are:

- I felt as if my mind and body were in different places.
- I felt as if I did not know myself.
- I felt that I was observing myself as if I was another person.
- I felt numb and immobilized as if I was in shock.

Growth and Discovery

> Loneliness may be seen as an experience of terror and devastation. However, it is positively valued as a force that may lead to inner growth.
> (Ettema, Derksen, and Van Leeuwen, 2010, p. 153)

This not so well-known dimension of loneliness was previously described by Moustakas (1961, 1975) and Sadler and Johnson (1980). They suggested that loneliness—just like pain—can be a beneficial force in one's growth and development. First, it directs one's attention inwardly as all pain does (an experience that the extroverted American way of life does not commonly encourage) and helps one take personal stock; evaluate relationships, goals, and values; and reorder one's priorities. Loneliness, just like the effect of intense fire on gold, can clear and purify our understanding of the human existence and enable us to avoid the common and mostly superficial elements of interpersonal relations. Out of the pain of loneliness we may emerge strengthened, becoming aware of new resources within us, feeling more content with our existence, and becoming more intensely involved in life. We may find within us creativity, personal strength, and meaning that we were not aware we had.

The following items in our questionnaire describe this process:

- I discovered a personal strength I was previously unaware of.
- I like and appreciate myself more than I did previously.
- Life seems richer and more interesting than it was previously.
- I have greater confidence in myself.

Moustakas (1961) relates his experience with his grief over his dying mother, an experience that held for him loneliness and feelings of guilt, helplessness, and separation. He found, however, that through that experience, he came to feel closely related to his mother, and he developed a sense of compassion and deep appreciation for close human relations.

Thus, loneliness may, rather than separate the individual from others, expand the person's perception, sensitivity, and sense of humanity. Consequently, Moustakas eloquently proclaimed that "in absolutely solitary moments, man experiences truth, beauty, nature, reverence, humanity. Loneliness enables one to return to a life with others with renewed hope and vitality, with a fuller dedication, with deeper desire to come to a healthy resolution of problems and issues involving others with possibility and hope for a rich, true life with others" (p. 102).

In his book *Love and Survival*, Ornish (1998) interviewed Rachel Remen, a clinical psychologist who commented that "Suffering is the great teacher of compassion. And being vulnerable is a doorway to compassion...We suffer not because we're in pain. The real suffering is that we feel we are in pain *alone*" (p. 204).

In discussing the personal growth that may follow traumatic experiences, Tedeschi and McNally (2011) suggested that it has been long known and recognized that "tragedy and suffering can trigger personal transformation...and struggles with adversity can foster psychological growth" (p. 19). Taku et al. (2008) found that adversity and trauma survivors may report renewed appreciation of life, improve their relationship with others and especially with their loved ones, and attain spiritual growth. This is very similar to what we discussed above. While loneliness has not been defined as traumatic per se, it may very well be a traumatic experience to those who experience it very intensely and for long periods. Tedeschi and McNally (2011) further clarify that while not everyone who has gone through trauma will attain personal growth, there are those who report it and may report the adversity as one of the best things that ever happened to them. This outcome therefore supports our observation that while loneliness is neither a pleasant experience nor one that we strive for, it can encourage self-development and personal growth that will have a positive and significant effect on one's life.

CORRELATES OF LONELINESS

Loneliness is such a painful and profound experience that it is unimaginable that it does not affect all facets of our lives. Research indicates that it affects us psychologically, emotionally, medically, and in our relationships in general and in intimate ones in particular.

Since social connectedness is so central to our survival, we may expect to find that loneliness may have adverse physical, emotional, and spiritual effects on us. Theeke (2009) noted that the physical correlates of loneliness include poor perceived health, physical symptomatology, hypertension, sleep disturbance, and, in older people, dementia. The negative psychological correlates include depression, negative self-assessment, diminished intimacy in marriage, general psychological distress, and psychological distress socially. When lonely we may suffer from a lower economic status, loss of friends, lack of religious affiliation, and even domestic violence.

Hawkley et al. (2003) further noted that depression that is correlated with loneliness has often been linked to greater perceived stress, poorer health behaviors, and obviously poorer personal interactions and relations. In general, they noted that loneliness may become self-reinforcing, experienced in such behaviors as more conflicts, arguments, hurt feelings, and dissatisfaction with life.

In the past decade or so, there has been a lot of emphasis on the role of social relations and health (Cohen, 2004). Regarding single parent households, Cacioppo et al. (2003) observed that as social isolation increased, the chance to get closer to others and have social needs fulfilled decreased, and of the sense of loneliness increased. This is considered a risk factor for broad-based morbidity and mortality (Seeman, 2000).

Hawkley and Cacioppo (2003) noted that social isolation may predict morbidity and mortality. The exact mechanisms by which our social connections impact our health, they maintained, have been elusive. Research has clearly documented the health hazards of social isolation: increased chance of carotid artery lesions (Knox et al., 2000), higher levels of stress (Cacioppo et al., 2000), and more individuals considering their daily lives more stressful, threatening, and demanding (Hawkley and Cacioppo, 2003). Seeman and McEwan (1996) have suggested that stressors can impair health by elevating hypothalamic-pituitary-adrenocortical (HPA) activation, which over time can cause significant damage.

Drageset et al. (2009) reported on studies that found that the risk of death for women who had low or no level of social support (and thus little or no reassurance, emotional closeness, or sense of belonging) was 2.5 times higher than women who had such support (Lyyra and Heikkinen, 2006). Löfvenmark et al. (2009) argued that lack of social support is a reliable predictor of hospital readmission, increased risk for heart disease, and even mortality.

Loneliness and lack of social support have been reported to be associated with impaired sleep, impaired mental health, cognitive sluggishness, increased vascular resistance, increased systolic blood pressure, and altered immunity (Hawkley and Cacioppo, 2010).

Loneliness was found to be associated with higher blood pressure, impaired immune function, cancer, morbidity and mortality, elevated mean cortisol levels (based on measures aggregated repeatedly several times per day), and depression (Adam et al., 2006; Doane and Adams, 2010; Pressman et al., 2005; Seeman, 2000). According to Geller et al. (1999), "Lonely people are four times more likely to die from such an event than those who are not lonely. They have been shown to be twice as likely to suffer from colds. A person's perceived interaction with others within a community may be a better predictor of health than smoking, cholesterol, or even genetics. We found significant association between a patient's loneliness score and total hospital visits" (p. 801).

Loneliness, in turn, may exacerbate conditions such as elevated blood pressure, increased vascular resistance, increased hypothalamic-pituitary-adrenocortical activity, impaired sleep, alcoholism, suicidal ideation and behaviors, and poorer physical health (Cacioppo et al., 2010; see also Adam et al., 2006; Wilson et al., 2007).

Loneliness is associated with communication apprehension, poor dating skills, minimal availability of social support, eating disorders, and some health-related problems such as high blood pressure. Loneliness was also correlated with diminished social contact and social support (Berg et al., 1981; Yeh and Lo, 2004) and domestic violence (Dong, Beck, and Simon, 2009). Segrin and Passalacqu (2010) further found that loneliness is negatively correlated with general health and positively correlated with stress, depression, and negative health behaviors (Cohen-Mansfield and Parpura-Gill, 2007; Minardi and Blanchard, 2004).

There is compelling evidence that social support and connectedness with others have a powerful impact on health and even on mortality. Loneliness seems to be lessened not by the *amount* of interaction with others but by the quality of that interaction with *close* friends and family members.

WHO ARE THE LONELY?

The eternal quest of the individual human being is to shatter his loneliness.
—Norman Cousins

Up to now, we discussed loneliness, social isolation, and the effects of a missing or weak social support system but who are the lonely? Are they individuals who feel disconnected, alienated, and all alone? How do they feel and behave? What are their characteristics? How do *we* know if we are lonely?

Today, social alienation is, unfortunately, a common experience. As Pappano (2001) so clearly observed, "We are losing touch. And we don't even realize it" (p. 1). Stivers (2004) echoes this view and suggests that people's desire to talk to people they hardly know, baring all on TV shows, and seeking crowds in shopping malls just so they are not alone are clear indications that the fear of being alone is terrifying to those who are lonely.

Due to the fact that loneliness is such a taboo topic and few people openly admit to being lonely, it is interesting to see what research says about them. As Rokach and Brock (1997b) and Heinrich and Gullone (2006) indicated, every person feels loneliness in a different way. There are, however, common affective, cognitive, and behavioral features.

Affective Features

Following an extensive literature review of studies that focused on children, adolescence, college students, and adults, Heinrich and Gullone (2006) found that, as Rokach's model indicates, loneliness invariably involves a host of negative and disturbing feelings. Among them are feeling unwanted, unloved, and rejected (Palotzian and Ellison, 1982); feeling sad and depressed; and perceiving oneself as unattractive, desperate, hopeless, and vulnerable (Rubenstein and Shaver, 1982). Other researchers found that the lonely experience anxiety (Hojat, 1983), social anxiety (Johnson et al., 2001), neuroticism (Neto and Barros, 2000), rejection (Hymel et al., 1999), and feelings of inferiority (Horowitz et al., 1982).

Cognitive Features

Low self-esteem has been suggested as the most prominent cognitive characteristic of lonely people (McWhirter, 1997; McWhirter et al., 2002; Pordham and Stevenson-Hinde, 1999). These researchers also suggest that low self-esteem may have a causal role in the development and maintenance of loneliness, where both reinforce each other. Thus, lonely people view themselves as inferior, worthless, unattractive, unlovable, and socially incompetent (Heinrich and Gullone, 2006). Loneliness was also found to be associated with self-consciousness and heightened self-focus (Jones, Freemon, and Goswick, 1981; Jones et al., 1985). Cutrona (1982) found that lonely people are more sensitive to rejection. They view others unfavorably and as untrustworthy (Ernst and Cacioppo, 1998), as less supportive (Vaux, 1988), and as less attractive and socially desirable (Jones et al., 1983). Sadly, as Heinrich and Gullone (2006) observed, lonely people feel powerless to change their predicament, because they attribute their loneliness to personal and regularly unchangeable characteristics (Koening and Abrams, 1999; Renshaw and Brown, 1993), and they tend to attribute their personal successes to luck or other external factors (Solano, 1987). All of this can contribute to feeling a sense of hopelessness and futility.

Behavioral Features

Studies have found that lonely individuals are socially inhibited and display behaviors that are ineffective (Cacioppo et al., 2000; Jackson, Soderlind, and Weiss, 2000). They are less willing to take social risks (Hojat, 1982; Moore and Schultz, 1983), are less assertive (Bell and Daly, 1985), have social skills deficits (Inderbitzen-Pisaruk et al., 1992), and have difficulty displaying friendly behavior, taking part in groups, and surrendering control. As a result of their social skills deficits, lonely people often display inappropriate patterns of self-disclosure (Sippola and Bukowski, 1999) and are pretty much self-focused (Jones, 1982), which may undermine developing relationships, furthering their feelings of loneliness. Lonely people have been found to adopt a more passive approach to coping with stress in general and loneliness in particular, than people who experienced loneliness infrequently (Van Buskirk and Duke, 1991). Cacioppo et al. (2000) found that the lonely deal with stress by disengaging, seeking guidance and assistance from others, and seeking emotional support.

Loneliness, according to Cacioppo and Patrick (2008), can make us demanding. Being very "hungry" for social contact and acceptance, lonely people are often more demanding of those around them. They end up wanting, expecting, and even demanding attention, acceptance, and social intercourse. Lonely people also tend to be more critical than others since, as we previously mentioned, the lonely may be depressed, be angry that they feel so alienated, doubt their ability to fit in, and see others as rejecting them so they become critical not only of themselves but of others as well. That critical approach stems from their doubt that others may mean well, may actually be sending them welcoming messages, and may even be interested in forging a relationship with them. Their deep doubt may result in their critical view of others, which will keep them isolated. They may end up criticizing and rejecting many of those who welcome their company and offer them "protection," because they may be concerned that if they allow others to get close to them, they may end up getting hurt. The lonely are also known for their social passivity and withdrawal. Those may result either from their depression, if they are indeed depressed, or from their disbelief that they are able to attract others. It is a kind of defeatist attitude that may be expressing their belief that "no one wants me, so why should I even bother?" (Cacioppo and Patrick, 2008).

Anthropomorphism is a term used to describe the projection of human attributes onto nonhuman entities. We commonly refer to our pets as happy, sad, or homesick. The lonely, however, may go one step further and anthropomorphize inanimate objects as well. For example, a friend of mine once told me that after her husband died, she put the chair he always sat in next to her chair when she ate supper, as if it were a friend sitting beside her.

Another good example of anthropomorphizing is the intense affection Tom Hanks's character felt for the volleyball in the movie *Cast Away*. He even gave it a name: Wilson.

Para-social interaction refers to the imagined intimacy that develops over time between TV viewers and a particular media persona. It is analogous to and resembles real social interaction (Horton and Wohl, 1956). Studies have indicated a connection between loneliness and para-social connections. Finn and Gorr (1988) found such a connection, and Eyal and Cohen (2006) found that lonely viewers became distressed over para-social breakups, as in the finale of *Friends,* the TV sitcom that their study focused on.

Baumeister and Leary's (1995) influential paper on the need to belong stated that the need to belong and to create meaningful social bonds underlies much of human interactive behavior. They asserted that a way to fulfill this fundamental human need is through frequent positive interactions, which would include mutual caring and concern. Greenwood and Long (2009) found that, while less optimal than real-life interactions, para-social interaction with media characters can partially satisfy the need to belong. Twenge et al. (2007) found that even writing about a favorite friend helped to reduce one's feelings of exclusion. Gardner, Pickett, and Kowles (2005) found that people with a high need to belong were more likely to report para-social connection to media characters.

LONELINESS ANXIETY

Moustakas (1972) was the first contemporary writer to develop the concept of *loneliness anxiety*, which is different from what he calls *existential loneliness*. Existential loneliness is the reality of being human, realizing and facing experiences of tragedy and upheaval, and accepting that one is born and dies a separate entity, all alone. Moustakas considers this condition the fate of every human being, everywhere.

Loneliness anxiety, on the other hand, is not true loneliness but the fear people have of being lonely. This is the same fear that creates the blind running away, the denial of pain, and the hectic social activity that are all aimed at one thing: relieving the fear of loneliness and blurring the realization of alienation. Due to the fact that the capacity to be lonely is so much a part of being human, and since in the course of living all people encounter separation or loss of some kind, we all grow to fear the agonizing pain of loneliness and its gnawing, saddening, and terrifying effects on us. As was previously mentioned and elaborated by Moustakas (1972), I, too, witness on a daily basis a heightened level of loneliness and anxiety among clients, friends, and acquaintances. While most people usually eat when they feel hungry, those unfortunate humans who in their history have experienced the excruciating suffering of prolonged hunger, later, upon leading a healthier and nourishing life, do not wait for hunger pangs to begin. They may eat continuously, store food unnecessarily, and be preoccupied with ensuring that they will never be without food again. They have become anxious about experiencing hunger and thus eat not so much to avoid hunger as to reduce their *anxiety* about being hungry. Loneliness has a similar effect on us. Since every human being has experienced it at some point in his life, many have acquired the dreadful loneliness anxiety.

Most people fear loneliness and the feelings of helplessness and hopelessness that are often part of the vicious cycle of loneliness. Lonely people are often deeply involved in desperate attempts to structure their lives and social involvement in such a way as to completely avoid the agony of loneliness and thereby maintain their denial of such feelings. As a result, we can often observe people accepting poor compromises, engaging in superficial social involvement, and engaging in a kind of clinging attachment to anyone who seems to be amenable to such attachment, grasping for any hope of companionship in order to assuage the suffering.

Lucas et al. (2010) observed that despite their heightened social sensitivity to the possibility of connecting with people, the lonely have problems initiating and maintaining social contact. Since they do not lack in social sensitivity, they suggest that lonely individuals' difficulty in social situations may be attributable not to social skills or social sensitivity (as they may possess those characteristics) but to social motivation. Indeed, they found that loneliness is more strongly correlated with social anxiety than with the more objective observer-rated social skills. Consistent with this social motivational model of loneliness, various other studies have shown that lonely individuals feel anxiety about their ability to perform in social interactions, fearing that they will be negatively evaluated by the other person. Given this anxiety, lonely individuals engage in overly careful interactional behavior or avoid social interaction altogether (see Cacioppo et al., 2006b; Nurmi and Salmela-Aro, 1997). Although these behaviors are aimed at minimizing the possibility of being negatively evaluated by others, they ironically undermine the lonely's ability to carry out social interactions (Stangier, Heidenreich, and Schermelleh-Engel, 2006).

Operating out of that defensive and self-protective paradigm can make lonely people appear less friendly, warm, and outgoing (Pilkonis, 1977; Stangier et al., 2006) and tends to minimize their motivation for social contact (Murray, Holmes, and Collins, 2006).

This combination of increased social anxiety with overly cautious social behavior has been termed the *prevention-focused* mind-set, which primarily involves motivations to maintain feelings of security and protect against negative outcomes (see Brewer, 2005; Higgins, 1997).

Most people are reluctant to admit, even to themselves, that they are lonely. We tend to deny the very same loneliness that is probably responsible for many of our thoughts, feelings, and behaviors. People seem to feel ashamed when they do admit to loneliness, which is socially stigmatized and is seen as a weakness in Western culture (Perlman and Joshi, 1987). As such, it is widely believed that loneliness should not affect normal, healthy, and strong people. We tend to identify it not with ourselves but with those who are considered marginal to the mainstream of our society: the elderly, the poor, the homeless, the handicapped, and criminals. We perceive these people as feeling unwanted, unloved, and alienated. That denial, although an expected reaction to pain, does not eliminate the loneliness. We still hurt, live with pain, and feel alienated at times. The drawback in our self-deception is that we cannot work through our loneliness because we refuse to recognize and accept it (see also Rokach, 1988a).

Despite our denial of loneliness, it is evidenced everywhere. All one needs to do is look around oneself, or even inside oneself, to see the painful evidence of loneliness and alienation (André, 1991; Moustakas, 1961; Rokach and Neto, 2000). The increased use of drugs and alcohol, the sale of pornographic material, the thousands of calls to distress hotlines, and the increasing number of suicides are some of the consequences of the pain of loneliness. The increases in stress management courses and clinics, divorces, and religious fads are other phenomena that are associated with loneliness.

Other areas of our life reflect the felt loneliness. We can see the motif of loneliness emerging in the renewed vigor in philosophy, art, literature, psychology, and religious and social thought. The pop arts, modern music, movies, literature, and popular magazines have covered and sometimes focused on the theme of loneliness. Bear in mind though, that even if there were no poets, no artists, no musicians, and no professional commentators to point out our loneliness, we would still know it and feel it within ourselves; the pain, agony, and suffering would be a constant reminder of its presence.

LONELINESS AND DEPRESSION

We frequently "taste" sadness or even depression when we are lonely, especially if we are lonely for a significant period of time. Consequently the two are often lumped together.

Loneliness and depression are closely related, and the strength of their association raises questions as to whether we are dealing with one or two separate concepts. One thing we do know is that *both* act in a synergistic effect to reduce well-being, yet they are different constructs that evoke different sets of responses. Cacioppo et al. (2006b) argued that based on theoretical and statistical grounds, loneliness and depression are distinct experiences. Loneliness promotes a desire to affiliate, together with a feeling of threat, which extends back to prehistoric times, when the one left behind or alone would soon meet extinction. Depression, on the other hand, consists of negative feelings such as sadness, difficulties making decisions, and repetitive and automatic thoughts, reflecting the theme of loss and revealing one's negative image of oneself, the world, and the future. While both loneliness and depression are aversive experiences, they are different. Loneliness is an alarm, motivating the individual to act in order to affiliate. Depression commonly results in inactivity. It results in a person who is apathetic, hopeless, and indecisive. It should be noted, argues Margalit (2010), that research demonstrated that loneliness does not cause depression. As Cacioppo and Patrick (2008) observed, "Loneliness reflects how you feel about your relationships. Depression reflects how you feel, period" (p. 83). While loneliness and the concern for our relationships may precipitate action and a forward movement, depression commonly results in apathy and inaction. Both, incidentally, share the diminished sense of control that may often lead to passive coping.

People who are chronically lonely, and consequently probably depressed as well, share the perception that they are doomed to social failure. They tend to withdraw, and that, of course, enhances future loneliness. The cynical worldview and little faith in others that they have adopted have been shown to contribute to their future loneliness.

It has been found that the relationship between loneliness and depressive symptoms is in the range of a large effect size ($r = .61-.62$). This was confirmed by a meta analysis conducted on 33 adolescents (Mahon et al., 2006; Yarcheski et al., 2006). Loneliness was found to predict depressive symptoms both within time (e.g., Hagerty and Williams, 1999) and across time (e.g., Heikkinen and Kauppinen, 2004). Cognitive theories posit that individuals commonly define their self-worth through their relationships, which makes them more vulnerable to depression in response to interpersonal difficulties (Blatt, 1990). Behavioral theories suggest that for certain individuals, poor social skills may increase their vulnerability to depression, making it difficult for them to elicit positive reinforcement from others and deal with relationship stressors (Lewinsohn, 1974). Empirical research confirmed these suggestions by showing an association between loneliness and depressive symptoms, both within (Mahon et al., 2006) and across time (Joiner, 1997).

THE LONELY CLIENT IN PSYCHOTHERAPY

Everyone is seeking companionship, yet most people seem to be having trouble finding it. People need intimacy and warmth, a sense of worth, and frequent confirmation of their identities. In most instances, the lack of quality human contact is so painful that people will go to great lengths to fulfill their need for others.

As was mentioned already, loneliness can cause a host of behavioral and emotional disturbances, including depression and social withdrawal, alcohol abuse and increased use of prescription medications, compulsive sexual involvement with many partners, anxiety attacks, and even hallucinations (Audy, 1980; Rokach and Brock, 1997a; Rook and Peplau, 1982). Mayer Gaev (1976), based on her clinical experience, suggested that one who experiences loneliness on a continuous basis, being chronically unable to relate meaningfully to others or himself, suffers from what she referred to as "pathological loneliness." Some clinicians and laypeople describe this condition as an abnormal and unnatural disease-like affliction, a very unhealthy and shameful ailment that needs to be treated before it becomes chronic. Traditionally, this had been done by declaring it a "mental problem" that confines its "sufferers" to psychiatric treatment (an approach I strongly oppose). I see loneliness as an existential phenomenon that is an integral part of being human, and I fail to comprehend how such a basic human experience, one that we all share, can be referred to as a "disorder" or "disturbance" (see also Moustakas, 1961). Fromm-Reichmann (1976) asserted that "loneliness in its own right plays a much more significant role in the dynamics of mental disturbances than we have so far been ready to acknowledge" (Fromm-Reichman, 1960, in Mayer-Gaev, 1976; p. 14). Mental health professionals often highlighted loneliness as an important factor that precipitates and maintains emotional problems (Hansson et al., 1986; Jones, Freemon, and Goswick, 1981). Mayer Gaev (1976) even claimed that almost all of her clients complain about loneliness as a problem. Interestingly, the overwhelming majority of people I treat, both in my private practice and in the jail with which I was associated, are struggling with loneliness, yet it is almost never presented as the problem troubling them when they come to see me.

"Veronica" (a composite "client" of mine), an attractive 29-year-old executive secretary, arrived for her first session smartly dressed, with her glasses and expensive purse accentuating her professional look. She was somewhat hesitant and appeared a bit nervous and guarded. We had spoken a week earlier on the phone, at which time she presented her problem as one of low self-esteem. She now inquired, almost unobtrusively, about my areas of specialty and nonchalantly asked if I see people for loneliness. I gave her some basic information about myself and the manner in which I conduct therapy. She then proceeded to tell me about herself and her background.

Veronica was born to parents who immigrated to Canada from France. They were loving and devoted but had very high expectations of her. Being a "good daughter," she had finished high school and went on to college to study engineering—something her mother had always wanted her to pursue. Veronica completed her freshman year and then dropped out. She was single, although she had dated a man who, after three years and an engagement ring, had left her for another woman. She consoled herself by attending evening courses in a community college and occasionally dating. Veronica claimed she was insecure and lacked confidence in both her personal and professional capacities, and she stated that, in general, she felt "pretty lousy" about herself. She later developed what she termed social phobia—that is, she experienced intense fear when she was around people or when interacting with them in supermarkets, banks, or on public transportation.

In later sessions, Veronica alluded to and finally directly addressed her loneliness. She grew up in a home with parents who, although loving and devoted, did not really communicate with her or teach her about human closeness. Her two younger brothers tended to play with each other and ignore her. Although she was never an outcast, Veronica was not very popular at school and usually had only one friend at a time, while interacting only superficially with the other students. In college, she met Richard, her first "serious" boyfriend, and they had an extremely close relationship, but it did not last. Although initially hardly noticeable, Richard became less warm and loving, and Veronica could not ignore it, even though she tried by remaining loving and devoted. It became clear during therapy that she had wanted to perceive herself that way, while in reality she was clinging to Richard because she was terrified of losing him.

After Richard told her he did not love her anymore, Veronica was devastated and felt completely heartbroken. She experienced deep depression, which necessitated antidepressants and a four-week leave from work. She would not allow others to get close to her emotionally, and she grew increasingly lonelier and more mistrustful. When she did find someone she liked and wanted to get close to, she would attempt it in such a clumsy and inappropriate manner that she would end up being repeatedly shunned. Veronica had also developed a moderate dependency on alcohol, and she took Valium once or twice a week. In the last two months she had gained 15 pounds, a situation that she found alarming and loathsome.

* * *

Drawing on the available literature and on observations I made while conducting psychotherapy, I will present a composite of a "typical" lonely client. What almost always strikes me first about lonely clients is their inability to admit to the therapist—and to themselves—that they are lonely. Generally, some clients want to discuss their discomfort, confusion, or immobilization, while others talk about a host of other issues that may be bothersome to them. Very rarely do I encounter a client who comes into my office and tells me outright, "I am in pain because I am terribly lonely." Lau and Gruen (1992) discussed the social stigma that prevents people form openly discussing and sharing their loneliness with others (see also Perlman and Joshi, 1987).

Most lonely clients appear to be depressed—not clinically or severely, but rather they feel sad, dejected, and hopeless. As was mentioned previously, depression and loneliness are sometimes confused. Although they frequently overlap, they are distinct experiences (Rokach, 1988a). Whereas lonely people, although dissatisfied with their social relationships, are quite content with other aspects of their lives, depressed people experience a more global pattern of negativity and discontent. They may be unhappy with their social relationships as well as experience dissatisfaction with schoolwork, finances, health, employment, and child-rearing practices in their home (Bragg, 1979; Horowitz, French, and Anderson, 1982).

I have also found the lonely client to be quite anxious about remaining alone and indefinitely desolate. This anxiety is often not recognized or expressed as being directly associated with loneliness but is instead presented as a fear of being among people in general (in public places, at social gatherings, etc.) or specifically related to a particular person, such as the fear of parental death and being abandoned even though parents are alive and well. Sometimes the client experiences a generalized anxiety that he can neither explain nor control.

Feelings of vulnerability, and at times panic, accompany anxiety (Rubenstein and Shaver, 1982). These feelings, along with depression, may provoke attempts to find respite through substance abuse. Among my clients are those who have been addicted to Valium, antidepressants or antihistamines, and alcohol. Those who preferred alcohol, however, regardless of their need for it, do not consider themselves alcoholics but just people in need of a "relaxant." For them, alcohol was simply a way to be in others' company as well as a habit that they planned to stop "one day." Drug abuse is becoming widespread among the lonely, as well as among the general population (Rokach and Brock, 1995). For those people, at least in their eyes, the problem then becomes one of substance dependency rather than the unthinkable: loneliness. Some users, on the other hand, are painfully aware of their feelings of isolation and loneliness, and claim that the drug or bottle is their "only friend."

I found low self-esteem, feelings of worthlessness, and self-deprecatory attitudes to be most salient among my lonely clients (see also Rokach, 1998). Initially, before attributing their distress to loneliness, clients may complain that they are not as "good," successful, or socially likable as others because of their seeming lack of abilities. Blaming oneself and one's shortcomings (whether real or perceived) for the loneliness one experiences and perceiving oneself as a failure in the social marketplace are common features of lonely clients.

Sometimes I see people who are lonely due to a divorce or the recent breakup of a relationship, or who are married and seeking therapy for marital difficulties. The couple may come to therapy together, but sometimes one partner comes alone because the other does not believe in therapy and refuses to join. Invariably I hear about disappointments, anger, emotional scars, and "empty-shell" marriages (see also Levinger, 1999). It becomes painfully clear to both the client and myself that loneliness—heavy daily doses of it—is the main issue with which the client is struggling. Almost without exception, the lonely person experiences varying degrees of stress that may be realized on a physical or behavioral level. To those unaware of its origin, their distress may appear related to work, school, or financial difficulties when actually it is a manifestation of their loneliness (Rokach and Brock, 1995).

> Many of the problems and much of the pain I felt came from trying to resist my loneliness. The moment we begin to build a wall against it, we have already lost...Before we can look at our loneliness, we must stop trying to resist it. We must stop blaming husbands or wives, children, or bosses for our feelings of loneliness and (the) alienation in our lives.
>
> (Schultz, 1976, p. 169)

This quote describes precisely what many lonely clients do; they run away, hide, or deny their loneliness, ashamed to admit that they are in pain (Moustakas, 1972; Rokach, 1990). If they do finally talk about their loneliness, however, they often go on a rampage, blaming everyone around them for it. My purpose then is to instill or develop in the client the courage to recognize and accept his loneliness, as well as take full responsibility for it. Once that has been done through nurturing within the therapeutic relationship, the client is on his way to lessening the pain. I say "lessening" even though all clients, as with the rest of us, want to *eliminate* pain. Life, however, will always include varying degrees of pain and loneliness, and to survive it, we need to learn to minimize and control the suffering as much as we can and to accept courageously that which we cannot overcome.

I was asked once to briefly describe how I help the lonely. I replied that I see myself as a father or a friend who is attempting to teach a child to swim while the child is terrified to even approach the water. That analogy, for me, encapsulated the trust the child must first have in order to place her hand in her father's hand—the courage the child needs to approach the water and the effort they both need to make so that the child can learn the coordinated movements that will help her swim.

Maintaining a close therapeutic relationship is central to successful psychotherapy with the lonely but it is not always easily attained. The people I see in my practice are those who have been beaten by pain, drained by suffering, and wounded by loneliness. They are at times very angry and often mistrustful or unwilling to open up for fear of further pain. At these times, I lend an ear and a shoulder along with my willingness to understand, share their burden, and offer whatever help I can.

* * *

Veronica, my client, responded to my approach with skepticism and anger. She could not believe I would not harm her if she allowed me to get emotionally close to her. Veronica was afraid to open up, to trust and truly relate to me, and I knew that persistence and patience on my part were crucial. I was there for her to hold her hand and give her the courage to trust in, relate to, and not run away from therapy. With the passing weeks and months, she calmed down, was more open, and began trusting me, while remaining constantly "on the lookout" to catch me slip and betray her trust.

We then concentrated on examining her experience of being loved throughout her life and on her frequent disappointments and loneliness, which I continuously encouraged her to face and accept. She refused, she cried, and she pleaded. I asked her to stop her fervent "running" both during and—in her numerous engagements—after working hours. I suggested that she think and write about her loneliness, not as a feared disease but rather as a painful part of her life. That acceptance and reflection, rendered by the solitude that she now chose rather than the past loneliness that was imposed upon her, provided insight and allowed her to again be close to herself. This intimacy encouraged healing and the rejuvenation of her soul and opening of her mind to believe that her future was brighter than she had imagined.

One day Veronica came into my office wearing a beautiful new suit that she said she had bought as a reward to herself for losing five pounds. I realized that this was one more indication that she was in the process of healing and of becoming more open and alive and less frightened and depressed. At this point, we began to work on what I call the "transition phase," where we structured her resources (see Rokach, 1990). We examined the behaviors and thinking patterns that may have sabotaged her connection with others. We worked on and changed her expectations of being rejected and guided her in exercising her listening skills and empathy. With time and help, Veronica came to understand and accept that love always goes hand in hand with pain. I worked with her on learning how to enjoy her own company and engage in solitary activities rather than solely depending on others to provide the essence to her life. Veronica also worked with me on curbing her drinking and eliminating her dependency on Valium—both of which, she now understood, were harmful and destructive crutches. She started to see the world as a more hospitable place and to see people as a source of love and joy, not only as causes of pain and sorrow.

Veronica was now ready to reach out and build social bridges, not as an attempt to be loved and accepted, but as a means of fulfilling a basic human wish to belong (see Rokach, 1990). She learned the importance of a social support network and, as a step toward developing one, asked that we devote some sessions to instruction in the basic principles of assertiveness.

Both Gordon (1976) and Schultz (1976) focused on the American "cultural imperative" of marriage and on the success that the Western "couple culture" attributes to married people. Consequently, individuals who are single, divorced, or widowed experience a sense of failure to fulfill societal expectations and remain dissatisfied and lonely. A prerequisite, therefore, to creating effective social contact may be assisting the client in examining his values regarding social roles, and encouraging him to reevaluate the "failure" stigma that he may have attached to his single status. Once the client is less pressured by cultural expectations, he or she becomes less self-centered and is better able to increase social relationships.

This is what happened with Veronica; she was now able to be with people rather than cling to them. She began interacting socially with men and women, took walks and went hiking with friends, and reentered family social functions. She truly enjoyed becoming an integral part of her family again without being ashamed of her "craziness" and without expecting more than her family could give. Veronica made strides at work as well, and she was promoted to assistant vice-president of a growing company.

After more than a year in therapy, Veronica and I felt that it was time to prepare for her departure. We gradually increased the time gaps between our meetings from a week to two, then three, and four weeks. It was time to say goodbye. I had truly grown to like, value, and appreciate Veronica, and she was grateful to me for teaching her how "to swim."

* * *

Unlike Veronica, other clients may need assistance in dealing with grief over an important loss they have suffered or with alienating personal characteristics, such as their aggressive or timid approach to others, fear of intimacy, or even poor personal hygiene that may be causing others to avoid them. Sometimes, when the "presenting problem," which may not be loneliness, is being addressed, the person feels relieved; his mood lifts, he may feel less lonely, and he is then ready to learn to actually enjoy solitary activities as well as social interactions (André, 1991). Some clients need to be encouraged to be less physically and geographically isolated by joining clubs, evening classes, and other activities where they may find people they can relate to (Blieszner, 1988).

Research indicates that a significant segment of the population lacks the skills necessary to initiate and maintain rewarding social interaction and, as a result, experience loneliness (see Jones et al., 1985; Rokach and Brock, 1995). According to this skill deficit hypothesis, socially anxious individuals have not learned the appropriate social skills or they may have learned inappropriate ones (Bandura, 1969; Jones, 1982). Experimental investigations support the effectiveness of social skills training in the reduction of dating anxiety (Curran, 1977). Consequently, proper instruction in initiating conversations, speaking fluently on the telephone, giving and receiving compliments, enhancing physical attractiveness, appropriate nonverbal communication, and handling physical intimacy may be successfully offered to lonely clients.

SOLITUDE

With some people solitariness is an escape not from others but from themselves. For they
see in the eyes of others only a reflection of themselves.
—Eric Hoffer

Imagine being alone—not in a desert or on an island, but at home for a whole day. Or imagine walking alone in a city or an area that you are not familiar with, or staying in a forest by yourself for a day. Some would do it if they needed to, but many would shudder at the thought and attempt to run away from that aloneness as fast as they could. There are still others, however, who'd welcome it, enjoy it, and grow from it.

Most people think about loneliness as aloneness, a geographical distance from other people—physical isolation from important others, but being lonely is not necessarily being alone (Hoff and Bucholz, 1996). Being alone is simply the objective reality of being without others, geographically being away from company. One can be alone physically or alone in a crowd and still not be lonely. Daydreaming, reliving past memories, or planning an upcoming trip are all examples of aloneness that is unrelated to the presence of others and is *not* loneliness. Therefore, being alone, as a state of being, is neither positive nor negative. It may be a purely cognitive experience, a geographical reality, or a crisis in one's life. Cacioppo, Hawkley, and Thisted (2010) captured the difference between *loneliness* and *solitude*. They observed that "the word *solitude* expresses the glory of being alone, whereas the word *loneliness* expresses the pain of feeling alone" (p. 453).

Long (2000), in an attempt to clarify the nature of solitude, catalogued undergraduates' experiences, and based on a factor analysis found nine different solitude types that he then combined into three factors: solitude of self-expansion (e.g., self-discovery, creativity), negative solitude (feeling lonely, needing a diversion), and solitude that is connected to feeling a connection to others (intimacy, spirituality). Although it is commonly accepted that loneliness and solitude are two separate constructs, it should be highlighted that solitude, not loneliness, provides people with opportunities for self-exploration and creativity (see Long et al., 2003).

Greenwood and Long (2009) found that self-expansion solitude predicted media involvement, where people who became involved with media characters and stories experienced a creative and transformative process that facilitated their personal growth.

It is not the environment that determines how we feel but our construction and interpretation of it that shapes our experiences. It is true that being alone when we crave human contact and belonging will be experienced as loneliness but being alone when we want to and need it is what constitutes solitude. When we need time to ourselves, wanting to get away from the constant bombardment of daily responsibilities, chores, demands, stimuli, and hassles, we find great pleasure in solitude. In being alone, at peace, we do what can only be done alone: think, meditate, reflect, write, walk in nature, play the piano, or paint. While we may enjoy and feel enriched when being with family and friends, solitude is a cherished time that can help us rejuvenate, refresh, and renew (see also Cacioppo and Patrick, 2008) ourselves. Commonly, solitude denotes a time of privacy or the ability to control how much others intrude upon our lives. It is a disengagement from the immediate demands of others, a state of increased freedom to choose one's mental or physical activities (Long and Averill, 2003).

Theologian Paul Tillich observed that "Loneliness can be conquered only by those who can bear solitude" (in Rubenstein and Shaver, 1982, p. 14). Although the words *alone* and *lonely* come from the same English root, meaning "all one," they are not synonyms. Many who live in unhappy marriages or with family or friends who "don't understand" them are much lonelier than others who live or exist alone but have close ties with friends and relatives. It is possible to be lonely without being alone and to be alone without being lonely.

Long (2000) found that solitude is often preceded by stress, a felt need to examine one's wishes, needs, and priorities—solving a problem, reflecting on the past, or preparing for the future. As a result of solitude, people reported increased self-understanding, self-renewal, creativity, and spiritual growth. Carl Rogers (1983), in addressing the child's natural creativity and the teachers' tendency to squash it by requiring compliance and conformity, equates creativity with people's tendency to achieve their full potential. Rogers, in fact, suggests that creativity is essential in our ability to cope with and survive in our ever-changing world. Maslow (1970) further saw the concepts of creativity, mental health, and self-conceptualization to be specific to human nature.

While Long et al. (2003) acknowledge that we are social animals and our survival depends on being with others, it is also true that we need time alone as relief from the constant bombardment of stimuli, to be away from social stressors so we can grow spiritually, creatively, and as people (Burger, 1998; Kock, 1994).

> In a society that is bombarded with billboards, cell phones, computer technology, iPods, and pocket-sized to wall-sized televisions—has the value for silence and solitude been replaced by a mass hysteria over more and more sound and sight stimulation?
>
> (Kock, 2004, p. 22)

It seems, at least at present, that the modern-day technological craze has challenged our capacity to be alone. Merton (2000) observed that solitude is not withdrawal from ordinary life and is not apart from it but is essential to living a meaningful life.

Feldman (2003) observed that silence and solitude lie at the heart of all the great spiritual traditions, and they serve as our vehicle in driving underneath words and ideas to discover the unspoken truths of being. Parse (2007) noted that the gifts of solitude offer comforting aloneness, visions for new horizons, and a sense of freedom. Mahler (2003) very eloquently observed that by doing nothing, "we stare into the potential of everything" (p. 65).

Historically, solitude was seen as a necessary condition for spiritual growth and creativity to occur. Many of the well-known religious leaders have spent significant amounts of time in solitude. Among them were Moses, Buddha, Jesus, and Mohammed. Long and Averill (2003) remind us that numerous spiritual, religious, creative, and artistic gains have resulted from solitary experiences that have, in turn, impacted countless social movements and practices. Over the past centuries, and today as well, nuns and monks of various religious affiliations continue to participate in collective devotional solitude, and solitary meditation is quite common (France, 1996). Writers such as Kafka, Gibbon, and Rilke wrote during their periods of solitude (Storr, 1988). Henry David Thoreau (1854/1981) poignantly wrote, "I never found the companion that was so companionable as solitude" (p. 205).

In some societies, solitude has been treated as a rite of passage in transforming boys into men. Boys were sent off into the jungle and ordered to remain there alone for varying periods ranging from overnight to several months. Later, when they returned to their village, they were accepted as men whose boyhood ignorance, dependence, and existential confusion were gone forever.

Storr (1988) observed that many of the world's greatest thinkers never formed close personal ties or reared families. They needed alone time, solitude, to create and become. Beethoven, for instance, became increasingly isolated as his deafness worsened. He then had great difficulty making close relationships.

> In his deaf world, Beethoven could experiment with new forms of experience, free from the intrusive sounds of the external environment; free from the rigidities of the material world; free, like the dreamer, to combine and recombine the stuff of reality, in accordance with his desires into previously undreamed-of forms and structures.
>
> (Storr, 1988, p. 52)

While Bowlby addressed attachment to parental figures and intimate others, Granqvist (2003), Shillito, Kellas, & Kirkpatrick (1999), and La Cour (2003) highlighted human attachment to the immaterial and the spiritual. The ability to be alone and experience spiritual development serves an important function in the capability to have healthy attachment to others. We know of many very creative people who could create and develop in their aloneness and did not have close attachments to others. Among them we could count Kafka, Kant, Hume, and Wittgenstein (Storr, 1988). Winnicot (1958) further highlighted the importance of being able to be alone by suggesting that it is a prerequisite to being able to have secure attachments. He introduced the distinction between attachment and dependence, and he conceptualized the capacity to be alone on the basis of the concept of the false self that would result in a person who, because he cannot be alone, desperately attempts to meet the needs of others. Winnicott (in Storr, 1988) links the capacity to be alone with self-discovery and becoming aware of one's deepest feelings, needs, and impulses.

Bucholz and Chinlund (1994) echoed that approach and added that solitude and aloneness are hard-wired into the human psyche because they are essential to normal growth. For instance, they describe the fetus as experiencing the first alone sensation in the uterus. This alone time then expands as the child grows, and the preschooler's need for time alone is expressed in her play time, fantasy life, and capacity for solitary play. The adolescent's self-imposed isolation and need for alone time is interwoven in her search for identity. The young adult aims to integrate intimate relationships with occasional alone time without creating conflict in order to coexist harmoniously in the course of human life. We need both, and with respect and nurturing, we can develop the skill to function both with others and alone.

While solitude is commonly seen as a positive experience, the ability to benefit from solitude requires a sense of self that can survive in the absence of social directions, expectations, and reinforcement (Larson, 1990). Modell (1993), referring to attachment theory, suggested that only the securely attached can freely surrender themselves to solitude and, when alone, can passionately pursue a commitment outside of the self, whether it be with God, an ideology, or a creative work. Storr (1988) observed that solitude, while hard to achieve in our cluttered and fast-paced modern culture, can lead to profound moments of thought and inner peace. The healing- and growth-promoting aspects of solitude have been extolled by Moustakas (1989), who highlighted our ability, while in solitude, to access our untapped resources, leading to unique realizations, increased awareness of ourselves and the world around us, and an improved ability to relate to others.

The Benefits of Solitude

> Aloneness can be as comforting as a soft, warm blanket on a cool fall day...[It] can be
> like a breeze, gently calling your name.
> (Schmidt Bunkers, 2008, p. 23)

As we have noted previously, solitude and engaging in solitary activities could be beneficial in several ways. Solitude relieves the individual of dependence on others for company, which may increase one's sense of personal control (Rook and Peplau, 1982). Increasing pleasurable solitary activities may help the lonely better cope with the depression that often accompanies particularly lengthy bouts of loneliness (Fuchs and Rehn, 1977; Lewinsohn, Biglan, and Zeiss, 1976). In fact, enhancing solitary skills has been recommended as part of the therapy offered to the lonely (Young, 1982) and may be particularly valuable in cases where social isolation imposed by external constraints cannot be easily modified.

Being alone could be very painful—experienced as loneliness and a time of utter despair. Being alone, on the other hand, allows one to "escape" the hectic pace of life and experience solitude. Solitude may serve as a time for writing, meditation, and other solitary activities, such as reflection, which is thought to promote individuality, creativity, and self-awareness (André, 1991; Garfield, 1986).

Turning loneliness into solitude, which is a recommended way to cope with its pain, can result in a beneficial, enjoyable experience. Experiencing solitude, we learn to take good care of ourselves by ourselves. We may get a better, deeper understanding of our needs as our increased self-knowledge contributes to a more focused and fulfilling life, and then we will be better equipped to have accepting and loving relationships with others (Brehm et al., 2002).

Solitude relieves the individual of dependence on others for company, which may increase one's sense of personal control (Rook and Peplau, 1982). Increasing pleasurable solitary activities may help the lonely better cope with the depression that often accompanies particularly lengthy bouts of loneliness (Fuchs and Rehn, 1977; Lewinsohn, Biglan, and Zeiss, 1976; Rokach, 1990). In fact, enhancing solitary skills has been recommended as part of the therapy offered to the lonely (Young, 1982) and may be particularly valuable in cases where social isolation imposed by external constraints cannot easily be modified. Hoff and Bucholz (1996) observed that solitude offers time for reflective, calm meditation and all in all is imperative to optimal functioning and creativity. Maslow (1970), in discussing self-actualization, wrote, "A musician must make music, an artist must paint, a poet must write, if he is to be ultimately at peace with himself. What a man can be, he must be. He must be true to his own nature" (p. 46); this nature can be discovered almost solely by engaging in solitude.

Long and Averill (2003) remind us that numerous spiritual, religious, creative, and artistic gains have resulted from solitary experiences that have, in turn, impacted countless social movements and practices. Tick (1988) eloquently observed that "loneliness accompanies creativity. It is necessary in that the creative person must differentiate him/ herself from the conforming majority, discover unique purpose, and gather the strength of sensibilities needed to create" (p. 131). Creative people are said to be different from the rest of us. They may have unique ways of seeing the world and think outside the box. It is not uncommon to see them struggling with loneliness or, having turned it into solitude, benefit from their distance from everyday life and using it to create and develop. Albert Camus (1970, in Tick, 1988) wrote in his composition, *The Plague*, that in order to find ourselves, we each withdraw from the rat race and confront our individual natures. This necessary withdrawal has been experienced by biblical and religious figures, as well as philosophers: Jesus' sojourn in the wilderness, the Buddha's forsaking of his throne and dedicating himself to meditation under the Bo Tree, Odysseus's solitary 10-year voyage of trials on the way to his homeland, and the German philosopher Nietzsche's solitude and his character Zarathustra's withdrawal to the mountain. Tick (1988) observed that "The person driven to create must withdraw from conformity. Only in such withdrawal will one's thoughts, emotions, and sensibilities be heightened to the pitch necessary to allow the world to flow through the self in artistic expression" (p. 133). Thomas Merton (1953), a poet and the child of artist-parents, lamented, "The integrity of the artist lifts a man above the level of the world without delivering him from it" (p. 11, in Tick, 1988). Lord Byron sang, "In solitude, when I am least alone," attesting to our ability to be alone and absorbed willingly in our own company and path.

Parkinson (1980) noted that solitude enhances the imagination and allows freedom for contemplation and exploration. Van Gogh used art to turn painful loneliness into the blissful solitude that provided him reflection, study, inspiration, and fantasy. Veith (1980) noted that the Coptic Church of Ethiopia placed its monasteries on nearly inaccessible mountaintops, believing that restricting access from the crowds and fostering solitude enhanced the monks' closeness to God. Henry David Thoreau removed himself to the remote Walden Pond for 26 months in order to find solitude, which he considered the best possible companion. His prolific writings were the result of a creative and well-directed solitude. Moustakas (1972) viewed solitude as a self-initiated capacity of humans. It comes and goes and serves a purpose when it exists. In solitude we are limitless and free. We renew contact with our self and discover another part of who we are.

> In being alone I can keep in touch with my own thinking and know more surely that my thoughts are coming from me and not from someone else. Hopefully, I can pursue my life in a way that will enhance my growth and lead to significant learning, based on the voices within rather than from without.
>
> (Moustakas, 1972, p. 19)

Solitude may help alleviate prolonged loneliness. Rubenstein and Shaver (1982) specifically mention solitude's calming effect on us, its enhancement of our ability to distinguish genuine from false needs for contact with others, and its central role in preparing us for social responsibility and intimacy (see also Rokach, 1988a). Recognizing the potential benefit of solitude, the Wilderness Act of 1964 (U.S. Public Law 88-577) mandated some designated areas "to preserve natural conditions, to provide opportunities for solitude, and to provide a primitive and unconfined type of recreation" (Shafer and Hammitt, 1995, p. 266).

Bucholz (1997) highlighted the importance of aloneness in the growth, development, and maturation of the individual. While agreeing with the accepted observation that we can advance and succeed specifically as a result of our attachment to others, Bucholz maintains that aloneness is just as essential. And while many equate aloneness with loneliness and view it as a necessary and dreaded part of human existence, Bucholtz (1997) appreciates aloneness as productive, creative, and essential for carrying out tasks that require aloneness, such as introspection, the development of intuition, and personal rejuvenation.

The comforting aloneness that solitude offers is a way to separate ourselves from our everyday demands and from various desires and strivings that consume our energy (Parse, 2007). Solitude can also offer what Schmidt Bunkers (2008) called a "Vision for New Horizons" that may include coming upon an idea for writing a poem, an insight on how to solve a difficult situation or problem, or a means of relaxation and innovation that may then enhance a vision of a new horizon. Goleman, Kaufman, and Ray (1992) report that Nolan Bushnell founded the very successful Atari company when he got inspiration for his phenomenally successful video game while idly flicking sand on a beach.

Merton (2003), in extolling the virtues of solitude and of those who can comfortably engage in it, posited that "very often it is the solitary who has the most to say; not that he uses many words, but what he says is new, substantial, unique" (p. 56). The gift of a sense of freedom is the third category of benefits that solitude may provide (Schmidt Bunkers, 2008). It refers to the sense of peace and security that solitude offers. It offers us an opportunity to discover within ourselves greater generosity, tolerance, and understanding (Feldman, 2003). True presence in the moment, mindfulness, can also be achieved in silence and solitude, when we can focus on just *being* (Hanh, 1991; Parse, 2007). Mahler (2003) observed, "Through the embrace of silence and solitude, we may enjoy the increasingly rare privilege of seeing things as they are, not as we wish them to be...and we can enjoy...a deeper understanding of the world we live in" (p. 75). Burton-Christie (2003) further noted that the self, once transformed by solitude, becomes more compassionate and a discoverer of new meanings in life.

Adults spend about 29% of their waking time alone (Larson, Csikszentmihalyi, and Graef, 1982), and many people may want even more time alone. One of the reasons is that solitude offers the person protection from overstimulation (Suedfeld, 1982). There is also a decreased self-consciousness when we are alone (Larson, 1990). Solitude enhances creativity, such as the scientist alone in the laboratory, the writer by herself in a cabin in the woods, or the painter in a secluded and empty studio. Engaging in fantasy, performing cognitive leaps from the present to the future and back—all of these are greatly enhanced by solitude.

Self-transformation is another benefit of solitude. Even intimacy, as paradoxical as it may sound, can benefit from solitude. Many people, while alone, experience feelings of intimacy, of connection with another person (Nisenbaum, 1984). Winnicott (1958) maintained that the person who as a child developed the capacity to be alone is never truly alone. Rather, he maintained, a presence that may unconsciously be equated with a parental care giving context is always available to him.

Spirituality is heightened by solitude and for the last several thousand years, monks and nuns have cloistered themselves in collective devotional solitude and in solitary prayers (France, 1997). "From the perspective of many spiritual traditions, solitude enhances one's ability to contemplate one's place in the universe and one's own thoughts and desires" (Long and Averill, 2003, p. 29).

While solitude is commonly seen as a positive experience where one can engage in selected activities alone and without the encumbrances and expectations of society, the ability to benefit from solitude requires a sense of self that can survive in the absence of social directions, expectations, and reinforcement (Larson, 1990). Modell (1993), referring to attachment theory, suggested that only the securely attached can freely surrender themselves to solitude and, when alone, can passionately pursue a commitment outside of the self, be it with God, an ideology, or a creative work.

> To transform the emptiness of loneliness, to the fullness of aloneness. Ah, that is the secret of life. —Sunita Khosla

Solitude over the Lifespan

Research has shown that from childhood to old age, people will experience more and more time alone, but interestingly, they will become better equipped to handle it as they age (Larson, 1990; Long and Averill, 2003).

During one's childhood years, playing alone is viewed by peers as deviant and by psychologists as indicative of insecurity (Rubin and Mills, 1988; Younger and Daniels, 1992). Preadolescents (seventh- to ninth-graders) show more affinity to loneliness than younger children, while adolescents may experience solitude even more positively, because they can make more constructive use of solitude due to their reasoning skills. Their environment is characterized by the pressure to conform, and solitude provides them an opportunity to deal with the issues of identity formation that they wrestle with during this period. Pines and Aronson (1988) highlighted the utility of "time out" as a known strategy to help children and youth reflect on their actions and how it may affect those around them, as well as a coping strategy for professionals who are involved in emotionally, mentally, or physically stressful work.

In adulthood, people spend more time alone and benefit from solitude. The elderly spend even more time alone, and when it is voluntary (unlike when they are ill, immobilized, or divorced or widowed), they benefit from and cherish their solitude.

To summarize, while we are social animals who must live in a group to survive, group living can by itself be a source of stress. Biology has provided us a need for solitude to counter the demands and pressures of the group. Some of us need or prefer more solitude than others. For all of us, we need to remember that being alone, engaging in solitary activities, and being with our self are akin to pampering ourselves, to listening to us and to our feelings, thoughts, and the whispers of our souls. Burnout comes to those who forget to or cannot allow themselves to be alone.

SOLITUDE

To sit on rocks, to muse o'er flood and fell,
To slowly trace the forest's shady scene,

Where things that own not man's dominion dwell,
And mortal foot hath ne'er or rarely been;
To climb the trackless mountain all unseen,
With the wild flock that never needs a fold;
Alone o'er steeps and foaming falls to lean;
This is not solitude, 'tis but to hold
Converse with Nature's charms, and view her stores unrolled.

But midst the crowd, the hurry, the shock of men,
To hear, to see, to feel and to possess,
And roam alone, the world's tired denizen,
With none who bless us, none whom we can bless;
Minions of splendour shrinking from distress!
None that, with kindred consciousness endued,
If we were not, would seem to smile the less
Of all the flattered, followed, sought and sued;
This is to be alone; this, this is solitude!

—Lord Byron

Chapter 3

DO WE EXPERIENCE LONELINESS THROUGHOUT LIFE?

We struggle against loneliness even before we know the adversary. As children, we sense we are alone when we discover that our parents are not omniscient and all-powerful. As adolescents we discover our own mortality, and this intensifies our awareness of loneliness. As adults we come to realize that we are not merely alone within our bodies, but alone in the world.

(Hartog, 1980, p. 1)

Loneliness is the very painful and agonizing longing to be related to, to connect to others, and to be accepted and valued. As many others who have gone through personal tragedies, loss, shattered dreams, and emotional upheavals, Moustakas (1975) whose daughter was gravely ill and he was called by her physicians to decide whether to allow her to undergo a life-threatening operation. He found himself at the center of others' attention and support, and still he felt totally alone as he himself had to make that potentially life altering decision.

If being alone and lonely is terrifying and painful, being lonely in a crowd is much worse. Having others around, being geographically close to other humans, and even relating to them socially is considered in our Western culture a remedy for loneliness. There is an expectation that in being with others, one would feel part of the group, belong, and be fulfilled. Hence, being with others and still being unable to connect to them, not belonging, and lacking the intimate closeness and acceptance that we all yearn for, evokes not only loneliness but self-doubt, anger, and shame (Rokach, 1998b).

In this section we explore whether we are always, from the cradle to the grave, able to experience loneliness and how it feels. As Rook (1984a) observed, age, life experience, maturation, and personal awareness no doubt affect our loneliness experiences.

As we tend to intuitively expect, loneliness was found to be relatively frequent among the very old (Holmen, Ericsson, and Winbald, 1992). Drennan et al. (2008), however, added that changes in the frequency of experiencing loneliness over time are not linear and strictly correlated with age, but are related to life events and transitions, marital status, and health status. Nexhipi (1983) noted that loneliness occurs at all age groups, and the relationship between age and loneliness is a curvilinear one, whereby the young and the old are especially prone to loneliness.

Loneliness prevalence studies indicate that a significant portion of the population has experienced loneliness at some point in their lives (Heinrich and Gullone, 2006). Let's look down the tunnel of time and examine those happenings and experiences at each developmental stage that may give rise to loneliness.

CHILDHOOD

Small children disturb your sleep, big children your life.
—Yiddish Proverb

Margalit (2010) observed that loneliness is not an uncommon experience for children. Up to 15% of children have reported feeling lonely. Previously, there were doubts about whether children could experience or even understand what loneliness is. Loneliness in children is not as well researched as loneliness in adulthood, and some even argue that loneliness in children was not even considered before the 1980s (Betts and Bicknell, 2011). Some researchers maintained that because children do not form intimate relationships like adults do, they could not experience loneliness (Dunn, 2004). Sullivan (1953) proposed that loneliness first emerged during the adolescence years, and Weiss (1973) similarly believed that loneliness could only be possible during adolescence, the period during which the youngster is searching for additional attachment figures besides parents. At present, however, there is wide agreement that loneliness, indeed, exists in childhood and moreover can have significant, and at times far-reaching, effects (Cassidy and Berlin, 1994).

Many of us experienced loneliness in school, even in the lower grades. We can still remember the disappointment felt from rejection and the bitter taste of alienation. Learning or figuring out that our child is lonely or rejected by his peers can be devastating. In fact, many parents and researchers refuse to believe that loneliness is experienced by young children.

Research has repeatedly shown that children have fundamental needs to be included, to have close relationships, and to feel related and to belong (Baumeister and Leary, 1995; Coplan, Findlay, and Nelson, 2004). There is a correlation between high levels of loneliness in children and physical health problems, depression, peer rejection, victimization, aggression and anxiety, low self-esteem, and low social status (Bakkaloglu, 2010; Qualter et al., 2010).

Studies have repeatedly found that children as young as 5 years old do indeed grasp the meaning of loneliness, that childhood loneliness can be measured, and that it relates to peer group behavior and acceptance, quality and quantity of friendships, and representations of the self and peers (Cassidy and Asher, 1992; Cassidy and Berlin, 1994; William and Asher, 1992). Lonely children have been depicted as less accepted, less popular, and more likely to be rejected by their peers (Cassidy and Asher, 1992; Crick and Ladd, 1993). A combination of withdrawal and peer rejection distinguishes lonely children from nonlonely ones (e.g., Parkhurst and Asher, 1992). Longitudinal associations have been found between loneliness and low perceived self-competence and self-worth (Hymel et al., 1999; see also Crick and Ladd, 1993).

Exploring childhood loneliness is important, since experiencing loneliness at this developmental stage may predispose the person to experiencing loneliness in adulthood. This can result in the individual experiencing some of the psychosocial consequences associated with loneliness (Betts and Bicknell, 2011; Hymel and Franke, 1985). A recent survey by

Stoeckli (2009) found that 38% of third- to sixth-graders reported having experienced loneliness in school. Galanaki (2004) suggested that up to a whopping two-thirds of children experience loneliness in school. Asher and Paquette (2003) found that loneliness in childhood has been associated with lower levels of school and psychosocial adjustment.

Weiss (1973) described loneliness in childhood as follows:

> The provisions of social integration are distinct from those of attachment in that neither can be substituted for the other. The small boy whose sniffles lead to his being kept in by his mother while the others boys are out sledding, or, even worse, who is told by older boys to go home and not bother them, will not find the presence of a maternal attachment figure to sustain his feelings of well-being. Nor can children be solaced for the protracted absence of parents by the attention of age mates. Children need both friends to play with and parents to care for them. Similarly, adolescents need both a social network to provide engagement and an attachment figure to provide security. (p. 148)

It was consistently documented in several countries that preschoolers were able to identify situations in which they felt lonely and were able to differentiate between loneliness and solitude (Galanaki, 2004). Children's descriptions of their lonely times indicated that it was associated with peer exclusion, poorer friendship quality, and school avoidance. Research has found that loneliness is related to developmental difficulties such as anxiety, shyness, aggression, and cognitive difficulties. Not surprisingly, lonely children relate to other children in a manner that indicates their expectation to be rejected or ignored. "Their [the lonely children's] interpersonal approach, communication style, and nonverbal cues reveal their alienation, self-concept, as well as their beliefs in their inability to change their distressing situation and to develop satisfying social relations" (Margalit, 2010, p. 49). In other words, the alienated children perpetuate their social isolation through their behaviors and expectations, which end up being borne out by reality.

Winnicott (1964) defined attachment as the interactive process that goes on between the infant and his caregivers (usually his parents), reflecting the emotional ties within the family unit. It signifies the intimacy and assured protection that is, or is not, present in the infant's life. As is intuitively obvious, infants have an innate need for a secure and protective relationship with their adult caregivers. Through that connection, the infant develops mental representation (or, as Bowlby (1969) called it, "internal working models") of people, relationships, and intimacy that may have significant influence on his ability to relate to others intimately (Raikes and Thompson, 2008).

Winnicott (1964) identified the interplay between attachment relations and the ability to stay alone to be at the root of loneliness. If the child has a secure base at home, knowing that he is loved and is reliably supported by his parents, he can explore his environment and stay alone. This gives him the opportunity to get in touch with himself and learn what he wants and how to express his feelings. The child would feel less alone than the one who lacks confidence in the availability of his caretakers, anxiously attempting to remain in their proximity (Bowlby, 1973). Such children commonly experience loneliness when separated from their caregivers. Thus, a child who repeatedly encounters insensitive or emotionally unavailable caregivers will construct negative working models and be more prone to loneliness.

Children, except maybe those raised in orphanages, are raised by and within a family. The structure, roles, members, and various experiences of the family have a significant effect, especially on young children. As Ginot, an Israeli pediatrician, once said, "Children are like wet cement. Whatever falls on them makes an impression" [undated].

Research has indicated that family structure and communication styles are predictors of the development of loneliness in the family. Lower levels of family cohesion and parental disagreement and quarrels are predictive of a child's loneliness (Holahan et al., 2007). Children who grew up in families that emphasized cohesion and intimate relations will develop emotional connections, feel content, and will not tend to feel socially isolated (North et al., 2008). It should be noted, however, that youngsters who grew up in families that valued what we would consider good and healthy behaviors, such as independence, achievement, and intellectual pursuits, may be at higher risk of loneliness. The stronger the focus on these factors, the more likely the child is to experience stress, anxiety, and loneliness.

> The breakdown of the nuclear family, the reduced involvement on the part of the several fathers, the rising divorce statistics, and the increasing mobility of modern society all contributed to increased loneliness until it reached epidemic proportions.
>
> (Margalit, 2010, p. 270)

Families play an important role in promoting a child's emotional and social health, but they were also found to be related to a child's loneliness (Junttila, Vauras, and Laakkonen, 2007). The family's interactions and patterns of communication are considered particularly important for the development of a child's feelings of relatedness and his interpersonal skills (Bowlby, 1988). It has been found that children who grew up in a loving, comforting, and stable home, where they experienced warm and secure relationships with their family members, were better prepared for the outside world, the one lying beyond the boundaries of their parental home (Vandeleur, Perrez, and Schoebi, 2007). For example, familial cohesion was found to be related to the child's well-being and satisfaction (Green et al., 1991). Family climate was shown to facilitate a positive response to stress (Minuchin, 1974) and personal resilience (Kashdan and Rottenberg, 2010; Olson, 1986).

School has almost as much effect on children's lives as family. Unfortunately, it is not uncommon to discover that the very same child who came from an alienating and unaccepting family is just as alienated in school. Children who are socially isolated often feel lonely in school. Beyond their relationships with their peers, however, it is their unsatisfactory relationships with their teachers, their level of classroom participation, and a tendency to withdraw into daydreaming that increase their vulnerability to experience loneliness. Similarly, expressions of aggressive or bullying behaviors have often resulted in loneliness. During recess, those children who do not initiate social contact, negotiate in a friendly manner, and play activities with their peers end up spending most of their time in school alone, slowly developing a passive attitude toward their school environment and experiencing loneliness and alienation. From there, the road to lowered academic performance, emotional difficulties, or behavioral problems seems short and straight.

Ladd (1996) focused on school adjustment and defined it as "the degree to which children become interested, engaged, comfortable, and successful in the school environment" (p. 371). Therefore, being lonely in school may reduce the child's comfort in the classroom, and that in turn may affect his school adjustment. In relation to that, it was found that the more positively a child feels about the school environment, the better the child's academic performance compared to children who do not harbor such positive feelings toward school (Donelan-McCall and Dunn, 1997; Valeski and Stipek, 2001). Brett and Bicknell (2011) observed that "Children who are lonely may be poorly adjusted to school because the children lack the peer support that aids their transition and integration in the school" (p. 12). Indeed, Kochenderfer-Ladd and Skinner (2002) found that lonely children are less likely than nonlonely children to be involved with classroom activities.

A child's poor academic performance is a concurrent issue. That, in turn, is related to a lonely child's school avoidance behavior (Ladd and Coleman, 1997). This reduces his engagement with school activities (Ladd et al., 2000). Researchers also pointed out that a child's loneliness is associated with his academic competence. In a study of 7- to 13-year-olds, Marcus and Gross (1991) found that loneliness was negatively associated with academic performance.

To conclude, loneliness in childhood has been linked to a myriad of adjustment problems. For instance, lonely children commonly experience poor peer relationships, feel excluded, and usually have low-esteem (Bullock, 1998). They reported lower social acceptance and peer support (Hawker and Boulton, 2000; Kockenderfer-Ladd and Skinner, 2002), anxiety, and a tendency to react aggressively if confronted (Coplan, Closson, and Arbeau, 2007). Lonely children have also been found to engage in solitary behavior and to lack sociability, more so than children who did not report loneliness (Qualter and Munn, 2002). Lonely children who also have poor relationships may display sadness and boredom (Bullock, 1998). They have been found to exhibit social withdrawal and (possibly as a consequence) have few friends and conceivably may not be satisfied with the *quality* of those friendships as well (Renshaw and Brown, 2000).

> Sex education may be a good idea in the schools, but I don't believe the kids should be given homework. —Bill Cosby

ADOLESCENCE

> Snow and adolescence are the only problems that disappear if you ignore them long enough. —Earl Wilson

Adolescence, the stage between ages 13 to 18, has been described as a period of "storm and stress" (Arnett, 1999). It is a tumultuous period of life characterized by conflicts with parents (Laursen, Coy, and Collins, 1998), mood disruptions or extreme emotions (Larson and Richards, 1994), increased substance abuse (Johnston, O'Malley, and Bachman, 1994), heavy reliance on peers and vulnerability to peer pressure (Arnett, 1999), and risky behaviors that Hall (1904) called "a period of semicriminality" (p. 404). Consequently, maintained Heinrich and Gullone (2006), loneliness is most prevalent during this unsettling period.

Cassidy and Berlin (1992) contend that adolescence, being a transitional period, culminates in early adulthood, where most individuals view their sexual or intimate partners, rather than their parents, as their principal attachment figures. As such, this period ushers in a vulnerability to experiencing what Weiss (1973) called "emotional loneliness," and if the adolescent has a steady dating partner, he may experience social loneliness if sociable relations with his peers are missing (Margalit, 2010). Those studies, however, do not break down the statistics according to age groups, and consequently it is unclear to what percentage each age group reports having experienced loneliness. In addition to not having clear data on the prevalence of loneliness in the various age groups, it is also interesting to find out how, if at all, that experience changes when we grow up.

Research suggests that while loneliness may occur at younger ages, it is mostly experienced by adolescents—those very youngsters who are transitioning from childhood to adulthood (Culp, Clyman, and Culp, 1995; Perlman and Landolt, 1999). Heinrich and Gullone (2006) maintain that as children move into adolescence, they develop greater expectations in regard to their social relations and go from just wishing to share activities (that they may have wanted as kids) to wanting loyalty, support, intimacy, and a set of shared values from their friends (Parker et al., 1999; Parkhurst and Hopmeyer, 1999). Adolescents are likely to develop a preoccupation with their status, and establishing intimate relationships becomes increasingly important during this period (Erikson, 1963). Being unattached could consequently induce loneliness (Neto and Barros, 2000). Rathus and Etaugh (1995) pointed to the dramatic increase in school violence committed by teenagers. The traumatic and highly publicized high school shootings in Columbine, and in 2012 in Aurora Colorado, and in Taber Alberta, Canada, as well as in universities in the U.S., called attention to youth and their attempts to deal with life stresses and pressures. In both of these cases, as no doubt in many others, the youths who opened fire and killed their classmates were later described in the media as lonely, alienated by other children, and not fitting in (Kenna, 1999; Liao, 2001).

Brennan (1982) reported that "adolescence is the time when loneliness first emerges as an intense recognizable phenomenon" (p. 269). Other writers report that contrary to the stereotype of the lonely elderly, adolescence is the developmental stage that is most frequently associated with loneliness and alienation, since being included, accepted, and loved is of such crucial importance in the formation of one's identity (Ostrov and Offer, 1978; West, Kellner, and Moore-West, 1986). Empirical data has shown that more adolescents experience loneliness than the elderly (Peplau and Goldston, 1984; Van Buskirk and Duke, 1991). Sullivan (1953) theorized that loneliness is experienced so intensely in adolescence as a result of the emerging interpersonal needs for intimacy. Brennan (1982) suggested that among the factors that contribute to adolescent loneliness are developmental changes, separation from parents, maturation, striving for personal autonomy, and the struggle for significance. Van Buskirk and Duke (1991) maintained that most research on loneliness has focused on college students or adults. One of the studies that examined loneliness in various life stages was carried out by Rokach and Brock (1995). They concluded that the loneliness of those aged 13 to 20 differed phenomenologically from the loneliness experienced in adulthood or old age.

Research has described lonely adolescents as passively sad and turned inward (Van Buskirk and Duke, 1991). They were shown to experience greater stress (Cacciopo et al., 2000) and high levels of social anxiety (Goossens and Marcoen, 1999) and to suffer from behavioral problems such as peer rejection and victimization (Boivin, Hymel, and Bukowski, 1995) and social withdrawal (Kupersmidt et al., 1999).

Our research has indicated that emotional distress and intense pain, inner turmoil, and feelings of hopelessness are the most salient elements of loneliness that adolescents experience. Other elements of their loneliness are social inadequacy and alienation, which address the feelings of being socially inept, inadequate, and unpopular. This is followed by attempts to distance oneself from others so as to not experience more rejections and heartache (Rokach, 2000). Loneliness is particularly painful and troublesome at this age, because it is when the budding adult's peers and his reference groups replace his parents and the family as his main social support, when his self-esteem is fragile and self-awareness very high.

Adolescence: A stage between infancy and adultery.
—Ambrose Bierce

YOUNG ADULTS

Young adults, aged 19 to 30, are fresh out of adolescence and are starting their life journey personally and professionally. This period lacks the turbulence, sharp mood swings, and frequent conflicts that are the characteristics of adolescence (Hatcher et al., 1994). During their twenties, young adults in the Western culture break away from their family and prepare themselves for life vocationally, academically, and socially (Coon, 1992). During that time, they have to make decisions about sexuality, marriage, children, career, friendships, social and civic interactions, and more. They undergo cognitive and intellectual changes, and those may affect their decisions. During that time period, their growth is completed, but "their potential for greater strength increases during early adulthood and reaches a plateau at about age 30" (Dworetzky, 1991, p. 374). Toward the end of the third decade of their lives, many young adults are said to experience a minor life crisis, and they question the essence of life and the wavering assurance about previous choices that are at the heart of that crisis (Coon, 1992). Erikson (1963) suggested that after establishing one's identity during adolescence, the individual experiences a strong need to "establish an essential quality of intimacy in his or her life" (p. 417) and share a meaningful love or deep friendship with others. Dworeytzky (1991) observed that during young adulthood, the formulation of close friendships and intimate relationships is vital to the healthy psychosocial development of young adults.

ADULTHOOD

Middle age is when your age starts to show around your middle.
—Bob Hope

Adulthood, from 31 to 64 years of age, is characterized as being at one's peak physical and mental abilities. Adults are at the height of their vocational experience, growth, and career building. They attend to their nuclear families and may experience various trials, tribulations, and triumphs; they will also attend to their family of origin, and they experience birth, growth, and their offspring's striving for independence. Adults also must deal with the "daily hassles of life" (Arnett, 1999; Smetana, 1988; Steinberg and Levine, 1997). As people move along adulthood toward middle age, they come to experience declining vigor, strength, and youthfulness, as well as letting go of their unrealistic dreams and aspirations (Coon, 1992).

Youth is idolized by the media and the public as a representation of vitality, health, and sexual viability. But middle age is often a time when the rewards of power, money, and prestige are more apparent. Although it's not uncommon for people to report some depression on their fortieth birthday, since culture reveres youth, it's the middle-aged who have the power.

(Dworetzky, 1991, p. 376)

Adults lose physical speed, strength, and endurance, but unless the adult is an athlete, those will usually pass almost unnoticed. Between the ages of 45 and 55, women pass through menopause, and the decrease in sex hormone levels may bring about some physical changes. Men also go through andropause, with some consequent physical and sexual correlates. Men may look and measure their adulthood years by their careers and achievements, while women commonly measure middle age by the trajectory of their children's growth, their leaving the nest, and the time they start a family of their own. A midlife crisis may be brought about when adults become aware that they have less time remaining to live than they already did and that they will have to give up those goals and aspirations that they have not yet fulfilled. The empty-nest syndrome, which we have evidenced and which has been extensively researched and written about, heralding the children leaving their parents' home, is now reportedly nonexistent as parents are afforded almost unlimited opportunities to live a life that is rich, satisfying, and unencumbered by their parental obligations (Dworetzky, 1991).

Research commonly finds that during the busy midlife years, loneliness is reduced as life is so full of goals, activities, and responsibilities (i.e., parenting, parental care, social life, and work life, to mention several), and when adults are alone, they perceive and welcome it as time for themselves, a welcome solitude (Keene and Quadagno, 2004; Putney and Bengston, 2001). Research has found, however, that adults who have smaller social networks whose structure and quality are unsatisfactory to the person are likely to report more daily hassles and negative interactions with their spouse and children (Antonucci, Hiroko, and Merline, 2001; Heckhousen, 2001).

Loneliness has been shown to partly mediate between interpersonal stress, depression, anxiety, and health in adults (Aanes, Middlemark, and Hetland, 2010). What are the life changes and events that may be happening in adulthood that may be related to loneliness? Some events (which were reviewed by Holmes and Rahe, 1967) include widowhood or death of a parent, for example. Women in particular may become widowed during this time, and the death of a parent usually occurs during this life period. Up to 75% of Americans report losing both parents by their early sixties (Aldwin, 1990). Other losses may include the injury or death of a child, job loss, or spousal death; these events may be particularly stressful for adults in the prime of their life (Aldwin, 1990).

Other, chronic stressors that arise subtly include problems associated with family relationships or person-environment issues that might be problematic and cause stress (Pearline and Skaff, 1995; Wheaton, 1991). Wethington, Kessler, and Pixley (2004) characterized the adulthood years as a time of change due to the multiple roles that people have during that period. Some events that they may undergo include the departure of their children, caretaking of their parents, illness or death of their parents or grandparents, and retirement (see also Willis and Reid, 1999).

Part of the reason for the ugliness of adults, in a child's eyes, is that the child is usually looking upwards, and few faces are at their best when seen from below. —George Orwell

THE AGED

There's one advantage to being 102. There's no peer pressure.
—Dennis Wolfberg

Moustakas (1961) noted that old age is "fertile soil for loneliness" (p. 26), and, indeed, as many as 50% of adults ages 80 and older experience loneliness (Dykstra, van Tilburg, and de Jong Gierveld, 2005). Loneliness increases with age, especially after the age of 75 (Dykstra, 2009; Jylhä, 2004). As people age, social support is essential in enhancing their health and security (Yeh and Lo, 2004). Traditionally, age 65 has been seen as the age at which one may be considered "old." In many countries, and especially in North America, the law mandated retirement at that age. The North American population of older adults is rapidly increasing and is expected to reach 71 million by 2030 (Centers for Disease Control and Prevention (CDC), 2003). People in their sixties and seventies encounter changes in their bodies, their functioning, and in their environment (Korporaal et al., 2008). Some of the changes that the elderly face include declining health, possible cognitive changes, retirement and lifestyle changes, death of a spouse, and other significant losses that may lead to loneliness and social isolation (Rokach et al., 2007; Tilvis et al., 2004). Eighty percent of the elderly experience at least one chronic health condition and up to 50% experience two or more (CDC, 2003). These can interfere with their daily activities, and they report feelings of loneliness, depression, anxiety, and stress (Capezuti et al., 2006; Walker et al., 2007). Examining loneliness by gender of the elderly, 30% of women, compared to 25% of men, reported loneliness (Holmen et al., 1992).

The elderly also experience social inadequacy, alienation, and interpersonal isolation more than emotional distress or self-alienation. Since, on average, ill health *increases* with advancing age, many activities decline because of increased frailty, and as social roles and relationships decline in number and change, it is apparent why the elderly experience loneliness as social isolation and interpersonal disconnect (Eshbaugh, 2009; Yeh and Lo, 2004). Research reported that up to 40% of the elderly experience loneliness (Cohen-Mansfield and Parpura-Gill, 2007).

Studies that were conducted in North America, Asia, and Europe reported rates of loneliness among the population aged 65+ to be in the 5% to 10% range (see Yang and Victor, 2011). In Southern Europe (i.e., Spain and Portugal), researchers found even higher rates of 10% to 14%, and Eastern Europe had the highest rates of elderly loneliness, including Poland (21%), Russia (24%), and Ukraine (34%) (see Yang and Victor, 2011). Research on centenarians—those aged 100+—found that a key issue they faced in their day-to-day lives was social isolation (Hawkley and Cacioppo, 2010), and this isolation is connected with a loss of social support (Martin, Hagberg, and Poon,1997). With advanced aging we can expect a myriad of losses, including loss of social status, loss of friends, loss of a spouse, and many times at that age, loss of health. Those losses and the impairments in health can interfere with communication with family members and others and reduce the ability to maintain social connections when they are especially needed. These losses may further contribute to the elderly's loneliness (Savikko et al., 2005).

Wilson et al. (2007) observed that loneliness was inversely related to levels of physical and cognitive activities. Loneliness was associated with a more rapid decline in global cognitive functioning, semantic memory, and perceptual speed in elderly with Alzheimer's disease. A number of factors have been identified as contributing to the loneliness of this age group. Among them are poor health status (Alpass and Neville, 2003), physical limitations (McWhirter, 1990), chronic illnesses (Alpass and Neville, 2003), and stress. Loneliness in older age has been shown to be correlated with variables such as living alone (Wenger et al., 1996), quality of the relationship with children (Long and Martin, 2000), quality of the marriage (De Jong Gierveld et al., 2009), personality (Newall et al., 2009), and self-perceived health (Kaasa, 1998) (for a metaanalysis, see Pinquart and Sörensen, 2001). Aartsen and Jylha (2011) found that increased feelings of uselessness, nervousness, and low mood led to a higher likelihood of becoming lonely in the future.

Having been linked to many aspects of life, loneliness may thus shed light on why the elderly may consider themselves to be lonely. Loneliness has been shown to be associated with the age, marital status, health condition, and related care needs of the elderly (Beeson, 2003). It is reported that more often than not, the aged, after widowhood or divorce, seem to prefer to continue living independently for as long as possible. While it has been established that marriage can help maintain social well-being, living alone is one of the main risk factors for loneliness (Allen, Blieszner, and Roberto, 2000; Dykstra and de Jong Gierveld, 2004).

Given the higher levels of institutionalization and solitary living in individualistic cultures (e.g., North America and Western Europe), Dykstra (2009) suggested that we may find lower levels of adult loneliness in these places than in more collectivistic cultures. She claims that people believe that the elderly are actually lonelier than the elderly themselves report. Becoming old is frequently equated with being lonely, however, Dykstra et al. (2005) concluded after conducting a longitudinal study that this is true only among the very old, ages 80 years and up. Overall, the elderly in collectivistic cultures (e.g., Italy, Greece, South America) are more used to living and closely interacting with the community. As a result, when that interaction is slowed down due to ill health or other causes, the elderly report being lonely to a greater extent than those living in Western Europe (Germany, Scandinavia, or the Netherlands) where aloneness is more familiar, and thus old age, with its decreased social intercourse, is not perceived as a lonelier period in life (Dykstra, 2009; Reher, 1998).

While we in the Western culture and Western psychology mistakenly assume that the older we grow, the more individualistic we become, Montagu (1962) observed that "the older a person grows, the more complex does the network of his social relationships become, and the more deeply involved does he become with society...He (thus) becomes less and less of an individual and more and more of a person" (p. 63).

In examining the loneliness of elderly who lived alone in the Chinese population, it has been suggested that the relationship between living alone and psychological well-being may be more salient in Chinese populations (Alexander and Baker, 1992) in which the collectivist culture places a strong emphasis on family togetherness and the interdependence of family members. Chinese traditional values still dominate the family system of modern Chinese communities today, and most elderly people prefer and are expected to live with their children (Chi, 1998). Thus, living alone may arguably have a particularly strong negative effect on the well-being of the elderly but that is mainly attributed to the loneliness of those who live alone.

Living alone is one of the main factors affecting the health of the elderly. The aged who live alone face increased risk of falling, dehydration, hypothermia, infections, and physical injuries (Yeh and Lo, 2004). It is not uncommon to find the elderly living alone who have fallen or died in their homes. It should be noted that research has repeatedly pointed out that older adults who are in poor health are most prone to loneliness. The level of social participation is related to the health situation of older adults. Thus, the increase in life expectancy that is occurring in the Western culture, the related increase in the length of time that the elderly live with disabilities, and the death of one's peers that most elderly experience increase the risks for shrinking social networks and increase their loneliness (for reviews, see Pinquart and Sörensen, 2001; Victor et al., 2000).

Johnson, Waldo, and Johnson (1993) reported that up to 62% of older Americans experience loneliness. Living alone and the absence of company, as well as the desolation that was brought about by bereavement, were found to be among the causes of loneliness in old age. Loneliness was not related to the level of contact that the elderly had with family members. Health status was found to be both a predictor and a consequence of loneliness (Fahey and Murray, 1994). A recent study by Luong, Charles, and Fingerman (2011) seems to confirm that assertion. They observed that social network size indeed decreases with age, but the quality of the interactions older adults have with those forming their social network was perceived as more satisfying as people aged (Lansford, Sherman, and Antonucci, 1998). Social network size does, indeed, place older adults at risk for loneliness and dissatisfaction with their social lives (van Tilburg, 1995). Research found that while social network size decreases with age, the interactions that the elderly have with friends and family are more satisfying (Lansford et al., 1998). Older adults also report experiencing more positive emotions when interacting with their social partners than do younger adults (e.g., Charles and Piazza, 2007).

Although the elderly experience the loss of close network members, the number of close confidants and the amount of social support they receive from them remain the same throughout later adulthood (see the review by Ertel, Glymour, and Berkman, 2009; Schnittker, 2007). Another interesting observation by Luong et al. (2011) was that the elderly seek relationships that are most rewarding and disband ties that are less so. Typically, people who are part of the most intimate social connections, such as romantic partners, close friends, and siblings, remain fairly constant across adulthood (Kahn and Antonucci, 1980). The elderly express a cognitive bias where they attend to positive and avoid negative experiences. This same bias is not observed in younger adults (Charles, Mather, and Carstensen, 2003). Research suggests that older age is associated with greater social expertise, which means that older adults make judgments about potential social partners that allow them to successfully avoid confrontations (Hess, 2005; Hess and Auman, 2001; Hess et al., 1999). Retired older adults seem to enjoy greater freedom in selecting their social partners and their leisure activities (Ginn and Fast, 2006; Rosenkoetter, Garris, and Engdahl, 2001); that helps decrease social conflicts and alienation and provides the elderly with a positive and enriching social experience.

Drennan et al. (2008) found *family loneliness* to be related to having lower income, being widowed, having limited contact with children and relatives, and having limited access to transportation. *Romantic loneliness* was related to older age, lower income, or being widowed, separated, or divorced. Other researchers repeatedly found that being in a romantic relationship provides an important source of both social and emotional support.

In my research (Rokach et al., 2007) I examined the qualitative aspects of loneliness in the elderly population. It is very interesting to note that the most salient element in the elderly population was the growth and development component. Older women in particular have been found to have larger and more multifaceted networks than men do in that they have more friends and provide and receive more support (Tomassini, Glaser, and Askham, 2003). Consequently, it stands to reason that the elderly—particularly women—who experience loss and loneliness and are thus more in need of support, assistance, and connection to others, may also greatly appreciate the support that they have and attribute their growth to the care and support they received. Yeh and Lo (2004) state, "As people age, social support is a key environmental factor enhancing health, participation, and security" (p. 130).

Men and women have been found to differ in their levels of isolation and need for social support, and while women were more interested in intimacy, men were more in need of friendship ties (Allen and Oshagan, 1995). Research indicates that while only 5% to 15% of seniors over the age of 65 experience loneliness, up to 50% of those older than 80 reported feeling lonely frequently (Prince et al., 1997; Smith and Baltes, 1993). Older women experience higher levels of loneliness than older men, although older women are more likely than men to interact with their adult children and receive support from them when they are in a crisis (Kaufman and Uhlenberg, 1998; Pinquart and Sorensen, 2001). Physical health problems, obviously, restrict the number and frequency of social contacts (Kline and Scialfa, 1996).

> I've finally reached the age where my wild oats have turned into All-Bran!
> —Tom Wilson

In a study of 711 men and women across all ages that I conducted in Canada, instead of exploring the intensity of the experience of loneliness (as psychological research often does), using the model described previously, I examined the qualitative aspects of loneliness and whether at different ages and life stages we experience it differently. As you may have intuitively guessed, the results confirmed that at different ages, people's loneliness is quite different. The next sections describe each element of loneliness, examining how the age groups experienced it, if they did at all.

We investigated the experience of loneliness across the life span by examining how it is experienced during adolescence, young adulthood, middle age, and the later years. To the best of my knowledge, no other research addressed the phenomenology of loneliness and its various facets and compared it across different age groups. The results from that study confirmed that loneliness, is indeed, experienced differently throughout the life cycle. Let us examine it more closely and see how the experience of loneliness differed at various life stages.

The *emotional distress* dimension captures the pain, emotional turmoil, sadness, helplessness, hopelessness, and feelings of emptiness that are such an integral part of experiencing loneliness. While the young adults had the highest score, the seniors scored the lowest on this element. Coon (1992) adopted Erikson's (1963) theoretical formulation and suggested that after establishing a stable identity during the adolescence period, a person experiences a strong need to "establish an essential quality of intimacy in his or her life" (p. 417). At that stage in one's life, one is prepared to share a meaningful love for deep friendship with others. In line with Erikson's view, Buchman and Johnson (1979) reported that 75% of all college-age men and woman ranked a good marriage and family life as their primary adult goal. During that stage in one's life, the formulation of close friendships and intimate relationships is vital to the healthy psychosocial development of young adults. It is not surprising that our research findings suggest that this group reported experiencing most acutely the pain and agony that loneliness at that age entails (Dworetzky, 1991).

The elderly, on the other hand, have been reported to experience less loneliness, and when they do encounter its pain, they may evaluate it differently and thus reduce its influence on them. Delisle (1988) noted that, in general, the majority of the aged lead a relatively active social life, and many of them are in contact with their children. The majority of the elderly in our study expressed satisfaction with the quality of their relationships with their loved ones (Delisle, 1988; Peplau and Perlman, 1982), and overall, "the ones suffering significantly from their isolation are in the minority" (Delisle, 1988, p. 364). Consequently, the pain of loneliness and the emotional turmoil it generates are lessened as we age. The elderly experience retirement, the death of loved ones, and a deterioration of their physical health and, at times, their cognitive functioning as well (Brown, 1996). In comparing themselves to their reference group—other seniors with similar losses—they likely see their hardships as a natural occurrence at that stage of life and consequently are able to regulate their emotions more effectively than younger people do (Rabasca, 1999).

The *social inadequacy and alienation* dimension addressed the perception of social isolation and the concomitant self-generated social detachment and self-deprecation that followed. We found that young adults experience this more intensely than the other age groups, while seniors had the lowest score. As we already mentioned, the elderly are indeed by and large less socially isolated than their stereotype might suggest (Delisle, 1988). Anthony (1998) brings numerous examples of seniors who are active, well connected socially, and productively create and contribute to society. In contrast, the young adults who are striving to establish themselves economically, educationally, and professionally; attempting to start a family, keep their childhood friends, or make new ones; and craving relationships, intimacy, and love (Coon, 1992) may be acutely aware of the possible shortcomings that may prevent them from achieving these goals or not achieving them at all. The majority of people break away from their families at this age. Leaving home is usually associated with building new friendships with other adults. These friends then serve as substitutes for the family and as allies in the process of breaking ties (Coon, 1992). Seeing other young adults who may be socially well supported and who may have achieved positions of power, prestige, social desirability, or marital and familial harmony could conceivably lead to self-attribution of social inadequacy, self-deprecation, and perceived social alienation.

Growth and discovery depict the beneficial effects of loneliness, including gaining a deeper understanding and appreciation of oneself, increasing the value one assigns to friendships and social support, and discovering the resources one has to cope with the pain of loneliness. As Moustakas (1961) so poignantly put it, "In absolutely solitary moments man experiences truth, beauty, nature, reverence, humanity. Loneliness enables one to come to a life with others with renewed hope and vitality (and) with a fuller dedication" (p. 102). This element, maybe more than other facets of loneliness, relates to one's cognitive appraisal of the experience and the maturity and daily lessons that were accumulated along the path of living. Intuitively, then, we can expect a positive correlation between age and the growth and discovery element. The present findings seem to support such a trend. The lowest score was reported in youths, while the seniors had the highest score.

Arnett (1999), in a meta analysis of the research on adolescence, noted that this "storm and stress" period, as Hall (1904) referred to it, "is not a myth that has captured the popular imagination but a real part of life for many adolescents and their parents in contemporary

America" (p. 324). Arnett contends that this is a period of life that is rife with conflicts with parents, mood disruptions, engaging in risky behaviors, and establishing one's identity. During this period, adolescents commonly break away from parental dominance and prepare for their future by dating, establishing friendships, and selecting a vocation or a future career. Clearly, such a turbulent and future-oriented stage is not amenable to the reflection and self-understanding that the more stable life changes could encourage. Adolescents possess the cognitive abilities to manipulate abstractions, to examine hypothetical ideas, and to generalize from concrete to abstract ideas (Dworetzky, 1991). They lack, however, sufficient self-knowledge, maturity, and life experience to fully appreciate the growth and discovery that loneliness can bring about.

The interpersonal alienation subscale highlights the sense of utter aloneness associated with the experience of being abandoned. It also addresses the absence of intimacy, having no satisfying meaningful intimate relationships. As was the trend with the previous subscales, here as well young adults scored the highest, while seniors scored the lowest.

Dworetzky (1991) contends that "young adults face many choices and predicaments in our society. They must make decisions about sexuality, marriage, children, career, friendships, social and civic interactions, and much more" (p. 383). During that period the individual experiences a need to achieve an essential quality of intimacy, being prepared to share meaningful love or deep friendship with others. As Coon (1992) observed, not all are fortunate enough to be socially accepted and find, or be able to maintain, meaningful and close relationships, and yet, even those who are married or sexually involved have no guarantee that intimacy will prevail; "Many adult relationships remain superficial and unfulfilling" (p. 417). Failure to establish intimacy with others may result in a deep sense of isolation. In light of our study, it appears that young adults experience interpersonal alienation significantly more than the elderly who were viewed as having gone through irreversible losses (Brown, 1996), suffered decreased physical capabilities and mental capacities, experienced lost social status, and suffered from isolation and interpersonal alienation (Kuypers and Bengston, 1973; Matras, 1990).

Recent research appears to shed light on the present results. Despite the inevitable losses that accompany old age, those healthy and independent seniors who can enjoy peer group support and the community of those who, as Fischer (1977) said, are "roughly alike" (p. 111) feel socially connected and valued. Brown (1996) reported that peer group participation is increasing among the aged throughout the world. In North America, the healthy aged may live independently in retirement communities and age-specific public housing (Malakoff, 1991). Under those conditions, and in light of Mroczek's (quoted in Rabasca, 1999) observation that seniors "gear their lives toward maximizing positive effect and minimizing negative effect" (p. 11), it stands to reason that they will experience interpersonal isolation to a significantly lesser extent than young adults who are not so generously socially supported.

Scoring on the *self-alienation* dimension varied widely among youths, young adults, and adults. It depicted self-detachment, which is often characterized by numbness, immobilization, and denial of the distress inherent in loneliness. While youths scored the lowest, young adults scored the highest on this subscale. As Hall (1904) and Arnett (1999) pointed out, adolescence is indeed a period of storm and stress, identity forming, rebelliousness, independence seeking, and mood disturbances. It is safe to argue that, especially during this period, the developing person is in touch with herself, is full of vigor and motivation to achieve and/or change unsatisfactory life situations, and may experience loneliness as a painful and distressing experience but not as an immobilizing event that results in self-detachment. The situation of the young adults is quite different. Those years are occupied with striving to prepare for a secure future; redefining familial relationships; building intimate friendships, marriage, and family planning; raising children; and caring for elderly parents (Blood, 1972; Doherty and Jacobson, 1982; Dworetzky, 1991; Glick, 1979). It is little wonder that very little time is left for young adults to engage in solitude (Larson, 1990) in order to get in touch with their deeper feelings and to reach a true understanding of the meaning and significance that life events have for them. Naturally, they will then experience self-alienation, numbness, and the familiar participation in the "rat race."

Although our study did not investigate the extent of the occurrence of loneliness in various life stages, present results indicate that with the exception of growth and development, young adults appear to experience most keenly and painfully the various facets of loneliness. It is interesting to note that only in the young adult group were significant differences found between men and women, with women scoring consistently lower than men on all subscales of our questionnaire. North American sex roles of women stress that they should be subjective and emotionally sensitive (Feldman, 1982). Consequently, it was observed that North American women are more at ease sharing their pain and anxiety (Rokach and Sharma, 1996). It is thus suggested that young adult women, in particular, experience less pain by openly expressing their emotional distress and attracting social support. Their male counterparts were not socialized to express their emotions openly and are more deeply involved in the early-adulthood tasks of laying the financial, vocational, and social foundations of their future (Geary, 1998). Irons (1979) observed that men throughout the world compete for cultural success to a larger degree than women do. That is, they compete for control of culturally important resources and for the establishment of social status. Thus, they are less apt to be reflective and expressive of their distress and experience loneliness more keenly and painfully. It is, however, unclear why gender differences exist only in that age group.

In examining each of the genders separately, while the men's scores differed significantly across age groups, the women's scores did not. This finding lends itself to the hypothesis that the North American socialization of men influences them to a lesser extent than it does women. Whereas men's experiences of loneliness change as they pass through life depending on their age, maturity, and life experiences, women's loneliness experiences appear to be more stable and somewhat less influenced by societal and situational factors. As Geary (1998) so aptly pointed out, "Men are not from Mars, and women are not from Venus, although there are many times when both sexes seem to be from different planets" (p. xi).

Chapter 4

LONELINESS OF MARGINALIZED GROUPS

Society is far from being homogeneous and if we, the people who are normative and doing relatively well, suffer the pain of loneliness, then the marginalized by definition, know it more intimately than we do. In this chapter we will review the loneliness endured by several of those groups.

THE HOMELESS

No one really cares if I die today or tomorrow because they are so consumed with making money, having power, and control, and even if I died today...people won't care...But one thing is for sure, sitting here all alone, cold and desperate to find a little bit of meaning to my life, I realize that really there isn't any. —Sonia, a homeless woman, quoted in Hill (2001)

It is (thankfully) safe to assume that most if not all the readers of this book probably do not have firsthand experience with being homeless. It may therefore be beneficial to take a closer look at homelessness. There is generally no accepted definition of *homelessness*. Farrington and Robinson (1999) suggested that homelessness means, literally, to be without a home. A more useful definition, however, is Kelling's (1991): "Homelessness is much more than rooflessness; it is the lack of a secure and satisfactory home" (p. ii). Moreover, some of the homeless even have a place to stay, but most are transient and move frequently from one living quarter to another (Kramer and Barker, 1996). That reminds me of something I myself evidenced. In the 1990s, I used to join a Salvation Army truck, and after we prepared coffee, sandwiches, and other necessities for those who did not have them, several of us boarded a specially equipped truck and drove around town at 4:00 a.m. in Toronto's darkened streets and alleys to feed the homeless. At one of our stops, a man wearing a jacket and tie, who looked like a middle-class citizen, came to the truck. He drank two cups of coffee and thanked us profusely for the socks and sandwich we gave him. After he left, I told the man who operated the truck that there was no harm in feeding this man who was probably on his way to work and just felt like having a cup of coffee. He replied that this man was actually a regular at the truck. He had lost everything in a nasty divorce, and although he had a job, he had no place to live and could barely afford to buy food with his meager salary.

Interestingly, whereas people once got most of their knowledge about the homeless from newspapers, TV programs, and movies, North Americans now see scores of homeless on the streets in their own cities (Hombs, 1994). In a study he conducted on the homeless in Canada, O'Reilly-Fleming (1993) found that homelessness is neither invisible nor far removed from the mainstream of society. He observed that the Canadian homeless are overwhelmingly average, drawn from all walks of life, represent all social and economic levels, are composed of males and females, are singles and entire families, and consist of young children and the elderly. It is estimated that out of a population of approximately 25 million Canadians, about 100,000 are homeless (O'Reilly-Fleming, 1993). Coates (1990) estimated the number to be 1 to 3 million in the United States.

WHO ARE THE HOMELESS?

It is reported that 55% of the homeless are unemployed, 52% receive social assistance, 33% are alcohol abusers, 15% are drug abusers, 20% are former mental patients, 9% have been evicted, and 3% have physical disabilities (O'Reilly-Fleming, 1993). An attempt by Rosenthal (2000) to classify the homeless resulted in three categories:

1. The "slackers": poor and lonely street dwellers who, in Rosenthal's words, are homeless as a result of their own "laziness, irresponsibility, and substance abuse" (p. 113)
2. The "lackers": those who lack competency to live a good life through no fault of their own, much as children, or those with mental and/or physical illness
3. The "unwilling victims": competent members of society who are caught by circumstances beyond their control, such as hard economic times, that may bring about plant closings, gentrification, and physical abuse in some cases. (The man in the truck incident belongs to this category.)

The daily survival of the homeless, which Sumerlin (1996) viewed as a "career," requires adaptation and focusing on food, clothing, and personal hygiene. As the duration of homelessness increases, daily routines develop and adaptation to street life progresses (Snow and Anderson, 1993). The homeless are not only burdened with issues of daily survival, violence, and social ostracism, but they also experience loneliness, depression, and fear (Coates, 1990; Hombs, 1994; O'Reilly-Fleming, 1993; Sumerlin, 1995). To support themselves, the homeless may try to find work, ask family or friends for money, panhandle, enter into prostitution, deal drugs, and steal (Greene et al., 1999; Hagan and McCarthy, 1997). It was found that society's negative feelings about homelessness led to homeless people's feelings of worthlessness, loneliness, social alienation, and even thoughts of suicide (Kidd, 2004).

Since homelessness is such a growing problem in North American society, and since the homeless are basically society's outcasts who are suffering but are shunned by society, loneliness is no doubt their loyal companion (see also Sumerlin, 1995; Layton, 2000). The stress that is caused when one is unable to secure such basic needs as food, shelter, employment, and some money coupled with the isolation and alienation that the homeless frequently experience can lead to depression, anxiety, and loneliness (Kidd, 2004; Lloyd-Cobb and Dixon, 1995).

Several years ago, I (A. R.) compared the loneliness of the homeless with the loneliness of the general population. The results of that study confirmed that the homeless did indeed, experience loneliness in a different way from the general population. In that study, I examined each of the five dimensions that denote the qualities or qualitative aspects of loneliness. Overall, it was found that the homeless had significantly higher scores on the interpersonal isolation and the self-alienation dimensions but they scored significantly lower on the growth and development one. These outcomes seem to be intuitively expected. Layton (2000) reported that on Toronto's streets, for instance, one homeless person dies every six days. Solarz and Bogat (1990) report that, "Living on the street day in and day out can take a psychological toll on a person. Isolation, alienation, and deprivation can create high levels of stress in the homeless" (p. 310). The homeless are subjected to aggression and victimization on the street (Whitbeck et al., 2000), and some struggle with psychiatric problems as well (Kidd, 2004; Solarz and Bogat, 1990).

Under such duress, it is quite clear that growth and development, even if experienced by the homeless, would not be noticed; its importance would be overshadowed by the challenge of survival, and they would most probably not report it as a positive aspect of loneliness. It is not difficult to see why being so stigmatized, isolated, shunned by society, and alone is not seen as having any positive dimensions to it.

Just to refresh, the interpersonal isolation dimension of loneliness addresses the feelings of alienation, abandonment, and rejection that are commonly related to a general lack of close relationships and/or the absence of primary romantic relationships. The homeless, as we could anticipate, scored higher than the general population on this subscale. The homeless may be one of the most stigmatized, isolated, and victimized groups in Western society (Layton, 2000; O'Reilly-Fleming, 1993).

Related to the social isolation that the homeless may feel is the social stigma that is so prevalent and intensely perceived by the homeless. This stigma can cause low self-esteem, loneliness, suicidal ideation, and feeling trapped. Feeling trapped, which arouses feelings of helplessness and hopelessness, has emerged as being central to suicidality among homeless youth (Kidd, 2004, 2006). Of these variables, the perceived stigma, suggested Kidd (2007), was most strongly associated with loneliness.

Being so burdened by a constant struggle for daily survival, and suffering the unrelenting impact of poverty, neglect, domestic violence, substance abuse, and stigma, it is easy to understand homeless people's profound sense of social isolation (Buckner and Bassuk, 1997; MacLean et al., 1999). Moreover, their living conditions, and the concomitant fear, sense of failure, stress, and possibly depression (Kidd, 2007; Lloyd-Cobb and Dixon, 1995; Sumerlin, 1995, 1996) also explain the sense of self-alienation, the detachment from one's self, which they experience. That self-alienation is characterized by immobilization and denial that they may use as defense mechanisms against their searing pain—pain with which the homeless are so familiar.

PHYSICAL DISABILITIES

When severe illness occurs, it seems like an unending nightmare that robs us of our
resources, insults our dignity, and often pushes us to the brink of desperation.
(Dell Orto, 1991, p. 333)

Most likely, when you think of marginalized groups, you would not consider those who
are dealing with illness and physical limitations to be among them. My research into the
loneliness of these people—the sick, the handicapped, and the terminally ill—may justify
their inclusion into this group. Here is a brief review of some illnesses and how the people
dealing with them cope with their social isolation.

The World Health Organization (WHO) distinguishes between *impairment, disability,*
and *handicap*. An impairment is considered the *loss* of function of a specific body organ or
system (e.g., muscular weakness). A disability is the inability to perform normal activities
(such as walking). A handicap is the result of impairment or disability, which consequently
prevents the individual from fulfilling a social role, such as an inability to work. This model,
which aids in understanding and identifying the physical, psychological, and social impact of
a disease, injury, or congenital disorder, has been widely used (Kennedy, 1999).

Disability applies to a multitude of medical and traumatic conditions, ranging from mild
to severe. Its trajectory may be sudden, such as a spinal cord injury that may occur as a result
of an accident, or gradual and slow, such as with multiple sclerosis (MS) or Parkinson's
disease. The disabled person is said to be disadvantaged in reaching personal and economic
independence and may be unable to function autonomously in one or more areas in life either
temporarily or permanently (Robinson, West, and Woodworth, 1995).

Depending on the organ or the bodily system affected, physical disabilities may cause
problems related to movement, vision, or hearing. Consequently, a person's ability to
communicate with others may be affected or diminished. The occurrence of the disability can
be a psychosocial shock (Thurer, 1991). Dell Orto (1991) pointed out the subjective
experience involved in every illness. He suggested that disabilities may bring out the best and
the worst in people and can deplete or create resources. He believes that coping with a
chronic disability is an ongoing process that may require all of a person's resources and
familial support. Throughout their lives, people experience varied "mini" losses, such as a
dent in their new car, the loss of valuable time when they are stuck in a traffic jam, or getting
into an argument with a friend (Robinson et al., 1995). Such *temporary* losses occur
throughout life and can cause anxiety and unhappiness yet they are, thankfully, reversible.
Serious and permanent losses like physical disabilities can, according to Robinson et al.
(1995), violate our identity and negatively affect our dreams and hopes.

One element that can make sick people feel marginalized is what Kennedy (1999) called
the "disabling environment" (p. 138)—the architectural and social inaccessibility of our
society that is geared toward able-bodied people. Kennedy saw chronic disability as
interwoven with emotional distress, turmoil, and pain, and he highlighted the emotional and
psychological distress that the disabled experience, including feelings of powerlessness,
helplessness, and social isolation. Radnitz and Tirch (1997) observed that adaptation to
everyday physical barriers can be quite challenging for those with physical disabilities, and
they consequently suffer stress and possibly embarrassment and social awkwardness. Kitto
(1988) further stated that "illness is something which affects the smooth working of our lives.

It stops our work pattern, interferes with our relationship, allows pain or distress to invade us, and stops us from pursuing our dreams" (p. 111).

Being different from able-bodied people, becoming dependent on others for what the rest of us may take for granted, and looking different physically can cause feelings of stigmatization, marginalization, and loneliness (Davis, 1995; Lupton and Seymour, 2000). According to Lupton and Seymour (2000), "While the person with a disability may not feel ill or be in pain, her or his body is coded as a dysfunctional body. It culturally exists as a transgression, a body that straddles boundaries and therefore is anomalous, 'matter out of place,' and threatening to the social order" (p. 1852). Prince et al. (1997), while not having focused on the disabled, found that loneliness was more common among people living alone, who lacked supportive neighbors, or who had little contact with friends, all of which could apply to those with a disability. Halvorsen (2000) asserted that social exclusion of marginal groups, including the disabled, drug addicts, the mentally ill, poor people, and immigrants, creates an overall poorer quality of life, more isolation, and increased loneliness (Blekesaune and Øverbye, 2000).

Due to the fact that health problems involve restrictions in the maintenance of someone's personal relationships, it can be expected that disability negatively influences one's social network and thus leads to loneliness (van Tilburg and Broese van Groenou, 2002). Disabling health problems can make emotional closeness and intimacy more difficult due to issues like a decrease in the number of activities shared with friends, lack of spontaneity, and problems with sexuality (Lyons et al., 1995). In addition, when the disabled person is married or in a long-term, intimate relationship, his irritability may lead to frustrations and anger in the well spouse, which can result in feelings of resentment in both partners and alienation from one another (Booth and Johnson, 1994; Cutrona, 1996).

Examining the effects of disability on the loneliness of the disabled individual or his spouse, Korporaal, Broese van Groenou, and van Tilburg (2008) found that for both men and women, disability is related to higher levels of emotional loneliness. For men, the effects were cumulative, while for women, the effects of their own and spousal disability slightly reinforced each other. The authors added that the effects of their own and spousal disability on emotional loneliness were not reduced or altered by the frequency of the emotional and instrumental types of support that were offered to the spouse.

Let us briefly examine several conditions that create disability and intensify one's feeling of alienation, because Thirsen and Clausen's (2008) study found a strong correlation between disability, loneliness, and depression.

Multiple Sclerosis

Multiple sclerosis (MS) is a progressive, demyelinating disease of the central nervous system. Its etiology is unknown, and there is no cure or effective treatment (Soderberg, 2001). MS afflicts three times as many women as men, and it is only second to stroke as the most common neurological disorder in the United States (Halper, 2001). Most patients, at least in the early stages of the disease, experience a relapsing/remitting course, in which a period of acceleration of the disease is followed by a period of remission and reduced or eliminated symptoms (Matthew and Rice-Oxley, 2001). Common MS symptoms include fatigue, visual abnormalities, bladder and bowel dysfunction, sexual dysfunction, reduced mobility, cognitive impairment, and emotional disturbance (Halper, 2001). Due to the fact that MS usually strikes during the productive years of life and because of its wide-ranging symptoms, issues related to employment and to connection to one's family and social support network are often prominent. Emotional difficulties, especially depression, may follow. As Kalb and Scheinberg (1992) observed, "Even though the range and severity of symptoms vary considerably among individuals, its impact will extend to work roles, economic status, relationship within the family, and relationship between the family and the large community" (p. 1). Kuebler et al. (2002) noted that the chronic nature of MS may erode and wear down the social support network of the patient, thus increasing the feeling of marginalization and loneliness.

Arthritis

Baker (1983) stated that, "Arthritis...is one of our oldest afflictions and the one we are least likely to escape" (p. 2). Those afflicted with arthritis include infants and people in their eighties. The word *arthritis* is derived from the Greek word *athron*, meaning "joint," and *itis*, meaning "inflammation." It is thus an inflammation of the joints, which causes pain that can range from mild to excruciating (Baker, 1983). Rheumatoid arthritis is an incurable disease of unknown etiology. Its onset is typically during the thirties or forties. As can be easy to determine, arthritis has a significant impact on one's life, draining the person of energy while causing joint and muscle pain. In the majority of cases, symptoms may take years to present themselves. In some cases the velocity of the illness is more rapid, and the person becomes severely disabled over a short period of time (Locker, 1983). In the United States, arthritis affects 43 million people (Millar, 2003). Although the level of pain may fluctuate, arthritis causes pain on a continuous basis, and it is often inescapable (Locker, 1983). As such, loneliness and social isolation, which are related to one's inability to fully partake in life's vibrant rhythm, characterize those afflicted with arthritis (see Liang and Daltory, 1985).

Osteoporosis

Osteoporosis is the most prevalent metabolic bone disease in North America, with half of its victims being older than 75 (Gold, 1999). Osteoporosis, which was once thought to be a normal part of aging, is now referred to as a "silent but crippling and deadly epidemic" (Hall Gueldner, 2000, p. 1). It is a systemic skeletal disease that is expressed by low bone mass and increased bone fragility. Osteoporosis is more common in women than in men, and it can change one's appearance and cause deformity (of which the most notable is kyphosis, or dowager's hump). That deformity is visible and over time affects other body structure, mobility, and range of movement (Hall Gueldner, 2000). One of its most powerful characteristics is pain (Melton, 1999). As pain and limitations of activity increase, so do the ill person's vulnerability to bone fractures, sadness, hopelessness, and their consequent decreased social activity (Falvo, 1999).

PSYCHIATRIC PATIENTS

In a recent survey in the United States, 1,300 people diagnosed with mental illness were asked to describe their situation and how it felt to be a psychiatric patient. They pointed out that they were worried that others would look on them unfavorably, were offended by mass-media messages about mental illness, avoided telling others about having a psychiatric problem, and were advised to lower their expectations in life. They felt shunned by others only because they had been labeled as having psychological problems (Thornicroft, 2006). Ottai, Bodenhausen, and Newman (2005) said, "In the Western culture, stereotypes of people with mental illness often suggest that they are dangerous, incompetent, unable to care for themselves, and childlike" (p. 100).

A definition of mental illness rests on a clinically significant behavioral pattern that leads to distress (e.g., a painful symptom), on disability (an impairment in an important life function), or a potential loss of personal freedom (American Psychiatric Association, 2000; Corrigan and Kleinlein, 2005). The general public commonly bases its inference that one may have mental illness on four signals: psychiatric symptoms, social skills deficits, physical appearance, and labels that were attached to some people (Corrigan, 1998).

Phillips (1990) suggested that society views psychiatric patients as damaged, defective, and less socially marketable than the general population. That perception of these people as damaged goods is what affects their social status and leads to stigmatization. Schizophrenia, the most severe psychiatric illness, may cause its sufferers to behave in what the public may perceive as "unpredictable," "strange," "dangerous," "bizarre," or "useless" ways and while some schizophrenics remain chronically ill and disabled, many, with the use of modern medications, show minimal impairment and their symptoms remit. Despite that, they are subjected to social discrimination, rejection, and alienation. Lai, Hong, and Chee (2000), who studied the social stigma of mental illness, indicated that, interestingly, in their study the stigma apparently was brought about by the psychiatric label and not from the presence of a chronic illness.

Among the symptoms of severe mental illness, people may encounter patients who display inappropriate affect, bizarre behaviors, language problems, and talking to oneself (Corrigan and Kleinlein, 2005). Such behaviors, together with body language and deficit in eye contact, inappropriate personal appearance, and lack of personal hygiene, tend to mark and stigmatize the person, who may then feel alienated and unwanted (Mueser et al., 1991; Penn et al., 1994; Penn, Mueser, and Doonan, 1997). Stigmatization of people with mental illness may be propelled by psychiatric labels, the patients' own labeling, or by association—for example, a patient coming out of an office in a mental hospital. Link et al. (2001) found that once members of the general public discovered the mental illness, they were quick to label and stigmatize the person even without any aberrant behavior. They found that psychiatric labels were closely associated with negative societal reactions, stigmatization, and consequent alienation (see also Thornicroft, 2006).

Recent data from the Substance Abuse and Mental Health Services Administration (SAMHSA) indicated that more than a whopping 60% of those with mental disorders are unemployed and up to 25% of this group lives under the poverty level (Willis et al., 1998). People with severe mental illness face stigma and discrimination in our society and consequently suffer harm and social status loss. The stigma they face brings about an insular support system, which relies mainly on family members, who themselves are affected by stigma. Psychiatric patients then adopt that social stigma, devalue themselves, and sometimes take it upon themselves and identify with the attitudes and negative approach that society holds toward them. In their study of the results of such stigma, Rishter and Phelan (2004) found that these patients suffered alienation and distress. Alienation, then, reduces self-esteem and may contribute to depression and loneliness. "Many people with disorders like schizophrenia suffer interpersonal, self-care, and cognitive deficits that prevent them from achieving their life goals. These persons are often unable to live independently, get competitive jobs, make a satisfactory income, and develop long-term intimacies. Persons with severe psychiatric disabilities typically rate their quality of life as poor" (pp. 201–202). People who suffer from a psychiatric illness often lack the appropriate social skills that could help them create a supportive social network. They face not only stigma (which is a public attitude) but also discrimination that is an outright behavior that excludes and rejects them. Discrimination, just like a stigma, results in a diminished social support network (Corrigan and Penn, 1998; Fisher, 1994).

Sufferers of mental illness may become increasingly withdrawn and consequently experience intense social anxiety that may lead to loss of friends and great difficulty in creating a social support system. It was found that frequent admissions to psychiatric services were positively correlated with the social isolation that is vital for one's rehabilitation and coping with one's mental illness (Bradshaw and Haddock, 1998). Erdner et al. (2005) suggested that the most significant consequence of the public's negative attitudes and stigmatization of the mentally ill is that they become an alienated population. Moreover, Erdner et al. (2005) found that psychiatric patients perceive themselves as undesirable, vulnerable, and clearly part of a marginalized group. Many have little hope about their lives changing, and they are worried about their future. Some experiences of people with mental illness are apparently so traumatic that the result is that they feel a need to completely stop doing what had previously been a very important aspect of their lives. The hurt, distress, embarrassment, or humiliation that they suffer when interacting with the public may completely curtail their attempts to form new relationships that could provide them the much needed support they crave or to find jobs (Thornicroft, 2006).

Borge et al. (1999) studied loneliness among psychiatric patients and indicated that about half of the patients studied felt lonely, and loneliness is one of the most a fundamental problems for psychiatric patients. The first sentence of their research article on psychiatric patients is, "Social isolation and loneliness are highly prevalent among people with mental illness...[and they] tend to remain isolated from the heart of their communities" (Elisha, Castle, and Hocking, 2006, p. 281). They added that social isolation makes it harder, sometimes much harder, for psychiatric patients to recover or even just cope with their mental problems. They suggest that there is an inherent clinical and psychosocial divide in the mental health system, which may address the patient's psychiatric and physiological needs, but not their psychosocial ones. An interesting study that focused on the psychosocial aspect of mental illness explored how people who befriend the psychiatric patients may affect them. Bradshaw and Haddock (1998) stated that their research indicated that "for clients who live alone, who are most often likely to experience loneliness and isolation, befrienders may form a link with the 'outside world,' providing valuable social contact and the opportunity to talk to someone" (p. 718). As is the case with other maladies that result in or bring about loneliness, a support system is vitally important and can empower the ill person to cope with and at times even overcome the illness.

LESBIAN, GAY, AND BISEXUAL ORIENTATION

Another marginalized group is comprised of those whose sexual orientation is different from the majority. It seems this group has its share of loneliness. Martin and Knox (1997) explored the extent to which urban gay men experienced loneliness. Results showed that their sample of urban gay men scored higher on the UCLA loneliness scale than college students, nurses, and the elderly (Russell, 1996). These findings lend credence to their hypothesis that loneliness experienced by gay men (and most probably lesbians and bisexuals as well) is associated with not just the intimacy of their personal relationships but also their perceptions of how supportive their community is.

Grossman, D'Augeli, and O'Connell (2002) studied older gay and lesbian individuals who grew up during a time when their sexual orientation was not as well tolerated as it is today. Therefore, in addition to the negative events related to society's homophobia, lesbians, gays, and bisexuals experienced stigmatization and discrimination as members of a sexual minority group in a primarily heterosexual society. That experience revolved around the incongruence between their culture, needs, and experiences and the greater societal structures (DiPlacido, 1998; Meyer, 1995). Accordingly, 63% of the participants experienced verbal abuse and 29% were threatened with physical violence. Moreover, more than 29% of the participants reported being victimized by a person who threatened to disclose their sexual orientation to others, thus shaming and humiliating them publicly. As indicated by Herek, Gillis, and Cogan (1999), stigma-based personal attacks on lesbian, gay, and bisexual adults occur more frequently and can affect their mental health even more than physical attacks.

Grossman et al. (2002) reported that 27% of their participants felt lonely and 52% reported that the responsibility for loneliness was perceived by them to be their own fault.

> The older lesbians, gay men, and bisexuals who participated in this study experienced their early identity development at a time when homosexuality was synonymous with abnormality, inferiority, and shame. As a result, many feared that identifying their sexual orientation would lead to humiliation, dishonor, and rejection, so they remained invisible. They tended to internalize society's **negative stereotypes** about them, developing feelings of unworthiness and self-hate. (Grossman, et al., 2002; p. 37)

Kuyper and Fokkema (2010) studied LGBs (lesbians, gays, and bisexuals) who grew up in Holland at a time when homosexuality was considered a sin or a sickness (Keuzenkamp and Bos, 2007; Schuyf, 1996). This situation may have made them quite susceptible to negative well-being outcomes. Kuyper and Fokkema (2010) asserted that one important aspect of well-being that causes severe distress among the general elderly population is loneliness (Loving, Heffner, and Kiecolt-Glaser, 2006). A study by Grossman, D'Augelli, and O'Connell (2002) of older LGBs in North America demonstrated that the situation in the United States is similar to that found in the Netherlands.

Since the beginning of the twenty-first century, societal attitudes have become more positive toward LGBs, but this is especially true among the younger generation (Adolfsen and

Keuzenkamp, 2006; van de Meerendonk and Scheepers, 2004). That means older LGBs are still likely to be surrounded by peers from the older generation, who most probably hold negative views about homosexuality.

It was repeatedly suggested that minority stress—the stress felt by a societal minority group whose needs, customs, and way of life may differ from that of the general population (DiPlacido, 1998; Meyer, 1995, 2003)—may be related to the loneliness felt by LGBs (Fokkema and Kuyper, 2010). Meyer (1995, 2003) stated that being an LGB individual can be stressful and lead to adverse mental health consequences.

Kuyper and Fokkema's (2010) study was conducted in order to examine whether minority stress processes can add to our understanding of the different levels of loneliness among older LGB adults and which specific minority stress processes contribute to loneliness the most. Their findings suggest that minority stress processes added strongly to the explained variance of models that predicted loneliness. They also found that three minority stressors contributed to general loneliness: experiences with discrimination, expectations of prejudiced reactions, and the LGB network. The authors stated that the positive relationship between loneliness and minority stress is in line with outcomes of other studies on social and health-related issues (e.g., mental health, relationship quality, sexual problems, domestic violence, HIV (human immunodeficiency virus) risky behavior, substance use, job stress, body image concerns) (Balsam and Szymanski, 2005; Hatzenbuehler, Nolen-Hoeksema, and Erickson, 2008; Zamboni and Crawford, 2007). Furthermore, Ueno (2005) pointed out the protective influence of LGB social support networks at school. Martin (2003) found that gay and lesbian adolescents are particularly vulnerable to social isolation and loneliness. Friendships among LGB adolescents, however, reduced psychological distress.

Abbott and Liddell (1996) found that lesbian and gay students reported being alienated among their heterosexual peers in college. The authors further stated that for lesbian and bisexual women, alienation is especially pronounced. That may have resulted in more than 50% of them having contemplated suicide (Bradford, Ryan, and Rothblum, 1994). Guyer et al. (1989) suggested that children's and adolescents' sexual orientations are greater predictors of the decision to commit suicide than other factors such as ethnicity, for example.

Westefeld et al. (2001) found that loneliness and depression were positively correlated and indicated that when such students are depressed/lonely, they have fewer reasons for living. They found that it was not sexual orientation per se but concurrent issues related to isolation, prejudice, and loneliness that explained this finding. They also found that homophobia was prevalent in many colleges.

In older LGBs, and not just during the college years, substance use, the number of sexual partners, negative affective states (e.g., depression, anxiety, loneliness), and a lack of social support have been consistently associated with sexually risky behaviors (Martin and Knox, 1997; Parsons et al., 2003; Semple, Patterson, and Grant, 2000). Several factors are associated with loneliness in gay men. One is their negative perception of their identity and lack of social support, which often results in loneliness. Social prohibitions against same-sex relationships cause many gay men to hide, ignore, and suppress their feelings (Martin and Hetrick, 1988), resulting in their identity development being strongly, negatively influenced in that they believe they are different, which in turn exacerbates isolation and feelings of loneliness (Flowers and Buston, 2001; Newman and Muzzonigro, 1993). The lack of social support that those from a marginalized group experience contributes to lower psychosocial functioning and increased loneliness.

Unlike other groups that are marginalized in society and that were also studied, a significant proportion of LGBs do not have familial support. Many LGBs report that they feel forced to choose between living an openly gay life without the support of their families or living a "double life" by hiding their sexual orientation out of desperation to retain their family's support (Caraballo-Dieguez, 1989; Chwee et al., 2003). Consequently, those who "come out of the closet" face the lack of an important source of social support that may increase their vulnerability to loneliness (Newman and Muzzonigro, 1993). For those who remain connected to their family but cannot be open about their sexuality, loneliness is exacerbated by the inability to express their true self or sexual identity. Many LGBs experience anxiety that they deal with in different ways. Compulsive sexual behavior is one way gay men, for instance, attempt to reduce their anxiety and the accompanying loneliness (Coleman, 1992). Individuals who engage in compulsive sexual behavior may do so as a way to relieve their anxiety and ease their loneliness (Hayden, 2000). The problem with using sex as a way to deal with anxiety is that it is often only a temporary solution, resulting in gays remaining anxious, isolated, and lonely.

INTELLECTUAL DISABILITIES

McVilly et al. (2006) reiterated that stable and rewarding interpersonal relationships are, most probably, the single most important factor influencing a person's quality of life (Kennedy and Itkonen, 1996). Evidently, the literature points out that relationships provide practical aid, emotional support, information, and assistance with decision making (Hughes 1999). Relationships are also important as safeguards against stress and psychological illness (Duck, 1991). It has been shown that there are clear mental and physical health benefits associated with the development of interpersonal networks and the loneliness associated with having unsatisfactory social networks (Bloom et al., 1978; Lynch, 1979; Stanfeld, 1999). Yet for many people with disabilities, satisfying interpersonal relationships are rare or nonexistent (Amado, 2004; Blum et al., 1991; Duvdevany and Arar, 2004; Fleming and Stenfert-Kroese, 1990; Rapley and Beyer, 1996).

People with intellectual disabilities especially suffer from loneliness (McVilly et al., 2006). In examining the social networks of people with intellectual disabilities, Hill, Rotegard, and Bruininks (1984) found a connection in only 36% of people in an institutional facility and in only 58% of those intellectually challenged in community residences.

Emerson and McVilly (2004) found in a large population-based study that adults with intellectual disabilities had little social activity, such as visiting friends or having friends visit them. Furthermore, they found that most activities the intellectually challenged engaged in with friends occurred in public places, with little or no opportunity for the privacy that would have encouraged closeness and intimacy. In a study examining students aged 11 to 16 years with mild intellectual disability, Heiman and Margalit (1998) found higher levels of self-reported loneliness than was reported by students without a disability.

McVilly et al. (2006) found that the lack of connection with a social network was a critical factor linked to the participant's experience with loneliness. This finding is consistent with the observation made by Pescosolido (2001) about the centrality of social networks in the lives of people with disabilities. Similarly, Krauss, Seltzer, and Goodman (1992) reported that 42% of adults with an intellectual disability living at home were found to have no friends outside of their immediate family. Clearly, those afflicted with intellectual disability are carrying an especially heavy burden; they cannot enjoy intellectual faculties as we know them, and they are usually lonely and not truly understood by others.

Chapter 5

LONELINESS, ILLNESS, HOSPITALIZATION, DISABILITY, AND DEATH

It is much more important to know what sort of a patient has a disease than what sort of a disease a patient has. —William Osler

Loneliness, which can involve both excruciating physical and mental suffering, is an ancient nemesis. Loneliness is implicated in numerous somatic, psychosomatic, and psychiatric diseases (McGraw, 2000). It is a mundane yet arcane human affliction that is often hazardous to health and hostile to happiness (Martens and Palermo, 2005, p. 298). In this chapter, I review the experience of loneliness as it affects us when we are not doing well, such as when we are ill, hospitalized, or terminally ill.

Sullivan (2003) observed that, "For the past 200 years, medicine has pursued the positivist goal of erasing the subject from medical perception. A fully objective view of disease was made possible when the autopsy was integrated into clinical medicine through clinico-pathological correlation...The observed body became the project of modern medicine" (p. 1596). An autopsy is done not for the deceased's sake but for the disease's and the cure's sake. The pathologist is not interested in the patient as a person but only as a source of data about the disease and its effects on the body so the idea of the health care system is to objectify its study and assessment of disease without much awareness of or emphasis on the person who has the disease: the one who suffers (Foucault, 1973). Modern medical science has always been focused on, and at times obsessed with, death. Death has provided medicine with a clear "enemy." Medical research has focused on conquering death-causing diseases. That goal gave medicine social prestige and a gigantic budget. Physicians were, and often still are, seen as possessing supernatural abilities in their fight against serious diseases and death (Sullivan, 2003). Only lately are we becoming more aware of the importance of considering *who* the patient is. This is what primary care medicine claims to do; first care for the patient and then focus on the disease the patient has. As such, it is in times of illness and hospitalization, and especially when we are near death, that we are most dependent on the love and support of friends and family.

Mijuskovic (1992) maintained that no one is completely self-sufficient, and the individual could not exist without the whole, the society in which he lives, and that his happiness is closely related to the community to which he belongs. Loneliness is a universal experience shared by all humans. Being a uniquely subjective experience, it is caused by the individual's personality, environmental and social changes, and his history (Rokach and Brock, 1996). That history includes, of course, the illnesses and the cultural context of those illnesses that one may have been afflicted with.

Geller et al. examined both loneliness and ill health and found that loneliness is a significant risk factor for many ailments. They also studied whether lonely people visited emergency rooms more often than nonlonely people. Their research demonstrated that while there was no positive correlation between illness and visits to the ER, there was indeed a positive association between loneliness and the number of times per year that an individual visited the ER. One of the lonely individuals in their study visited the ER nine times in one year. Let's examine the association of illness, hospitalization, and death with loneliness and alienation.

ILLNESS

The biggest disease today is not leprosy or tuberculosis, but rather the feeling of being unwanted. —Mother Teresa

In our research on loneliness and illness, I have reviewed several chronic and debilitating conditions and examined how those who are afflicted with them are affected by loneliness. Examining first the effects of loneliness on the body and the immune system, Cohen (1985) observed that life events, including separation, loss, and feelings of hopelessness, that are associated with the experience of loneliness affect the endocrine system through abnormal secretion levels from the pituitary and adrenal glands. That may adversely affect the immune system and therefore decrease the body's ability to fight illness and/or result in an increased risk of cancer. The deterioration in health through this process is most probable in people with already compromised immune functioning, especially people with Acquired Immune Deficiency Syndrome (AIDS), an immunosuppressive disease (Kiecolt-Glaser and Glaser, 1992). Research has found that high loneliness scores are also correlated with significantly lower levels of natural killer cell activity, which are the lymphoid immune cells that play a role in cancer protection and appear to have antitumor and antiviral capabilities (Kennedy, Kiecolt-Glaser, and Glaser, 1988).

Leventhal and his colleagues (Benyamini, Leventhal, and Leventhal, 2000; Leventhal, Leventhal, and Cameron, 2001) suggested that there are five components to how people conceptualize illness:

1. The *identity of the disease* is very important for the patient's behavior, since the symptoms themselves are not sufficient to initiate help-seeking behavior, but labeling could make the difference. For instance, chest pains that are labeled "heartburn" will cause a very different behavior than those labeled "heart attack." It is obvious that an individual will experience less emotional arousal when the label of their illness indicates a minor physical problem than if it is a more serious illness. The label carries with it information about the problem, a projection as to the length of sickness, and the possible treatment course.

2. The *timeline* may not always correspond with the diagnosis. For instance, people with hypertension, a chronic condition, tend to view it as acute and that will affect their adherence to treatment and the manner in which they will cope with the illness.

3. *Determination of cause* is important. After a diagnosis, most of us would want to know the cause of the problem, which will affect how we seek treatment and how we will comply with the instructions of the health care professional. For instance, being told the pain in our leg is a result of a fall would generate a completely different reaction than if we are told it might be bone cancer.

4. While we would expect the *consequences of the disease* to be clear once a diagnosis is made, people may incorrectly understand the diagnosis and that may affect the treatment they seek. For instance, many consider a diagnosis of cancer a death sentence, so they will assume the situation is hopeless and will not seek treatment.

5. The *controllability of a disease* has to do with how people view the possibility of treating and controlling the disease. If they, for instance, view the situation as beyond hope, they may not seek treatment, while those who believe medical science can help them will take much more interest in their course of treatment.

Psychological variables, including loneliness, have been associated with changes in immune functioning and may weaken the body's capacity to fight disease (Kennedy, Kiecolt-Glaser, and Glaser, 1988). The immune system protects the body from illness through the recognition and destruction of antigens, disease-causing substances like bacteria, viruses, and cancer cells. Once an antigen enters the body, lymphocytes (T cells or B cells) multiply in order to combat the antigens; B cells create immunoglobulins that act as antibodies that combine with and neutralize harmful antigens (Barlow and Durand, 1995). Kiecolt-Glaser et al. (2002) pointed out that more and more research now indicates that psychological factors are clinically significant and are correlated with immune-related health outcomes, including infectious diseases, cancer, autoimmune diseases, and HIV.

Hagerty et al. (1996) observed that the nature of people's interconnections with others and their perceptions of such relationships can have a strong influence on physical and mental health. Research has repeatedly demonstrated that those with social support systems were much healthier (Glaser et al., 1992), whereas those with fewer social ties had increased susceptibility to illnesses (Cohen et al., 1997). In general, when close relationships are discordant, they are often associated with immune deregulation (Kiecolt-Glaser et al., 2002). It has been suggested that people who have well-established social supports seem to be better able to cope with stress and chronic pain. Moreover, social isolation rivaled other well-established risk factors such as cigarette smoking, high blood pressure, obesity, and sedentary lifestyle, as factors in poor health (Brannon and Feist, 2004). It was also found that people with higher rates of social support have better health and lower rates of mortality. In that study it was observed that participants who had the fewest social ties were two to four times more likely to die than those who were well supported (Berkman and Syme, 1979).

Lynch (2000) described a study carried out by two researchers at Johns Hopkins University between 1948 and 1964. The researchers followed 1,185 healthy and relatively young medical students and asked them a variety of questions about their families, health, and lifestyle. Later, when those students became physicians, some started to develop serious health problems and others died prematurely. The investigators went back to their data and discovered that the medical students who had developed various cancers prematurely had described their parents as cold and aloof. A similar study that was carried out at Harvard University found that people who rated their parents as cold and their relationships with them as strained experienced significant increases in poor health. It was found that an astonishing 91% of those who reported they were not close to their mothers while growing up developed serious medical problems in midlife, including coronary heart disease, hypertension, ulcers, and alcoholism. Even more remarkable was the finding that 100% of those who reported that both of their parents were cold and aloof had developed medical problems by midlife. Of those who were close to their parents, only 47% had serious medical problems by the same age (Russek and Schwartz, 1997).

LONELINESS ASSOCIATED WITH MEDICAL DIAGNOSIS

Many of us are familiar with the feelings of anxiety and loneliness following the diagnosis of a disease or illness. Just as distressing, however, is the experience associated with awaiting a diagnosis or procedure (see, for example, Chappy, 2004). A few studies have focused on this particular experience. Patients undergoing diagnostic processes are prone to feelings of uncertainty and anxiety (Liao et al., 2008). Mishel (1988) delineated the "uncertainty in illness" theory, which describes uncertainty as a cognitive state in which a person is unable to determine the meaning of illness-related events. Uncertainty is experienced when one does not have sufficient information to categorize an event. This can have an effect on one's psychological state, often manifested as anxiety, because feeling uncertain about one's fate and feeling helpless are considered threatening (Mishel, 1988).

Several studies have examined women's experiences with abnormal mammograms or women who were told they might have breast cancer. Breast cancer is one of the most common and deadly cancers in women. Women experience anxiety from the time a breast lump is discovered or an abnormal mammogram report is received, and it increases right up to the surgery (Chappy, 2004). Thorne et al. (1999) interviewed women who were waiting for a diagnosis after an abnormal mammogram. Many described the time from the mammogram until the diagnosis as being "in limbo." Many of the women described serious disruptions to their daily activities, insomnia, panic attacks, inability to concentrate at work, inability to plan, and preoccupation with fear. They considered themselves suspended from their participation of normal living. In addition, some of the women's coping strategies involved keeping their abnormal mammogram results a secret from loved ones. Such disconnection from normal daily routines and from loved ones may promote feelings of isolation and loneliness. Cancer patients may experience difficulties in interpersonal relationships as a result of these constraints and restrictions. As the ability to cope with the disease decreases, the quality of cancer patients' social interactions also decreases (Bloom and Spiegel, 1984; DeHaes and Van Knipperberg, 1985). Feelings of hopelessness, helplessness, and fear of death are present in the minds of patients fearing a diagnosis of cancer, and they typically lack the social and emotional support they desperately need, which may lead to feelings of loneliness (Cohen, 1985; Friedman, Florian, and Zernitsky-Shurka, 1989).

Similar research with men awaiting a prostate cancer diagnosis has been performed. Prostate cancer is one of the most common malignancies affecting men. Men who are undergoing screening for prostate cancer report anxiety levels that are significantly higher than baseline levels experienced by men in the general population (Dale et al., 2005).

Other studies have focused on the experiences of patients awaiting medical procedures, particularly radiologic procedures. Compared to many other types of medical procedures and surgeries, image-guided diagnostic procedures are often cutting edge and less invasive. Patients awaiting these procedures report anxiety, fear of the unknown, anxiety about further interventions, destruction of body image, disruption of life plans, loss of control, and disability (Johnston, 1980; Viegas, Turrini, and da Silva Basts Cerullo, 2010). Many medical professionals may assume that such minimally invasive diagnostic tests create less distress than more risky invasive approaches, but such diagnostic procedures still cause uncertainty and stress (Mishel, 1984). Flory and Lang (2011) conducted a study comparing the distress levels in women awaiting large core breast biopsy for diagnosis of suspicious lesions with the distress levels of women undergoing invasive, potentially risky treatment of diagnosed malignancies of the liver and uterus. All of the groups in the study experienced abnormally high levels of perceived stress and depressed mood, but only the women awaiting breast biopsy experienced abnormally high anxiety levels. The authors concluded that the invasiveness of the procedure has less influence on patients' distress, and most probably feelings of alienation, than does the uncertainty of outcome. Similar research exploring patients' anxiety associated with interventional radiology procedures supported the notion that patients experience considerable anxiety prior to undergoing interventional procedures, many of which are considered, by their physicians, easy procedures for the patients (Mueller et al., 2000). Those procedures may be followed by a diagnosis of an illness—possibly a serious one—that no doubt causes the patients to feel alone as they await an answer that could impact the rest of their lives.

A phenomenological study by Brown et al. (2006) examined the waiting period for liver transplantation. Patients with end-stage liver disease who were accepted for liver transplantation must wait anywhere from 210 days to 3.5 years (Brown et al., 2006). The waiting process for liver transplantation is a difficult period that is filled with uncertainty and loneliness. Patients worry they may never find a donor or that there will be complications from the surgery (Brown et al., 2006; Streisland et al., 1999). Brown et al. (2006) discovered that while waiting for liver transplantation, patients experienced large fluctuations in their emotions and had difficulty retaining a positive outlook. This period also involved a loss of important roles and increasing disability that were associated with a sense of isolation and loneliness. Patients noted difficulty in meeting social obligations and maintaining relationships as well as lack of reassurance, comfort, and consistent information from the transplant teams as factors that contributed to their sense of social isolation. They also reported feeling lonely in a turbulent situation, not knowing what is to come, and evidencing that others cannot truly understand their experiences (Brown et al., 2006). Much research has focused on patients' psychological state after diagnosis. In fact, many of the resources in the hospital and health care field are focused on helping patients deal with their diagnoses once they have them. To our knowledge, there are not many support infrastructures designed to help patients cope while they are awaiting diagnoses, which, as described above, can be equally distressing. This time period harbors feelings of uncertainty, anxiety, fear, disconnection from daily living, and difficulty maintaining social relationships, all of which contribute to feelings of isolation and loneliness.

Illness may be a crisis for the ill person as well as for her family. Chronic illness may cause a redefinition of one's identity, and the relationship between married partners and between parents and children can be affected (Christ et al., 1993; Palmer, Canzona, and Wai, 1984). Families of young children who are ill suffer even more, because in addition to the heartache in seeing their child ill, they must also continue their relationship and manage the host of problems related to caring for a sick child (Knafl and Deatrick, 2002). In addition, there may be concerns about the financial demands of the treatment, of absence from work, and of the future, should the ill have a terminal condition.

Cancer

Cancer was described as early as 1500 BC in the Ebers Papyrus. Later, Hippocrates designated the name "cancer," and the Greek physician Galen first described and named tumors. Cancer is not a single disease but a group of diseases that have in common the unregulated growth and spreading of cells. After scientists were unable to find any parasite or infectious agent, the theory of mutation developed to explain the cause of cancer. This theory holds that cancer develops because of a change in the cell, a mutation, which results in the cell growing in a mutated form until a tumor is formed. The most common characteristic of all cancers is the presence of neoplastic tissue cells that grow rapidly and rob the host organ of nutrients. If the tumors are malignant, they metastasize, spread much more rapidly to other organs. That in turn results in the tumor becoming like a parasite and taking priority when it comes to consuming nutrients, damaging body functions (Brannon and Feist, 2004). Brannon and Feist (2004) explain, "Although some people may have a genetic predisposition to cancer, the disease itself is almost never inherited. Behavior and lifestyle are the primary contributors to cancer" (p. 252). Loneliness is prominent among them in both causation and cure.

Due to the constraints and restrictions of the illness, cancer patients often experience difficulties in interpersonal relationships (Dunkel-Schetter, 1984; Engleberg and Hilborne, 1982; Revenson, Wollman, and Felton, 1983). As the disease progresses and their ability to cope with it decreases, so do the quality of their social interactions (Bloom and Spiegel, 1984; De Haes and Van Knipperberg, 1985). Weisman (1979) proposed four psychosocial stages that cancer patients experience: (1) the "existential plight" stage, a period of about 100 days beginning with the diagnosis and extending through primary treatment; (2) the "mitigation and accommodation" stage, when the patient is behaving in the psychosocial equivalent of having the disease, even during remission; (3) the "decline and deterioration" stage; and (4) the "preterminality and terminality" stage. Feelings of hopelessness, helplessness, and fear of death are present in the minds of patients during each stage, and they typically lack the social and emotional support they desperately need, which may lead to feelings of loneliness (Cohen, 1985; Friedman, Florian, and Zernitsky-Shurka, 1989).

A factor that may lead to or increase one's loneliness is that cancer often produces physical changes that may be adverse to others (Wortman and Dunkel-Schetter, 1979). For example, during treatment, patients may experience bleeding tendencies, hair loss, mouth sores, and unattractive skin reactions (Stearns et al., 1993). People are known to have fears about contracting the disease from others, and they may consequently shy away from the ill at the time when they are most needed and their friendship is crucial (Cohen, 1985; Mages and

Mendelson, 1979). Furthermore, some believe that avoiding speaking openly about the disease, on the part of the patients themselves, their family members, or medical personnel, to avoid further distress may only contribute to the lack of social interaction, or at least a meaningful and open one (Cohen, 1985; Holland, 1977; Schwartz, 1977; Silberfarb and Greer, 1982). Being hedonistic creatures, Singer (1983) asserted, it is part of human nature to avoid pain, so cancer patients and their families often experience tremendous difficulty relating to each other and working with the problem at hand in a constructive way. Finally, as the cancer progresses, opportunities for social activities decrease due to the disabilities caused by the disease (Bloom and Spiegel, 1984). Friedman et al. (1989) observed that approximately 50% of their 60 subjects felt that their loneliness was associated with illness or illness-related situations. Unfortunately, while cancer patients may be facing a monumentally distressing life event, they also face a decrease in their social support resources or even adverse and unhelpful support, which further increases their feelings of being misunderstood and unaccepted (Friedman et al., 1989; Koopman et al., 1998; Martin et al., 1994).

> Don't defy the diagnosis; try to defy the verdict.
> —Norman Cousins

HIV and AIDS

AIDS, a result of exposure to the human immunodeficiency virus, is the disorder in which the immune system becomes ineffective, leaving the body defenseless against bacterial, viral, parasitic, cancerous, and other opportunistic diseases. As a result, the body cannot protect itself and succumbs to the disease without a chance of recovery. Therefore, infections and other illnesses that normally can be treated and cured lead to death in those with AIDS. While some researchers believe that AIDS has been around for thousands of years, it was discovered and identified in the beginning of the 1980s (Corbitt, Bailey, and Williams, 1990).

AIDS is considered the deadliest plague in history, and as of 2001, an estimated 40 million people have been infected. When those people die, HIV will surpass the number of victims of the bubonic plague of the fourteenth century (Lamptey, 2002).

Research investigating the psychosocial experience of people with HIV and AIDS indicated that people afflicted with that disease not only suffer from the physical disease process, but they also suffer from the emotional agony that is created because there is no cure for AIDS and from the public's fear and suspicion that results in blaming the victim. Many believe some infected people deliberately infect others, either intentionally or because they refuse to practice safe sex (Hellman, 1994).

The social stigma attached to HIV and AIDS leads to the rejection of these patients, and it has been argued by Sontag (1988) that in the North American culture, where cancer was once the disease of fear and shame, today this position has been replaced by HIV and AIDS, since many of these patients' experiences parallel those of cancer patients. As Cherry and Smith (1993) observed, "The body of social knowledge that explains cancer as a dreaded disease, a curse, or a punishment now has been transferred to HIV (and AIDS) patients" (p. 189).

Surveys indicate that a large percentage of AIDS patients live alone. In many cases they do not have an intimate relationship, or they reported that their partner had died of the disease (Christ, Wiener, and Moynihan, 1986; Nokes and Kendrew, 1990). Most frequently, the individual loses both a job and the social contacts associated with employment. In many cases, alienation from the self and society intensifies the pain of loneliness (Cherry and Smith, 1993). People in the North American culture have been socialized into fearing the process of death and dying so individuals with AIDS suffer the ultimate aloneness as they face an inevitable death (Bascom, 1984; Cherry and Smith, 1993).

This experience is common to both cancer and AIDS patients, as well as those with terminal diseases in their final stages of illness (Bascom, 1984). Kaye (1991, quoted by Vachon, 1998) further stated that "ultimately one is alone with the diagnosis with the need to receive treatment, and with the reality of one's life being threatened. Nothing another contributes, no matter how valuable, can change this" (p. 37).

> Sometimes I have a terrible feeling that I am dying not from the virus but from being untouchable. —Amanda Heggs

Parkinson's Disease

Parkinson's disease was first described in the beginning of the nineteenth century by the English physician James Parkinson in his work, *An Essay on the Shaking Palsy*. Parkinson's is a slowly progressive disorder of the central nervous system. It involves extensive degenerative changes in the basal ganglia and the loss of, or a decrease in, the levels of neurotransmitter dopamine in the brain. It is unknown what causes this disease. The symptoms of Parkinson's include disorders of movement, tremor, muscle rigidity, and abnormalities of postural reflex (Falvo, 1999). Additionally, Parkinson's may cause cognitive changes as well as apathy, depression, and loss of initiative. There is no cure for Parkinson's, and the stricken individual must continuously readjust each time as additional functional capacity is lost. The activities of daily living are often altered, and help from others, even for such basic activities as bathing or other aspects of self-care, may become necessary. The patient with Parkinson's disease may have a reduced attention span, visuospatial impairment, and even personality change. Up to 20% of people afflicted with Parkinson's may suffer profound dementia (Kuebler et al., 2002). As the literature pointed out, the disabled endure pain, physical limitations that keep on progressing up to the patient's total dependence on others, emotional upheaval, and a markedly decreased ability to socialize, connect with others, and later even speak to them. Social isolation and loneliness inevitably result.

> When severe illness occurs, it seems like an unending nightmare that robs us of our resources, insults our dignity, and often pushes us to the brink of desperation.
> (Dell Orto, 1991, p. 333)

HOSPITALIZATION

A hospital should also have a recovery room adjoining the cashier's office.
—Anonymous

The hospital is where we go (or are taken) when we are sick, in pain, in a medical emergency, or in need of immediate and extensive medical attention. The modern hospital environment is supposed to provide a safe and healing environment for people inflicted with a variety of illnesses, be it for short-term visits and minor health problems or more serious conditions requiring long-term treatment and care. Upon entering the health care system, patients in the Western hemisphere receive the most contemporary care available, benefiting from modern technology and the expertise of professional staff who are armed with the most current information about the human body and the variety of treatments that are available (Rollins, 2004). In view of this, although the modern hospital facility might be geared to be the "safety residence," hospitalization can be one of the most distressing events people experience in their lifetime (Hughes, 2001). Brannon and Feist (2004) observed, "When a person enters the hospital as a patient, that person becomes part of a complex institution and assumes a role within that institution. That role includes some difficult aspects: being treated as a 'nonperson,' tolerating lack of information, and losing control of daily activities" (p. 64). When people become hospitalized, they become identified by their illness. It is not uncommon to hear a physician telling the nurse to "attend to the multiple fractures in room." Patients' identities, comments and questions, and emotional needs are often ignored by the hospital staff (Yarnold et al., 1998).

Let's look at the case of a woman when she is admitted to the hospital. First, hospitalization means the disruption in her daily routines, a change in her living environment, and having to adjust to the hospital environment. She must resign herself to the care of doctors and nurses and get used to unfamiliar surroundings and, often, unpleasant experiences associated with the course of treatment. She will most probably live now in a state of constant worry, and she must have complete faith in the medical professionals (Hallstrom and Elander, 2007; Paul and Rattray, 2007). The reality of this situation is that an individual and her family are not only subject to the debilitating aspects of the physical illness but also to the added stressors inherent in the experience of being hospitalized (Rokach and Matalon, 2007; Williams and Irurita, 2005).

> For efficiency of the organization, uniform treatment and conformity to hospital routine are desirable, even though they deprive patients of information and control.
> (Brannon and Feist, 2004, p. 65)

Illness is a major stressor on one's life (Sellick and Edwardson, 2007). Various symptoms put the body into a state of continuous stress that may include pain, fatigue, and, in more severe cases, immobility and even loss of bodily functions and control (Rowe, 1996). Being hospitalized, individuals experience a wide range of consequences and effects (Incalzi et al., 1991; Pressman et al., 1997). In general, it is not only the physical suffering and distress that puts the body into a state of continuous stress, but factors that negatively affect the patient's psychological state as well (Rattray, Johnston, and Wildsmith, 2005). These include perceived threat to one's life, the uncontrollable and unpredictable nature of one's condition, and the state of apprehension and hopelessness, which can have a considerable effect on the patient's thoughts, emotions, and behaviors (Mishel, 1997; Raps et al., 1982; Seeman and Seeman, 1983).

In more extreme circumstances of life-threatening illnesses, which require intensive, isolated care and nursing, the combination of these factors is enhanced and might even alter their previously held perception of themselves and their sense of how they are perceived by others. Sensing a lack of identity and confidence in who they truly are, these people might feel disorganized and disengaged (Parkinson, 2006). Indeed, the lingering, long-term psychological effects such as anxiety, depression, and post-traumatic stress disorder commonly occur in response to critical illnesses (Eddsleston, White, and Guthrie, 2000; Mayou and Smith, 1997; Scragg, Jones, and Fauvel, 2001).

> In hospitals there is no time off for good behavior.
> —Josephine Tey

Current psycho-physiological research has provided evidence on the alarming possibility of the adverse effects of hospitalization stress on the patients' already deteriorated physical health and marked interference with their recovery (Huges, 2001). In addition, it was observed that simple features inherent in the design of hospital environments may negatively influence the process of the patients' recovery (Rollins, 2004). In general, adapting to a hospital environment and routine is often stressful. Having to eat hospital food or having to sleep on different beds may bring about emotional discomfort, as patients no longer "feel at home," and as such have minimal personal control over their choices (Williams and Irurita, 2005; Williams, Dawson, and Kristjanson, 2008).

Uncontrollable noise is a significant source of stress for most people (Kramer, Trejo, and Humphrey, 1995). Research has demonstrated that the continuous noise and activity in most hospitals can lead to increased sensitivity to pain and increased need for painkillers in patients (Topf, 2000), as well as disruptions in the quality of sleep (Topf, 1992). Consequently, it may have an adverse effect on the patients' well-being, healing, and recovery. Inadequate lighting or the absence of well-designed windows to allow exposure to adequate natural sunlight is yet another factor that has been shown to get in the way of the patients' recovery by increasing the occurrence of depression, agitation, and sleep disruptions (Walch et al., 2005).

The round-the-clock care, in addition to severe pain and discomfort render patients in intensive care units (ICU) immobilized, confined to bed, and often connected to multiple intravenous devices. These patients are exposed to a monotonous and uncomfortable environment of sensory overload over an extended period of time (Baker, 1984). Many other factors related to the design of the hospital, such as double occupancy rooms that impede the patients' privacy and quality of rest, and the lack of fresh air and poor ventilation systems, can increase the patients' physical and emotional discomfort (Rollins, 2004; Williams et al., 2008).

In addition to the technical aspects of care in the hospital, the attitudes and behaviors of the medical staff toward the patients appear to be key factors in perceived quality of care and whether the patients can successfully cope with the stress of hospitalization (Attree, 2001; Thomas and Bond, 1996). This is essentially due to the fact that, with the exception of the (limited) visiting time of their family and friends, the hospitalized patients' social contact is limited to interaction with the medical staff. These interactions are unbalanced as well. On one side, you have the patient, who is powerless, passive, weak, and dependent, and on the other side, you have the doctors, nurses, and supporting staff, who are in complete control of almost every aspect of the patient's care, with all the knowledge, authority, and power (Hughes, 2001).

As a consequence of this enormous gap in power and control in relation to the medical staff, patients may feel even more hopeless and emotionally distressed, particularly in settings where the doctors and nurses treat the patients in a mechanical, insensitive, or distant manner (Attree, 2001). For instance, one indicator of such a power differential is the frequent use of complex medical jargon by the medical staff that patients are unable to understand (Phillips, 1996). In such situations, many patients may experience heightened levels of anxiety because they feel deprived of control over and knowledge about their health and recovery (Raps et al., 1982; Williams and Irurita, 2005). For instance, quantitative research data on a sample of hospitalized women indicate that between 10% and 40% were subjected to stress at times when the hospital staff disregarded their need for communicating adequate comprehensive information about many aspects of their care (Polimeni and Moore, 2002). It is not uncommon for patients to feel invisible and to perceive their care as lacking kindness, concern, and sensitivity (Attree, 2001). More specifically, they might feel "dehumanized," since it is not uncommon for health professionals to treat their bodies while ignoring their human spirit and the wholeness of their existence (Hughes, 2001). Such perception can result in considerable distress and feelings of helplessness and loneliness in patients (Polemini and Moore, 2002). Emotional distance and depersonalization of the patients might be the medical practitioners' natural reactions in dealing with the harsh reality of the hospitalized patients' ill fate and the enormous demands of their responsibilities; it is the only way for them to do their job without feeling burned out or becoming unable to concentrate on treatments (Tattersall, Bennett, and Pugh, 1999).

THE DYING

Death is not the greatest loss in life. The greatest loss is what dies inside us while we live.
—Norman Cousins

As Rando (1984) so poignantly indicated, death "is not romantic. It is not graceful. It is not beautiful. In fact, death stinks—literally and figuratively! It is clammy, too. It can sound bad, and it often is ugly" (p. 272). Consequently, people with terminal illnesses may be spending the more advanced stages of their illness in a hospice. Palliative care may be provided in a hospice or at home, with the goal of achieving the best possible quality of life for the dying patients and for their families and to provide them with dignified treatment and lower their distress for their final days (Faull and Woof, 2002; Tang, McCorkle, and Bradley, 2004). Van Bommel (1992) eloquently observed that palliative care provided physical, emotional, spiritual, and informational support geared toward enhancing the quality of life of the dying, while recognizing the patient and family as the principal decision makers. Palliative care, thus, takes a holistic view and integrates the psychological, physical, social, and spiritual aspects of a patient's care. It centers on offering a support system that encourages patients to live as actively as possible until death, and it helps the family cope (during the patient's illness) with bereavement, anticipatory, and postmortem grief (Faull and Woof, 2002).

> The good die young—because they see it's no use living if you've got to be good.
> —John Barrymore

The Dying Patient

People who are ill and dying may impose particular demands on their caregivers. The patient may be difficult because of her pathology, which may affect her behavior or personality, such as in the case of brain tumors, cerebrovascular disease, or concurrent illnesses like hypothyroidism. Pharmacological agents such as over sedation or tardive dyskinesia may exacerbate the situation. Psychological factors and psychiatric disorders may result in a patient who is very demanding and difficult to please. Patients may exhibit anger, mistrust, fear, shame, depression, or paranoia. Such emotions can even disrupt the lives of healthy people and the lives of those close to them. The patient's symptoms also contribute to a patient being difficult to care for. Those may include gross disfigurement, malodor, poor response to symptom management, and somatization (Twycross, 2003).

Rokach and Rokach (2005) presented a multidimensional model of the needs of dying patients, including the following:

1. *Physical/medical needs*: These include pain and symptom management, the need to have a warm and caring environment, and the patient's need to have a sense of control with regard to his or her treatment.
2. *Social needs*: These items include completing unfinished business, the needs to love and to be loved, to forgive or be forgiven, and to sustain trusting and intimate relationships.
3. *Emotional/psychological needs*: These include maintaining a sense of control, affirmation of one's existence, searching for meaning, and finding the courage to "let go" and bring closure to one's life.
4. *Spiritual/religious needs*: These needs include having a sense of hope and inner peace and being able to participate in cultural observances and prayers.

Loneliness has been documented to be an integral part of ill health for both the patient and her caregivers. One of the most excruciating elements of death is the leaving of everything the patient owned, had, and knew behind. Separating from friends and family is not only one of the most heartwrenching aspects of dying, but it is also a precursor to loneliness and aloneness (see Doka, 1997; Rokach et al., 2007).

> Death ends a life, not a relationship.
> —Robert Benchley

OUR STUDIES

We have conducted research that compared the qualitative aspects of the loneliness of the groups mentioned above to that of the general population. The various dimensions of loneliness are addressed.

Arthritis, Parkinson's disease, multiple sclerosis, and other physical disabilities have been shown to have a significant emotional and social impact on the disabled. Liang and Daltroy (1985) noted that physical disabilities limit one's level of activity and social integration, and maintaining contact with one's social support system is naturally affected. Displaced feelings (as well as anger and fear), difficulty in communicating with others (for those whose cognitive or speech abilities are impaired by the disease), and the resultant social withdrawal and alienation (Bennett, 2000) clearly highlight the reasons why those with physical disabilities scored higher than the nondisabled on social inadequacy and alienation and emotional distress. These, as Bennett (2000) and Clemmons (2002) suggested, are expressed via the depression, anxiety, fear, and frustration that the disabled feel about being unable to control their body. The disabled experience grief reactions that can occur or recur with exacerbation of the illness. Such reactions include shock, numbness, and disbelief (Bennett, 2000). The same emotional reactions apply to self-alienation, such as estrangement from one's self, feeling that one's mind and body are separate, and attempts to distance oneself from the pain of alienation. It is fairly obvious why both ill and healthy participants from the general population did not differ significantly on the interpersonal isolation subscale. While the social inadequacy and alienation element addresses one's negative perception of one's characteristics and ability to attract others and socialize (a perception that many of the disabled no doubt have), the interpersonal isolation subscale addresses a situation where the person is geographically isolated and does not have others who care for him or her. Since almost by definition the disabled are not alone and must be cared for by others, their experience of loneliness is not affected by social isolation to a different degree from the general population.

Our results indicated that the nondisabled, general population had significantly higher mean subscale scores on the growth and discovery subscale (describing one's growth and personal development as a result of loneliness) than did the disabled. Here, again, the nature of the disabilities, their unrelenting progression, and continuous effect on every aspect of everyday life, clearly suggests that most of the disabled did not find in loneliness, opportunities for growth, self-awareness, and positive aspects beyond what their illness may have provided them with. Krueger's (1984) observation that the physically disabled endure such emotions as shock, denial, depressive reaction, reaction against dependence, and dealing with the devastating loss of one's ability to independently navigate through life's trials and tribulations seems to support the perception that the loneliness that accompanies such a dramatic experience like chronic physical disability is not perceived in positive terms.

Comparing each of the homogeneous subgroups in the disabled sample (i.e., MS, Parkinson's disease, arthritis, and osteoporosis) helped to clarify which of the groups contributed to the significant differences that were found in this study. First, we address the difference between the initial findings and when we compared the disabled subgroups to each other. These groups did not differ significantly on interpersonal isolation (this element refers to the sense of utter aloneness associated with the—perceived—lack of social support and the painful feelings of rejection one feels in light of the realization that one does not connect with and cannot rely on others), and there was similarly no significant difference on the emotional distress element (agony, turmoil, feelings of anguish and internal upset, emptiness and hopelessness, and the lack of control one feels when lonely). As was mentioned earlier, a physical disability invariably carries with it emotional turmoil, distress, and heartache. It is unclear why no significant difference was found, although the difference in mean subscale scores between the general population and osteoporosis approached the significance level (p < .05).

A significant difference between these two groups (the nondisabled, general population and osteoporosis) was found on the social inadequacy and alienation subscales. Dennison and Cooper (2004) define osteoporosis as a skeletal disorder where we may find low bone mass and deterioration of bone tissue, with increase in bone fragility and increased susceptibility to fracture. A patient described the effects of the disability and stated, "Then there was the dramatic height loss and resultant rearranging of my figure to deal with. When the spine shrinks so drastically, it causes the abdomen to protrude in a most unsightly fashion and the waistline completely disappears. This, coupled with a noticeable curvature of the upper spine, made me dread looking in the mirror" (Horner, 1989, p. 9). This clarifies the profound effect that it may have on one's self-esteem, perception of one's abilities and social attractiveness, and on one's belief that one is as socially acceptable as others. Hall Gueldner (2000) further echoed this self-description by observing that concomitantly the one afflicted with osteoporosis may suffer not only skeletal changes and deformities but also vertebral fractures that limit social activities and may lead to the perception of social inadequacy and alienation. It is suggested that while the physical effects of osteoporosis are clear and visible, the data that was collected from the other groups in the present study may have included symptoms that were not easily observable and pronounced; these symptoms may have been the ones that would render the disabled into feeling socially inadequate at that particular point of their illness trajectory.

Rheumatoid arthritis is an incurable disease that produces swelling and inflammation of the supporting tissues of the joints throughout the body (Locker, 1983). Baker (1983) noted that "the pain associated with arthritis can run the gamut from mildly disturbing to agonizing. It varies from person to person and from case to case...[but] the one thing that every arthritis sufferer in the world will agree on, however, is that when it hurts, it really hurts; the pain can be excruciating" (p. 2). Needless to say, such pronounced pain can hardly be seen to contribute to growth and discovery as was indicated.

The nondisabled sample had the lowest mean subscale score of all the six groups on the self-alienation element. As the literature on physical disability and its effects on the sufferer indicate, the reason for that is quite obvious. Locker (1983) indicated that the pain, unrelenting progress, and variable and at times unpredictable pattern of those illnesses add to the psychological and emotional effects that the illness has on the sufferer. Many individuals experience grief for their lost health, their eroding independence, and their increased dependence on others. That grief usually includes shock, denial, numbness, and an overpowering sense of futility. Those experiences are very similar to what the self-alienation subscale captures. Consequently, it stands to reason that those with physical disabilities will experience more self-alienation and will attempt to dissociate from the agony and to dull the pain more than the nondisabled do.

To conclude, it was found that physical disability, with its profound emotional and psychological impact, affects the quality of loneliness. When compared to a sample of the general population, those with physical disabilities scored higher on all but the growth and discovery and the interpersonal isolation subscales.

We examined the loneliness of people on their deathbed in a hospice and compared it to the one experienced by their caregivers. Life is a journey and death is its final destination. Rainer and McMurry (2002) said, "For many individuals, death comes as a universally unwelcome event...The mental, spiritual, social, and emotional adjustments may make this event overwhelming" (p.1421).

Death is not only distressing and overwhelming, but it is accompanied by loneliness for both the dying and those who care for him (Chentsova-Dutton et al., 2000). Our study examined that very loneliness, the loneliness of the dying and of his caregivers. What we focused on was not the quantity or level of loneliness, but rather its qualitative aspects. Our results indicated that loneliness is experienced differently in or out of the hospice, the place where the patients and their caregivers were recruited. That difference was confined to the growth and discovery and the self-alienation elements. In both instances, the general population scored significantly lower than the other two subgroups. It is intuitively apparent, and easier to explain, the higher mean subscale scores of the patients and their caregivers. The pain, emotional turmoil and the sense of terror that both death and loneliness may evoke could mobilize a reaction akin to fainting which is a physical response to acute pain. Self-alienation may be present as a reaction to loneliness and to the individual's impending death. Rando (1984) pointed to the need of the patient and the caregiver to have at least some control of the dying process. She goes on to observe that the patient often feels powerless in the midst of a progressive and debilitating illness. Connor (1998) observed that people respond differently to their impending death. Most often their behavior is characterized by ambivalence—"fearful avoidance and the desire for release" (p. 46). Results of the present study thus indicate that in the midst of that ambivalence—that most probably is experienced by the patient and the caregiver—self-alienation may be the dimension of loneliness that they most acutely experience. Indeed, a form of distancing and numbing may be needed in facing the end of life and the impending separation from loved ones.

The growth and discovery higher scores are not intuitively expected, though they can be explained in light of the "moments of truth," the shirking of social "niceties" and expectations, and the order that the dying are putting to their affairs (see Rokach and Rokach, 2005). It is thus suggested that in the atmosphere of a hospice and in attending to the dying, both the patient and the caregiver may find the strength, inner resources, and personal capabilities to deal with loneliness and with the impending separation and loss.

Chapter 6

SO WHY ARE PEOPLE LONELY?

Bob, a 32-year-old single man, came to see me (A.R.) due to what he described as "anxiety." He, indeed, appeared anxious, nervous, and unsettled. In our sessions, he was often rambling, strayed from the main points that he attempted to make, or from my questions, and while he seemed to and said that he liked to come to our sessions, because they helped ease his great pain, he was not motivated to find out why he felt it. Bob's parents were in their late 40s when he was born. Being an only child, they had very high expectations that he would attend university, and then inherit his father's large business. While his mother was a housewife and attended to his (almost) every whim, his father was a very busy business executive who had little time for his son; especially, when that son was not the brightest of students, nor good at sports, something his father had hoped his son would be. As he grew up and his parents realized that he would not be the son that they hoped for, one that would bring them the pride they could share with all their friends, Bob slowly started to realize that he was not what he wanted to be. He was not what his parents hoped that he would be. He felt that the children in school did not like him, and his teachers mostly ignored him and often punished him. Bob had difficulties dating, had one or two friends whom he was not close to, and was mostly alone and painfully lonely. He sought therapy to ease his pain, to learn how to be less alone, and to gain the skills necessary to find a lover. Mostly he sought therapy to start to and believe in himself, something that his parents had robbed him of.

The public commonly believes that being alone or without an intimate partner results in loneliness. That is not necessarily so. As we discussed under the heading of "*Solitude*," there are times when we want and need to be alone, and when we are—the solitude affords us a relief from daily pressures and gives us time to renew and recharge. Being without an intimate friend (romantic or otherwise) does often result in loneliness but is that it? Is loneliness just evoked when we are friendless? Not so. To find out what may cause loneliness, I embarked on research to explore that issue. Before I describe my own research, however, I will, briefly, review what other researchers and clinicians said about the causes of loneliness. These various approaches are presented in chronological order, so that we can examine the evolution of thinking on that experience.

Although Freud himself did not write about loneliness, he did address fear of the dark (Freud, 1941). Mijuskovic (2012) extrapolates on Freud's writings and suggests that children are not, initially, afraid of death because they cannot grasp its finality. They are, however, afraid of the dark, which gives them the feeling of being separated from all around them and which introduces fear upon their time to go to sleep. Similarly, contends Mijuskovic, we are not so much afraid of death as we are terrified of loneliness, of being alone, of being isolated from all that we know, which is the fate of the dead. Possibly one of the first articles about loneliness was published by Zilboorg (1938) who believed that loneliness reflects infantile feelings of narcissism, megalomania, and hostility. The origins of loneliness go, as far as Zilboorg was concerned, back to the crib, where the infant learns how small and weak he is, and how dependant on others he will be for his survival. Sullivan (1953) saw the human drive for intimacy as the cause of loneliness. We spend, according to Sullivan, our entire lives looking to be loved and accepted, and since that can rarely be fully realized, we end up mostly lonely and feeling dejected. Fromm–Reichman (1959), another psychodynamically oriented writer, agreed with Sullivan's view but additionally saw loneliness as leading to psychotic states. She maintained that what she referred to as premature weaning from a mother's love and affection was at the root of it. Carl Rogers (1961) believed that when people view their real selves (rather than the self they present to the world) as unlovable, they experience emptiness and rejection, and thus loneliness. Therefore, Rogers viewed loneliness as a manifestation of maladjustment, and like the rest of the therapists we reviewed, as originating from within the person.

Moustakas (1961), in his ground breaking book, came out against those assumptions and explained why loneliness is not a character blemish and is not necessarily caused by one's unloving mother or by our understanding of how small we are in the universe. Loneliness, as Moustakas saw it (and I fully support his view), is an existential part of being human. Once man recognizes his stature in the world, his separation (physically and emotionally) from others, he is prepared by his nature to experience loneliness. Needless to say, that Moustakas, unlike some of those who wrote about loneliness before him, sees this experience as a natural, normal, and even welcomed aspect of being human, definitely not an aberration or a character flaw. Weiss (1973), who wrote a major book on loneliness, viewed loneliness as essentially caused by being alone, separated from those we love and want to be with, and especially separated from an intimate loving relationship. Social integration and emotional intimacy were the causes of loneliness as Weiss saw it.

Bowlby (1973) and Parkes (1973) saw loneliness as a proximity promoting, survival mechanism, in that it is caused by our need to be with others. That need originated in earlier days when man could only survive, deal with harsh environmental conditions, and not be consumed by animals by sticking together with the group. Wandering off could mean death. It is evolution, they maintained, that instilled in us anxiety as a response to being away from the group, and that anxiety brings about loneliness which, in turn, motivates us to rejoin the group. Mayer Gaev (1976) supports this view and sees loneliness as being caused by our need and longing to be part of a larger group, feeling closeness and protection.

Potthoff (1976) believes that deep within us is a great need to be accepted, to belong, and to be loved. Potthoff was among the first people to suggest that loneliness antecedents may be composed of a combination of the internal need to belong and deprivation of a loving intimate relationship. He suggested that the loneliness that comes from within may be precipitated by our difficulties in relating to and communicating with others and is characterized by withdrawal, building walls that separate us from others, and by fearing physical and even more, emotional closeness to others. In addition, loneliness may also be caused by others who may be unaccepting, uncaring, and indifferent towards us.

Rolheiser (1979) differentiated the loneliness experience into five types. A review of the causes that he saw for that experience include feeling alienated from and emotionally unconnected to others, feeling fear, having a low self-esteem, being selfish, having a fear of rejection, and having physical and geographical separation from others. In other words, anything that increases physical and emotional distance between humans and blocks the potential for the development of closeness and intimacy could be a cause. Other reasons that Rolheiser named as causes of loneliness included man's need to achieve, his desires, and the difference between who we think we are and who we truly may be. Rolheiser further maintained that man's geographical movement from one country and region to another is the root cause of loneliness, as uprootedness is known to create longing and alienation.

Peplau, Miceli, and Morasch (1982) viewed loneliness as a subjective, cognitively modulated experience. They maintained that in labeling themselves as lonely, people use cognitive, affective, and behavioral cues. The affective cues include the diffused state of unhappiness and emotional distress that is so often reported by the lonely. Behavioral cues include low levels of social contacts, disruptions in established relationships, or an unsatisfying relationship that we may have and cannot change. The cognitive cues have to do not so much with the person's actual social contacts, as much as with his desired frequency and quality of social relations. Peplau et al. (1982) further suggested that causality of loneliness is commonly explained by people as emanating from being without supportive and intimate relationships and as consequences of their personality and characteristics such as aggression, passivity, lack of social skills, being uninteresting, etc.

In general, most researchers believe that desired but unfulfilled social and emotional needs for support and caring are the most salient causes of loneliness. Heinrich and Gullone (2006) suggested that the various loneliness antecedents could be divided into three categories: (1) social needs approach, (2) cognitive discrepancy approach, and (3) the interactionist approach.

SOCIAL NEEDS APPROACH

The social needs perspective is the most popularly held and was proposed by the early writers on loneliness (Fromm-Reichman, 1959; Sullivan, 1953; Weiss, 1973). They maintained that the cause of loneliness is the absence of needed relationships that may be either intimate or more casual, but which allow the individual to meet such social needs as attachment, social integration, nurturance, reassurance of worth, and guidance (Heinrich and Gullone, 2006; Dykstra, 2009; VanderVoort, 1999).

COGNITIVE DISCREPANCY APPROACH

This perspective proposes that the main cause of loneliness is the discrepancy between our views and our present wishes and the kind of interpersonal relationships and social connections that we wish to have (Peplau and Perlman, 1982). This approach also holds that our thoughts about ourselves and others, influence the likelihood that we may, or may not, form satisfying relationships. Our cognitions impact not only our behavior while we interact, but also on how we interpret those interactions. In explaining the causality of their loneliness, lonely people are likely to blame themselves, and thus believe that since they may be dull, boring, or unlovable, others do not and will not desire their company (Murphy and Kupshik, 1992; Solano, 1987). Moreover, Shaver et al. (1985) found that chronically lonely people hold very high expectations for interpersonal interactions; those expectations may further enhance their loneliness.

INTERACTIONIST APPROACH

The interactionist perspective holds that loneliness arises from what Rook (1984) termed person-situation factors (see also Weiss 1982). Accordingly, loneliness antecedents are made of characterological factors (such as shyness, introversion, and social anxiety), which may interact with cultural or situational forces and result in one's reduced ability to develop or maintain social relations (Heinrich and Gullone, 2006). Among the situational determinants that have been identified are relocation, social conflict, imprisonment, poverty and low income, and hospitalization (Blai, 1989; Hymel et al., 1999; Mahon and Yarcheski, 1992).

One such interactionist approach is my own (Rokach, 2003) model of loneliness antecedents that is composed of five factors. The first and most salient antecedent to emerge in our study of more than 600 people is *Personal Inadequacies*. This factor recognizes the relationship between an individual's perception of herself and her experience of loneliness. Negatively perceived characteristics, such as feeling that one does not fit in or is personally or socially inadequate in the company of others, initiate or sustain feelings of low self-esteem that induce and eventually reinforce social withdrawal and interpersonal distancing.

The emergence of *Personal Inadequacies* as the most central antecedent of loneliness is supported by a review of the literature, which indicates that loneliness is generally attributed to either personal factors or situational constraints, or their interaction (Rook, 1988). Regarding personal factors, loneliness has been inversely related to self-esteem (Jones et al., 1981; Russell et al., 1980), and was found to be strongly related to measures of shyness and social anxiety (Jones and Carpenter, 1986; Moore and Shultz, 1983) and sensitivity to rejection (Jones et al., 1985; Russell et al., 1980). In addition, Goswick and Jones (1982) discovered that loneliness was associated with negative perceptions relating to one's body, sexuality, and appearance.

As verified in our study, it would appear that certain personality correlates are central to loneliness in that they seem to hinder the development and maintenance of healthy and fulfilling relationships, which are fundamental to a supportive and empowering social support network. Further, as noted previously (Jones and Moore, 1987; Shaver et al., 1985), there is sufficient evidence to tentatively conclude that the personality configuration and shortcomings of the lonely—whether actual or perceived—precede and contribute to the development of loneliness rather than vice versa.

The following is an account of loneliness antecedents that was reported by one of our study participants.

I cannot really mention any one experience where I've felt lonely since this feeling of loneliness is always present with me, whether at that moment I'm aware of it or not. Social alienation seems to occur a lot when I'm with people—seem to be so different from myself and I feel unable to become a part of their group, e.g. I may not enjoy the bar scene, or at times people seem too superficial for me to become interested in their company. Many things have resulted in my feelings of loneliness such as leaving my job, going through a relationship breakup, lack of intimate friends, shyness, fear of being rejected or hurt, distrust of people. It seems like the main reason for my loneliness is that I haven't found anyone with whom I can have an intimate friendship, someone of like mind/soul. So, in certain ways, I'd therefore rather be alone. Coping-withdrawal, distrust, accepting my life as a "loner," though looking for close friends when I feel I have found them…

The second antecedent, *Developmental Deficits*, which also appeared in the original study, addresses the developmental and familial causes of loneliness. This factor accounts for the effects of growing up in an inadequate or dysfunctional home that is characterized by emotionally distant or rejecting parents, psychological or physical abuse, and/or an atmosphere that is generally marred by upset and unhappiness. Such a home provides neither the environment (e.g. security, caring, and sense of belonging) nor the real-life modeling that is necessary to prepare an individual for healthy, meaningful, and trusting adult relationships. As Perlman and Duck (1987) observed, "our childhood roots matter…The general assumption of attachment theorists is that disruptions in childhood relationships lead to emotional and interpersonal difficulties [including loneliness] in adulthood. [Conversely], secure attachment, if established in childhood, is believed to lead to persisting capacities for warmth and closeness in social bonds" (p. 22).

A 40-year-old married man, who participated in our research, related the loneliness he felt as a 9-year-old boy who experienced illness and pain and was "greeted" by cold adult indifference.

> I was in great pain at age nine. I was told by everyone around me that there was nothing wrong with me. Doctors said I didn't want to go to school so I faked this pain I felt. After I experienced a blackout, a doctor was called to the house and he picked me up and took me to the hospital in his own car.
>
> Apparently, my appendix was bursting and caused the blackout. My hospital experience was horrible. This, by the way, was a very old hospital in England, dreary and stark. The nurses had no compassion towards a crying, lonely child. I was slapped for crying. My mother couldn't visit, as there were four other children she had to attend to. When my mother did visit and brought candy, the nurses took it away and I didn't see any of it. I was in hospital approximately three months. My sisters and brothers were not allowed in the hospital. I remember waving to them. They were quite a distance away.

Studies that examined the potential influence of early experiences on subsequent loneliness (particularly the type and quality of parental contact) suggest a relationship between loneliness and early life experiences of parental disharmony and divorce (Shaver and Rubenstein, 1980; Hazan & Shaver, 1994). Loneliness was also found to be correlated with retrospective accounts of parents as cold, distant, non-nurturing, remote, punishing, and absent and lacking in warmth and emotional support (Bergenstal, 1981; Hojat, 1982; Koski & Shaver, 1997; Paloutzian and Ellison, 1982). Further credence was lent to the notion that problematic parent-child relationships contribute to the later developmental of loneliness by Lobdell and Perlman (1986) who found that parental loneliness correlated with the loneliness scores of their adult children (see also Mikulincer et al., 2001). Finally, Peplau and Goldston

(1984) observed that "lonely adolescents reported higher levels of parental rejection, more parental use of rejection as a form of punishment, and greater dissatisfaction with their choice of friends. Lonely offspring, furthermore, felt their parents gave them very little encouragement to strive for popularity" (p. 24).

The third antecedent to emerge, *Unfulfilling Intimate Relationships*, acknowledges the importance and impact of the failure of intimate (particularly romantic) relationships on the development of loneliness. This factor addresses relationships, both ongoing and those that had ended in separation and divorce, which were reported as disappointing and hurtful due to disharmony, lack of emotional support, and/or emotional or physical abuse.

Numerous studies have demonstrated that loneliness is related to deficiencies in intimate relationships, particularly the lack of support from friends and partners during a time of crisis (Jones and Carver, 1991). Loneliness was shown to be inversely correlated to marital satisfaction (Lobdell and Perlman, 1986), having a steady dating or romantic partner among non-married respondents (Jones et al, 1985), and to the proportion of a respondent's social network that was comprised of intimate confidants (Levine and Stokes, 1986). Rook (1988) observed that while studies indicate that the lonely do not necessarily have fewer social ties or less frequent social contacts than the nonlonely, it is the quality of these relationships that decides whether loneliness is reported. "Such findings suggest that dissatisfaction with the existing social relationships, rather than the lack of relationships per se, contributes to feelings of loneliness for some people" (p. 577). Self-reported evaluations indicated that the relationships of lonely respondents are characterized by lower levels of intimacy and reciprocity than those reported by nonlonely respondents (Cutrona, 1982; Jones et al., 1981; Rook 1987; Shaver and Hazan, 1985; and Solano, 1986). Finally it is noted that loneliness may result from a "mismatch" between one's actual relationship and what is wanted or needed (Blai, 1989).

The following account typifies such a situation:

> I think my most profound loneliness happened when my two older children were 1 and 3 years of age. I felt inadequate as a parent, trapped as a social being and lonely as a wife. I sought religious growth as a means of boosting my rather poor self-esteem. This proved to be a most difficult task as I had to re-examine all my past teachings and experiences in my faith. Of necessity, this is a solitary search on a solitary journey as it is ultimately a personal growth, change, and personal commitment. The little "help" I had via friends was adequate only to a point.
>
> My husband didn't support this "search." My religious pursuit became a wedge between me and my husband in our marriage, while my friends who were pursuing their religious journey did it as couples. This negated my social functions within the spiritual milieu and I began to resent my husband, envy my friends, and eventually, jealousy reared its ugly head.
>
> After reaching a point in my "journey" where I felt I could carry on outside the spiritual milieu of these friends, I withdrew from the group, and focused on solidifying a good marriage to make it even better. I found my spiritual re-birth and loneliness dissipated from my marriage.

The fourth antecedent, *Relocation/Significant Separation,* captures the effects of the changes that occur to, and often the loss off, important relationships as a consequence of mobility and relocation. Blai (1989) observed that separation from and/or the ending of an important relationship is most often cited as one of the primary causes of loneliness, and asserts that those who have moved recently and who have experienced significant changes to their social support networks are at particular risk of feeling lonely.

The importance of the relationship between separation and loneliness was noted previously by Weiss (1973), who coined the term "social loneliness" to distinguish that type that results from a deficient or lacking social network of friends, neighborhood acquaintances, and organizations that normally form a cohesive social group. In keeping with Rolheiser's (1979) and Sadler and Johnson's (1980) models of loneliness, Shultz (1979) further observed that loneliness is experienced primarily while traveling, during periods of transition, and under circumstances that are marked by a state of flux (see also Rokach & Brock, 1996). This is because these times, although temporary in nature, lack—or disrupt—the dependable and familiar social environment that is so essential to a secure social support network. In an attempt to understand the aspect of human nature that makes this possible, Bowlby (1973) suggested that loneliness became part of the human response pattern as a result of its usefulness to human survival. He maintains that the possession of "proximity-promoting mechanisms," such as loneliness, was essential to the survival of our ancestors in that such behaviors assured them against isolation from others, thereby decreasing their vulnerability to extinction by nature, animals, or other human enemies.

The fifth and final antecedent, *Social Marginality,* addresses the actual or perceived social reaction and distancing that is experienced by criminals, the unemployed, and people who are separated or estranged from loved ones, particularly their children, such as hospitalized patients (Rokach and Brock, 1996). Here, participants reported, "I felt ugly because of cancer treatments," "I had a facial scar," "I was unemployed and all my friends worked," or "When people hear that I was in jail, they do not want anything to do with me." Blai (1989) observed that "individuals who are marginally or chronically cut off from social contacts, such as the unemployed, imprisoned, etc.; individuals who live alone; and persons who are severely ill or chronically disabled" (p. 165) are at heightened risk of experiencing loneliness. Given the societal emphasis on appearing successful and "fitting in" (i.e. displaying a "normative" lifestyle), it is not surprising that those who do not fit in feel cut off, alienated, and eventually, lonely. After reviewing the literature, Rook (1988) observed that while membership in a social network increases the opportunities for social support and belonging, it also increases the responsibilities and efforts necessary to maintain that relationship in good standing (Margulis, Derlega, and Winstead, 1984); activities that are not generally encouraged or readily accessible to incarcerated, debilitated, or unemployed individuals.

A 20-year-old single woman, a participant in our study, suffered from chronic loneliness and painful experiences when she attempted to end her alienation.

I cannot really mention any one experience where I've felt lonely since this feeling of loneliness is always present with me, whether at that moment I'm aware of it or not. Social alienation seems to occur a lot when I'm with people—it's like I'm separate from everyone and looking at them from the outside. They seem to be so different from myself and I feel unable to become a part of their group, e.g., I may not enjoy the bar scene, smoking up drugs, drinking, or at times people seem too superficial for me to become interested in their company. Many things have resulted in my feelings of loneliness such as leaving my job, going through a relationship breakup, lack of intimate friends, shyness, fear of being rejected or hurt, distrust of people. It seems like the main reason for my loneliness is that I haven't found anyone with whom I can have an intimate friendship, someone of like mind/soul. So, in certain ways, I would therefore rather be alone.

Regarding the duration of loneliness, I support the conceptual distinction between chronic or trait and situational or state loneliness previously offered by Shaver and his colleagues. They proposed that loneliness for some people is an enduring trait, while others experience it as a time-limited state resulting from situational changed (Rubenstein and Shaver, 1982; Shaver, Furman, and Buhrmeister, 1985; Heinrich and Gullone, 2006). The findings of our study suggest that the factors comprising Cluster I, Characterological and Historical: *Personal inadequacies* and *Developmental deficits*, characterize the loneliness that is experienced on a stable or chronic basis, while the factors of Cluster II, Experiential and Situational: *Unfulfilling intimate relationships*, *Relocation/significant separations*, and *Social marginality*, depict loneliness experiences that are situation-specific and relatively shorter. It is clear, though, that there is usually more than one antecedent to the loneliness we feel, and it may come from within, from without, or be a combination of both.

Chapter 7

LONGING AND BELONGING

> Humans are obligatorily gregarious...The average person spends nearly 80% of waking hours in the company of others...and their survival depends on their collective abilities, rather than on their individual might. (Distel et al., 2010, p. 480/481)

Humans are fundamentally social creatures. Our quality of life depends on others. We thrive on social intercourse and consequently, when we become socially disconnected our psychological, physiological, and even spiritual well-being may be negatively affected (Pond, Brey, and DeWall, 2011). While we seek to satisfy our inherent need to belong, it is not the just relationships that we are after; we also need mutual concern and caring for those relationships in order for them to be satisfactory and growth promoting (Shaver and Buhrmeister, 1983).

Between the two ends of the continuum, composed of loneliness and solitude, is our yearning to belong. Our whole survival depends on it. Ornish (1998) reviewed numerous studies that suggested that "anything that promotes a sense of isolation often leads to illness and suffering. Anything that promotes a sense of love and intimacy, connection and community, is healing" (p.14). Cacioppo et al. (2011) maintained that "Human evolutionary heritage has endowed us with the capacity to feel the pain of social isolation and the rewards of social connection. Importantly, it has also endowed us with the capacity to feel others' pain and the compassion to care for the sick and the elderly far beyond their reproductive or instrumental utility" (p. 43).

Psychology, while showing growing interest in loneliness, has not devoted much attention to the need to belong. "As social beings most humans live in a matrix of relationships that, to a larger extent, define their identity...and our personality" (Mellor et al, 2008, p. 213) and those connections transcend cultural differences (see Heine, Lechman, Markus, and Kitayama, 1999). Such reliance on belongingness explains the resultant loneliness and psychological health issues that may arise when those needs remain unfulfilled.

People in mutually nurturing relationships report higher satisfaction than those who do not get that caring and nurturance (Baumeister, Wottman, and Stillwell, 1993). Interestingly, and as with other basic needs (e.g. food), once people feel that they belong, say in a romantic union, they are less likely to search for another one (DeWall, Baumeister, and Vohs, 2008). "The desire for social acceptance is universal and instinctive. Humans respond to a lack of social connectedness, independently of the circumstances that caused them to feel isolated" (Pond et al., 2011, p. 108). In fact, contends Leary and colleagues (1995), there may be an "internal gauge" that they termed the "Socio-meter," which helps us constantly monitor the environment for clues to changes in our inclusionary status. For it is so important to us, that as we become aware of it, we may endeavor to improve it (see also Leary and Springer, 2001).

Ornish (1998) stated at the very beginning of his book, *Love and Survival*, "Our survival depends on the healing power of love, intimacy, and relationships. Physically. Emotionally. Spiritually. As individuals. As communities. As a culture. Perhaps even as a species" (p. 1). Weil (1997) asserted that the human species is comprised of highly social, communal animals that are meant to live in families, tribes, and communities, and when we lack those connections we suffer. Our Western industrialized society, however, glorifies individualism and independence and fosters a spirit of "Every Man for Himself." Weil further maintained that many people pride themselves on their independence and seem to habitually distance themselves from others. Some may indulge in isolation as a defensive strategy due to emotional pain, while others may never have learned how to meaningfully connect to anyone beyond themselves. Kohut (1977) asserted that establishing and maintaining relatedness to others is a pervasive human concern, believing that "through interpersonal interactions people survive, develop and grow" (Hagerty, Williams, Coyne, and Early, 1996, p. 235).

Another indication of the centrality of belongingness is the old practice of ex-communication that was the Church's most severe social reprimand and the solitary confinement used in jail to punish unruly criminals. Furthermore, it was suggested that physical and social pain systems are closely linked (MacDonald and Leary, 2005), so much so, that people even use the same terms to describe rejection as they do to describe physical injury. We have all heard of feeling "hurt" or "crushed," just as two examples (Leary and Springer, 2001). Such words appear in all languages and are used all over the globe (Pond et al., 2011). A study by DeWall and Baumeister (2006) suggests that people respond similarly to physical and social pain producing events. When, for instance, we are interpersonally rejected, we experience a sort of numbness (similar to the physical analgesia that is usually the initial response to trauma) that protects us from distressing emotional reactions. Eventually, this analgesic effect will fade away and the social (or in the other case, physical) effects will be experienced (Pond et al., 2011).

Both loneliness and belonging share the subjective perception of connectedness to others. Mellor et al. (2008) found that those who reported a higher need to belong also reported increased loneliness, while satisfaction with one's social network was moderately negatively correlated with loneliness. Unsatisfied belongingness needs may thus lead to social isolation, alienation, and loneliness. It is generally the discrepancy between the *need to belong* and the degree in which that need is satisfied that is crucial in ushering in the experience of loneliness, and that, indicates their research, applies both to those who live alone and to those who are living with others.

In support of the evolutionary perspective to belongingness, Olds and Schwartz (2009) observed that socially connected people, indeed, live longer, have more robust immune systems, are better equipped to respond to stress, and are generally better off. Medical research, according to Olds and Schwartz, has demonstrated that social connection is good and important to our health, or put even more poignantly, "Human beings, both as a species and as individuals, survive only through attachment to one another...we are designed to become attached to one another" (Olds and Schwartz, 2009, p. 57)

Weiss (1974), recognizing the need to belong, asserted that social relations are a rich source of:

1. Attachment—which is a result of good relationships that may provide us with security and commitment.
2. Social integration—which may be felt when our social relationships offer us companionship and shared activities.
3. Opportunity for nurturance—which results from relationships that provide us with a sense of being needed, and possibly being responsible for someone else's well-being.
4. Reassurance of worth—may result when relationships provide us with a sense of competence and of being valued.
5. Reliable alliance—relationships that provide a stable source of assistance and support.
6. Guidance—when relationships allow us to receive trustworthy advice and tried and true wisdom.

Weiss (1974) further noted that no one relationship can satisfy all the types of relational provisions, and thus we need, and commonly draw upon, various relationships to satisfy our connection needs.

> Anyone who either cannot lead the common life or is so self-sufficient as not to need to,
> and therefore does not partake of society, is either a beast or a god.
> (Aristotle, as quoted by Erber and Erber, 2001a)

Weil (1997) unequivocally stated his concern that the widespread isolation in our Western society is unhealthy—physically, emotionally, and spiritually. "I do know for sure that connectedness is necessary to well-being. You can eat as much salmon and broccoli as you can, take anti oxidants for the rest of your life, breath terrifically, and walk all over the earth, but if you are disconnected (from others), you will not achieve optimum health" (p. 153).

WHAT IS THAT SENSE OF BELONGING THAT WE ARE AFTER?

In the past, especially for the "Great Depression" generation, one's work was seen as the valued means of self-fulfillment; it was about "bread winning" through a career or a job for men, and for women, it was about the creation of a home and family. Ours, however, is the age of relationships. We believe in the importance, uniqueness, and availability of methods of relating to others, thinking that we know how to conquer the barriers against closeness that we ourselves have erected. At present, relationships appear to be the main avenue, and perhaps the only means, by which self-esteem can truly be affirmed. As Gordon (1976) so poignantly observed, "To be alone is to be different, to be different is to be alone, and to be in the interior of this fatal circle is to be lonely. To be lonely is to have failed" (p. 15). We seem to be living in a "Noah's Ark" society where everything goes two by two, and if you are lonely, you are out of place. This same society, however, creates and maintains a paradox. We yearn for close, intimate relationships, but social conditions today are not conducive to the development of human relations. Our present lifestyle, which was developed in the last 25 years, creates and reinforces isolation, making loneliness even more difficult to cope with.

Hagerty, Lynch-Sauer, Patusky, Bouwsema, and Collier (1992) observed that the sense of belonging has received minimal attention in the field of mental health. They defined it as, "The experience of personal involvement in a system or environment so that persons feel themselves to be an integral part of the system or environment" (p. 173). It is a significant predictor of depression and is related to anxiety, loneliness, and suicidability (Hagerty and Patusky, 1995). When asked in one study which of their social activities was most enjoyable, the participants pointed to their intimate relationships and activities that promote bonding and high quality relationships; commuting and working were seen as the less enjoyable (Distel et al., 2010).

> In principle, people could find meaning in communing with nature or with divinity, engaging in philosophical or religious contemplation, pursuing scientific, artistic or technological innovation or other potentially solitary pursuits. Life's meaning does not obviously or inherently depend on social relations. Yet in practice it seems that people find meaning in their social relations.
>
> (Stillman et al., 2009, p. 686)

Social support-a-la-Cohen (2004) refers to a "social network's provision of psychological and material resources intended to benefit an individual's ability to cope with stress" (p. 676). We can group together the various kinds of support into three categories: *Instrumental support*, which involves the provision of material and practical help; *Informational support*, giving information that could aid the receiver in coping with difficulties or current problems; and *Emotional support*, involving the expression of empathy, caring, trust, and reassurance that could be an invaluable assistance at times of need or crisis. Social integration is the construct that includes the *behaviors* that one engages in, in order to be integrated into and feel part of the community (Brisette et al., 2000). The current literature suggests that the critical factor that may buffer stress is not the social support one has, but the *perception* that one is cared for, supported, and can rely on someone for help when the need arises (Cohen, 1988; Uchino et al., 1996). When one feels supported, one may change one's appraisal of the situation and that by itself may reduce the level of stress and dampen the emotional and physiological response to the event (Willis and Cleary, 1996). Substantial evidence points out that the perceived social support can buffer the negative impact of stress on psychological distress, depression, and anxiety (Kawachi and Berkman, 2001). Additionally, social support may alleviate stress by, for example, providing a solution to the problem or it may facilitate healthful behaviors, such as exercise, personal hygiene, proper nutrition, and rest (House, 1981). In general, people who are part of a social network are naturally subjected to social controls and peer pressures that influence normative health behaviors (Cohen, 2004). By abiding to those normative social expectations, one may get a sense of identity, predictability, stability, belonging, and self-worth (Cohen, 2004; Thoit, 1983; Willis, 1985).

Alternatively, research indicates that social isolation, and the concomitant loneliness it may cause, is itself a stressor that may decrease one's sense of control and self-esteem, and there is the possibility that it could increase neuroendocrine and cardiovascular responses, suppress immune function, and interfere with practiced health behaviors (Cacioppo et al., 2002; Uchino et al., 1996). A person commonly feels that she belongs when she feels valued, needed, and important to a group of people with whom she feels that she fits (Friedman, 2007).

As the loneliness literature indicates, a sense of belonging is not dependent on participation with or proximity to others, but to the perception of the quality of those social interactions. Friedman (2007) highlighted the centrality of the sense of belonging to the development of the self and to identity building.

What is a community then? Community has been viewed in a variety of ways. In the past, it was associated with physical space and a social network that existed in that space over time. More recently, however, it was suggested in the psychological literature that the definition of community is closely related with that of a sense of belonging. Blow and Timm (2002) viewed community as a network of significant relationships that are characterized by caring, understanding, mutual valuing, and commitment. It is a network of people who are committed to each other and interact on an ongoing basis. It also includes a feeling of fitting in, of belonging, of being valuable to others. Community includes belonging plus a sense of genuineness and love (Friedman, 2007). It has been mentioned earlier that today's society is not as cohesive, close-knitted, and involved in its members' lives as it was in yesteryears but the longing to belong and be part of a community still exists because it is an integral part of being human. In our digital age, Facebook has provided a partial answer to this paradox, where we want to belong and be connected, but seem to prefer to do it "the long distance way," via the Internet and writing, versus the face-to-face interaction that was such an accepted part of life in the pre-Internet days. That is precisely the reason that Facebook has become an empire, a mega institute, in only five years!

SOCIAL CONNECTION, BELONGING, AND HEALTH

Earlier researchers also focused on the role of social support in relation to both physical and mental health (Cohen and Syme, 1985; House, Landis, and Umberson, 1988). Others have explored the effects of loneliness on health (Hagerty et al., 1996; Lynch, 1979; Russell, Cutrona, Rose, and Yurko, 1984) on social integration (Case, Moss, Case, McDermott, and Eberly, 1992), on attachment (Sperling, Berman, and Fagan, 1994), and on mortality (Carpenter, 2001). Ornish (1998) reviewed numerous studies that suggested that "anything that promotes a sense of isolation often leads to illness and suffering. Anything that promotes a sense of love and intimacy, connection and community, is healing" (p. 14).

Commenting on the importance of community to our well-being, Lewis, Amini, and Lannon (2000) observed that "with results like these backing the medical efficacy of mammalian congregation, you might think that treatments like group therapy...would now be standard. Guess again. Affiliation is not a drug or an operation, and that makes it nearly invisible to Western medicine" (p. 80). Ornish (1998, 2007) echoes this sentiment.

Emile Durkheim (1951), sixty years ago, focused on social dynamics as contributing to individual pathology. He argued that people are bonded to society by attachment and regulation, and the latter implies the extent to which an individual is held within society, its values, beliefs, and norms. Consequently, it became an acceptable observation that self-destruction is a consequence of one's failure to integrate into society. Since Durkheim's seminal book, research has confirmed that social support and connectedness are among the most important contributors to our well-being.

Some research has extolled the power of social integration and support by suggesting that they rival, in their positive influence, cigarette smoking, obesity, elevated blood pressure, and physical inactivity, which are all well-established biomedical risk factors (House, Landis, and Umberson, 1988). Berkman (1995) in his large scale longitudinal study concluded that those who had a supportive social network at the beginning of the study were less likely to die in the following nine years through which the study was conducted. Moreover, social support does not only affect our capacity to ward off loneliness, but it may also affect the rate of recovery from a variety of illnesses (Cassell as cited in Pillisuk and Hillier Parks, 1986).

Research has found that sudden separation or the disruption of social and emotional bonds may affect our immune system and reduce our body's ability to remain or become healthy (Pilisuk and Hillier Parks, 1986). Putnam's (2000) study echoed those findings and suggested that the more integrated we are with our communities, the better are our chances of avoiding colds, heart attacks, cancer, strokes, and premature death. Those who are well integrated within their community are less likely to experience sadness, loneliness, low self-esteem, insomnia, and eating disorders. Putnam further found that social embeddedness may reduce the likelihood of mental illness. Depression, which has been shown to be rampant in North America, is inhibited by social connection (Hagerty and Williams, 1999). Pilisuk and Hillier Parks (1986) found that more disturbed people had fewer reciprocal network relationships. Even combat related stress—and hence PTSD—was found to be moderated by belongingness (Baumeister and Leary, 1995). To summarize it all—if you want to increase your chances of living and being healthy, you should belong to a group, to any group that will value you.

> Intimate attachments to other human beings are the hub around which a person's life revolves, not only when he is an infant or toddler or schoolchild, but throughout his adolescence and his years of maturity as well, and on into old age. From these intimate attachments a person draws his strength and enjoyment of life, through what he contributes, he gives strength and enjoyment to others.
>
> (Bowlby, 1980, p. 442).

Social support networks have been shown to be important in enhancing the recovery process (Pernice-Duca, 2010). Social networks consist of one's family, friends, and others who provide support that, as Milardo (1988) observed, "leads one to believe that he or she is cared for, loved, valued and belongs to a network with mutual obligations" (p. 13).

Social scientists have concluded that those support networks relate to measures of effective coping strategies, self-efficacy, and overall quality of life (Berkamn, Glass, Brissette, and Seeman, 2000). Being diagnosed with a serious mental or physical illness, however, commonly results in a serious disruption of those interpersonal social ties with devastating consequences (see our previous discussion, as well as Grofein and Owens, 2000; Pernice-Duca, 2010). Inadequate or limited social support may exacerbate pre-existing psychiatric symptoms (Resnick, Rosenheck, and Lewman, 2004).

Dean Ornish, in his recent book, *The Spectrum* (2007), observed that "Medicine today focuses primarily on drugs and surgery, genes and germs, microbes and molecules. Yet love and intimacy are at the root of what makes us sick and what makes us well. If a new medication had the same impact, failure to prescribe it would be malpractice" (p. 30). He contends that social connections can not only affect our *quality* of life, but the length of it as well. Ornish maintained that many studies that were conducted throughout the world have shown that those who feel lonely and depressed are many times more likely to die prematurely than those who have a strong sense of love and intimacy, connection and community. He further believes (and I join him in this) that the most powerful motivating force in the world is love. Love is even more powerful than survival. For instance, almost all parents would suffer, or even sacrifice their lives, to help to or keep their children safe and away from harm's way.

Australian researchers (Price et al., 2001) interviewed 514 women who required breast biopsies. About half of them were later diagnosed with malignant breast cancer, and the other half with benign tumors. The researchers concluded that the women who were experiencing a highly threatening stressor and faced it without intimate emotional and social support had a nine fold (!) increase in their risk of developing breast carcinoma. Mate (2003) maintained that since infancy, we have very little, if at all, capacity for self-regulation, and our internal biological states such as heart rates, hormone levels, and nervous system activity, depend completely on the infant's relationship with her caregivers. Those emotional and social relationships remain important beyond infancy and childhood. "Human beings as a species did not evolve as solitary creatures but as social animals whose survival was contingent on powerful emotional connections with family and tribe. Social and emotional connections are an integral part of our neurological and chemical makeup" (p. 189). He further states that social support helps reduce physiological stress, and people who are more isolated are more prone to illness. In three studies of the elderly that he reviewed, he noted that mortality risk was shown to be directly related to social integration. Social ties and support, he concluded, are significant predictors of morbidity and mortality, independent of other risk factors.

The 1998 movie, *Patch Adams*, (about a noted physician by that name) centers on the community that this physician has created where he hospitalizes, treats, and heals the sick. He does so not in a detached, efficient, and modern hospital, but in a house that he bought, and later in his Gesundheit Institute, which he created, where the sick are tended to by physicians free of charge, and in turn contribute to the maintenance of the institution by tending (socially and emotionally) to other patients, helping wherever they can and creating a society that takes care of its members: in the operating rooms, the nursing, the garden, and the kitchen. He continues to live among us and preaches that the healing that the ill patients need, involving caring for their physical, mental, and emotional needs, is best done in a caring community.

THE CENTRALITY OF THE "SELF," RATHER THAN THE COMMUNITY, IN PSYCHOLOGY

Lewis et al. (2000) described the impact of Freudian theory on the field of psychology and on understanding pathology by observing that it casts a long shadow on our present understanding and conceptualization of the psychological working of man. "Freud," he maintained, "is delivered anew to each generation. His conclusions permeate our culture in a multitude of ways, and his assumptions have endured for so many years that they are mistaken for facts" (p. 6). Cognitive Behavior Therapy seems to have furthered the emphasis on the individual. Its focus was correcting "errors in thinking" or challenging "irrational beliefs" as Ellis advocated Beck's approach (Oltmanns and Emertym, 1998) and while the humanistic movement in psychology originally developed to counteract the seemingly mechanistic and deterministic views of the psychodynamic and behavioristic approaches, it also focused on the individual, suggesting that as individuals, although we live and wish to be connected to a society, we have the responsibility of finding meaning in our own lives (Oltmanns and Emertym, 1998). The fields of clinical, personality, and developmental psychology are thus dominated by the psychology of the *individual*. Cushman (1995) sadly observed that "theorists often hold ideas aloof from any social context, claiming a privileged epistemological position uncontaminated by the rough and tumble of the local values and politics of their respective eras" (p. 7).

Generally speaking, that trend in theoretical psychological formulations continues today. Seligman (1988) similarly noted, "Let the self reflect upon itself, talk to itself and find out what it's doing wrong, change and improve the self—and participate in the act of self-creation" (p. 52).

In contrast to the individualistic approaches of those theoreticians that were mentioned, were others who while not as influential, did raise the flag of societal and cultural influences that help shape who we become. Adler, who believed that the community played a central role in the health of humans, proclaimed that the highest destiny of people's existence is their realization of a kind of an everlasting community (Rychlak, 1981). Karen Horney, Harry Stack Sullivan, and Eric Fromm formed the "cultural wing" of the psychoanalytic approach and highlighted our basic needs, as people, to engage in and be supported by satisfying interpersonal relations (Pilisuk and Hillier Parks, 1986). Horney (1937) wrote about cultural difficulties and conflicts that inherently are expressed in individual psychic problems. Sullivan (1953) believed that the individual can be understood and fully appreciated only when he is examined within his community and with regard to his relationships with others. Like Sullivan, Fromm (1970) sought to examine the political and cultural influences on the individual and his personality development and evolution.

Maslow (1970) extolled love, affection, and the need to belong as basic and poignant human needs—needs that have been experienced since the dawn of time in themes found in novels, autobiographies, poems, plays, and sociological literature. Psychology is slower to embrace this truth that we have a strong need to belong, to be part of and valued by a larger group, be it a family, our community, our working colleagues, or all of the above.   We live in a highly individualistic age, and psychology reflects that culture (Pipher, 1999). Freud, the so-called father of modern psychology, focused on intrapsychic conflict, which ultimately lies within the individual. To Freud, the motive of belonging was but a sexual (libidinal) drive. Thus, he viewed psychopathology as a result of inner conflicts, urges, and self-deceptions. Consequently, concluded Horney (1937), to Freud, culture is not a result of various social processes, but merely the result of repressed biological drives. Miller (1976) and Gilligan (1982), representing Feminist theory, observed that what applies to both men and women is the need to connect and belong rather than the need to separate; these are the primary forces in human growth and development.

Non-Western cultures and psychological and sociological viewpoints hold a similar view. The Japanese experience of the self centers on one's interdependence on a larger social unit, on engagement and harmony with others, and on open-hearted and sensitive cooperation (Hamaguchi, 1985; Markus and Kitayama, 1991). Consequently, while the Western approach regards the failure to *separate* as a developmental setback, in Japan, a failure to *connect* is cause for concern.

It was Bowlby's (1969) attachment theory, and later Minuchin's (1974) family systems therapy, that redirected our psychological and clinical attentions to viewing the family as a dynamic primary system that has a crucially important role in influencing, molding, and even shaping individual functioning. Anderson (1982), in addressing the impact of social networks on family functioning, further highlighted the importance of social embeddedness by suggesting that the family's healthy functioning and ability to weather life's storms and stresses, are related to the way the family is connected to the larger society within which it exists. Sarason (1974) even proposed creating a discipline within psychology that would address the "psychological sense of community," the community that humans belong—or may wish to belong—to and that provides support and a dependable structure to operate from (see also Bess, Fisher, Sonn, and Bishop, 2002). Baumeister and Leary (1995) picked up on that trend, and after conducting an extensive literature review, asserted that "belongingness can be almost as compelling a need as food and that human culture is significantly conditioned by the pressure to provide belongingness" (p. 498).

James Billings, who has degrees in clinical psychology, epidemiology, and divinity, was interviewed by Ornish (1998) for his book Love & Survival. He commented on psychology and human nature and how we miss the mark. It moved me deeply and seemed to validate what I felt for a long time. I frequently share it with my students, who I am always worried may be frowned upon by their teachers (and in the future, once they complete their degrees, by their colleagues, just as I was) for seeing love as a cornerstone of our existence.

Billings said the following very wise things:

> Western psychology, which is a little more than a hundred years old, really redefined man by developing a new paradigm of what is normal and what is abnormal. The focus shifted almost completely to the individual. The very idea that someone was dependent on another person was diagnostic of any number of pathologies. In my dissertation I followed a group of people for five years after they were hospitalized for attempting suicide. I was surprised to find that people in therapy were killing themselves at a substantially higher rate than the others! [What I then understood after further investigation] was that [the] people killing themselves in treatment were seeing an analyst therapist who maintained a detached distance from them—they would lie on a couch, not able to see the therapist, who would say very little to the patient during the session. The patient was having an enormous need to make contact with the therapist and to have him or her respond in a nurturing, caring way, when the therapist didn't, the patient often ended up attempting suicide or actually killing himself or herself.
>
> These people were usually the ones who were often depressed, who were feeling isolated, abandoned, and they were having a hard time getting someone to respond to their condition...so we have a world full of people who have a genetic predisposition to affiliation, the need to belong, and we still have a psychological development theory that defines what is normal as making sure that people are not dependent in their relationships. It says that affiliation is pathological, that what you really need to be healthy is not to need anyone. These psychological constructs define what is normal in ways that are at odds with our biology, that thwart affiliation and add to the demise of the family...We need a place where we belong,

where we are seen, we are visible, we feel welcome, a place where we can talk easily, and we can listen easily (p. 225-6).

SO WHAT IS PSYCHOLOGY TO DO THEN?

THERAPEUTIC IMPLICATIONS

Many of the emotional difficulties for which people seek professional help are related to unsatisfied belongingness needs. Baumeister and Leary (1995) poignantly observed that "a great deal of neurotic, maladaptive, and destructive behavior seems to reflect either desperate attempts to establish or maintain relationships with other people or sheer frustration and purposelessness when one's need to belong goes unmet" (p. 521). Beck and Malley (1998) even suggest that the social alienation that is now rampant among today's youth contributes to drug and alcohol abuse, rising violence and gang membership, and depression and suicide.

Consequently, Friedman (2007) advocates that therapy explores those needs and their impact on clients' lives. That, she hastens to remind us, should not come instead of attending to the intrapsychic world, but in addition to it. "The challenge then, is to embrace both the interpersonal realm and the wider multidimensional intrapersonal experiences of one's life...viewing sense of belonging as a framework through which to examine a client's life inherently links the individual with the community that defines and supports her" (p. 77).

Social work and sociology are, indeed, cognizant of the importance of community and social forces on the individual. Psychotherapy, on the other hand, often overlooks an exploration of the client's place in the community and helping the client cultivate a strong sense of belonging to that community. Rokach (1986) highlighted the crucial importance of the therapeutic rapport to the help that the client may derive from therapy. Rogers' (1959) Client-Centered Therapy focused on fostering a warm and genuine relationship between the therapist and her client. The therapeutic relation can thus model the importance of connection and support, and may empower people to reach to others and connect (Blow and Timm, 2002).

Therapists need to stop implicitly valorizing the isolated, separated, and self-sufficient individual and rather encourage social integration and interpersonal connection. Friedman (2007), among a list of proposed suggestions for therapists in order to achieve this goal, highlights the need to query the client, and if needed, address his number of significant community experiences and community building efforts, addressing the present disconnection of the client from his own family and the community, and encouraging, empowering, and guiding the client in rebuilding his damaged relationships or creating ones that could enrich his life.

Ornish (1998) repeatedly found that what we are all after, especially those who go for therapy, is a caring person to listen to us, to validate our need to belong, and to help us achieve the fulfillment of that very basic human wish—to belong, to matter, to be seen, to be valued, and to be loved. We need to follow this practice in therapy, teach our children to do so, and allow ourselves to accept the notion that love is good. Love helps us grow. Actually, love is essential for survival!

Cacioppo et al. (2011) put forth a new concept of "Social Resilience," thus suggesting that it is something that can be developed if we lack it or enhanced if we already possess it. What, then, is social resilience? In their words, it is "the capacity to foster, engage in, and sustain positive relationships and to endure and recover from life stressors and social isolation. Its unique signature is the transformation of adversity into personal, relational, and collective growth through strengthening existing social engagements, and developing new relationships, with creative collective actions" (p. 44). Social resilience is the person's ability to work with others and help the group achieve its goals. It is working with others towards common goals while taking individual differences into account and recognizing and valuing the bond with one's peers. The concept of social resilience is applicable to all forms of human connection, including dyads, families, communities, and cultures. Cacioppo et al. (2011) enumerated nine ingredients, or resources, that foster social resilience.

1. The capacity and wish to perceive others with accuracy and empathy.
2. Feeling a connection to other people and to collectives—being part of a larger group, and giving and receiving to members of that group.
3. The ability to communicate caring and respect to others. That may help one become more socially desirable, and thus be sought after by others.
4. Perceiving others' regard for themselves, and thus learning to value myself. For if I do not value myself, such as the case with anxious, depressed people with low self-esteem, I may become shy, avoidant, and remain alone.
5. Valuing and promoting the welfare of myself and those I care for.
6. The ability to respond appropriately to social problems, because an inappropriate response will help to isolate the individual since others may find it difficult to relate to him. The socially resilient person will then promote helpful problem solving strategies and with them will avoid any social pressure that may hinder open communication.
7. The ability to express empathy and social emotions, such as gratitude, compassion, forgiveness, respect, and even loneliness, in constructive ways that will endear the person to others.
8. Trusting, believing that others can be relied upon and are benevolent. Thus, one will be ready to cooperate and connect.
9. Tolerance and openness to others' different values, background, beliefs, and wants. Tolerance implies the ability to coordinate cooperative efforts while incorporating the diversity of others into the solution.

We may thus suggest that the theoretical model from Cacioppo et al. (2011) is the first step in helping people learn how to become accepted and feel a sense of belonging. Helping those who feel lonely and wish to belong learn how to become more socially involved and endear themselves to others will increase their ability to become part of a larger group and be nurtured by it.

> We can never get a re-creation of community and heal our society without giving our citizens a sense of belonging. —Patch Adams

Chapter 8

COPING WITH LONELINESS

Obviously, there can be no promise for any permanent "cure" for this affliction…there can be no final escape from, or transcendence beyond, loneliness so long as man is alive…[it is not] that man is unable to temporarily alleviate his sense of loneliness, but rather that the relief can never be permanent or long lasting.

(Mijuskovic, 2012, p.1)

"Carolyn" is a 24-year-old pre-school teacher who participated in an evening course which I taught at a community college. We met one evening after class, and she recounted her loneliest experience. At first, she played nervously with her coffee cup, but as she talked, Carolyn became serious and her eyes misted over. Her most intense nonverbal communication was displayed when she discussed her alarmed reaction to the realization that she had been rejected and felt lonely.

My loneliest experience came about when my boyfriend and I were—ummmm…experiencing problems. After three years—he decided he didn't want a full-time relationship—although he said that he still loved me. Going skiing, to movies, or dinner, phone calls at least once a day; all these were a routine in our three year relationship. All of a sudden it all came to a stop. He didn't call me for about two or three weeks and I felt like pulling out my hair. I became isolated from others. I invited him to go out with me on a Saturday night. Of course I waited by the phone all day until he finally called at 6 o'clock and told me he was doing something else. I was shocked, heart broken, enraged. That night I felt so lonely—my roommate was with her boyfriend at his house, so there I was pacing my apartment—all by myself. I phoned several friends hoping to be able to join them. However, doing it so late on Saturday night I found that people had already made plans. All my friends were busy. That's when it dawned on me that I was lonely!!

I believe that loneliness is part of being human. Everyone has experienced it at some point, and no one wants or likes it. Since loneliness is so painful, however, we would most commonly want to prevent it, or once we experience it, we want to find ways to lower the pain it causes and stop feeling alienated, isolated, and in turmoil. Although common to all people, the nature of loneliness as a subjective experience varies from person to person, occurring under many conditions with a multitude of causes, results, and consequences (Rokach, 1988b, 1989). Attempts to survive this agonizing experience are similarly varied and coping strategies are numerous.

Researchers have described a variety of strategies for coping with loneliness. Some accounts were philosophical in nature (e.g. Moustakes, 1961; Sadler and Johnson, 1980), while others were based on personal observations and surveys of the existing literature (Gordon, 1976). In my research, the focus was on the qualitative aspects of coping strategies. The literature, as well as the public, can name a variety of ways that are thought to be effective in warding off the pain of loneliness. Although possibly popular, how do we really know that these solutions actually "work" and are helpful? To find that out, I conducted a study that involved more than 600 people drawn from all walks of life. I gave them, essentially, an empty piece of paper and asked that they indicate the *helpful* strategies that they utilized to cope with loneliness. Statistical analyzes grouped the multitude of strategies into six distinct factors, or as we will refer to them here, dimensions.

The first dimension identified was *Acceptance and Reflection*, focused on using the opportunity of being by one's self and becoming aware of one's fears, wishes, and needs as the most salient means of coping with loneliness. This dimension can be divided, conceptually, into two themes: facing and accepting loneliness, and self-intimacy and inner search. This would appear to support Rook's (1984b) suggestion that an inability to spend time alone may precipitate and/or exacerbate the experience of loneliness, and it would also back Young's (1982) contention that many lonely people are actually afraid of being alone but are often able to initiate friendships more easily once they overcome this fear (see also Hazan and Zeifman, 1999).

Several of the items that were included in this dimension are:

- I turned loneliness into a time for reflection.
- I came to accept how I felt.
- I came to view being alone as an opportunity to think things through.
- I set new goals for myself.

Mate (2003) maintained that "Acceptance is simply the willingness to recognize and accept how things are. Acceptance does not demand becoming resigned to the continuation of whatever circumstances may trouble us, but it does require a refusal to deny exactly how things happen to be now…Acceptance implies a compassionate relationship with oneself" (p. 264). Awareness, the ability to let ourselves evidence what we feel and what we experience, is an essential part of this dimension (Mate, 2003). Those who will not allow awareness to guide them may attribute their pain to other reasons, and thus be unable to address their pain and distress in a helpful, healthy way. Full awareness, maintained Mate (2003), means that we would regain the capacity that we many have lost as children to perceive emotional reality and that we are ready to dispose of the paralyzing belief that we are not strong and capable enough to face the reality of our lives, as painful as they may be.

Moustakes (1972) and Mayer Gaev (1976) described loneliness as including a feeling of inner void, a detachment from one's self, and an alienation from one's core identity. As such, the most salient coping strategy to emerge, reflection and acceptance, maintains that one cannot deal effectively with loneliness without having an encounter with one's self that involves a direct and straightforward facing of one's loneliness. As indicated by our study, such an encounter requires the willingness to experience fear, anger, agony, and/or disillusionment. Thus, loneliness may precipitate a "joyous experience of self-discovery, a real meeting of self-to-self...it includes a sense of harmony and well-being... [and a way] of advancing life and coming alive in a relatively dead or stagnant world" (Moustakes, 1972, p. 21).

Andre (1991) referred to this coping strategy as *positive solitude*, which he described as the antidote to the sometimes desperate attempts of some people to "find someone." Contemporary belief holds that being alone is related to unhappiness, depression, and failure; consequently, the ability to think positively about being alone—and to be content living alone—is not well developed in North America. A particularly pernicious belief, observed Andre, is that finding relationships, friends, or partners may cure loneliness. Being alone, it is assumed, means that people cannot really conquer their loneliness (Andre, 1991). Andre believes that "only when we learn to live alone, and even to love alone—when we face our alienation, our vulnerability, our creativity, our uniqueness, our humanity, and our desires—will the problems of finding others and finding community become less urgent" (p. xix).

Solitude (i.e. welcomed aloneness), which we may learn to engage in instead of the mad rush to find company, can aid in coping effectively with the pain of loneliness in that it stops attempts to deny loneliness, thereby promoting its acceptance as an existential and, at times, unavoidable human condition. Solitude, once we can allow ourselves to experience it, facilitates a redirecting of one's inner resources towards greater understanding of ourselves, learning to enjoy our own company, and taking the time and space to plan ways to overcome the conditions that precipitated the experience of loneliness. Solitude is said to promote individuality, creativity, and self-awareness by allowing the opportunity for contemplation, self-exploration, and insight.

Mijuskovic (2012) suggested that man has the ability to, what he termed, "extro-reflect," meaning to concentrate on the external world, to remain preoccupied with diversions, amusements, sports, projects, tasks, "causes," people, popularity, or seeking power. As long as man is directed and attentive "outwardly," he is quite secure from confronting his loneliness. This only means, however, that while being lonely, he is not fully aware of it and is unable to confront and deal with his loneliness.

Coping can be successful and beneficial only after loneliness has been accepted as an integral, natural, and common experience of human existence. Unsuccessful coping is often the result of "loneliness anxiety," which is the unresolved fear of being lonely (Moustakas, 1972). An example of a typically unsuccessful coping strategy is forming a new relationship before a previous one has been completely terminated and dealt with. This approach usually proves not only unsuccessful, but pain-producing as well. Attempting to cope without having first resolved one's loneliness anxiety may help to mask pain temporarily, but ultimately, the individual is left quite vulnerable to the very thing he is trying so desperately to avoid—recurrent bouts of loneliness. In accepting loneliness, however, the fear of its pain no longer reigns as the motivator and driving force for coping. Instead, the individual becomes fully aware of himself as a human being by realizing his inner strength, resources, and ability to survive despite the anguish of loneliness (Moustakas, 1972). Thus, the individual is not desperate for intimate relationships; he does not *have* to be with others, but can exert control over his life and become involved with others at will. Being free to *choose* rather than *need* a relationship is a major contributing factor to a person's independence. Not clinging to a mate allows one to be more appreciative of human relations and thus be able to offer more of oneself to another. Paradoxically, this independence results in closer and longer unions, and exonerates loneliness to a situational and temporary occurrence.

The next dimension, *Self-Development and Understanding*, addresses the increased self-intimacy, renewal, and growth that are often the results of active participation in organized focus groups (Parents Without Partners, Alcoholics Anonymous, dating clubs, etc.) and of receiving professional help or support and guidance from the clergy.

A sample of items that formed this dimension is:

- I sought professional help from a medical doctor.
- I went back to work after years of being at home.
- I enrolled in personal development seminars.
- I joined a support group.

When we decide to consult a mental health professional, we bring a new brand of connection into our lives—a connection with someone who can help us feel and function better. Soon, client and therapist—provided they have established good rapport—are deeply involved in a unique relationship that is geared to help one of them, the client, benefit from the discussions with the therapist who has the ability and lengthy training to provide the client with reliable attention and understanding, keeping the focus on the client's world and his problems.

Therapy can help the lonely in many ways. First, via therapy, the lonely is relieved as she is able to talk with another human being about important issues in her life. Another benefit is that the lonely can share strong, painful emotions without needing to censor himself or worrying about the effect it may have on his relationship with the therapist. That alone may contribute to the client not feeling alone, and at times even feeling that she is reentering the human race. The hope is that it will jump start the client's other relationships and will aid in social intercourse. Therapy will also assist the lonely to examine his life and past, and resolve issues that keep him unhappy, lonely, and not belonging.

In keeping with the general belief that humans often experience loneliness as a response to the absence of relationships that provide intimacy, attachment, warmth, and caring, the third dimension, *Social Support Network*, addresses the reestablishment of a social support network that provides the means for helping one feel connected to and valued by others. A sample of the items in this dimension includes:

- I renewed old friendships.
- I went to more parties and social functions.
- I corresponded with friends/family more frequently.

Baumeister (1991) found four criteria to people's meaningful life. First, having a sense of purpose; this is a result of realizing that present activities contribute to future outcomes. Second is the sense of efficacy that people feel when they perceive that they have control over the outcomes. Third is when people perceive that their actions have a positive value or are morally justified. Fourth, people want a sense of self-worth; they want to feel that they possess some positive traits and that they are as good as or better than others.

The formation and maintenance of positive social relations is one of the major motivations of humans (Buss, 1990; Maslow, 1968). Baumeister and Leary (1995) described it as the need to belong.

Social contentment, being comfortable with our social support system, contributes to our ability to be generous, optimistic, and resilient. Moreover, such a behavior will, most often elicit warmth and good-will from others, and thus help us develop, maintain, and increase our social network (Cacioppo and Patrick, 2008).

It is widely accepted by laymen and researchers alike that rebuilding one's social network and establishing close relationships are among the most effective ways of coping with loneliness. Blieszner (1988) observed that having a support network, which may be constituted in a variety of ways, from attending impersonal social events to being involved in deeply personal relationships, provides the feeling that one belongs and is loved and valued. Weiss (1974) described a well-functioning social support network as one that encourages feelings of attachment, social integration, opportunities to be nurturant, reassurance in one's worth, and guidance from the people who form the network. Due to the fact that relationships tend to be specialized and each typically fulfills a different need, a variety of relationships are necessary to avoid the distress of loneliness. The items included in this dimension suggest relational diversity ranging from increased time spent with people, to reestablishing relationships with friends and family members, to initiating romantic connections.

Humans obtained most of what they need from their fellow man, and consequently during their evolution they have developed the ability to socialize and connect with others for the sake of their survival. Hence, the inability to connect with others, be it because of social isolation or otherwise, would be perceived as a threat to people's existence and decrease their life's meaning.

Social support is basically a communication that is a critical component of the maintenance, or disruption, of mental and physical health (House, Landis, and Umberson, 1988). It is, naturally, related to loneliness, though it is the quality rather than the quantity of support offered that is the important element (Cacioppo et al., 2006b). Cacioppo and colleagues, in series of studies, found that chronic loneliness is deleterious to health. Loneliness, they theorized, reduced our resilience over time so that as we age our resilience is lowered and we become more susceptible to health problems (Hawkley and Cacioppo, 2003, 2007).

"In effect, many of the risk factors for poor health, such as ineffective health behaviors and exaggerated sensitivity to stress, are more prevalent among people who are lonely in comparison to those who are not" (Segrin and Passaccacque, 2010, p. 313). The authors found that loneliness is negatively associated with general health and in relation to that, they found that social support from a significant other, from friends, or from family is associated with better health.

It seems that the lonely, in comparison to the nonlonely, perceive their life circumstances as more stressful, unpredictable, and overwhelming. That creates, over time, wear and tear on the body's nervous system and physiology, thus increasing one's susceptibility to health problems and illness. Sleep, which has a major recuperative function, is disturbed in lonely people, leading to health and emotional problems, e.g. anxiety and depression.

Social support has been long known to positively affect our physical health and to work as a stress buffering agent that is essential for its helpful properties; it supplies the perception that others will provide necessary resources to help us cope with and lower our stress level (Uchino et al., 1996). Beyond the perception that one is helped by others, support may alleviate the effects of stress by providing solutions to the difficulty that precipitated the stress or by providing a distraction to the problem. It is also known to influence one's sense of self and one's emotional tone. While people get support and engage in social interaction, they are guided by a common set of expectations about how people should act in different roles, and they thus gain a sense of identity, predictability, and self-worth (Willis, 1985; Cohen, 1988). In addition, social intercourse has been found to increase the positive affect of and help limit the intensity and duration of negative affective states (Cohen, 1988).

Sociability was associated with greater resistance to developing colds when people were experimentally exposed to a cold virus (Cohen, Doyle, Turner, Alper, and Skoner, 2003). Social support also buffered the effects of the psychological stress of depression.

> At the beginning of a new millennium social worlds are changing. Developments in the physical environment, scientific and technological innovations, the reorganization of work or leisure and the impact of globalization and global capitalism have varyingly influenced the nature of the world in which we now live. Social engagement and relationships, however, remain important at any age and their quality is a key element contributing to the quality of life of older people.
>
> (Bond and Corner, 2004; Bowling et al., 2005)

> Framed by networks of kin and friends, participation in activities and hobbies, the enactment of social roles and the nature of social relationships is shaped and modified by experiences along the life course through the dynamic interaction of time and place.
>
> (Olds and Schwartz 2009, p.1)

Although increased social participation may not ultimately offer lasting, deeply personal, and intimate relationships, such participation may provide company, a sense of belonging, and guidance and advice that one gets from acquaintances and friends. Jones, Cavert, Snider, and Bruce (1985) believed "relational stress" to be a major contributor to the development of loneliness; this can be defined as (a) emotional threats to relationships, such as arguments or failure to live harmoniously; (b) social isolation, which is related to being left out or having few or no friends; (c) social marginality, felt when one is with people with whom there is little in common; and (d) romantic conflicts. As Jones, Rose, and Russell (1990) reported, relational stress appears to increase feelings of dissimilarity between and distance from others. Therefore, effectively coping with loneliness should involve decreasing the social gap between oneself and others while increasing the similarity of one's experiences and skills with those of others.

Distancing and Denial, the next dimension of coping, addresses this issue and confirms the connection found between loneliness and alcoholism, drug abuse, and other behavioral disorders or deviant behaviors (Rook, 1984). Some of the items that formed this dimension are:

- I purposely built walls around myself.
- I drank alcohol in excess.
- I denied to myself that anything was wrong.

Considerable diversity appears to exist among the coping strategies of the lonely (Rook, 1988), and people differ in their readiness to recognize or admit (to themselves and to others) that they are in pain because they feel lonely (Booth, 1983; Rook and Peplau, 1982). Feared stigma and loneliness anxiety, i.e. defending against the fear of experiencing loneliness (see

Moustakes, 1972), may result in attempts to deny the experience either outright or by distancing oneself from the pain, feelings of failure, and restlessness and desperation that loneliness entails (Rook, 1988). Although previous writers (i.e. Moustakes, 1961, 1972; Rokach, 1990) emphasized the need to face and accept loneliness as the initial step of coping with its pain successfully, it is interesting that participants in our studies found that such denial was beneficial in some respect and for a limited time.

Self-generated social detachment (e.g. "I purposely built walls around myself") or the purposeful avoidance of interacting with others was identified as an important facet of this dimension. It has been suggested (Sullivan, 1953; Weiss, 1973) that loneliness is actually a driving force that motivates people to initiate social interactions, and intuitively one may agree that this could be beneficial in attempting to end loneliness. Participants in the present study, however, found that the acute pain, suffering, upheaval, and agony suffered when lonely was so disturbing and unsettling that they felt they could not comfortably associate with others. On the contrary, they reported that the pain and vulnerability they experienced caused them to maintain some "space" or detachment from people, both as a measure for protecting their vulnerable self and as an attempt to minimize further hurt that might be caused by failed attempts to associate with others.

When we started to explore loneliness and how people cope with it, we did not expect that religiosity and attending religious services would be prominent among the strategies that are used to address the pain of loneliness. The *Religion and Faith* dimension, suggests that individuals need to feel connected to and/or worship a divine entity, God, or supreme being. Through affiliating with religious groups and practicing their faith, individuals gain strength, inner peace, and a sense of community and belonging. The items included here are:

- I sought answers to my problems in prayer.
- My attendance at religious services increased.
- I felt strengthened and comforted by my faith in God.

Andre (1991) suggested that one may successfully deal with loneliness by finding solace, that "emotional experience of a soothing presence. In a turbulent world solace calms us. In the face of adversity it gives us composure" (p. 108).

Andre observed that ritual is an important source of solace in that it provides rewarding connections to the past and the future and anchors the individual to time and space. Thus, religion and faith may not only provide the person with connectedness to other worshippers but also with the solace that comes from feeling related to a protective and powerful supreme being. In the dawn of the 21st century, this has been termed a "New Age practice," but it seems that the public, in reaction to the Western money and capital oriented culture, are addressing the alienation that our individualistic culture promotes by increasing their attendance in religious services and developing their spirituality. It is also safe to assume that at least part of those attending religious services are there not so much out of religious "duty," but in order to be among people, to feel part of a group, and to partake in common practices and beliefs.

Spirituality, which is different from religiosity, is seen as the belief in something bigger than ourselves and is the recognition that we are part of a magnificent universe, which runs according to its own rules, to which we also must adhere. Pargament and Sweeney (2011) defined spirituality as "the continuous journey people take to discover and realize their spirit, that is, their essential selves…for as long as people engage in these various means with the intent to enhance their search to discover and realize their essential selves, they are participating in spiritual quest" (p. 58-59). It has been reported that people who engage in spiritual quests may grow from them while taking different paths including nature, work, exercise, intimate relationships, religion, art, or philosophy (Dalton, Eberhardt, Bracken, and Echols, 2006). Those who attain spiritual growth are better able to accept the reality of the situation, develop creative coping strategies, find meaning in their trauma or stressful situation, grow from adversity, and generate the motivation to access their social support network (Pargament and Sweeney, 2011; Tedeschi and Calhoun, 2004). Spiritual struggles and quests, along with the questions, conflicts, and tensions about matters that may be of deepest meaning to the individual, have led to profound personal growth, an increased ability to make meaning out of a situation and one's experience of loneliness, and engagement in positive problem solving actions (Pargament, 2007; Pargament, Murray-Swank, Magyar, and Ano, 2005; Park, 2005).

Suggesting ways for the seriously ill to help their body heal, Mate (2003) recommended the affirmation of people's confidence in their traditional faith or their communion with nature. Just like in addressing the emotional pain of loneliness, dealing with illness and its consequent physical pain involves seeking the way to the light within and without us. Spirituality is often embraced by the sick and those who understand that we as humans have more than one dimension. We are a body, a psyche, and a spirit. Psychologist Thomas Plante, quoted in Azar (2011), maintained that religion helps us see people as more whole. Religion, and the way we think of spirituality and the supernatural (i.e. God), reiterates that we are whole people. All our aspects are connected—the biological, psychological, social, cultural, and spiritual. It is suggested that having spiritual beliefs may help us enjoy a more peaceful, longer, and healthier life but more than that, "Religion…allows people to live in large, cooperative societies…religion is one of the big ways that human societies have hit on as a solution to induce unrelated individuals to be nice to each other" (p. 55).

The distress of loneliness has also been described as "paralyzing hopelessness and unalterable futility" (Fromm-Reichman, 1959, in Rokach 1988, p. 540b). Such immobilization in response to the pain and anxiety of loneliness is akin to the shock that one experiences following a traumatic event, such as the death of a loved one or being involved in a car accident (Rokach, 1988b). The coping strategies identified as helpful in the *Increased Activity* dimension appear to counteract the immobilization associated with loneliness. Rather than be immersed in pain, helplessness, and sadness, lonely people may actively pursue not only their daily responsibilities but also leisure and fun-filled solitary or group activities as well, thus creating new opportunities for activity and social contact. Increasing their repertoire of rewarding activities may be useful to the lonely for several reasons. First, it may decrease their dependence on others and may consequently increase their sense of personal control (Rook and Peplau, 1982); second, pleasurable and satisfying activities may aid in lifting the sadness or depression that often accompanies loneliness (Fuchs and Rehn, 1977; Lewinsohn, Biglan, and Zeiss, 1976). The items that make up this dimension include:

- I took up a new hobby.
- I immersed myself in work.

- I took up a new sport.

Health is improved by religious and spiritual activities. The person who is part of a religious community often participates in supportive social activities and is shown to be less lonely and have a less stressful life. Research has further demonstrated that spiritual activity is life prolonging and illness-preventing (Seeman et al., 2003).

We divided the conception of coping with loneliness into three clusters. The first, which could be termed *Acceptance and Resource Development*, included the Reflection and Acceptance, Self-Development and Understanding, and Religion and Faith dimensions. The salient feature of this cluster is the person's increased awareness of his thoughts and feelings, and at times, reflections on his standing in the universe. This sort of reflection seems to naturally go along with a wish to connect to a higher power and find the meaning to life and explanation of universal "truths."

Once we have accepted loneliness as a real part of our life, there is a greater readiness to surrender to the experience and endure its pain and terror (see also Moustakas, 1961). During the phase of acceptance, while withstanding lengthy periods of solitary activities, the lonely person may become involved in self-exploration. Using loneliness as a time for reflection, the lonely may evaluate and assess life, their goals, and the people around them. As a result of enduring the pain, they emerge stronger, with a clearer understanding of themselves and a renewed commitment to cope with their loneliness. This renewed commitment is not borne out of fear or the perception that loneliness is a "disease" or "unacceptable phenomenon," but of the pain that was replaced with the pleasure of having survived the ordeal.

"Jim" is a 52-year-old father of six who experienced his loneliest moment after separating from his wife. He found the strength to cope and survive after accepting loneliness as his inescapable companion.

> I faced loneliness like I have faced all other problems I have had in my life. First there is pain and then fear and then you face the problem itself and decide what to do about it. I understood and accepted that I am alone and made use of the time I had—learning about who I am and what I like to do. I read a great deal, I think a great deal. I enjoy my own company. I have learned in my solitude to be a good listener, and there are many people who just want someone to listen to them. While I don't always enjoy their company I feel a sense of satisfaction from just being with them.

The second conceptual cluster, *Building Social Bridges*, included the Social Support Network and the Increased Activity dimensions that may be useful if they occur after the person has done the preparatory work: looked into himself, understood *and* accepted his loneliness, embellished those skills he needed to polish in order to increase his chances to create satisfying social or romantic relationships, and possibly developed his spirituality, which will in turn enhance his contact with and knowledge of himself.

Both of these clusters emphasize the intention and concerted effort to build social bridges through which a lonely individual can reconnect to others. By developing a social support network, one's chances, at least statistically, of finding people to relate to, become closer to, love, and be loved by are increased.

Distancing and Denial formed the third conceptual cluster of dealing with loneliness by succumbing to loneliness anxiety—the inability to face loneliness and the overwhelming need to deny it and avoid a full awareness of its pain. Although this approach may successfully block the pain of loneliness in the short run, it probably would not suffice to deal with it on an ongoing basis. For, as Moustakes (1961) observed, in order for it to be resolved, loneliness must be faced and courageously accepted, and its pain endured. The consequences of using some of these methods will undoubtedly result in further problems.

"Howard," a 26-year-old heavy machinery operator who had recently separated from his wife, described his struggle with loneliness in an eloquent manner. His pain was followed by denial and culminated with the realization that he was, indeed, all alone.

> I suppose the most intense period of loneliness I ever experienced was after my wife and I separated. For the first couple of months I tried to deny that it was happening. Anger became my constant companion. For days my thoughts drifted from blaming her to blaming myself until finally acceptance came. Along with the acceptance I realized that no matter who was right or who was wrong it was over. The anger and resentment subsided and I started to recall some good memories. I knew I had to make a life for myself without her. Working kept me occupied and kept my feeling of loneliness at bay. The thought of leaving work at the end of the day was the hardest part, because I knew no one would be waiting for me at home. At 4 o'clock I'd hit the street and catch a bus. I felt totally alone, even in the crowded bus. People were like objects and I was hardly aware of them. When I arrived home to an empty house, often I would cry and sometimes even call her name. I knew then that I was alone and lonely.

The conditions under which distancing from loneliness may be helpful need to be explored. We suggest that such an approach may have been reported as successful either by individuals who were in the throes of attempting to deal with loneliness or by those who had experienced brief loneliness that dissipated as a result of a change in their life circumstances. Thus, these individuals could indulge in "clouding" their perception and distorting their alienation when, without making any effort to address their loneliness directly, it was resolved. It should also be noted that isolating oneself and/or engaging in illegal or harmful activities may indeed ward off loneliness but it is safe to presume that even if this is the case, the long-term personal and social costs far outweigh any possible gains from such an approach.

I wish to close this chapter with a quote from Ornish's (1998) book, where he discussed what a strong and overwhelming need for belonging may cause a person to do. "When people are unable to experience the feeling of connection and community in healing ways, they will often find it in ways that are dark and destructive…Joining a gang is becoming a popular way of getting a sense of community and family, even if you have to rob or to kill somebody to join the gang…In San Diego, thirty nine people chose to commit suicide together in 1997, many of whom already had undergone surgical castration in order to be part of that community" (p. 19). And all that, to be part of a community.

Chapter 9

ON LOVE AND LONELINESS

> Loneliness, or more correctly, the drive to avoid it, a sense of isolation, actually constitutes the dominant psychic force underlying all human consciousness and conduct.
> (Mijuskovic, 2012, p.4)

People are social animals. As we have repeatedly observed in this book, there is a basic human need to belong, to be part of an intimate, lasting, caring relationship with a partner who is close and deeply concerned about us (Miller, 2012). In order to fulfill that need, we are driven to establish close contact with others and participate in intimate relationships. Research has demonstrated that people live happier, longer, healthier, and more fulfilling lives when they are closely connected to others (Koball, Moiduddin, Henderson, Goesling, and Besculides, 2010). More poignant indications can be seen in the observation that people holding their lover's hand felt supported and their brain's response to a threatening situation was reduced (Coan, Schaefer, and Davidson, 2006). Even pain was reported to be less potent when one was doing something as little as looking at a *photograph* of one's loved one.

On the contrary, people who have less than the needed quantity and quality of intimacy in their lives risk a variety of health problems, loneliness, and mortality (Cohen, 2004; Berkman and Glass, 2000). Happy, contented partnerships lead to greater well-being than unhappy ones do, yet many people feel more fulfilled in an unhappy relationship than they do when they're completely alone, preferring a bad relationship to utter loneliness (Miller, 2012). Segrin (1998) observed that those with unsatisfying ties have a higher probability than those in intimate and satisfying relationships to experience depression, alcoholism, and eating disorders. Lack of intimacy may be both the cause and the enhancer of emotional problems (Miller, 2012).

THE NATURE OF INTIMACY

Intimacy is a multifaceted concept and is composed of *knowledge, caring, interdependence, mutuality, trust, and commitment* (Miller, 2012; Ben-Ari and Lavee, 2007; Prager and Roberts, 2004). An intimate relationship indicates that the partners have extensive personal, confidential, and private *knowledge* about each other. That rich information, which the partners share, may include their histories, preferences, feelings, and desires that they would commonly not reveal to other people. Intimate partners *care* about each other, feeling affectionate towards their partner to a greater extent than they would to someone else. Intimate partners' lives are intertwined and they affect each other continually. Interdependence between them, i.e. the extent to which they need and influence each other, is frequent; it impacts meaningfully on the other and does so in many areas of life, in different ways, and over long periods of time (Berscheid et al., 2004; Miller, 2012). Intimate couples often exhibit *mutuality*, thinking of themselves as "us" (Fitzsimons and Kay, 2004) and seeing themselves as overlapping in various respects. It almost goes without saying that intimacy means *trust*, where the partners know that it is safe to open up and that their partner will be there to support and respond to their needs (Reis et al., 2004). Finally, being in such a unique and protective relationship, intimate partners are *committed* to their relationship; they expect them to go on indefinitely and to reach that goal, they are ready to invest time, effort, and the resources at their disposal. Miller (2012) asserts that "none of these components is absolutely required for intimacy to occur, and each may exist when the others are absent" (p. 3).

While many complain, after years of togetherness, that "love went out the window," some couples, and we may want to learn from them, do continue to feel passionately in love, but that love changes over time (Walster and Walster, 1978). Such people, even 10 or 20 years into their relationship or marriage, when they see a picture of their loved one, experience activation of the reward centers in their brains just as they did when they were falling in love years earlier (Acevedo et al., 2011). Research suggests that even when desire and caring remain, the sometimes obsessive preoccupation with the loved one tends to fade away (Acevedo and Aron, 2009). While it seems that passion may decline over time, intimacy and commitment actually increase with age (Ahmetoglu et al., 2010). Consequently, it has been observed that compassionate love is more stable than romantic love (Sprecher and Regan, 1998).

LOVE: A BRIEF HISTORICAL PERSPECTIVE

Historically there was a "double standard" as far as sexuality was concerned (Hatfield et al., 2008). Many older adults would interpret "passionate love" to mean sexual love. In the Victorian era, men loved sexually but women did not. Older women actually prefer the relational aspects of sexual activities, such as talking and uttering love words, to the sexual act itself. Men, on the other hand, view sexual activities (such as body caressing, masturbation, and intercourse) to be the most important aspect (Johnson, 1997; Peterson, 2007).

Traditionally, women depended on their husbands for status and economic well-being so their emotional yearnings had to be controlled in order to please "Mr. Right"—the man who came from the proper social background and had a promising financial potential. Men, on the other hand, did not need to engage in all those "calculations" and had the luxury of marrying a woman they passionately loved. Therefore, women passively waited for the right match, while men were free to initiate a relationship with those they loved (Safilios–Rothschild, 1977).

Today, when women depend less on marriage for status and financial well-being, when they can pursue education and career opportunities, it is acceptable that they actively seek men to whom they are attracted (Peplau, 2002). In this day and age, and especially in the Western culture, both genders insist on a "love match" regardless of the practical implications or potential (Allgeier and Wiederman, 1991).

WHAT ARE RELATIONSHIPS INFLUENCED BY?

Intimacy and love are considered a universal experience (see also Xu et al., 2011). It should be noted, however, that relationships and intimacy are, indeed, influenced by the times and the culture in which they occur. A brief examination of the relational patterns in the U.S. reveals interesting trends:

a) Fewer people got married in the dawn of the 21st century than ever before. While in the 1960s, 94% of people married at some point in their lives, only 85% of today's young adults are expected to marry (Cherlin, 2009). Taking into account separation, divorce, widowhood, and those who never married, only 52% of the U.S. adult population is presently married (Mather and Lavery, 2010).

b) People marry now at an older age. On average women are 26 and men are 28 years old when they first marry (Jayson, 2010). Up to 46% of Americans reach their mid-30s without being married.

c) Babies are regularly born now to unwedded parents, while in the 1960s, for instance, it was a rare (and often shameful) occurrence. It has been reported that in 2009, up to 41% of children were born to unwed mothers, the highest rate ever recorded in North America (Taylor, 2010).

d) A whopping half of all marriages now end in divorce (Cherlin, 2010). What was once a sacred institution, one that was to last until people were separated by death, is now but an excursion at life together until the common ship hits an iceberg and the couple either drowns or jump to safety, each swimming in a different direction.

e) Up to 40% of children live in a single parent home (Taylor, 2010). As they grow up, they often witness their single parent attempting to reestablish intimate connections and find a mate, which means that a variety of adults may come and go through their homes and lives affecting them in enumerable ways—good, bad, and sometimes harmful (Cherlin, 2010).

f) While in the 1960s, for example, 75% of mothers stayed home during their children's pre-schooling years, only 40% of them do so now (Taylor, 2010). Presently most mothers work, and while we do not refer to them as "latchkey kids" any longer, there are more of them now than in the past.

Miller (2012) observed that "once upon a time, everyone married within a few years of leaving high school and, happy or sad, they tended to stay with their original partners. Pregnant people felt that they *had* to get married, and cohabitation was known as 'living in sin'. But not so anymore" (p. 8-9).

Do these changes matter? Apparently, they do. Acitelli et al. (2011) highlighted the close connection between cultural standards and intimate relationships, or for that matter—relationships in general. Cohabitation is a relatively recent development in relational trajectories and is assumed to help the couple adjust to each other, so when they later marry, they will have a chance at a happier union. Research, in fact, indicates that if a subsequent marriage—following a period of cohabitation—does occur, it has an *increased* chance to end in divorce (Jose et al., 2010).

Another influence on people's intimate relationships is the American individualistic culture with its emphasis on personal expression and fulfillment, and self-realization, which causes people to focus on themselves and their needs at the expense of their relationships and of caring for the good of their relationships (Twenge and Campbell, 2010). So why should it matter to us? Why is it important that intimate relationships have been and are still changing?

Lynch (2000) observed that mortality rates for all causes of death in the U.S. are found to be consistently higher at all ages for divorced, single, and widowed people regardless of their gender or race. This finding is very striking since death rates in unmarried individuals may be as high as ten (!) times the rate of married individuals of comparable ages (see also Kraus and Lillienfeld, 1959). Forty years after Kraus and Lillienfeld's observation, the relative disparity in life span for the married and non-married has grown even larger (Lynch, 2000). As if to confirm the above finding, Medalie and Goldbourt (1976) found in a large scale study of men that those who later experienced myocardial infractions reported a higher incidence of dissatisfaction with their marital lives and did not feel supported by their wives.

Ornish (1998) described a very large scale research study that looked at ten thousand married men with no prior history of heart related complaints. In general, men who suffered from significant risk factors such as elevated cholesterol, high blood pressure, age, diabetes, or electrocardiogram abnormalities were found to be twenty times more likely to develop chest pain (angina) over the next five years. The men were asked, by the researcher, a simple question, "Does your wife show her love?" Those who answered in the affirmative had suffered from significantly less angina, even when they had high levels of the risk factors mentioned previously. Men who did not receive such love and care from their partner showed a substantial increase in angina. The researchers found that those men, who had anxiety and family problems, conflicts, and concerns, had increased levels of chest pain.

LOVE AND ATTACHMENT

Classical psychoanalytic and Pavlovian behavioral systems viewed emotional bonds that develop between the infant and its parent as a secondary effect of feeding. As we have previously reviewed it, we will briefly mention that Bowlby (1969, 1982) and Harlow (1959) rejected that psychoanalytic view and described infants as innately relationship-seeking and orientated toward what Harlow termed, "contact comfort," naturally inclined to seek proximity to their caregivers. Bowlby extended that view and observed that the caregivers, or attachment figures, need to provide a "safe haven" in times of need and a safe environment that the infant can then explore comfortably. Shaver, Hazan, and Bradshaw (1988) extended Bowlby's conceptualization of attachment figures into adulthood. Thus, adult romantic bonds are actually emotional attachments that are reminiscent of the bonds an infant had with his caregivers. Shaver et al. claimed that "for every documented feature of attachment there is a parallel feature of love, and for most documented features of love there is either a documented or a plausible infant parallel" (p. 73). Interestingly, pointed out Shaver and Mikulincer (2002), love in infancy as well as in adulthood is expressed similarly in activities such as crying, clinging, a desire to be comforted by the other person (relationship, partner, or primary caregiver), and experiencing such negative emotions as anger or anxiety at a separation, and conversely, happiness upon a reunion. In both kinds of relationships, when the partner (or primary caregiver) is *not* available or does not respond to the other person's proximity bids, the one seeking closeness may become "obsessed" with getting it and become hypersensitive to signs of rejection or disapproval.

Hazan and Shaver (1987) utilized the same three attachment modes that were described by Ainsworth, Blehar, Waters, and Wall (1978) to illustrate their adult attachment versions. These are:

> *Secure*: I find it relatively easy to get close to others and am comfortable depending on them and having them depend on me. I don't worry about being abandoned or about someone getting too close to me.
> *Avoidant*: I am somewhat uncomfortable being close to others; I find it difficult to trust them completely, difficult to allow myself to depend on them. I am nervous when anyone gets too close, and often others want me to be more intimate than I feel comfortable being.
> *Anxious*: I find that others are reluctant to get as close as I would like. I often worry that my partner doesn't really love me or won't want to stay with me. I want to get very close to my partner, and this sometimes scares people away.
>
> (Berscheid, 2006, p. 39)

Hazan and Shaver (1987) researched these hypothesized relationship styles and concluded that frequencies of attachment styles in adulthood are similar to those expressed by infants. Moreover, they found that in their romantic relationships, adults tend to display the same attachment style that they displaced during infancy so *securely* attached adults, perceived their love relationships to be friendly, warm, and supportive. Intimacy was the core of their romantic relationships, and they believed that love can be maintained over a long period of time. *Avoidant* attachment style individuals had romantic relationships that they described as low in warmth or friendly interactions and lacking in emotional involvement. In their experience, love fades over time, and the kind of love depicted in novels and movies is simply unrealistic. People who display an *anxious* attachment style characterized their romantic involvement as containing strong physical attraction, a desire to merge with their partner, and proneness to fall in love somewhat indiscriminately. Their lovers were depicted by them as untrustworthy and unsupportive, and rejection or abandonment aroused in them intense bouts of jealousy and anger.

Romantic relationships, love, and sex are significantly affected by the three parameters named by Shaver and Mikulincer (2002): attachment to one's partner, the care giving behavior that they both display, and their sexual relationships. They maintained that these three "ingredients are important for understanding romantic love, because the system's smooth functioning brings relationship partners together, increases physical and emotional closeness, and heightens feelings of love and gratitude toward the partner as well as feelings of being loved and esteemed by the partner" (p. 49).

Research has demonstrated that people with a secure attachment style enjoy higher levels of relational stability and satisfaction in their dating and marital unions (see Mikulincer, Florain, Cowan, and Cowan, 2001), higher levels of intimacy and commitment (Collins and Read, 1990; Simpson, 1990), and they employ positive expectations about their partner's behaviors and conflict resolution skills (Baldwin, Fehr, Keedian, Seidel, and Thompson, 1993). There is also accumulating research evidence that care giving behavior, as well as sex that gratifies, contribute to relationship satisfaction and stability (see Collins and Feeney, 2000; Sprecher and Cate, 2004) and heightened feelings of love (Sprecher and Regan, 1998; Waite and Joyner, 2001).

ON LOVE

I used to feel loved because I was special. Now, I feel special because I am loved and because I can love   (Ornish, 1998, p. 91)

What is love is a question that is probably as old as humanity. Writers, philosophers, poets, and sculptors have attempted to describe and capture its meaning for centuries, but it is only relatively recently that social scientists have shown interest in researching and writing about love (Fehr, 2006).

Ancient Views of Love

"What 'tis to love?" asked Shakespeare in *As You Like It* (in Fisher, 2006, p. 87), and, indeed, since the time of the ancient Greeks to our time, there have been literally hundreds of theories that aimed to describe and explain love; that emotion that "we know when we feel it" but are hard pressed to define (Fehr, 1988; Fisher, 2006; Lee, 1988).

Knox and Schacht (2010) maintain that our present day notions of love stem from early Buddhist and Greek writings. The Buddhists conceived of two forms of love: a) self-love, the unfortunate kind of love, and b) the creative spiritual attainment, which to them was the "good" kind of love. This was the "love of detachment," not as in withdrawal from emotional connections, but in accepting people the way they are and not expecting them to be different in order to get friendly affection. That is the best love to a Buddhist.

The Greeks introduced three kinds of love: phileo, agape, and eros. *Phileo* is love that is based on friendship and can be found between family members, friends, and lovers. *Agape* is love that has at its core the concern for the well-being of others. It is a spiritual and not a sexual kind of love. It is altruistic and requires nothing in return. Such love is based on generous "giving," but is not always reciprocal. *Eros* is sexual love. It is a love that seeks gratification and sexual expression. In the days of Plato, this kind of love was reserved for marriage, and even more so for homosexuals, which were considered to possess the highest form of love, because their love existed independent of their procreation instinct and bonds of matrimony (Knox and Schacht, 2010).

Love in the 1100s was influenced by economic, political, and family structure (Hatfield et al., 2008). During those times, love was not tied to marriage but was based on the adoration of physical beauty and served as a spiritual and romantic endeavor. It could occur between married partners or unmarried people. Thus, romantic love was mainly found in extramarital love rather than between spouses (Trachman and Bluestone, 2005). Later on, in Medieval times, marriage was less of a way to connect on the basis of politics or finances and this is when marriage started to be based on love.

The first psychologist to write extensively about love was Rubin (1970, 1973) who defined it as an attitude that causes one to think, feel, and act in particular ways towards the love object. Rubin further suggested that love has three components: intimacy, need/attachment, and caring (see also Steck, Levitan, McCane, and Kelley, 1982). Berscheid and Walster's (1974) model of love was the next major contribution to the study of love. They differentiated between compassionate and passionate love, and while compassionate love is characterized by friendly affection and brings about caring, trust, honesty, and respect similar to what one feels towards one's close friends and family (Hatfield and Walster, 1978; Brehm, 1992), passionate love—on the other hand—is often characterized by emotional extremes, physiological arousal, and sexual attraction (Fehr, 2006).

Hendrick and Hendrick (1986) and Lee (1973) have drawn a typology of six different love styles, described below. They include agape (altruistic love), storge (friendship-based love), ludus (game-playing love), mania (obsessive, dependent love), pragma (practical love), and eros (romantic, passionate love) (Fehr, 2006). Sternberg (1986) proposed the triangular theory of love, with passion, intimacy, and commitment as the vertices. Eight different kinds of love (see below) result from the various combinations of these three elements. Finally, a conceptualization of love as attachment was offered by Hazan and Shaver (1987). The three different attachment styles that humans display in infancy are also evident in people's relation with an adult romantic partner.

Fehr (1988) wanted to find out what ordinary people think about love. She asked laypeople (represented by university students) what was love to them. Features that were listed frequently included honesty, trust, and caring, while dependency, sexual passion, and physical attraction were listed infrequently. Fehr concluded that laypeople perceive love to encompass both compassionate and passionate loves. More specifically, she observed that laypeople regarded compassionate love as central to love, whereas passionate kinds of love were considered peripheral (see also Fehr, 2006).

Hegi and Bergner (2010) saw investment in the well-being of the other for his own sake as a central and critical characteristic of love. Singer (1984) observed that in the Western culture, "The lover takes an interest in the other as a person, and not merely as a commodity…He bestows importance on her needs and her desires, even when they do not further the satisfaction of his own…In relation to the lover, the other has become valuable for her own sake" (p. 6). Rankin Williams and Hickle (2010) observed that while humans, from adolescence and on, are intensely involved in the exploration of intimacy, little is known about what romantic love holds.

To conclude, we bring an eloquent definition of love that was offered by Gottschall and Nordlund (2006), who exclaimed that "To love someone romantically is …to experience a strong desire for union with someone who is deemed entirely unique. It is to idealize this person, to think constantly about him or her, and to discover that one's own life priorities have changed dramatically. It is to care deeply for the person's well-being, and to feel pain or emptiness when he or she is absent" (p. 450).

IS LOVE BLIND? IS IT THE SAME EVERYWHERE?

Research involving fMRI (magnetic resonance) scans of the brains of those who reported to be in love demonstrated that the experience of romantic love, in those people, has been correlated with the deactivation of brain centers responsible for critically assessing others and for making moral judgments. That research lends credence to two claims:

1.   That love is blind, and thus, when in love, we tend to overlook the loved one's follies (Fisher and Aron, 2002).
2.   That love is most probably universal and is part of human nature; thus it can be traced to our neural connections (Fisher, 2005).

The Universality of Love

> J. H. Newman, cardinal and philosopher, noted that we tend to fear less that life will end, but rather that life will never begin. His point targets the importance of love in one's life that provides an unparalleled richness, meaning, and happiness. (Knox and Schacht, 2010, p.44)

Love is universal and transcends cultural and geographical borders. Someone once said that love does not make the world go round, but it makes the ride worthwhile.

It is also universally accepted that love can be distinguished as passionate or compassionate (Hatfield, Rapson, and Martel, 2007). Buss (2000) declared that love is universal. Whether experienced or not, man has the capacity to feel love, regardless of his culture, gender, or age. One example of its universality can be gleaned from the attempt of the Oneida society, in the nineteenth century, to banish romantic love since they believed that it was but a deceit, covering up for sexual lust. The Shakers provide another example. They sought to banish love since they saw it as undignified and a threat to the larger society. The Mormons, also in the nineteenth century, viewed love as a disruption in one's life and sought to banish it. In all those societies, however, romantic love persisted and flourished, hidden from the harsh eyes of the group's elders. Love can actually be fueled by others' attempts to deny or suppress it. "Lovers have no choice; they can quell their feelings temporarily, or muffle the expression, but they cannot excise them entirely" (Buss, 2006, p. 67). The same thing happens in cultures that impose arranged marriages and permit polygamy (see also Miller, 2012).

While love is universal, however, its expression may be culturally bound. Persons (1992) claimed that love is culturally bound; if not the emotion itself, then certainly the consequent behavior and the importance of love in people's lives are expressed in a culturally condoned manner. Persons contends that the fact that love is actually absent in some cultures indicates that love is culturally bound. Bloch (1991) even claimed that love is a cultural invention and can be traced back to 12th century France. Gottschall and Nordlund (2006), citing the literary theorist Culler, claimed that "the notion of romantic love [and its centrality in the lives of individuals] is arguably a massive literary creation" (p. 451).

Love itself is said to be experienced identically in the U.S. and say, in China (Xu et al., 2011), and romantic and compassionate love are also recognized as distinctly unique across cultures (Shaver et al., 2001). There are, however, some cultural nuances that are interesting.

Americans, when describing their experiences of falling in love, seem to emphasize the similarities between themselves and their partner, and possibly, the latter's good looks while Chinese people describe their partner's desired personality, their opinions, and their own physical arousal (Riela et al., 2010). Romantic fantasies—which color love in warm, cozy tones with the hope that it will last, in happiness, forever—are more common in America, while the Chinese tend to view such love as a mixed blessing (Jackson et al., 2006). Finally, the requirement of love as necessity for marriage is much more pronounced in the Western, individualistic, countries than in the East (Levin et al., 1995). College students in China are commonly guided by their parents when they seek a partner to marry, whereas in America the choice of a future spouse is seen as the choice of the one who will marry him (Zhang and Kline, 2009).

Attempting to Understand Love

> I believe that love is a felt word, spoken in our flesh and blood, which can only have meaning in the interpersonal context of human dialogue. It is not a rational or objectively quantifiable construct whose essential meaning can be gleaned from a dictionary, learned on the Internet, or observed in a microscope. It is, instead, a word first taught to us by others in dialogue, which helps to bind separate bodies together in shared dialogue.
>
> (Lynch, 2000, p. 197)

Theorists and social researchers have attempted, for quite a long time, to explain what love is. The conceptualization of this central feature in humanity's life, however, has eluded them. One of the reasons for this state of affairs was highlighted by Murstein (1988) who pronounced that "the word *love* is bandied about more promiscuously than almost any other word in the English language" (p. 13). In other words, the word *love* is used in an astounding number of situations, to describe a large variety of attitudes, behaviors, and feelings. Consequently, argues Berscheid (2006), because love has so many meanings, it cannot have one definition. People use the word "love" in a variety of ways. We hear people say, "I love ice cream," and they most probably mean something very different when they utter, "I love you." Berscheid (2006) believes that people usually know what *love* means, since the context in which that word is used establishes its meaning.

Gender Differences in Love

Love exists and seems to have a clear evolutionary goal. In addition, it feels good and is invigorating, so it is something that (a) people wish to feel, but (b) it can be exploited and ruthlessly manipulated. For instance, in order to gain sexual favors, men deceive women about the depth of their love or their willingness to commit to their relationship (Haselton, Buss, Oubaid, and Angleitner, 2005). Ovid, hundreds of years ago, already declared that "love is…a sexual behavior sport, in which duplicity is used in order that a man might win his way into a woman's heart and subsequently into her boudoir" (in Buss, 2006, p. 72). While men may use "love" to get sex, women may deceive men by using sex as a means of getting love (Buss, 2003). Both sexes have developed, along the years, defenses to detect and protect against deception and so "(t)he arms race of deception and detection of deception, of strategies and counter strategies, continues with no end in sight" (Buss, 2006, p. 73).

In his review of the human mating literature, Buss (1989, 2003) found that men place a greater premium than women on physical appearance. That can be explained in terms of evolutionary demands. Physical appearance provides the man with information about the woman's youth and health, and thus the chances of having healthy offspring with her. Women as well value physical appearance because this dimension provides cues of one's youth and reproductive ability; that is more important to women than to men. Buss (2006) further detailed the physical features that support the "attractiveness–fertility" links: "clear skin, smooth skin, slim, lustrous hair, long hair, symmetrical features, absence of open sores, pustules or lesions, relatively small waist, relatively large breasts, and a low waist-to-hip ratio" (p. 68-69). Women, on the other hand, value qualities that cannot be assessed by one's appearance; these include a man's ambition, his industriousness and ability to produce, and status trajectory, all of which are qualities that are related to resource acquisition (Buss and Schmitt, 1993). These are all qualities that men and women look for when choosing a mate for a long-term relationship, and since love is said to be an emotion that belongs and develops in long-term mating, it is interesting to note that men, more than women, report falling in love at first sight. Cultural stereotypes indicate that women generally love men more than they are loved in return. It should be noted, however, that while the stereotype has been recycled by psychologists, sociologists, and feminists, there is little research to support this stereotype. There are gender differences in love, but they are closely related to the kind of love under consideration, people's age and stage in life, and how that love was measured. As far as *passionate* love is concerned, sometimes women are found to be more passionate, while other studies find that it is actually men who are more passionate. Men, however, may have more a romantic or passionate *view* of love than women do (Hatfield and Rapson, 1993; Rubin, 1970) but it would seem that women *feel* more passionately than men do (Hatfield and Rapson, 1993). As for *compassionate* love, results are more clear cut. Here, the cultural stereotype that holds that women are more loving is supported. Women love compassionately more than they are loved (Hendrick and Hendrick, 2006).

Love as a Commitment Tool

Elementary economics, posits Buss (2006), would clearly demonstrate that the one holding valuable resources does not give them away indiscriminately. That leads us to the question, how does one know that one's partner is going to be there through thick and thin, through sickness and health? Frank (1988), an evolutionary economist, maintained that love is, in part, a solution to that quandary, for regardless of the supposedly "rational" reasons that may have been responsible for one being chosen as a mate, commitment can be maintained when the "partner is blinded by an uncontrollable love that cannot be helped and cannot be chosen, a love for only you and no other, then commitment will not waver…Love overrides rationality. It is the emotion that ensures that you will not leave when someone more desirable comes along" (Buss, 2006, p. 71).

Ornish (1998) highlights the evolutionary fact that humans are "touchy-feely" creatures of community. Those humans who learned along the way to care for and love each other, to nurture each other, and keep close—physically and emotionally—over the past hundreds of thousands of years, were more likely to survive than those who did not. In our individualistic cultures, we have neglected caring for each other, and this may imperil our survival. Love is not only soul nourishing, but it can physically heal as well. Ornish (1998) stated it quite powerfully when he wrote that "I have found that perhaps the most powerful intervention— and the most meaningful for me and for most of the people with whom I work, including staff and patients—is the healing power of love and intimacy, and the emotional and spiritual transformation that often result from these" (p. 2).

TAXONOMIES OF LOVE

Love is elusive, and those caught in its spell cannot define it. Love may, at times, be confused with lust and infatuation (Knox and Schacht, 2010) so let us examine them separately. While *love* is about deep, passionate feelings, *lust* is taken to represent sexual desire. *Infatuation* indicates those emotional reactions that are based on very little actual exposure to the love object. Sternberg (1986) developed the "triangular view of love," which focuses on three basic elements: intimacy, passion, and commitment. The love we experience, asserted Sternberg, depends on the presence or absence of those three elements. The various types of love that he enumerated include:

1. *Non love* – two strangers looking at each other. There is no intimacy, passion, or commitment here.
2. *Liking* – a new friendship is usually based on liking, where there is intimacy between the two people, but no passion or commitment.
3. *Infatuation* – passion without intimacy or commitment. Two people who flirt with each other experience infatuation.
4. *Romantic love* – intimacy and passion without commitment. Example: love at first sight.
5. *Conjugal* (compassionate) love – intimacy and commitment without passion. A couple, in a long time marriage, is said to experience this kind of love.
6. *Fatuous love* – passion and commitment without intimacy.
7. *Empty love* – as the title implies, it may describe a couple who stays together for financial or legal reasons but have no spark or emotional sharing between them. It is commitment without passion or intimacy.
8. *Consummate love* – this, a-la-Sternberg, is the ultimate love. It includes all three: intimacy, passion, and commitment.

Hamilton (2006) attempted to highlight what love is, by observing that it is not just what we *feel*, but also how we *behave*. Due to the fact that it is used in an almost infinite contexts and meanings, Berscheid (2006) presented a taxonomy of loves. She highlighted four varieties of loves that each may be associated with different behaviors and causes. Since the capacity for experiencing these types of love is, according to Berscheid, innate, she believes that it also transcends culture. She named four kinds of love:

A) Attachment love. The attachment system was described by Bowlby (1969) and Harlow (1958). Its historical cause lies in the infant's need to remain in close proximity to its caregiver and protector in order to survive (see our previous description).

B) Compassionate love. The salient feature of this type of love is another's welfare and one's attempt to promote it, regardless of any future gain to the self. Berscheid (2006) termed this kind of love "altruistic love," "charitable love," "brotherly love," or "agape" (p. 176). This kind of love has been theorized to also be innate, since the infant's attachment would not enhance its survival if it was not complemented by that care giving behavior. Humans are born immature, vulnerable, and weak. They need, for their survival, the care giving and the protection of stronger and wiser adults. Later on, as we grow, such behaviors as care giving, social support, and prosocial behaviors are expressed when we perceive that someone else is in distress.

C) Compassionate love. Berscheid called this type "friendship love." Other names that were given to it are "philias," "affection," "affiliation," and "pragmatic love" (Berscheid, 2006, p. 177). This type of love is said to be related to, and dependent upon, the reward-punishment paradigm. We like those who reward us, and dislike those who punish us. That is to say, that we like those who are familiar to us, who are similar, who are physically attractive in our opinion, and who like us. That makes our interactions with that person more rewarding than it would be with people who do not possess those characteristics. Compassionate love, on the other hand, is a much less intense emotion. It includes feelings of commitment, attachment, and intimacy. It is the affection and tenderness that we tend to feel for those whose lives are intertwined with ours, those close and meaningful to us (Hatfield and Rapson, 1993). Hatfield and Walster (1978) observed that "passionate love is a fragile flower—it wilts in time. Compassionate love is a sturdy evergreen; it thrives with contact" (p. 125).

D) Romantic love. This is the type of love that laypeople and theorists alike are most interested in. Other names for this type of love include such terms as "passionate love," "addictive love," and "erotic love." Sexual desire (i.e. "lust") is a necessary condition for romantic love. Hatfield and Rapson (1993) defined the powerful emotional state of passionate love, as: "A state of intense longing for union with another. Passionate love is a complex functional whole including appraisals or appreciations, subjective feelings, expressions, patterned physiological processes, action tendencies, and instrumental behaviors. Reciprocated love (union with the other) is associated with fulfillment and ecstasy. Unrequited love (separation) is associated with feelings of emptiness, anxiety, and despair" (Hatfield and Rapson, 1993, p. 5).

Romantic love, which has a unique constellation of emotions, behaviors, and motivations (Harris, 1995; Leibowitz, 1983), first evolves when an individual regards another as special or even unique. The lover then intensely focuses on the preferred person, aggrandizing his or her better traits and minimizing or even ignoring flaws. Fisher (2004) described the lover's exaltation that many of us may be familiar with: extreme energy, euphoria, sleeplessness, impulsivity, and mood swings—all motivated to win the beloved's heart. Once won over, lovers become emotionally dependent on their relationship, and are ready to reorder their daily activities in order to maximize their proximity, and may experience separation anxiety when they part. Rejected lovers may experience such intense hurt and emotional turmoil that they may experience depression, rage, and despair, and engage in extraordinary and even inappropriate efforts to win back their sweetheart (Fisher, 2004). Romantic love has been said to be involuntary, difficult to control, and impermanent (Harris, 1995; Tennov, 1979). While it is said that romantic love changes over time, Miller (2012) echoes Shaver and Hazan's observation and suggests that romantic love does indeed evolve. He found that when asked about their love, after several years of marriage, most of those who manage to stay married get lower scores on passionate and love scales. Moreover, research demonstrated that the decrease in romantic love may be rapid, and that only two years into the marriage, married couples are 50% less affectionate to their partner than they were before they were married (Huston and Cohrost, 1994). Divorces throughout the world occur more frequently in the fourth year of marriage than at any other time (Fisher, 1995; Miller, 2012).

An analogy of a color wheel was used by Lee (1973) when he conceptualized his typology of love. The three primary love styles (eros, ludus, and storge) paralleled the three primary colors on the wheel, while mixture of the three primary loves yielded the secondary ones: pragma, mania, and agape.

Hendrick and Hendrick (1990) researched Lee's "color wheel of love" and created the LAS (Love Attitude Scale); they described the six types of love in everyday language, containing observable behaviors (all of the following are quotes from Hendrick and Hendrick, 2006, p. 153).

Eros – "Strong physical attraction, emotional intensity, a preferred physical appearance, and a sense of inevitability of the relationship define the cultural core of the Eros."

Ludus – "Love is a game to be played with a diverse set of partners over time. Deception of the partner and lack of disclosure about self and other partners are prime attributes of Ludus."

Storge – "This is love as friendship. It is quiet and compassionate. The fire of eros is alien to storge."

Pragma – "Love is a shopping list of desired attributes (e.g. fitting into the family, good parents, etc.). Computer dating is a good metaphor to describe pragma."

Mania – "This style might be called 'symptom' love. Mania is intense, alternating between ecstasy and agony. Mania love, when strongly felt, usually does not end well."

Agape – "This style is sacrificial, placing the loved person's welfare above one's own. In romantic love, pure agape is manifested only sporadically. In settled relationships, agape is ordinarily reduced by the demands of equity in long-term relationships and increased by life events such as one partner's illness."

We may wonder whether love changes over time. In general, asserted Hatfield et al. (2008), love is the greatest source of marital satisfaction. They found that many men and women claim that "being in love" is the most important factor in achieving marital success.

For couples who are fortunate, their passionate love evolves into compassionate love, a love that may last a lifetime (see Sternberg, 1998). There are theorists, however, who disagree with that linear progression of passionate love. They opine that once passionate love declines and becomes compassionate love, even that love declines over time, along with relational satisfaction (Karney and Bradbury, 1995; Tucker and Aron, 1993). In a five year longitudinal study, Sprecher (1999) confirmed that observation and found that when asked, couples *reported* that their love was increasing over time. Their *ratings*, however, indicated that their love actually declined year by year.

LOVE AND LONELINESS: TROUBLE IN EMOTIONAL PARADISE

We all want love,
And when we can't get it
We settle for sex
(Anonymous)

Rokach (1988a, 1989) previously observed that being in a love relationship, where we expect to be cared for, and for our lover to share her experiences with us, could also be terribly lonely. Love and loneliness, by definition, are not supposed to go together, but many times they do. How can someone who is loved feel lonely?!

Gordon and McKinney (2010) maintained that much of the dream, what they referred to as torrential romance, is related to the lovers' attempt to sustain the intensity of the relationship by introducing some sort of crisis; in this way, they mention provocations to jealousy, outbursts of anger, marked withdrawal, etc. If that is what lovers do in order to keep the flame alive, then they may end up withdrawing emotionally from one another and feel hurt, unimportant to their lover, alienated, and lonely.

Shaver and Hazan (1987) maintained that romantic love is fueled by a mixture of sexual attraction and its continuous gratification, reduced feelings of loneliness, and excitement, which is often related to the exploration of the novelty of one's partner. With time, they maintained, sexual attraction wanes, attachment anxieties may lead to conflict or mutual withdrawal, familiarity replaces novelty, and lovers either find themselves securely attached and caring deeply about each other or experiencing such distress as boredom, disappointment, or loneliness.

The *anxiously* attached feel, according to Shaver and Mikulincer (2005), chronically frustrated since their immense need for demonstrations of love and support from their partner cannot be satisfied. They consequently appraise conflicts with their partners as catastrophes in the making, doubt their partner's good-will, and intensify their emotional, as well as behavioral reactions to even minimal signs that may indicate their partner's unavailability or disinterest (Collins, 1996; Simpson, Ickes, and Grich, 1999). As a result of such a behavioral approach by the anxiously attached, his partner may feel engulfed by the partner's desire for intense closeness, frequent suspicions, and hypervigilance. These feelings may end up causing the partner to distance herself from the demanding person who is likely to intensify her insecurity and feelings of alienation (Shaver and Mikulincer, 2002).

A deactivation of the attachment system can be seen in *avoidant* type individuals. This reduces a person's emotional involvement, commitment, and consequently, their intimacy (Shaver and Brennan, 1992) and may result in feeling frustrated, as her attempts at intimacy and bids for affection are being ignored. Additionally, the avoidant person's great difficulty in discussing relational problems may hasten the breakup of this union (Scharfe and Bartholomew, 1995).

The Wear and Tear of Love

Love and relationships can be harmed and damaged, not only by the process of time, as we have indicated above, but also due to various pitfalls, stumbling blocks, and hazards such as hurt feelings, ostracism, jealousy, lying, and betrayal (De Paulo et al. 2009; Vangelisti, 2009). We like to be liked, we want to be loved by our intimate partners, and we hope that our relational value—the degree to which our partner considers our intimate relationship valuable, important, close—is as high as we perceive it to be. It is painful if our partner perceives it as lower than we would like it to be perceived. Should relational devaluation occur, that is, that we were, but are no longer, thought of as positively as before, we experience pain, anger, hurt, and loneliness. "Psychological wounds can cause real distress, and the sense of injury that characterizes hurt feelings—the feeling that relationship rules have been broken and that one has been damaged, shattered, cut or stabbed—makes hurt feelings a distinct emotional experience" (Miller, 2012, p. 309; see also DeWall, 2009; DeWall et al., 2010).

People, even in a close, intimate relationship may experience ostracism when their partner gives them the "cold shoulder" and ignores them. Ostracism, explain the ostracizers, is commonly utilized to punish the other, to help the ostracizer remain calm, or in order to help the ostracizer cool down after a conflict (Sommer et al., 2001). Ostracism can be very painful, because it threatens our basic social needs (Williams, 2007), and it is dehumanizing (Bastian and Haslam, 2010). The "silent treatment" not only threatens our need to belong, but may also damage our feelings or self-worth, and reduce our perceived control over the interactions. Usually the ostracized partner does not even get an explanation for the cold shoulder, nor does he know what to expect further. When their belongingness is threatened and when their feelings of alienation intensify, people may either work hard to regain their partner's regard, or start looking somewhere else (Miller, 2012; Williams, 2007).

Jealousy is an age old relationship spoiler. It is said that the three emotions that define jealousy are hurt, anger, and fear (Guerrero et al., 2005). Hurt follows the perception that our partner may not value us enough to honor their commitment to the relationship, and fear and anxiety are the result of the dread one feels at the prospect of being abandoned, losing the relationship, and being left alone and lonely. Consequent anger may even turn to violence, which may, in some cases, be fatal (Buss, 2000).

There are two types of jealousy. *Reactive jealousy,* which occurs at the awareness of an actual threat to the relationship, or *suspicious jealousy,* which may even occur while one's partner has not misbehaved and without any indications that the relationship may be threatened (Bringle and Buunk, 1991). Suspicious jealousy often results in mistrustful vigilance and following or spying, as the jealous partner is attempting to validate his suspicions. Some react to their suspicion with mild fantasies; others may demonstrate outright paranoia (Miller, 2012). Sometimes, a reactive jealousy (to a partner's affair) may end up with suspicious jealousy thereafter (Guerrero, 1998).

Deception and *lying* can also spoil a good and loving relationship and result in intense loneliness. Deception is conceptualized as an intentional behavior that "creates an impression, in the recipient, that the deceiver knows to be untrue" (Miller, 2012, p. 323), while *lying* is one form of deception, people may—as part of their deception—simply conceal information or divert attention from vital facts in order to avoid discussing what they consider "touchy" subjects. Another form of deception is telling half truths that are misleading (Vrij et al., 2010). Lies may be used to benefit the liar, to ward off embarrassment or guilt, or to seek a partner's approval (Haselton et al., 2005). Research indicated that men are more likely to lie about their income or to claim that they are committed to a relationship when they are not, while women may promise, but not provide, sex; cry out in fake pleasure during sex; or engage in the well-known practice of faking an orgasm (Brewer and Hendrie, 2011; Miller, 2012; Muehlenhard and Shippee, 2009).

Betrayals are probably the most hurtful of relationship spoilers, and they are the ones most closely related to loneliness. Betrayals are defined as "disagreeable, hurtful actions by people we trusted and from whom we reasonably did not expect such treachery. Sexual and emotional infidelity and lying are common examples of betrayal" (Miller, 2012, p. 328) but so is every other behavior that our loved one exhibits that violates the norms of kindness, loyalty, respect, and support that relationships, especially intimate ones, are believed to uphold (Metts, 1994). When it occurs, the betrayal causes a drop in our perceived relationship value, where we end up feeling that we and our relationship are less important to our partner than we would like to believe. Jones et al. (2001) found that betrayal of some form occurred in half of all the intimate relationships, and thus concluded that it is common in close relationships.

Men and women do not differ in their tendency to betray others. Men, however, are likely to betray their romantic partners and business associates, while women betray their friends and family more often than men do. What is the downside to betrayal, aside from deeply hurting one's partner and endangering the relationship? Betrayers, contend Couch and Jones (1997), were found to be unhappy, maladjusted, resentful, vengeful, and suspicious people. They are jealous and cynical and do not trust others much, which is possibly an indication of projecting on others their own needs and mistrust. They are lonely and miserable.

Other reasons for loneliness in loving or intimate relationships can be divided into personal and situational ones.

PERSONAL REASONS

a) As we mentioned earlier, those with an *attachment style* that is not secure, i.e. anxious or avoidant (Bowlby, 1973), cannot just "throw" themselves into the situation, love and be loved, and actually trust that their lover truly values, respects, wants, and loves them. The anxious type just waits for signs that her lover is untrustworthy, that he is not committed to their union, or that being told that she is loved is not a true representation of how her partner feels. Consequently, rather than bask in their love and friendship, she is anxious and lonely. Feeling that while she may be with a loving partner, she feels alone—and if her partner is still with her and is loving—it is only a matter of time (she is convinced) before he will cease loving her.

   The *avoidant* type may fall in love, but soon thereafter withdraws emotionally and does not allow the emotional guard to come down. Hence, what started as love may end up as an isolated, lonely journey in the land of a relationship—a journey, that is neither fulfilling, nor reminiscent of true love.

b) *People who cannot love.* I once had a friend who, after she divorced, started a relationship with a single man, who was kind to her and to her two young sons. The couple decided to live together and become a family. I later asked my friend whether her partner loved her. She replied with a resounding, "No!" I was intrigued and inquired about it. She explained that at the age of 16, her partner fell head over heels in love with his high school classmate, who rebuffed him. He was devastated and vowed to never again fall in love, so no one would hurt or reject him. He remained, while in a relationship with my friend, loveless and lonely, yearning for love, but unable to give or receive it. Fear of intimacy, that terror that some experience and that inhibits them from getting intimately close to others or falling in love, inevitably causes loneliness and a feeling of disconnection and alienation.

SITUATIONAL REASONS

a) *A love relationship that includes a perversion, a twisted way of loving.* One such example is abusive relationships with a repeated cycle of tenderness and abuse that leaves the loved and loving partner confused, wounded, and lonely (see also Rokach, 2007). Since love is inextricably bound to tenderness, caring, giving, and even sacrificing, an abusive relationship—be it physical, sexual, or emotional—hurts doubly. Love makes us vulnerable, lowers our defenses, enhances our trust especially in the ones we love, and consequently may leave us lonely and hurting when that love brings with it pain and hurt.

b) *Romantic relationships are dynamic* (Keller, 2000). Partners change over time, and so does their relationship, as we just described. Research presented in this chapter suggested that romantic relationships tend to evolve over time to compassionate love or may even be replaced by other feelings that are not as intimate and binding as love is. If romantic partners change, and they do so in concert with their lover, then they are on the same trajectory and are together on the same life journey. If their personal growth is bidirectional, however, meaning that they grow at different rates and in different directions, they may end up feeling isolated from the one they love and feel left behind, resentful, and lonely. Thus, love that changes may transform the relationship, and potentially leave one or both partners lonely.

c) *Relationships are never smooth sailing into the horizon.* We encounter disappointments, anger, frustrations, unfulfilled wishes, and a returned love from our partner, which does not provide us with what we need. Thus, although love–loneliness may be an oxymoron, it is not an infrequent occurrence that people are in love and feel lonely—longing for more, waiting to be closer and be understood, and unable to evade the loneliness that they experience when the love they receive is not what they need.

Keller (2000) described the ideal romantic love as a situation where the one I love, loves me back since "out of all the people she could love, she chooses to love me. That suggests that the reason why she loves me should be to do with the things that set me apart from others" (p. 163). When those feelings seem to change, when I stop feeling so valued and special to my partner, it may lead to my feeling neglected, unappreciated, and thus, lonely. When I am not as important to my lover as I know I was in the past, it ushers in loneliness, sadness, and longing to recreate what was, what made me feel so good and special in the first place.

> I have loved, and I have been loved, and all the rest is just background music.
> —Estelle Ramey

Chapter 10

MARRIAGE EDUCATION:
PREPARATION AND PREVENTION

A hard man is good to find.
—Mae West

Marriage, at least in the Western culture, is an institution that is supposed to guard and protect us from loneliness. As we previously indicated, numerous studies clearly showed that marriage can indeed offer that protection—and a good, loving, and soul nourishing union may not only diminish loneliness, but increase our resistance to illness and result in a longer life with greater quality than that enjoyed by singles or divorced people. Ties to one's spouse and children simply add meaning to life. Marriage is often seen as central to create what may be referred to as the "good life," and the intimacy that is offered by marriage is seen as a major source of support (Stack, 1998). Both married men and women report that their spouse is their chief confidant, and consequently Stack observed that those who are married enjoy higher levels of both physical and mental health and well-being than their unmarried counterparts. Additionally, compared to unmarried people, those who are married have lower levels of depression, higher levels of happiness, lower rates of mortality, and lower levels of suicide (Stack, 1998).

The creation of a marital union is one of the most important transitions across a person's life span development (Carter and McGoldrick, 1999). Upon entering into a martial relationship, most people possess a deep desire to form an ideal, lifelong marriage in which one can feel safe, loved, happy, and satisfied (Gordon, 1993). The increased rate of divorce in the United States, however, has challenged this idealistic conceptualization of the "until death do us part," "happily ever after" marital relationship (Amato and Irving, 2006). This means that viewing marriage as a lifelong and satisfying relationship between two closely bonded partners represents a cultural ideal more than it describes the social reality. Amato and Irving (2006) indicate that "people are no longer willing to remain married through the difficult times, for better or for worse, until death do us part. Instead, marital commitment lasts only as long as people are happy and feel that their own needs are being met" (p. 51).

As indicated above, the divorce rate is extremely high in the United States. Current estimates show that in spite of a slight decline shown in recent years (U.S. Bureau of Census, 2000), 40-50 percent of first-time marriages will end up in divorce (Gottman, 1999a; Carroll and Doherty, 2003). Divorce does not only have adverse effects on the couple's physical and emotional well-being, but on their children and their well-being as well (Sanders, Nicholson, and Floyd, 1997).

For the many others that for various reasons do not divorce, the marriage that was intended to be a source of intimacy, happiness, and satisfaction ends as an enduring source of pain, anguish, and despair (Karney and Bradbury, 1995). Research also showed that approximately two-thirds of the couples who divorce do so within the first 10 years of marriage (Clark, 1995). In addition, a review of marital development research shows a noticeable decline in the quality and satisfaction of marital relationship during the early stage of marriage (Kurdek, 2000). Nonetheless, despite these findings, the vast majority of American young adults possesses positive views and attitudes toward marriage and would like to marry (Amato, Booth, Johnson, and Rogers, 2007). Amato et al. (2007) add to the positive view of marriage their observation that "demographers project that most young adults (in the U.S.) eventually will marry...Marriage may have lost much of its former status, but it still has much to offer" (p. 2).

It appears that parental divorce influences their offspring and increases the risk that they will end up divorcing their spouse as well. It is suggested that marital disharmony may be transmitted across generations (Wolfinger and Nicholas, 1999).

O'Leary and Cascardi (1998) reviewed studies that examined disharmonious marriages and suggested that violent parental marriages made it more likely that their children's marriages would be violent.

Caspi and Elder (1988) found that conflicted parental marriages increased the likelihood, of children's behavioral problems, which later as adults, resulted in those children exhibiting problematic interpersonal style that affected the quality of their marriages. More recently, Conger, Cui, Bryant, and Elder (2000) studied 193 families and confirmed that parents' interpersonal behavior during their offspring's childhood influenced the children's approach and relationship with their intimate partner. Thus, parental marriages that were characterized by discord, disharmony, and dissatisfaction were reflected in their children's own intimate unions.

When marital relationships are dissatisfying and conflicted, they can cascade into depression, anxiety, and loneliness or enhance problems at work or socially (Flora and Segrin, 2000).

While marital or intimate relationships are supposed to offer support, which may buffer loneliness, about half of all married couples report that they experience loneliness often or sometimes (Flora and Segrin, 2000; Tornstam, 1992). The impracticality of marital dissolution—due to factors such as children, religion, or economic status—may keep people married but dissatisfied and lonely. Loneliness, observed Flora and Segrin (2000), "is particularly distressing in intimate relationships because it is inconsistent with expectations about such a relationship" (p. 815). In their own study, Flora and Segrin (2000) found that relationship satisfaction was negatively correlated with loneliness (loneliness in romantic relationships is discussed in chapter 16 of this volume).

Marriage counseling and other therapeutic interventions seem to be effective in reducing marital difficulties and distress (Jacobson, 1991; Ward and McCollum, 2005). In many cases, however, couples turn to counseling and therapy when they are excessively distressed and emotionally disengaged, thus it is too late to repair their troubled marriage (Markman, Renick, Floyd, Stanley, and Clement, 1993). Moreover, couples who are severely distressed and who are on the verge of dissolution and divorce do not necessarily consider the option of counseling, and in most cases, they are lacking the commitment to one another and to the therapeutic process.

Markman et al. (1993) suggested that rather than wait until the marriage starts to deteriorate, it is much better to provide preventive intervention while the couple is happy, or alternatively, when the distress is in its initial stage. The advanced stage of marital research makes it possible to identify personal and interactive components that impact on marital success and stability, making it relatively easy to target couples who are at risk to develop marital distress for preventive programs (Rodrigues, Hall, and Fincham, 2006). It goes without saying that by employing preventive measures, practitioners can utilize ways to protect couples from marital deterioration by enhancing the couple's relationship. Like in other areas of mental health, marital preventive intervention programs focus on the identification of both protective and risk factors and then provide preventive interactions to promote and enhance the relationship, which in turn immunizes the relationship from the threatening risks of deterioration (Rishel, 2007). This philosophy is the guiding conceptual framework of the various premarital preparation programs and marital enrichment programs (Carrol and Doherty, 2003).

To encourage marriage and family counselors to incorporate preventive measures in their interventions with couples, the Code of Ethics of the International Association of Marriage and Family Counselors (2002) issued a statement that indicates that counselors "should pursue the development of clients' cognitive, moral, social, emotional, spiritual, physical, educational, and career needs, as well as parenting, marriage and family living skills, in order to prevent future problems" (cited by Murray, 2005, p. 27). Fraenkel, Markman, and Stanley (1997), in stressing the importance of professional marital preventive intervention, consider it "the wave of the future" (p. 257). The promise of enhancing and promoting marital health has also been recognized by policy makers. The U.S. Federal Government allocated some 750 million dollars to the Healthy Marriage Initiative program to be used during five years for the promotion of marriage stability and satisfaction through preventive modalities (Roberts, 2005).

The practical implications of marital research on premarital preventive intervention were examined by Story, Rothman, and Bradbury (2002). The authors argue that an applied approach to research has to focus on generating positive change in spouses' functioning, adding that this approach "has far greater relevance to the goals of preventive intervention than to marital therapy" (p. 469). Whereas marriage counseling and therapeutic modalities are better served by individual case studies, prevention programs on the other hand, can help newlyweds to learn critical skills without necessarily referring to the couple's unique difficulties, concerns, and history (Story, Rothman, and Bradbury, 2002). Another practical advantage of preventive programs is that they provide educational and counseling remedies during the early stages of marriage, when couples are in a better position to acquire adaptive patterns of relational interactions and skills.

Primary intervention modalities are offered to couples either premaritally or to newlywed spouses. Programs for both target populations provide basic resources and skills with the purpose of preventing future marital difficulties and distress. Primary intervention programs concentrate mainly on effective interpersonal communication and conflict resolution skills (Rodrigues, Hall, and Fincham, 2006; Sayers, Kohn, and Heavy, 1998). The focus placed on communication skills training and in relationship and marriage preparation programs is based on the notion that relational communication is dynamic, acquired, and changeable.

Also, effective couple communication is central to marital quality and satisfaction (Halford, Wilson, Lizzo, and Moor, 2002), and poor communication skills predict negative marital outcomes especially during the early stage of marriage (Kurdeck, 1998). Kouneski and Olson (2004) constructed a model of relational intimacy in which communication and conflict resolution skills are incorporated. According to these authors, these very skills are said to be taught in most marriage and couples education programs. The emphasis there is on building competencies for healthy and intimate relationship. Kouneski and Olson (2004) view healthy communication as composed of the partners' ability to talk to each other openly and assertively in an atmosphere that promotes support, understanding, and validation. Effective communication is the foundation for the development of effective conflict resolution strategies.

MARRIAGE ENHANCEMENT PROGRAMS

Laurenceau et al. (2004), observed that in light of the variety of stressors on marriage and intimate relations, premarital intervention programs as well as marriage enrichment workshops are becoming more popular and are gaining community (McManus, 1993), political (Ooms, 1998), and scientific (Stanley et al., 2001) attention.

Addressing premarital education programs, Laurenceau et al. (2004) observed that their goals—applying as wellness programs offered to already married couples—aim to reduce the well-documented erosion of marital harmony and satisfaction that may occur early in the marriage, and thus reduce divorce rates (Clements, Cordova, Markman, and Laurenceau, 1997).

The Prevention and Relationship Enhancement Program (PREP) is an example of an evidence-based, primary, and proactive premarital prevention program that has been successful at incorporating specific predictors of marital distress and dissolution into its structure (Christensen and Heavey, 1999; Markman et al., 1993; Markman, Markman, Stanley, and Blumberg, 1994). Based on the cognitive-behavioral model of change, PREP has taken into consideration the various marital interactive components that affect marital outcomes (Markman et al., 1993). The basic premise underlying the PREP prevention program is that various kinds of negative interactions are known to be corrosive to the intimate bond between partners, and therefore, they represent key factors for marriage preparation (Prado et al., 2001). In light of this fact, the program targets the promotion and enhancement of protective marital interactions (commitment, friendship, effective communication, and conflict management) and the decrease of risk factors (Stanley, Markman, St. Peters, and Leber, 1995).

PREP intervenes with couples upon their transition to marital life, when the motivation to learn effective interactional skills, commitment, and friendship are relatively high, focusing on protective factors related to marital well-being and durable health and interactive components that can be changed and enhanced through education (Stanley and Markman, 1998). PREP is about:

1. Promoting protective relational factors by training premarital couples in effective communication and conflict resolution skills

2. Encouraging couples to express, clarify, and evaluate their expectations regarding marriage so that they are better prepared to develop a durable relationship. This clarification and refinement of marital expectations is likely to prevent future conflicts and disagreements relating to relational beliefs, values, and attitudes

3. Offering participants strategies that couples can use to evaluate, reveal, and restructure their commitment and the role it plays in their close relationships

4. Enhancing constructive aspects of close relationships and concentrating on friendship, sensuality, and fun (Chrestensen and Heavy, 1999; Monarch, Hartman, Witton, and Markman, 2002)

As noted above, PREP identifies premarital communication and conflict solving as a reliable predictor of future marital success or failure. As such, "One of the most intensive focuses of the program lies in helping couples to first identify negative patterns of interaction, followed by communication skills training designed to reduce these detrimental behaviours" (Rodrigues, Hall, and Fincham, 2006, p. 101).

Following this conviction, PREP consists of a series of six sessions, lasting between 6 and 16 hours, conducted in a group format (Monarch et al., 2002). A central, hands-on component of PREP is the "Speaker-Listener" experience.

The speaker-listener technique of interactive skills training is designed to promote in couples effective communication. Couples are asked to discuss a topic relevant to their current life. The discussion is conducted in a manner that enables partners to speak freely and uninterruptedly. When one partner speaks (the speaker), the other is instructed to listen attentively (the listener). The speaker yields the floor when he feels his views and opinions were fully expressed and listened to. At this point in the discussion, the floor is switched to the listener who is now the designated speaker, while the other is now the listener. This exchange continues until the partners feel their views were well expressed, listened to, and fully understood. According to Monarch et al. (2002), "use of the speaker-listener technique slows down escalation in heated discussions, allowing both partners to hear and validate each other's point of view. This validation is thought to be essential for healthy communication" (p. 244). In addition to the use of the speaker-listener approach, partners are instructed to follow some discussion ground rules, such as not to assume what the other's intentions or thoughts are but rather to have the other explain what he is thinking. Another important ground rule that partners are asked to establish is that either partner is free to ask for "time-out" when tension is escalated. These ground rules seem to prevent destructive interactive behaviors during discussion (Monarch et al., 2002). Such a communication-based training format also helps partners regulate negative emotions so as to prevent negative reciprocity (Story, Rothman, and Bradbury, 2002).

According to Laurenceau, Rivera, Shaffer, and Pietromonaco (2004), using this speaker-listener communication technique enhances relational intimacy. Encouraging couples to openly discuss their thoughts and feelings and receiving their partner's validating and accepting response improves relational intimacy. In addition, the listener's validating response to the speaker's expressions encourages partners to engage in a more self-disclosing, interactive exchange, thus improving relational emotional closeness and intimacy (Laurenceau et al., 2004). Laurenceau et al. (2004) argue that "the speaker-listener technique, used as a central couples communication exercise in the Prevention and Relationship Enhancement Program (PREP), focuses on the role of self-disclosure and responsiveness in couple's communication. The PREP program teaches couples how to express emotions about problems and how to respond to such expressions in a way that promote[s] understanding and validation, ultimately leading to problem solving and resolution" (p. 66). PREP, being based on the cognitive-behavioral tradition of change (Stanley and Markman, 1998), is highly suitable to train premarital and newlywed couples in the skills of emotional expression and the adequate manner for self-disclosure of personal thoughts and feelings. At the same time, the skills of attentive listening and empathic responsiveness are also acquired (Laurenceau et al., 2004). Improving such skills is likely to promote, enhance, and maintain emotional closeness and intimacy between relational partners (Fitzpatrick, 1987; Markman, Stanley, and Blumberg, 2001).

As noted, empathic responsiveness to a partner's revealing personal thoughts and emotions is important to the development, enhancement, and maintenance of close, intimate couple's relationships (Roberts and Greenberg, 2002). There is empirical evidence to suggest that self-disclosure is also an important interactive component of a stable, successful, communal relationship (Mills and Clark, 2001). Expanding the concept of relational empathy, Simpson, Ickes, and Orina (2001) presented their "Empathic Accuracy Model" that essentially relates to the degree to which a person in close relationships is able to accurately infer his partner's thoughts and feelings. A high level of empathic accuracy is important to the promotion of intimacy and it can be attained mainly through effective communication and attentive listening and responsiveness. The essential elements in this interactive process are: (a) "The partners' respective levels of readability (the degree to which each partner displays cues that reflect his or her true internal states), and, (b) the partners' respective level of empathic ability (the degree to which each partner can accurately decipher the other's valid behavioral cues)" (Simpson, Ickes, and Orina, 2001, p. 30).

Due to its focus on communication and interactive skills training, PREP (and other similar marital prevention programs) is likely to be effective in training couples in both self-disclosing interaction and accurate emphatic responsiveness. Achieving these goals, couples can ensure effective communication that has the potential to promote, enhance, and maintain a successful marital relationship. Training premarital couples to openly express feelings, thoughts, and desires, as well as acquire attentive listening, sensitive, validating, and accurate empathic ability, can offer preemptive maintenance to relationship closeness and stability (Simpson, Ickes, and Orina, 2001; Laurenceau et al., 2004). PREP strategies can also focus on decreasing specific patterns of relational deteriorating interactions (Rodrigues, Hall, and Fincham, 2006). Attesting to the success of PREP in preventing marital discord and dissolution by promoting relational positivity, Rodrigues, Hall, and Fincham conclude that "It appears that both the principles and practices of PREP have been successful in integrating empirical findings regarding marital dissolution with a practical prevention for couples" (p. 101).

PREP has been created based on a theoretical foundation and has specific and measurable goals (Monarch, Hartman, et al., 2002). This is the case in regard to several other prevention programs, such as Relationship Enhancement (RE) that has been extensively evaluated through empirical research (Monarch, Hartman, et al., 2002).

Relationship Enhancement, like PREP, is a skill-based, prevention program aimed at promoting and enhancing intimate relationships (Monarch et al., 2002). The program was originally developed by Guerney (1977). Participants in RE programs reported improvements in communication, the ability to respond empathically to one's partner, increased disclosure of personal feelings and thoughts (Avery, Ridley, Leslie, and Milholland, 1980; Heitland, 1986), increased feelings of relational trust, and genuine warmth and closeness (Ridley, Jorgensen, Margan, and Avery, 1982).

The primary goal of RE is training couples in interpersonal communication interactive behaviors in order to prevent relational distress and dissolution. The training format of RE is based on Carl Rogers' communication approach that emphasizes the expression of empathy, support, and acceptance to one's relational partner (Monarch et al., 2002).

The RE prevention education program provides training to couples in three basic communication behaviors: (a) expressing feelings openly and clearly so as to generate understanding from one's partner as opposed to expressing feelings in a way that might evoke negative responses of anger and belligerence and (b) responding empathically by conveying acceptance of their partner and by validating their partner's feelings, opinions, and thoughts. This set of communication behaviors taught in RE "involves moving from the role of expression to that of empathic listener in a way that maximizes mutual understanding, satisfaction, problem solving, and conflict resolution" (Monarch et al., 2000, p. 241). Studies that evaluated the effectiveness of the RE enrichment program found that couples showed significant improvements in communication, empathy, and self-disclosure (Christensen and Heavey, 1999).

PREPARE/ENRICH COUPLE PROGRAM

As with other similar marital prevention and enrichment programs, PREPARE/ENRICH's theoretical assumption is based on vast empirical research that shows that marital outcomes can be predicted by premarital variables (Larsen and Olson, 1989; Olson and Olson, 1999). In order to develop a sound and effective prevention program, Olson and his colleagues developed the Premarital Inventory PREPARE (Olson and Olson, 1999; Fowers, Montel, and Olson, 1996) that consists of 11 scales that assess premarital variables that are related to marital relationship quality (Fournier and Olson, 1986). Based on empirical research that examined the PREPARE/ENRICH Inventory, Olson and Olson (1999) concluded that premarital prevention programs should cover at least six relational areas:

1. *Exploring, assessing, and sharing relational strengths, growth, and enhancement areas.* Couples participating in the premarital prevention workshop are asked to raise and discuss areas they perceive as relationship strengths, and others that they feel are relational growth and improvement areas. This exercise helps couples to identify the positive features of their relationship and the areas that both partners are encouraged to further develop and strengthen.
2. *Communication skills.* Here couples are helped to be more effective in their communication and interactive behavior, concentrating mainly on assertiveness and active listening. Partners are trained to be more effective in the manner in which they discuss issues that are raised in their relationship. Program leaders encourage participants to identify three wishes they would like their partners to achieve (i.e. things they would like done more frequently). Couples are trained to be open and

assertive in regard to the needs and wishes they would like to accomplish while learning how to be better listeners.

3. *Conflict resolution.* Couples learn how to effectively resolve inevitable disagreements and conflicts. The PREPARE/ENRICH format consists of 10 steps that include setting proper time for conflict discussion; clearly defining the conflictual issue to be discussed; examining personal responsibility for the problem that was raised (i.e. in what way partners contribute, personally, to the problem); raising attempts that were made, in the past, to resolve the conflict; jointly brainstorming possible resolutions to the conflict being addressed; evaluating solutions that were identified and raised to ascertain the level of their feasibility and appropriateness; jointly choosing a solution that partners both feel comfortable with; discussing how each of them will contribute to the success of the resolution agreed upon; setting up a follow-up meeting to discuss and evaluate the implementation of the resolution; and, finally, offering positive feedback and rewards for each other's contributions (Olson and Olson, 1999).

4. *Issues related to family of origin.* Couples participating in the PREPARE/ENRICH program start the program by taking various assessment inventories of which two relate to family of origin, aimed at assessing family cohesion and family flexibility. Taking these scales helps couples to better understand their relationships with their families of origin that in turn reflects on the couple's relationship. During workshop interventions, counselors explore with participants the similarities and changes they see between their relationship and the relationships they experienced in their respective families. The couples are encouraged to discuss interactions and behaviors they would like to make in their own relationships.

5. *Financial planning and family budget issues.* The issue of financial planning and budgeting is raised in many marital relationships and in many cases these issues are presented as an area of conflict and difficulties (Olson and Olson, 1999). Program counselors help couples to plan their budgets realistically and suitably for their needs.

6. The final relational area of intervention in the PREPARE/ENRICH program is focusing on personal, couple, and family goals. The purpose of this segment of the program is to have couples develop and share their life goals so as to promote intimacy and closeness. Couples are encouraged to work on an action plan to facilitate the fulfillment of some of their goals.

In conclusion, the PREPARE/ENRICH premarital prevention program is designed to strengthen and enhance a couple's interactive relationship. One of the main goals of the program is to provide participants with the essential relationship skills of assertive communication, conflict resolution, and financial and budgeting planning and management. In addition, the program raises a participant's awareness of his close relationship's growth areas as well as areas that require improvement. There are some research findings to attest to the effectiveness of the program in impacting upon positive marital outcomes and reducing divorce dissolutions (Fowers, Montel, and Olson, 1996; Olson and Olson, 2000).

TRAINING IN MARRIAGE ENRICHMENT (TIME)

Like the previously discussed programs (PREP and RE), Training in Marriage Enrichment is a skill-based, marital education program for couples who are motivated to enrich and enhance their marital relationships. TIME was developed by Dinkmeyer and Carlson (2003), who designed their program mostly to help marital spouses to improve on various fundamental skills that are important for the development of happy, supportive, and well-adjusted marriages (Bowling, Hill, and Jencius, 2005). Carlson and Dinkmeyer (2003) outlined in their book, *Time for a Better Marriage* (used as a workbook for couples participating in TIME), the various skills they found to be needed for couples who wish to enrich their marriages. The various essential skills were found to characterize couples in happy and successful marriages, and they are taught to participants during sessions. These are:

1. Assume and accept individual responsibility for one's respective interactive behavior
2. Identify personal goals one wishes to accomplish and make an attempt to align them with the goals that are important to the marriage
3. Interact with each other in an encouraging manner
4. Choose to communicate feelings and thoughts in an open, honest, and authentic manner
5. Be an attentive, active listener to one's partner expressing inner feelings and thoughts
6. Offer an empathic listening to one's partner
7. Make an effort to closely understand one's partner and the factors that positively affect the marriage so as to act upon them
8. Admire and value each other and demonstrate acceptance to each other so as to enhance mutual self-esteem
9. Make choices in a communal manner, namely so that choices that are made are pro-relational, as opposed to self-centered. The marital benefits come first
10. Support the achievement of marital goals in thoughts, actions, and investments
11. Do not avoid dealing with disagreements and conflicts. Instead, make an attempt to adequately manage conflicts as they come up
12. Commit to the success of one's marriage through enhancement and maintenance activities (Carlson and Dinkmeyer, 2003)

The TIME program is conducted in 10 weekly sessions that provide participating couples with hands-on opportunities to promote, enhance, and practice the above mentioned relational skills.

Research examining the effectiveness of the TIME program shows positive results (Bowling, Hill, and Jencius, 2005).

COMPASSIONATE AND ACCEPTING RELATIONSHIPTHROUGH EMPATHY (CARE)

The Compassionate and Accepting Relationship through Empathy program was developed at the University of California at Los Angeles (Cobb and Bradbury, 2003). CARE places great attention on the promotion and enhancement of protective factors to prevent marital distress (Monarch et al., 2002). More specifically, CARE's main intervention approach is the enhancement of pro-relational interactive behaviors that are known to produce positive marital outcomes such as mutual support, empathic understanding, and emotional expression. The promotion of these relational components is conducted by CARE within the framework of three marital processes: social support, conflict interaction, and forgiveness. The fundamental interventions of CARE are based on Integrative Behavioral Couple Therapy—IBCT (Dimidjian, Martel, and Christensen, 2008) that posited that marital distress and disharmony are caused by the destructive ways that couples respond to areas of inevitable incompatibilities. In contrast, happy marital couples engage in solving conflicts and disagreement with empathic understanding, acceptance, and support (Dimidjian, Martell, and Christensen, 2008).

CARE trains couples in skills that promote better, more effective ways to handle inevitable daily stresses on their marriage to prevent relational erosion. One of those skills is aimed at providing effective social support in order to reduce conflict and to enhance suitable resolution of differences and disagreements. Social support in this context is defined as "responsiveness to another's needs…which involves acts that communicate caring, that validate the partner's worth, feelings, or actions, and that help the partner cope with life's problems" (Monarch et al., 2002, p. 246). There is evidence to suggest that social support promotes marital commitment, greater loving relationships, and marital relationship satisfaction (Arriaga, Goodfriend, and Lohman, 2004). This focus on empathy through social support in marital relationships brought Cobb and Bradbury (2003) to view CARE through an attachment theory lens. This is due to CARE's focus on key relational interactive processes that promote secure models of relational attachment (empathy through social support, acceptance, and forgiveness).

Another skill taught by CARE is to show one's partner empathy through acceptance. In this context, acceptance is defined as "the capacity to experience some offensive, unacceptable, or blameworthy action by the partner as understandable and tolerable if not necessarily desirable, or even as something worthy of appreciation" (Monarch et al., 2002, p. 246). It should be noted that the partner's acceptance is in no way a sign of giving-up on marriage problems and difficulties, but rather, showing some tolerance and accommodation to the partner's destructive behavior. Using empathy through acceptance promotes more positive and effective engagement in the process of conflict management. The element of acceptance in CARE's conceptualization is an important feature of integrative behavioral couple therapy (Jones, Doss, and Christensen, 2001).

The third main area of empathy training conducted through the CARE prevention program concentrates on forgiveness. Marital forgiveness predicts better, more effective conflict resolution (Fincham, Beach, and Davila, 2007). Consequently, CARE teaches participating couples various skills that promote understanding and forgiveness as opposed to blaming, attacking, and retaliating in a punitive manner (Monarch et al., 2002).

SELF-REGULATED POSITIVE RELATIONSHIP EDUCATION PROGRAM (SELF-PREP)

In order to achieve high marital quality and satisfaction, partners are required to attend to and mind their relationship and work on their marriage to make it stable and well-functioning (Halford, Wilson, Lizzio, and Moor, 2002). The construct of relationship self-regulation is used as a central component of the Self-Regulated Positive Relationship Education Program. Halford and Moor (2002) reviewed relevant research on the effectiveness of skills training marriage education programs to conclude that "the prediction and promotion of relationship satisfaction and stability need to be focused on a broader concept of what is adaptive for promoting satisfying and stable relationships" (p. 498) as opposed to concentrating mostly on skills training (i.e. communication and conflict resolution skills). Thus, Halford et al. (2002) suggest that an effective marriage prevention and enhancement program should focus on encouraging couples to effectively work at their relationships as opposed to managing specific interactive behaviors. The authors added that in their conception, working at a relationship indicates that partners are attending to the relationship and the various possible influences on that relationship, and are engaging in behaviors that promote relationship satisfaction (Halford et al., 2002). In order to achieve this goal the Self-PREP program encourage participants to focus on developing relational self-regulation through a process of self-directed changes by both relational partners (Halford and Moor, 2002). This is done in addition to active, hands-on experiential training in fundamental skills needed for well-functioning and satisfying marriage (communication and conflict solving skills).

The structure of the Self-PREP marriage enrichment program consists of six educational modules, the first of which focuses on relationship goal setting (Halford and Moor, 2002). Special attention is given, during this module, to the identification of core interactive behaviors that promote and enhance relational emotional connectedness and intimacy. The end result of this process is for couples to develop a clear, well-formed, shared goal initiative, specified in a self-directed goal attainment manner. The couple's agreed upon relational vision of expectations is used as a foundation upon which the partners progress toward the practical achievement of the identified relational goal and vision (Halford et al., 2002).

The second module in Self-PREP constitutes effective communication and conflict resolution skills training. Couples are guided to evaluate their current communication patterns so that they are able to identify elements in their communication behavior that they would like to change. The enhancement achieved in a couple's communication skills is then used to teach them how to effectively manage inevitable conflicts and marital difficulties. After couples identify their usual pattern of conflict interaction, they are encouraged to select goals that may assist them in achieving better, more adaptive conflict resolution interactive patterns (Halford and Moor, 2002). Additional sessions of Self-PREP review the closeness and intimacy enhancement goals of participating couples, goal-setting for enhancing sexual functioning and enjoyment, enhancing partner emotional support, and finally, encouraging partners to prepare for effective handling of possible life changes they may encounter. This includes life events such as the transition to parenthood, stressful events such as an illness or losing a job and the like (Halford and Moor, 2002).

Association for Couples in Marriage Enrichment (ACME)

Mace and Mace (1975), considered pioneers of the marriage enrichment movement in the U.S., (Bowling, Hill, and Jencius, 2005) defined, developed, and shaped the Association for Couples in Marriage Enrichment program (Mace, 1979; Mace and Mace, 1975). The program is aimed at helping couples to enhance and enrich their marital relationships and to prevent marital distress. The program introduces participating couples to the fundamental concepts of relational growth and the developmental processes of marriage enrichment. The process of ACME marriage education shares three key theoretical elements with other similar endeavors: providing an empathic, accepting atmosphere to promote growth and learning and practicing modalities to teach couples basic relational skills (communication and conflict resolution skills) to encourage positive outcomes through the use of group processes that provide a safe environment for effective learning (Hoff and Miller, 1981).

The ACME program consists of a five-stage process, the first of which is aimed at helping participating couples to develop comfort and security in their environment in the group process. The need for this initiation process is based on Mace's (1975) observation that "many couples, while eager to improve their relationship, have difficulty in involving themselves in programs for this purpose, because they are aware of resistances within themselves, both, to acknowledging their need for help, and to communicating their need to others" (p. 171). This psychological inhibition and restraint is gradually reduced as a result of couples engaging in icebreaking group processes that help them to open up and become more comfortable in further participation in the program (Mace, 1975). Following this initial, warming-up, group process, participants are encouraged to develop self and couple awareness of their marital relationship by identifying strength and improvement issues, and raising suggestions for positive change. The third stage in this education program is devoted to developing skills for effective, improved communication and conflict management and improving emotional closeness and intimacy. During the fourth stage of the program, couples set up both personal and relational goals for marriage enhancement and enrichment. In addition, couples discuss and develop plans to achieve the fulfillment of the goals identified. During the first and final stages of the program, participants reaffirm their strengthened commitment to their partners and to their marriage, show mutual gratitude for the success of the enriching experience and terminate the intervention (Bowling et al., 2005).

Bowling et al. (2005) reviewed various research studies that examined the efficacy of the ACME program. In general, the results attest to significant benefits achieved by participating couples in this program. Couples who took the ACME program "demonstrated improved marital satisfaction, sexual intimacy, and intellectual intimacy" (Bowling et al., 2005, p. 89).

What, then, should be included in a marital enrichment program? We have reviewed the variety of available programs and compiled, below, a list of some important ingredients that were based on the needs of couples experiencing some marital problems or were shown to be helpful in preventing marital disharmony and distress.

MARITAL ENRICHMENT PROGRAM

1. *Helps couples examine their values and priorities and how motivated they are to improve their relationship/marriage.* Examining any disagreements of those priorities that the couple may have and discussing ways to bring about mutual support for embarking on an enrichment process is a good launching point for improving and enhancing a relationship that needs some "life" to be added to it.

2. *Examines the couple's strengths and weaknesses as a unit,* encouraging strength related behaviors, and highlighting the price they pay for allowing the unsatisfactory behaviors to continue.

3. *Becomes aware of their gender role socialization, or their present division of tasks,* as well as the options they chose to consider.

4. *Identifies attitudes, beliefs, and behaviors that may be an obstacle to change.*

5. *Helps the couple develop effective communication and negotiation skills.*

6. *Teaches couples to express thoughts, feelings, perceptions, and expectations to a receptive and supportive partner.*

7. *Teaches active listening,* how to support and encourage openness.

8. *Teaches the difference between wants and needs.* Becoming aware of cognitive approaches to change "wants" and acceptance if they cannot be fulfilled.

9. *Addresses power issues in marriages,* including needs for control, direct and indirect control, decision making power, competitiveness, and power imbalance.

10. *For dual careers couples, teaches the common pitfalls of such a working arrangement,* the superwoman phenomena, perfectionism, taking on too much, or feeling competitive with regard to their partner's achievements.

11. *Teaches how "to do" quality time.*

12. *Teaches the importance of love,* tenderness, how to show deep caring, sexuality that will satisfy both partners, and reintroduces romance, excitement, and interest in otherwise boring marriages.

13. *Teaches how to fight* while respecting one's partner, and then knowing how to make up to minimize lasting scars that fights may otherwise leave.

Marriage preparation and enrichment programs suffer from "underwhelming participation" (Duncan, Holman, and Yang, 2007). It is of interest, especially in light of low participation, to inquire about the characteristics of those who do attend such programs. Duncan et al. (2007) found that those who attend enrichment programs valued their marriage, were kind and considerate, and acted maturely (rather than impulsively) to a greater extent, than those who did not participate.

Duncan and Wood (2003) found that couples who participate in marriage preparation and enrichment programs tend to be at lower risk for marital distress and separation (see also Sulliven and Bradbury, 1997). While in past years scholars suggested that low participation in such programs may stem from the programs' failure to answer the clients' needs (Katz, 1988). Recently, a marketing perspective was utilized to understand and utilize clients' perceptions of the programs.

Katz (1988) suggested that four dimensions be used when analyzing marketing decisions. Those applied to the marketing of marriage enrichment services, are:

a) *Product* – which is the package of professional services that are delivered to the client. A person must realize that he faces a genuine problem and that the product offered may provide a good solution to the problem. That means that research—and later marketing—should examine the clients' perceptions of their problems and how important it is for them to do something about it (Weinrich, 1999).

b) *Price* – includes financial cost for the services, but also various intangible "costs" that clients may have to pay (e.g. giving up of secondary gains that they may be enjoying) in order to receive the benefits that the program has to offer.

c) *Place* – describes the location where the program is offered. Client convenience is a key issue. These locations may include offices, shopping malls, at-home education (e.g. the internet, videos, etc.), or even mass media.

d) *Promotion* – is the method used to bring awareness of the service to the service user. It includes advertising, word of mouth, public relations, promotions, media advocacy, personal selling, and entertainment approaches.

Which marriage preparation and enrichment program would be most attractive to clients? Research found that inexpensive, private (versus in group) programs that are held close to home, which are relatively brief, led by skilled and well-known professionals, offered at traditional educational settings such as colleges, freely chosen (not mandated), promoted through friends and parents, as well as programs that use various methods to address self and other awareness, are the most preferred ones (Duncan and Wood, 2003; Koval, Wong, Emery, and Granoff, 1992).

CHARACTERISTICS OF ATTENDEES OF ENRICHMENT PROGRAMS

Duncan and Wood (2003) investigated the characteristics of those who attended such programs and found that females were more motivated to attend than males were. Parental divorce seemed to heighten men's motivation to attend, but lowered females' motivation. It appears that both males and females who experienced lower parental marital happiness were less optimistic about their own marriages (see Amato and Rogers, 1999; Dostal and Langhinrichsen-Rohling, 1997).

Duncan et al. (2007) highlighted two implications for professionals offering enrichment programs and who wish to reach as many attendees as they can. Accordingly, they should:

1. Approach the "likely to attend" demographic, especially those females who place a high value on marriage. It is possible that the "high risk" couples need it the most, but the "likely to attend" couples will be the ones that will enroll.

2. Employ great marketing strategies that will aim at the "less likely to attend" group. This group consists of couples who do not highly value marriage and possess fewer intra- and interpersonal skills.

Chapter 11

MARRIAGE AND THE FAMILY

A major function of marriages and families is to provide us with intimacy and social support, thus protecting us from loneliness and isolation. (Strong et al., 2011, p.13)

MARRIAGE

A 19-year-old single woman, who participated in my [A.R.] study, wrote about her pain and consequent confusion and her denial of her desperate struggle with loneliness.

My ex-boyfriend and I broke up. I wasn't prepared for the trauma and it took about four months until I healed completely. We were going out for 11 months and I was used to the "routine" of seeing him. He was my first love. I was 18 years of age when we broke up. I felt empty, weak and I couldn't think straight. I went out and pretended to be content, but I was hurting so much inside. I had mixed feelings. One minute I was praising the relationship we had and the next minute I was putting it down. I took a new man in my life to heal my wound completely. Now what is left is just memories and no feelings. That was the only experience I've had of loneliness.

About sixty percent of adults (60% of males and 57% of females) aged 18 and older in the U.S. are married, while overall 72% have experienced marriage and may, thus, be married, divorced, or widowed (Strong, DeValut, and Cohen, 2011).

"A marriage is a legally recognized union between two people generally a man and a woman, in which they are united sexually, cooperate economically, and may give birth to, adopt, or rear children. The union is assumed to be permanent (although it may be dissolved by separation or divorce)" (Strong et al., 2011, p. 7). Marriage, or long-term intimate commitment, has changed in the last generation and has a smaller chance to succeed but is still the most preferred lifestyle of living adults.

De Jong Gierveld and Havens (2004) assert that people with partners, whether they are married or not, are happier and better protected from unhappiness and loneliness than those without a partner. Loneliness is a common visitor of those who divorced or were widowed. Remarriage and entering new relationships seems to improve the situation to a certain extent. Ample research has demonstrated the protection afforded to people by marriage (e.g., De

Jong Gierveld et al., 2009; Dykstra and De Jong Gierveld, 2004; Pinquart and Sörensen, 2003; Stevens and Westerhof, 2006a), and alternatively, has highlighted the increased risks of loneliness for divorced and widowed men and women (Dykstra and Fokkema, 2007; Guiaux, Van Tilburg, and Broese van Groenou, 2007).

It is well documented that when marital relationships hit a snag and are distressing, those negative relational states may escalate and lead to depression, anxiety, and loneliness, or difficulties at work or with the rest of the family (Beach et al., 1987; Clements et al. 1997; Flora and Segrin, 2000). Lynch (2000) pointed out that "It is a striking fact that the U.S. mortality rate for all causes of death, and not just heart disease, are consistently higher at all ages for divorced, single, and widowed individuals of both sexes and all races" (p. 97).

Relational trajectories refer, according to Flora and Segrin, to the path of growth or decline that a relationship may undergo over time. The angle of a relational trajectory is affected by behavioral, cognitive, and affective responses that the partners have to their relationship.

Flora and Segrin (2000) found that relational satisfaction was negatively correlated with loneliness. While those who are in a relationship are less prone to mental and physical health problems (Argyle, 1991), those in dissatisfying relationships may suffer worse consequences (Wickrama, Lorenz, and Conger, 1997).

Romantic relationships develop and change and those stages are affected by the individual characteristics of the couple, the one-on-one interactions that the couple has with one another, and the larger environment in which they operate, including the friends and family to which they are related. There is growing evidence that couples who have a large percentage of shared friends (versus individual friends) tend to have happier and better relationships. After some time of being together, people may become bored in their relationship suggests Slatcher (2010a). For such couples, intense self-disclosure with another couple may be a novel way to heighten feelings of closeness towards one's partner.

Slatcher's (2010b) study confirmed previous findings that the closer women felt to their partner; the more they have experienced positive affect. The same was found for men as well.

LOVE

Nothing could be more reasonable or natural than that people who are isolated and lonely should seek sociability and love wherever they think they can find it.
(Horton and Wohl, 1956, p.223)

Love has been talked about, examined, and extolled since the beginning of time (Hazan and Zeifman, 1999). Love relationships between adults, unlike mother and infant love, involve two adults who seek protection, comfort, and closeness. They offer each other support and, at times, sexual gratification. In such a relationship, the couple's qualities and the unique combination between the two of them influence their emotions, behaviors, and the outcome of their unique relationship (Schachner, Shaver, and Mikulincer, 2003). More poignantly, "the profound joy and gratitude, deep affection, self-protective anxiety, deadening boredom, corrosive anger, uncontrollable jealousy, and intense sorrow" (Schachner et al., 2003, p. 19) are hallmarks of that very special relationship.

Franklin Jones, an American businessman once remarked that "Love doesn't make the world go round, love is what makes the ride worthwhile" (in Strong et al., 2011, p. 138) and Americans share this sentiment. We can see it in the way we seek partners, the music we listen to, and the books we read; even in the movies we watch including love stories is very popular. American families place high value on love and getting married, being fulfilled in the relationship with one's spouse or partner, and the relationship between parents and children—all of these are based on love. Why, then, is love so central in our lives? As Maslow (1970) confirmed in his hierarchy of needs, the only needs more important than love are our physiological and safety needs. That places love, our need to connect and yearning to belong, pretty high up in the hierarchy of human needs and the millions of stories, songs, and essays that have written in an attempt to explain, understand, and learn about it is a confirmation of the centrality of love in our lives.

Emotional Closeness

Emotional closeness is the cornerstone of love relationships. It is described as a close relationship that commonly is seen to include sex, but that even more importantly includes emotional intimacy: "having someone to talk to, to share our selves, to give and receive love, affection, personal validation, trust, and revealing of personal feelings (Hook et al., 2003; Strong et al., 2011).

Strong et al. (2011) suggested that intimate relationships buffer us against loneliness, may positively affect our self-esteem, and were shown to be related to happiness, contentment, and a sense of well-being. In close relationships, intimacy can be expressed in a variety of ways including sharing with each other, listening to one's partner, being open and honest, and trusting each other. Intimacy has been rated as more important in relationship satisfaction than autonomy, individuality, freedom, agreement, or sexual satisfaction (Hassebrauck and Fehr, 2002). "When asked what is most important in life, older men and women in the Netherlands rate a good marriage second only to good health" (Hassebrauck and Fehr, 2002). Attachment theory starts from the premise that in childhood, parents or primary caregivers are the most important figures with whom a child bonds (Bowlby, 1969). Attachment and care giving are central, interrelated components of love relationships (Feeney and Noller, 1996).

Addressing intimacy and love calls for examining attachment. Unfortunately, our Western culture has pathologized attachment and dependency and exalts separateness, autonomy, and self-sufficiency. As Mackay (1996) noted, marriage and family therapy has neglected the dimension of support and nurturance, in favor of focusing on power, control, and separateness. Bowlby, the originator of attachment theory, emphasized emotional accessibility and responsiveness in all attachment relationships. "Seeking and maintaining contact with significant others is an innate, primary motivating principle in human beings across the lifespan. Dependency…is an innate part of being human rather than a childhood trait that we outgrow…proximity to a loved one tranquilizes the nervous system…and is a natural antidote to feelings of anxiety and vulnerability" (Johnson, 2003, p. 5). Secure attachment provides a secure base from which individuals can explore and experience their world, and that encourages adaptability to our surrounding environment and cognitive openness (Mikulincer, 1997). The emotional engagement and the trust that this engagement holds are crucial.

Schachner, Shaver, and Mikulincer (2003) suggested that people who are *securely attached* (i.e. exhibiting low anxiety and avoidance) tend to enjoy long, satisfying, and stable romantic relationships characterized by trust, friendship with their loved one, and a relationship that they are highly invested in. Their described style of love is selfless and they are open to sexual exploration with their partner. Attachment security contributes to mutual, high levels of self-disclosure, and mutual expression and negotiation during conflicts.

Those who are *insecurely attached,* if they are high on anxiety and low on avoidance, tend to be preoccupied with their romantic relationship. They tend to be unsatisfied with their relationship and thus experience a high rate of breakup. They may experience passionate love, but tend to show a dependent, obsessive style of relating to their partner. Attachment insecurity is associated with destructive "tracking" of the partner's behavior, and that may be interpreted as a threatening behavior (Feeney, 2002). These people are less likely to fall in love, and they hold positive attitudes toward casual, "one night" sex. Bogaerts, Vanheule, and Desmet (2006) found that a relationship between insecure attachment and feelings of loneliness does indeed exist (see also DiTommaso et al., 2003; Matsushima and Shiomi, 2001).

In comparison to the two previous styles of attachment, the *avoidant type* is less interested in romantic relationships, especially long-term stable ones. These people's relationships are characterized by low satisfaction and a high breakup rate, and by relatively low intimacy. Their insecurity increases their negative memories and negative expectations of their close relations (see Collins, 1996; Collins and Read, 1990; Hazan and Shaver, 1987; Madsen, 2000).

Emerging adulthood is a stage where romantic relationships are explored and the timing of marriage planned (Crockett and Bingham, 2000). In their study on university students, Mohr et al. (2010) found that those who expressed high attachment anxiety when asked to imagine future romantic relationships were more likely than others to imagine it including high levels of aversive communication and arguments that would negatively affect how the partners felt about the relationship. Those who had high attachment avoidance imagined that their future relationships would be characterized by a high degree of dissatisfaction and aversive communication. While those with high attachment anxiety referred to their fear of abandonment, the other group did not.

This adaptive system that we refer to as "attachment," emerged over the course of evolution to ensure that humans have an increased likelihood of survival, reproduction, and supportive relationships. Although the attachment system is most critical during the early months and years of life, Bowlby (1988) claimed that it is active throughout our lifespan and is expressed especially during times of stress. "We assume" suggested Schachner, Shaver, and Mikulincer (2003), "that it is an important component of romantic love and marital commitment, and that meeting needs for a felt sense of security is one of the primary reasons for marriage" (p. 22).

Especially when aging—but not only then—a supportive network and a good marriage can help maintain social well-being and protect from loneliness (Dykstra and de Jong Gierveld, 2004). Research indicated that marital quality increases with age, but is inversely related to the length of marriage (Umberson, Williams, Powers, Hui, and Needham, 2005). That, naturally, may contribute to loneliness.

Loneliness is viewed by de Jong Gierveld et al. (2009) not as caused by lack of social contacts, but by dissatisfaction with existing relationships, or a lack of relationships.

Consequently, dissatisfaction with the marital relationships may lead to loneliness. Hence, evaluative judgments of marital quality have been investigated and indicate changes in the quality of communication later in life (Herman, 1994). Research on adult attachment to peers also indicates that insecure attachment patterns correlate strongly with loneliness (DiTommaso, Brannan-McNulty, Ross, and Burgess, 2003).

The existence and quality of intimate relationship has a strong influence on health and general well-being (Burman and Margolin, 1992; Heene, Buysse, and Van-Oost, 2007). Competence in being alone may indicate well-being and may contribute to a high quality marital relationship (Knoke, Burau, and Roehrle, 2010; Patrick, Keen, Canevello, and Lonsbary, 2007).

Research on the variables that predict marital satisfaction indicates that a low level of neuroticism is correlated with a better relationship (Caughlin, Huston, and Hout, 2000). Age, sex, and length of the relationship are the most important factors in marital quality. Marriage at a young age, remarriage, and parental divorce significantly contribute to marital instability (Umberson, Williams, Powers, Liu, and Needham, Heaton 2002; Amato and Rogers, 1999).

In general marital satisfaction draws a curvilinear course with high satisfaction in young adulthood, a decline in middle age, and increases after the childbearing years (Gagnon, Hersen, Kabacoff, and Van-Hasset, 1999). It is possible that positive integration in later years is an important contributor to that increased satisfaction.

Age was shown to be positively correlated to the quality of a marital relationship. Emotional loneliness as well is an important factor influencing the stability and quality of the couple's relationship. It is suggested that those who lack closeness and intimacy report inadequate communication, affection, mutuality, and marital bliss. Their relationships are, consequently, of limited duration (Knoke, Burau, and Roehrle, 2010).

The Benefits of Marriage

In marriage we see greater economic security, the promotion of health-related behaviors, and the higher levels of social support that married vs. unmarried people have; married people are less prone to loneliness. In marriage, people find companionship, nurturance, and care (Joung et al., 1997; Ross, 1995).

Married people are reported to experience less loneliness than unmarried people (Pinquart, 2003). That, however, does not preclude the married from experiencing loneliness. Tornstam (1992) found that 40% of married people in Sweden experienced more loneliness than unmarried people (Sorenson, 2001). "Marriage seems to fulfill fundamental needs for belonging, companionships and support (i.e. embededness), thereby decreasing motivation to engage in other kinds of relationships" (Stevens and Westerhof, 2006, p. 714) but loneliness is not uncommon in marriages. Tornstam (1992) found that 40% of married Swedes felt lonely sometimes or even often. As we may have intuitively understood, or even experienced, Stevens and Westerhof (2006) found that, as other researchers indicated, men relied primarily on their wives for support, but unlike women, worried less about their partners. Women, on the other hand, utilized their connection with children, other family members, friends and other people as sources of emotional support. Research has consistently demonstrated that the risk of loneliness is closely related to marital status. Those living alone seem to be at a higher risk of being lonely than the married, although an unsatisfying marriage may also produce loneliness. While women are more prone to emotional loneliness, which indicates a longing for a close, intimate friend or partner; men mostly experience social loneliness, stemming from the absence of a broader social network, which commonly includes friends, colleagues, and neighbors.

It is now well established that religious involvement tends to positively affect marital quality. It benefits romantic relationships through discouraging negative ones (Wolfinger and Wilcox, 2008).

Edin and Kefalas (2005) contended that religion and spirituality guard against infidelity, drug use, or criminal activity. Additionally, they may be associated with the "sanctification" of the marriage, adding meaning and structure to support the intimate relations (Mahoney, Pagament, Murry-Swank, and Murry-Swank, 2003). How does partner support buffer the effects of stress? Brock and Lawrence (2008) found that perceived support moderated chronic stress and marital satisfaction for wives and helped them cope with stress, leading to increased marital satisfaction (Fincham and Beach 2010).

Slatcher (2010a) observed that there is a relatively long tradition of research that linked marital status to health. It was approached from two theoretical angles:

1. The main effect model:
    Here, the main idea is that high levels of social support are health promoting regardless of one's stress level (Cohen, 2004). This model predicts that positive marital dimensions directly affect physical health. Similarly, unhappy marriages are theorized to cause health problems, regardless of other stressors, such as work stress. Marital strength, the positive dimension of marriage, is presumed to influence health throughout its effects on positive psychological states that are in turn proposed to be beneficial for physical health (Cohen, 1988; Danner, Snowdon, and Friesen, 2001; Pressman and Cohen, 2005). "The findings from these studies demonstrate that the quality of people's marital relationships is linked to cardiovascular functioning, neuroendocrine output, immunity, and health outcomes including morbidity and mortality" (Slatcher, 2010b, p. 462).

2. The stress buffering model:
    Advanced by Cohen (1985), this model focuses on describing how stress that occurs outside of the marriage is lowered by the social support that one gets. Social support is beneficial because it provides the psychological and material resources needed to cope with stress. It predicts that those who are going through a stressful period will benefit—health wise—from social support.

A marriage that is characterized by a distanced, non-intimate partnership and emotional inhibition is particularly detrimental to health (Laurenceau, Barrett, and Rovine, 2005). For example, a large sample of women from the well know Framingham Heart Study indicated that those who self-silenced (i.e. inhibited their emotions) during conflicts with their spouse had a 400% greater risk of dying within 10 years compared to women who did not inhibit their emotions or their expression (Eaker, Sullivan, Kelly-Hayes, D'Agostino, and Benjamin, 2007). Conversely, positive behaviors are linked to physiological changes (Heffner, Kiecolt-Glaser, Loving, Glaser, and Malarky, 2004). There was a strong link found between marital adjustment and physical health, particularly with cardiovascular disease (Baker et al., 2000,

Kulik and Mahler, 2006). High quality marriages buffer the effects of stress on physiology, morbidity, and mortality (Slatcher, 2010a).

Intimacy and Health

We know, and many of us have even experienced, that actively holding back thoughts, feelings, or actions can exacerbate physiological problems, such as increased cortisol production, and may suppress our immune system (Traue and Deighton, 1990). Mental openness and a higher level of self-disclosure (which is the building block of intimacy) are associated with better health (Laurenceau et al., 2005; Manne et al., 2004). Feeling understood, validated, and cared for after self-disclosure by one's partner is critical to relationship success, to greater intimacy, and to enhanced sharing of the couple's personal goals (Gable, Gonzaga, and Strachman, 2006; Feeney, 2006).

Couple's Communication

Stress affects marital quality through the couple's communication, the spouses' psychological and physical well-being, and the quality of time that the marital partners spend together (Bodenmann, 2000). There is evidence that the couple's communication particularly buffers marital quality from the negative effects of marital problems (Ledermann and Macho, 2009; Lederman, Bodenmann, Rudaz, and Bradbury, 2010).

> Overheard during a couple's argument. The wife says to her husband, "When I talk and you answer me, it disturbs the dialogue between us…"

Gender Differences in Marriage and in Loss

Women who are socialized to tend or befriend in the marriage provide most of the support that their partners get and develop their skills in attentiveness, disclosure, and empathy; all of these aspects may contribute to the stability of a marriage (Becker, 1991). Therefore, each gender contributes to the marriage what he can do best. Wives nurture and provide support while husbands perform instrumental functions. Consequently, men tend to find, more than women do, emotional fulfillment in marriage. Generally, women are reliably there to provide support, but they get their own support mainly from their women friends.

Subsequent marriages, those occurring after separation, divorce, or widowhood, are more complex than first marriages. In a second marriage, the person carries more emotional baggage, children may be present as soon as the relationship begins, and problems related to the previous relationship may still linger.

From a social support network point of view, the result of a remarriage is the bringing together of the previously separate family networks and that contributes to the expansion of social ties, where loyalties and responsibilities need to be renegotiated.

Remarried men are significantly less lonely than remarried women. The number of children and the quality of contact with them are closely related to social loneliness. The less satisfactory their contact with their children is, the higher their loneliness (De Jong Gierveld et al., 2009). As Buber and Engelhardt (2008) observed, a high frequency of contact with children indicates an appropriate degree of social integration. Of course, that is central to alleviating or even warding off loneliness. In remarriage, Dykstra and de Jong Gierveld (2003) found that women experience higher levels of social loneliness than men do. Participation in sports and hobby clubs, political movements, and senior citizens' organizations assist men in warding off social loneliness. For older men, unlike women, those out of the home engagements serve to generate in them the feeling of belonging and being part of the community. Women may not be socially integrated, may focus on attending to their husbands, and while their spouses are involved in social activities and clubs, they may feel left behind and experience loneliness.

The loss of one's partner's support, which is an inevitable result of divorce or the death of a spouse, may increase the likelihood of psychological problems (Gove and Shin, 1989). Divorce, unlike widowhood, leads to lower levels of emotional loneliness because it occurs following an unhappy or dissatisfying union, but it also results in greater social losses (Stevens, 1989). While friends and family join forces to support the bereaved, to help, comfort, and assist in a marital breakup may force people to side with one of the partners (Broese van Groenou, 1991), and that will obviously lead to disruptions in the social network that is available to the separated or divorced partners.

Marriage in the 21st Century

It is reported that the average age of first marriage has steadily increased over the last several decades, and the median age of first marriage for men has gone from 23 years in 1964 to 28 years in 2008; for women, it has similarly increased from 21 years in 1964 to 27 years in 2008 (U.S. Census Bureau, 2008a) This data indicates that adults are on average single for a longer period of time, contributing to the overall increase in singlehood rates. Interestingly, despite the high rates of singlehood in the United States, 93% of Americans report that they hope to marry (Waite and Gallagher, 2000).

Marriage as a social institution has now become less dominant in North America than at any other time in history (Cherlin, 2004). Fewer people are marrying and divorce rates are increasing throughout the world (Adams, 2004). Divorce now replaces death as the end point of a marriage (Fincham and Beach, 2010; Pinsof, 2002).

Diversity in marriage has increased markedly in the beginning of the 21st century, thus changing the ethnic makeup of the population and substantially increasing the religious heterogamy of couples (Myers, 2006). There is now increased recognition of same-sex marriages and same-sex relationships (Kurdek, 2006; Biblarz and Savci, 2010).

Remarriages

This is a union where at least one of the partners was previously married. Following their separation, women treat their "divorce time" as essential for their personal development as individuals, because they utilize their wide social support to grow and develop, while men hope to get that kind of support through remarriage. While men have higher remarriage rates than women, women's remarriage rates are quite significant. Fifty four percent of women are remarried within five years following a divorce and a staggering 75% remarry within 10 years (Bramlett and Mosher, 2002). Cohabitation after divorce is quite common. Remarried people are as satisfied in their second marriage, as they were in their first. Remarried couples, however, are more likely to divorce (Coleman et al., 2000).

Remarriages that include children have been termed "blended families," "stepfamilies," "reconstituted," "reconstructed," or "remarried families." The present trend indicates that there may soon be more stepfamilies than any other family form in North America. While many expect stepfamilies to be like their primary, intact family—this is an impossibility. There are several reasons for it; almost all the stepfamily's members have experienced the significant loss of a parent, a spouse, or a child and one biological parent no longer lives with the rest of the original family. The stepparent's roles have not been clearly delineated by society, and the last reason is that the children in stepfamilies have at least six, if not more, grandparents.

WHAT IS A FAMILY?

We may, or may not, feel part of it, consider it supportive or abusive, good or inhibiting of our growth, but we are all part of it—our family of origin. While there are significant differences in what a family is across cultures, there are also common threads. Universally, a family consists of at least one parent and one child with grandparents and in-laws as extended members. The family is a unit whose members are connected biologically, psychologically, and spiritually. Moreover, while individuals within the family are unique, a family provides a sense of togetherness. This bond is unique to all families and has to do with emotions and common experiences (Paterson, Blashko, and Janzen 1991).

Why do we actually live in families and remain forever connected to them? Evolution may provide the answer. For thousands of years, we have been given emotional security and support by our families. Our strongest bonds are commonly with our family. These bonds can be forged from loyalty, love, attachment, obligation, or even guilt. Lasch (1977) observed that as society has become more industrialized, bureaucratic, and impersonal, it is within the family that we find support and strength, because it is "heaven in a heartless world" (in Strong et al., 2011, p.12).

The extended family consists of the parents and child, who are connected to relatives such as in-laws, grandparents, aunts and uncles, and cousins. While most households in the U.S. are nuclear in structure, the number of multigenerational households is increasing, especially those with strong ethnic identification.

The social network is seen as the total of interpersonal ties that consist of family, friends, or others who provide support that lead the person receiving it to believe that she is cared for, valued, and belongs to a network of people (Milardo, 1988; Pernice-Duca, 2010). The family system is of prime importance in providing support. Pernice-Duca (2010) asserted that it is the quality, rather than quantity, of the contact with the family that was related to one's satisfaction with the support provided (see also Corrigan and Phelan, 2004). Equity in personal relationships is as important as is reciprocity of support, which helps increase self-esteem and self-efficacy (Bracke, Christiaens, and Verhaeghe, 2008).

"The architecture of families has changed under the influence of changing fertility and mortality patterns...visualized as family tress, 'beanpole' families have become more prevalent" (de Jong Gierveld and Dykstra, 2008, p. 272). Due to increased life span, family relations are longer lasting and it is not uncommon for parents and their children to be alive together for half a century or even longer. It is common now for those in middle or early-old age to occupy a middle position in a three or four generation family (Matthews and Sun, 2006) and it consequently is not uncommon for those in midlife to provide support to several generations. That very support may be stressful for the providers as it requires their time, efforts, and even goods. It may be true that providing support has its "costs" (see Thibault and Kelley, 1959), but the act of giving also has its rewards (Batson, 1998), such as being respected, appreciated, and valued by others, and that may have positive effects on the givens of physical and mental health (Consendine and Magai, 2005; Musick and Wilson, 2003; Van Willigen, 2001).

Loneliness is experienced by all people at some point in their lives, although it differs with age and one's life experiences (Rokach, 2000). It was found that one's family of origin and lack of social support network may significantly contribute to loneliness and alienation (Rook, 1988). In general, social support benefits our physical, emotional, and even spiritual well-being (Barker and Pistrang, 2002; Helgeson and Cohen, 1996). Social support is intended to help the individual cope with stress and has been viewed as consisting of three types: *emotional* support, which involves communicating verbally and nonverbally, caring, and showing concern; *informational* support, which includes giving advice or providing helpful information; and *instrumental* support, which is providing material goods such as money, physical assistance, etc. (Antonucci, 1985; Cohen, 2004; Hogan, Linden, and Najarian, 2002; House and Kahn, 1985).

Ornish (1998) in his book, *Love and Survival*, maintained that we all need that support within and without our nuclear family if we are to not only remain healthy emotionally and physically but to survive as a species. Hogan, Linden, and Najarian (2002), among other researchers, have emphasized the pivotal role of one's family in the provision of such support. Growing up among one's parents and siblings and in later years one's spouse and friends are all important, if not essential, sources of social support. Internal family dynamics, however, coupled with societal norms may prevent the North American family from being the hoped for "powerhouse" of support.

Studying the recovery attitudes and beliefs of "consumers" from 15 community treatment programs that centered on psychosocial rehabilitation by helping people with mental illness in their transition from living in hospitals to community life, Pernice-Duca (2010) found the quality, rather than the quantity, of support that was offered by the family was more instrumental to the development of positive recovery attitudes and beliefs. It was reported that the larger the family network, the more satisfied one was with the support received (Corrigan and Phelan, 2004). Pernice-Duca (2010) found that reciprocal support, receiving support from the family as well as reciprocating, and thus feelings of value and being of assistance to others, was most beneficial. Reciprocity of support was found to increase one's self-esteem and self-efficacy (Brack, Christiaens, and Verhaeghe, 2008), and the family's emphasis on giving and not just receiving were related to increased optimism about recovery.

American Families across Time

A striking difference between families in the 21st century and earlier American families is the diversity of their lifestyles. Let us briefly review the evolution of the family in North America in the past 400 years.

The colonial era (1607-1776): During that decade, we can see several diverse cultures, family roles, and traditions that marked that time span.

Native American families were the cornerstone of the two million Native Americans who populated the continent at that time. Some groups were patrilineal, whereby the power and consequently, the property, followed from the father, while others (such as the Zunni, Hopi, and Iroquois) were matrilineal—where power and property descended from the mother.

Most Native American families were small; child mortality was high and mothers breastfed their infants. During that time they abstained from sexual intercourse. Children were rarely physically disciplined, and instead were taught by example, by praise, or by shaming words. They began working at a young age and specific ceremonies, such as menstruation for girls and killing of the first large animals for boys, marked their transition to adulthood (see also Olds and Schwartz, 2009).

Colonial families were ethnically diverse. Colonial America was made up of explorers, soldiers, traders, pilgrims, servants, and slaves. The European colonists attempted to replicate their families of origin. These families emphasized patriarchy, where the household was ruled by the father or oldest son, women's subordination, and sexual restraints. The family's life revolved around agriculture, making their own clothes, and caring for the necessities of life. As a social unit, the family cared for its members, looked after the sick and the aged, and was responsible for teaching the principles of religion to its children. Hunting, entertaining, and politics provided the greatest pleasure. Marriage was not based on love but was prearranged by parents because it had major, profound economic and social consequences. Love came *after* marriage as it was a person's duty to love his or her spouse (Coontz, 2005).

Both the church and the larger community accepted and reinforced patriarchy (Mintz, 2004). The father's authority was based on his ownerships of the land and family's property. Wives were expected to submit to their husbands and were but helpmates rather than equal partners in marriage. Women bore and raised children; there were up to six children in a family and they did all the household chores.

African American Families

In 1619, a Dutch man docked at Jamestown in need of supplies. He had 20 Africans whom he captured from a slave trader and sold them as servants. By 1664, the British gained New Amsterdam from the Dutch and found that those 20 Africans had, in a matter of 45 years, become 40% of the colony's population. During the 17th and 18th centuries, Africans and their descendants were prohibited, *by law*, from getting married; they did succeed, though, in creating their own families.

Children's experiences in that era were harsh and bitter and included separation from their parents, who were sold at the whim of their owner. The African American slave culture was based on strong family bonding and discouraged casual sexual relationships. Parents named their offspring after themselves in order to maintain family identity and cohesiveness (McAdoo, 1996).

Nineteenth Century Marriages and Families

The 19th century was the era of industrialization, which transformed the social fabric in America. Many families moved from the farms to cities and found employment in ever expanding factories and businesses; the family shifted from being a production unit to a consumer and service oriented unit. Men began working outside the home in factories or offices and became identified as the family's breadwinner. Thus, men's work became the "real" work vs. the women's unpaid housework.

The family became the hub of emotional support and well-being. Love became the main reason for marrying and creating a family (Coontz, 2005). Women gained the power to decide whom they would marry and choose the mates they viewed as most compatible with them. Middle class 19th century women were mainly identified as housewives and mothers, whose role in the family was central. Between the years 1800 and 1900, fertility rates declined by 50% and so, having fewer children, and doing so earlier in their lives, allowed women to concentrate on mothering. A strong emphasis was consequently placed on children, and the belief in childhood innocence was widely accepted. Thus, protecting the child from the evils of the world was a widely accepted role of parents and adults in the family. Unlike in earlier centuries, at the end of the 19th century and beginning of 20th century, children did not work and were kept economically dependent on their parents. They were expected to attend school until their mid-teens, and the tumultuous period of adolescence was recognized and highlighted by the teens' reluctance to enter the adult world. Schools, rather than the family, became responsible for children's education. At school, the child sometimes learned things that conflicted with parental and family values, and the peer group increased in influence.

By the 19th century, slave families were more integrated into the North American social landscape, though they still lacked autonomy and economic importance. Slave marriages were not legally recognized and so it was still up to the white owner to decide the fate of slaves and their children. Slave children endured material deprivation, were forced into hard labor at ages as young as five or six, and suffered illness and mortality at young ages. Many young children were separated from their parents, mainly their father, who may have died or lived on another plantation. Despite all that oppression and those harsh conditions, many were resilient and survived, relying on their families for support and strength. In 1865, slavery became outlawed. Members of the African American community looked for their kin, as they were now free to travel, and renewed their marital vows that were now legally recognized. Until the last quarter of the 20th century, African American families remained poor, exploited, and segregated (see also Olds and Schwartz, 2009).

Immigration

The 19th and 20th centuries saw great waves of immigration, mainly from Europe. Today, Americans are the product of a melting pot, and they can trace their roots almost all over the globe. Native Americans were incorporated into society as well as the Latino population.

Most immigrants arrived in America without skills or money. Immigrants congregated in large neighborhoods where they spoke their own tongue, consumed their ethnic foods, and practiced religion as they did in their homelands. Kinship groups were central to their survival in the new, and not always hospitable, country. Family members cooperated economically and being poor saw mothers working outside the homes, just like fathers did.

The Twentieth Century

This century ushered a major change in the functions of American families. Food was produced outside the home; children were educated, not by the family, but often in state run schools; and the sick were cared for in and by hospitals. Thus, the family developed as the main source of emotional support to its members, leading to self-centered individualism, where one's well-being became more important than that of the family. During this era, men and women began sharing household chores and responsibilities and decision making marriages centered on romance, love, and sexual fulfillment. Children were raised more democratically, and the expression of their feelings gained importance. Both the Great Depression and the two World Wars had a profound effect on the family's economic resources, causing mothers to become an appreciable segment of the work force and children were turned into "latchkey" kids (Mintz, 2004). For many families, survival depended on the mother's and children's earnings, on help from the extended family, or on public assistance, especially when men, the major earners, were deployed in war.

The 1950s came to symbolize the family stability that occurred after half a century of economic instability and bloodshed. Youthful marriages, low divorce rates, and the "Baby Boom" characterized this era. The economy prospered and many couples were able to buy a home that was occupied by the man as the breadwinner, the wife as the housewife, and their children. The post war economy prospered and was supplemented by governmental assistance, which allowed many married couples to reach the middle-class family dream home. Later on, in the 20th century, the economic boom had leveled and people married later, postponed producing children, and curbed their fertility. Women went out to work in droves and gender roles became more similar, though far from equal (see also Friedman, 2007).

The Family and How It has Changed

> Nobody has ever before asked the nuclear family to live all by itself in a box the way we do. With no relatives, no support, we've put it in an impossible situation.   —Margaret Mead

In the past "family" was a "fixed" unit, which was often large and included two parents and then children, and was embedded in the extended family that often lived close by. As such, the family unit was the main provider of social support, many times from one's birth to one's death (Pilisuk and Hillier Parks, 1986).

Following the significant changes in the American social and economic structures, including the Women's Liberation Movement, mobility, and one-parent families, the family unit began to unravel. As the Industrial Revolution took work out of the home, it made the worker "a mass of undifferentiated equals, working in a factory or scattered between the factories, the mines, and the offices, bereft forever of the feeling that work was a family affair, done within the household" (Lewis et al., 2000, p. 225). In the 1960s, women shed their narrowly defined roles as the "homemaker" and many times the hub of the family, in favor of work outside the home, personal development, self-sufficiency, and independence (Putnam, 2000). Mate (2003) observed that "The nexus previously based in the extended family, village, community and neighborhood has been replaced by institutions such as daycare and school, where the children are more oriented to their peers than to reliable parents or parent substitute" (p. 223).

The 1980s marked the strengthening of what was referred to as the "me generation," an enhanced attempt by people to do "their own thing," look after their needs and wishes, sometimes at the expense of others, and search for personal fulfillment. All of which led to an increasing number of people becoming what Cushman (1995) referred to as "isolated, self-contained individual(s)" (p. 6). That has resulted in an endless search for community, belonging, and human contact.

Since then, there has been a shift in the composition of family households, with the traditional two-parent, married couple and their children becoming less common. In the 1930s, the average household size was 4.1 members; this changed to 2.8 members in 1980 (Pilisuk, 1986). In 2004, it was further reduced to 2.4 (American Community Survey, 2004). As recent statistics indicate, more than half of first marriages end in divorce and projections indicate that a whopping 67% of all recent first marriages may dissolve (Mills, Sprenkle, and Douglas, 1995). Family diversity is another component that, in a significant way, affects the familial landscape in America. The diversity includes more common gay and lesbian families, cohabiting families, and biracial families (Friedman, 2007). The multitude of familial changes surveyed above are believed to lead to a host of social problems, paramount among them are social isolation and loneliness, and as Brehm (1987) observed, "in the face of extensive geographical mobility, smaller nuclear family size, and a fifty percent divorce rate, the modern American family is a fragile social organization" (p. 34). Such overwhelming social and familial changes, inevitably, lead people to search for ways to compensate for the loss of community support and for the emptiness that they may feel.

Contemporary 21st Century Families

Families in the dawn of the new millennium are diverse and include various categories: families where there is a breadwinner (usually but not always, the man), a homemaker, and a child or children; two-earner couples with children; single parent households with children; married couples without children; cohabiting (unmarried) couples with or without children; blended families; and gay and lesbian couples with or without children. According to the U.S. Census (cited in Strong et al., 2011) in 2008a, more than 100 million Americans, 18 years of age or older, were single, meaning that they had never been married, divorced, or widowed. That figure represents 47% of all U.S. citizens 18 years or older. The U.S. Census Bureau (2008a) indicates that there are more single women than men, and they make up about 45% of all unmarried Americans. Examining singlehood by race indicated that 65% of African Americans, 37% of Asians, 47% of Hispanics, and 42% of non-Hispanics whites were unmarried.

The varieties of lifestyle of the single or unmarried people are numerous and include:

- The never married
- The divorced
- Young, middle-aged, and old
- Single parents
- Gay, lesbians, and bisexuals
- Widows and widowers
- Up to 5 million (in 2008) were separated people, living apart from their spouse

The changes in the family constellation compared to previous generations are profound. Economic changes, technological innovations, demographics, and gender roles and opportunities for women are all seen as facilitators of familial transformation.

The Family Varieties

A dramatic shift has occurred—from the days of a lifetime marriage and an intact nuclear family, to a new pluralistic family system that consists of:

- Intact nuclear families
- Single parent families
- Stepfamilies

While there is no need to describe the intact nuclear families, let us review the other two varieties.

Single Parent Families

These families consist of one parent and one or more children. No other family type has increased in number, in North America, as much as the single parent family. Between 1970 and 2008, there has been an increase from 17% to 26% of children living in single parent families. Single parent families existed in the past, but they were commonly a result of widowhood rather than divorce or non-marriage. While, in the past, women experienced a life pattern consisting of marriage-motherhood-widowhood, in the dawn of the 21st century their life pattern often includes marriage-motherhood-divorce-single parenthood-remarriage-widowhood.

For those who are not married when their child is born, the sequence may look like this: dating or cohabiting-motherhood-single parenting-marriage-widowhood. Single parent families are a result of divorce, births out of wedlock, or the death of a spouse. Some are created intentionally by, say, artificial insemination or adoption, and most are headed by women.

Binuclear Families

These are post-divorce families with children (Ganong and Coleman, 1994). They consist of two nuclear families: the maternal nuclear family, which is headed by the mother, and the one headed by the father. Divorce dissolves the marriage, but not the family so regardless of whether the parents (who are now ex-spouses) relate well to each other, or are at war, they are still connected with their children, who are part of the original family system.

Remarriage

This is a union where at least one of the partners was previously married. Following their separation, women treat their "divorce time" as essential for their personal development as individuals; they utilize their wide social support network to grow and develop, while men hope to get that kind of support through remarriage. While men have higher remarriage rates than women, a woman's remarriage rate is quite significant. Fifty four percent of women are remarried *within* five years following divorce and a staggering 75% remarry within 10 years (Bramlett and Mosher, 2002). Cohabitation after divorce is quite common. Remarried people are just as satisfied in their second marriage as they were in their first. Remarried couples, however, are more likely to divorce (Coleman et al., 2000).

The present trend indicates that there soon may be more stepfamilies than any other family form in North America. While many expect stepfamilies to be like their primary, intact family—the reality is quite different. Almost all the stepfamily's members have experienced the significant loss of a parent, a spouse, or a child and one biological parent no longer lives with the rest of the original family. The stepparent's roles have not been clearly delineated by society, and such a living situation is further complicated by the fact that the children in stepfamilies have at least six, if not more, grandparents.

> Family: A social unit where the father is concerned with parking space, the children with outer space, and the mother with closet space. —Evan Esar

PARENTHOOD

Since the 1960s, major changes in society have significantly influenced parental roles. What does parenthood mean to each of the parents then?

Mothers may feel that their feminine identity is confirmed, especially if they do not work outside of the house or have few marketable skills. "Unlike their wealthier sisters, who have the chance to go to college and embark on careers...poor young women grab eagerly at the surest source of accomplishments within their reach: becoming a mother" (Edin and Kefalas, 2005, p. 46). The ideology of intensive mothering portrays mothers as the essential caregivers, who should be emotionally, financially and in all other respects, fully absorbed in childrearing, and put the child's needs first while they invest much of their time, emotion, intellect, and labor into raising the child. While those stay-at-home mothers may be able to follow those directives or expectations, working mothers clearly cannot. Instead such expectations and social messages may provoke self-doubt, guilt, and low self-esteem. Factors that *increase* a mother's time with the child depend on whether she is employed, her level of education, her economic status, and the number of children she has (Kendig and Bianchi, 2008).

Fathering is more ambiguous than mothering. Fathers today, at least in North America, participate more actively and intensely than they did in the past in child rearing. Cultural expectations significantly affect what is expected from the father. There are conflicting opinions on what fathering includes now at the dawn of the 21st century. The person who came to be known as the "nurturant father" now participates in most parenting practices. Fathering activities may include communicating, teaching, giving care, protecting, and sharing affection with their children (Palkovitz, 1997).

Due to lack of sufficiently evolved models of desirable parenting, fathers end up being confused about their role expectations and fathering valued behaviors. It is clear, however, that many fathers are more involved with their children than their parents were with them (Strong et al., 2011).

A model of familial dynamics that I (A.R.) have developed highlights the effect that the family may have on one's support, connectedness, and belonging in an attempt to provide a heuristic device for examining the dynamics of the nuclear family within that of the community. In addition, this model may contribute to the identification and assessment of isolation and alienation of family members and thus assist therapists in choosing a treatment modality that aims at integrating the isolated member into the family and the community.

The model depicts the family in the center, surrounded by a supportive social network.

The family is composed of two subsystems: (1) the parents, and (2) their children. The *social network* is composed of peers and intimate friends, the extended family, and the community at large. Community involvement for adults commonly takes place when leisure activities are carried out with other community members via club membership and engaging in volunteer work. Children become involved with the community through attending school or joining the scouts or other clubs that offer leisure time activities.

Inter-Relationships

The model depicts three inter-relationships: a) connection, which describes the possible relationship between family members and part of or the entire social network. "Connection" indicates a family that is well rooted in the community, maintains close and satisfactory relations with extended family members, and whose members are also in contact with friends and with those whom they have developed intimate friendships. The b) coalition symbolizes the intra-unit relationship between the parents' subsystem or among the children's subsystem. Here too, we can find various levels of relationships that have a bearing on marital satisfaction, intra-familial dynamics, and the personal growth of family members. The existence of coalition in the family indicates that its members have close, open, and meaningful relationships. The c) alliance represents the inter-unit relationship within the family system. Various levels of relationships between the two subsystems may exist and they may or may not affect the intra-unit relationships. When alliance is present, however, there is closeness, caring, and a positive relation between the subsystems.

The family may be represented by a three dimensional cube with *connection, coalition, and alliance* as factors representing the suggested relationships. A family unit may experience part or all of these relations. It is quite safe to suggest that when such a situation exists (where the three kinds of relationships are present), family members will most probably not experience loneliness, rejection, or alienation within the family.

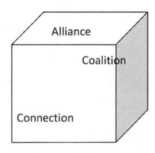

Figure 1. A schematic representation of intra-familial relations.

Unfortunately, and despite what children's stories and TV programs may depict, a well developed connection-coalition-alliance is not common in the Western culture. A more detailed examination of loneliness in the family will highlight the causal factors that prohibit these relationships from taking place.

FAMILY DYNAMICS

Coalition-Alliance: A Close-Knit Family

In this situation, the parental subsystem is strongly and closely connected in experiencing full coalition, and thus, they enjoy mutual caring, sharing, and interdependency and allow growth to occur. The children's subsystem forms a coalition as well. Its members are supportive, helpful, and care for each other, providing a sense of belonging and cohesion to the siblings.

The above scheme describes a situation where there is an alliance between the parental and the children's subsystems. Acceptance, support, and sharing are conveyed bi-directionally between the parents and their children. Bengnston and Schrader (1982) described a wider model, which refers to the above dimension as the "Intergenerational solidarity model" (Krauss Whitbourne, 2001, p. 282). The phrase "home sweet home" and nostalgic memories about childhood and adolescent years probably originate from such intra-familial, tight-knit, caring, and emotionally close families that this depicts.

Alliance-Non Coalition

Here we find a family that does not display coalition within its two subsystems. Relationships between parents are not supportive or satisfactory and marital, sexual, and emotional difficulties may be expected. The children's subsystem in this scheme is in a non-coalition state as well. The siblings' relationships with each other are marked by sibling rivalry, competition, and lack of caring and support. Each child may live in his own world that can be entered only by one or two of his parents (alliance). Such a situation, where one or two parents are the only figures in the family that the child feels close to, may foster increased dependency of the child on the adults in the family. In addition, competition for the parents' time and affection, and possible interference of the children in the intra-parental unit relationships, may result in a lack of cohesion and the disorientation of the family unit.

Coalition-Non Alliance

Here we find strong relationships between parents, as well as within the children's subsystem. The relationship between the two subsystems, however, is "weak" and unsatisfactory. While individual members may get support from other members of their subsystems (e.g., a parent from the other parent or a child from her siblings), the inter-relationship between the subsystems is lacking, and hence a sense of alienation within the family unit may be experienced.

Families that are prone to experience the coalition-non alliance condition, usually have full time working parents, parents who are much older than their children, families with a large number of children, or families where the children are all teenagers. Krauss Whitbourne (2001) termed it "developmental schism" (p. 280), which she described as the discontinuity between generations, a schism that results in tension.

Non Coalition-Non Alliance: A Disintegrated Family

A family that experiences both non coalition and non-alliance is most probably markedly distressed and disturbed and its members experience a sense of alienation, rejection, and loneliness. Here, there is minimal support within and between the subsystems. Marital difficulties are commonly present and the parents may devote their energy and attention to getting gratification from the wider social network. In their attempt to fulfill their own needs, they may fail to fulfill their children's needs for closeness and love. Feeling alienated by their parents, the children may experience a high level of stress with which they cannot cope. As a result, they might turn against one another, just like monkeys that were put in stressful conditions were shown to do. Alternatively, they may withdraw from the rest of the family and experience loneliness and rejection, which could aggravate any existing personal problems that they may experience.

THE FAMILY AND THE SOCIAL NETWORK

Mate (2003) sees people as part of an intergenerational family system, where what affected our ancestors is carried in the "family genes" and dynamics and is expressed by our parents and then by us as well. Parents and children, however, are also part of a larger whole: that of the culture and the society in which they live. "The functioning of human beings can no more be isolated from the larger social context than can that of a bee in a hive" (p. 223).

The terrifying and unpleasant experience of loneliness, the feeling of being unwanted, unneeded, alienated, and isolated is generally perceived as incompatible with the concept of the *family* (see Rokach and Brock, 1997b). The nuclear family unit is often viewed (at least in its ideal state) as a close-knit, secure, and supportive system, which allows its members to experience both the belonging that is so fundamental to a healthy mental adjustment (Olds and Schwartz, 2009; Sullivan, 1953) and the individualization and personal growth that makes a family member distinctly separate from other family members. With the present staggering divorce rates (Erber and Erber, 2001), however, comes the awareness that "all is not well in the family unit," and that the closeness, the feeling of being part of a stronger system, and the feeling of being a functional member of that system may be replaced by feelings of isolation, hopelessness, and loneliness for one or more of the family members.

The nuclear family unit is usually connected to members of the larger community. Among those many ties, one can find the general category of *peers,* or the more specific group of intimate friends. Another category of out-of-the-nuclear-family connection is the extended family. The feeling of belonging and of being part of a larger and stronger system may be enhanced by ties with members of the *extended family. Community involvement* may also enhance one's feelings of being rooted, connected, and engaged in the give and take of human relations.

A close-knit family is one that is rooted in its social environment, develops ties with the community, and enables its family members to be in contact with other individuals within the community (Gordon, 1976: Rokach, 2000; Schultz, 1976). Consequently, adults get their feeling of belonging and of relatedness from their work place, through joining professional or quasi-professional clubs, by devoting time to volunteer work, or by joining social groups. Children also seek to belong to groups, and hence are part of the educational system through their participation in school, where they may join social or ideological groups (e.g., scouts) or clubs that offer leisure time activities.

Family Support

The most important social relations usually involve long lasting, significantly close relationships such as a marital relationship, the relationship between parent and child, and the sibling relationship (Pinquart, 2003). According to Canton's (1979) hierarchical compensatory model of support, the key factor that determines the utilization of a specific source of support is the primacy of the relationship. Consequently, spouses are the primary source of support, followed by adult children, and then other close relatives, and only after all of them come one's friends. The unmarried adults first approach of all their children for support (Reinhardt and Fisher, 1988). The children of divorced parents, however, may offer varying degrees and quality of support depending on their relationship with that parent. Similarly, siblings of the unmarried are an important source of support (Wilson, Calsyn, and Orlofsky, 1994).

De Jong Gierveld and Dykstra (2008) found that those middle-aged family members, who engaged in balanced exchanges, i.e. gave and received support, with parents, siblings, and children, were the least lonely. Examining the pattern closer, it appears that those who gave more to their siblings had generally lower levels of loneliness, but the opposite was found for those who gave to their offspring in larger measures than they received.

> In time of test, family is best.
> —Burmese Proverb

Chapter 12

A DEVELOPMENTAL PERSPECTIVE
ON MARITAL RELATIONSHIPS

All families change over time. Many of these changes are obvious and typical: a family is formed; children are born; they grow up, go to school, and eventually leave home to form their own families. Others, such as divorce or remarriage, are not as predictable but still common, in modern family life. Each transition requires the family to change, to test priorities, and to reorganize to meet the challenges of the new life cycle stage.

(Gerson, 1995, p.91)

Marriage, being referred to as a unique, unduplicated, distinctive, "of its own kind" phenomenon, progresses through various developmental stages. Viewed through the lens of developmental perspective, the marital union, from its conception and birth, throughout its life span, goes through a growth process that resembles human development (Nichols and Pace-Nichols, 2000). As such, the marital cycle has discreet, identifiable stages, each involving interactive patterns and developmental tasks that must be mastered to ensure a healthy, well-functioning, successful marital system (Nichols, 1988). From the moment of its emergence, the "newborn infant" marriage is launched upon an intensive, day-to-day process of development and growth. Just like human development, in order for a marital dyad to adequately proceed, it must successfully accomplish and complete certain marital tasks in each of its developmental stages. Although each marital union is unique, most enduring marriages develop through similar sequential stages. In this sense, Nichols (1988) views marriage development as an unfolding process and "embodied in the process are progressions as well as sameness and static conditions, stability as well as change, and continuity as well as discontinuity" (p. 18).

This chapter focuses on the earlier developmental stages of the marriage that are highly important to the creation, growth, and enhancement of the marital union.

There is a distinction between two categories of tasks that marital spouses are to accomplish as their marriage unfolds and develops: internal marital relationship tasks and external marital relationship tasks. Both sets of tasks need to be accomplished sufficiently well by the spouses to ensure marital success and stability (Nichols, 1988).

Marriage is a mistake every man should make.
—Quoted by Sir George Jessel

INTERNAL MARITAL TASKS

Internal marital tasks are those tasks that involve relationship components that are within the inner boundaries of the marriage. Included under this heading are central elements such as developing and strengthening marital commitment; developing interpersonal communication and problem solving skills; expressing of love, care, and affection; attending to a partner's needs; developing a foundation for intimacy; working on an agreeable balance of power and influence; developing mutual trust; and developing agreeable sexual closeness.

EXTERNAL MARITAL TASKS

External marital tasks are those tasks that exist outside of the marital boundaries, involving individuals, systems, and subsystems that are connected to the marital spouses. To ensure the successful development and maintenance of the marital relationship, spouses are required to accomplish various external tasks. This starts at the early stage of the relationship formation when "partners need to begin establishing a firm enough and yet penetrable enough set of boundaries around their relationship and between them and friends, family of origin, and, in some instances, occupation or career" (Nichols, 1988, p. 21). The most important task for couples from the early stage of marriage is to establish a workable balance between intrinsic and extrinsic marital needs.

PREMARITAL FACTORS RELATED TO MARITAL QUALITY AND STABILITY

Premarital education and counseling programs are based on the well founded understanding that some premarital factors are associated with the later marital developmental course.

The interest of marriage and family scientists in this area is related to the high rate of marriage discord, dissolution, and divorce in the United States (Larson and Holman, 1994). This state of affairs has challenged marriage scholars to study the premarital factors that affect the developmental process of marital quality and stability and to utilize the knowledge to provide effective counseling and education programs for premarital couples (Larson and Holman, 1994; Carroll and Doherty, 2003).

From a developmental point of view, studying premarital predictive variables of marital success is founded on the conviction that the premarital partners' individual characteristics and a couple's interpersonal components are the foundations of later marital success (Holman, 2001).

Another conviction is that individuals have the capacity to change the premarital nature of their relationship to positively influence the development of their marriage (Renick, Blumberg, and Markman, 1992). This conviction is supported by evaluative research that has been conducted on the impact of premarital prevention education on marital quality, stability, and satisfaction (Halford and Moor, 2002).

Keep your eyes wide open before marriage, half shut afterwards.
—Benjamin Franklin

Following a review of the literature on premarital predictors of marital outcomes (quality, stability, and dissolution), Holman (2001) developed four broad conceptual categories of premarital factors that affect later marital development. These are: (a) family of origin background variables; (b) partners' intrapsychic, individual traits and characteristics; (c) couple's interpersonal, interactional qualities and dynamics; and (d) social contextual variables.

FAMILY OF ORIGIN INFLUENCE

Premarital predictors of marital outcomes that relate to the influence of family of origin are considered "fixed markers" (Story, Rothman, and Bradbury, 2002). This is because these variables cannot be altered or manipulated through counseling interventions. Family of origin "fixed markers" are variables such as the quality of one's parents' marital relationship, degree of family cohesion, parental divorce, and so forth (Story et al., 2002).

Accumulating empirical evidence suggests a convincing and steady positive association between family of origin functioning and a person's marital success. Positive family of origin experiences promote a person's later marital satisfaction, whereas negative family of origin experiences decrease the likelihood of his marital success.

Family of origin predictors consist of background factors that describe one's parents' marital interaction, degree of conflict and negativity, parents' communication and conflict resolution patterns, parents' way of expressing feelings and affection, and other interactive behaviors that characterize parental marriage (Holman and Linford, 2001; Larson, 2003).

Larson (2003) developed various questionnaires to be used by premarital couples to identify and assess risk factors that may affect the course of their marital development, including those that are connected to family of origin influences.

Premarital and newlywed partners are presented with various items that evaluate their family of origin experiences, and their perceptions of their parent's marriage. Positive experiences are those that describe secure, comforting, supporting, and loving family relationships. In contrast, negative family of origin experiences are those that describe conflicted, tense, anxious, criticizing, and unrewarding family interactions. Other components of family of origin assessment relate to one's parents' marriage qualities. A stable, well-functioning, and successful parental marriage has a positive influence on one's marriage preparation process and functioning. There is empirical evidence that shows that an individual's family of origin experiences and the quality of the parental marriages assessed premaritally affect later marital outcomes (Holman, 2001).

Story, Rothman, and Bradbury (2002) examined the impact of family of origin factors on the marital outcomes of 60 newlywed couples. The authors replicated other studies that showed intergenerational transmission of marital outcomes. Their results indicated that parental marital negativity and divorce predicted the newlyweds' marital outcomes. A parental divorce's influence on newlywed marital outcomes was also found to be higher for wives than husbands.

Story et al. (2002) used multiple instruments to get aggregated measures of newlywed partners' family background (parental marital satisfaction, family of origin conflict, and an overall measure of family functioning). The results led the authors to conclude that men and women of negative family of origin characteristics (divorce, marital negativity) are likely to bring to their marriages maladaptive interactive behaviors that are linked to negative marital development. This assertion presents a challenge for marriage counselors and educators to target these at risk individuals for premarital prevention programs (Story et al., 2002). Proper prevention education programs can break the chain of intergenerational transmission of marital negativity.

Individual Traits that Predict Marital Outcomes

Holman's (2001) second conceptual category of premarital factors that affect marital developmental processes is individual traits. Research on the association between a partner's individual traits and his marital functioning has focused mostly on personality characteristics and mental health factors (Larson and Holman, 1994). Individual factors that predict marital outcomes consist not only of personality attributes but also values and attitudes regarding marriage, realistic expectations, interpersonal skills, individual coping strategies, emotional health, and attachment security (Larson and Holman, 1994; Holman, 2001).

The five-factor model of personality has been used to identify and characterize personality attributes that are associated with marital development (Shackelford and Buss, 1997). This model presents five major bipolar factors of personality structure (Digman, 1990). These factors are: openness, conscientiousness, extraversion, agreeableness, and neuroticism. According to Shackelford and Buss (1997), a partner's low ratings on emotional stability (the bipolar factor of neuroticism), conscientiousness, and agreeableness are associated with negative marital development. These marital partners are characterized by a combination of personality attributes that predict marital distress, such as emotional instability, anxiety and irritability, impulsive behavior, a lack of self-efficacy, distrust, inconsideration of others, and an unwillingness to compromise. Woman married to men who rate low on the factor of agreeableness (trusting, kind, prosocial, considerate, and generous) describe their spouses as being condescending, unreliable, neglecting of the spouse's needs; emotionally, their spouses are inconsiderate, abusive, and self-centered (Buss, 1991; Shackelford and Buss, 1997).

Larson (2003) identified six personality characteristics that affect marital development and predict negative relational outcomes. These are:

1) Excessive vulnerability to stress that relates to emotional instability, anxiety, and irritability.
2) Excessive impulsiveness, characterized by low impulse control and emotional regulation and stability. Impulsivity is associated with marital instability and distress (see also Kelly and Conley, 1987).
3) Exorbitant anger and hostility that create an atmosphere of negative affect and emotional distance between spouses. It can also lead to physical and emotional partner abuse.

4)   Untreated depression manifested by a lack of excitability, emotional expressiveness, low energy, pronounced disengagement, and emotional distancing. Depression has been found to predict negative marital outcomes (Larson and Holman, 1994).

5)   Anxiety, in the form of emotional instability, excessive irritability, emotional reactivity, excessive worry, anger, and sadness. In many cases, depression and anxiety occur simultaneously (Larson, 2003).

6)   Self-consciousness, manifested by a person's constant need for reassurance from his partner, and low self-esteem.

Basic trust is another attribute that contributes to marital development. Trusting people are more likely to be prosocial, to behave benevolently, and to be considerate and friendly toward their partners, thus promoting marital success. Partners who are trusting and have strong faith in the goodness of their relational partner are more likely to adopt communal norms in their marriages. Since trust is a basic attribute of secure attachment style (Hazan and Shaver, 1987; Clark et al., 2002), it is reasonable to suggest that "secure people ought to be especially adept at following communal norms and at retuning to the use of such norms when they have been abandoned. People who are avoidant, in contrast, may be likely to switch to some other rule for allocating benefits more readily, and more likely to stick with that rule over time" (Clark et al., 2002, p.169).

Interpersonal, Interactional Traits

Holman's (2001) third category of premarital factors that are associated with marital development is a couple's interactional traits. Premarital communication and conflict resolution skills are considered strong and reliable interactional traits that affect marital development outcomes (Larson and Holman, 1994; Holman, 2001). Gottman, Carrere, and Swanson (1998) found negative affect reciprocity to be detrimental to latter marital outcome. This maladaptive interaction can be detected and treated premaritally to avoid later martial distress. The amount of positive affect that premarital couples exercise during conflict interaction is associated with later marital stability and success. This assertion conceptualizes the marital communication process as a complex interactional process in order to include the quality and nature of the affect that accompanies verbal exchange (Holman, 2001). Premarital and newlywed couples that possess communication and conflict resolution skills that create positive affect are likely to behave this way later in marriage. In contrast, negativity displayed in premarital and newlywed couples' communication, especially during conflict, is predictive of later marital distress (Markman, 1991; Gottman, Coan, Carrere, and Swanson, 1998). Gottman et al. (1998) examined the kinds of negative interactional processes in newlywed couples that are detrimental to later marital stability and satisfaction. The amount of positive affect maintained by couples during conflict was found to predict later marital outcomes (stability and satisfaction).

Markman (1981, 1984) conducted a longitudinal study to examine premarital communication processes and the extent to which they predict later marital satisfaction. The results showed an association between positive premarital communication positivity and later marital satisfaction. This positive association was found 5 ½ years after the premarital rating of a couple's perceived positivity with regard to their communication patterns. We again indicate that findings of this nature have bearing on marital development since they can be detected and dealt with prior to marital quality decline and distress.

Larson (2003) developed a model for marital relationship evaluation and enhancement. This model can be used by premarital as well as by newlywed couples. Relating to marital communication, the author states that "communication is the heart of a marriage, it determines how well the rest of the marriage functions. That is, with good communication skills, individual problems can be overcome, stresses dealt with in a healthy and efficient manner, disagreements resolved to both spouses' satisfaction, love expressed, and other matters discussed frankly and objectively" (p. 58). Following the developmental process suggested by Larson's (2003) model, premarital partners can engage in a communication evaluation process in which they record a discussion on a conflictual issue they currently have (e.g. budgeting expenses, in-laws).

Following this recorded discussion, partners score their respective communication interactive behavior on a scoring form that consists of items such as: "I expressed a thought, feeling or intention in a respectful way" or "I made positive suggestions to resolve our disagreement." Negative items included, "I tried to force my solution to the problem on my partner." Other items refer to positive and negative listening skills ("I ask my partner for his or her opinion" or "I was intolerant or judgmental about my partner's point of view"). In addition, partners rate themselves on items relating to nonverbal interactive behaviors (maintaining eye contact), empathic communication skills ("I understand my partner's feelings"), their partner's empathic interactions ("My partner understands my feelings"), and other components such as criticism, contempt, stone-walling, intimacy, affect expressivity, and so forth. Based on the scores received on the various communication and conflict resolution measures, partners can identify areas of improvement and for the enhancement of their interaction behavior prior to marriage.

SOCIAL CONTEXTUAL FACTORS

The fourth broad conceptual category of premarital factors that predict later marriage success or failure consists of social-contextual variables (Holman, 2003; Larson and Holman, 1994). According to Holman (2003), "Relationships are embedded in their larger contexts, and these large contexts influence the quality and stability of relationships" (p. 57). Social contextual factors that affect marital relationships consist of variables such as age and education at marriage, gender, social network (family, close friends) support of the marriage, and alternative attraction. Several studies examined the association between social contextual variables and marital outcomes (see Holman, 2003, for a detailed literature review). Among the variables studied are age at marriage and social network support.

> Marriage at a young age was found to be linked to marital distress, instability, and dissolution. White concluded that "age at marriage is the strongest predictor of divorce in the first five years of marriage" (White, 1990, p. 906, in Holman, 2003, p.58).

Social network support for mate selection for marriage and for premarital and newlywed couples is a positive predictor of later marital success and stability (Surra, 1990). Holman (2003) stated that "the psychological network's (family) interference or support appears to be more closely associated with decreasing or increasing the stability of the (dyadic) relationship than the interactive network (friends, co-workers), which may not include many important and close relationships" (p. 123). Moreover, social network support (especially from significant others) for one's mate selection and dyadic relationship was found to be positively related to feelings of love, emotional intimacy, relational commitment, satisfaction, and stability. In contrast, social network rejection and discouragement of one's dyadic relationship is predictive of later marital negative outcomes, including distress, dissolution, and even divorce (Surra, 1990, in Holman, 2003). Concluding the results of the studies that examined social network support's impact on premarital couple's later relationship, Holman (2003) stated that "parents and extended social networks have an influence on relationships, and that support can be effective in developing greater relationship quality for a couple over time" (p. 124).

TRANSITION TO MARRIAGE: THE UNATTACHED ADULT

This premarital stage requires that the young adult separates emotionally from his family of origin in order to be able to invest in the development of long-term, intimate relationships. This is an important life passage for a mature, independent young adult to further develop and crystallize his self-identity and determination. It requires not only the acceptance of separation from the family of origin but also the development of a sense of identity and the establishment of a well-differentiated self, capable of forming and investing in a committed, prolonged, intimate relationship. Entering marital relationships without sufficient self-differentiation may cause difficulties in forming, securing, and maintaining intimate marital bonds.

Nichols (1988) outlined the internal tasks to be accomplished by premarital couples, including the development of an initial commitment to each other, examining whether there is sufficient caring to "justify" wedlock, creating a shared sense of intimacy, beginning to establish workable patterns of communication, and conflict resolution skills. In addition, partners need to clarify their "contract" and their expectation of each other and the relationship. Nichols (1988) also stresses the importance of the development of mutual caring upon which the premarital mating couple can enter a further stage, the transition to marriage stage.

Most family changes are listed by Holmes and Rahe (1967) as typical major life stressors. The transitions from one stage to another are not clear cut, may take as long as several years, and tend to merge into one another. All families, and this has been so since the beginning of time, must organize to cope with the multiple entrances (births) and exits (deaths) of its members (Gerson, 1995).

THE TRANSITION TO THE MARRIAGE STAGE: COUPLE FORMATION

According to Erikson (1968), in the early stage of young adulthood, people seek to form intimate, loving relationships with others. More specifically, during this developmental stage (intimacy vs. isolation, the sixth of the eight-stage developmental process), people become capable of forming and developing intimate relationships with a significant other, making the necessary commitment, sacrifices, and compromises that this process requires. Viewed through a family life cycle lens, entering into this developmental stage through marriage is considered a transitional stage—the transition into the marital stage (Morris and Carter, 1999). Although the transition to marriage is anticipated and voluntary, it still has the potential to be stressful and threatening to the relationship (Carter and McGoldrick, 1989). Some view this transition as a complex and most difficult passage despite the romanticized notion of the joy embedded in the blissful bonding of two people. Apparently, marriage, with all the joy and intimacy it provides, is a complicated merger of two nearly strangers that have to create a third, combined entity—the marital unit (Carter and McGoldrick, 1989).

DEVELOPING A SENSE OF INTIMACY AND TOGETHERNESS

Developing a sense of intimacy, togetherness, and belonging is an important internal task to be accomplished during the initial stage of marriage. Relational intimacy develops gradually in a dynamic, interactive process. As partners invest in the marriage and become more committed, they get intimately closer.

McCarthy, Ginsberg, and Cintron (2008) observed that during the first two years of marriage, the couple faces the task of developing a strong, resilient marital bond of respect, trust, and intimacy. Benign neglect is the couple's most "dangerous" enemy. Addressing the problems that the couple faces while adjusting to one another in an efficacious manner is much more advantageous than denying them.

Reis and Shaver (1988) developed an interpersonal process model of intimacy development, suggesting that intimacy develops through marital interactions in which the revelation of personal feelings and thoughts is met with sensitivity, acceptance, and an empathetic response by the listening partners. Accordingly, intimacy is created, developed, and enhanced through the partners opening up to one another, disclosing personally relevant information, and responding positively to one another's disclosure.

Closely linked to intimacy development for newlywed partners is their ability to express love and affection to each other as a measure for the development of strong, stable marital foundations. Roberts and Greenberg (2002), attesting to the importance of affectional expressions, indicate that "the regular enactment of behavioural exchange that lead to experiences of relational intimacy will serve to maintain the climate of security, trust, and acceptance that characterizes well-functioning relationships" (p. 120-121).

One of the most cited theories that portrays and describes relationship development, especially during the initial stage of marital development, is the Social Penetration Theory (SPT) (Altman and Taylor, 1973). Using the metaphor of an onion, the theory suggests that when one explores one layer of information about an intimate partner, there is another, deeper layer to be "peeled off." As two partners become acquainted, their relationship develops by becoming broader and deeper, thus, the relationship gradually moves to more enhanced levels of intimacy over time. According to SPT, at first, partners at the early stage of relationship creation tend to exchange impersonal information, not allowing entrance into more intimate, personal issues. As they come to know and trust each other, a greater intimacy is achieved through their willingness to explore more topics (breadth) and share more personal, intimate information (depth). Revealing and disclosing personal thoughts and feelings is one important channel through which couples achieve breadth and depth in their unfolding intimate relationship. As self-disclosure progresses in breadth and depth, so does intimacy between the two bonding partners.

As indicated previously, there is a set of personal and interpersonal tasks that involves both internal and external dimensions that need to be achieved during the initial stage of relationship formation. One of the most important internal tasks is to establish constructive patterns of effective communication, especially during conflict. Koski and Shaver (1997) reviewed attachment styles of marital couples and their relation to marriage satisfaction. Their findings showed the important role of effective, constructive communication on marital satisfaction. Couples that manage at this early stage to fulfill the task of developing effective communication skills are likely to establish a strong foundation of a healthy and long lasting marriage. High quality communication manages to mediate the negative association between a partner's insecure attachment style (that many individuals possess at this early marital developmental phase) and relationship satisfaction. Kelly, Fincham, and Beach (2003) indicate that spouses view their marriage as successful when they experience mutual, rewarding, interactive communication. This is true particularly for couples in the stage of marital formation. A progressive decline in marital satisfaction at this developmental stage is experienced when partners interact destructively. It is well known that when distressed couples talk about relationship issues, what starts as a discussion can rapidly turn into an escalated, furious argument. Among other things, this occurrence is attributed to a lack of communication skills (Noller and Feeney, 1998).

ACCOMMODATION

It is inevitable that couples, even in the early stage of their marital formation, may engage in conflicts and difficulties. Rusbult, Bissonnett, Arriaga, and Cox (1998) suggest the use of accommodation in marital transaction in order to strengthen the foundations of marriage. According to these authors, "interaction sequences involving accommodative behavior are initiated when one partner engages in potentially destructive acts, such as behaving in a thoughtless manner, saying hurtful things, yelling at the partner, or worse. Accommodation refers to an individual's willingness, when the partner has enacted a potentially destructive behavior to (a) inhibit impulses to react destructively in turn and (b) instead behave in a constructive manner" (p. 74). Behaving in an accommodative manner is important to the development of strong mutual marital commitments and marital quality and satisfaction (Rusbult and Buunk, 1993). Thus, it is especially important for couples in the marital formation stage to start practicing accommodative interactions due to the tension prevention impact of accommodation.

A high level of commitment, developed in the early stage of relationship formation, is central to later marital success and stability and is associated with partners' accommodative behavior (Rusbult, Zembrodt, and Gunn, 1998).

Rusbult, Zembrodt, and Gunn (1982) suggested an accommodative response to dissatisfaction and the destructive partner's behavior in their EVLN (Exit-Voice-Loyalty-Neglect) typology. If partners want to be productive in their reaction to a partner's negativity, they should choose the *voice* or *loyalty* construct of the EVLN model. "Voice" refers to the active, constructive response when discussing a problem and focuses on calming the partner so as to de-escalate tension and improve the situation. Choosing loyalty refers to passively waiting for things to improve and supporting the partner in the face of criticism (Rusbult et al., 1998). Learning to interact in an accommodative manner is relatively easy for newlywed couples due to the closeness, romantic love, and intimacy characterizing this stage of marriage. It is easier to develop constructive interactive behaviors in such an atmosphere. Once developed and established, constructive, accommodative interactions become natural and habitual assets of the relationship. Rusbult et al. (1998) concluded that marital relationships can be well functioning, persist successfully, and be satisfying if partners adhere to mutual accommodative interactions.

SETTING BOUNDARIES

Shaping the marital union from its very early stage of marital formation requires the development and maintenance on the part of the couple of semi permeable boundaries between their marriage and other subsystems in their lives (parents, in-laws, friends, and work). The boundaries foster the alignment that occurs as the bond between the spouses is developed. It has been shown that families of origin and close friends commonly accept this newly developed bond in its creation and stabilization. Boundaries also help to promote a sense of loyalty and commitment between the young spouses who become the "significant other" to each other (Nichols, 1988). This "inner circle" created by the couple and supported by the appropriate boundaries they set is the foundation for the development and enhancement of emotional and physical marital intimacy. Moreover, the development of the couple's "marital identity" depends to a great extent on how successful the couple was in establishing boundaries between their marriage system and the rest of their surrounding world (Nichols, 1988).

CREATING AND FORMING THE "MARRIAGE CULTURE"

One of the main tasks to be accomplished by the newlywed couple is the creation and formation of their "marriage culture," the story of their marital relationship and identity (Gottman, 1999a). This process consists of a wide range of transactions, such as repetitive interactions of fondness, marriage maintenance activities, attending to each other's needs, solving disagreements effectively, being benevolent to each other, sharing joyous time together, and so forth. Generally, the newlywed partners' attention and energies are to be focused and invested into the relationship's development. With that happening, the couple "sculpts" their love story, find common purposes, learn how to show and express love and affection, and continually invest personal resources to benefit each other and the relationship. Through this ongoing process of interaction, the newlywed spouses increase their knowledge of each other and show interest in, and care for, each other. This interactive pattern of positive exchange enables the partners to develop and sustain a positive marital climate (Gottman, 1999a; Gottman, 1999b). Daily talks are also important for a couple's development of closeness and intimacy, which is achieved through continuously learning each other's deep thoughts, ideas, feelings, personal philosophy of life, needs, wants, and desires. From this accumulation of knowledge "springs not only love but the fortitude to weather marital storms" (Gottman, 1999b, p. 48).

CONFLICT RESOLUTION SKILLS

Another important task for newlywed couples to accomplish is the development of effective conflict and disagreement resolution skills. Personal skills and effective interpersonal patterns of interaction during conflict are essential to marital success, especially during the initial stage of marriage formation (Birchler, Doumas, and Fals-Stewart, 1999; Nichols, 1988). Birchler et al. (1999) developed a behavioral systems model that they incorporated in working with couples on acquiring and enhancing conflict resolution skills. The authors suggested a model that consists of: (1) developing a focused, well-defined, and mutually accepted agenda for problem identification and discussion focused on resolution; (2) developing an open communication interaction for partners to freely share their personal perspectives, definition, and understanding of the conflict under discussion; (3) developing a creative process, thereby allowing partners to generate solutions in a brainstorming fashion; (4) developing a plan for the implementation of the agreed upon solution; and (5) evaluating the solution while leaving room for possible modifications. Birchler et al. (1999) indicated that this five-step process can be taught to newlywed couples as a preventive measure to enhance and maintain their marriage. Research demonstrated that marital quality is enhanced when partners possess cooperative conflict resolution skills (Masuda and Duck, 2002).

EXPANSIONS STAGE: TRANSITION TO PARENTHOOD

Marital quality, stability, and satisfaction may be affected by major life events and passages, the most important of which is the transition spouses make to the role of parenthood (Shapiro and Gottman, 2005). This stage in the marital development cycle is characterized by the disequilibrium experienced by first-time parents facing new situations, expectations, and challenges (Levy-Shiff, 1999). Research has consistently shown that the transition to parenthood, with the joy and happiness of having a first-born child, is generally associated with a decline in marital satisfaction for both spouses (Helms-Erickson, 2001). Some even consider this stage a major life stressor, requiring many adaptations (Rholes, Simpson, Campbell, and Grich, 2001). As such, one can understand the decrease in marital satisfaction associated with this stage.

Rholes et al. (2001) conducted a study that examined the impact of the transition to parenthood on marital functioning and satisfaction with different attachment orientations. Data was collected from both husbands and wives during two periods of time, 6 weeks prior to the birth of the first child and 6 months postpartum. The findings, discussed through an attachment theory lens, showed that when the wife perceived her husband's support before birth, it mediated the insecure attachment orientation of the husband's. In other words, a wife's marital satisfaction was influenced mostly by her husband's support. In contrast, a deficient husband's emotional support predicted a decline in the wife's perceived marital satisfaction.

With the transition to parenthood, the marital dyad is transformed into a familial triad, with the expectation that the couple, now holding the new status of parents, will shift a great amount of time, attention, and energy from each other to the newborn baby. Considering the importance of this stage for both spouses and their child, the U.S. Department of Health and Human Services invested a substantial amount of money for the development of intervention programs for new parents (Mitnick, Heyman, and Slep, 2009). This implies that spouses experiencing the transition to parenthood face the risk of marital distress and even dissolution (Mitnick et al., 2009). According to Shapiro and Gottman (2005), the decline in marital quality during this stage may also have a negative impact on the newborn child.

Summarizing relevant literature, Shapiro and Gottman (2005) outlined the following effects of the transition to parenthood on marriage:

1) There is the likelihood of a significant increase in the amount and level of conflict interaction between spouses.
2) Between 40-60% of marital couples experience a decrease in the quality of their marriage during the first year of the birth of the first-born child.
3) Marital satisfaction is found to reach a high point in the last trimester of pregnancy and thereafter show a decline.
4) Well adjusted new parents, who manage to maintain high relationship quality, are more likely to interact more effectively with their child.

Based on these and other research findings, Shapiro and Gottman (2005) suggest that the transition to parenthood can be partially associated with statistics showing that half of all divorces occur in the first seven years of marriage. During this early stage of marital development, most of the transitions to parenthood occur, which can possibly and partially account for these divorce statistics.

What is it about the transition to parenthood that makes this marital developmental stage detrimental to marital quality and satisfaction? Apparently, there are various changes that couples experience as they become parents for the first time. This transition was found to be characterized by intensive physical and emotional energies devoted to the baby. The associated anxieties and worries, reduction in perceived intimacy and love, and reduction in time for social, fun activities may all have a negative impact on marriage (Peterson, 2010). Also, the transition to parenthood requires changes in the division of household labor and assignments that may lead to increased tension, husband-wife conflicts, and fatigue (MacDermid, Huston, and McHale, 1990). These changes may negatively affect the expression of intimacy, both physically and emotionally. Indeed, a person's expression of love, fondness, and admiration toward his spouse, and greater, more sensitive awareness and responsiveness to relational needs, buffer against the decline in marital quality and satisfaction (Shapiro, Gottman, and Sibil, 2000).

The findings of Tucker and Aron (1993) present strong evidence of the importance of investment in marital intimacy and closeness, especially during the transition to parenthood. They found that becoming parents for the first time has a negative impact on the partners' romantic feelings and on their expression of passionate love. Compared to the impact of other marital passages, the transition to parenthood has a greater negative effect on intimacy and the expression of love and closeness. Similar findings were presented by Woollett and Parr (1997) who studied postpartum couples who reported a decrease in their feelings of intimacy and sexual satisfaction.

The transition to parenthood transforms spousal identity to include the identity of a parent. The "parent aspect of self" takes a meaningful and central place in the lives of the partners who are becoming parents (Cowan et al., 1985). Cowan et al. (1985) asked first-time parents to describe how they perceived their identity and role in life (by dividing a circle "pie" in accordance with their perceived roles). As expected, the parental identity (the "parent aspect of self") showed a noticeable increase for both spouses. The piece of the "pie" representing women's parental identity and role, however, increased twice as much as it did for men. Also, as the parental self identity grew larger, the partner identity (friend, lover) decreased significantly for both spouses. This, according to Cowan et al. (1985), can explain the drop in marital satisfaction associated with the transition to parenthood. Similarly, Belsky, Lang, and Rovine (1985) found that this transition is characterized by a decrease in the emphasis placed by couples on the romantic aspects of their lives, and a greater emphasis on partnership and parenthood. The authors further indicated that during the transition to parenthood, "the marital relationship becomes more focused on instrumental functions and less on emotional expressions" (p. 863).

In support of this finding, Belsky and Rovine (1990) reported that couples who scored high on the index of romance and intimacy showed greater marital satisfaction upon becoming parents for the first time than couples who scored lower on these measures. MacDermid, Huston, and McHale (1990) reported that first-time parents interact and are engaged in more joint activities than childless couples. It should be noted, however, that when one excludes from the joint activities those activities that relate to caring for the new baby, new parents showed less romantic, intimate involvement. Commenting on the decrease in romance and intimacy found in new parents, Glenn and McLanahan (1982) indicated that it may be that in our highly individualistic and hedonistic society, in which marriage is expected to involve a high degree of emotional and sexual intimacy and to be the spouses' primary source of companionship, children seem to lower marital happiness and satisfaction regardless of whether or not the children are planned and wanted. Children tend to lessen the spontaneity of sexual relations, and their presence creates the potential for jealousy and competition for affection, time, and attention between the partners.

Nichols (1988) argued that the transition to parenthood (the family expansion stage) "begins psychologically with pregnancy or, in some cases, with the decision to have a child" (p. 29). In his opinion, a couple's preparation for the transition to parenthood should take place earlier, before the pregnancy starts. Pregnancy is a sensitive, and for many, anxiety provoking occurrence, especially for first-time parents (Entwisle and Doering, 1988). Anxiety is attributed to stresses that pregnancy, delivery, and parenthood impose on the mother and father to be (Shapiro and Gottman, 2005). Lower levels of anxiety during pregnancy, childbirth, and parenthood are related to the partners' self-efficacy and belief in their ability to become effective parents (Biehle, 2009; Coleman and Karraker, 1998). Feelings of confidence in the mother's competence and capabilities to adequately execute parental roles and functions are associated with parental well-being and positive parenting outcomes (Jones and Prinz, 2005). Stated in another way, the normal and adaptive anxiety and stress inherent in bringing into the world and adequately raising a child depends to a large extent on the parents maintaining a positive view of themselves as "good enough" parents.

PARENTAL SELF-EFFICACY

Some researchers expanded on Bandura's (1995, 1997) self-efficacy model and examined the impact of the transition to parenthood on couples. Rooted within Bandura's social cognitive perspective, self-efficacy is seen to provide the foundation for human motivation, achievement, and accomplishments. According to Bandura (1995), "self-efficacy is the belief in one's capabilities to organize and execute the course of action required to manage prospective situations" (p. 2). Stated even more sharply, "people's level of motivation, affective states, and actions are based more on what they believe than on what is objectively true" (p. 2). In line with the self-efficacy perspective, Colman and Karraker (1998) found that parental competence and satisfaction with the parental role are associated with the self-efficacy beliefs held by parents. How confident a parent feels about his child caring abilities is determined by his level of parental self-efficacy. Parents holding high parenting self-efficacy engage in better parenting and care giving behaviors, and thus experience less anxiety and stress, which may be related to the transition to parenthood (Halpern and Mclean, 1997). Teti and Gelfand (1991) examined parental self-efficacy in clinically depressed and non-depressed mothers of infants 3 to 13 months old. It was found that the parental self-efficacy held by the mothers significantly related to the mothers' competence, anxiety, depression, and marital satisfaction. These relations were found to be independent of the possible impact of variables such as social and marital support. The authors concluded that the results of their study suggest that maternal self-efficacy mediates between maternal "ingredients" and psychological variables and may play a crucial role in influencing parenting behavior and an infant's psychological development (Teti and Gelfand, 1991).

The positive impact of parental self-efficacy was also found during pregnancy. High parental self-efficacy predicted the strength of the emotional mother-infant attachment and adaptation to the stressful transition to parenthood (Williams, Joy, et al., 1987).

As indicated previously, in Nichols' (1988) view, the developmental stage of family expansion begins cognitively and emotionally during a first-time pregnancy. Therefore, proactively preparing couples for pregnancy, childbirth, and parenthood is an important preventive measure.

Based on this premise, Shapiro and Gottman (2005) developed and examined the impact on marriage of a psycho-communicative-educational intervention program for couples in the transition to parenthood. The program consists of several elements such as developing and strengthening personal and relational resources, recognizing and appraising the potentially stressful upcoming events, providing program participants with professional information regarding the transition to parenthood, developing preliminary coping capabilities to adequately and effectively function as parents, and so forth. In Shapiro and Gottman's (2005) pregnancy and parenthood preparation program, attention is given to the necessary shifts and changes in gender roles that are needed for better coping. Special attention is specifically given to promoting greater involvement on the part of new fathers with regard to their newborn babies. This is due to the potentially detrimental influence of husbands' lack of active involvement with the process of pregnancy and more importantly, with the newborn child (Cowan and Cowan, 2000). Shapiro and Gottman (2005) argued that "in the transition to parenthood much of the marital conflict centers on the inequities in [the] father's verses [the] mother's involvement with the family" and that "there is growing evidence that the father's continued involvement with his infant bodes well for the future of the marriage and for the infant's intellectual and emotional development" (p. 4). These remarks are based on what is generally accepted by family scholars, that is, that marital effectiveness and parent-child interactions are interrelated (Shapiro and Gottman, 2005). High quality marital relationships are significantly associated with sensitive, responsive, and effective parenting (Krishnakumar and Buehler, 2000). In contrast, poor quality marital relationships can cause an escalating cycle of negativity between the parents and consequently, negatively affect the parents' and the infant's bond (Halford and Petch, 2010).

Shapiro and Gottman's (2005) pregnancy and parenting preparation program is a two-day workshop for couples who are in the transition to parenthood stage; it is designed to make this transition positive and more functional. The workshop (the Bringing Baby Home workshop) consists of lectures, role-play simulations, videotape presentations, and various communication exercises. The general aim of this workshop is to enhance the participants' marital relationship and maintain an adequate level of friendship and a shared-meaning system as new parents. More specifically, the workshop was designed to accomplish several objectives:

- Prepare couples to better adjust to stresses and difficulties associated with the transition to parenthood
- Strengthen and facilitate both parents' involvement with the newborn babies and expanding family needs
- Provide basic information regarding the psychological developments of a newborn baby, offer couples some basic tips and suggestions as to how to raise their baby

Shapiro and Gottman (2005) examined the effectiveness of their Bringing Baby Home workshop with a sample of expectant and new parents. In their concluding remarks, the authors indicated that the data collected proved the workshop to be effective in achieving its proposed objectives.

Chapter 13

INTIMATE RELATIONSHIPS: GROWTH AND DEVELOPMENT

I think...therefore, I'm single.
Lizz Winstead

Establishing and maintaining close, intimate relationships with a significant other has been recognized as a fundamental human motivation (Baumeister and Leary, 1995; McCarthy, Ginsberg, and Cintron, 2008). In that context, marriage is perceived as the most intimate adult bonding, serving as a primary source of affection, love, and support (Laurenceau, Feldman, Barrett, and Rovine, 2005; Strong, DeValut, and Cohen, 2011). Long-term, committed intimate relationships are essential to physical and emotional well-being. This health enhancing property of intimate relationships has been repeatedly documented (Cohen, Gottlieb, and Underwood, 2000; Lynch, 2000). Attesting to the health benefits of intimate relationships, Prager (1995) indicated that intimate relationships seem to buffer people from the pathogenic effects of stress. It was documented that people who are in intimate relationships suffer from fewer stress-related symptoms, experience faster recoveries from illness, and usually have a lower probability of relapse or reoccurrence of stress than those who do not have intimate relationships (see also Flora and Segrin, 2000). Intimacy, being a close relational phenomenon, is first and foremost a reciprocal interactive experience and as Kouneski and Olson (2004) put it, "either both partners are intimate or neither is" (p. 131).

Prager and Roberts (2004) conceptualized intimate relations by considering two fundamental, interrelated phenomena: intimate interactions and intimate relationships. The reason for this distinction is that partners in intimate relationships interact with each other in a variety of ways, some of which cannot be characterized as being intimate (e.g. partners, at times, argue, inform, consult, and even ignore), yet the partners may nevertheless have an intimate relationship. On the other hand, some intimate interactions may temporarily occur between people who are not in an intimate relationship (e.g. disclosing personal thoughts and other intimate information to a stranger). These are the reasons Prager (1995) concluded that intimate interactions and intimate relationships are best conceptualized as separate phenomena.

For an interaction to be intimate, it has to fulfill three fundamental conditions; it has to include self-disclosure, positive involvement between partners, and shared understanding.

These three conditions distinguished between a couple's intimate and non-intimate interactions. When these three necessary components exist between partners, it is likely that some degree of intimate interaction is present in the relationship (see also Slatcher, 2010a, b) *Self-disclosure* has long been identified as a basic feature of intimate interaction (Prager and Roberts, 2004). A deep feeling of intimate closeness and connectedness can hardly be developed, let alone maintained, without partners revealing to each other their personal emotions and thoughts (see a more detailed discussion of the concept of self-disclosure and its relation to intimate relationship, later in this chapter).

POSITIVE INVOLVEMENT

The second fundamental condition for an interaction to be considered intimate is that the interacting partners need to be positively involved with each other (Frager and Roberts, 2004). Involvement refers to the partner's attentional focus on the developing interaction, rather than providing only a divided or intermittent attentional focus as non-intimate partners may offer (Prager and Roberts, 2004). Positive regard in an intimate interaction is a central behavioral component of the positive involvement element of intimate interaction. Also, intimate relating, as we would intuitively know, precludes attacking, defensive distancing, or alienating behavior (Prager and Roberts, 2004,). Positive involvement in intimate interaction can be related through verbal and nonverbal communication. Nonverbal positive involvement can be achieved through decreasing physical distance between partners, increasing eye contact, touching and hugging, facial expressions that display closeness, and other physical gestures.

SHARED UNDERSTANDING

The third condition for an interaction to be identified as intimate depends on the couple's shared understanding of each other's self (Prager and Roberts, 2004). Partners in intimate interaction know or understand some aspects of their partner's inner experience, which may include private thoughts, feelings, habits, or even sexual fantasies and preferences (Prager and Roberts, 2004, p. 45). In other words, the two "selves" get to be closely familiar with each other. Gathering knowledge about one's partner can be achieved explicitly, through verbal communication, or implicitly, through other, nonverbal cues. For example, a partner may know the other's sexual preferences without necessarily talking about it.

To sum up, Prager and Roberts (2004) indicate that when self-disclosure, positive involvement, and shared understanding are part of the couple's behavioral repertoire, then the couple interact intimately to some degree. "The degree and quality of intimacy in any given interaction varies widely as a function of the depth of self-exposure, the intensity of positive involvement and the extent of the shared personal understanding" (p. 46).

SUPPORT IN INTIMATE RELATIONSHIPS

An extensive literary study on social support demonstrates why people seek contact and closeness with others when they are in distress (Reis et al., 2010). Columbia University social psychologist Stanley Schachter (1959) found that people in stressful circumstances tend to affiliate with others in order to achieve the following: (1) to escape a feeling of distress, which they may achieve through talking to others; (2) to gain greater cognitive clarity by talking to others ; (3) to direct anxiety reduction, which may be achieved through people's emotional support; (4) to partake in self evaluation, which is achieved through comparison with others with regards to one's anxiety level and allows for self-assurance and comfort; and (5) to talk to others about non-stressful subjects, which results in indirect anxiety reduction (in Reis et al., 2010).

More recent studies that examined social support show that people in distress seek proximity to others in order to get support for various reasons such as relieving distressing thoughts and feelings, eliciting resources to better cope with the distress, and in order to gain comfort and reassurance (Reis et al., 2010). These findings have all been for seeking support under negative affect but what about seeking closeness to others in order to share positive thoughts and feelings? Rime (2007) showed that people are just as likely to recount and share positive emotions and events with others, and that plays an important role in close, intimate relationships (Argyle and Henderson, 1984).

Sharing positive emotions and events serves different objectives than sharing negativity. Whereas the latter is motivated by the need to reduce anxiety or alleviate stressful events, the former involves "savouring, embellishing, retaining, and further benefiting from the event" (Reis et al., 2010, p. 31). In other words, sharing positive experiences, especially with an intimate listener, maximizes the significance of the event to one's self and provides additional, expanded, and enhanced pleasure, a motive that Langston (1994) termed, "capitalization" (Reis et al., 2010, p. 311). Gable et al. (2004) examined the intrapersonal and interpersonal benefits of sharing positive experiences. The authors found that a relationship's well-being was higher among subjects that perceived their partners' response to their capitalization attempts to be more actively enthusiastic. Langston (1994) found three functions that are related to capitalization attempts that were made when sharing positive experiences with one's partner: (1) sharing positive experiences makes them more memorable to the speaker, (2) letting others know about the positive events builds social resources and support, and (3) sharing maximizes the events, thus expanding personal resources of strength and enhancements. The self-worth of the one who shares positive experiences is especially enhanced when he receives a positive response, e.g. validation or approval (Gable and Reis, 2006). Apparently, people prefer to socially affiliate with those that approve of their world view and emotional experiences.

Sharing positive emotions and events with a relational partner is likely to initiate an interaction sequence in which further positive effects are experienced and shared by partners (Reis and Gable, 2003; Rime, 2007). Sharing positive experiences in intimate relationship enhances the speaker's self only if the listener is aware of the importance of the sharing to the speaker and is willing to listen attentively in a supportive manner (Reis et al., 2010). This sharing interaction also provides an opportunity for both partners to show each other awareness, recognition, and a willingness to support (Reis, 2007). According to Aron and

Aron (1997), committed, intimate partners "may even bask in reflected glory by including the other's good news in the self, one sign of cognitive and behavioural interdependence in close relationships" (Reis et al., 2010, p. 313).

When partners in romantic relationships perceive each other as caring and supportive of positive emotions and experiences related to them, it is likely that their relationship is high on measures of commitment, intimacy, and satisfaction (Gable et al., 2004). Furthermore, it is highly likely for people in intimate relationships to be willing to confide in their partner when they expect a supportive, accepting response (Reis and Patrick, 1996). An enthusiastic response to a partner's sharing of positive experiences fosters trust and strengthens the perception that the relationship is valued and respected by the listening partner (Reis et al., 2010).

Reis et al. (2010) conducted four experiments and a diary study in order to examine the underlying mechanisms of capitalization. In the diary study, participants were asked to provide a description of the "best thing that happened to you today" and the kind of response they received from their listeners. Based on their results, Reis et al. (2010) concluded that "when capitalization process goes right, it allows relationship partners not only to savour their own good fortune but to share in that of the partner" (p. 327). If sharing a good experience does not evoke a rewarding and enhancing response from the listening partner, however, it may result in changing the positive feeling to a negative one. The authors believe that sharing of positive feelings and experiences and receiving enthusiastic responses from the listening partner promotes the further development of relational intimacy.

Pinel, Long, Landan, and Psyszcynski (2006) introduced the concept of "I-sharing" as an important phenomenon to relational connectedness and intimacy. I-sharing is a subjective belief, understanding, or feeling that one's partner has had a similar subjective experience at a given moment. Since there is no way to directly experience the world exactly as another person, I-sharing refers to the subjective sense that another person has experienced a given stimulus or situation similarly. In other words, anytime one person senses, or perceives that he has an identical experience (feeling, thought) with another person, it constitutes an I-sharing instance, regardless of whether or not the experiences are actually identical. The conclusion is that when one I-shares an experience with another person, one contributes significantly to a strong feeling of connection, liking, and intimacy. In this sense, I-sharing is so powerful that it might even cause those who repeatedly experience it to consider themselves "soul mates" (Pinel et al., 2006). In conclusion, I-sharing has an important impact on the promotion of enhanced closeness and intimacy between partners.

SELF-DISCLOSURE

Feelings of relational closeness and intimacy are developed and enhanced through intimate interactive transactions (Laurenceau et al., 2005). Reis and Shaver (1988) developed the interpersonal process model of intimacy to explain and describe the relational interactions that contribute to closeness and intimacy. According to this model, the dyadic intimacy process consists of two interplaying components: self-disclosure and partner responsiveness. Self-disclosure is related to a person's sense of openness in disclosing (sharing) to her partner personal feelings and thoughts and personally vulnerable aspects of herself, thus encouraging emotional involvement between the partners. Responding by being sensitive and supporting the partner's revealing disclosure is the second component of the dyadic intimacy process (see also Miller and Berg, 1984).

Intimacy, as a developing, dynamic process, is initiated when one partner (the speaker) reveals personal feelings or thoughts to the other (the listener) who in return responds in a validating, accepting, and benevolent manner. Such a response shows caring and support to for speaker. For this interaction to be experienced as intimate, it is important that the revealing partner subjectively perceives the response as actively demonstrating validation and acceptance (Laurenceau et al., 2010). A benevolent response to one's partner's disclosure of personal information communicates to the speaker that she is valued and cared for by the listener. This intimate interaction reinforces and encourages further, deeper, more personal disclosures from the speaker. Greater intimacy is achieved when the listener, aside from her positive responsiveness, also reveals to the speaker her personal feelings and thoughts. Thus, added interaction contributes to the speaker's perception of a meaningful, more expanded responsiveness. It is clear that the process of intimacy development is a dynamic, fluid, and ongoing one where both partners play interrelated, exchangeable roles (Laurenceau et al., 2010). Due to the transactional nature of the process of intimacy development, the experience of relational intimacy is enhanced as partners' selves become revealed and validated interchangeably. In contrast, marital disillusionment reflects a diminished perception of one's partner as positively responsive and affectionate (Huston et al., 2001). Additionally, in distressed, dissatisfied marital relationships, it is very probable that one will find invalidated disclosures of feelings made in the course of marital interactions (Laurenceau et al., 2005). When feelings and thoughts regarding marital problems are revealed but receive invalidating responses, they erode the impact of the positive interactions and eventually create a negative atmosphere and marital dissatisfaction (Clements et al., 1997).

POSITIVE EMOTIONS IN INTIMATE RELATIONSHIPS

Positive emotions bring partners in romantic relationships closer. The interpersonal benefits of positive emotions, like joy, love, happiness, and commitment, are well known and documented (Waugh and Fredrickson, 2006). Diary studies with partners in close relationships showed that positive emotionality motivates greater and more involved prosocial activities (Burger and Caldwell, 2000). Also, positive emotions promote friendship and enjoyable interpersonal interactions that bring people closer to each other (Waugh and Fredrickson, 2006). Thus, positive emotions cause people to be more sociable and their interactions to be open and beneficial. The existence and expression of positive emotions facilitates revealing self-disclosures of personal and emotional information even to a stranger, let alone to an intimate partner (Cunningham, 1988; Waugh and Fredrickson, 2006).

There are various theoretical accounts to explain the effect of positive emotions on interpersonal interactions. Isen (2002) presents a neuropsychological theory suggesting that "feeling positive affect activates the dopaminergic system in brain areas responsible for executive control and flexible thinking" (Waugh and Fredrickson, 2006, p. 94).

Accordingly, positive emotions expressed in close relationships soften cognitive processes, making thinking more flexible, which leads interactive partners to take broader and more flexible perspectives. This emotional-cognitive-behavioral dynamic results in increased and expanded intimacy (Isen, 2002). A different theoretical direction has been taken by Forgas (1995, 2002). The author makes use of the Affect Infusion Model to theorize that in social, interpersonal interactions, positive emotions promote the priming of positive memories and past rewarding experiences, which in turn produce communal, prosocial behaviors. This process brings interactive partners to feel intimately closer.

Waugh and Fredrickson (2006) contributed a unique perspective regarding the role that positive emotions play in forming and conducting interpersonal, close relationships. The authors suggest that when people feel positive emotions, eventually those positive emotions become associated with greater feelings of "oneness" with others, and this broadened sense of self may enhance a more complex understanding of others. Waugh and Fredrickson (2006) based their perspective on Fredrickson's Broaden-and-Build model of positive emotions (Fredrickson, 1998, 2001, 2003). The Broaden-and-Build model theorizes that positive emotions (e.g. joy, happiness, interest, love, contentment, etc.) broaden one's repertoire of cognitive processes, feelings, and behaviors. This expansion goes beyond typical patterns of thinking to achieve greater, deeper awareness, which in return sparks and encourages novel, creative, and more open and flexible exploration of cognitive-behavioral repertoires. In contrast, negative emotions (e.g. sadness, anger, frustration, anxiety, etc.) narrow a person's thought-action possibilities, emphasizing specific responses for immediate adaptive thoughts and behaviors (fear and anxiety lead to narrow, fight-or-flight possible actions).

Fredrickson (1998) argued that positive emotions not only affect the momentary thought-action repertoire, but in the long run, they also build stronger personal resources. In other words, positive emotions broaden and build durable physical, cognitive, and social resources of a thought-action nature. In time, enduring, more stable psychological resources and cognitive-behavioral capacities are developed, broadened, and built. This cumulative impact of positive emotions on cognitive, intellectual, and action properties and capacities may explain why the propensity to experience positive emotions has become such a ubiquitous feature of human nature. Positive emotions are said to promote individual and collective well-being and health (Fredrickson, 1998).

The Broaden-and-Build model of positive emotions (Fredrickson, 2004) has clear implications for helping partners in romantic relationships to regulate experiences of the negative emotions that are inevitable. In this way, positive emotions possess the potential to significantly decrease, and even undo, the impact of negative emotions from a partner's interactive behavior—what Fredrickson (2004) called the "undo hypothesis." By broadening a person's thought-action repertoire, even if "only" momentarily, positive emotions undo or preempt and free the mind from negative emotions, which paves the way to more positive perspectives and actions. Fredrickson's (2004) "undo hypothesis" predicts that partners experiencing positive emotions will show a reduction and even a recovery from the impact of previously experienced negative feelings, thus broadening their thought-action repertoire. In Fredrickson's (2004) words, "By broadening a person's momentary thought action repertoire, a positive emotion may loosen the hold that a negative emotion has gained on that person's mind and body by specific action" (p. 1371). Expressing positive emotions in close relationships reduces the resonance left by previous destructive interactions. Cultivating ongoing experiences of positive emotions enhances intimate partners' psychological well-being and strengthens their abilities to better cope with inevitable stressful events in their life (Fredrickson, 2004).

It has been documented that by concentrating on positivity, by finding positive meanings in day-to-day events and experiences, people can be aided in coping with adversity (Moskowitz, 2003). There is a reciprocal nature embedded in the Broaden-and-Build conception, which suggests a complementary upward spiral movement evoked by positive emotions. This is contrary to the downward spiral movement that characterizes negative, depressive emotions. Positive emotions create this upward spiral movement by fostering and enhancing personal resilience and by strengthening coping, action oriented strategies to overcome stressogenic events (Aspinwall, 1998).

To conclude, Fredrickson's Broaden-and-Build model emphasizes the importance of positive emotions in general, and in romantic relationships in particular. Positive emotions broaden people's attention, awareness, thinking processes, and sensitivity, building stronger cognitive-behavioral capacities to better cope with stressful events, undo lingering negative emotional arousal, strengthen psychological well-being and resilience, build consequential personal resources, trigger upward spiral movements toward greater personal capacities, and fuel optimal functioning, growth, and robustness. Cultivating positive emotions in romantic relationships has a flourishing impact on closeness and intimacy, allowing couples to become more benevolent, generative, enthusiastic, and communal with each other. Moreover, positive emotions prime access to positive information and joyous experiences stored in one's memory (Forgas, 2011). Thus when partners in close relationships express positive emotions or engage in joyous, playful activities, it causes selective access to positive memories of past happy events, which in turn increases the likelihood of more prosocial and supportive interactions. Positive emotions also create greater emotional involvement between couples in intimate relationships (Sanderson and Evans, 2001).

Intimacy Goals

There is research evidence to suggest that partners with intimacy goals are likely to experience enhanced relational quality and satisfaction. Partners who are emotionally engaged in their relationship and who are particularly focused on developing and enhancing relational intimacy are likely to experience greater satisfaction than those who do not show such a focus (Sanderson and Evans, 2001). Consequently, partners who develop intimacy goals structure their thoughts and activities in such a manner so that they engage intensively in actions and behaviors that fulfill their intimacy goals; therefore, they will behave benevolently toward their partners, create more opportunities to spend quality time, and engage in intimate interactions and shared activities (Reissman, Aron, and Bergan, 1993). They may engage in intimacy-enhancing thoughts, focusing on positive experiences they enjoy through their relationship (Cate et al., 1995). In addition, intimacy goal-oriented partners may be more dependent on their partners for affection and support, expecting their partners to be equally dependent on their resources (Fincham and Bradbury, 1990). This interdependence fosters intimacy by enhancing their reliance on the relationship (Sanderson and Evans, 2011).

Sanderson and Evans (2001) demonstrated that partners with a strong intimacy goal orientation enjoy greater relational satisfaction. Intimacy goals encourage people to engage in intimacy-enhancing interactions with their partners (e.g. provide support, act benevolently).

Additionally, individuals with strong intimacy goals tend to perceive their partners as also having intimacy goals. They "see their partners through intimacy-colored glasses" (Sanderson and Evans, 2001, p. 471), thus projecting their own intimacy goal orientation onto their partners. This perception of intimacy leads partners to perceive and interpret their partner's behavior through a positive lens, which leads to an enhancement of the relationship quality and satisfaction. Finally, there exists a reciprocal dynamic between intimacy goals and relational satisfaction. When one experiences high relational satisfaction, one expands one's intimacy goals, which in turn increases relational satisfaction (Sanderson and Evans, 2001).

ASSESSING INTIMACY

Laurenceau, Barrett, and, Rovine (2005) used Reis and Shaver's (1988) Interpersonal Process Model as a framework for conceptualizing and assessing intimacy in the ongoing, daily interaction of marital couples. The authors used a daily diary methodology whereby spouses independently completed a structured diary on a daily basis over a period of 42 days.

This method allows participants to accurately report detailed, focused accounts of daily, actual, real-life interactions, capturing the dynamic nature of intimacy processes. In addition, the participants completed questionnaires measuring their overall relationship intimacy and satisfaction. The results of this study clearly confirmed that self-disclosure and the partner's disclosure predicted ratings of intimacy in marital daily interactions. The importance of the partner's positive responsiveness to the other's self-disclosure was also indicated. It was shown that a perceived sense of positive responsiveness (validation, caring, supporting) is clearly linked to a couple's intimacy. The finding reported by Laurenceau et al. (2005) is consistent with clinical intervention research that showed that various couple's counseling and therapy approaches emphasize the mutual exchange of self-disclosure and supporting responsiveness. These two interactive components (self-disclosure and the partner's supporting responsivity) are used in couple's therapy for the purpose of developing and enhancing relational intimacy (Laurenceau, Feldman, and Rovine, 2005). Similar findings were reported by Johnson and Greenberg (1995) who stress that mutual disclosure of hidden, unexpressed feelings, needs, and wishes in the presence of non-judgmental and validating partner's responsivity leads to an enhanced experience of closeness and intimacy. Couples counselors and therapists encourage and facilitate engagement in self-disclosure and partners' positive responsivity through the development of expressive communication and supportive listening skills.

As indicated earlier, Prager and Roberts (2004) conceptualized intimacy in their model by considering two basic, interplaying components: intimate interactions and intimate relationships. As these authors showed, intimate interactions provide the infrastructure upon which intimate relationships are developed and enhanced. As noted, the essential blocks of intimate interactions are self-revealing (self-disclosing) communication, partners experiencing positive involvement with one another, and achieving shared understanding. Thus, an intimate relationship is necessarily a result of the partners experiencing multiple interactions characterized by these three elements. The degree of intimate relationship achieved through the operating impact of intimate interactions is determined by the extensiveness of the couple's intimate relating, which stems from the frequency, degree, and quality of interactional intimacy (Prager and Roberts, 2004). In other words, a higher level of relational intimacy is achieved through frequent intimate interactions.

INTIMATE RELATIONSHIPS: MAINTENANCE AND ENHANCEMENT

Harvey and Wenzel (2001) indicated that one of the most daunting issues confronting researchers and practitioners in the area of close relationships concerns the dynamics of how people maintain and enhance their intimate relationships. The intensive interest in studying the necessary ingredients for the maintenance and enhancement of intimate relationships was a response to societal concern regarding the staggering increase in divorce rate in the United States over the last three or more decades (Harvey and Wenzel, 2001). Consequently, we have witnessed an intensive development of theoretical models and empirical research devoted to the investigation of the dynamics that take place in the process of maintaining and enhancing intimate relationships. There are several theories and conceptual models that were developed to describe the characteristics of relational maintenance and enhancement, some of which are described in this section.

The Communal Relationship Model

Mills and Clark (2001) extended their theoretical conceptions on communal relationships to the understanding of relational maintenance and enhancement (Clark and Mills, 1993; Mills and Clark, 1986). The authors consider close, intimate relationships to possess a communal nature and characteristics because each partner is concerned with the welfare of the other. The main component of an intimate relationship that follows communal interaction is that the partners provide benefits to each other without expecting a reward in return. In other words, the key to a communal-based, intimate relationship is that both partners are committed to be truly concerned for each other's welfare and both are highly motivated to the fulfill needs and expectations of the other without keeping score. Maintaining and enhancing intimate relationship depends on the extent to which partners meet the needs of each other without expecting any benefits in return. Following these communal behavioral strategy results, according to Mills and Clark (2001), both intimate partners feel cared for, supported, and satisfied. Following the communal interactive strategy increases relational quality and satisfaction resulting in a situation where each member of the couple feels secure in the relationship.

The mutual attraction that commonly exists between partners in intimate relationships serves as a strong motivation to adhere to the communal rule (caring for the other's needs without expecting benefits in return). Attraction leads partners to turn toward each other by showing care and support and by being deeply concerned about the other's well-being (Mills and Clark, 2001). Mutual attraction, however, cannot remain the sole motivation for a couple's adherence to communal interactive behavior. In time, the intimate relationship "may change from one in which the communal rule is followed as a result of the initial mutual attraction to one in which there is a feeling of obligation to be good communal partners and place importance on meeting the needs of the other" (Mills and Clark, 2001, p. 16).

Therefore, maintaining and enhancing intimate relationships depends on the persistence and continuity of the partners' motivation to behave with each other communally in their day-to-day interactions. Mills and Clark (1986) identified various attitudes and behaviors that are contrary to communal relationships demeanor that result in the partners feeling exploited and dissatisfied. These include any behavior that minimizes the other's needs and expectations or ignoring the other's needs all together. This is similar to Gottman's (1999a) conception of partners turning towards each other as opposed to turning away. The turning toward attitude is one in which partners pay attention to each other's needs, behaving in a friendly and benevolent manner, being supportive and helpful to each other, and so forth. In contrast, partners' turning away interactions are those that show lack of true interest in each other's welfare and ignoring each other's needs and expectations; these behaviors that do not follow one another's bids for closeness and attention or they may reflect emotional distance and lack of intimacy.

In order for partners in intimate relationships to behave communally, both need to be familiar with and show understanding of each other's needs and expectations. Thus, disclosing needs, desires, and expectations clearly and assertively is essential to the maintenance and enhancement of intimate relationships (Clark, Mills, and Corcoran, 1989). Revealing personal information regarding one's needs and desires is a strong characterizing feature of a mutually satisfying communal relationship. It is only when partners in romantic relationships clearly understand each other's needs that they can effectively and accurately respond to them.

Preemptive Relationship Maintenance and Enhancement

The idea of preemptive relational maintenance and enhancement (Simpson, Ickes, and Orina, 2001) is based on several modalities. First, it is based on the notion that relational maintenance and enhancement can be done preemptively, as a preventive measure, and not when relationship discord has already occurred. For example, relationship maintenance is done preemptively when intimate partners attempt to avert a potential problem in their relationship. Harvey and Omarzu's (1997) observation that intimate partners who are continuously "minding" each other and the relationship are able to maintain and enhance a satisfying relationship. "Minding" includes a range of cognitive, and interactive behaviors such as communicating empathy, acceptance, appreciation, and respect; engaging in revealing personal thoughts and feelings; making significant investments to the relationship and to each other; making relationship-enhancing attributions; developing an optimistic view of the relationship's future; and so forth (Harvey and Omarzu, 1997).

According to Simpson et al. (2001) preemptive relational enhancement and maintenance occurs when intimate partners utilize behavioral or cognitive tactics that help them avoid or minimize potential threats or problems that, if left unaltered, could destabilize or even destroy their relationship. The authors differentiated between preemptive interactive behaviors that are aimed at preventing the emergence of relational difficulties and problems and those aimed at restabilizing a relationship after problems have set in. Whereas the former are deliberate and premeditated actions, the latter are reactive, post emptive behaviors. Accordingly, most preemptive interactive behaviors are premeditated and they are manifested in various forms, such as:

1. When partners in intimate relationships know and understand each other well enough so that they can anticipate each other's needs, desires, and moods before the eruption of relational problems and misunderstandings.

2. When partners engage in clam and open discussions to prepare the other for any disturbing information or event, so as to avoid or avert anger, frustration, or disappointment.

3. When partners make a thoughtful attempt to solve relational problems or conflicts that may have a troubling impact on the other or that the other may find difficult to deal with effectively.

4. Preparing suitable, acceptable explanation to present to one's partner in order to avoid or minimize the threatening consequences of a troubling act or event.

5. Partners routinely take the time to discuss and deal with day-to-day occurrences and minor potential problems, not letting problems accumulate and escalate into major discord.

Another preemptive tactic that contributes to relationship enhancement and maintenance is found in the Empathic Accuracy Model developed by Simpson et al. (1995, 2001). Empathic accuracy is "the extent to which partners in a relationship can accurately infer each other's thoughts and feelings during an interaction episode" (Simpson, Ickes, and Blackstone, 1995, p. 629). There are some factors that were identified as contributing to empathic accuracy between partners in close relationships. For example, couples who aim to directly and openly resolve conflicts and disagreements are more likely to develop emphatic accuracy than couples who avoid conflicts (Simpson et al., 1995). It is possible that open, direct engagement in ongoing discussions promotes the partners' knowledge of each other's thoughts and feelings through information that becomes available during these discussions. There is evidence to suggest that empathic accuracy contributes to relationship maintenance and enhancement (Simpson et al., 2001). There are findings to show that satisfied marital couples tend to be more empathically accurate (able to correctly identify one partner's sensitivities and feelings) than couples in unhappy marriages (Noller and Ruzzene, 1991).

Through accurate empathy, partners can recognize and perhaps even anticipate potential threats to their relationship. By so doing, they can protect their intimate relationship by either avoiding danger zones in their interaction (not raising sensitive issues) or by preparing adequately to deal with sensitive topics so that they avoid or minimize threats to the relationship (Simpson et al., 2001). These qualities make accurate empathy a preemptive relationship maintenance mechanism.

THE MINDING THEORY OF INTIMATE RELATIONSHIPS

Another model of relational maintenance and enhancement relevant to the promotion of intimacy is the Minding Theory of intimate relationships (Harvey and Omarzu, 1997; Omarzu, Whalen, and Harvey, 2001). According to Harvey and Omarzu (1997), the use of the word "minding" in this model emphasizes the central role of cognitive elements (the mind) in forming, developing, and maintaining intimate connectedness. The theory suggests that various expectations, interactive behaviors, and cognitive processes are centrally necessary to the development, maintenance, and enhancement of well-functioning and satisfying intimate relationships.

There are five major components in the minding model:

1. An effective degree of minding in intimate relationship requires that partners enact interactive behaviors that facilitate knowledge of each other. This includes devoting quality time for one's partner, revealing personal feelings and thoughts, and listening attentively and supportively to such disclosures. Minding involves sharing experiences and past personal narratives. In this regard, Harvey and Omarzu cite Aron and Aron (1996), who describe their concept of relational intimacy as a process of self-expansion. This process is described as "when people first fall in love there is often a rapid, exhilarating expansion of self. People (partners in intimate relationship) stay up all night talking, sharing, and just doing everything they can to merge selves" (Aron and Aron, 1996, p. 340). This sharing of feelings, thoughts, and experiences and consequently, the expansion and merging of the partners' selves, contributes to a sense of relational meaning, thus promoting and strengthening connectedness and intimacy. Partners in an intimate relationship ought to go beyond acquiring bilateral knowledge of each other. In a minding-based intimate relationship, partners also show empathic understanding and non-judgmental acceptance of what they find out about each other's feelings, thoughts, and past experiences. Omarzu and Harvey (2001) underlined the importance of acceptance and respect for individual differences by saying that "accepting and respecting the inevitable differences in opinions, values, and habits prevent partners from falling into the trap of criticism which can handicap intimate relationships" (p. 346).

2. The second component of relational minding behavior relates to the intimate partners' attributions regarding their interactive behavior with each other. In well-minded intimate dyads, the partners use relationship-enhancing attributes (e.g. attributing a partner's negative behavior to external, situational causes).

3. Reciprocity is another major component of relationship minding. Minding cannot be one-sided, involving one partner only. In order for the behavioral and cognitive aspects of minding to promote and enhance intimacy, they are to be reciprocal. That is, self-disclosure, and sensitive and supporting listening should be reciprocal, involving both partners. The same goes for positive, relationship-enhancing attributions and all other elements of minding.

4. For minding behavioral patterns to be intimacy enhancing, they must be continuously operative in an ongoing relationship. This component means that "partners must continue to find out about each other, respect individuality, and make attributions that encourage positive feelings within the relationship. It is this continuity of minding that ensures continuity of relationship satisfaction. This is the key component that promotes long-lasting close relationships" (Omarzu et al., 2001, p. 346).

SELF-EXPANSION THEORY

The self-expansion theory developed and empirically examined by Aron and Aron (1996, 1997) provides "an overreaching conceptual framework for understanding cognition and motivation in close relationships" (Aron, Norman, and Lewandowsk, 2002, p. 178). The theory originated from the conceptualization of self and consciousness in ancient Eastern psychology (Vedic psychology, in particular) and views the purpose of human life as a continuing drive for knowledge and the expansion of awareness beyond its boundaries for higher self-growth and development. The theory also has roots in various modern fields of self-psychology, love, intimacy and attraction, human motivation, and social cognition (Aron and Aron, 1986, 1996).

The theoretical construct of self-expansion consists of two basic propositions; first, the desire for self-expansion is a fundamental human motive. The need to achieve and the yearning to expand one's boundaries of knowledge, awareness, spirituality, intellect, and other psychological resources are essential human motivations. Consequently, in order to achieve self-expansion, people inherently look for and explore new intellectually challenging activities and experiences (Aron and Aron, 1986). The second proposition of the construct of self-expansion is that one common way to achieve expansion of the self is by forming close relationships, in which the other is "included in the self" in the sense that one's partner's resources, perspectives, and identities are to some extent treated as one's own (Aron, Norman, Aron, and Lewandowski, 2002). In other words, one of the most important sources of self-expansion and growth derives from and is incorporated through close, intimate relationships (Aron and Aron, 1996; Aron and Fraley, 1999). Through intimate connectedness and ongoing interactions, one's own sense of self assimilates some of the intellectual and psychological resources, qualities, and uniqueness of the partner. In intimate relationships, this assimilation and incorporation process is dynamically reciprocal. An integration of these key propositions of self-expansion theory strongly suggest that when intimate partners engage in joyful, exciting, new, and challenging joint activities, they are likely to mutually expand their sense of self, increase intimacy and connectedness, and improve both their personal self and the combined dyadic-self (Aron, Norman, and Aron, 2001).

Aron and Aron (1997) used a metaphor to capture the inner experience of intimate relationship vis-a-vis the phenomenon of self-expansion:

> A sense of expansion in the heart or the chest is a common bodily experience associated with deeply felt positive experiences, such as when people fall in love, or [are] looking at their sleeping child. A bodily experience of having the other included in the self can occur when one's own muscles move while watching a beloved partner perform, or when one receives news that would please or upset the other were she or he be there, and one feels the physical signs of joy or grief that the other would feel. Most striking, perhaps, are descriptions of losing a partner being like having a part of one's body ripped out or die.
>
> (Aron and Aron, 1997, p. 254)

As noted, ongoing intimate relationship transactions facilitate the expansion of one's self through the partner's knowledge, expertise, life perspectives, and other human resources that become a conjoined entity. This joint self-expansion process creates relational positive affect and the shared activities and experiences that are associated with self-expansion become appreciated and desirable in their own right (Aron, Mashek, and Aron, 2004).

Aron, Norman, and Aron (2002) argue that during the initial stage of relationship formation, a period associated with infatuation, arousal, and excitement, there is commonly an initial exhilaration as the couple engages in heart-to-heart conversations with considerable risk-taking and self-disclosure. This period is one in which the partners are gaining knowledge, feeling an increased self-efficacy, and many times, feeling that they are including the other in the self. Since this exhilarating, infatuation stage is time-limited, however, most couples experience an inevitable decline in what earlier was experienced as a rapid self-expansion. According to Aron et al. (2002), this may explain the possible decrease in relationship satisfaction being attributed to boredom, apathy, and habituation, and explain the decrease in time spent together (Reissman, Aron, and Bergen, 1993). Accordingly, Aron and Aron (1997) strongly suggest that couples in intimate relationships who have passed through the early stage of rapid self-expansion keep a relatively high level of relationship satisfaction by spending time together in self-expanding activities (novel, exciting, and arousing activities). The desired experience of self-expansion acts as a positive reinforcing agent for both the relationship and the activities (Aron, Norman, and Aron 2001; Reissman, Aron, and Bergin, 1993).

The research consistently supports the self-expansion model led Aron, Norman, and Aron (2001) to its present, practical implications. An important clinical implication aimed at couples and marriage therapists is to encourage couples to engage in self-expanding activities to improve relationship intimacy. Shared participation in self-expanding activities prescribed in a therapeutic process is an easily managed intervention that has the potential to improve a couple's relationship quality. My (A.S.) clinical experience with distressed couples has shown that it is usually counterproductive to have couples engage in self-expanding activities during the initial phase of therapy, when the partners are still flooded with negative emotions. Clinical use of self-expansion intervention is usually productive in producing relationship outcomes only when couples are somewhat calm and the tension between them has been de-escalated.

SELF-EXPANSION MEASUREMENT

To concretize the seemingly abstract nature of the concept of self-expansion, Lewandowski and Aron (2002) constructed and tested the Self-Expansion Questionnaire (SEQ). This measurement consists of 14 items assessing the extent to which a person experiences a relationship partner as facilitating increased knowledge, skills, abilities, mate value, positive life changes, and novel experiences.

The following are sample items from the SEQ:

- "How much does being with your partner result in your having new experiences?"
- "How much does your partner increase your ability to accomplish new things?"
- "How much does your partner help to expand your sense of the kind of person you are?"

Studies conducted to examine the validity and reliability of the SEQ showed that the SEQ is internally consistent and unifactorial and thus represents a coherent construct (Aron and Aron, 2006).

INCLUSION OF THE OTHER IN THE SELF MEASUREMENT

As indicated previously, inclusion of a partner's self is a central component of the self-expansion theory, regarded as the essence of intimate relationships (Aron and Aron, 2006). Aron and colleagues developed and tested the Inclusion of Other in the Self Scale (IOS Scale) (Aron, Aron, and Smollan, 1992). This measurement assesses the degree of closeness perceived by partners in close relationships. The IOS Scale consists of seven diagrams of pairs of circles overlapping to various degrees. The participant is instructed to select the pair of circles that best describes the closeness that exists between him and his partner. The participant's choice of a pair of circles is taken as a measure of the degree of closeness he perceives in his intimate relationship (Agnew et al., 2004). Greater overlap of the circles is thought to indicate a greater perceived closeness in the relationship. The IOS Scale has been used in numerous studies that showed the scale's high level of reliability convergent (high correlation with other relevant measurements) and predictive validity (Aron and Aron, 2006).

The Michelangelo Phenomenon

Drigotas, Rusbult, Wiselquist, and Whitton (1999) described an interactional process commonly found in intimate relationship that they termed the Michelangelo Phenomenon (MP). The MP "describes a congenial pattern of interdependence in which close partners sculpt one another in such a manner as to bring each person closer to his or her ideal self" (p. 321). Due to the interdependent nature of intimate relationships, partners, through interactions and mutual experience, actually "sculpt" each other's self, affecting and modifying personal dispositions, attitudes, beliefs, values, and behavioral tendencies (Rusbult, Kamashiro, et al., 2005). This process is very much like real sculpting; as viewed by one of the greatest artists of all times, Michelangelo "described sculpting as a process, whereby the artist released a hidden figure (the "ideal form") from the block of stone in which it slumbered" (Drigotas et al., 1999, p. 294). The sculptor's task is to extract the "ideal form" from the stone. Drigotas et al. (1999) argue that the ideal self is the human representation of the "ideal form" in the sculpting metaphor. The "ideal self" is the self that one aspires to develop and maintain.

Due to the interdependent nature of intimate relationships, partners are in a position that offers vast opportunities to have an impact on each other's self. The mutual influence that partners have on each other's "self sculpting" materializes through behavioral adaptations in which the partners adjust to one another as a result of extended interaction; they develop some qualities and inhibit others (Kumashiro, Rusbult, et al., 2007). Over time, and through extended partners' transactions, such adaptations become a stable component of the self (Rusbult et al., 2005). In other words, partners in intimate relationships adapt to one another's self throughout the course of the interactive processes in which the partners respond to each other's needs and expectations. Partners' affirmation, another behavioral component of the

MP model, also plays a role in the partners' "sculpting" one another's self, i.e. helping each other move closer to gratifying their ideal selves (Kumashiro et al., 2007). Partner's affirmation is the degree to which one's perceptions and behaviors are congruent with his ideal self. These mutual movements that partners enact to feel closer to their ideal selves, characterize well-functioning, successful intimate relationship (Rusbult, Kumashiro, et al., 2009). In contrast, in distressed relationships, partners, instead of promoting one another's ideal self accomplishments, inhibit one another's movement toward ideal self goals and achievements through destructive, unrewarding interactions.

Accommodation in Intimate Relationships

Involvement in romantic and intimate relationship (including, but not only, through marriage) brings partners inevitably to encounter circumstances of disturbing, dissatisfying interactions during which one or both partners enact destructive behaviors, such as insulting, attacking, hurting, or yelling. Within such an atmosphere, partners are inclined to fight fire with fire (Finkel and Campbell, 2001), reciprocally attacking each other (Kilpatrick, Bissonnett, and Rusbult, 2002). This reciprocal interaction tends to escalate anger, tension, and conflict. Partners, especially in distressed and unhappy relationships, exchange insults, thoughtless remarks, nasty retorts, and so on. In order to de-escalate this increasingly heated exchange of negativity, however, partners are required to accommodate each other so as to reduce or even eliminate the destructive chain of interactions and soothe heated emotions (Kilpatrick, Bissonnett, and Rusbult, 2002).

Accommodation in intimate relationships is defined as "the willingness, when a partner has engaged in a potentially destructive behaviour, to (a) inhibit tendencies to react destructively, and, (b) instead, engage in constructive responses" (Finkel and Campbell, 2001, p. 264). Accommodative interaction comes to the rescue when a person in a romantic relationship is inclined to resolve conflict or a destructive behavior from one's partner by avoiding gut-reaction negative reciprocity and moving toward reconciliation and reduction of the escalating tension (Rusbult, Wieselquist, et al., 1999). The inclination to reciprocate negatively to a partner's destructive behavior is considered an immediately available defensive reaction to a personal attack (Kilpatrick et al., 2002). According to this view, responding constructively, in a communal manner, rather than reciprocating an attack, is not the natural human inclination; it requires a person to forgo a gut-level inclination.

According to the Interdependence Theory of close relationships (Kilpatrick et al., 2002; Finkel and Campbell, 2001) there is a distinction between two interactive behavioral preferences. *Given preference* refers to an immediate response derived from self-centered impulse, whereas an *effective preference* relates to directing behavior in a more suitable, effective, pro relational manner. The cognitive process that enables a person to accommodate, namely, to behave constructively to a partner's destructive behavior was termed *transformation of motivation* (Rusbult, Wieselquist, et al., 1999; Kilpatrick et al., 2002). In this context, Rusbult, Wieselquist, et al., (1999) suggested that moving away from a self-interested, given situation preference is the consequence of a process that leads individuals to relinquish immediate self-interest and act on the basis of broader considerations. In other words, transformation of motivation may yield effective preference for pro relational behavior (accommodative behavior) to replace the immediate preference, the gut-level, negative reciprocating response to a partner's destructive behavior (Yovetich and Rusbult, 1994).

Arriaga and Rusbult (1998) propose that the inclination to take one's partner's perspective during conflict enhances positive emotions and benign interpretations of the partner's potentially destructive act, thereby bringing about increased motivation to accommodate (Arriaga and Rusbult, 1998). In contrast, narrowing perspective to one's own self-centered point of view creates more defensive, stressful emotions, yielding the inclination to respond destructively rather than in an accommodative behavior. In such an event, the partner's interaction is likely to spiral into a repetitive chain of reciprocated negativity, creating an emotional disengagement and distance between the partners (Arriaga and Rusbult, 1998).

There is an association between partners' willingness to accommodate and the degree of relational commitment that exists between the partners (Rusbult, Wieselquist, et al., 1999). The greater the personal commitment between partners, the higher their willingness to accommodate when faced with a partner's destructive behavior. Unsurprisingly, a high degree of accommodative behavior has been found to characterize well-functioning, intimate marital relationships (Margolin and Wampold, 1981; Rusbult, Olsen, Darvis, and Hannon, 2001).

Partners' Willingness to Sacrifice

Another commitment and enhancement-derived motivation in marital interactions is a partner's willingness to sacrifice (Rusbult, Olsen, et al., 2001). Marital partners may inevitably experience circumstances in which one's preferences are incompatible with the partner's preferences, creating non corresponding situations (i.e. what is good for one is objectionable for the other). When partners' preferences do not correspond, one has to show the willingness to resolve the conflict between the self and the partner's interests by sacrificing for the benefit of the partner's and the relationship's well-being (Van Lang, Rusbult, et al., 1997).

Van Lang, Rusbult, et al. (1997) adopted the interdependence model to examine the impact of sacrifice on close relationships. The authors indicated that "situations of conflicting interests are potentially disruptive to the health and vitality of a relationship. To deal with such situations, requires some inclination towards a pro-relationship transformation of motivation, yielding increased willingness to sacrifice" (p. 1373). The model of interdependence analysis of the willingness to sacrifice in close relationships distinguishes between passive and active modes of sacrificial interactions (Van Lang, Rusbult, et al., 1997). Passive sacrifice entails refraining from behaving in a way that is beneficial and desired whereas active sacrifice is shown when one acts in a way that is initially undesirable (see also Finkel and Campbell, 2001).

A non-corresponding relational situation (conflict between one's self and one's relationship interests) presents a person with a dilemma: engaging in pro-relationship behavior is likely to yield better relational rewards than if one acts selfishly for immediate self-centered interests. The other side of a non-correspondent situation is that one's immediate self-centered interests are likely to be better achieved when one acts selfishly (Van Lang, Rusbult, et al., 1997). Non corresponding relational situations present an important challenge to a relationship's functioning and well-being, thus the willingness to sacrifice is important for the progression of the partners from *given preferences* (acts directed by immediate self-centered interests) to the more pro-relational, *effective preferences* (acts directed by relational considerations and interests). Partners in successful marriages understand and accept the willingness to forgo personal, immediate interests and desires for broader relationship well-being (Impett, Gable, and Peplau, 2005).

Some argue that sacrifice is not always a beneficial behavioral strategy; sometimes it can even be costly (Impett et al., 2005). This is because sacrifice depends on the inner motivation that drives the individual to forgo her immediate self interests so as to enhance the well-being of the other. In this context, the authors make a distinction between an "approach motivation" and "avoidance motivation" of sacrifice motivation. Accordingly, an individual may forgo personal interests and act sacrificially in order to obtain benevolent, rewarding outcomes (approach motivation), such as making one's partner happy, promoting relational intimacy, improving problem solving strategies, enhancing marital satisfaction, feeling good out of behaving benevolently, and so forth. In contrast, acts of sacrifice, such as denying one's own desires and needs so as to avoid negative relational consequences (avoidance motivation), may result in negative, undesirable personal outcomes.

Impett, Gable, and Peplau (2005) applied the approach avoidance model of motivation to the study of relationship sacrifice. They concluded that the inner perceived motivation behind the sacrificial acts determined the value attached to the outcomes that result from the sacrifice. An individual is likely to generate positive relational outcomes when he sacrifices for approach motives (to promote greater intimacy, make partner happy). In contrast, an individual may sacrifice for avoidance motives in an attempt to avoid tension or conflict or out of a fear of rejection. When partners sacrifice for approach motives, they are more likely to experience positive feelings and greater relationship satisfaction than if the sacrifice is motivated by avoidance motives.

In addition, the authors found that when recipient partners perceive that their partner's sacrifice is emerging out of approach motivation, they also experience significantly more positive feelings and enhanced relationship satisfaction. In contrast, when recipient partners felt that their partner's sacrifices were avoidance motivated (avoiding conflict, tension), they experienced more negative feelings and a decreased level of relationship satisfaction.

Whitton, Stanley, and Markman (2007) studied the downside, harmful impact of sacrifice in close relationships. Results from a cross sectional study of 145 couples showed that the perceived impact of sacrifice to self and relationship was associated with relationship indices such as commitment and a couple's functioning. Perceived negative outcomes of sacrifice were significantly more noticeable in couples with lower relationship commitment and function. Similarly, Stanley, Whitton, et al. (2006) predicted that partners in close relationships would have a greater willingness to sacrifice for the relational well-being if they saw a future for it (e.g. strong long-term commitment). In this sense, sacrificial behaviors are perceived as an investment in an important and desirable relationship. The results of the study showed that a high willingness to sacrifice discriminated between distressed, unsatisfied couples and those who were well-functioning and satisfied. Also, individuals with a greater willingness to sacrifice for their partners reported feeling more intimacy, more effective problem solving strategies, and more shared quality activities (Impett and Gordon, 2008).

Attribution in Marital Relationship

The role of cognition in general and causal attribution, in particular, on close relationships has been the focus of empirical research (Fincham and Bradbury, 1992; Sillars, Leonard, Roberts, and Dun, 2002). Robust empirical evidence generally suggests that partners in well-functioning, satisfying, and intimate relationships use different cognitive strategies to manage relational conflicts and difficulties than those who are distressed, unhappy, and lacking relational intimacy. Happy and satisfied couples tend to use positive and benevolent cognitive strategies that minimize the destructive implications of their negative interactions and enhance and maintain their relationships (Fincham and Bradbury, 1992). Applying positive causal attribution to explain partners' destructive behavior is an example of such benevolent cognition (Karney, McNulty, and Frye, 2001).

Simply defined, attributions are the various explanations and interpretations that partners make for events they experience in their close, marital relationships (Sillars et al., 2002). A large body of empirical evidence indicates that the attributions that partners make for relational events and a partner's behaviors are closely related to the level of their relational intimacy and satisfaction. Therefore, partners in distressed relationships are more likely than non-distressed partners to attribute relational problems and negative partner behavior to stable characteristics of the partner and to view the partner as behaving intentionally in a self-serving manner (Bradbury, Fincham, and Sullivan, 1994). Fincham and Bradbury (1992) indicated that whereas distressed couples use maladaptive causal attributions that accentuate negativity and minimize the positivity of relational events, non-distressed couples do the opposite. These authors presented an example to illustrate their observation: a woman who is happy and satisfied in her marriage is likely to attribute her husband's lack of sexual interest to his work tension and pressures. In contrast, an unhappy and dissatisfied woman is likely to attribute this event to her partner's lack of love for or sexual attraction to her (Bradbury and Fincham, 1992).

The basic premise of attribution theory (Heider, 1958; Kelley, 1973) that makes it applicable to marital interactions and intimacy is that a person's attributions have an impact on her partner's subsequent feelings and reactions. Fincham and Bradbury (1992) examined the associations between attributions and marital interactions in a broader Contextual Model, which "emphasizes that behaviors exchanged in an interaction can mean different things, depending on other events occurring in the interaction...when one spouse behaves, the partner attends to and perceives that behavior, assigns some meaning to it, and then exhibits a behavior of his or her own" (p. 614). The cognitive process that affect a spouse's interactive response to the other's behavior is rapid in its occurrence, and in most cases is not done with full conscious awareness (Fincham and Bradbury, 1992). Given the intensive dynamics of day-to-day marital transactions, husband-wife interactions are viewed as having a great amount of cognitive-behavioral sequences in which a husband's behavior is processed by his wife who then responds back. The husband processes his wife's response and enacts his behavior in return. This processing-behaving sequence can go on and on.

According to Fincham and Bradbury (1992), this processing is influenced by a wide range of variables such as the nature of the marital relationship, the couple's degree of marital commitment, the level of their marital intimacy and satisfaction, and so forth (see also Gottman, 1999). Attributions, according to the Contextual Model, relate to the meanings and causal interpretations assigned by partners to each other's interactive behavior. Fincham and

Bradbury (1992) found that attributional processes in marriage occur mostly, and have greater impact, when the events and behaviors that are subject to attributional explanation and interpretation are destructive and threatening to the relational balance. The attributions made by marital partners to destructive events and behaviors "are assumed to derive from an accumulation of experiences in interaction with the partner, and in subsequent situations when the negative behavior or difficulty occurs it is likely to be understood or interpreted in terms consistent with that attribution" (Fincham and Bradbury, 1992, p. 614). It is clear that one's reaction to a partner's behavior depends on, and is colored by, the nature and direction of the attribution assigned to the behavior. Thus, the attribution serves as a foundation upon which reactive behavior is based.

Adaptive benevolent attributions will evoke constructive, pro-relational responses, leading towards resolving conflicts, de-escalating tension, and improving intimacy. In contrast, maladaptive attributional processes will give rise to a destructive reaction that is likely to add to the persistence of relational tension, distress, and emotional distance (Karney and Bradbury, 1995). This pattern of maladaptive attribution that evokes a destructive response is likely to perpetuate rather than reduce relational negative affect, thus affirming and confirming the initial attribution, adding to the further reciprocal exchange of negativity. Over time, this reciprocal attribution-behavior chain results in a decrease in marital quality, intimacy, and satisfaction (Fincham and Bradbury, 1992).

Gottman (1999a) presents several attributional categories seen in relational interactions. These are:

1. Locus: this category relates to attributing events and behaviors to a partner's internal, dispositional characteristics, such as personality traits or attitudes. The locus of the attribution can be external when the causes of events and behaviors are attributed to situational or conditional factors in which the behavior took place and was observed by a partner.
2. Stability: this attributional dimension refers to the tendency to view and interpret a partner's action as being changing in accordance with varied conditions and circumstances, and temporary as opposed to stable.
3. Range: this attributional factor describes whether the observed destructive act affects several marital components or is limited in its impact range to a particular incident.
4. Intentionality: this attributional category is the tendency to assume self-centered, selfish, intentional, and blameworthy causes for a partner's destructive behavior or to assume that a partner's destructive behaviors were unselfishly motivated, giving the partner the benefit of doubt.

Gottman (1999a) reviewed the research relevant to the effect of negative attributions on marital relationships to conclude that: "for attributions about negative events, all of the studies reviewed supported significant differences between happily and unhappily married couples on the two dimensions of range and intentionality" (p. 72).

Manusov (2002) examined connections between attributional patterns and the nonverbal behavior of intimate relationship patterns such as facial expressions, head nods, posture, vocal pleasantness, and the like. Manusov found that nonverbal affect cues made by partners were associated with the attributions provided to them (whether nonverbal cues were perceived positively or negatively). A positive correlation was found between relationship-enhancing attributions and positive nonverbal cues (e.g. facial pleasantness). The results also showed a positive association between distressed negative attributional patterns and negative nonverbal behaviors. Manusov (2002) concluded that her findings "suggest that a large range of affect cues may result from, or be associated with, the attributions made for a spouse's behaviour...people do respond to a partner in part on how they make sense of their spouses' non-verbal action" (p. 27, 28).

Trust in Intimate Relationships

Recent developments in relational and marital research reflect the importance of trust for the maintenance and enhancement of marital quality, intimacy, and overall satisfaction (Holmes and Rempel, 1989). Rusbult, Olson, et al. (2001) relate trust as a core component that has a central functional value in marital relationships and is viewed as an implicit gauge of spouses' commitment to marriage. Personal commitment of spouses to one another and to the relationship cannot be established unless it is founded on basic and mutual trust (Rusbult, Wieselquist, et al., 1999).

One of the earliest definitions of relational trust was offered by Deutsch (1973). He accorded trust an esteemed value, viewing this phenomenon as being based on the "confidence that one will find what is desired from another rather that what is feared" (Rempel, Holmes, and Zana, 1985, p. 95). Trust in marital relationships is unlikely to immediately and suddenly emerge at an early stage of the marriage, but rather, it is a developed and dynamic phenomenon that requires relationship time to be established (Rempel, Holmes, and Zanna, 1985). Trust needs a meaningful span of relational experience to be developed, and it is often positioned by relationship scholars in conjunction with love and commitment (Wieselquist, Rusbult, et al., 1999). The initial stage of relationship formation that is characterized by romantic love progresses gradually to a more mature companionship love in conjunction with the development of trust (Remple, Holmes, and Zanna, 1985). Larzeler and Huston (1980) found a link between intimacy and love, and trust in a close relationship. The authors view trust as one's perceived notion that the partner is genuinely interested in her welfare and that the other is motivated to maximize relational outcomes.

Trust is also linked to partners' honesty, which is the extent to which one's intentions regarding the future of her relationship involvement are reliable and believable (Larzeler and Huston, 1980). Similarly, Holmes and Remple (1989) argue that trust should not be viewed as an enduring personal disposition or trait, but rather as a relationship interacting phenomenon. In other words, trust is "a relationship-specific phenomenon, defining trust-level as the expectation that a given partner can be relied on to behave in a benevolent manner and be responsive to one's needs" (Rusbult, Olson, et al., 2001).

Holmes and Rempel (1989) found that trust in close relationships is composed of three basic elements: predictability, dependability, and faith. According to this model, predictability is a specific and concrete component that signifies one's inner, perceived belief that his partner's benevolent and rewarding interactive behavior is enduringly consistent and not transient. The degree to which a partner's interactive behavior is predictable depends on the consistency of its appearance in the couples interactions (Rempel, Holmes, and Zanna, 1985). Predictability is affected by the reward contingencies that follow behavior. It is more likely that a person's benevolent behavior would appear again if the partner responds constructively than if the response is destructive (Rusbult et al., 2001). When a partner's past interactive experiences show stability and consistency, the trust element of predictability is promoted and becomes an integral part of the relational exchange.

The component of dependability in relational trust development relates to one's conviction and belief that his partner can be counted on to be reliable, to behave in a pro-relational, benevolent manner. To illustrate the hierarchal nature of trust development, Remple et al. (1985) indicate that as relationships progress, there is an inevitable shift in focus away from assessing the partner's behaviors to an evaluation of the characteristics attributed to the partner. Consequently, trust is located and identified in a person as a whole, not in her specific actions and demeanors. Developing such global dispositional assessment of a partner relies on an accumulation of interactional and transactional experiences from one's partner. Accumulating experiences that show that one's partner is honest, reliable, and can be counted on to be supportive and benevolent promote relational trust.

Finally, the third developmental stage in Rempel, Holmes, and Zanna's (1985) model of trust is faith, which goes beyond partners' interactive behavior or the accumulation of positive relational experiences. This means that "faith reflects an emotional security on the part of individuals, which enables them to go beyond the available evidence and feel, with assurances, that their partner will be responsive and caring despite the vicissitudes of an uncertain future" (p. 97). The faith component of relational trust is a strong and fundamental conviction that one's partner's motivation to be supportive, positively responsive, and benevolent comes intrinsically from within the person and is not a vehicle to achieve self-centered rewards and gratifications. The partner's pro-relational behavior in and of itself intrinsically generates its own positive incentives and rewards (Holmes and Rempel, 1989; Rusbult, Kumashiro, et al., 2002).

How do partners in intimate relationships develop the kind of trust that possesses predictability, dependability, and faith? It has been suggested that trust development is founded on the manner in which partners are perceived to act during interdependence dilemmas (when self and relational interests or benefits conflict). In such situations, one has to make a choice between acting benevolently for pro-relational interests (achieving relationship benefits) or acting to achieve self-centered rewards (Holmes and Rempel, 1989; Rusbult et al., 2001; Rusbult et al., 2002). As trust is progressively developed in a given intimate relationship, the partners become increasingly dependent on one another. That is, as trust increases, the partners become more satisfied in their relationship and they are more willing to intrinsically enhance their involvement with one another and the relationship (Rusbult, Olsen, Davis, and Hannon, 2001).

Rusbult, Olsen, et al. (2001) conceptualize intimate partners' relational commitment and trust to be interdependently regulating the relationship. As partners become increasingly dependent on each other, their commitment to each other is promoted and enhanced. In turn, this development yields a stronger willingness to invest in the relationship and to engage in mutual benevolent behaviors (i.e. forgo personal interests and benefits to fulfill the partner's desires). Trust is developed and enhanced as a result of this enduring pro-relationship behavior and the strengthening of commitment (Rusbult, Olsen, et al., 2001). Enhanced trust in return develops greater interdependence between the partners, increases relational satisfaction and intimacy, and promotes more willingness for greater investment in the relationship. According to Rusbult, Olsen, et al. (2001), "this brings us full circle, in that enhanced dependence yields increased commitment. Thus, relationships to some degree are internally regulated via the process of adaptation to evolving patterns of interdependence, changes in each person's actions and motives [that] trigger complementary changes in the partner" (p. 109). Accordingly, the strength of a partner's trust is basically a reflection of the strength of one's personal commitment and dedication to one's partner and the relationship.

Commitment and trust contribute to the overall quality of intimate relationships (Rusbult, Wieselquist, et al., 1999). This reciprocal sequence that exists between relational, interdependent commitment and trust is illustrated in a model developed by Rusbult, Kumashiro, et al. (2002) called the *mutual cycling growth* that suggests that one's trust in one's partner is essentially the mirror-image of the partner's commitment. Moreover, when trust and commitment are high, partners are more willing to forgive each other for destructive behaviors (Rusbult, Kumashiro, et al., 2002). Forgiveness is perceived as both a cause and consequence of committed and trusting intimate relationships. Due to the fact that trust in one's partner triggers benevolent and pro-relationship interactions, it promotes greater a tendency and willingness to forgive. This is because trust triggers the benevolent interpretation of a partner's betrayal so that forgiving becomes easier. Full-hearted forgiveness of a partner's destructive behavior (betrayal) leads to greater trust development "in that earlier acts of benevolen[ce]—such as forgiveness of betrayal—may yield increased trust, along with enhanced commitment and increased inclinations toward pro-relationship motives and behaviours" (Rusbult, Kumashiro, et al., 2002, p. 274).

To summarize this chapter on the development and growth of intimate relationships, we may that partners in a happy couple is one that trusts each other; can depend on, share, be supported, and nurtured by their partner; and knows that they have the other's love, commitment, and dedication.

Chapter 14

INGREDIENTS OF A SUCCESSFUL MARRIAGE: HOW TO ACHIEVE ONE, AND WHAT TO STAY AWAY FROM

The secret to a happy marriage remains…a secret.
—Henry Youngman

Considerable scholarly attention, both theoretical and empirical, has been devoted to the question of why some marriages are well adjusted, successful, and happy while others are dysfunctional, unsuccessful, and miserable (Gottman and Notarius, 2002; Fincham, Stanley, and Beach, 2007). As early as 1938, Terman, Butterweiser, Ferguson, Johnson, and Wilson raised and examined the question of, "what is fundamentally different about happily and unhappily married couples?" (Gottman and Notarius, 2002, p. 159) These authors concentrated mainly on examining personality traits that are related to marital success. They used self-report methodology to assess personality traits and their impact on marriage. The study, however, failed to show an optimal personality make-up for a successful marriage. Nonetheless, these authors' studies have had great influence on the conceptualization of constructs and components of research in this field (Chung, 1999). Since the pioneering work of Terman et al. (1938), the field of marital research has enjoyed remarkable developments and advances in innovative technologies and methodologies used to collect relevant information (Karney and Bradbury, 1995; Fincham and Beach, 1999). One important advance is credited to Gottman and Levenson (1992) who conducted and reported the first prospective longitudinal study, using the lab observational data of couples in an attempt to predict marital outcomes (divorce). For example, it was found that partners' interactions and their physiological responses (physiological arousal during conflict discussion) that form more negativity than positivity predicted marital dissolution. Based on their empirical work, Gottman (1999a) has identified several interactive behaviors that threaten marital relationships and lead to marital deterioration, dissolution, and divorce. Four of these components, that Gottman (1999a) calls "the four horsemen of the apocalypse" (p. 29), are particularly corrosive. These are criticism, contempt, defensiveness, and stone-walling.

CRITICISM

According to Gottman, criticism is "any statement that implies that there is something globally wrong with one's partner, something that is probably a lasting aspect of the partner's character" (Gottman, 1999a, p. 41). Apparently, criticism, especially when it attacks one's spouse's personality, or threatens one's self-esteem, is destructive and is likely to cause tension arousal, emotional distance, and insecurity (Koski and Shaver, 1997). Criticism in marital interactions has been identified as a major behavioral component that characterizes couples in distressed marriages (Hojjat, 1997). Also, criticism is an ineffective communication pattern of spouses who are coping with disappointments and unmet marital needs (Vangelisti and Alexander, 2002). Gottman (1994b) argued that "on the surface, there may not seem to be much difference between complaining and criticism. But criticism involves attacking someone's personality or character rather than a specific behavior" (p. 73). The author views complaining (i.e. expressing one's disappointment concerning an unmet standard) as a healthy marital behavior as long as it does not assault one's partner. Expressing disagreement, disappointment, and even anger, even if unpleasant, still strengthens the relationship in the long-run. This approach is by far more effective than suppressing disappointments, which has a negative effect on marriage.

Along this line, Vangelisty and Alexander (2002) found that the manner in which partners express disappointments concerning their unmet needs is likely to have greater impact on marital outcomes than the expression itself. Expressing disappointment regarding a partner's behavior, as opposed to his character, is beneficial, contributing to marital enhancement (Vangelisty and Alexander, 2002). A complaint is usually a specific, behavior-centered statement expressed by disappointed partner. For example, "I'm upset that you did not call to say you'll be late for dinner." The complaining partner was focusing on an event, act, or behavior that upset her. The complaint was addressing a specific behavior as opposed to attacking the person. Criticism, on the other hand, attacks the partner's character, as in, "you're always late for dinner, you're so selfish and inconsiderate, and you never care about me." As one can note, this criticizing statement was stated in global terms, using words like "you always" or "you never." According to Gottman (1999a), this global manner of expression can easily transform feelings of being upset and disappointed into attacking criticism. Complaints escalate to criticism and personal attacks when one feels that time and again his complaints are not positively responded to by the partner.

In my (A.S.) marriage therapy practice, I encourage criticizing spouses to identify the hidden unmet needs and wants that commonly are disguised by criticizing and blaming interactions. This therapeutic intervention usually redirects destructive behaviors and results in a more soothing affect and greater cooperative interactions that were missing in their distressed marriage. Also, this intervention is likely to lead couples to discuss changes they desire to accomplish. A woman criticizing her husband for being self-centered, being inconsiderate, and being interested only in his work, is implying, "I'd like to have you around more, spend more time with you, feel you care about me, make me feel like I belong and am wanted." I have found that previously criticized partners respond much more positively to statements relating to core marital needs (like feeling appreciated and loved, feeling wanted). Employing this strategy of expressing feelings and unmet needs usually results in positive outcomes, demonstrated by the previously criticized person transforming her motivation to comply with what is needed by the partner. At this point, what was previously considered a risk factor (criticism) to the relationship has been transformed into a developmental, enhancing factor (expressing feelings and unmet needs). Also, the expression of feelings and unmet needs and desires that replaces criticism reduces partners' display of aggression and the negative effect on the partners' interactions during conflict.

CONTEMPT

Contempt is another destructive behavior that is associated with marital distress (Gottman, 1994a, 1999a; Hojjat, 1997). According to Gottman (1999a), contempt is "any statement or nonverbal behaviour that puts oneself on a higher plane than one's partner" (p. 45). Contemptuous interactions tend to deflate the partner's worth, indicating hostility and rejection (Roberts and Greenberg, 2002). The intent in contemptuous behavior is to communicate to the partner that he is deemed worthless by, and unimportant to, the speaker. Accordingly, "what separates contempt from criticism is the intention to insult and psychologically abuse (one's) partner" (Gottman, 1999b, p. 79). Contempt is evoked by the negative feelings that are harbored by the speaker about his partner (e.g. she is incompetent, lazy, or uncultured). There are various manners by which contempt is delivered in marital interactions: through insults and name calling, using hostile humor, putting down a partner through sarcastic mockery, and through more subtle, nonverbal facial expressions. To illustrate the destructive power of contemptuous facial expressions, Gottman (1999a) found that "certain contemptuous facial expressions by husbands were predictive of their wives infection illnesses over the next four years" (p. 46). It was also found that contemptuous interactions predict marital dissolution and divorce better than all other destructive behaviors; it has to be treated with an attitude of zero tolerance, namely, it has to be banned completely from the marital relationship.

Roberts and Greenberg (2002) argue that in order to understand marital success, there is a need to examine not only negativity (conflict, contempt) but also positivity, i.e. how do couples establish and maintain intimate connectedness. Roberts and Greenberg (2002) asserted that "relational harmony may depend on the successful enactment of positive behavioural interchanges in the context of intimate marital interactions" (p. 119). Thus, although negativity suggests decreased positive marital exchange, and the development of marital distress, the inception of this negativity is the absence of marital intimate interchange. This intimacy deficiency eventually leads to the development of negative interactions of criticism, contempt, and distress (Roberts and Greenberg, 2002). In other words, couples that invest in relational development and enhancement (promoting intimacy) are likely to be immune against the development of negative transactions. In Roberts and Greenberg's (2002) own words: "The regular enactment of behavioral exchanges that lead to experiences of relational intimacy, will serve to maintain the climate of security, trust, and acceptance that characterize well-functioning relationships" (p. 120). Maintaining intimate and caring marital relationships enables spouses to adequately resolve conflicts and marital problems without resorting to criticism and blame as a getaway route. Conversely, couples who neglect this important relational task of developing and maintaining intimate connectedness are exposed to the threatening effects of negativity. According to Gottman (1999a, b) the antidote to contempt is praise, pride, and admiration. The existence of contemptuous interactions results in pain, anger, resentment, and distress, whereas mutual praising and admiration of one's partner promote and enhance emotional closeness and relational intimacy.

As indicated, contempt is found mostly in distressed, emotionally flooded marital couples, and it is hardly found in successful, well-functioning marriages. Once contempt find its way in marital interactions, appearing repeatedly during conflict, the relationship is bound to deteriorate. This deterioration presents a clear predictive component of continuing discord and dissolution (Gottman, 1994a, 1999a). Contempt is likely to induce destructive reactions that causes the escalation of negativity and distress and eventually results in the couple becoming emotionally disengaged. Gottman (1999a) views emotional disengagement as a major problem of highly distressed couples who are entrapped in negative affect reciprocity. Gottman adds that "what is very clear in these marital interactions is the absence of positive affect," and that "such couples appear not to make any emotional connection, and there is no humour, affection, or even active interest in one another" (Gottman, 1999a, p. 48).

Couples in happy and successful marriages manage to develop and maintain a strong foundation of friendship and positive affect through frequent and spontaneous expressions of "fondness and admiration" (Gottman, 1999a, p. 106). Couples high on fondness and expressions of admiration, develop and maintain strong, successful, and happy marriages. In contrast, one of the most significant manifestations of marital distress is the lack of these components in the partners' interactions. As Gottman (1999b) puts it, "fondness and admiration are two of the most crucial elements in a rewarding and long-lasting romance" (p. 63). Furthermore, a positive view of one's marriage and the appraisal of one's partner protect the relationship against deterioration even during crises and bad times.

DEFENSIVENESS

Defensiveness is identified as the third "Horsemen of the Apocalypse" (Gottman, 1999a). It is another marital destructive interaction, defined as "any attempt to defend oneself from a perceived attack" (p. 44). For the outside observer, defensiveness may be seen as a legitimate, understandable reaction to feeling criticized and attacked. There is something about the attitudinal front displayed by defensiveness, however, that tends to escalate conflicts and negative affect. Defensiveness adds to marital difficulties by being a major link in the chain of interactive patterns that characterize distressed couples and predict dissolution and divorce (Hojjat, 1997). It is quite common for distressed couples in marital therapy to be emotionally flooded with negative affect and to display mutual blame, criticism, and defensiveness (Cordova and Jacobson, 1997). Defensive postures have several possible forms of presentation: denying responsibility when faced with complaints or criticism, making excuses by indicating that it is not one's fault with regard to things one is being blamed for, and cross-complaining, namely meeting one's partner's complaints with a complaint or blame of one's own (Gottman, 1994b). Identifying the negative impact of defensiveness, Gottman (1999a) indicates that "defensiveness usually includes denying responsibility for the problem, and this fuels the flames of marital conflict because it says the other person is the culprit, the guilty party" (p. 45). This is the reason this interactive pattern is associated with the escalation of negativity and, in the long run, why it is linked to decline in marital satisfaction and relationship dissolution (Whisman, 1997).

STONE-WALLING

Stone-walling is another destructive marital interactive behavior that occurs when one partner withdraws from a discussion that turned into an argument. In couples that interact in a functional, well-adjusted manner, "there is [a] marvellous dance of nonverbal behavior between speaker and listener that, in effect regulates turn-taking in conversations and shows the speaker that the listener is fully present. Speakers do such things as to look away from the listener as they begin talking, while listeners maintain a steadier gaze until they switch roles" (Gottman, 1999a, p. 46). This positive interaction hardly exists in distressed couples where stone-walling occurs regularly during conflicts. Instead, distressed couples use brief glances, maintain a stiff neck, vocalize very minimally, and in general convey the stance of an impassive stone wall.

Stone-walling is likely to occur when a discussion, especially on sensitive topics, begins with a harsh start-up, and the couple's interaction is loaded with criticism, blaming, contempt, and defensiveness (Gottman, 1999a; Gottman, 1999b). This negative exchange escalates to the point that one partner stone-walls or withdraws from the argument (e.g. by leaving the room). Observations and codings of couples' discussions during conflict show that men stone-wall much more than women (Gottman, 1999a). Physiological differences between men and women seem to be the reason for this observed discrepancy. Since men in distress react physiologically more intensely (a rise in pulse and blood pressure, among other physiological signs), turning away and withdrawing have a protective, soothing effect on stone-walling men. This gender difference in physiology can also explain the reason men may take longer to calm down and bring their physiology to a baseline level. Women that are left behind during conflict by stone-walling husbands, feel deeply hurt, neglected, lonely, and worthless. These accumulating negative effects, experienced as a result of partner's stone-walling behavior, escalate tension and threaten marriage stability. Stone-walling interactions also leave conflicts and disagreements unsolved, thus creating an ongoing accumulation of frustration, anger, and emotional distance.

Gottman (1994b) described the sequence of a negative interactive chain that characterizes distressed couples as one in which harsh blaming and criticizing lead to contempt, which leads to defensiveness, resulting in the listener's withdrawal from the emotionally flooded interaction. This destructive interaction sequence creates a continuing cycle of negativity, the accumulation of which is predictive of the negative marital outcomes of discord and dissolution. Gottman (1994b) developed a self-test instrument to identify stone-walling interactions during conflict. Some of the items in this self-test are: "When my partner complained I felt that I just wanted to get away from this garbage," "When we have a big blow-up I just want to leave," and "I withdrew to try to calm down" (p. 96).

Stone-walling in Gottman's model of the "Four Horsemen of the Apocalypse" is somewhat similar to the active-destructive Exit response in Rusbult's (1993) EVLN model. "Exit" is a partner's walking away or leaving the room during conflictual argument.

As noted, the frequent occurrence of destructive interactions (criticism, contempt, etc.) is significantly lower in well functioning, successful marriages. Commenting on the reason for this finding, Gottman (1999a) suggests that successful couples (what he calls "masters") use effective repairs in their interactions during conflict and disagreement. Effective repairs result in lowered tension occurring more often even when the interaction becomes tense. Gottman (1999b) views repair attempts as "the secret weapon of emotionally intelligent couples" (p. 22). Repair attempts are those behavioral mechanisms employed by couples during conflict in order to calm down, soothe, and de-escalate a heated interaction. These behaviors and gestures occur much less in distressed couples. Also, due to the emotional flooding that characterizes a distressed couple's conflict interactions, they fail to de-escalate negativity.

To help couples evaluate the effectiveness of their repair attempts of negativity, Gottman (1999a) developed a 20 item Repair Attempts Questionnaire that may help couples and marriage practitioners to identify partners' abilities and skills in de-escalating tension, especially during conflictual situations and arguments. Clinical interventions with couples in therapy can be based on couples' ratings on this questionnaire. The instrument includes items such as: "We are good at taking breaks when we need them"; "When I apologize, it usually gets accepted by my partner"; "My attempts to repair our discussions when they get negative are usually effective," or, "When emotions run hot, expressing how upset I feel makes a real difference" (Gottman, 1999a, p. 385). Marriage counselors and therapists encourage couples to develop effective repair mechanisms to de-escalate tension and prevent negative affect reciprocity. Again, the importance of negativity repairs to marital well-being has been supported by research findings showing that the lacking of this component characterizes dysfunctional marriages and predicts dissolution and divorce (Gottman, Driver, Yashimoto, and Rushe, 2002).

MARITAL SUPPORT

Close, intimate marital relationships are an important and major source of emotional support, especially at times of stress; intimacy is an integral part of stable and well-functioning marital relationships (Iida, Seidman, et al., 2008). Moreover, getting needed support from outside of the marriage does not adequately compensate for the lack of one's spousal support (Barry et al., 2009). At the same time, being in close marital relationships does not imply giving and receiving mutual support (Iida, Seidman, Shrout, Fujita, and Bolger, 2008). Nonetheless, a partner's perceived emotional support is among the most significant predictors of marital satisfaction and well-being (Molden, Lucas, et al., 2009).

Social support is defined in marital relationships as: "one partner's coping assistance for a problem the other is having" (Gable and Reis, 2001, p. 179). Support between marital spouses has been said to play a most important role in a relationship's well-being and stability. This is mostly due to the characteristics of support in close relationships that evoke, in the recipient of support, warm and comforting feelings, e.g. being cared for and feeling worthy, loved, and valued, and feeling secure that one can count on getting support whenever it is needed (Sarson and Sarson, 2001). Partners who receive support when in need view their marriage as satisfying and well adjusted, while the lack of a partner's support predicts marital distress and dissolution (Kelly, Fincham, and Beach, 2003). A distinction is made between received support, the amount and quality of support perceived by the recipient during a support interaction, and the actual act of support provision (Barry, Bunde, Brock, and Lawrence, 2009). Apparently, for a support interaction to be benevolent and beneficial to the recipient, supportive behavior must be enacted, but more importantly, it must be perceived and received as such (Barry et al., 2009). More specifically, while a spouse may provide support, the intended support recipient may not necessarily recognize it as supportive. Thus supportive behaviors that are not perceived as such by the recipient partner may not produce positive outcomes. Not only that, but a person may believe that she invests in providing support whereas her partner may perceive the behavior to be unsupportive (Gardner and Cutrona, 2004). Also, a support interaction may be well intended by the provider, but may be perceived as inadequate, inappropriate, or excessive by the recipient (Iida et al., 2008).

There is a distinction made between the two sets of factors relating to support provision and reception in close relationships. The first, "Recipient Factors," are variables relating to the partner in need of support, and the second, "Provider Factors," are variables referring to the person that responds to the partner who is in need for support (Iida et al., 2008). In order for support to be effectively and appropriately provided, the partner in need should make a direct request for support, specifying the manner by which he would like to be supported. The direct, specific request for support is likely to avoid ambiguity and ensure the receiving of timely and appropriate support (Iida et al., 2008). This support transaction, characterizing successful marriages, increases the beneficial potential of the support and is likely to result in positive personal and relational outcomes.

Another component relating to the recipient of marital support is the degree of recipient distress. Accordingly, we would expect that greater recipient distress would motivate increased support provision by the support provider since intimate relationships tend to highlight communal norms (Iida et al., 2008). A communal relationship is characterized by partners who are concerned with the welfare of each other and are motivated to provide benefits (support) to one another when needed (Mills and Clark, 2001). Following communal norms maintains and enhances marital relationships and improves marital quality and satisfaction. The attraction that exists in successful marriages motivates the partners to behave communally by supporting each other, especially when one partner is in distress. Reducing a partner's distress through caring and supporting behavior is an important goal for partners in successful, well-adjusted marriages.

There is some empirical evidence to suggest that not all support transactions are associated with positive personal and or dyadic outcomes (adjustment and comfort). Not only that, some support interactions are negatively related to marital well-being (Gable, Gonzaga, and Strachman, 2006). Gable et al. (2006) posit that receiving social support may have neutral or detrimental effects on the relationship, as it may be a signal to the recipient that she is unable to cope with the stressor, which may threaten her sense of self-worth and self-esteem. The authors added the perception of a diminished self-worth in the eyes of one's intimate partner may be especially problematic to the relationship. If this sequence of events and emotive transaction occurs, however, it is a sign of a relationship that is low on personal commitment, satisfaction, well-being, and love for one's partner (Murry et al., 2005).

Provider factors of support transactions consist primarily of the level of the provider's motivation to render support to his partner. Noticing a partner's need for support and being motivated to provide it, depends on the quality of and the mood that exists in the relationship and the level of marital satisfaction (Iida et al., 2008).

The enhancing component of providing and perceiving support is not restricted only to support provided in times of distress. The role of perceived support from one's partner in achieving personal goals (self-expansion and self-actualization) has also been studied. Feeney (2004) found that support in the form of encouragement to achieve personal goals received by a marital partner, enhances the recipient's self-esteem and promotes relational positive affect. Perceived support for the accomplishment of personal goals and aspirations is an important contribution not only to recipient's well-being but also to the relationship's success and marital satisfaction (Drigotas, 2002).

The role of marital support has also been studied in relation to one's supportive responses to her partner sharing positive events and emotions. Benevolent expressions of support to positive feelings and events experienced and shared by a partner promote relationship positivity, well-being, and satisfaction (Gable, Gonzaga, and Strachman, 2006). This positive interactive process has been called "capitalization" (Langston, 1994). Thus, capitalizing on good things that were experienced by an intimate partner contributes to relationship enhancement and maintenance, independent of the positivity of the feelings and events that were shared. The effect of capitalization, however, depends to a great extent on the quality of the responsivity of the partner with whom the sharing was made. Gable et al. (2006) assert that "the targets of capitalization are almost always [a] close relationship partner," and "research has shown that when close relationship partners, especially romantic partners, regularly respond to positive event disclosures in a supportive manner, disclosers report feeling closer, more intimate, and generally more satisfied with their relationships than those whose partners typically respond in a nonsupportive manner" (p. 904). In view of this finding, it is clear that the dynamics and development of successful marriages emerge in the context of dyadic sharing of positive emotions. The important role of the capitalization processes with regard to marital outcomes is added to the enhancing effect of social support discussed earlier (supporting a partner in distress).

Gable, Gonzaga, and Strachman (2006) categorize responses to a partner's capitalization attempts (sharing positive feelings and events) along two dimensions: constructive vs. destructive and active vs. passive.

Based on this model, responses can be divided into four groups of responses:

1. Active constructive responses that reflect enthusiastic, happy, cheerful support.
2. Passive constructive responses characterized by quiet or minimal expressions of support (a smile, saying, "That's nice").
3. Active-destructive response that demeans or ridicules the positive feelings expressed by one's partner.
4. Passive-destructive responses shown by ignoring the expressed feelings or events, or changing the subject.

There is empirical evidence to suggest that only responses that were perceived to be active and constructive were correlated with personal well-being and higher relationship quality and satisfaction. The other three types of responses were negatively associated with relationships' well-being (Gable et al., 2006). Apparently, active constructive responses to capitalization attempts (sharing positive feelings and events) project and convey to the disclosing partner that the feelings and events she has experienced are important and significant not only to her, but also to the responder. Additionally, it conveys that the responder has a close intimate knowledge of what is important and exciting to his partner.

In conclusion, Gable et al. (2006) indicate that "sharing personal positive events provides prime opportunities to obtain understanding, validation and caring" (p. 906). In Reis and Shaver's (1988) transactional model of intimacy, this process is called "perceived partner responsiveness to the self" (p. 368). This interactive process consists of three overlapping elements:

1. Strengthening the beliefs regarding the partner's understanding and accepting of one's qualities, emotions, self-worth, and personal needs and goals.
2. Perceived positive responsiveness invokes cognitions regarding the degree to which the responder values, respects, supports, and validates the receiver partner's self.
3. The support provided by the responder promotes in the partner the perception that she is valued and cared for.

Gable, Gonzaga, and Strachman (2006) add another contribution to the self of partners who share positive events and emotions. They indicated that when individuals share positive events with their partners, they are sharing their strengths with their "best friend." Perceiving that their partner validates a strength could be quite beneficial for their feeling of self-worth, which promotes and strengthens relationship security, marital commitment, and satisfaction. In addition, Canvello and Crocker (2010) concluded that "people who perceive others as responsive become responsive themselves and perceive their partner as more responsive" (p. 100), thus creating a supportive and enhancing interactive cycle. This interactive reciprocal dynamic is closely related to Fredrickson's (2001) Broaden-and-Build model of positive emotions, which stipulates that experiencing and expressing positive emotions in marriage, broadening the scope of a partner's cognition, encouraging creative processing and behavior, and also building coping abilities and social-interpersonal resources are all important actions. In return, these broader capacities are associated with increased positive emotive experiences (Fredrickson and Joiner, 2002).

This chain of reciprocal exchange and emotional development creates what Gottman (1999a) calls the "Positive Sentiment Override (PSO)." PSO characterizes marital couples that manage to develop, enhance, and maintain successful, well-functioning relationships; they enjoy an ongoing presence of positive affect to the point that "even negativity by the partner is interpreted as information rather than as a personal attack" (Gottman, 1999a, p. 164). PSO is the accumulation of day-to-day positive interactions between partners that produces a well-balanced, communal relationship that promotes effective resolution of conflicts and disagreements. The high degree and constant presence of positive affect allow couples to override destructive and irritating behaviors. PSO protects happily married couples from being entrapped into a cycle of negative affect reciprocity that characterizes distressed couples. In contrast, continuous accumulation of negative interactions between partners such as blaming, criticizing, and personal attacks creates perpetual marital conflict and distress, a composition that may evolve into Negative Sentiment Override (NSO) (Gottman, 1999a). This emotional atmosphere is likely to override positive, constructive gestures that may occasionally occur. In addition, in NSO, even a neutral interaction is perceived as an attacking and threatening communication.

Two evidence-based components of successful marriages were the foundation of Gottman's (1999a) intervention model, which he entitled the "Sound Marital House." These are:

1. The importance of developing and maintaining an overall atmosphere of marital positive affect
2. The positive impact on marital relationship of the couple's ability to reduce negative affect during conflict, thus de-escalating tension to allow effective resolutions.

Accordingly, in order to create a lasting change in troubled marriages, therapeutic interventions need to increase the level of positive affect in both non conflict and conflict contexts. In other words, the foundation of the Sound Marital House is the development of a communal, friendly marital relationship, leading to the promotion and enhancement of positive sentiments that may override occasional negativity and promotes the effective resolution of conflicts.

Three developmental processes are needed in order to establish the marital foundation of friendship:

1. Developing and enhancing the dimension of marital "love maps."
2. Couples' investment into fondness and admiration.
3. Encouraging marital partners to turn toward each other as opposed to turning away or ignoring one's partner when he is in need of attention, of time together, for sharing feelings, thoughts, and events, and when he is bidding for closeness and support. The following is an elaboration and expansion of these three processes (Gottman, 1999a).

LOVE MAPS

Happily married couples share time together talking and getting to know each other intimately. The depth and breadth of the knowledge they accumulate and the mere fact that they spend quality time in close togetherness are important components of a successful marriage. The construct of "Love Maps" refers to the amount of cognitive room partners have for the knowing of one's partner's psychological world, and being known as well (Gottman, 1999a; Gottman, 1999b). Successful partners make the effort to know each other deeply and extensively by encouraging each other to open up and share inner thoughts and feelings in an empathic and accepting atmosphere. Through that, partners convey to each other, verbally and nonverbally, that they are interested in each other, wanting to deepen the knowledge they have for one another's personal world. By being intimately familiar with each other's psychological world, partners thereby promote, enhance, and maintain closeness and friendship. In Gottman's words, "From knowledge springs not only love but the fortitude to weather marital storms. Couples who have detailed love maps of each other's world are far better prepared to cope with stressful events and conflicts" (Gottman, 1999b, p. 48).

Examining Gottman's (1999a, p.379) Love Map Questionnaire provides input concerning the concept of cognitive room for knowledge of a partner's personal world. The 20 item questionnaire includes items such as: "I can name my partner's best friends," "I can tell you some of my partner's life dreams," "I know my partner's major current worries," and the like. By creating cognitive room (Love Maps) for relational knowledge, partners promote and enhance the creation of their love and affection for each other. This may include storing positive mental representations of what first attracted them to one another; positive, joyful experiences they have had together; the partner's greatest strength that make him unique and special; and things the couple enjoy doing together. Naturally, successful couples make it a point to increase and expand the knowledge they have of each other, which in and by itself enables them to retrieve memories and mental representations of good times, exciting and joyful mutual experiences, and positive qualities of one another. By doing so, their relationship is likely to be enhanced and maintain positive affect.

The *fondness and admiration system* is another important dimension found to be important for the development of well functioning, successful marriages (Gottman, 1999a). Frequent and spontaneous experiences of love, fondness, and admiration were found to be vitally important for the development of viable, exciting, and happy marriages. Successfully married partners are high on the expression of fondness and admiration, a condition that strengthens the couple's marital immune system (Carrere, Gottman, and Ochs, 1996). In contrast, one of the most noticeable manifestations of distressed couples is that fondness and admiration no longer exist in their relationship.

Roberts and Greenberg (2002) developed the Intimate Interaction Coding System to code, analyze, and describe interactive processes in a couple's intimate expressions. The authors identified four basic themes discussed in the interactions of couples who were observed and coded: shared enjoyable memories; feelings of respect or admiration for the partner; feelings of security, comfort, and trust in the relationship; and feelings of attraction and desire for the partner. It was clearly demonstrated that successful, satisfied spouses related more frequently and extensively on these interactive dimensions than couples in distressed marriages.

In his book *Seven Principles for Making Marriage Work*, Gottman (1999b) suggested some exercises for couples who are motivated to improve and nurture their marital fondness and admiration toward each other. One of these exercises guides partners to recall positive mental representations of their love. The exercise requires partners to answer questions such as how the partners first met, what did they see as being special about each other, and the impressions each of them had at their first meeting. Other questions relate to the dating period, such as the type of activities they shared and how each of them felt during that period. Other memories that the partners are asked to recall relate to the decision to marry and call for a description of the wedding and the honeymoon. Couples in this exercise also reflect on the first stage of their marriage, happy moments they shared, the ups and downs they have had, and so forth. Based on his experience in working with couples in therapy and workshops, Gottman (1999b) indicates that most couples find that recalling their past together helps to rejuvenate their relationship in the here-and-now. Answering these questions often reminds couples of the love and great expectations that they initially had that motivated them to marry in the first place.

The third important developmental dimension for the establishment of marital friendships is for the partners to turn to each other instead of away from one another (Gottman, 1999a, 1999b). This concept reflects the degree of emotional closeness or distance that exists between couples. When one conveys active interest in her spouse, bidding for attention, acknowledgment, or help, the emotional movement conveyed is of a "turning toward" type. If a person ignores his partner's request for consideration, assistance, attention, or acknowledgment, he communicates a "turning away" attitude. Couples who turn toward each other remain emotionally engaged and stay married; those couple that do not eventually drift apart.

COMMITMENT

In spite of the high rate of divorce in America (Byrd, 2009), the increased emphasis on personal self-determination, the pursuit of personal fulfillment, and the various alternatives to traditional marriage, social expectations of a lifelong, committed marriage remain strong (Thornton and Young-DeMarco, 2001). Relating to the changes regarding the state of marriage in America, Andrew Cherlin wrote, "the interesting question is not why so few people are marrying, but rather, why so many people are marrying, or planning to marry, or hoping to marry, when cohabitation and single parenthood are widely acceptable options" (Cherlin, 2004, p. 845).

Thompson-Hayes and Webb (2004) defined marital commitment as "the extent to which spouses experience mutual desire to remain in their marriage as a function, in part, of their interaction" (p. 250). They view commitment as a dynamic relational component that is created and recreated throughout marital communication; that commitment, due to its dynamic, developmental, and changeable nature, "waxes and wanes" over time. The notion that commitment is constructed, developed, and maintained through dyadic communication is based on Duck's (1995) assertion regarding the role of dyadic discourse on relationship development. Accordingly, dyadic communication and interactions create partners' beliefs and attitudes regarding their relationship, including the commitment that exists between them. Realizing the unique perspective offered by dyadic communication to the study of commitment, Thompson-Hayes and Webb (2004) indicated that most of the definitions of commitment they reviewed are individual-focused definitions, paying "scant attention to how married couples construct and reconstruct the experience of commitment" (Thompson-Hayes and Webb, 2004, p. 250). Thus, instead of concentrating on the individual's desire and intention to commit to one's marriage, the authors conceptualize commitment as anchored in the dyad. Since marriage itself is a "twosome," dyadic union, commitment being so central to marriage, should also be viewed and conceptualized through a dyadic lens. Accordingly, commitment was described by them as a dyadic, continuous variable that is based on the couple's mutual desire and is sustained through interaction.

The Dyadic and Communicative Model of Marital Commitment developed by Thompson-Hayes and Webb (2004) consists of three components that have an impact on commitment: (1) communication maintenance behaviors (CMB), which relates to the ability of spouses to effectively use specific interactive activities that sustain the relationship and repair negativity. This component is based on empirical evidence that suggests that in successful romantic relationships, partners engage in communication interactions that enhance and maintain their marriage and promote marital commitment. The (2) marital quality component refers to the perception that partners hold regarding the quality of their marriage and its unique and noticeable features that they value. Additionally, the partners are convinced that compared to other relationships, theirs is an outstanding and superior marriage, and they do not expect to have a better relationship elsewhere. Accordingly, the level of marital commitment is related to the quality of the relationship. As the level of marital quality and satisfaction increases, so does the strength of the commitment. (3) Projected longevity refers to the extent to which partners imagine their marriage remaining stable and long-lasting. Accordingly, "it seems reasonable to assume that the more marital partners' projections of the future contain each other, the more they will engage in behaviours that sustain their marriage" (Thompson-Hayes and Webb, 2004, p. 258). Thus, when projected longevity in marital relationship enhances, it is likely that the personal commitment to the marriage will increase. Moreover, increased projected longevity has a positive impact on the partners' dependence on each other and on the marriage, and as a result, commitment increases.

In a similar fashion, Agnew et al. (1998) present data showing that commitment and a couple's interdependence mutually influence each other. That is, when marital partners imagine themselves growing together, it results, in part, from their future-oriented dialogues (talks they have about the future of their marriage and its longevity). Through this discourse, partners solidify and strengthen their union and their commitment to their marriage in that they share a vision and a future plan for the course they wish their life together to take (Dickson, 1995).

Byrd's (2009) articulation of a theoretical framework of marital commitment presents a multidimensional view that emphasizes multifaceted components. These are the (1) value rational component and the (2) practical component. Participants in Byrd's study viewed marital commitment through the value relational component, which captured marriage as being a desired and valued resource for social status and identity, an expected life course to be implemented, and a core religious or moral dictate to follow. Those viewing marriage through the practical prism of commitment referred to the obstacles to attaining commitment. This conceptualization focuses on the barriers that restrain and obstruct partners' development of marital commitment and how to overcome these barriers (Byrd, 2009).

Levinger (1999) outlined a guiding paradigm for marital stability and commitment that suggests the notion that forces leading toward the maintenance of marital relationships, or its dissolution, come from attraction, barriers, and alternative availability. Levinger calls his model "the attraction-barrier model of relational cohesiveness" (p. 41). Basically, there are positive and restraining motivational forces that encourage or deter a person's movement towards or away from a partner and a relationship. The attraction component of a relationship consists of behavioral interactions and emotions that if sufficiently present will strengthen and maintain commitment. Attraction forces in a marital relationship are linked to the rewards that partners perceive they are getting from the marriage, including love, respect, nurturance, security, and consensual validation (Levinger, 1999).

The dimension of the barriers that impact relational commitment is an accumulation of the restraining factors that deter a spouse from dissolving an unsuccessful and dysfunctional marital union. Barriers take the form of socio-cultural pressures to remain in an unrewarding marriage, threats of social stigma against being divorced, high financial expenditures of divorce processes and procedures, the children's well-being, and a lack of potential alternatives that seem to be more rewarding. Irretrievable resources invested in the marital relationship are also considered a barrier against leaving an unfulfilling marital relationship (Johnson, 1991). As can be easily noted, commitment to a marriage that is motivated by attraction forces is of a personal nature, indicating that one wants, wholeheartedly, to remain in the marriage out of strong attraction to, and out of love for, one's partner. In contrast, commitment to marriage that is based on barriers against divorce indicates that one is trapped in the relationship without any better, more rewarding relational alternatives.

Michael Johnson (1999) has articulated the definition, meaning, and construct of commitment using a three-part model to specify and describe three essential types of marital commitment. These three types of commitment are: *personal commitment, moral commitment,* and *structural commitment* (Johnson, 1999; Johnson, Caughlin, and Huston, 1999).

Personal Commitment

Personal commitment is basically the sense of wanting to stay in a relationship. This dimension is close to Levinger's (1999) notion of the attraction force of commitment, and it reflects a person's dedication and attachment to the partner, a motive that draws married couples emotionally closer to each other. This subjective psychological experience of partners' bonding and attachment, reflected in personal commitment, generates in couples a positive drive and energizes them to strengthen, enhance, and maintain their marriage.

Johnson (1999) identified three elements of personal commitment. In doing so, he makes a distinction between one's attraction toward a partner and one's attraction towards the relationship he is in. Both directions of attraction point to the individual wanting to stay in a marital relationship and to continue his personal involvement and investment in the relationship so as to maintain, enhance, and improve it.

The third component of personal commitment is what Johnson calls "relationship identity" or "couple identity" (Johnson, Caughlin, and Huston, 1999). It means that when one is personally committed to one's marriage, it becomes integrated into one's self identity and concept. This personal involvement in one's close relationship is a forceful drive to want to stay in the relationship.

Moral Commitment

Moral commitment relates to one's feeling that one is morally obligated to stay in a marital relationship even if it is not personally rewarding or satisfying (Johnson, 1999). Thus staying in such an unrewarding marriage is not so much a personal choice, but rather a dedication to a moral, socially sanctioned vow that must be kept. Obviously, a moral commitment is not the creation of a loving, self-fulfilling, close attachment that exists between two lovers, but rather the result of a set of values regarding dissolution and divorce. Marriage, according to the moral commitment type, ought to last "till death do us part" (Johnson, 1999).

Structural Commitment

Structural commitment stems from socio-cultural or familial pressures and constraints prohibiting an individual from dissolving a nonrewarding relationship. This sense of constraint erects barriers to withdrawing from unsatisfying marriages.

Structural commitment becomes salient when the cohesive impact of personal and moral commitments reaches a low point. In such a case, "the components of a structural commitment will become salient and contribute to a sense of being trapped in the relationship and/or a feeling of being constrained by the costs of dissolution to remain whether one wants it or not" (Johnson, 1999, p. 75). Johnson's conceptualization of construct commitment consists of four components, the first of which is the attractiveness of an alternative to the current marital relationships that an individual perceives to be available for her, if and when she dissolves the primary relationship. Johnson (1999) relies on Thibaut and Kelley's (1959) model of Comparison Level of Alternatives, referring to the best alternative available to a person outside her current, primary marriage. Accordingly, one may decide to stay in an unrewarding marriage if the best relational alternative is worse than the current one. Aside from the availability and attractiveness of an alternative partner, one's decision to stay or leave a primary relationship also depends on economic issues, housing, child custody arrangements, and other constraining factors.

The second constraining component of structural commitment is the socio-cultural and familial anticipated pressures, which may cause one to feel trapped in an unrewarding relationship; "to the extent that such pressures come from people whose opinion matter, one may feel constrained to continue a relationship even where one feels little moral or personal commitment" (Johnson, 1999, p. 76). The difficulties and complexities of the processes required to end a marital relationship is another, third, component of constraint against leaving a relationship.

Finally, the fourth component of constraint involves what Johnson (1999) called irretrievable investments, which relate to the perceived sense that one has about the enormous investment put into the marriage that would be wasted if the marriage dissolves. Some people may be reluctant to leave even an unsatisfying relationship because they would then see their initial "investment" in the relationship as having been wasted (see also Lund, 1985).

Each of the three types in Johnson's (1999) model of relational commitment may impact marital persistence and continuity. Which of these three dimensions of commitment is salient at a certain point in time, however, determines marital quality and satisfaction. Adams and Spain (1999) observed that "even though the spouses may indicate that their motivation to remain together derives from their personal desire for union, structural commitment may also be growing around the relationship, forming a barrier against dissolution" (p. 167). This view is somewhat different from Johnson's (1999) conclusion that structural commitment becomes relevant to and is implicated in decisions to maintain or dissolve a relationship only when both personal and moral commitments decline significantly. In other words, when a marriage deteriorates and become distressful, and the personal commitments of the spouses is considerable questioned, only then might the awareness of the spouses be transformed to other commitment types that still have the power to sustain even an unrewarding relationship.

A prominent conceptualization of marital commitment is found in Rusbult's (1983; Rusbult, Wieselquist, Foster, and Witcher, 1999) Investment Model, which includes principles and theoretical constructs of Independence Theory (Kelley, 1983; see Rusbult et al., 1999 for major components of the Independence Model). The investment model suggests that commitment is a major motivation in marital relationships that promotes pro-relationship behaviors, such as one's "willingness to depart from immediate self-interest for the good of a relationship" (Rusbult et al., 1999, p. 433). Strong marital commitment motivates relationship persistence and longevity as well as inclinations to engage in a variety of costly and effortful relational maintenance. Commitment level is an assessment of the extent to which one shows intent to persist in a marriage and becomes emotionally attached to one's spouse. Moreover, commitment is a psychological state that globally represents the experience of dependence on a relationship, representing feelings of attachment to a partner and a desire to continue and maintain the relationship for better or worse. Thus, commitment is a subjective state, including both cognitive and emotional components, which, in turn, influence a wide range of behaviors in an ongoing relationship (Rusbult and Buunk, 1993; see also Arriaga and Agnew, 2001).

Rusbult's Investment Model of marital commitment (Rusbult, 1983; Rusbult et al., 1999) consists of three core determinants: satisfaction level, quality of alternative, and investment size. The first component, satisfaction level, refers to the degree of gratifying personal benefits and rewards that one receives from one's marital relationship and the extent to which core needs are fulfilled (e.g. love, belonging, affection, appreciation, companionship, and sexual needs). A person's satisfaction is high when the outcomes resulting from the marital interactions and involvement are gratifying.

Quality of alternatives, the second component of the Investment Model, is the perceived desirability and availability of alternatives to the current unrewarding, unsatisfying marriage one is in. One will stay in an unrewarding marriage when there are no suitable alternatives available or if the alternatives are poor and unattractive compared with the current relationship.

The third component of the Investment Model of relationship commitment is investment size, referring to the amount and value of resources that one has invested in one's marriage. The greater the investment (time, material, and emotional resources; raising children; etc.) that went into the union, the more likely it is that one will remain in the relationship.

Rusbult et al. (1999) maintained that commitment is a key component in inducing communal, pro-relationship motivation and behavior. The authors outlined several features that are found in marital commitment that account for the pro-relationship behavior of partners. Firstly, the enhanced pro-relationship behavior found among highly committed marital partners stems from the interdependent nature of their interactions and the mutual need they have for their marriage .As discussed earlier, being interdependent indicates that both partners invested personal and other resources into the relationship that provide both with desirable benefits and rewards. Since highly committed individuals need their relationships, we can expect that they would be more willing to forgo immediate self-interests and engage in costly relationship building behaviors in order to sustain the union.

Secondly, committed partners hold persisting, long-term visions and orientations of their marriage, considering not only immediate relationship situations, but looking beyond them into the future well-being of their marriage. This long-term futurist involvement induces and aids in developing pro-relationship patterns of motivation and behavior in order maximize long-term marital outcomes.

The third feature found in the pro-relationship behavior of committed partners is that it involves deep, emotional attachment to the other, to the extent that self-interest and the partner's interest become inseparable. In other words, a strong personal commitment is associated with communal orientation, motivating one to be willing to invest and endure personal costs and even discomfort, so as to respond positively to one's partner's needs without the score-keeping that counts what one receives in return.

Adams and Spain (1999) view relate relational commitment as a developing, dynamic construct that is manifested by variability throughout the course of the marital life cycle. When examining marital commitment, they observed, one has to examine the ways in which the various dimensions of the commitment interact in order to promote relationship stability.

Reviewing the preceding commitment models, Adams and Spain (1999) found a shared theme indicating that commitment is not simply a state in which those who are romantically involved find themselves when their relationship becomes more intimate. Rather, it is dynamic, evolves over the course of a relationship, and seems to change, grow, or decrease as spouses get closer together or drift farther apart.

In the conceptual framework developed by Stanley and Markman (1992; Stanley, Lobitz, and Dickson, 1999), commitment is viewed as a two-factor phenomenon consisting integratively of personal dedication and constraint commitment elements. The model views personal dedication as the desire to maintain or improve the quality of a given relationship for the benefit of both participants (Stanley et al., 1999). Two identified, interrelated elements are involved in the personal dedication component; these are the persistence on continuing the dyadic relationship and the willingness to invest in the relationship and to sacrifice for it so as to maintain and enhance the partner's and relationship's welfare. In addition, personal dedication is characterized by linking one's personal needs, life goals, and achievements to the relationship and by behaving communally toward one's spouse (Markman et al., 1999).

In contrast, the constraint component of commitment is related to the forces that constrain people to remain in relationships regardless of how dedicated they are to them (Stanley and Markman, 1992). Factors that encourage spouses to remain in a relationship regardless of its quality and the extent of one's personal dedication arise from external or internal pressures (economic and emotional costs of divorce and social and familial pressure to maintain an unrewarding marriage).

The dimensions incorporated in Stanley and Markman's (1992) conceptualization of personal dedication come from various existing models. These are:

1. *Relationship agenda.* Referring to how strongly one personally wants one's marriage to persist over the long run. This aspect of commitment stems from positive feelings that one has toward one's partner based on a strong attachment bond, mutual attraction, and intimacy (found also in Levinger's (1999) Attraction-Barrier model of commitment).

2. *Primacy of relationship.* This component "refers to the priority level that the relationship holds in a person's hierarchy of activities" (Stanley and Markman, 1992, p. 596). Personal dedication and commitment to marriage motivates spouses to put their relationship on top of their priorities, working together as a team for the benefits of their relationship so as to constantly improve and enhance its quality and stability.

3. *Couple's identity.* This source of the personal dedication component of commitment refers to the degree to which an individual thinks of the relationship as a team rather than as two separate individuals, who are each trying to maximize their individual gains. The team approach to marriage shows both partners playing a significant role in developing and shaping a unique identity of togetherness and we-ness.

4. *Satisfaction with sacrifice.* This component of commitment relates to the feeling of satisfaction that a partner senses in acting benevolently for the benefit of his spouse, even if it requires sacrificing his personal interests. This dimension of relational

commitment can be found in a communal marital relationship where partners look after each other and care for each other's welfare, and both spouses show strong motivation to be responsive to each other's needs (Mills and Clark, 2001).

5. *Alternative monitoring.* Describes the partners' examination of potential alternatives to their marriage. The existence of an attractive potential alternative for a partner in an unrewarding marriage is likely to reduce one's personal dedication to a current relationship.

6. *Meta-commitment.* This final attribute of personal dedication refers to one's commitment to commitment. This is unrelated to a particular relationship but is a value the individual may bring to a relationship (Stanley and Markman, 1992).

Stanley et al. (1999) conducted a thorough review of the literature in support of the personal dedication aspect of commitment. They found personal dedication to be associated with marital quality and satisfaction, the amount of investment made by partners, and their confidence in being able to handle the future in the right way as a couple. The authors concluded that the personal dedication component of commitment is a more reliable predictor of future relationship quality, satisfaction, and stability than the constraint component of commitment. This is due to the nature of personal dedication to one's marriage, which is associated with marriage enhancing interactive behaviors and attitudes.

Commitment and Attachment

According to attachment theory, romantic partners' feelings of love, intimacy, attraction, and relational commitment are all a reflection of attachment-related mechanisms (Morgan and Shaver, 1999). Adults in close marital relationships exhibit the same major attachment behavioral patterns found in a person's early years of life (see review by Feeney, 1999). Simpson (1990) examined the impact of attachment style (secure, anxious, avoidance) on subjects' experience of commitment to a romantic relationship. The findings show that securely attached partners experience and show stronger relational commitment, whereas those with high avoidant attachment style were found to be significantly less committed. Anxious attachment was also found to be associated with a lesser commitment level. Similar findings are reported by Pistol, Clark, and Tubbs (1995). Rusbult (1983) also views relational commitment through an attachment model lens, indicating that commitment is the partners' intent to stay in a close relationship, a motivation rooted in one's emotional attachment to the relationship. Sacher and Fine (1996) support Rusbult's (1983, 1991) view by indicating that relational commitment, by definition, is one's attachment to a partner that produces a desire and intent to stay in a relationship and continue to maintain and enhance it. Following a thorough review of research studies, Morgan and Shaver (1999) concluded that attachment style is closely related to people's approach to marital commitment, with anxious people tending to make commitments quickly and easily, while people who experienced avoidant attachment in their past showed hesitation to invest fully in relationships. Consequently, commitment level and relational endurance and longevity can be predicted by attachment mechanisms. Also, commitment and attachment are two relational variables that are interrelatedly reciprocal. This means that major changes in relationship quality and status (e.g. divorce) may have an impact on attachment style "with people in committed relationships tending to move toward security, and people experiencing a divorce or breakup becoming less secure" (Morgan and Shaver, 1999, p. 122). Also, securely attached people are likely to enter close, romantic relationship with a tendency to comfortably accept the interdependent nature of the relationship and to relate intimately with their partners (Simpson, 1990). Hazan and Shaver (1987), in a similar direction, found that securely attached individuals are likely to be involved in relationships characterized by a close, intimate interplay of emotions, trust, and friendship.

Individual Traits Affecting Marital Success

There is a wide range of individual traits and personality characteristics that contribute to marriage outcomes. Some act as a liability to marriage, in that they predict marital dysfunction, while others are an asset, in that they foster and enhance marital quality and success. There is growing empirical research that suggests that partners' psychological problems are intricately associated with marital discord (Whisman, Uebelacker, and Weinstock, 2004). As early as 1938, Terman and his associates posited that certain personality characteristics predispose a person to having low relational satisfaction (Terman et al., 1938). In general, individual characteristics associated with marital outcomes consist of personal traits (anger, impulsivity, dependence); attitudes and values regarding marriage and intimacy; flexible and realistic expectations; skills in coping with stress; interpersonal skills; and emotional functioning and stability (neuroticism, anxiety, depression, self esteem) (Larson, 2003). Amato and Previty (2003) found that personality factors are the cause of divorce in 10% of people from U.S. National data collected during 1980-1997.

Another personal component affecting marital relationships is Bowen's (1978) differentiation of the self-concept. This concept refers to the individual's ability to actively and reactively immerse in an intimate marital relationship while maintaining the sense of one's self intact. Detachment from one's family of origin in order to develop an intimate, committed relationship is an important component of Bowen's differentiation of the self-concept. A mature and adequate differentiation, however, does not mean a complete detachment from one's family of origin. It is within a person's ability to develop and maintain autonomy while being emotionally involved with a romantic partner. Mature, intimate connectedness involves one's ability to be emotionally involved with, and intimately close to, one's partner without losing one's self-identity (Lester and Lester, 1998). This implies that self-awareness and identity development are crucial ingredients in one's capacity for partaking in intimate relations (Patrick et al., 2007). Couples with high self-differentiation are better capable of developing successful and satisfying intimate marital relationships. They are also capable of adequately managing inevitable conflicts and problems in their marriages (Patrick et al., 2007).

Beach, Kamen, and Fincham (2006) found two out of the "five-factor" personality model to be associated with marital outcomes: (1) *conscientiousness*, which relates to a person's self-discipline, orderliness, responsibility, and persistence when temporary obstacles are encountered; concentration on the task at hand; prioritization of self-regulation; and lastly, goal attainment over other competing wishes and demands (Mikulincer and Shaver, 2007b).

This self-control, regulating capacity of the conscientiousness personality factor promotes a person's ability to attain important life goals, such as facilitating the accomplishment of a well-functioning, well-adjusted marital relationship (Bouchard et al., 1999). In contrast, deficient conscientiousness leads to marital dysfunction and discord. For example, men who are low on conscientiousness have a higher tendency to be verbally and physically abusive and to resort to alcoholism in the face of marital conflict or difficulties, which in turn increases the level of conflict, tension, and marital discord (Hart, Dutton, and Newlove, 1993).

(2)The second personality factor, found by Beach et al. (2006) to be associated with marital outcomes, is *neuroticism*. This factor relates to a person's generalized tendency to experience negative moods, distress, sadness, anxiety, discomfort, and disturbing emotions of anger, guilt, and dissatisfaction (Karney and Bradbury, 1997). As expected, a high degree of neuroticism is associated with low marital quality and dissatisfaction and with marital dissolution and divorce (Kurdek, 1993).

Individual traits that predict marital outcomes such as marital success can also be viewed through the lens of attachment theory, which has been extensively utilized in the study of close relationships (Collins, Guichard, Ford, and Feeney, 2004). Most of the research in this field has focused on individual differences in attachment style and their impact on relational outcomes. There is consistent and strong empirical evidence that shows an association between attachment insecurity and lower commitment to marital relationship and marital distress (see review in Mikulincer and Shaver, 2007b). Pistol, Clark, and Tubbs (1995) found differences between anxious and avoidant individuals regarding the degree of their investment in close relationships. Although partners with both anxious and avoidant styles showed relatively low levels of relational commitment, anxious partners invested significantly more in the relationship than avoidant partners. Mikulincer and Shaver (2007b) suggested that this implied that anxious people's lack of commitment stems from the disappointment, pain, and frustration that they have encountered, whereas avoidant people's lack of commitment stems from their unwillingness to invest in an enduring relationship.

Larson (2003) found that vulnerability to stress and deficient stress management skills, excessive impulsivity (acting without proper thinking about the consequences of the actions on the other), anger and hostility shown through hurting one's partner's feelings regularly, and untreated depression, anxiety, and low self-esteem, are all personal traits that may predict marital dissatisfaction.

RELATIONAL INTERACTIVE TRAITS AFFECTING MARRIAGE

Communication in Marriage

A considerable amount of empirical evidence attests to the importance of communication for marital success and stability (Fincham, 2004). Marital functioning and success is defined by many as a reflection of partners' communication quality (Whisman, 1997; Vangelisti, 2004). Effective communication skills distinguish between distressed and nondistressed couples, and poor conflictual communication, especially during conflict, is linked to poor immune system response and elevated stress-related hormonal reaction (Kelley, Fincham, and Beach, 2003).

Carroll, Badger, and Young (2006) presented a multidimensional model of marital competence, comprised of two core domains: intrapersonal competence and interpersonal competence. The former is composed of individual capacities such as the ability to love, adequate self-esteem, ability to emotionally regulate, and ability to form a secure attachment. The interpersonal competence domain consists of what the authors call "effective negotiation" capacities such as conflict resolution skills, ability to clearly express of ideas and feelings, and listening skills.

A high level of communication competence is considered a marital protective factor, whereas deficient communication competence is a marital risk factor (Markman, 1979). Gottman (1999a) observed that "in ailing marriages people generally communication very clearly, but what they communicate is mostly negative" (p. 16). Gottman (1994b) found that the interactive communication behavior of distressed, unhappy, couples showed enhanced levels of negative interaction and affect, less humor and laughter, fewer agreements and compliance, and more disagreement, criticism, and put downs. Similarly, Pick and Sillar (1985) observed that marital communication is conceived "in terms of the contingent relationship between acts. That is, getting along is less a matter of how you act than how you respond" (p. 303). Distressed couples' communication during conflict is characterized by cross-complaining interactive sequences (complaint-counter-complaint sequences), thus escalating conflict, while happy and successful couples tend to communicate in a manner that resolves conflicts adequately, thus soothing and de-escalating conflict and tension.

Ballard-Reisch and Weigle (1999) identified several relationship enhancement behaviors that characterize a positive and effective marital communication environment. These include the couple's attempts to avoid destructive interactions, attempts to repair stressful situations, acting in a manner that rejuvenates the marriage, and keeping the relationship at a high satisfaction level. Ballard-Reisch and Weigle concluded that fundamental to the achievement of these marital enhancing goals is an effective communication process.

Sexual Satisfaction and Marital Communication

Longitudinal research shows positive association between partners' sexual enjoyment and satisfaction and communication (Litzinger and Gordon, 2005). It was found that when couples learned to communicate, their sex lives improved (Chesny et al., 1981). Litzinger and Gordon (2005) describe potential links between marital sexuality and communication with a special emphasis devoted to interactive communication during conflict. It appears that unresolved conflicts, which arise from poor communication skills, are a source of sexual dissatisfaction and dysfunction, which in turn increase marital relationship conflict.

Communication Measures

There are various measurements used in research and clinical practice to assess communication components. Examining these measurements provides additional understanding of what is considered an effective and ineffective communication in couples' relationships. DeTurck and Miller (1986) developed the conjugal understanding measure that conceptualizes social cognition in marital communication. Through this 12 item instrument, communication is assessed by the level of openness that exists in a couple's interactions and the confidence they share in raising and discussing personal, intimate feelings and thoughts. A sample of items that measure this component includes: "I find it hard to tell my husband (wife) certain things because I am not sure how he (she) will react," "I feel confident that I know how my husband (wife) would react if I told him (her) the most intimate details about myself," and "My spouse and I cannot talk about our communication problems."

Cognitions related to marital communication are measured by items such as, "To really know a person you have to be aware of all his (her) values and beliefs," or "In order to understand why a person feels the way he (she) does about things, it is vital to get to know the person as an individual."

Ease, comfort, and openness in expressing feelings is an important component of the ENRICH (1993) effective communication skills program. Items that measure these communication variables are: "It is very easy for me to express all my true feelings to my partner," "I am sometimes afraid to ask my partner for what I want," and "I wish my partner was more willing to share his/her feelings with me." Another aspect of marital communication depicted in this measurement is the partner's response, demonstrated in items such as, "My partner sometimes makes comments which put me down" or "I do not always share negative feelings I have because I am afraid he/she will get angry."

The Kansas Marital Goals Orientation Scale (2000) is another communication measurement instrument. This scale focuses mainly on the frequency through which partners communicate with each other to discuss relationship related issues, such as the future of their marriage, changes that ought to be made to enhance the relationship, and agreements on long-term goals. These and other topics are evaluated by items such as: "How often do you and your husband discuss the primary objectives you have for your marriage," "How often do you and your husband make a deliberate effort to learn more about you so he can be more pleasing to you," and "How often do you and your partner discuss the primary objectives for your marriage?"

Powers and Hutchinson (1979) constructed the Personal Report of Spouse Communication Apprehension (PRSCA). This 30 item instrument reveals the various areas of communication difficulties and limitations a couple might encounter. PRSCA covers the following communication points of concern:

1. The degree of apprehension or hesitation that marital couples may encounter that inhibits open, assertive communication. This is covered by items such as: "I feel strained and unnatural when trying to maintain a conversation with my spouse," "I feel no apprehension at verbalizing my intimate reaction to my spouse," "I am hesitant to develop a 'deep' conversation with my spouse," and "I don't hesitate to tell my spouse exactly how I feel."

2. The willingness and motivation to communicate, is covered in representative items such as: "I look forward to expressing my opinion to my spouse on controversial topics," "I look forward to discussing with my spouse those aspects of our relationship most important to me," and "I usually come right out and tell my spouse exactly what I mean."

3. Openness that exists in the marital communication is depicted by items such as: "I feel that I am more fluent in talking with my spouse than most other people are" and "I never find it difficult to express my true feelings to my spouse."

Feeney, Noller, and Ward (1997) developed the Quality of Dyadic Interaction Scales that yielded five factors. Relevant to our present discussion, it was noted that the quality of communication effectiveness "was generally seen as a particularly crucial aspect of marital relationship" (p. 187). The items loading highest on the factor of communication effectiveness relate to partners being very understanding of each other and partners being able to relate to one another's feelings and thoughts. Sample items are: "My partner is unable to relate to my thoughts and feelings" and "My partner and I are able to communicate effectively with one another."

Noller and Feeney (1998) identified four components that constitute quality communication: marital couples engage openly in self-disclosure (revealing to each other personal feelings and thoughts), partners recognize each other's points of view when communicating, partners' satisfaction with their interactive behavior, and partners accept and validate the other's position throughout a discussion.

Conflicts in Marital Relationships

Another predictor of marital outcome is spouses' interactive behavior during conflicts and disagreements. Of all the factors that Larson (2003) presents and discusses in his book, *The Great Marriage Tune-Up Book*, communication and conflict resolution skills are considered two of the most important predictors of marital outcomes.

Three assumptions have guided researchers in the field of marital conflict (Ridley, Wilhelm, and Surra, 2001).

1. Conflicts and disagreements occur inevitably from time to time even in the most gratifying, congenial relationship. Spouses face conflictual situations as a normative facet of normal, day-to-day interactions.
2. Conflicts are neither negative nor positive in nature, and they can be dealt with constructively or destructively.
3. Conflict is conceptualized as an interactive process. It is studied in terms of its marital relationship outcomes, whether or not conflicts are resolved, the manner of conflict resolution, and the extent to which conflict processes increase or decrease closeness and intimacy between spouses.

Cahn (1992) also views marital conflicts as a process and not incompatibility between partners or partner opposition. A marital conflict is an enduring or persistent element of interaction that develops over time. It is thus a process rather than a onetime occurrence. Cahn (1992) reviewed the relational outcomes of various conflict management strategies and their relative contributions to intimate relationships, and observed that marital successes is related to open, effective communication in managing conflicts. Couples in successful marriages, compared to distressed couples, are more likely to openly discuss conflicts and difficulties and are less likely to disengage conflictual issues or stop talking about them. In addition, the direct, assertive resolution of conflicts tended to promote marital interdependence and emotional closeness and intimacy.

Combs and Avrunin's (1988) model of conflict progression illustrates conflict as a process. The model encompasses three identifiable stages: (1) when a rupture in marital consensus occurs, partners are experiencing a conflict resulting from a choice between incompatible options and (2) the conflict becomes real and noticeable when the partners reveal out in the open their opposing needs, desires, or opinions. At this stage, the partners are under the impression that their differences are resolvable. (3) At a certain point in the discussion, when the partners realize that there is no mutually acceptable resolution, the unresolved conflict becomes a threat to the relationship balance. At this stage of conflict progression, relational interests are replaced by self-centered interest. This leads partners to a power struggle and to the polarization of opinions. This progression views conflicts as exhibiting relational distress that is more closely related to how a couple manages conflict regardless of its actual content, thus providing the basis for the deterioration of the marriage (Ridley et al., 2001). It is commonly accepted that one of the most salient reasons for marital distress is spousal aversive response to conflictual situations and deficient conflict resolution skills (Fincham and Beach, 1999). For example, when partners respond to a conflictual event in a positive, functional manner, it promotes intimacy and increases the likelihood of adequate conflict resolution (Cahn, 1990). In contrast, a destructive response to conflicts and disagreements is likely to create negative effects on the relationships (Fincham and Beach, 1999).

Coercion and manipulation interactive responses to conflict were also found to result in negative relationship outcomes. According to Paterson and Hope (1972), "coercion involves the simultaneous operation of positive and negative reinforcement. One partner applies aversive stimulation to the other until the other complies" (Christensen and Walczynski, 1997, p. 256). More specifically, coercion (the use of threats, rewards, intimidation, rejection, and disapproval to create feelings of guild) develops when one partner behaves negatively to achieve personal benefits, and the other, due to "emotional blackmail" is coerced and complies involuntarily, contrary to her wish. Repeating this interactive exchange over time results in both partners becoming habituated to the coercive and manipulative interaction (Christensen and Walczynski, 1997). Additionally, repeated coercive exchange results over time in the relationship becoming increasingly marked by tension and emotional distance. To add insult to injury, partners who become habituated to coercive interactions also develop negative attributions to explain the causes of the negativity in the other (Christensen and Walczynski, 1997). Eventually, the cause of the conflict that started this negative exchange is set aside and the couple expands their escalating argument to motives and personal vilification of one another's characteristics. Coercive and vilifying exchange cause partners to polarize their positions of the conflict. As one partner is deprived of achieving what he wants, he escalates the tension by becoming more insisting, more pressing. The deprived need (e.g. going to a social event) becomes more intensively and forcefully elaborated on and justified.

In response to the increased pressure by the seemingly deprived partner, the other partner is compelled to more strongly defend and justify her view on the conflict at hand. As a result of the initial coercive exchange and the accompanied vilification and polarization processes, partners may appear even more opposing than they were initially (Christensen and Walczynski, 1997). This is how unresolved marital conflicts set the stage for the escalation of conflict and tension. As indicated previously, a rupture in marital consensus creates a conflictual situation to be dealt with by the partners. The resulting conflict, manifested by differences in opinions or perceptions, might potentially create tension as an argument escalates to a bitter fight. If constructively motivated, partners are likely to resolve the conflict through proactive and respectful interaction. Again, conflicts, in and of themselves, do not necessarily damage the relationship but rather it depends on how the spouses manage their conflicts (Canary, Cupach, and Messman, 1995).

One pattern of interactive exchange during conflict that tends to result in tension escalation is the demand-withdraw pattern (Eldridge and Christensen, 2002). This interactive pattern is characterized by one spouse who criticizes, blames, and presses demands on the other who in return withdraws (usually to avoid confrontation) and becomes defensive (Eldridge and Christensen, 2002).

An example for such exchange is when one partner repeatedly complains to the other about not having enough time together so that they may enjoy closeness, adding how must he resents the other being distanced and uncaring. Raising this demand for increased closeness may start a "demand-withdraw" cycle in which the other (whose behavior was just criticized) withdraws, thus being perceived as even more distant. Usually, demand-withdraw interaction is a repetitive pattern as opposed to an isolated behavior. Research attests to the potential destructive nature of the demand-withdraw interactive exchange on marital relationships (Eldridge and Christensen, 2002). Roberts and Krokoff (1990) examined demand-withdraw interactions among married couples and found that in distressed marriages, men's withdrawing behavior during conflict was predictive of women's display of negative affect and hostility.

Conflict Management Styles

Cahn (1992) presents five conflict management styles representing alternative strategies for managing conflicts in close relationships. These are:

1. *Avoiding*: this is a lose-lose situation that results from partners avoiding conflicts instead of engaging in an interactive process to try and resolve them. Avoiding mode stems from both partners realizing that their desired interests cannot be accomplished by a discussion, therefore both of them acquiesce.
2. *Accommodating*: when one partner accommodates the other by yielding her self-centered interest to benefit the other, or the relationship (or in most events, both). This conflict management mode is operated when partners perceive that by continuing the conflict they cannot gain any positive outcomes.
3. *Competing*: this management style occurs when partners perceive they can gain individual benefits through the conflict. This mode eventually results in one partner forcing the other to give in so that she wins the desired benefits.
4. *Compromising*: when a partner sacrifices some self-centered outcomes in a certain conflict so as to gain other benefits not necessarily related to the current conflict. One settles for a compromise by losing potential rewards now in order to win some later in some other occasion.
5. *Collaborating*: both partners engage in the conflict, knowing they will end up resolving the conflict in a manner that both partners get the outcomes they desired.

Rusbult's adaptation of the Exit-Voice-Loyalty-Neglect model provides some insight into conflict management patterns found in marital relationships (Rusbult et al., 1998). This typology of possible reactions to dissatisfaction can also be used to better understand the interaction processes enacted by partners during conflict. The EVLN categorizes how partners behave when a threat to the relationship is imminent (Simpson, Ickes, and Orina, 2001). The model represents actual interactive behaviors representing response strategies that differ on two primary dimensions: (1) constructiveness vs. destructiveness and (2) activity vs. passivity (Rusbult et al., 1998). These key dimensions create four response categories, each representing a different behavior enacted by partners during conflict. These four categories are:

1) Exit (a destructive-active response) involves direct negative and avoiding actions during conflict, such as leaving the room; vilifying, harming, or abusing the partner; stone-walling; or threatening to leave.
2) Voice (constructive-active response) involves partners engaging the conflict, discussing possible solutions, attempting to influence a change through communal behaviors, and accepting influence by the partner throughout the attempt to find an adequate solution.
3) Loyalty (constructive-passive response) occurs when partners passively wait for the conflict or the problem to improve.
4) Neglect (destructive-passive response) involves avoiding the conflict and refusing to openly discuss issues relating to the conflict.

Partners' constructive responses (voice and loyalty) during conflict predict positive marital relationship outcomes such as marriage quality and satisfaction (Simpson, Ickes, and Orina, 2001). In contrast, using destructive responses (exit and neglect) is ineffective in managing conflicts and is associated with marital distress and dissolution. Moreover, "the EVLN model assumes that constructive behavior (voice and loyalty) can be used as preemptive relationship maintenance tactics to solve current problems, lessen their severity, or reduce the likelihood of future conflicts. In contrast, destructive behaviors (exit and neglect) are not regarded as preemptive tactics" (Simpson et al., 2001, p. 41). Rusbult (1993) found that using voice and loyalty responses in dealing with conflicts and marital disharmony promotes closeness and enhances the quality of the marriage.

Pietromonaco, Greenwood, and Feldman-Barrett (2004) take a positive view of dyadic conflicts, indicating that conflicts can be viewed not only as potential threats to marriage, but conflict also may provide an opportunity for enhancing marital intimacy and for improving a couple's communication. Disagreements give partners in successful marriages an opportunity to learn more about each other, a process that may enhance their closeness. In addition, open discussion about disagreements and conflicts may enhance a sense of marital stability and interpersonal security. This can be achieved when spouses manage conflicts in a communal manner by accepting each other's point of view despite their differences, and by revising thoughts, personal interests, and goals in order to promote harmonious interaction (Pietromonaco et al., 2004). Just as the perception of a conflict as a threat characterizes couples in distressed marriages, successful, well-functioning couples view conflict as a challenge to their relationship. We can also predict that partners in distressed marriages are guided by different goals when faced with conflicts than partners in happy marriages. Distressed couples are likely to be guided by self-centered, self-reliance goals for achieving personal, as opposed to relational outcomes (rewards, benefits). In contrast, partners in successful marriages are likely to be guided by relational goals for achieving outcomes that enhance and maintain relational closeness and intimacy (Noller and Feeney, 1998).

In this chapter, we attempted to illustrate that a successful marriage does not necessarily require that both partners be "heavenly angels" who are perfectly suitable and compatible for each other. What we would like to convey, both as researchers and clinicians, is that contrary to the common belief that marital incompatibility necessarily leads toward separation and divorce, partners can, indeed, become compatible by utilizing the variety of techniques and learning some of the behaviors illustrated above.

> There's only one way to have a happy marriage, and when I find it I will get married
> —Clint Eastwood

Chapter 15

MARITAL SATISFACTION

A man is incomplete until he is married. After that, he is finished.
—Zsa Zsa Gabor

Marriage, undoubtedly, is one of the most unique and sought after human experiences, entailing intimate connectedness, expectations, and interactional processes that can hardly be found in any other close relationship (Schoen and Weinick, 1993; Talbot, 1997). Marital happiness and satisfaction, however, are not a given considering the high rate of divorce and dissolution (Kitson, 2006). Paradoxically, the issue of divorce is raised and discussed as an option even in marriage counseling and therapy procedures (Lebow, 2008). Intuitively, the impact of marital satisfaction on dissolution seems well founded. In fact there are accumulating research findings that show a positive relationship between marital satisfaction and marital quality and stability (Rodrigues, Hall, and Fincham, 2006). Even with these results, though, there are many couples who remain in unhappy and unsatisfied marriages due to various intermediate variables such as insecure attachment styles, duration of marriage, religious and moral considerations, lack of alternatives, and other barriers against divorce (Johnson, 1999; Rodrigues et al., 2006).

The construct of marital satisfaction has been defined and measured in various ways (Fincham and Beach, 2006). A privileged position has been given to viewing marital satisfaction as a summative, subjective evaluation of the fulfillment of needs and desires that one receives from a close relationship (Levinger, 1997; Koski and Shaver, 1997). Another definition of relational satisfaction concerns a general, subjective partner's evaluation of the quality of his or her intimate relationship (Huston and Vangelisti, 1991).

The scientific study of the factors that contribute to marital satisfaction has occupied the attention of marriage and family scholars for several decades (Bradbury, Fincham, and Beach, 2000). As indicated, the intensive research that investigated the components of marital satisfaction stem primarily from the increased rate in dissolution and divorce. Another reason for studying marital satisfaction relates to the centrality of marriage's functioning to individual and family health and stability and the need to develop effective preventive marriage education programs and clinical interventions for couples counseling and therapy (Bradbury et al., 2000).

Clements, Cordova, Markman, and Laurenceau (1997) pointed at a paradox faced by relationship scholars. On one hand, there exists a common human need for love and romantic bonding yet there are so many close relationships that start with high mutual attraction and commitment and after awhile are a source of pain and dissatisfaction. Karney and Bradbury (1995) reviewed and analyzed over 120 published empirical studies that attempted to resolve this paradox by assessing a wide range of psychological, interactional, and contextual variables relating to marital satisfaction and the longitudinal course of its development, stability, and erosion (Halford and Moor, 2002). Some of these studies provide us with an understanding of the relational development processes that affect marital satisfaction.

Longitudinal studies of marital quality show that a spouse's satisfaction is universally quite high early in the marriage, gradually declining across the first five years of marriage (Kayser and Rao, 2006; Halford and Moor, 2002). Despite this typical decrease in marital satisfaction, a remarkable variability has been noted among couples, from those who develop a lifelong happy and stable relationship, to others living in distress, to yet others who separate and divorce (Halford and Moor, 2002). This trajectory in marital satisfaction emphasizes the importance of providing premarital education programs and counseling intervention for couples in the early years of marriage (Rodrigues, Hall, and Fincham, 2006).

Halford and Moor (2002) discussed some key factors that have an impact on marital satisfaction trajectory, one of which they called Adaptive Couple Processes (ACP). ACP relates to cognitive, behavioral, and affective processes in close relationship interactions. Deficits in these processes predispose couples to relational distress and dissatisfaction. For example, a dysfunctional couple's communication and maladaptive conflict management are identified as predictive of deterioration in marital satisfaction over time (Halford and Moor, 2002). Similarly, Kayser, and Rao (2006) found that conflict occurrence and the manner by which spouses engage in it are critical components in the development of marriage satisfaction. The authors caution that conflicts should be openly addressed by partners. Avoiding engagement in conflict resolution processes creates resentment, anger, and emotional distance between partners, which in turn threatens marital satisfaction and stability. More specifically, conflict interactive behaviors such as manipulation, criticism, coercion, and avoidance are detrimental to marital satisfaction (Kayser and Rao, 2006). Another set of interactive patterns predictive of marital dissatisfaction relates to spouses who display contempt, negativity, and withdrawal (Halford and Moor, 2002; Gottman, 1999a; Gottman and Levenson, 1992).

Working with couples in therapy, practitioners base part of their interventions on this reciprocity effect that exists between partners' investment in the relationship and marital commitment and satisfaction. For example, Gottman (1999a) made use of the concept of an "emotional bank account" (EBA) to encourage couples to invest positively in each other and in the relationship in order to promote positive exchange and a better, more enhancing marital climate and satisfaction. Generally, a "deposit" to a partner's EBA is any interaction that makes the other feel good, wanted, and appreciated. Gottman (1999a) refers to "deposits" in one's EBA as a way to promote positive exchange between spouses, outlining several interactional behaviors that can achieve this goal, such as showing genuine interest in one's partner, communicating, showing acceptance and understanding, listening attentively to a partner, validating the partner's feelings, and so forth. These positive interactive behaviors reveal good-will and a friendly turning toward one's partner as opposed to turning away from him. According to Gottman (1999a), these positive interactions are the foundation of marital relationship satisfaction that is based on fondness, admiration, and friendship, all of which create an exchange of positive affect in everyday interactions.

Observations from the interactive behavior of marital partners discussing disagreements or conflicts have been used by researchers to distinguish between satisfied and dissatisfied couples (Weiss and Heyman, 1990).

In general, as predicted, distressed and dissatisfied couples' interactions are much more negative in nature, exhibiting criticism, personal attacks, and blaming (Gottman and Levenson, 1992). Gottman and Levinson (1992) coded interaction behaviors of couples discussing conflictual relational issues. Based on these ratings, two groups of couples were identified: "regulated couples" in which both partners displayed positivity during conflictual interaction and "unregulated couples," where one or both partners displayed negativity during interaction. Participating couples were evaluated four years later and it was found that "regulated couples" were more satisfied in their marital relationship than "unregulated couples." The latter not only were less satisfied, but were also more likely to talk about and consider the option of divorce and showed higher rates of separation.

Gottman (1999a) observed and coded interactional behaviors of newlywed couples discussing conflict issues for 15 minutes. The results of this longitudinal study showed that the amount of positive interactions displayed by the observed couples was predictive of marital satisfaction six years later. Relating to what he called the "Positive Affect Model," Gottman (1999a) concluded that what characterizes happy and satisfied couples is their ability to display positive affect during conflict (showing care, affection, and interest; engaging in active listening, etc.)

It was also found that positive affect interactions during conflict discussion had a soothing and conflict de-escalating affect, changing the atmosphere during conflict discussion to be less negative. These positive affect interactions are more likely to exist among couples who are satisfied with their marital relationship.

Another well-established association between marital interactive behavior and marital satisfaction relates to negative affect reciprocity, an interaction in which a destructive behavior by one partner is followed by a negative response by the other (Weiss and Heyman, 1990). In dissatisfied couples, it is highly probable that a person's negative affect (attacking, blaming, vilifying) is evoked immediately after a destructive behavior is exhibited by her partner. In satisfied couples, this reciprocity of negativity hardly exists.

RELATIONAL INTIMACY AND SATISFACTION

Intimacy is a strong social goal sought after mostly in close marital relationships. A high degree of goal-directed activity in romantic relationships is focused on obtaining and enhancing relationship intimacy (Gable and Reis, 2001). Sanderson (2004) presented empirical evidence that shows a strong association between intimacy and relationship satisfaction. She noted that partners who engage in revealing personal feelings and thoughts to each other (promoting intimacy) experience high relationship satisfaction and stability. In contrast, couples who are lacking closeness and intimacy are likely to be dissatisfied. Undoubtedly, intimacy in marriage predicts relational satisfaction (Sanderson, 2004).

Sanderson and Cantor (1995) developed a 13 item self-report measurement scale to examine an individual's pursuit of intimacy goals in close relationships. Items relating to goals of intimacy were polled from the literature regarding self-disclosure, interdependence, and emotional attachment. Data was collected from 44 married couples to study the association between partners pursuing intimacy goals and relational satisfaction.

The results showed that partners who strongly focus on achieving intimacy goals experience higher levels of relational satisfaction than those with less focus on intimacy. This association between intimacy goals and relational satisfaction was found to exist regardless of the amount of time the partners spend together.

Individuals who rated high on relational intimacy goals provide more social support to their marital spouses, have greater influence on relational plans and goals, and have more positive thoughts about their partners and their relationship, thus promoting relational satisfaction. In addition, married people who focus strongly on relational intimacy goals are likely to feel satisfied from providing social support to their partners, more so than by receiving support (Sanderson, 2004). Also, people who show stronger intimacy goal orientation experience higher relational satisfaction partially due to their better ability to manage conflict in their relationship more effectively and in a benevolent manner (Sanderson, 2004).

Sanderson and Evans (2001) argue that individuals who focus on relational intimacy goals are likely to perceive their partners as having similar intimacy goal orientation. This is due mostly to the tendency to project one's traits, images, and perceptions on the partner (Sanderson and Carter, 1995). Association between this projection process and relationship satisfaction suggests that people who place high importance on the pursuit of intimacy goals are likely to be motivated to see their partner as having similar desire for intimacy. This perception enables partners to feel comfortable and safe in engaging in vulnerable disclosure of personal feelings, which in turn increases marital satisfaction (Sanderson and Cantor, 1995). Apparently, people who possess high intimacy goals are so intensively focused on promoting intimacy to the point that they view their partners through an intimacy lens. Again, this process enhances relational satisfaction. Empirical research supports this three layer association, i.e. strong intimacy goal orientation, perceiving partner as sharing intimacy goal, and relational satisfaction. It was found that women in close, romantic relationships who have strong intimacy goals projected these orientations upon their partners, a trend that predicted relational satisfaction (Sanderson, 2004). These results were also found in a sample of married couples, indicating that people who concentrate on achieving intimacy goals in their marital relationships perceive their partners as having a similar intimacy-focused desire. This reciprocity accounts for the association between intimacy goals and marital satisfaction (Sanderson, 2004).

Relational satisfaction can be promoted and enhanced not only through intimate verbal interactive transactions (e.g. self-disclosure of inner feelings). Apparently, there are other relational activities that are conducive to relational intimacy (therefore, also to satisfaction), such as partners sharing activities (Berscheid, Snyder, and Omoto, 2004). The amount of time marital partners spend together engaging in shared activities and interests is vitally important for promoting relational intimacy, quality, and therefore, satisfaction (Hill, 1988; Berscheid et al., 1989).

MARITAL COMMITMENT AND SATISFACTION

Adams and Jones (1999) suggest a three dimensional view of commitment of which one, the attraction dimension is related to marital satisfaction. As discussed earlier in this volume, the attraction dimension of commitment refers to a voluntary intention to remain in a (marital) relationship and a desire to promote and enhance it. The attraction aspect of relational commitment reflects a personal attraction to one's partner, who is viewed and perceived as a source of intimacy, love, and needs fulfillment (Adams and Jones, 1999) and with whom one enjoys a satisfying relationship.

The attraction dimension of marital commitment is associated with the rewarding and satisfying side of marriage that draws spouses together out of companionship, love, intimacy, and sexual enjoyment (Johnson, 1999; Levinger, 1999). Rusbult, Olson, Davis, and Hannon (2001) offer a model of relational commitment and satisfaction, depicting the strong and well founded association between marital quality and satisfaction and the attraction dimension of commitment. These authors use the Investment Model to suggest that when partners become interdependent on each other and on their relationship, they are likely to increasingly promote and enhance their attraction dimensional commitment. With increasing interdependence, marital spouses are motivated to intrinsically commit to each other; they develop a dyadic identity and strong emotional attachment, and they envision their marriage to persist well into the foreseeable future, all of which is highly connected to marital satisfaction (Rusbult et al., 2001). Also, partners become increasingly interdependent (and increasingly invested in one another and the relationship) when marital satisfaction is high (Adams and Jones, 1999). Thus, the link between and impact of these two commitment-related components (investment and satisfaction) are reciprocal. Namely, when marital satisfaction is high, it is highly likely that the partners would increase their investment (and their interdependence) in each other and in the relationship. In turn, a high investment level and high level of marital satisfaction are two key elements of marital commitment (Rusbult, Olsen, Davis, and Hannon, 2001; Davis, 1999).

ATTACHMENT PERSPECTIVE ON RELATIONAL SATISFACTION

Attachment theory as applied to adult romantic relationships (Hazan and Shaver, 1987) provides a well-documented framework to the understanding of individual, attachment-related needs (security, love, sexuality) that ought to be fulfilled to render relational satisfaction (Koski, and Shaver, 1997; Simpson, Campbell, and Weisberg, 2006).

Marital partners that provide sensitive, empathic, and supportive response to each other, especially in times of need, promote relational security and satisfaction (Collins, Guichard, Ford, and Feeney, 2006). Understanding and responding to the attachment needs of one's partner (providing felt security, a secure base, a safe haven) play a fundamental role in promoting and enhancing a high quality and satisfying marital bond (Koski and Shaver, 1997).

For example, a strong sense of relational felt security provides the necessary atmosphere for partners' exploratory activity, e.g. pursuing a career, fulfilling personal goals, engaging in leisure activities (Hazan and Shaver, 1990; Carnelley and Ruscher, 2000; Feeney, 2004).

When exploratory needs are generously met by a supporting and encouraging attachment figure (e.g. a marital partner), it promotes relational closeness, stability, and satisfaction (Feeney and Collins, 2004).

Attachment styles were found to be associated with marital quality and satisfaction (Koski and Shaver, 1997). Cohn, Silver, Cowan, Cowan, and Pearson (1992) found that couples with an attachment secured husband were better functioning and satisfied than couples with husbands with insecure attachment.

Also, the presence of one partner with a secured attachment style enhances the constructive marital interactions and marital satisfaction. Similarly, Hazan and Shaver (1987) found support for the predicted association between the partner's attachment style and romantic relationship satisfaction. Securely attached individuals described their experiences in close, romantic relationships as happy, friendly, and satisfying.

In contrast, insecure individuals characterized their close relationships by fear of intimacy, fear of abandonment, mistrust, and as dissatisfying. Kobak and Hazan (1991) measured two dimensions of attachment: reliance on one's partner and the partner's psychological availability, in relation to the quality of communication and marital satisfaction. Their results showed that a husband's and wife's reliance on each other and their ratings of their partner's psychological availability were linked to constructive communication and marital satisfaction.

Koski and Shaver (1997) outlined some implications for marital partners and couples therapists for promoting and enhancing marital satisfaction based on attachment constructs. These are:

1) Availability and sensitive responsiveness, which in turn enhances marital satisfaction.
2) Provide a partner a strong, secure base from which he can explore and undertake self-enhancing and challenging activities, and a safe haven to turn to at times of distress when he is in need of care and support. When marital spouses can rely on each other to provide both a secure base and safe haven, a felt security is promoted, leading to high relational quality and satisfaction.

Philosophy of Life and Relational Satisfaction

Hojjat (1997) developed a model of close relationship satisfaction in which the construct of *"Philosophy of Life"* (POL) plays a major role. POL is defined as the overall value system and basic beliefs and attitudes that a person possesses about the world, about one's self, and the interaction between the two. The basic premise of Hajjot's model is that "the satisfaction of partners in an intimate relationship is primarily related to the similarity in their basic beliefs and assumptions about the world around them, and also to the similarity in their beliefs about themselves relative to the world" (Hojjat, 1997, p. 103). Integral parts of a person's general POL regarding close, romantic relationships are the following components:

1) Beliefs and assumptions that a person holds as true regarding close, intimate relationships (e.g. women are more romantic than men, expressing feelings reflects weakness).

2) A person's view of the qualities of a desirable relationship (e.g. the importance of a partner's care giving and support).

3) Behavioral dictates regarding close relationships (e.g. leaving an unrewarding relationship). The POL model of relational satisfaction proposes that a partner's dissimilarity in basic beliefs, values, and assumptions regarding life and intimate relationships are detrimental to relational satisfaction. In other words, marital spouses who are similar to each other in terms of their POL are more likely to be happy and satisfied than those who are not. The association between partners' similarity in POL and relational satisfaction was supported by empirical research (Kenny and Acitelli, 1994; Craddock, 1994).

Another central component of the POL model is that the construct of relational satisfaction is not a static, one time partner's judgment. Rather, relational satisfaction is a dynamic, constantly developing, and changeable process that partners are actively involved in shaping. This view has been supported by more recent studies (Fincham and Beach, 2006). In view of the ever changing, dynamic maturation of close relationships, Hojjat (1997) concluded that "partners in satisfied relationships, who start their union with more congruent POLs will eventually develop a joint POL together" (p. 117). This is possible through ongoing, constant, interactive transactions between the relational partners.

Partner Support and Relational Satisfaction

There is growing research evidence that underlies the importance of a partner's supporting interactions for relational satisfaction (Berscheid and Reiss, 1988; Pasch, Bradbury, and Bradbury, 1998; Kurdek, 2005). Individuals receiving high measures of adequate support from their partners report high levels of relational satisfaction (Katz, Beach, and Anderson, 1996). A distinction is made between two measures of support: structural and functional. Whereas structural support refers mostly to objective, instrumental measures of a partner's supportive activities, functional support relates to psychological and emotional support provided by one's partner (Cohen and Wills, 1985). Berscheid and Reis (1988) offer a three-dimensional typology of relationship provisions: emotional partner's support provided through affection, intimacy, and love; appraisal support, which includes the provision of advice, helpful information, and feedback; and instrumental support, provided by material resources. All of these provisions are linked to marital satisfaction (see also Baxter, 1986; Cutrona, Russell, and Gardner, 2005).

Cutrona, Russell, and Gardner (2005) developed a Relationship Enhancement Model of social support that conceptualizes and examines the impact of support on the enhancement of the recipient's health and well-being within a close relationship context. According to this model, the health and well-being benefits gained by the recipient of support are influenced by the relational satisfaction associated with that support.

In other words, support enhances relational satisfaction and stability which in turn promotes the health and well-being of the support recipient partner. The model distinguishes between the amount of support interactions and the perception and interpretation of the support received by a partner. Accordingly, only supportive acts that are perceived as contributing and beneficial promote individual and relationship well-being and satisfaction.

This conception goes beyond the simple examination of the amount of support provided within the context of a close relationship to the evaluation of the adequacy of support transactions.

Love and Relational Satisfaction

Hendrick and Hendrick (1997) introduced love in their holistic conception of relational satisfaction. The authors suggest that Eros (passionate love characterized by emotional intensity, attraction, and high commitment) is associated with relational satisfaction in the early stages of relational development. Compassionate love (mature, steady, friendship-based love) is more likely to be linked to long-term marital bonding and satisfaction. The authors find compassionate love to be important for the development of connectedness, commitment, and intimacy, which are integral parts of relational satisfaction.

Sokolski (1995) examined 161 married couples on various variables (e.g. intimacy, communication, support, and love style) in order to explore predictors of marital satisfaction. As expected, Eros was found to be highly correlated with marital satisfaction for both men and women. The challenge that marital couples face is how to strengthen and keep their love so as to maintain a high level of satisfaction. Based on research data, Hendrick and Hendrick (1997) concluded that both passionate and compassionate love styles are the most salient predictors of relationship satisfaction.

Barnes and Sternberg (1997) studied the association between the construct of love and relationship satisfaction. The authors developed an integrative hierarchical model of love, using methodology that combined factor analysis and hierarchal analysis. Two clusters, described as compassionate love and passionate love, were assigned a superior rank:

1) The compassionate love clusters were Trust, Sincerity, Mutual understanding, Fulfillment, and Compatibility.
2) The passionate love clusters were Sexuality, Intimacy, and Mutual need. The results of Barns and Sternberg's (1997) study showed that all of the above listed clusters (describing compassionate and passionate love styles) were associated with relational satisfaction.

Fricker and Moor (2002) examined various love styles' impact on relational satisfaction. Their results showed that passionate love (Eros) had a positive effect on relational satisfaction, while the Ludus love style had a negative effect on relational satisfaction.

The Erosion of Relational Satisfaction

Christensen and Walczynski (1997) consider conflicts between couples to be an important variable that affects marital satisfaction. The frequency of conflictual situations and interactions between distressed and unsatisfied couples is much higher than in satisfied couples (Fincham, 2003). A distinction is made between two elements of conflict: (1) The structure of conflict, relating to the partners' incompatible needs, interests, or desires that create a conflict and (2) the process of conflict that is the interactive behavior enacted by the partners in dealing with the conflict or disagreement (Christensen and Walczynski, 1997).

Clements, Cordova, Markman, and Laurenceau (1997) found in longitudinal studies a steady decline in marital satisfaction over time. This decrease in marital satisfaction was found for both husbands and wives. The authors suggest that the decline in marital satisfaction over time relates not only to transitional stages in the family life cycle (e.g. the transition to parenthood) but more distinctly to the partners' patterns of interaction. Observational studies were conducted in an attempt to identify dysfunctional couples' interactive behaviors, especially during problem solving and conflict discussions (Fincham, 2003; Karney and Bradbury, 1995; Fincham and Beach, 1999).

Christensen and Walczynski (1997) consider conflicts between couples to be an important variable that affects marital satisfaction. The frequency of conflictual situations and interactions between distressed and unsatisfied couples is much higher than in satisfied couples (Fincham, 2003). A distinction is made between two elements of conflict: (1) the structure of conflict, relating to partners' incompatible needs, interests, or desires that create conflicts and (2) the process of conflict that is the interactive behavior enacted by the partners in dealing with the conflict or disagreement (Christensen and Walczynski, 1997).

In view of this line of empirical findings, Clements et al. (1997) developed their erosion theory of marital satisfaction. The author's conceptualization of the theory is based on the following assertions:

1) The first stage of marital relationship formation is commonly characterized by a high degree of love, attraction, commitment, intimacy, and satisfaction.
2) In time, all marital couples experience inevitable conflicts and disagreements in various relational areas (e.g. degree of closeness and intimacy, sexuality, family budgeting, child rearing, etc.).
3) The seeds of the erosion in relational satisfaction are to be found in the manner in which couples handle and manage conflicts and disagreements.
4) Distractive interactions during conflict erode the positive factors of marital satisfaction. Variables associated with destructive interactions predict marital outcomes (dissatisfaction) considerably better than components that characterize positive interactions.

In addition, Clements et al. (1997) outline several couples' interactive behaviors (some of which were previously discussed in this volume) that are detrimental to marital success and have an erosive impact on satisfaction. These are:

1. Discussions and arguments during conflicts and disagreements that escalate to heated fights with mutual criticism, blaming, vilification, and contempt.
2. Lack of partners' respect, acceptance, and validation of the other's feelings, needs, and desire.
3. Negative attributions of a partner's actions and viewing a partner's actions more negatively than she intended.
4. Partners deal with problems and difficulties as if they are on opposing, fighting teams, not as partners on the same friendly team.

5. Partners fearing criticism and invalidation refrain from sharing and disclosing personal thoughts, opinions, and feelings.
6. Partners seriously think about alternatives that are more attractive to their current marriage.
7. Partners feeling emotional loneliness within the marital relationship. That is, although being officially married, they feel emotionally neglected, unsupported, and all and all, alone and lonely.
8. The cycle of conflict and tension escalates due to a partner's withdrawal during arguments.

The erosion in marital satisfaction and stability gradually develops when these destructive interactive behaviors are repeatedly present in the marital relationship (Clements, et al., 1997). When this negativity accumulates over time, erosion in the positive elements of marital satisfaction (love, attraction, trust, commitment) is most likely to occur.

Schema-Focused View of Relational Satisfaction

The basic elements of the Schema-Focused Model (SFM) (Young, 1994; Young, Kloska, and Weishaar, 2003) were applied by Young and Gluhoski (1997) to the understanding of relational satisfaction. According to the model, a person develops relational schemas that include beliefs and mental representations regarding the self, the other (partner), and the interpersonal representations linking the self and the other (Waldinger, Diguer, Guastella, Lefebre, Luborsky, and Hauser, 2002; Baldwin, 1992). In other words, relational schemas are cognitive structures of internalized beliefs, perceptions of the self and the intimate partner, and patterns of interpersonal relatedness representations. Personal schemas of the self develop as a consequence of the fulfillment of core needs, beginning at an early age with further development over the lifespan. Unmet core needs develop Early Maladaptive Schemas (EMS) that lead to dysfunctional and maladaptive relational interactive behaviors, which in turn cause a decline in relational satisfaction (Young, 1994).

As noted, core needs fulfillment is a key element in the SFM of relational satisfaction. The core needs are categorized into various domains (Young, 1994), of which six were adopted for the SFM or relational satisfaction (Young and Gluhosk, 1997). These are:

1. Basic safety and stability: This domain relates to the needs of security, consistency, and predictability of the other's behaviors, resulting in the basic experience of trust and reliability. This domain relates to attachment theory that based the development of attachment styles (secure, anxious, avoidant) on early experiences with caregivers, which develops internal working models of close, intimate relationship (Feeney and Collins, 2004). People whose domain of safety and security is well met are likely to develop committed, secure, and satisfying close relationships with their partners.
2. Close connection to another is a domain that relates to a person's feelings of being well nurtured, cared for, and accepted during childhood and the degree to which one received physical affection from warm, compassionate, and loving parents. Adults whose need for close connection to another was adequately met are likely to be involved in and promote close relationships that involve affection, loving care,

warmth, and empathy. These individuals tend to be emotionally expressive, comfortable in showing love and affection to close partners, enjoy the company of a partner, and easygoing at giving and receiving love. These tendencies contribute to relational richness, stability, and above all, to relational satisfaction.

3. Self-determination and self-expression is the third domain in the SFM of relationship satisfaction. This domain consists of one's ability to freely and assertively express personal needs, desires, and preferences in daily interpersonal transactions. People with such abilities are likely to be self-determined and independent, capable of making decisions with strong sense of competence. People who possess these capacities tend to enter relationships with partners that respect and value their contributions and the decision making processes. They know they can freely express emotions and thoughts without intimidating their partners, knowing they will be supported by them. These qualities contribute to relational satisfaction and stability.

4. The fourth domain, self-actualization, reflects a person's autonomy to pursue interests and aspirations without being frustrated by others. Partners who encourage each other's need for self-actualization share a sense of mutual freedom and independence that increases emotional closeness and relational satisfaction.

5. Acceptance and self-esteem reflect a core need for unconditional regard, appreciation, and acceptance. Partners who fulfill these core needs for acceptance and self-esteem promote a sense of relational security, well functioning, and satisfaction.

6. The final domain of SFM is realistic limits and concern for others, which reflects a person's ability to show empathy, consideration, and understanding to one's partner. In addition, this domain consists of the willingness to compromise when in a conflict of interests. Within this domain, "partners behave in a way that is considerate and respectful of each other, for example, they are consistently faithful and honest" (Clements et al., 1997, p. 359).

The fulfillment of the above mentioned core needs within the context of close relationships is highly important for promoting and enhancing relational quality and satisfaction.

Sexual Satisfaction

Sexual satisfaction and overall relational satisfaction are closely related to each other. Partners who enjoy gratifying and satisfying sexual experiences are likely to be satisfied with their intimate, marital relationships (Karney and Bradbury, 1995; Sprecher and Cate, 2004; Holmberg, Blair, and Phillips, 2010). This association between sexual satisfaction and overall relationship satisfaction was found in premarital couples (Sprecher, 2002), newlywed couples (Young, Denny, Young, and Luquist 2000), as well as in couples in later, more advanced stages of marriage (Yeh, Lorenz, Wickrama, Conger, and Elder, 2006; Ashdown, Hackathorn, and Clark, 2011). Sexual intimacy and satisfaction are also closely linked to passionate and compassionate love experiences with partners (Grote and Frieze, 1998; Hendrick and Hendrick, 2004) and to the level of existing marital commitment and stability (Sprecher, 2002). The association between sexual satisfaction and overall relationship satisfaction is dynamic so that changes in one are likely to evoke changes in the other (Sprecher and Cate, 2004).

Stephenson and Meston (2011) found inconsistencies in the conceptualization and measurement of the construct of sexual satisfaction. The authors relate these inconsistencies to the few validated theories that offer a foundation upon which sexual satisfaction can be studied adequately. Nonetheless, Lawrance and Byers (1992) developed and validated such a theoretical framework, the Interpersonal Exchange Model of Sexual Satisfaction (IEMSS). This model is based on the social exchange theory of close relationships (Rusbult, 1983; Byers and MacNeil, 2006). The social exchange model posits that in close relationships partners strive to maximize the rewards they receive from the relationship (love, affection, sex, services) while minimizing the costs (investing time, money, efforts). Similarly, IEMSS suggests that the construct of sexual satisfaction is defined in accordance with a person's perceived balance of sexual rewards enjoyed by the relationship and the sexual costs imposed by the relationship. Other components of the IEMSS relate to the degree to which rewards and costs are in line with one's expectancy, partners' subjective perception of the equality of rewards and costs that exist between them, and, finally, the overall quality of the nonsexual transactions (Byers and MacNeil, 2006; Stephenson and Meston, 2011). In this context, sexual rewards are activities that are pleasurable and gratifying to one's partner, whereas costs are sexual interactions that require physical and emotional efforts, or cause disappointment, anxiety, discomfort, or pain (Byers and MacNeil, 2006). The validity of the IEMSS model was empirically demonstrated in that "individuals were more sexually satisfied if they experienced a more favorable balance of sexual rewards and sexual costs in their relationship, if this balance compared favorably to their expectations, if they perceived themselves and their partners to experience approximately equal levels of sexual rewards and costs, and if they were satisfied with the nonsexual aspects of the relationship" (Byers and MacNeil, 2006, p. 54).

The IEMSS highlights the role of the history of partners' sexual experience as an important factor that affects sexual satisfaction as opposed to current sexual exchanges (Lawrance and Byers, 1992; Byers and MacNeil, 2006). Accordingly, sexual satisfaction is more a function of the long-term history of satisfaction experienced by the couple than of partners' satisfaction at a particular point in time in their relationship.

Communication and Sexual Satisfaction

Effective communication has been identified as an important component of marital success and satisfaction (Feeney, Noller, and Ward, 1997; Carrere and Gottman, 1999). Whereas a considerable body of research examined the associations between interpersonal communication and marital success and satisfaction, very little has been done to study the impact of communication on sexual satisfaction (Litzinger and Gordon, 2005). Marital couples who participated in a communication skill-based educational program, however, reported an improvement in their sexual satisfaction (Markman, Renick, Floyed, Stanley, and Clements, 1993). Metz and Epstein (2002) suggest an inter-relationship existence between sexual functioning and satisfaction and marital communication relating to conflict and disagreements. Negative marital interactions during conflict are destructive to sexual functioning and well-being, which in turn creates sex-related tension and added conflict. This increased conflictual distress further precipitates the decline of marital quality and satisfaction.

Litzinger and Gordon (2005) explored the joint, interdependent effect of communication and sexual satisfaction on marital satisfaction. 387 community couples were assessed on a subscale relevant to sexual satisfaction, which adopted from the Inventory of Specific Relationship Standards, the Communication Patterns Questionnaire, and the Dyadic Adjustment Scale. The results indicated that sexual satisfaction and effective communication patterns were strongly associated with marital satisfaction. Results also showed that high couples' sexual satisfaction compensates for destructive communication patterns, thus softening its impact on marital satisfaction. In other words, marital satisfaction can be maintained even when the level of constructive communication is not high, providing the couple enjoys a high degree of sexual satisfaction. Thus sexual satisfaction acts as a protective buffer for poor spouses' communication patterns, which results in higher marital satisfaction. It should be noted, however, that when partners' communication patterns are constructive, sexual satisfaction does not contribute considerably to marital satisfaction. Litzinger and Gordon (2005) identified a possible marital risk that stems from their findings. High levels of sexual gratification and satisfaction may distract spouses from engaging in solving communication problems, a pattern that may threaten marital satisfaction at a later point in time. Also, being supported by high gratification associated with sexual satisfaction may cause spouses to persist in an ineffective, unhealthy marital relationship without getting counseling until it is too late.

The previous discussion stressed the importance of effective couples' communication as a predictor of sexual satisfaction. Partners communicate on various topics, one of which is their sex lives (Cupach and Comstok, 1990). The importance of sexual communication for satisfying sexual relationships has been stressed by many authorities (Masters, Johnson, and Kolodny, 1986; MacNeil and Byers, 2005; Sprecher, 2006). It is through open and assertive sexual communication that partners can expand and deepen their knowledge and sensitivity about each other's sexual interests, desires, and preferences. The disclosure of such information promotes sexual enjoyment and satisfaction (Cupach and Comstock, 1990; Sprecher and Cate, 2004). My (A. S.) clinical experience as a couples and sex therapist has shown me that the more partners know about each other's sexuality (desires, preferences, erogenous zones, etc.), the better they are in fulfilling each other's sexual and intimacy needs. Sex therapists encourage open discussion of sexual issues between partners as an integral aspect of the therapeutic process aimed at promoting relational and sexual satisfaction (Montesi, Fauber, Gordon, and Heimberg, 2010).

Sprecher and Cate (2004) observed that in spite of the importance of sex-related communication and its impact on marital and sexual satisfaction, empirical research in this area is sparse. The authors suggest two reasons for this state of affair. First, sexual communication is not so accessible to direct observational research methodology since it is mostly done during sexual interactions. Second, a great deal of sexual communication is subtle, revealed through facial expressions and other nonverbal communication channels. Nonetheless, most authorities accept the notion that the more partners openly talk about sexual desires, preferences, and needs, the greater their satisfaction with both the sexual and nonsexual aspects of their marital relationships (Sprecher and Cate, 2004).

Effective, high quality sexual communication is positively associated with not only sexual outcomes but also with overall relational adjustment and satisfaction (Cupach and

Comstock, 1990). Evidence in support of this association was proposed by Banmen and Vogel (1985) who found a strong positive association between skilled, high quality, sex-related communication and marital adjustment and satisfaction. In contrast, inhibited sexual communication was strongly correlated with marital distress and dissatisfaction. Based on their data, Banmen and Vogel (1985) recommend therapists apply therapeutic interventions for the improvement and betterment of both sexual and overall marital interactive behavior.

MacNeil and Byers (2005) outline two pathways by which sexual communication promotes and enhances sexual and relational satisfaction: the expressive pathway and the instrumental pathway. The expressive pathway relates to partners revealing to each other personal and sensitive information about their sexual desires, preferences, likes, and dislikes. This self-disclosure promotes greater relational closeness, intimacy, and satisfaction, which in turn contributes to increased sexual satisfaction. The instrumental pathway of the impact of sex-related communication on sexual satisfaction suggests that revealing sexual information enhances a partner's sexual scripts through greater understanding of the partner's sexual preferences. Well developed partners' sexual scripts improve sexual interaction, enjoyment, and satisfaction.

Sexual scripts are socio-cultural learned guidelines that provide direction regarding sexual attitudes, behaviors, and the appropriate, acceptable manner of sexual expression (Sprecher and Cate, 2004). Miller and Byers (2004) suggest that a couple's sexual script is influenced by the partners' perceptions of one another's sexual preferences and desires. It is important for partners in close relationships to accurately perceive each other's sexual scripts so as to increase the likelihood of mutual sexual satisfaction (Purnine and Carey, 1997). Being knowledgeable and understanding of a partner's sexual script (e.g. what he likes and desires sexually) is central to a couple's sexual satisfaction mainly because it facilitates the partners' ability to gratify and satisfy each other sexually (MacNeil and Byers, 1997). In support of this notion, Purnine and Carey (1997) found that a high level of men's understanding of their female partners' sexual preferences accounted for 65% of the variance in women's sexual satisfaction.

Sexual Frequency and Sexual Satisfaction

Another variable associated with marital couples' sexual satisfaction is the frequency of their sexual activity (Yabiku and Gager, 2009). It has been established by empirical research that couples whose sexual activity is more frequent report more general sexual satisfaction than couples with a lower frequency of sexual activity (Sprecher and Cate, 2004). Call, Sprecher, and Schwartz (1995) examined predictors of sexual frequency among marital couples. The authors analyzed data collected by the National Survey of Families and Households from 6,785 participants. Their results showed that age was the strongest variable associated with frequency of marital sexual activity. Marital quality and satisfaction was the second strongest variable predicting sexual frequency. In other words, satisfied marital couples have sex more frequently than dissatisfied couples. Donnelly (1993) reported similar findings. Young and Luquist (1998) used a sample of 797 married couples to examine and identify correlates of sexual satisfaction. The results showed that sexual satisfaction correlated positively with the frequency of marital sexual activity. Yabiku and Gager (2009) suggested that reduced frequency of sexual activity affects marital satisfaction indirectly.

When marital partners encounter unresolved conflicts and difficulties, it reduces emotional closeness and intimacy, which in turn results in decline in sexual activity and sexual satisfaction.

Orgasmic Experience and Relational Satisfaction

Another factor that contributes to relational and sexual satisfaction is orgasmic response and frequency of orgasm occurrence. The occurrence and frequency of female partners' orgasmic response was found to be positively related to both sexual quality and satisfaction in marital relationships (Young, Denny, Young, and Luquis, 2000; Young and Luquis, 1998). Sprecher and Cate (2004) observed that most of the research on orgasmic response in sexual activity has dealt with women. This is "Because they exhibit much more variation than males in the likelihood of having an orgasm during sexual interaction" (p. 244). Sexual satisfaction is related to the frequency of the female orgasmic response during sexual intercourse (Birnbaum, Glaubman, and Mikulincer, 2001; Young et al., 2000). For example, Birnbaum et al. (2001) found that higher orgasmic frequency is related to a stronger sense of relational love and affection (loving one's male partner and feeling loved by him) and a greater perceived feeling of interdependence with a partner.

Sprecher and Cate (2004) proposed two explanations to the dynamics of the association between orgasmic response and sexual satisfaction. The authors' first causal link is based on the social exchange model, suggesting that women who consistently experience orgasmic pleasure gain higher levels of sexual rewards, which in turn enhance sexual satisfaction. The second causal link proposes that partners' high sexual satisfaction promotes and enhances orgasmic response because sexually satisfied individuals compared to those who are dissatisfied are more open and willing to engage in non-coital sexual activities (e.g. oral-genital stimulation and extensive foreplay), thus increasing the likelihood of orgasm (Sprecher and Cate, 2004).

The female partner's orgasmic response and consistency is also associated with the quality of partners' communication (Kelly, Strassberg, and Turner, 2004). Poor and inhibited sexual communication between partners is associated with the female's inhibited orgasmic response (Barbach, 1980; Kelly, Strassberg, and Kircher, 1990). Comfort in and a willingness to openly express to one's partner what is sexually pleasing and arousing is essential to an effective female response and orgasmic release (MacNeil and Byers, 1997). Women with inhibited orgasmic response reported discomfort in communicating to their partners how they like to be stimulated as compared to orgasmic women (Kelly, Strassberg, and Turner, 2004). Inhibited sexual stimulation prevents effective sexual stimulation, which results in the lack of sufficient arousal to reach an orgasm (Pierce, 2000). Inhibited orgasmic response can negatively affect marital relationship quality and satisfaction and evoke emotional distress (Mah and Binki, 2004).

Sexual Conflicts and Sexual Satisfaction

Conflicts over sexual issues are inherent and inevitable in long-term relationships (Long, Cate, Fehsenfeld, and Williams, 1999). Therapists rated sexual conflicts among the most frequent problems presented by marital couples in therapy (Geiss and O'Leary, 1981). Little empirical attention has been given to the association between sex-related conflicts and marital and/or sexual satisfaction (Sprecher and Cate, 2004). It has been established, however, that increased conflict over sexual issues negatively affects both general relational satisfaction and sexual satisfaction (Long, Cate, Fehsenfeld, and Williams, 1996). Unresolved incompatibility and conflicts about the frequency of sexual activity were found to decrease sexual satisfaction (Sprecher and Cate, 2004). The pressure to comply with a partner's desire to engage in sexual activity is also predictive of sexual and relational dissatisfaction. Lower sexual satisfaction is reported by married women whose husbands are aggressively demanding of sexual activity. On the other hand, husbands are sexually dissatisfied when their wives refuse to engage in sexual activity (Buss, 1989). From an evolutional perspective, "When women withhold sex (a strategy to increase reproductive fitness), it leads to emotional upset due to interference with men's reproductive strategies. For women, they are dissatisfied with aggressiveness by their husbands because it does not signal that husbands are committed to supporting their offspring" (Sprecher and Cate, 2004, p. 248).

Chapter 16

LONELINESS IN ROMANTIC RELATIONS

> Being lonely and alone is painful and disturbing…being lonely in a crowd, while being surrounded by others, is both painful and frightening…however, the deepest, most painful and the most culturally unacceptable is loneliness in marriage…[which] if not addressed, destroys it.
>
> (Rokach, 1998, p. 8)

The book that you are reading addresses two main areas in human relations: loneliness and its causes and consequences, and romantic relations, which are commonly thought of as the antidote to loneliness. This chapter is a combination and the interweaving of the two. Written by two clinicians, we have addressed the two forms of loneliness as they are expressed in intimate relationships. The first one deals with *essential loneliness*, which is so primal that it becomes part of one's personality. By drawing on our experience with couples, we have shown how such loneliness may affect the intimate connection. We then addressed *transient, reactive loneliness*, which is usually triggered by the dynamics of the couple's interactions and as such, can be coped with and ameliorated through changes and improvements to the very same interactions that may have initially caused it.

Transient, reactive loneliness is also identified and was referred to as social loneliness, in contrast to emotional loneliness, which is close to the essential type of loneliness. At the core, emotional loneliness is the absence or loss of an attachment bond that provides a deep sense of felt security and belongingness. A romantic relationship that deprives partners of a deep sense of support, emotional closeness and intimacy, and basic security is likely to result in disengagement, and eventually, in emotional loneliness. Thus, although marriage is supposed to protect partners from loneliness, the absence or loss of marital pair bonding, the essence of close attachment and felt security, is actually the cause of emotional loneliness. In other words, a high quality, successful marriage is a protective agent against loneliness, and in contrast, an unhappy, emotionally empty marriage is the main cause of emotional loneliness.

George was hesitant when he started speaking with me [A.R.] on the phone. He was asking for help for himself, for Nancy, his wife, and for their marriage. A week later, they both showed up to our scheduled appointment. They were both in their mid-forties, of middle class, and desperately in search for help—help for their six year marriage, which they felt was in danger despite their love, devotion, and adoration of each other. I saw them together for the first time so that we could decide how to proceed. The picture that emerged was a perplexing one. Yes, their love and affection for each other were evident in the manner in which they gently touched each other, looked at one another when their partner spoke, and nodded when their partner described good times. George and Nancy, however, were quite unhappy and seemed depressed. Taking in their personal and then their couple history crystallized the fact that while they loved each other, they felt alienated, alone, and frequently disconnected from one another. While George started feeling that way some four years ago, Nancy had felt lonely and disconnected since she could remember.

Nancy and George, a composite of clients of mine (A.R.), are examples of the types of loneliness that we may experience, one that is inextricably intertwined into being human. Rokach (1988) elaborated on this and pointed out that while loneliness is such a basic human experience, what we all have is actually the *potential* to experience it, like having a recessive gene. Loneliness comes to fruition, or is openly expressed, under the "right" circumstances. There are two types of such "right" circumstances that may give rise to loneliness:

a) Life's journey, trials and tribulations, and situations where we find ourselves isolated and disconnected. We could term this experience, *Transient Loneliness*.

b) *Essential Loneliness* denotes an experience of almost constantly feeling cut off, disconnected, and not belonging. These feelings are an essential part of the person and are experienced in almost all situations, including those that would *not* give rise to such feelings in most people. Hojat (1987) referred to it as "loneliness of early detachment experiences." He suggested that the other type of loneliness is reactive, transitory loneliness. "Chronic loneliness resulting from early disruption of [the] affectional bond is out of the individual's control…its cause and origin being unknown to the sufferer. It carries with it some deep-seated emotional loads, usually subconscious, originating from unfulfilled contact, intimacy, emotional and social needs very early in life" (Hojat, 1987, p. 97).

In our chapter on the causes of loneliness, we illustrated a model, which is based on research exploring the antecedents of loneliness. While such factors as unfulfilling intimate relationships (the kind that Nancy and George complained about), relocations and separations from significant others, or living on the fringe of society could obviously explain the cause of Transitory Loneliness, Essential Loneliness is caused by personality and developmental factors that the person experienced during childhood. Those include a low self-esteem, strong and lasting feelings of inadequacy that were reinforced at home and in school, and repeated failure in getting close to others or remaining in intimate relationships with parents, friends, etc. Additionally, those suffering from Essential Loneliness have also frequently, grown up in unwelcoming families and had parents that resented them; that were unavailable physically or emotionally; that were cold, depressed, and in an unhappy marriage; or that used their children as "boxing bags"; they were kids that were unwanted, unloved, resented, and punished harshly and frequently. Those who grew up in such homes may develop essential loneliness—the realization, which they adopt, that they are unwanted, not valued, and unlovable. As Bowlby (1973) and other developmental theorists since Freud noted, those early and often traumatic experiences imprint in our souls the message that will accompany us throughout our lives.

Back to Nancy and George, George, a bank's assistant manager is successful professionally, highly regarded by his friends, and has a good relationship with his and

Nancy's parents. George is not frequently sad or depressed; he loves Nancy very much and is looking forward to the time that they will be parents, something which they have discussed and are planning for in the next 1-2 years. He is unhappy with their marriage, or more specifically, with their level of intimacy. While they both work, and then grocery shop and visit family and friends together, he feels that they are not emotionally close. Nancy, he said, can speak about her work as an interior designer and about some of her friends, but aside from that he finds it almost impossible to get close to her. George wants to be able to speak openly and intimately about his life, wishes, and heartaches with his wife, the one he sees as his best friend. In contrast, Nancy is pleasant, can listen, and provides wise advice, but she cannot herself open up. George told of times when he initiated discussions between them only to hear from Nancy that she does not feel like talking, she is very busy and has no time, or worse—he said—they started talking and shortly thereafter Nancy would change the subject or become teary and offended if George shared with her some of his frustrations about his unsuccessful attempts to get close to her. He initiated couples therapy due to his concern that they will continue to grow apart, something that he tried very much to prevent. George is obviously experiencing Transitory Loneliness. It is quite clear that because he has not been sad or lonely frequently in the past, since he showed no other pathology and because he reported a variety of good and emotionally satisfying intimate relationships he will most likely not experience loneliness again once his relationship with Nancy becomes closer, more intimate, and mutually nourishing.

Nancy is the younger of two daughters born to a business man and his homemaker wife. There is an eleven year difference between Nancy and her older sister. Nancy, a pleasant, gentle, and well-dressed interior designer, realizes that her husband's concerns are valid but has great difficulty facing the situation. When I ask her to talk a bit about herself, her marriage, and her own concerns, she bursts out crying. When she regains her composure, Nancy talks about her successful career, her professional achievements, and the painting and drawing course that she has recently started to attend. It quickly becomes clear that Nancy can, indeed, discuss a variety of issues, but not those that have anything to do with her feelings or that may display weakness on her part.

Nancy grew up in the sixties in a traditional home where her father, a driven businessman brought home the bacon. He was a peripheral parent as he hardly saw his daughters, and when he did see them, he was too tired and busy to even notice them. Nancy's mother, Jane, was a homemaker who, though she officially took care of the children, was too busy with her social network to spend much quality time with them. Nancy remembered that when she and Jane interacted, it was mainly concerning Nancy's clothes (they had to be clean, and always expensive and from brand name companies), about Nancy's inability to do what was expected of her, and about Nancy's cognitive abilities. While Nancy had no cognitive shortcomings and probably had average or above average intelligence, her mother downplayed her abilities, did her homework ("so she could get good grades"), and frequently pointed out Nancy's shortcomings. In school, both in elementary and high school, Nancy was an average student with very few friends. She was not socially popular, was shy, very insecure, and felt unlovable and obviously unwanted. At home, Nancy did not experience much warmth or acceptance. Both of her parents were busy and fulfilled by their separate lives (her father in business, her mother with her friends) and were emotionally distanced and mostly unavailable to Nancy and her sister.

In several subsequent individual meetings with Nancy, where I wanted to create the safest, non-threatening environment so that she could open up without her husband's presence (in case it prevented her from speaking what was on her mind), Nancy described herself as being successful professionally, but quite unhappy socially and in her marriage.

Nancy feels sad, she is convinced that she has very few friends, simply because she cannot be a good friend, and does not "know" how to keep in touch. Despite being an attractive woman, she described herself as unattractive, as very vulnerable to criticism, and as desperately lonely. Nancy, since childhood, found it extremely difficult to speak in public, to partake in any group programs (such as those offered by community centers or by nearby colleges), and in any way be the center of attention. She was terrified of being criticized. Actually she was terrorized of being found out as the "nobody" that she believed she was; the woman who was not even loved by her parents. She mentioned, on several occasions, that she finds it very difficult to openly express her love for George, although she can talk about his wonderful qualities and how much she values him inside her head, she cannot actually say it to him.

When there are disagreements between her and George, she invariably gets flustered, is unable to listen to George for fear that she will be criticized, and cannot articulate her own point of view. She feels George's love for her and knows that she loves this kind man who adores her, but she cannot *feel* love. She cares deeply about him, but feels lonely, isolated, and unable to knock down the walls of fear, inadequacy, low self-esteem, and fear of rejection and intimacy that were instilled in her since a young age; these walls seem to now "protect" her from the world, giving her a false protection from pain, but efficiently separating her from a loving and soul nourishing relationship with her husband. Although, like her husband, Nancy wishes to be a mother, she is deeply concerned that while she will certainly be an attentive mother, she may feel the same disconnect with her children. She is afraid she will not know how to express love to them and how to be emotionally open and available to them. Before we ended our several individual meetings, so that we could resume couple therapy, Nancy bashfully offered that while she has regular sex with her husband—whenever, mostly, he initiated it—she cannot orgasm, nor can she allow him to penetrate her. Physically he does and they have close physical contact with a lot of cuddling, yet Nancy cannot open herself up, cannot let George become emotionally and intimately one with her, or allow herself to orgasm. Nancy has never orgasmed, nor has she ever masturbated, as that is not what "nice girls" do; she has not done so even in their own bedroom.

A loneliness model developed by Hawkley and Cacioppo (2010) draws a portrait of a relational interactive process they called the Self-Reinforcing Loneliness Loop (SRLL) (Hawkley and Cacioppo, 2010, p. 220). The perceived emotional isolation and separation expressed by lonely individuals gives rise to constant tension and increased awareness and sensitivity to their relational surrounding. They are constantly "on guard," carefully scanning for potential sources of added threatening signs.

This hyper vigilance (enhanced state of sensory sensitivity and alertness) is accompanied by increased vulnerability to the point that "lonely individuals see the social world as a more threatening place, expect more negative social interactions, and remember more negative social information" (Hawkley and Cacioppo, 2010, p. 220). These maladaptive social cognitions (expecting negativity) are self-reinforcing and act as a self-fulfilling prophecy by evoking and confirming attitudes and interactive behaviors from others, e.g. the marital spouse (Snyder, 1992; Snyder and Stukas, 1999). It is quite possible that when a marital spouse feels emotionally lonely, as a result of relational distress and disengagement, she (most likely it is the wife) construes the interaction as threatening. This is coupled with holding negative expectations and interpretations of partner's behavior. This social cognition is followed by the lonely spouse reciprocating negatively to the other, thus adding to the marital distress and negativity, which in turn deepens the feeling of loneliness. In other words, it is possible that the lonely spouse may contribute to her own loneliness' existence by perpetuating the Self-Reinforcing Loneliness Loop (Hawkley and Cacioppo, 2010).

Therefore, here we have a couple, George and Nancy, who love and are devoted to each other but at the same time feel lonely and alienated from one another. There is George, who cannot get emotionally close to Nancy and Nancy, who has always experienced loneliness and even a loving husband cannot change that.

> When we fall in love and get married to the special someone we cherish and want to share our lives with, we hope to live happily ever after. Newlyweds can be easily recognized not only by the glow on their faces and the loving glances they share with one another, but by the hope and excitement they radiate—hope for maintaining a satisfying, nurturing, intimate, and caring relationship. By committing ourselves to the other person, we often also implicitly state our expectation that our "one and only" will fulfill our needs. We have high expectations and sometimes unrealistic ones of our loved one. He should be honest, loving, entertaining, be able to express love repeatedly, fit in with her friends, and get along with the in-laws.

It is clear that Nancy and George have a loving, yet lonely relationship. As much as it may be an oxymoron, their relationship, which started out as a loving union, progressed to the point where both felt alienated from each other, unfulfilled emotionally, and unnourished or replenished.

As we review the various "ingredients" of a relationship, we will point out whether they are present in Nancy's lonely marriage.

> *Getting together for the right reasons* – it is intuitively understood that couples do not fit each other's wishes completely. People have quirks and shortcomings and imperfections. If we know ourselves, if we have an idea of what we need and want, and if we have the psychological insight and wisdom to know who is suitable to be our partner and share the future with us—we have a better chance of creating, together, a harmonious relationship. When marriage is used as a solution to loneliness, it becomes a negative bond between the couple who together defend against being lonely (Gordon, 1976). A marriage that is based on the fear of loneliness implants it at its core, and may unite two lonely people, who remain lonely in their union (see also Flora and Segrin, 2000; Tornstam, 1992). Moustakas (1972) maintained that a marriage that started out as the couple's attempt to run away from loneliness usually ends in loneliness (which is felt, for instance, in separation), and often there is a lot of loneliness in between. A marriage that is based on the fear of loneliness, fear which serves as the glue that bonds the couple together, is bound to crumble.

Nancy and George met and married as a panacea for their loneliness anxiety. George experienced transient loneliness after high school, had some difficulty dating, and was quite fearful of the "dreadful loneliness" as he described it. Nancy, on the other hand, knows loneliness well and intimately. Much as she has almost always experienced it, however, the pain of loneliness is very frightening to her. During her years growing up—as a child, an adolescent, and as a grown up woman—she did whatever she could to avoid it. As a child, she had imaginary friends, tended to dogs and a couple of budgies at home, and often convinced herself that she was the one who did not want to befriend the other children. As she grew and matured, she experienced the fear of loneliness, accompanied by her inability to get—and feel—close to others. Meeting George after several years of grieving her previous romantic engagement gave Nancy hope, hope of escaping a future of disconnection and alienation, of being able to overcome the loneliness that she hated so much.

The result was a marriage of two people who did not take the time to examine whether their chosen partner was the right one for them, and whether they could offer what was required by that person. While George loved Nancy, he also knew that a close relationship was not supposed to include loneliness; Nancy, who was highly anxious about the prospect of finding herself alone and lonely, hung on to the marriage and to George, and while she attempted to escape loneliness, she found herself lonely and alienated—just as she has always been.

Intimate sharing and involvement – the hallmark of an intimate relationship is the sharing of intimacy, not only physical, but mainly emotional. Feelings, wishes, fears, and self-revealing are shared and received by a supportive partner, who is non-judgmental, is listening without interrupting his partner with a caring attitude, wishes to help when such is requested, and above all, accepts his loved one (See also Prager and Roberts, 2004; Reis et al., 2010). The partner might not necessarily agree with all that she says, but he has a solid acceptance of the other, offering unconditional love. Rokach (1998) observed that "as anyone who has ever been involved in a relationship surely knows—relationships are never perfect. They evolve, people change and daily life's little problems all contribute to frustrations, anger and disappointments. Dealing with them, they become part of our history and may teach us how to avoid the anger/frustration arousing situations in the future. But if we accumulated grudges and bitterness, if we allow the anger to become part of our make up, it eventually comes between our partner and us. A gap filled with resentment, dissatisfaction and discomfort is created, inviting emptiness and loneliness to replace it" (p. 10).

While George opened up to his wife, she would listen half-heartedly, mainly to see whether she was blamed for any "wrong doings." She would then, when George finished talking, simply redirect the discussion to another topic, fearing to be seen as "taking sides" if she offered her opinion on a topic. George was frustrated and shared with her his need for feedback, for active support, and his yearning for her openness. He wanted to know why she would suddenly become quiet, taken by day dreaming and thinking, why she occasionally—when she did open up and shared—claimed to be so lonely, while he poured love and attention on her. As time went by, and it became clearer to George that Nancy is not able to open up, he gradually stopped sharing with her. He wanted and needed to talk to his best friend, but understood that Nancy may be his wife but not his best friend, so their closeness "cracked" and the distance between them widened.

Mutual positive involvement – is one of the things that make couples feel connected and close to each other, and helps them grow, develop, and cement their union. Psychologists and other mental health professionals have been trained to do provide this in therapy. It allows for a safe environment where one feels cared for, listened to, and when needed—rejuvenated (see also Gable and Reis, 2006). Roberts and Greenberg (2002), attesting to the importance of affectional expressions, indicate that "the regular enactment of behavioural exchange that lead to experiences of relational intimacy will serve to maintain the climate of security, trust, and acceptance that characterizes well-functioning relationships" (p. 120-121).

George seemed to be able, at least in the past, to provide that kind of caring and undivided attention. Now, however, seeing that Nancy is so closed off, so distanced and unable to open up, unable to actively listen and show involvement when he discussed his fears, hopes, and disappointments, he gradually spoke less, learned not to be as open, and the emotional distance between them grew.

Resolving relational conflicts – no couple is immune from disagreements, arguments, and even fights (not physical, of course). These are normal, expected, and may even be helpful, as they allow the couple to share those things that bother, irritate, or concern them. It is said that couples who know how to fight know how to love. When the fight does not include physical insults, does not involve harsh language, or personal and characterological "digs," it may create a situation where one partner can vent, exclaim, and even scream out his frustrations, and his partner, rather than take offense, will help the hurt or angry one resolve the situation and rebuild what may need rebuilding. An appropriate conflict resolution in a romantic relationship can not only allow venting, but can actually bring the couple closer, if they allow each other the time and space to express their feelings, and if they are ready to listen non defensively and make amends when those are called for. Personal skills and effective interpersonal patterns of interaction during conflict are essential to marital success, especially during the initial stage of marriage formation (Birchler, Doumas, and Fals-Stewart, 1999; Nichols, 1998).

Nancy was unable to fight with George. She told him, when they met, that he "would not be able to fight with me." George imagined a smooth sailing marital union without disagreements or hard feelings. That was, of course, not the case. When George was angry or hurt, he shared with Nancy his frustrations and indicated what he needed. Nancy listened and did not have much to say. She later revealed that hearing George complain was very painful for her, as she perceived him claiming that she was inappropriate, was not a worthy wife, and was in danger of losing him. George felt that Nancy was not listening, may not even care about how he feels, and soon thereafter stopped sharing his frustrations with her. Nancy, on the other hand, did not tell George how she felt, felt unheard, and her issues remain unresolved. Both ended up in their own corner, feeling that it was not safe, or productive, to share their negative emotions with each other.

Interdependence – is that optimal relational stage, between a high level of dependence that some couples may experience, and a high level of independence, which may beg the question—why are the two people together?! Interdependence is the combination of those two. While there is a union cemented by love, marital goals, and deep caring, partners who are in such a relationship realize and respect the fact that, in essence, they are two separate human beings, rather than a reflection of each other. They rejoice at their partner's qualities and may gently help him change the behaviors or goals that are disturbing or harmful to the relationship. Above all, however, they share a deep respect for their individuality. Based on principles of independence theory, Rusbult, Bissonnett, Arriaga, and Cox (1998) suggested the use of accommodation in marital transaction in order to strengthen the foundations of marriage.

It is the partner who does not feel that she is worth much, the one who does not think that she can "survive" without the other's continual fulfillment of his needs, or the one who is focused on one source for satisfying her wishes and aspirations, that is the one who becomes dependent on her partner. A high degree of dependency by one partner on the other, or by both on each other, is nothing but pathological and destructive. Obviously, if two people decide to experience life together they will, at least to some degree, depend on one another for love, caring, support, and the partial fulfillment of their needs but when all our worth, value, and aspirations center around that one specific person and he becomes enormously essential for our emotional survival—so much so that we cannot afford to lose him, his attention, or his love–then there is a problem. We become demanding, we expect love and approval, and we cling to that person with all our might. Being in a relationship because we need and have to, rather than because we want and choose to, is deadly. It kills affection and creates a gap between the partners; they either cling to one another without ever feeling secure in each other's love or one clings while the other tries to flee and both are unhappy (Schultz, 1976).

Since Nancy had experienced Essential Loneliness, she regularly withdrew from people, because she felt that others did not understand or appreciate her, and that it was futile to get close to people since experience taught her that she would remain lonely anyways. George initially thought that he was in an interdependent relationship. While he was his own person, he depended on Nancy for support, for her wisdom and advice when he felt that he needed it, and for her friendship and company, as a close, dear, and loving friend. Nancy, who was always feeling lonely, was very dependent on George, asked for frequent declarations of his love and devotion to her, wanted to spend all the time with him, and resented it when George wanted to meet with his childhood friends, whom he cherished. Nancy was satisfied with going to work and then being continuously with George even though she was unable to open up, be his friend, or actually believe that he loved and was devoted to her, despite his numerous attempts to convince her of it.

Preemptive relational enhancing interactions – are those couple interactions that help improve the relationship and attempt to prevent, or at least minimize, potential disagreements or difficulties that the couple could be facing. This is one of the adjustments and refinements of their interaction that a couple may engage in, in order to reduce potential friction and to anticipate the other person's needs, desires, and wishes (see also Amato, Booth, Johnson, and Roger, 2007; Markman et al., 1993). McCarthy, Ginsberg, and Cintron (2008) observed that benign neglect is the couple's most "dangerous" enemy.

Nancy was too involved in her thoughts, concerns, and internal struggles to be able to do it. Even when George, who occasionally engaged in such preemptive behavior, mentioned to her that she could have prevented disagreements and friction by engaging in such preemptive behaviors, she was not able to bring herself to actually do so. It was not because she did not love George but because of her loneliness; it made her feel unable to reach out and connect and distracted her from preparing appropriately for the possibility of future frictions. It may be that had Nancy been less lonely, more connected to the here-and-now, and had increased awareness of her ability to positively influence their interaction, that she would actually want to do so.

In couple therapy, people sometimes say to me (A.R.), "Look at us. We were so close and alike when we started our relationships years ago, and now we hardly know each other." People are commonly mystified by their inability to connect with their long-term partner, since initially that very connection is what got them together. It has been my observation that bidirectional growth explains that relational change.

Avoiding bidirectional growth – is one of the best ways to prevent distancing and loneliness in romantic relationships. Enhancing one's partner's personal growth is a sign of a healthy, respectful, and nourishing relationship, however, when only one partner develops and grows, he then experiences the world differently and may change to such a degree that the two may no longer "speak the same language" or want the same kind of relationship. Their needs, desires, and social connections change as they themselves grow and change. When the two change at a similar pace and in a similar direction (e.g. he attends cooking classes and she a book club) then the relational equilibrium is maintained. If that is not the case, though, the growth of only one member of the couple may alienate them from one another since they will have less common topics to discuss, their interests may change, and their outlook on themselves and on life.

Nancy, being so deeply lonely, was mostly sad, and suffered from low energy. She simply did not have much energy to spare outside her work. George, being interested and excited about psychology, recently enrolled in an evening introductory psychology class. He would afterwards go home and excitedly want to discuss with Nancy what he learned, show her the textbook, and even asked her to join him once in a class, so that she could evidence what and how he studied. Nancy was not interested. She was not interested in meeting new people, did not particularly care about psychology, and was threatened by the other women who might attend that evening course with George. Instead, she spent those hours when George was in school mindlessly watching TV programs and waiting for George to return home so that they could go to sleep. Their distance widened. George, who desperately needed a friend that could understand his experiences and share his excitement, could not find it in Nancy. They loved each other, but lived in a marriage that was unfulfilling and loneliness enhancing.

Up to now, we discussed the interaction of loneliness and intimate/marital relations, when loneliness "was there first." In other words, we reviewed essential loneliness and how it impacts the marriage and intimate relation of the couple. The following is a review of what happens when the couple gets into their intimate relationship with love, hope, and good intentions, but things change and erode those feelings along the way. We are addressing the marriage, which rather than being protective of the couple, is the very reason that introduces loneliness into their lives.

TRANSIENT LONELINESS IN MARITAL RELATIONSHIPS

The expanded literature on loneliness has placed great emphasis on the social isolation experienced by lonely people and on their perception of the adequacy of their social relationships as a basic component of this construct (Hawkley, Browne, and Cacioppo, 2005). Social isolation coupled with the absence of a meaningful relational connectedness is at the core of experiencing loneliness (Hughwa, Waite, Hawkley, and Cacioppo, 2004; Hawkley and Cacioppo, 2010). The individual's perceived deficiency of her social or romantic relationship significantly affects her sense of loneliness (Hawkley, Hughes, Waite, Masi, Thisted, and Cacioppo, 2008).

De Jong Gierveld (1998) presented a multidimensional conceptualization of loneliness as a social-emotional phenomenon. One of the dimensions relevant to this discussion is viewing loneliness as an emotional deprivation associated with the absence of an intimate attachment bond. This deprivation results in feelings of emptiness, abandonment, and rejection. The core of this dimensional construct of loneliness is the absence of an attachment bond that provides a deep sense of relational cohesion, felt security, and belongingness that are known to shield against loneliness (de Jong Gierveld, 1998). Described negatively, being in a romantic, marital relationship that deprives a partner of these basic relational quality components (support, emotional closeness, and security) is likely to result in loneliness (Olson and Wong, 2001). Although marriage is known to protect partners against the painful feeling of loneliness (Dykstra and Fokkema, 2007), it is the quality of the relationship that counts (Essex and Nam, 1987; Olson and Wong, 2001; Hawkley et al., 2008). Relating to the importance of an attachment bond as a preventive measure of loneliness, Cacioppo and Hawkley (2009) asserted that Bowlby, in his monumental work on attachment, "Heralds the beginning of [a] theoretical conceptualization of loneliness" (p. 227).

Weiss (1973, 1974) was one of the first scholars to argue that deficiencies in attachment bonding contribute to the feeling of loneliness. Weiss categorized loneliness into two distinct types: social loneliness and emotional loneliness. This typology distinguishes between the two types of loneliness on the basis of the characteristics of the social network and relational deficits perceived by the individual. Social loneliness (called social isolation by Weiss) is felt when there is a perceived discrepancy between a person's desired and actual social connections and relationships. Emotional loneliness, on the other end, results from the individual's perceived experience of the absence of a close, intimate attachment bond with another person, e.g. marital partner (Russell, Cutrona, Rose, and Yurko, 1984). The underlying premise of Weiss's typology of loneliness is that different types of relational interactions fulfill different human needs, called "social provisions." Accordingly, when a person is deprived of a particular relationship, the resulting feeling depends on the provisions (social, emotional) that are to be provided by that relationship. For example, a woman in a distressed and unsatisfying marriage is deprived of the social provisions she desires such as a partner's support, emotional closeness, sexual intimacy, and so forth.

Weiss presented six distinct social provisions that are supplied by interpersonal relationships (in Russel, Cutrona, Rose, and Yurko, 1984). Provisions that are relevant to loneliness in romantic relationships are as follows:

1. *Social provisions supplied within an attachment bond.* This may include the provision of a secure base depicted by the partner's support, that enables personal exploration and growth in secure conditions (Feeney and Collins, 2004) and a safe haven that provides reassurance and support at times of need or when one is in stress, desiring proximity to an attachment figure, e.g. one's romantic, marital partner (Hazan, Gur-Yaish, and Campa, 2004).
2. *Provision of nurturance* in the form of affectionate care and support.

Provision of nurturance is quite similar to the provisions offered by marital couples who maintain and enhance their marriage by viewing it as a communal relationship (Mills and Clark, 2001). In communal relationships, both partners share a strong concern for each other's well-being and "both are strongly motivated to benefit the other when the other is in need" (Mills and Clark, 2001, p. 15). In a communal relationship, priority is given to the other's needs and welfare even at the expense of one's personal interests. Partners' caring for each other's welfare promotes trust, emotional closeness, and intimacy. Deficits in attachment-related provisions (felt security, reassurance, and support) and perceived deficits in the provision of nurturing and affectionate care are associated with emotional loneliness (Russell, Cutrona, Rose, and Yurko, 1984). Again, although marriage has been documented as a protective agent against emotional loneliness, this is only true if the relationship provides both partners with attachment bond provisions of security, mutual support, and caring for each other's welfare. In the absence of this provision, emotional loneliness is likely to develop (Ernst and Cacioppo, 1998; Russell et al., 1984).

Closely related to this position are the results of a study that examined distal and proximal factors relating to loneliness in a sample of 229 married or cohabiting participants (Hawkley et al., 2008). Loneliness measures were obtained by the revised UCLA Loneliness Scale. One of the proximal factors examined was the quality of the participants' relationships. This factor was determined by the degree to which the participants perceived their relational partner as a close source of support and as being a confidant with whom they could openly discuss important matters. The degree of enjoyment and satisfaction the participants experienced with their partners was also assessed. The ratings of these three attributes were accumulated to form a measure of overall relational quality. The results showed that having a spouse who is a confidant was significantly associated with lower ratings of emotional loneliness. Moreover, being married to a spouse who was not perceived as a supportive confidant was not protective against loneliness. Finally, a high quality marital relationship mediated and minimized the impact of other loneliness related factors such as chronic work stress and poor health. Based on their data, Hawkley et al (2008) concluded that being married is positively linked to loneliness only when a partner is perceived and serves as a confidant. If the partner is not a confidant, being married is not more protective against emotional loneliness than not being married at all. This happens when the partners are not close to one another.

This conclusion corresponds to the findings reported by Olson and Wong (2001), who examined emotional loneliness in relation to marital cohesion, satisfaction, and dyadic agreement on values. The results of this study underlined the importance of emotional intimacy and communication (marital cohesion) in protecting against marital loneliness. Barbur (1993) studied loneliness among 467 marital couples and found that 20% of the wives and 24% of the husbands rated considerably high on loneliness measurement. Loneliness correlated negatively with various indices of marital quality such as the level of perceived emotional closeness and intimacy, marital functioning, and the overall level of dyadic satisfaction. Loneliness intensity was higher among those that reported lower levels of intimacy and satisfaction.

Mikulincer and Segal (1999) applied a phenomenological methodology to examine the emotional construct of loneliness. Based on their analysis, the authors identified four types of loneliness, of which only one, "depressive loneliness" seems relevant to our discussion.

Depressive loneliness is characterized by the experience of the absence of close, intimate ties. It also includes one's sense of being misunderstood, rejected, and secluded; being a target of criticism and hostility; and lacking love, affection, and intimacy from a significant other (e.g. marital spouse). In a prolonged state of depressive loneliness, the individual's motivation for connectedness, intimate affiliation, and proximity seeking might be impaired, producing an increased feeling of being rejected and pushed away. In turn, this regressive cascade deepens the level of loneliness. The cognitive interactive patterns associated with depressive loneliness may create a "self exacerbating cycle of loneliness" (Mikulincer and Segal, 1999, p. 227). A similar perpetuating cycle experienced by emotionally lonely individuals was described by Weiss (2006), who made observations on members of the Parents without Partners Organization. Weiss (2006) found that individuals who were not in a committed, romantic pair bond relationship reported being emotionally lonely. Loneliness was experienced by these individuals in spite of active social connections, which did not compensate for the void and emotional emptiness experienced in the absence of an attachment bond. Weiss (2006) found that this (emotional) loneliness was accompanied by distress and restlessness and an inability to give attention to anything other than the painful feelings one experienced. Some of the parents without a romantic partner described feeling "empty inside...constriction in their throats" (Weiss, 2006, p. 606). It is likely that these emotional compulsions (despair, dispirited self-doubts, and distress) displayed by attachment-deprived, lonely people may deplete their energies, thus restricting their abilities to improve their situation. This in turn might deepen their distress and perpetuates their emotional loneliness, increasing their isolation and feelings of being unwanted, undesirable, and rejected (Tornstam, 1992; Flora and Sergin, 2000).

The circular mechanism associated with the bidirectional affect that exists between relational distress and loneliness is similar to the erosive perspective of depression suggested by Joiner (2000). In an attempt to explain the persistent and reoccurring nature of depression, the author suggested that central to the erosive element of depression is "that a depressive episode erodes personal and psychological resources, such that episodes may be lengthened and, upon recovery, the formerly depressed individual is left with fewer buffers to protect against future depression" (Joiner, 2000, p. 203). In a similar fashion, it is reasonable to propose that a prolonged loneliness in the context of marital relationship erodes the person's psychological resources to effectively deal with the marital relationship problems that are associated with the loneliness (e.g. the partner's withdrawal, diminution of support, decreased attachment bonding). Upon recovering from even a transient episode of loneliness (usually coupled with depression and anxiety), the individual's psychological stamina is weakened, which in turn may limit his abilities to cope with the loneliness that is causing the marital problems.

Such loneliness, coupled with a distressed and dissatisfying marital relationship, is particularly depressing and painful because it is completely disharmonious with the joyous bliss expected from a rewarding and enhancing marriage. Apparently these are people who are locked into distressed, dissatisfying, and loneliness-evoking marriages, unable to break away due to the barriers to dissolution. This situation is likely to compound and perpetuate emotional loneliness (Flora and Segrin, 2000). Barriers to marital dissolution and divorce are various restraining factors (moral commitment, loss of irretrievable investment, children's welfare) that keep a person from leaving a distressed and dissatisfying marital relationship (Levinger, 1999). As noted, married individuals who have constraints on leaving a discordant, painful relationship are at high risk to develop intense emotional loneliness evoked by the prolonged absence of a pair bonding. This is especially true for women (Tornstam, 1992; Olson and Wang, 2001).

Loneliness and Belonging

Intimately close romantic relationships enhances partners' well-being by fulfilling various vital psychological needs, e.g. intimacy and the need to be attended to and cared for, understood, accepted, and valued. Positive, high quality relationships, such as a marriage, is a major integrating psycho-emotional structure that offers partners a high degree of safety, cohesion, and a deep sense of belongingness (Hawkley et al., 2008; de Jung Gierveld, 1998). Belongingness is one of the most important needs that romantic relationships can potentially and ultimately fulfill for partners (Baumeister and Leary, 1995; Gottman, 1999; Hendrick, 2004). The need to belong and be loved was placed in Abraham Maslow's hierarchy of needs close to the biological and safety needs in order to stress its importance as a core, highly essential human need. Belongingness is an innate human motivation manifested by the longing to form, develop, and enhance a mutual, reciprocal attachment bond with a significant other (e.g. marital spouse) (Maslow, 1968). Not being able to fulfill the need to belong due to marital distress might cause negative consequences to a person's psychological and emotional welfare (Baumeister and Leary, 1995). One of these consequences is the painful feeling of exclusion and loneliness (Hendrick, 2004). Loneliness is related to the need to belong to such a degree that "If people did not have a fundamental need to belong, loneliness, as we know it, would not exist" (Hendrick, 2004, p. 9).

According to the belonging hypothesis presented by Baumeister and Leary (1995), belongingness, as a core human motivation, consists of two basic components: (1) the desire to form a lasting, quality relationship that includes frequent emotional interactions with a partner who is pleasant and rewarding and (2) the desire for this affectionate and benevolent relationship to be stable and enduring over time. Given the central role of the belongingness motive as part of the evolutionary make up of human survival (Baumeister and Leary, 1995), people are motivated to develop gratifying pair bonds to shield against exclusion, loneliness, and alienation. To protect against the devastating emotional loneliness, one needs a close, affectionate partner with whom one can engage in an ongoing, enduring, and satisfying relationship (Bogarts, Vanheule, and Desmet, 2006; Flora and Sagrin, 2000; Hawkley and Cacioppo, 2009; Hendrick and Hendrick, 1995). In its most basic, broadest form, such a relationship serves as an antidote to loneliness and evolves mutual, reciprocal physical and emotional connectedness between two romantic partners, who feel strongly attached to each other. This physical and emotional proximity between romantic partners is an essential condition, necessary to the mutual fulfillment of the need to belong and be loved.

Whereas belongingness is fulfilled through a supportive and enhancing attachment bond, the absence or loss of a deep sense of belongingness is equally potent, resulting in distress and loneliness (Hendrick and Hendrick, 1995). One of the main reasons for marital partners to feel lonely is when their need for belongingness is not sufficiently met within their romantic relationship. Having large social network and connections, without the essential feeling of romantic belongingness does not buffer against the anguish accompanied by loneliness. Paradoxically, people in marital relationships who feel lonely spend little time, if any, with partners who are ordinarily the most likely people to fulfill their psychological need to belong.

The continuum that reflects the level of relational loneliness places belongingness and togetherness on one end and disengagement, isolation, and loneliness on the other. Gottman (1999) describes what he calls the "Distance and Isolation Cascade" underlying the deteriorating course of marital distress that eventually leads to disengagement, isolation, and loneliness. The first identifiable landmark is when a partner feels emotionally flooded as a result of constant negativity (e.g. criticism, emotional negativity). Prolonged flooding results in the conviction that the marital problems are so severe that any attempt to discuss problems will get nowhere. According to Gottman (1999), this conviction is a major step in the marital partners turning away from the marriage and eventually living parallel lives. In this advanced stage of the distance and isolation cascade, the partners are emotionally distanced and there is an absence of affect expression. The couple is in a state of emotional disengagement. Both are married to an emotionally unavailable partner. A partner's sense of not belonging, isolation, and emotional loneliness are, in this stage, inevitable. According to Perlman and Peplau (1998) this "empty-shell" marriage, characterized by the lack of belongingness, emotional disengagement, and indifference is a common antecedent of loneliness. It's the feeling of being de facto separated while de jure still married. Depicting her empty-shell marital loneliness, a patient of mine (A.S.) said, "I married, but I feel like not having a husband."

Gottman (1993) developed descriptions of five different types of marriages, one of which, the hostile/detached type describes an empty-shell marriage. The main attribute of the hostile/detached union is that partners' emotional distance reaches a point of complete uninvolvement, disengagement, and loneliness. Another well-documented typology of marriage was described by Olson and Fowers (1993). One of these marital types, the *Devitalized Couples*, closely resembles the empty-shell marriage, which is associated with loneliness. Devitalized couples are pervasively dissatisfied with their marriage and they are likely to divorce or remain in a marriage characterized by indifference, emotional emptiness, and loneliness.

Since emotional flooding has been identified by Gottman (1999) as an antecedent factor of marital disengagement and loneliness, the author constructed a 15 item instrument to assess flooding. Reviewing the items of this questionnaire gives a clear picture of the emotional flooding that may precipitate loneliness. Some of the recognizable features of flooding are: when discussions often turn to heated, hard to calm down arguments; when partners keep emotional distance, especially after arguments; when partners are overwhelmed by the constant atmosphere of fighting and tension; and when it is difficult to think clearly and rationally as a result of the hostility expressed during arguments.

To assess the degree of emotional disengagement and loneliness, Gottman (1999) constructed a 20 item questionnaire that provides some insights as to how loneliness is reflected. Some of the features of this questionnaire are: when one very often feels disappointed from one's spouse, when one is expecting less and less from the relationship, when one is feeling lonely from time to time, and when one's feelings don't get a sensitive response or attention. Other features of marital disengagement and loneliness are when one restricts one's self from expressing inner feelings and thoughts, when one feels like walking on eggshells, when intimacy and closeness are scarce, when one feels emptiness and let down by constant disappointment, and when one feels gradually separated, emotionally disconnected, and above all, feels emotionally lonely.

Maladaptive Social Cognitions

Earlier, we discussed the strenuous impact of the emotional loneliness associated with marital distress. In addition, there is a high degree of coexistence between the distressing phenomenon of loneliness and other constructs such as depression, anxiety, anger, and frustration (Mikulincer and Segal, 1990; Flora and Segrin, 2000; Hawkley and Cacioppo, 2009). These features of loneliness result from the antecedent negative marital characteristics of loneliness, such as: a decrease in marital quality and satisfaction; emotional disengagement; a partner's neglect, withdrawal, and inattentiveness; and indifference and emotional emptiness. Remaining untreated through marital counseling, this set of relational circumstances might be self-perpetuating.

A loneliness model developed by Hawkley and Cacioppo (2010) draws a portrait of a relational interactive process they called the Self Reinforcing Loneliness Loop (Hawkley and Cacioppo, 2010, p. 220). The perceived emotional isolation and separation expressed by lonely individuals gives rise to constant tension and an increased awareness and sensitivity to their relational surrounding. They are constantly "on guard," carefully scanning for potential sources of additional threatening signs.

This hyper vigilance (enhanced state of sensory sensitivity and alertness) is accompanied by increased vulnerability to the point that "lonely individuals see the social world as a more threatening place, expect more negative social interactions, and remember more negative social information" (Hawkley and Cacioppo, 2010, p. 220). These maladaptive social cognitions (expecting negativity) are self-reinforcing and act as a self-fulfilling prophecy by evoking confirming attitudes and interactive behaviors from others, e.g. marital spouse (Snyder, 1992; Snyder and Stukas, 1999). It is quite possible that when a marital spouse feels emotionally lonely, as a result of relational distress and disengagement, she (most likely it is the wife) construes the interaction as threatening. This is coupled by holding negative expectations and interpretations of a partner's behavior. This social cognition is followed by the lonely spouse reciprocating negatively to the other, thus adding to the marital distress and negativity, which in turn deepens the feeling of loneliness. In other words, it is possible that the lonely spouse may contribute to her own loneliness existence by perpetuating the Self Reinforcing Loneliness Loop (Hawkley and Cacioppo, 2010).

The clinical implications of this model consists of a two-phase interventions, with the phases being: (1) breaking the self-reinforcing loop of loneliness by transforming the lonely partner's cognitions and eliminating negative affect reciprocity and (2) working with the couple on improving their relationship by reducing distressing interactions and developing and enhancing foundations for a high quality, more satisfying marriage. Clinicians ought to include relational factors in the understanding of marital loneliness so as to ameliorate dysfunctional, maladaptive cognitions and interactive behaviors in order to alleviate loneliness. At the same time, it is necessary to take a prophylactic approach to eliminate the potential of future loneliness episodes. This therapeutic process is rather complicated and requires the marital partners to fully commit to it. Several circumstantial and developmental factors contribute to the complexity and possible obstacles to therapeutic success:

1) The intricacy of dealing with the enduring chronicity of the marital distress and dysfunctional interactive behaviors that preceded the loneliness and the anguish and pain it causes.

2) Overcoming the self-reinforcing loneliness loop, described earlier, that perpetuates the dysfunctional interactive behaviors that in turn intensify distress. The spouse exhibiting loneliness symptoms ought to be highly motivated to go through cognitive transformation and behavioral changes in order to break away from the loneliness loop. This is not an easy task, considering the devastating impact of loneliness.

3) It is likely that couples who reach this deteriorated level in their marriage hold a rather low level of personal commitment to the marriage. A considerably low level of marital commitment is a challenging imposition to therapy.

4) Overcoming the long-lasting marital distress that erodes relational resources in order to be able to cope with future stresses and conflicts. Following a prolonged marital distress, partners are left with fewer and weaker buffers to deal with problems and to protect against inevitable future conflicts.

Prolonged distress tends to erode cognitive and emotional stamina; it is unsurprising that it would erode optimism and hope.

5) It is known by therapists that disengaged couples who are seriously affected by the unpleasant loneliness loop do not respond positively to marital therapy. It is mostly because these couples pursue therapy when their marriage has seriously deteriorated (Gottman and Gottman, 1999). It is for these reasons that marriage therapy with disengaged, lonely couples is complicated, presenting a unique challenge to therapists and couples. We should also note that romantic disengagement, characterized by emotional distance, indifference, and loneliness, is a common reason for couples to seek therapy (Barry, Lawrence, and Langer, 2008).

Case Illustration

Rita, a 29-year-old pre-school teacher, and David, a 30-year-old graduate student at a theological seminary came to my (A.S.) clinic for therapy because they both felt they were alienated from each other and their marriage was emotionless. Although they have reached a point of emotional indifference, living parallel lives, they have not considered divorce due to moral and religious restrictions. Rita, pointing to the severity of their marital predicament said, "Although legally we are still married, emotionally we are divorced. I have a husband but deep inside I feel all alone and lonely."

Rita and David were married for seven years and had two children, a 5-year-old son, and, a 3-year-old daughter, described as "wonderful, healthy kids that we do not want to harm." Throughout the initial assessment Rita and David hardly looked at each other, seemed isolated, remote, and withdrawn. They seemed very sad. This interaction reflected their basic marital problem. Upon my probing, they reported a seven-year marital history that was divided into two distinctly different periods. During the first 4 years they were happy and satisfied. They were drawn lovingly toward each other, being affectionate, close, and intimate, spending a lot of time talking, getting to know and appreciate each other—all in all having a good time together. In complete contrast, the last 3 years were marked by them being less and less involved in each other's life, feeling progressively emotionally distanced from each other. Now they hardly talk, and when they do, it is only in regards to domestic, household issues. Upon Rita's request, they have not made love for almost a year. Rita said, "I can not make love to him when I feel so empty emotionally, so very uncared for and lonely." David has accepted Rita's sexual banning mostly because he has felt very much the same. He has also lost interest in and the desire for sexual closeness.

This couple's marital problems started after the birth of their second child. Being particularly sensitive and vulnerable, Rita felt for the first time that David had become distant, showing less interest in being with, or in supporting, her. Instead, David has become increasingly immersed in his studies, spending less and less time at home. Rita had complained about David's absence and the more demanding she became for his attention and closeness, the more withdrawn and distant he became. The little time David spent at home turned into loud and fierce arguments, leaving both of them angry and frustrated. Rita's needs for comfort, safety, and reassurance were not met by David, who became gradually less and less available and responsive to Rita's attachment needs, leaving Rita flooded by anxiety of being forsaken, abandoned, losing her secure bonding. Rita's criticism, anger, and personal attacks left David feeling unloved and unappreciated. Rita's fears of abandonment coupled with David feeling unloved and neglected got the couple into a reinforcing cycle of pursuing-distancing interactive communication. On one side of this interactive equation was Rita pursuing David for closeness, intimacy, and affection, and on the other side, David was withdrawing and distancing himself from Rita. The overriding therapy goal for this couple was for Rita and David to restore their ailing, distressed relationship, to look for and find what they have lost, namely, their attachment bonding. This is the only known and effective antidote to emotional loneliness. When asked about their commitment to therapy and how motivated they were to make positive relational changes, Rita said, "In my mind I know that I need to commit to the process…but emotionally I'm not there yet…I need to be assured that there is a chance to go back to what we were." David said, "I feel very much the same, but I know that divorce is not an option…we have no alternative so I guess I'll do my best to change things around."

To conclude, a marital union has a cohesive and protective function that affects partners' emotional well-being. Although marriage is likely to protect against the painful emotional injuries of loneliness, we should not be deceived and misled to believe that marriage is a constant and stable guarantee against loneliness. Generally, those who are utterly unhappy with their marriage, and who do not perceive their spouses as their closest friend and confidant, are highly vulnerable to emotional loneliness. The absence or loss of a trustworthy attachment figure (spouse) results in severe deficiencies in the provisions of a safe haven and a secure base and is a known to cascade into an interactive process that leads toward marital loneliness. In contrast, the formation, enhancement, and maintenance of a supportive, safety providing attachment bond protects against the deleterious effects of loneliness.

Although loneliness may be perceived as an adverse, distressing, and painful condition, it can, at the same time be adaptable, in that it may motivate couples in lonely marriages to modify and repair their relationships (Masi, Chen, Hawkley, and Cacioppo, 2011). It is only through the restoration of the attachment bonding that couples can alleviate emotional loneliness.

In the absence of a marital distress model of Transient Loneliness, we suggest the adoption of the stress generation model that describes the bidirectional pattern that exists between marital discord and depression (Beach, Dreifuss, Franklin, Kamen, and Gabriel, 2008; Devila, Bradbury, Cohan, and Tochluk, 1997). Hammen (1991, 2005) was the first to describe the construct of stress generation, which is "the process by which depressed people contribute to the occurrence of stress in their lives and thereby contribute to their experience of depression" (Davila et al., 1997, p. 849).

In other words, depressed people exacerbate their own stress through the negative cognitions and behaviors that they display (greater negativity, avoidance), which in turn result in more severe depression. An expansion of Hammen's framework was made by Beach et al. (2008) to suggest a bidirectional causal coexistence between marital distress and depression.

Accordingly, depressed individuals (as a consequence of marital distress) generate an added stress through negative relational interactions, which in turn exacerbate marital distress, leading to deeper depression.

Since loneliness has been associated with depression (Hojat, 1998; DiTommaso, Brenner-McNulty, Ross, and Burgess, 2003; Erozkan, 2011), it is reasonable to suggest a similar coexistence between marital distress and Transient Loneliness. Accordingly, loneliness caused by marital distress generates stress through negative interactive behaviors, which in turn exacerbates and maintains marital discord, leading to heightened loneliness. For couple therapy to get started, the therapist ought to conduct a thorough evaluation of the bidirectional causal effect that exists between marital distress and emotional loneliness. Once the marital distress and its resultant Transient Loneliness have been evaluated and established, partners are then to be challenged to enter a process of restoring marital cohesion and attachment bonding. This is to be done by the therapist emphasizing mutual acceptance, tolerance, and compromise to help the couple eliminate the impact of the vicious cycle caused by the bidirectional causal links between their distressed relationship and loneliness.

There are no couple-based therapeutic processes that are especially designed for the treatment of emotional loneliness in marriage. Intuitively, we suggest that any intervention that improves and enhances marital quality and satisfaction can potentially alleviate loneliness (Flora and Segrin, 2000). More specifically, interventions that promote and strengthen emotional connectedness, intimacy, and relational safety and support are likely to decrease the stressful sense of loneliness. Restoring a couple's cohesion seems to be an important purpose in this direction. Cohesion can be achieved by challenging partners to spend greater amounts of quality time together and engaging in shared enjoyable activities and joint projects.

Emphasis is also to be placed in marital therapy aimed at loneliness reduction in order to increase opportunities for the spouses to be in self-disclosing interactions. Self-disclosure is a particularly important factor associated with intimacy and emotional engagement in romantic and marital relationships.

One of the interactive behaviors missed by emotionally lonely spouses is the opportunity to talk about personal feelings and thoughts with a supportive partner (Solano, Batten, and Parish, 1982). Challenging couples in therapy to engage in self-revealing communication may prove to be a potent antidote to loneliness. Disclosure of inner feelings to one's supportive and accepting partner relates positively to marital quality and satisfaction (see chapter 10 in this volume). Enhancing self-disclosing interactions in lonely marital spouses is quite challenging due to the lonely individuals' tendency to withdraw and avoid interaction with one's partner, let alone expressions of inner feelings and thoughts.

Moreover, a therapeutic effort has to be directed at interrupting the stress generation vicious cycle associated with loneliness, especially when it is coupled with possible depression. As noted, marital cohesion and emotional closeness interact with loneliness in both cause and effect directions. A significant decrease in cohesion and intimacy creates disengagement and loneliness due to the absence of attachment bonding.

In return, loneliness, coupled with emotional distress and depression, exacerbates marital discord through the further reduction of cohesion and intimacy. Therapists should encourage and motivate couples to interrupt this cycle by re-investing in cohesion and intimacy promoting interactions and activities. Promoting marital cohesion and emotional connectedness is likely to restore the attachment safety, a vital component that protects against further emotional loneliness. We should bear in mind that the loss of attachment bonding is the most salient factor that creates emotional loneliness in the first place, thus restoring this loss is likely to reduce loneliness.

A couple's therapist is likely to detect in lonely spouses deficiencies in relational skills, i.e. inappropriate communication and conflict resolution skills. It is likely that during the initial phase of treatment, the partners will be emotionally remote, criticizing, blaming, and vilifying each other. These interactive behaviors are not conducive to an effective communication and problem solving processes. At this stage, the partners' problem solving and conflict resolution strategies are characterized by high levels of conflict, tension, and overt hostility, avoidance, and withdrawal interactions. These longstanding, counterproductive relational patterns are to be "pictorially" drawn by the therapist to evoke a thorough understanding in the couple concerning their relational predicament. This is to be followed by enlisting the couple to actively participate in the process of restoring their attachment bonding.

This chapter, being the concluding chapter of this volume, is, in our opinion as clinicians and researchers, perhaps the first attempt to bring together and discuss the inter-relationship between loneliness and romantic relations, which are commonly referred to separately. This chapter, thus, in focusing on the clinical aspects of the cases which we presented, integrated the theoretical and empirical aspects that were presented throughout this book. While working on this volume, we became aware of the scarcity of empirical research in studying loneliness in marital/romantic relationships. Furthermore, we would like to highlight that there is lack of any assessment instruments to evaluate loneliness in romantic relationships. Additional research focusing on both issues is essential for academic and clinical purposes.

REFERENCES

Aanes, M. M., Middlemark, M. B., & Hetland, J. (2010). Interpersonal stress and poor health: The mediating role of loneliness. *European Psychologist, 15*(1), 3-11

Aartsen, M. & Jylha, M. (2011). Onset of loneliness in older adults: results of a 28 year prospective study. *European Journal of Ageing*, (8), 31–38.

Abbott, E., & Liddell, D. L. (1996). Alienation of students: Does sexual orientation matter? *College Student Affairs Journal, 16*, 45-55.

Acevedo, B. P., & Aron, A. (2009). Does a long-term relationship kill romantic love? *Review of General Psychology, 13*, 59-65.

Acevedo, B. P., Aron, A., Fisher, H. E., & Brown, L. L. (2011). Neural correlates of long-term intense romantic love. *Social Cognitive and Affective Neuroscience*. doi: 10.1093/scan/nsq092

Acitelli, L. K., Wickham, R. E., Brunson, J., Nguyen, M. (2011, January). *When couples read stories about other couples' relationships*. Poster presented at the meeting of the Society for Personality and Social Psychology, San Antonio, TX.

Adam, E. K., Hawkley, L. C., Kudielka, B. M., & Cacioppo, J. T. (2006). Day-to-day dynamics of experience: cortisol associations in a population-based sample of older adults. Proceedings of the National Academy of Science of the United States of America, 103, 17058e17063.

Adams, B. (2004). Families and family study in international perspective. *Journal of Marriage and Family, 66*, 1076-1088.

Adams, J.M., & Jones, W.H. (1999). Interpersonal commitment in historical perspective. In J.M. Adams, & W.H. Jones (Eds.). *Handbook of interpersonal commitment and relationship stability*. New York: Kluwer Academic/Plenum Publishers (pp. 3-36).

Adams, J.M. & Spain, J.S. (1999). The dynamics of interpersonal commitment and the issue of salience. In J.M. Adams & W.H. Jones. *Handbook of interpersonal commitment and relationship stability* (pp. 165-179). New York: Kluwer Academic/Plenum.

Adler, M. J., & Doren C. L. (1972). *How to Read a Book*. New York: Simon and Schuster.

Adolfsen, A., & Keuzenkamp, S. (2006). Opinieonderzoek onder de bevolking [Attitude studies among the population]. In S. Keuzenkamp, D. Bos, J. W. Duyvendak, & G. Hekma (Eds.), *Gewoon doen. Acceptatie van homoseksualiteit in Nederland [Act normal. Acceptance of homosexuality in the Netherlands]* (pp. 27–57). Den Haag: SCP.

Agnew, C.R., Van Lange, P.M.R., Rusbult, C.E., & Langston, C.A. (1998). Cognitive interdependence commitment and the mental representation of close relationships. *Journal of Personality and Social Psychology.* 74, 939-954.

Ainsworth, M. D. S., Blehar, M. C., Waters, E. & Wall, S. (1978). Patterns of attachment: A psychological study of the strange situation. Hillsdale, NJ: *Erlbaum.*

Aldwin, C. M. (1990). The Elders Life Stress Inventory (ELSI): Research and clinical applications. In P. A. Keller & S. R. Heyman (Eds.), *Innovations in clinical practice: A source book, Vol. 10* (pp. 355-364). Sarasota, FL: Professiona Resource ress/Professional Research Exchange.

Alexander, S., & Baker, K. (1992). Some ethical issues in applied social psychology: The case of bilingual education and self-esteem. *Journal of Applied Social Psychology,* 22(22), 1741-1757.

Allen, R. and Oshagan, H. (1995). The UCLA Loneliness Scale invariance of social structural characteristics. Personality Individual Differences, 19, 2, 185–95.

Allen, K. R., Blieszner, R., & Roberto, K. A. (2000). Families in the middle and later years: a review and critique of research in the 1990s. *Journal of Marriage and the Family, 62,* 911-926.

Allgeier, E. R., & Weiderman, M. W. (1991). Love and mate selection in the 1990s. *Free Inquiry, 11,* 25-27.

Alpass, F., & Neville, S. (2003). Loneliness, health and depression in older males. *Aging & Mental Health, 7*(3), 212-216.

Altman, I. & Taylor, D.A. (1973). Social penetration: The development of interpersonal relationships. New York: *Holt, Rinehart, & Winston.*

Amado A. (2004) Lessons learned about promoting friendship. *Connections 30, 8–12.*

Amato, P.R. (2000). *The consequences of divorce for adults and children. Journal of Marriage and Family* 62, 1269-1287.

Amato, P.R., Booth, A., Johnson, D.R., & Rogers, S.J. (2007). Alone together: How marriage in America is changing. *Cambridge, Mass: Harvard University Press.*

Amato, P.R. & Irving, S. (2006). Historical trends in divorce in the United States. In M.A. Fine & J.H. Harvey (Eds.) *Handbook of divorce and relationship dissolution.* (pp. 41-57). New York: Rutledge.

Amato, P. R., & Rogers, S. J. (1999). Do attitudes toward divorce affect marital quality? *Journal of Family Issues, 20*(1), 69-86.

Amato, P.R., Previty, D. (2003). People's reasons for divorcing: Gender, social class, the life course, and adjustment. *Journal of Family Issues,* 24(5), 602-626.

American Community Survey (2004). *United States Census Bureau.* Retrieved July 8, 2007, from http://www.statemaster.com/graph/lif_ave_hou_siz-lifestyle-average-household-size.

American Psychiatric Association (2000). *Diagnostic and Statistical Manual of Mental Disorders (4"Ed.).* Washington, D.C.:Aulhor.

Anderson, C. (1982). The community connection: The impact of social networks on family and individual functioning. In A. Walsh (Ed.), *Normal Family Processes, 425-445.* New York: Guilford Press.

André, R. (1991). Positive solitude: A practical program for mastering loneliness and achieving self-fulfillment. NY: Harper Collins.

Anthony, T. (1998, Jan. 29). Young at heart. *The Toronto Star,* E6.

Antonucci, T.C (1985). Personal characteristics, social support and social behaviour. In: R.H. Binstock, & E. Shanas (Eds.), *Handbook of aging and the social sciences* (pp. 94-128). New York: Van Nostrand-Reinhold.

Antonucci, T. C., Hiroko, A., & Merline, A. (2001). Dynamics of social relationships in midlife. In M. E. Lachman (Ed.), *Handbook of midlife development* (pp. 571-598). Hoboken, NJ: John Wiley & Sons.

Argyle, M. & Hendersen, M. (1984). The rules of friendship. *Journal of social and personal relationships,* 1, 211-237.

Argyle, M., & Martin, M. (1991). The psychological causes of happiness. In F. Strack, M. Argyle, & N. Schwarz (Eds.), Subjective well being: An interdisciplinary perspective (pp. 77–100). Oxford: Pergamon.

Aristotle (2004). Politics, Book I. Translated by Benjamin Jowett. Belle Fourche, South Dakota, USA: *NuVision Publications.*

Arnett, J. J. (1999). Adolescent storm and stress, reconsidered. *American Psychologist, 54(5),* 317-326.

Aron, A. & Aron, E.N. (1986). Love as the expansion of self: Understanding attraction and satisfaction. New York: *Hemisphere.*

Aron, A. & Aron, E.N. (2006). Romantic relationship from the perspectives of the self-expansion model and attachment theory. In M. Mikulincer & G.S. Goodman (Eds.) Dynamics of romantic love: Attachment, care giving and sex (359-382). New York: *The Guilford Press.*

Aron, A. & Aron, E.N. (1996) self and self-expansion in relationship. In G.J.O. Fletcher & J. Fitness (Eds.) Knowledge structures in close relationships: A social psychological approach (pp. 325-344). Mahwah, New Jersey: *Lawrence Erlbaum.*

Aron, A. & Aron, E.N. (1997). Self expansion motivation and including others in the self. In W. Ickes (2nd Ed.) & S. Duck (Ed.) *Handbook of personal relationship* (2nd Ed; Vol 1, pp. 251-27). London: Wiley.

Aron, A., Aron, E.N., & Smollan, D. (1992). Inclusion of other in the self scale and the structure of interpersonal closeness. *Journal of Personality and Social Psychology,* 63, 596-612.

Aron, A. & Fraley, B. (1999). Relationship closeness as including others in the self: Cognitive underpinning and measures. *Social Cognition,* 17, 140-160.

Aron, A., Norman, C. C., & Aron, E. N. (2001). *Shared self-expanding activities as a means of maintaining and enhancing close romantic relationships.* (pp. 47-66). Mahwah, NJ, US: Lawrence Erlbaum Associates Publishers, Mahwah, NJ.

Aron, A., Norman, C.E., Aron, E.L., & Lewandowski, G. (2002). Shared participation in self-expanding activities: positive effects on experienced marital quality. In P. Noller & J.A. Feeney. *Understanding marriage: Developments in the study of couple interaction. Cambridge University Press* (pp. 177-194).

Arriaga, X.B., & Agnew, C.R. (2001). Being committed: Affective, cognitive, and conative components of relationship commitment. *Personality and Social Psychology Bulletin,* 27, 1190.

Arriaga, X. B., Goodfriend, W., & Lohmann, A. (2004). Beyond the individual: Concomitants of closeness in the social and physical environment. In D. J. Mashek & A. Aron (Eds.), *Handbook of closeness and intimacy* (pp. 287 – 303). Mahwah, NJ: Erlbaum.

Arriaga, X.B. & Rusbult, C.E. (1998). Standing in my partner's shoes: Partner perspective taking and reactions to accommodative dilemmas. *Personality and Social Psychology Bulletin,* 24, 927-948.

Ashdown, B.K., Hackathorn, J., & Clark, E.M. (2011). In and out of the bedroom: Sexual satisfaction in the marital relationship. *Journal of Integrated Social Sciences,* 2011,2,1, 40-57.

Asher, S. R., & Paquette, J. A. (2003). Loneliness and peer relations in childhood. *Current Directions in Psychological Science, 12*(3), 75-78.

Aspinwall, L.G. (1998). Rethinking the role of positive affect in self-regulation. *Motivation and Emotion,* 22, 1-32.

Attree, M.(2001). Patients' and relatives' experiences and perspectives of `Good' and `Not so Good' quality care. *Journal of Advanced Nursing, 33*(4), 456-466.

Audy, R.J. (1980). Man the lonely animal: Biological roots of loneliness. In J. Hartog, J.R. Audy, & Y.A. Cohen (Eds.), *The anatomy of loneliness* (p. 111 - 128). NY: International Universities Press.

Avery, A.W., Ridley, C.A., Leslie, L.A., & Milholland, T. (1980). Relationship enhancement with premarital dyads: A six-month follow-up. *American Journal of Family Therapy,* 3,23-30.

Azar, B. (2011). A reason to believe. *Montior on Psychology, 41,* 11, 52-56.

Baker, P. (1983). *Coping with arthritis: A comprehensive guide for sufferers and care-givers.* Toronto, Ont. Clarke Irwin pub.

Buss, D. M. (1990). The evolution of anxiety and social exclusion. *Journal of Social and Clinical Psychology, 9,* 196-210.

Bakkaloglu, H. (2010). A comparison of the loneliness levels of mainstreamed primary students according to their sociometric status. *Procedia – Social and Behavioural Sciences, 2*(2), 330-336.

Baldwin, M.W. (1992). Relationships schemas and the processing of social information. *Psychological Bulletin,* 11,3, 461-484.

Baldwin, M.W., Fehr, B., Keedian, E., Seidel, M., & Thomson, D.W. (1993) An exploration of the relational schemata underlying attachment styles: Self-report and lexical decision approaches. *Personality and Social Psychology Bulletin,* 19, 746-754.

Ballard-Reisch, D.S. & Weigle, D.J. (1999). Communication process in marital commitment. In J.M. Adams & H.J. Warren (Eds.) *Handbook of interpersonal commitment and relationship stability* (pp. 407-449). New York: Kluwer Academic/Plenum Publishers.

Balsam, K. F., & Szymanski, D. M. (2005). Relationship quality and domestic violence in women's same-sex relationships: The role of minority stress. *Psychology of Women Quarterly,* 29, 258–269

Bandura, A. (1969). *Principles of behaviour modification.* NY: Holt, Rinehart & Winston.

Bandura, A. (1995). Self-efficacy in changing societies. New York: *Cambridge University Press.*

Bandura, A. (1997). Self-efficacy: The exercise of control. New York: *Freeman.*

Banmen, J., & Vogel, N.A. (1985). The relationship between marital quality and interpersonal sexual self-disclosure. *Family Therapy,* 12, 45-58.

Barbach,L. (1980) Women discover orgasm: A therapist's guide to a new treatment approach. New- York: the free Press.

Barbur, A. (1993). Research report: Dyadic loneliness in marriage. *Journal of Group Psychology, Psychodrama & Sociometry,* 46, 2, 70-73.

Barker, C., & Pistrang, N. (2002). Psychotherapy and social support: Integrating research on psychological helping. *Clinical Psychology Review*, 22(3), 361-379.

Barlow, D. H., & Durand, V. M. (1995) *Abnormal psychology.* London: Brooks/Cole.

Barnes, M.L., & Sternberg, R.J. (1997). A hierarchical model of love and its prediction of satisfaction in close relationship. In R.J. Sternberg & M. Hojjat (Eds.). *Satisfaction in close relationship.* (pp.79-101). New York: The Guilford Press.

Barry, R., Bunde, M., Brock, R.L., & Lawrence, E. (2009). Validity and utility of multidimensional model of received support in intimate relationships. *Journal of Family Psychology,* 23(1), 48-57.

Barry, R.A., Lawrence, E., & Langer, A. (2008). Conceptualization and assessment of disengagement in romantic relationships. *Personal Relationships,* 15, 297-315.

Bascom, G. S. (1984) Physical, emotional, and cognitive care of dying patients. *Bulletin of the Menninger Clinic*, 48, 351-356.

Bastian, B., & Haslam, N. (2010). Excluded from humanity: The dehumanizing effects of social ostracism. *Journal of Experimental Social Psychology, 46*, 107-113.

Batson, C. D. (1998). Who cares? when? where? why? how? *PsycCRITIQUES, 43*(2), 108-109.

Baumeister, R.F. & Leary, M.R. (1995). The need to belong: Desire for interpersonal attachments as a fundamental human motivation. *Psychological Bulletin, 117*(3), 497-529.

Baumeister, R.F., Wotman, S.R., & Stillwell, A.M. (1993). Unrequited love: On heartbreak, anger, guilt, and scriptlessness, and humiliation. *Journal of Personality and Social Psychology*, 64, 377-394.

Baxter, L.A. (1986). Gender differences in the heterosexual relationship rules embedded in break-up accounts. *Journal of Personality and Social Psychology,* 3, 289-306.

Beach, S.R.H., Dreifuss, J.A., Franklin, K.J., Kamen, C., & Gabriel, B. (2008) couple therapy and the treatment of depression. In A.S. Gurman (Ed.) *Clinical handbook of couple therapy* (pp. 545-566). New York: Guilford Press.

Beach, S. R. H., Jouriles, E. N., & O' Leary, K. D. (1985). Extramarital sex: Impact on depression and commitment in couples seeking marital therapy. *Journal of Sex and Marital Therapy, 11*, 99-108.

Beach, R.H., Kamen, C., & Fincham, F. (2006). Marital dissatisfaction. In F. Andrasic (Ed.) Comprehensive handbook of personality and psychopathology. *Adult psychopathology* (Vol II, pp. 450-465). New York: Wiley

Becker, G.S. (1991). A treatise on the family (Enlarged ed.). Cambridge, MA: Harvard University Press.

Beeson, R.A. (2003). Loneliness and depression in spousal caregiving of those with Alzheimer's disease versus non-caregiving spouses. Archives of Psychitaric Nursing, 17, 135-143.

Bell, R.A., & Daly, J.A. (1985). Some communicative correlates of loneliness. *Communication Monographs*, 52, 218-235.

Belsky, J., Lang, M.E. & Rovine, M. (1985). Stability and change in marriage across the transition to parenthood: a second study. *Journal of Marriage and the* Family, 47, (4), 855-865.

Belsky, J. & Rovine, M. (1990). Patterns of marital change across the transition to parenthood. Pregnancy to three years postpartum. *Journal of Marriage and the Family, 52*, 5-19.

Ben-Ari, A., & Lavee, Y. (2007). Dyadic closeness in marriage: From the inside story to a conceptual model. *Journal of Social and Personal Relationships, 24*, 627-644.

Bengston, VL. & Schrader, S.S. (1982). Parent-child relations. In D.J Mangen & W.A. Peterson (Eds.), *Research instruments in social gerontology 2,* 115-185. Minneapolis: University of Minnesota Press.

Bennett, J. A. (2000). Mediator and moderator variables in nursing research: Conceptual and statistical differences. Research in Nursing and Health, 23, 415–420

Berg, S., Mellström, D. Persson, G., & Svanborg, A. (1981). Loneliness in the Swedish aged. *The Journal of Gerontology, 36*(3), 342-349.

Bergenstal, K. W. (1981). The relationship of father support and father availability to adolescent sons' experience of loneliness and separation anxiety. Dissertation Abstracts International, 2024-2025.

Berkman, L. (1995). The role of social relations in health promotion. *Psychosomatic Medicine, 57,* 245 – 254.

Berkman, L. F., & Glass, T. A. (2000). Social integration, social networks, social support and health. In L. F. Berkman & I. Kawachi (Eds.), *Social epidemiology* (pp. 137-174). New York: *Oxford University Press.*

Berkman, L.F., Glass, T., Brissette, I., & Seeman, E.A. (2000). From social integration to health: Durkheim in the new millennium. *Social Science and Medicine*, 51, 843-857.

Berkman, L.F. & Syme, S.L. (1979). Social networks, host resistance and morality: A nine-year follow-up study of Alameda County residents. *American Journal of Epidemiology,* 109, 186-204.

Berscheid, E. (2006). Seasons of the heart. In M. Mikulincer & Goodman G.S. (Eds.), Dynamics of romantic love: Attachment, caregiving and sex. NY: *Guilford Press.*

Berscheid, E, Snyder, M., & Omoto, A. M. (2004). Measuring closeness: The relationship Closeness Inventory (RCI) revisited. In D. J. Mashek & A. Aron (Eds.), *Handbook of closeness and intimacy* (pp. 81-101). Mahwah, NJ: Erlbaum.

Berschied, E., Snyder, M., & Omato, A.M. (1989). The relationship closeness inventory: Assessing the closeness of interpersonal relationships. *Journal of Personality and Social Psychology,* 57, 792-809.

Berscheid, E., & Reis, H.T. (1988). Attraction and close relationships. In D.T Gilbert & S.T. Fiske (Eds.). *The handbook of social psychology* (Fourth Ed.) (pp. 193-281). New York: *McGraw Hill.*

Berscheid, E. & Walster (Hatfield) E. (1974). A little bit about love. In T.L. Huston (Ed.), *Foundations of interpersonal attraction* (pp. 355-381). NY: *Academic Press.*

Bess, K.D., Fisher, A.T., Sonn, C.C. & Bishop, B.J. (2002). Psychological sense of community: Theory, research and application. In K.D. Bess, A.T. Fisher, C.C. Sonn & B.J. Bishop (Eds.*), Psychological sense of community: Research, Applications and Implications,* 1-22. New York: Kluwer Academic/Plenum.

Betts, L.R. & Bicknell, A.S.A. (2011). Experiencing loneliness in childhood: Consequences for psychological adjustment, school adjustment, and academic performance. In: Bevinn, S.J. (Ed.). *Psychology of loneliness* (Pp. 1-27). NY: Nova Science Pub.

Biblarz, T. J. & Savci, E. (2010). Lesbian, gay, bisexual, and transgender families.

Birnbaum, G., Glaubman, H., & Mikulincer, M. (2001). Women's experience of heterosexual intercourse: Scale construction, factor structure, and relations to orgasmic disorder. *Journal of Sex Research,* 38, 191-204.

Biehle, S.N. (2009). Preparing for parenthood: Individual and couple models of anxiety and marital satisfaction. Masters Thesis, Kent State University.

Birchler, G.R., Douman, D.M., & Fals-Stewart, W.S. (1999). The family journal: Counselling and therapy for couples and families, 7, 3, 253-264.

Blekesaune, M. & Øverbye, E. (2000). *Uførepensjonisters material living conditions and social affiliation.* NOVA Report 7/2000. Oslo: Norwegian Institute for research on welfare and aging.

Blai, B. (1989). Health consequences of loneliness: A review of the literature. Journal of American College Health, 37, 162−167.

Blatt, S. J. (1990). Interpersonal relatedness and self-definition: Two personality configurations and their implications for psychopathology and psychotherapy. In J. Singer (Ed.), *Repression: Defense mechanisms and personality* (pp. 299–335). Chicago: University of Chicago Press.

Blieszner, R. (1988). Individual development and intimate relationships in middle and late adulthood. In R.M. Milardo (Ed.), *Families and social networks,* (p.147-167). Newburg Park, CA: Sage.

Bloch, H. (1991). Medieval misogyny and the invention of Western romantic love. Chicago, ill: University of Chicago Press.

Blood, R. O. (1972). *The family.* New York: Free Press.

Bloom B., Asher S. & White S. (1978) Marital disruption as a stressor. *Psychological Bulletin* 85, 867–894.

Bloom, J. R., & Spiegel, D. (1984) The relationship of two dimensions of social support to the psychological well being and social functioning of women with advanced breast cancer. *Social Science and Medicine,* 19, 831-837.

Blow, A.J., & Timm, T.M. (2002). Promoting community through family therapy: Helping clients develop a network of significant relationships (Electronic version). *Journal of Systemic Therapies, 21,* 1-14.

Blum R., Resnick M., Nelson R. & St Germaine A. (1991) Family and peer issues among adolescents with spina bifida and cerebral palsy. Pediatrics 88, 280–285.

Bodenmann, G. (2000). *Stress und Coping bei Paaren [Stress and coping in couples].* Göttingen: Hogrefe.

Bogarts, S., Vanheule, S., & Desmet, M. (2006). Feelings of subjective emotional loneliness: An exploration of attachment. *Social Behaviour and Personality,* 34(7), 797-812.

Boivin, M., Hymel, S., & Bukowski, W. M. (1995). The role of social withdrawal, peer rejection, and victimization by peers predicting loneliness and depressed mood in childhood. *Development and Psychopathology,* 7, 765–785.

Booth, R. (1983). Toward an understanding of loneliness. *Social Work,* 23,116–119.

Booth, A.,&Johnson, D. (1994). Declining health and marital quality. *Journal of Marriage and the Family, 56,* 218-223.

Borge, L., Martinsen, E.W., Rudd, T. Watne, Q., & Friis, S. (1999). Quality of line, loneliness and social contact among long-term psychiatric patients. *Psychiatric services, 50,* 81-84.

Borys, S., & Perlman, D. (1985). Gender differences in loneliness. *Personality and Social Psychology Bulletin, 11,* 63-74.

Bouchard, G., Lessier, Y., & Sobourin, S. (1999). Personality and martial adjustment: Utility of the five-factor model of personality. *Journal of Marriage and the Family*, 61(3), 651-660.

Bowen, M. (1978). *Family therapy in clinical practice*. New York: Aronson.

Bowlby, J. (1969/1982). Attachment and loss, vol. 1, Attachment, 2nd ed. NY: Basic books.

Bowlby, J. (1969). Attachment and loss. *Vol.1: Attachment*. New York: Basic Books.

Bowlby, J. (1973). Affection bonds: their nature and origin. In R. S. Weiss (Ed.) *Loneliness: The experience of social and emotional isolation* (Pp. 38-52). Cambridge Mass: The MIT Press.

Bowlby, J. (1980). Attachment and Loss: Vol. 3. Loss. New York: Basic Books.

Bowlby, J. (1988). A secure base: Clinical applications of attachment theory. London: *Routledge*.

Bowling, T.K., Hill, C.M., & Jencius, M. (2005). An overview of marriage enrichment. *The Family Journal: Counseling and therapy for couples and families*, 13, 1, 87-94.

Bracke, P., Christiaens, W., & Verhaeghe, M. (2008). Self-esteem, self-efficacy, and the balance of peer support among persons with chronic mental health problems. *Journal of Applied Social Psychology, 38*(2), 436-459.

Bradbury, T. N., Fincham, F. D., & Beach, S. R. (2000). Research on the nature and determinants of marital satisfaction: A decade in review. *Journal of Marriage and the Family*, 62, 964-980.

Bradbury, T. N., & Karney, B. R. (2004). Understanding and altering the longitudinal course of marriage. *Journal of Marriage and Family*, 66, 862 – 879.

Bradford, J., Ryan, C., & Rothblum, E. D. (1994). National health care survey: Implications for mental health care. *Journal of Consulting and Clinical Psychology, 62, 228-242*

Bragg, M.E. (1979). A comparative study of loneliness and depression. *Dissertion Abstracts International, 39*, 79-137.

Bramlett, M.D. & Mosher, W.D. (2002). Cohabitation, marriage, divorce and remarriage in the United States. *Vital Health Statistics, 23*, 22.

Brannon, L. & Feist, J. (2004). *Health psychology: An introduction to behaviour and health*. Toronto, Canada: Thomson Wadsworth.

Brehm, S. S. (1987). Social support and clinical practice. In J. E. Maddux, C. D. Stoltenberg & R. Rosenwein (Eds.), *Social processes in clinical and counseling psychology* (pp. 26-38). New York: Springer-Veriag.

Brehm, S.S. (1992). Intimate relationships. 2nd Ed. NY: McGraw-Hill.

Brehm, S.S., Miller, R.S., Perlman, D. & Cambell, S.M. (2002). *Intimate relationships* (3rd Ed.). New York: McGraw Hill.

Brennan, T. (1982). Loneliness at adolescence. In: L.A. Peplau & D. Perlman (Eds.) (1982). *Loneliness: A source book of current theory, research and therapy* (pp. 269-290). New York: John Wiley & Sons.

Brewer, M. B. (2005). The psychological impact of social isolation: Discussion and commentary. In K. D. Williams, J. P. Forgas, & W. von Hippel (Eds.), *The social outcast: Ostracism, social exclusion, rejection, and bullying* (pp. 333-345). New York, NY: Psychology Press.

Brewer, G., & Hendrie, C. A. (2011). Evidence to suggest that copulatory vocalization in women are not a reflexive consequence of orgasm. *Archives of Sexual Behavior, 40*, 559-564.

Bringle, R. G., & Buunk, B. P. (1991). Extradyadic relationships and sexual jealousy. In K. McKinney & S. Sprecher (Eds.), *Sexuality in close relationships* (pp. 135-153). Hillside, NJ: Erlbaum. Brock, R. L., & Lawrence, E. (2008). A longitudinal investigation of stress spillover in marriage: Does spousal support adequacy buffer the effects? *Journal of Family Psychology, 22*(1), 11-20.

Broese van Groenou, M.I. (1991). Gescheiden Netwerken: De Relaties met Vrienden en Verwanten na Echtscheiding (Separate networks: The relationships with friends and kin after divorce). Unpublished dissertation, Universiteit Utrecht.

Brown, A. S. (1996). *The social processes of aging and old age.* Upper Saddle River, N. J.: Prentice Hall.

Brown, J., Sorrell, J., McClaren, J., & Creswell, J. (2006). Waiting for a liver transplant. *Qualitative Health Research*, 16(1), 119-136.

Buber, M. (1958). *I and thou* (R. G. Smith, Trans.). New York: Charles Scribner's Sons. (Original work published 1923)

Buber, I. & Engelhardt, H. (2008). Children's impact on mental health of their older mothers and fathers: Findings from the survey of health, ageing and retirement in Europe. *European Journal of Ageing, 5*, 31-45.

Buchman, G.J. & Johnson, L.D. (1979). The freshmen. Psychology Today, 13, 78-87.

Bucholtz, E. (1997). *Alone time is a world of attachment.* NY; Simon & Shuster.

Buckner, J.C., Bassuk, E.L. (1997). Mental disorders and service utilization among youths from homeless and low-income household families. *Journal of the American Academy of Child and Adolescent Psychiatry*, 36, 890–900.

Bullock, J.R. (1998). Loneliness in young children. *ERIC digest*, EDO-PS-98-1.

Burger, J. M. (1998). Solitude. In *Encyclopedia of mental health* (Vol. 3, pp. 563-569). San Diego, CA: Academic Press.

Burger, J. M., & Caldwell, D. F. (2000). Personality, social activities, job-search behavior and interview success: Distinguishing between PANAS trait positive affect and NEO extraversion. *Motivation and Emotion, 24*(1), 51-62.

Burman, B., & Margolin, G. (1992). Analysis of the association between marital relationships and health problems: An interactional perspective. *Psychological Bulletin, 112*, 39-63.

Burton – Chrisite, H. (2003). *An empirical investigation of the interrelationships of organizational culture, managerial values, and organizational citizenship behaviors. Dissertation Abstracts International: Section B: The Sciences and Engineering*, 1532-1532.

Buss, D. M. (1989). Sex differences in human mate preferences: Evolutionary hypotheses tested in 37 cultures. *Behavioral and Brain Sciences*, 2, 1-14.

Buss, D. M. (1990). The evolution of anxiety and social exclusion. *Journal of Social and Clinical Psychology, 9,* 196-210.

Buss, D.M. (1991). Conflict in married couples: Personality predictors of anger and upset. *Journal of Personality*, 59, 663-668.

Buss, D.M. (2000). Prescription for passion. *Psychology Today,* May/June, 54-61.

Buss, D. M. (2000). The dangerous passion: Why jealousy is as necessary as love and sex. New York: Free Press.

Buss, D. M. (2003). The evolution of desire: Strategies of human mating. (rev. ed.). NY: *Basic Books.*

Buss, D. M. (2006). The evolutionary genetics of personality: Does mutation load signal relationship load? *Behavioral and Brain Sciences, 29*(4), 409-409.

Buss, D.M. & Schmitt, D.P. (1993). Sexual strategies theory: An evolutionary perspective on human mating. *Psychological Review,* 100, 204-232.

Byers, E.S., & MacNeil, S.A. (2006). Further validation of the interpersonal exchange model of sexual satisfaction. *Journal of Sex and Marital Therapy,* 32, 53-69.

Byrd, S.E. (2009). The social construction of marital commitment. *Journal of Marriage and Family,* 71(2), 318-336.

Cacioppo, J.T., Ernst, J.M., Burleson, M.H., McClintock, M.K., Malarky, W.B., Hawkely, L.C., et al. (2000). Lonely traits and concomitant physiological processes: The MacAthur social neuroscience studies. *International Journal of Psychophysiology,* 35, 143-154.

Cacioppo, J. T., Hawkley, L. C., & Berntson, G. G. (2003). The anatomy of loneliness. *Current Directions in Psychological Science, 12,* 71-74.

Cacioppo, J.T., & Hawkley, L.C. (2009). Loneliness. In M.R. Leary & R.H. Hoyle (Eds.). *Handbook of individual differences in social behavior* (pp.227-239). New York: Guilford.

Cacioppo, J.T., Hawkley, L.C., Crawford, E., Ernst, J.M., Burleson, M.H., Kowalewski, R.B., Malarkey, W.B., Cauter, E.V., & Berntson, G.G. (2002). Loneliness and health: Potential mechanisms. *Psychosomatic Medicine, 64,* 407-417.

Cacioppo, J. T., Hawkley, L. C., Ernst, J. M., Burleson, M., Berntson, G. G., Nouriani, B., & Spiegel, D. (2006a). Loneliness within a nomological net: An evolutionary perspective. *Journal of Research in Personality, 40,* 1054-1085.

Cacioppo, J.T., Hawkley, L.C., & Thisted, R.A. (2010). Perceived social isolation makes me sad: 5-Year cross-lagged analyses of loneliness and depressive symptomatology in the Chicago health, aging, and social relations study. *Psychology and Aging, 25*(2), 453-463.

Cacioppo, J. T., Hughes, M. E., Waite, L. J., Hawkley, L. C., & Thisted, R. A. (2006b). Loneliness as a specific risk factor for depressive symptoms: Crosssectional and longitudinal analyses. *Psychology and Aging, 21,* 140–151.

Cacioppo, J.T. & Patrick, W. (2008). *Loneliness: Human nature and the need for social connection.* New York: W.W. Norton.

Cacioppo, J.T., Reis, H.T., & Zautra, A.J. (2011). Social resilience: The value of social fitness with an application to the military. *American Psychologist,* 66(1), 43-51.

Call, V., Sprecher, S., & Schwartz, P. (1995). The incidence and frequency of marital sex in a national sample. *Journal of Marriage and the Family,* 57, 639-652.

Cahn, D.D. (1992). Conflict in intimate relationships. New York: Guilford

Cahn, D.D. (1990). Confrontation behaviours, perceived understanding and relationship growth. In D. Cahn (Ed.) *Intimates in conflict* (pp.153-166). Hillsdale, New Jersey: Erlbaum

Canary, D.J., Cupach, W.R., & Messman, S.J. (1995). Relationship conflict in parent-child friendship and romantic relationships. *Thousand Oaks*, CA: Sage

Canton, M. (1979). Neighbors and friends: An overlooked resource in the informal support system. *Research on Aging, 1,* 434-463.

Canvello, A. & Crocker, J. (2010). Creating good relationships: Responsiveness, relationship quality, and interpersonal goals. *Journal of Personality and Social Psychology,* 99 (1), 78-106.

Capezuti, E., Boltz, M., Renz, S., Hoffman, D., & Norman, R. (2006). Nursing home involuntary relocation: Clinical outcomes and perceptions of residents and families. *Journal of the American Medical Directors Associations, 7*(8), 486-492.

Caraballo-Dieguez, A. (1989). Hispanic culture, gay male culture, and AIDS: Counseling implications. *Journal of Counseling and Development, 68*(1), 26–30.

Carlson, J. & Dinkmeyer, D. (2003). TIME for a better marriage. Atascadero, CA: Impact Publisher.

Carnelley, K., & Ruscher, J. (2000). Adult attachment and exploratory behavior in leisure. *Journal of Social Behavior and Personality,* 15, 153-165.

Carpenter, S. (2001) An interdisciplinary group of scientists argues that we know behavior is crucial to health—and its time health research and interventions reflect that. *Monitor on Psychology,* 32(8), 34-35.

Carrere, S. Gottman, J.M., & Ochs, H. (1996). The beneficial and negative influence of marital quality on the immune functions. *Paper presented at the thirty-sixth Annual Society for Psychophysiological Research Meeting.* Vancouver, B.C.

Carroll, J.S., Badger, S., & Young (2006). The ability to negotiate or the ability to love? Evaluating the developmental domains of marital components. *Journal of Family Issues,* 27(7), 1001-1032.

Carroll, J.S.& Doherty,W.J.(2003).Evaluating the effectiveness of premarital prevention programs:A meta analytic review of outcome research. Family Relations,52,2, 105-119.

Carter, B. (1995). Focusing your wide-angle lens. *The Family Therapy Networker,* 19(6), 31-35.

Carter, B. & McGoldrick, M. (1989). Overview: the changing family life cycle: A framework of family therapy. In B. Carter & M. McGoldrick (Eds.) The changing life cycle: A framework for family therapy (2nd Ed.) (pp. 3-28). Boston: Allyn & Bacon.

Carter, B. & McGoldrick, M. (1999). Overview: The expanded family life cycle: Individual, family, and social perspectives. In B. Carter & M. McGoldrick (Eds.) *The expanded family life cycle: Individual, family, and social perspectives* (3rd. Ed.) (pp. 1-24). Needham Hights, MA: Allyn & Bacon.

Case, R. B., Moss, A. J., Case N., McDermott, M. & Eberly, S. (1992) Living alone after myocardial infarction: Impact on prognosis. *Journal of the American Medical Association,* 267, 515-519Caspi, A. & Elder, G.H.J. (1988). Emergent family patterns: The intergenerational construction of problem behaviour and relationships. In R.A. HINDE and J. STEVENSON-HINDE (Eds), Relationships within families: Mutual influences (pp. 218 – 240). Oxford: Clarendon Press

Cassidy, J. & Asher, S.R. (1992). Loneliness and peer relations in young children. *Child Development,* 63(2), 350.

Cassidy, J., & Berlin, L.J. (1994). The insecure/ambivalent pattern of attachment: Theory and research. *Child Development,* 65, 971-991.

Cate, R.M., Koval, J., Lloyd, S.A., & Wilson, G. (1995). *Assessment of relationship thinking in dating relationships,* 2, 77-95.

Centers for Disease Control Prevention. (2003). Public health and aging: Trends in aging – United States and worldwide. *Morbidity and Mortality Weekly Report, 52* (6), 101-106.

Chappy, S. (2004). Women's experience with breast biopsy. *AORN Journal,* 80(5), 885-901.

Charles, S.T., Mather, M., & Carstensen, L.L. (2003). Aging and emotional memory: The forgettable nature of negative images for older adults. Journal of Experimental Psychology: General,132, 310–324.

Charles, S. T., & Piazza, J. R. (2007). Memories of social interactions: Age differences in emotional intensity. *Psychology and Aging*, 22, 300–309.

Chentsova-Dutton, Y., Shucter, S., Hutchin, S., Strause, L., Burns, K., Dunn, L., ... Zisook, S. (2002). Depression and grief reactions in hospice caregivers: From pre-death to 1 year afterwards. Journal of Affective Disorders, 69, 53–60.

Cherlin, A. (2004). The deinstitutionalization of American marriage. *Journal of Marriage and Family, 66*, 848-861.

Cherlin, A. J. (2009). *The marriage-go-round: The state of marriage and the family in America today.* New York: Knopf.

Cherlin, A. J. (2010). Demographic trends in the United States: A review of research in the 2000s. *Journal of Marriage and Family, 72*, 403-419.

Cherry, K., & Smith, D. (1993) Sometimes I cry: the experience of loneliness for men with AIDS. *Health Communication*, 5, 181-208.

Chesny, A.P., Blackeney, P.E., Chan, M.S., & Cole, C.M. (1981). The impact of sex therapy on sexual behaviour and marital communication. *Journal of Sex and Marital Therapy, 70*, 70-79.

Christ, H. (1988). Psychosocial issues for patients with AIDS - related cancers. *Recent Results in Cancer Research, 112*, 84-92.

Christ, G. H., Siegel, K., Freund, B., Langosch, D., enderson, S., Sperber, D., et al. (1993). Impact of parental terminal cancer on latency-age children. *Journal of Orthopsychiatry*, 63, 417-425.

Christ, G., Wiener, L., & Moynihan, R. (1986). Psychosocial issues in AIDS. *Psychiatric Annals, 16*, 173-179.

Christensen, A. & Heavey, C.L. (1999). Intervention for couples. *Annual Review of Psychology, 50*, 165-190.

Christensen, A., & Walczynski, P.T. (1997). Conflict and satisfaction in couples. In R.J. Sternberg & M. Hojjat (Eds.) Satisfaction in close relationships (pp. 249-274). New York: Guilford.

Chung, H. (1999). Research on the marital relationship: A critical review. *Family science review, 1*, 41-64.

Chwee Chang, C., Wong, F., Park, R., Edberg, M., & Lai, D. (2003). A model for understanding sexual health among Asian American/Pacific Islander men who have sex with men (MSM) in the United States. *AIDS Education and Prevention, 15*(1), 21.

Clay, R.A. (2000). Linking up on line. *Monitor on Psychology, 31*(4), 20-23.

Clark, S.C. (1995). Advance report of final divorce statistics, 1989 and 1990. *Monthly Vital Statistics Report, 43* (Suppl. 8), pp. 1-20.

Clark, M.S. & Mills, J. (1993). The difference between communal and exchange relationships: What it is and is not. *Personality and Social Psychology Bulletin, 19*, 684-691.

Clark, M.S., Mills, J., & Corcoran, D. (1989). Keeping track of needs and inputs of friends and strangers. *Personality and Social Psychology Bulletin, 15*, 533-542.

Clements, M. L., Cordova, A. D., Markman, H. J., & Laurenceau, J. P. (1997). The erosion of marital satisfaction over time and how to prevent it. In R. J. *Sternberg* & M. Hojjat (Eds.), *Satisfaction in close relationships* (pp. 335-355). New York: Guildford Press.

Clemmons, D.C. (2002). Multiple Sclerosis- a medical overview. In R.T. Fraser, D.C. Clemmons & F. Bennett (Eds.). *Multiple Sclerosis; Psychosocial and vocational interventions* (p. 1-16).

Coan, J. A., Schaefer, H. S., & Davidson, R. J. (2006). Lending a hand: Social regulation of the neural response to threat. *Psychological Science, 17*, 1032-1039.

Coates, R. C. (1990). *A street is not a home: Solving America's homeless dilemma.* Buffalo, NY: Pometheus Books.

Cobb, R.J. & Bradbury, T.N. (2003). Implications of adult attachment for preventing adverse marital outcomes. In S.M. Johnson & Whiffen, V.E. (Eds.). *Attachment Processes in couple and family therapy* (pp. 420-435). New York: Guilford.

Cohen, I. S. (1985) Psychosomatic death: voodoo death in modern perspective. *Integrative Psychiatry*, 16, 46-51.

Cohen, J. (1988a). *Statistical power analysis for the behavioral sciences* (2nd edn). Hillsdale, NJ: Lawrence Erlbaum.

Cohen, S. (1988b). Psychosocial models of social support in the etiology of physical disease. *Health Psychology, 7*, 269–297.

Cohen, S. (2004). Social relationships and health. *American Psychologist.* Special Issue: Awards Issue 2004, 59, 676-684.

Cohen, S., Doyle, W. J., Skoner, D. P., Rabin, B. S., & Gwaltney, J. M., Jr. (1997). Social ties and susceptibility to the common cold. *Journal of the American Medical Association, 277*, 1940–1944.

Cohen, S., Doyle, W. J., Turner, R. B., Alper, C. M., & Skoner, D. P. (2003). Sociability and susceptibility to the common cold. *Psychological Science, 14*, 389–395.

Cohen, S., Gottlieb, B.H. & Underwood, L.G. (2000). Social relationships and health: Challenges for measurement and interventions. *Advances in Mind-Body Medicine, 17*, (2), 129-141.

Cohen, S., & Syme, S. L. (1985) Issues in the study and application of social support. In S. Cohen & S. L. Syme (Eds.) *Social support and health* (Pp. 12-23). San Diego, CA: Academic Press.

Cohen, S. & Wills, T.A. (1985). Stress, social support, and the buffering hypothesis. *Psychological Bulletin, 98*, 310-357.

Cohen-Mansfield, J., & Parpura-Gill, A. (2007). Loneliness in older persons: A theoretical model and empirical findings. *International Psychogeriatrics, 19*(2), 279-294.

Cohn, D.A., Silver, D.H., Cowan, C.P., Cowan, P.A., & Pearson, J. (1992). Working models of childhood attachment and couple relationships. *Journal of Family Issues, 13*, 432-449.

Coleman, E. (1992). Is your patient suffering from compulsive sexual behavior? *Psychiatric Annals, 22*(6), 320–325.

Coleman, M., Ganong, L. & Fine, M. (2000). Reinvestigating remarriage: Another decade of progress. *Journal of Marriage and the Family, 62*(4), 1288-1307.

Coleman, P.K. & Karraker, K.H. (1998). Self efficacy and parenting quality: Findings and further applications. *Developmental Review, 18*, (1), 47-85.

Collins, N.L. (1996). Working models of attachment: Implications for explanation, emotion and behavior. *Journal of Personality and Social Psychology, 71*, 810-832.

Collins, N.L. & Feeney, B.C. (2000). A safe heaven: An attachment theory perspective on support seeking and caregiving in intimate relationships. *Journal of Personality and Social Psychology, 78,* 1053-1073.

Collins, N.L., & Feeney, B.C. (2004). An attachment theory perspective on closeness and intimacy. In D.J. Mashek & A. Aron (Eds.) *Handbook of closeness and intimacy. Mahwah,* New Jersey: Lawrence Erlbaum Associates, Publishers (pp.163-187).

Collins, N.L., Guichard, A.C., Ford, M.B., & Feeney, B.C. (2006). Responding to need in intimate relationships: Normative processes and individual differences. In M. Mikulincer, & G.S. Goodman (Eds.). *Dynamics of romantic love: Attachment, caregiving, and sex.* New York: The Guilford Press (pp. 149-189).

Colins, N.L., Guichard, A., Ford, M.B., & Feeney, B.C. (2004). Working models of attachment: New developments and emerging themes. In W.S. Rholes & J.A. Simons (Eds.) *Adult attachment: Theory, research, and clinical implications* (pp. 196-239). New York: Guilford Press.

Collins, N. L., & Read, S. J. (1990). Adult attachment, working models, and relationship quality in dating couples. *Journal of Personality and Social Psychology, 58,* 644-663.

Combs, C.H. & Avrunin, T.L. (1988). *The structure of conflict. Hillsdale,* New Jersey: Erlbaum

Conger, R.D., Cui, M., Bryant, C. M., & Elder, G. H., Jr. (2000). Competence in early adult romantic relationships: A develop-mental perspective on family influences. *Journal of Personality and Social Psychology, 79, 224-237.*

Connor, S. R., (1998). Hospice: Practice, pitfalls, and promise. Washington, DC: Taylor & Francis

Coon, D. (1992). *Introduction to psychology: Exploration and application* (6th ed.). New York; West publishing.

Coontz, S. (2005). *Marriage, a history: From obedience to intimacy, or how love conquered marriage.* New York: Viking.

Coplan, R. J., Findlay, L. C., & Nelson, L. J. (2004). Characteristics of preschoolers with lower perceived competence. *Journal of Abnormal Child Psychology, 32*(4), 399-408.

Coplan, R.J., & Closson, L.M., & Arbeau, K.A. (2007). Gender differences in the behavioural associates of loneliness and social dissatisfaction. *Journal of Child Psychology and Psychiatry,* 48, 988-995.

Corbitt, G., Bailey, A., & Williams, G. (1990). HIV infection in Manchester, 1959. *Lancet,* 336, 51.

Cordova, J.V. & Jacobson, N.S. (1997)Acceptance in couple therapy and its implications for the treatment of depression. In R.J. Sternberg & M. Hojjat (Eds.). Satisfaction in close relationships (pp. 307-334). New York: *The Guilford Press.*

Corrigan, P. W. (1998). The impact of stigma on severe mental illness. *Cognitive and Behavioral Practice,* 5, 201-222.

Corrigan, P. W., & Phelan, S. M. (2004). Social support and recovery in people with serious mental illnesses. *Community Mental Health Journal, 40*(6), 512-523.

Corrigan, P. W., & Kleinlein, P. (2005). The impact of mental illness stigma. In P.W. Corrigan, *On the stigma of mental illness: Practical strategies for research and social change.* Washington, DC: American Psychological Association.

Couch, L. L., Jones, W. H. (1997). Conceptualizing levels of trust. *Journal of Research and Personality, 31,* 319-336.

Craddock, A.E. (1994). Relationships between marital satisfaction and privacy preferences. *Journal of Comparative Family Studies, 25*, 371-382.

Cowan, P., Cowan, C., Heming, G., Garret, E., Coysh, W., Curtis-Boles, H., & Boles, A (1985). Transition to parenthood, his, hers, and theirs. *Journal of Family Issues, 6*, 451-481.

Crick, N.R. & Ladd, G.W. (1993). Children's perceptions of their peer experiences: Attributions, loneliness, social anxiety, and social avoidance. *Developmental Psychology, 29*, 244-254.

Crockett, L. J., & Bingham, C. R. (2000). Anticipating adulthood: Expected timing of work and family transitions among rural youth. *Journal of Research on Adolescence, 10*, 151-171.

Culp,A.M.,Clyman, M.M.,&Culp, R. E. (1995).Adolescent depressed mood, reports of suicide attempts, and asking for help. *Adolescence, 30*, 827−837.

Cunningham, M.R. (1988). Does happiness mean friendliness? Induced mood and heterosexual self-disclosure. *Personality and Social Psychology Bulletin, 14*, 283-297.

Cupach, W.R. & Comstock, J. (1990). Satisfaction with sexual communication in marriage: Links to sexual satisfaction and dyadic adjustment. *Journal of Social and Personal Relationships, 7*, 179-186.

Curran, J.P. (1977). Skills training as an approach to the treatment of heterosexual-society anxiety: A review. *Psychological Bulletin, 84*, 140-157.

Cushman, P. (1995). *Constructing the self, constructing America: A cultural history of psychotherapy.* Cambridge, MA: Perseus Publishing.

Cutrona, C. E. (1982). Transition to college: Loneliness and the process of social adjustment. In L. A. Peplau & D. Perlman (Eds.), Loneliness: A sourcebook of current theory, research, and therapy (pp. 291-301). New York: Wiley Interscience.

Cutrona, C. E. (1996). *Social support in couples: Marriage as a resource in times of stress.* Thousand Oaks, CA: Sage.

Cutrona, C.E., Russell, D.W., & Gardner, K.A. (2005). The relationship enhancement model of social support. In T.A. Revenson, K. Kayser & G. Bodenman (Eds.). *Couples coping with stress* (pp. 3-23). Washington D.C.: American Psychological Association.

Dahlberg, K. (2007). The enigmatic phenomenon of loneliness. International Journal of Qualitative Studies on Health and Well-being, 2, 195−207.

Dale, W., Bilir, P., Han., M, & Meltzer, D. (2005). The role of anxiety in prostate carcinoma. *Cancer, 104*(3), 467-478.

Dalton, J.C., Eberhardt, D., Bracken, J. & Echols, K. (2006). Inward journeys: Forms and patterns of college student spirituality. *Journal of College and Chaacter, 7*(8), 1-22.

Danner, D. D., Snowdon, D. A., & Friesen, W. V. (2001). Positive emotions in early life and longevity: Findings from the nun study. *Journal of Personality and Social Psychology, 80*, 804.

Darwin, C. (1959). *The origin of the species by means of natural selection: Or, the preservation of favored races in the struggle for life.* London, England: John Murray.

Davila, J., Bradbury, T.N., Cohan, C.L., & Tochluk, S. (1997). Marital functioning and depressive symptoms: Evidence for a stress generation model. *Journal of Personality and Social Psychology, 73*, 4, 849-861.

Davis L. (1995). *Enforcing Normalcy: Disability, deafness and the body.* New York: Verso.

Davis, K.E. (1999). What attachment styles and love styles add to the understanding of relationship commitment and stability. In J.M. Adams & Jones (Eds.). *Handbook of interpersonal commitment and relationship stability.* New York: Kluwer Academic/ Plenum Publishers (pp. 221-238).

de Jong Gierveld, J. (1998). A review of loneliness: Concepts and definitions, determinants and consequences. *Reviews in Clinical Gerontology, 8,* 73-80.

De Jong Gierveld, J. & Dykstra, P.A. (2008). Virtue is its own reward? Support giving in the family and loneliness in middle and old age. *Ageing & Society, 28,* 271-287.

De Jong Gierveld, J., Broese van Groenou, M., Hoogendoorn, A. W., & Smit, J. H. (2009). Quality of Marriages in Later Life and Emotional and Social Loneliness *The Journals of Gerontology Series B: Psychological Sciences and Social Sciences, 64B,* 497-506.

De Jong Gierveld, J. d. J., & Havens, B. (2004). Cross-national comparisons and social isolation and loneliness: Introduction and overview. *Canadian Journal on Aging/La Revue canadienne du vieillissement, 23*(2), 109-113.

De Haes, J. C. J. M., & Van Knipperberg, F. C. E. (1985) The quality of life of cancer patients: a review of the literature. *Social Science and Medicine, 20,* 809-817.

Delisle, M. A. (1988). What does solitude mean to the aged? *Canadian Journal of Aging, 7*(4), 358-371.

Dell Orto, A. E.(1991). Coping with the enormity of illness and disability. In R.P. Marinelli & A. E. Dell Orto (Eds.). *The psychological and social impact of disability.* (Pp. 333-335). New York: Springer.

DeTurck, M.A. & Miller, G.R. (1986). Conceptualizing and measuring social cognition in marital communication: A validation study. *Journal of Applied Communication Research,* 14(2), 69-85.

Deutsch, M. (1973). The resolution of conflict: Constructive and destructive processes. *New Haven,* CN: Yale University Press.

DeWall, C. N. (2009). The pain of exclusion: Using insights from neuroscience to understand emotional and behavioral responses to social exclusions. In M. J. Harris (Ed.), *Bullying, rejection, and peer victimization: A social cognitive neuroscience perspective* (pp. 201-224). New York: Springer.

DeWall, C.N. & Baumeister, R.F. (2006). Alone but feeling no pain: Effects of social exclusion on physical pain tolerance and pain threshold, affective forecasting, and interpersonal empathy concern. *Journal of Personality and Social Psychology,* 91, 1-15.

DeWall, C.N., Baumeister, R.F., & Vohs, K.D. (2008). Satiated with belongingness? Effects of acceptance, rejection and task framing on self- regulatory performance. *Journal of Personality and Social Psychology, 95,* 1367-1382.

DeWall, C. N., MacDonald, G., Webster, G. D., Masten, C. L., Baumeister, R. F., Powell, C., Eisenberger, N. I.(2010). Acetaminophen reduces social pain: Behavioral and neural evidence. *Psychological Science, 21,* 931-937.

Dickson, F. (1995). The best is yet to be: Research on long-lasting marriage. In J.T. Wood & S. Duck (Eds.) Understanding relationships: off the beaten path (pp. 22-50). *Thousand Oak CA: Sage.*

Digman, J.M. (1990). Personality structure: Emergence of the five-factor model. *Annual Review of Psychology,* 41,417-440.

Dimidjian, S., Martel, C.R. & Christensen, A. (2008). In A.S. Gurman (Ed.). *Clinical handbook of couple therapy* (pp. 73-103). New York: Guilford.

Dinkmeyer, D. & Carlson, J. (2003). Training in marriage enrichment. *Bowling Green,* KY: CMTI Press.

Distel, M.A., Rebollo-Mesa, I., Abdellaoui, A., Derom, C.A., Willemsen, G., Cacioppo, J.T., & Boomsma, D.I. (2010*). Familial resemblance for loneliness. Behavioural Genetics, 40,* 480-494.

DiPlacido, J. (1998). Minority stress among lesbians, gay men, and bisexuals: A consequence of heterosexism, homophobia, and stigmatization. In G.M. Herek (Ed.), *Stigma and sexual orientation: Understanding prejudice against lesbians, gay men, and bisexuals* (pp. 138-159). Thousand Oaks, CA: Sage.

DiTommaso, E., Brannan-McNulty, C., Ross, L., & Burgess, M. (2003). Attachment styles, social skills and loneliness in young adults. *Personality and Individual Differences*, 35, 303-312.

Ditzen, B., Hoppmann, C., & Klumb, P. (2008). Positive couple interactions and daily cortisol: On the stress-protecting role of intimacy. Psychosomatic Medicine, 70, 883–889.

Doane, L. D., & Adam, E. K. (2010). Loneliness and cortisol: Momentary, day-to-day, and trait associations. *Psychoneuroendocrinology, 35*, 430-441.

Doherty, W. & Jacobson, N. S. (1982). Marriage and the family. In B. B. Wolman (Ed.), *Handbook of Developmental Psychology* (pp. 667-680). *Englewood Cliffs,* N. J.: Prentice Hall.

Doka, K.J. (1997). When illness is prolonged: implications for grief. In: K.J. Doka (Ed.) *Living with grief when illness is prolonged* (Pp. 5-16). Washington, D C: Hospice Foundation of America.

Donelan-McCall, N. & Dunn, J. (1997). School work, teachers, and peers: The word of first grade. *International Journal of Behavioral Development*, 21, 417-427.

Donnelly, D. (1993). Sexually inactive marriages. The Journal of Sex Research, 30, 171-179.

Dong, X., Beck, T., & Simon, M.A. (2009). Loneliness and mistreatment of older Chinese women: doe social support matter? *Journal of Women and Aging, 21*(4), 293-302.

Dostal, C., and Langhinrichsen-Rohling, J. (1997). Relationship specific cognitions and family of- origin divorce and abuse. *J.*

Divorce Remarriage 27: 101- 120.

Drageset, J., Eide, G. E., Nygaard, H. A., Bondevik, M., Nortvedt, M. W., & Natvig, G. K. (2009). The impact of social support and sense of coherence on health-related quality of life among nursing home residents- A questionnaire survey in Bergen, Norway. *International Journal of Nursing Studies, 49*, 66-76.

Drennan, J., Treacy, M., Butler, M., Bryne, A., Fealy, G., Frazer, K., & Irving, K. (2008). The experience of social and emotional loneliness among older people in Ireland. *Aging & Society, 28*, 1113-1132.

Drigotas, S.M. (2002). The Michelangelo phenomenon and personal well-being. *Journal of Personality, 70*, 59-77.

Drigotas, S.M., Rusbult, C.E., Wieselquist, J., & Whitton, S.M. (1999). *Journal of Personality and Social Psychology, 77*, (2), 293-323.

Duck S. (1991) Understanding Relationships. The Guilford Press, New York.

Duck, S. (1995). To be means to communicate: Living and talking in a social world. *Psyccritiques, 40*(1), 16-17.

Duncan, S. F., Holman, T. B., & Yang, C. (2007). Factors associated with involvement in marriage preparation programs. *Family Relations: An Interdisciplinary Journal of*

Applied Family Studies, 56(3), 270-278. doi: http://dx.doi.org/10.1111/j.1741-3729.2007.00458.x

Duncan, S. F., & Wood, M. M. (2003). Perceptions of marriage preparation among college-educated young adults with greater family-related risks for marital disruption. *The Family Journal, 11*(4), 342-352. doi: http://dx.doi.org/10.1177/1066480703255044.

Dunkel-Schetter, C. (1984) Social support and cancer: findings based on patient interviews and their implications. *Journal of Social Issues, 40,* 77-98.

Dunn, J. (2004). Children's friendships: The beginnings of intimacy. Oxford: Blackwell Pub.

Durkheim, E. (1951). *Suicide: A study in Sociology.* New York: W.W. Norton.

Duvdevany I. & Arar E. (2004) Leisure activities, friendships and quality of life of persons with intellectual disability: foster homes vs community residential settings. *International Journal of Rehabilitation Research* 27, 289–296.

Dworetzky, J. P. (1991). *Psychology (4th Ed.)* NY: West Publishing Co.

Dykstra, P. A. (2009). Older adult loneliness: Myths and realities. *European Journal of Aging, 6,* 91-100.

Dykstra, P.A., & de Jong Gierveld, J. (2003). Gender and marital-history differences in emotional and social loneliness among Dutch older adults. *Canadian Journal on Aging/La Revue canadienne du vieillissement, 23*(3), 141-155.

Dykstra, P. A., & De Jong Gierveld, J. (2004). Gender and marital-history differences in emotional and social loneliness among Dutch older adults. *Canadian JournalAging/ La Revue canadienne du vieillissement, 23,* 141-155.

Dykstra, P. A., & Fokkema, T. (2007). Social and emotional loneliness among divorced and married men and women: Comparing the deficit and cognitive perspectives. *Basic and Applied Social Psychology, 29,* 1-12.

Dykstra, P.A., van Tilburg, T.G., & de Jong Gierveld, J. (2005). Changes in older adult loneliness: Results from a seven-year longitudinal study. *Research on Aging, 27,* 725-747.

Eaker, E. D., Sullivan, L. M., Kelly-Hayes, M., D'Agostino, R. B. Sr, & Benjamin, E. J. (2007). Marital status, marital strain, and risk of coronary heart disease or total mortality: The Framingham Offspring Study. Psychosomatic Medicine, 69, 509–513.

Eddleston, J. M., White, P. &, Guthrie, E.(2000). Survival, morbidity, and quality of life after discharge from intensive care. *Critical Care Medicine, 28*(7), 2293-2299.

Edin, K. & Kefalas, M. (2005). *Promises I can keep: Why poor women put motherhood before marriage.* Berkeley: University of California Press.

Eisenberger, N. I., Lieberman, M., & Williams, K. D. (2003). Does rejection hurt? An fMRI study of social exclusion. *Science, 302,* 290–292.

Eldridge, K.A. & Christensen, A. (2002). Demand-withdraw communication during couple conflict: A review and analysis. In P. Noller & J.A. Feeney. *Understanding marriage: Developments in the study of couple interaction* (pp. 289-322).. Cambridge: Cambridge University Press

Elisha, D., Castle, D. & Hocking, B. (2006). Reducing social isolation in people with mental illness: the role of the psychiatrist. *Australian Psychiatry,* 14(3), 281-284.

Emerson, E., &McVilly, K. (2004). Friendship activities of adults with intellectual disabilities in supported accommodation in Northern England. *Journal of Applied Research in Intellectual Disabilities, 17,* 191-197.

Engleberg, L., & Hilborne, L. (1982) Psychosocial social aspects of cancer. In D. M. Prescott & A. S. Flexer (Eds.), *Cancer, the misguided cell.* Sunderland MA: Sinauer Associates. Pp. 211-234.

Entwisle, D. & Doering (1988). The emergent father role. *Sex Role,* 18, 119-141.

Erber, R., & Erber, M. W. (2001a). Mood processing: A view from a self-regulation perspective. In L. L. Martin & G. Clore (Eds.), *Theories and mood cognition: A users guidebook* (pp. 63-84). Mahwah, NJ: Erlbaum

Erber, R., & Erber, M. W. (2001b). The role of motivated social cognition in the regulation of affective states. In J.P. Forgas (Ed.), *Handbook of affect and social cognition* (pp. 275-290). Mahwah, NJ: Erlbaum.

Erdner, A., Magnusson, A., Nystrom, M. & Lutz'en, K. (2005). Social and existential alienation experienced by people with long-term mental illness. *Scandinavian Journal of Caring, Science,* 19, 373-380.

Ernst, J. M. & Cacioppo, J. T. (1998). Lonely hearts: Psychological perspectives on loneliness. *Applied and Preventive Psychology,* 8, 1–22.

Ernst, J. M., & Cacioppo, J. T. (1999). Lonely hearts: Psychological perspectives on loneliness. *Applied and Preventive Psychology,* 8, 1–22.

Ertel, K. A., Glymour, M. M., & Berkman, L. F. (2009). Social networks and health: A life course perspective integrating observational and experimental evidence. *Journal of Social and Personal Relationships,* 26, 73–92.

Erikson, E. H. (1963). *Childhood and society.* New York: Norton.

Erikson, E. H. (1968). *Identity: Youth and crisis.* Oxford, England: Norton & Co., Oxford.

Erozkan, A. (2011). The attachment styles bases of loneliness and depression. International *Journal of Psychology and Counseling,* 3, 9, 186-193.

Essex, M., & Num, S. (1987). Marital status and loneliness among older women: The differential importance of close family and friends. *Journal of Marriage and the Family,* 49, 93-106.

Ettema EJ, Derksen LD, Van Leeuwen E. (2010). Existential loneliness and end-of-life care: a systematic review. *Theor Med Bioeth, 31,* 141–169. Eyal, K., & Cohen, J. (2006). When good *friends* say goodbye: A parasocial breakup study. *Journal of Broadcasting and Electronic Media, 50,* 502-533.

Falvo, D.R. (1999). *Medical and psychosocial aspects of chronic illness and disability.* Gaithersburg, MD: Aspen Pub.

Farrington, A. & Robinson, W.P. (1999). Homelessness and strategies of identity maintenance: A participant observation study. *Journal of Community and Applied Social Psychology, 9,* 175-194.

Feeney, J.A. (1999). Adult romantic attachment and couple relationships. In J. Cassidy & P.R. Shaver (Eds.) *Handbook of attachment: Theory, research and clinical application* (pp. 355-377). New York: Guilford.

Feeney, B.C. (2004). A secure base: Responsive support of goal striving and exploration in adult intimate relationships. Journal of personality and Social Psychology, 87, 631-648.

Feeney, J.A. (2002). Attachment, marital interaction and relationship satisfaction: A diary study. *Personal Relationships,* 9, 39-55.

Fenney, J. A. (2006). Parental attachment and conflict behaviour: Implications for offspring's attachment, loneliness, and relationship satisfaction. *Personal Relationships, 13,* 19-36.

Feeney, J. A., & Noller, P. (1996). *Adult Attachment.* London: Sage Publications.

Feeney, J.A., Noller, P., & Ward, C. (1997). Marital satisfaction and spousal interaction. In R.J. Sternberg & M. Hojjat (Eds.) *Satisfaction in close relationships* (pp. 169-189). New York: Guilford.

Fehr, B. (1988). Prototype analysis of the concepts of love and commitment. *Journal of Personality and Social Psychology, 55,* 557-579.

Fehr, B. (2006). A prototype approach to studying love. In R.J. Sternberg & K. Weis (Eds.), *The new psychology of love* (pp. 225-246). New Haven, CT: Yale University Press.

Feldman, L. B. (1982). Sex roles and family dynamics. In F. Walsh (Ed.), *Normal family processes* (pp. 354-382), New York: Guilford Press.

Feldman, C. (2003). *Silence.* Berkeley, CA: Rodmell Press.

Fincham, F.D. (2004). Communication in marriage. In A.L. Vangelisi (Ed.) *Handbook of communication* (pp. 83-104). Mahwah, New Jersey: Erlbaum.

Fincham, F.D. (2003). Marital conflict: Correlates, structure, and context. *Current Directions in Psychological Science, 12,* 1, 23-27.

Fincham, F.D. & Beach, R.H. (1999). Conflict in marriage: Implications for working with couples. *Annual Review of Psychology, 50,* 47-77.

Fincham, F.D., & Beach, S.R.H. (1999). Marital conflict: Implications for working with couples. *Annual Review of Psychology, 50,* 47-77.

Fincham, F.D. & Beach, S.R.H. (2006). Relationship satisfaction. In D. Perlman & A. Vangelisti (Eds.). *The Cambridge handbook of personal relationships* (pp.579-594). Cambridge: Cambridge University Press.

Fincham, F. D., & Beach, S. R. (2010). Marriage in the new millennium: A decade in review. *Journal of Marriage and Family, 72,* 630-649.

Fincham, F.D., Beach, S.R., & Davila, J. (2004). Forgiveness and conflict resolution in marriage. *Journal of Family Psychology, 18,* 72-81.

Fincham, F.D., & Bradbury, T.N. (1990). Social support in marriage: The role of social cognition. *Journal of Social and Clinical Psychology, 9,* 31-42.

Fincham, F.D., Stanley, S., & Beach, S.R.H. (2007).Transformative processes in marriage: An analysis of emerging trends. *Journal of Marriage and the Family, 69,* 275-292.

Fincham, F.D., & Bradbury, T.N. (1992). Assessing attributions in marriage: The relationship attribution measure. *Journal of Personality and Social Psychology, 62,* (3), 457-468.

Finkel, E.J. & Campbell, W.K. (2001). Self control and accommodation in close relationships: An interdependence analysis. *Journal of Personality and Social Psychology, 81,* (2), 263-277.

Finn, S., & Gorr, M. B. (1988). Social isolation and social support as correlates of television viewing motivations. Communication Research, 15, 135–158.

Fischer, D. H. (1977). *Growing old in america.* Oxford, England: Oxford U Press, Oxford.

Fisher, H. (2004). Why we love: The nature and chemistry of romantic love. NY: Henry Holt.

Fisher, H. (2006). Broken hearts: The nature and risks of romantic rejections. In A. Booth& C. Crouter (Eds.), *Romance and sex in adolescence and emerging adulthood: Risks and opportunities* (pp. 3-29). Mahwah, NJ: Erlbaum.

Fisher, D.B. (1994). Health care reform based on empowerment model by people with psychiatric disabilities. Hospital and Community Psychiatry, 45, 913-915.

Fisher, H. (1995). The nature and evolution of romantic love. In W. Jankowiak (Ed.), *Romantic passion: A universal experience?* (pp. 23-41). New York: Columbia University Press.

Fisher, H.E. & Aron, A. (2002). Defining the brain systems of lust, romantic attraction, and attachment. *Archives of sexual behaviour, 30*(5), 413-419.

Fisher, H.E., Aron, A. & Brown, L.L. (2005). Romantic love: An fMRI study of a neural mechanism for mate choice. *Journal of Comparative Neurology, 493*, 58-62.

Fitzpatrick, M.A. (1987). Marriage and verbal intimacy. In V.J. Derlega & J. Berg (Eds.), *Self-disclosure: Theory, research, and therapy* (pp. 131-154). New York: Plenum.

Fitzsimons, G. M., & Kay, A. C. (2004). Language and interpersonal cognition: Causal effects of variations in pronoun usage on perceptions of closeness. *Personality and Social Psychology Bulletin, 30*(5), 547-557.

Fleming I. & Stenfert-Kroese B. (1990) Evaluation of a community care project for people with learning difficulties. *Journal of Mental Deficiency Research* 34, 451–464.

Flora, J., & Segrin, C. (2000). Relationship development in dating couples: Implications for relational satisfaction and loneliness. *Journal of Social and Personal Relationships, 17*(6), 811-825.

Flory, N., & Lang, E. (2011). Distress in the radiology waiting room. *Radiology, 260*, 166-173.

Flowers, P., & Buston, K. (2001). "I was terrified of being different": Exploring gay men's accounts of growing-up in a heterosexist society. *Journal of Adolescence, 24*(1), Special issue: Gay, Lesbian, and Bisexual Youth, 51–65.

Fokkema, T.,&Kuyper, L. (2009). The relation between social embeddedness and loneliness among older lesbian, gay, and bisexual adults in the Netherlands. Archives of Sexual Behavior, 38, 264-275.

Forgas, J. P. (1995). On seeing a bear that isn't there: Affect and perception. *PsycCRITIQUES, 40*(11), 1057-1058.

Forgas, J. P. (2002). Toward understanding the role of affect in social thinking and behavior. *Psychological Inquiry, 13*(1), 90-102.

Forgas, J.P. (2011). Affective influences on self-disclosure: Mood effects on the intimacy and reciprocity of disclosing personal information. *Journal of Personality and Social Psychology, 100*, 449-461.

Foucault, M. (1973). *The birth of the clinic*. New York: Pantheon.

Fournier, D.G. & Olson, D.H. (1986). Programs for premarital and newlywed couples. In R.F. Levant (Ed.) *Psychoeducational approaches to family therapy and counselling* (pp. 194-231). New York: Springer.

Fowers, B.J., Montel, K.H., & Olson, D.H. (1996). Predicting marital success for premarital couple types based on PREPARE. *Journal of Marital and Family Therapy*, 22, 103-119.

Fraenkel, P., Markman, H., & Stanley, S. (1997). The prevention approach to relationship problems. *Sexual and Marital Therapy,* 12, 249-258.

Frank, R. (1988). Passions Within Reason: The Strategic Role of Emotions. New York: W.W. Norton.

France, P. (1996). *Hermits: The insights of solitude*. New York: St. Martin's.

Fredrickson, B.L. (2001). The role of positive emotions in positive psychology: The broaden-and-build theory of positive emotions. *American Psychologist,* 56, 218-226.

Fredrickson, B.L. (2004). The broaden-and-build theory of positive emotions. *Phil Trans. Royal Society Lond B,* 359, 1367-1377.

Fredrickson, B.L. (1998). What good are positive emotions? *Review of General Psychology,* 2, 300-319.

Fredrickson, B.L. & Joiner, T. (2002). Positive emotions trigger upward spiral toward emotional well-being. *Psychological Science, 13*, 172-175.

Friedman, R. L. (2007). Widening the therapeutic lens: Sense of belonging as an integral dimension of the human experience. *A Dissertation submitted to the Wright Institute Graduate School.*

Friedman, G. & Florian, V., & Zernitsky-Shurka, E. (1989) The experience of loneliness among young adult cancer patients. *Journal of Psychosocial Oncology, 7*, 1-15.

Friend, R. A. (1990). Older lesbian and gay people: A theory of successful aging. *Journal of Homosexuality, 20*, 99-118.

Fricker, J., & Moor, S. (2002). Relationship satisfaction: the role of love styles and attachment styles. *Current Research in Social Psychology-an electronic Journal, 7*, 182-204.

Fromm, E. (1941). *Escape from freedom.* New York: Rinehart.

Fromm – Reichman, F. (1959). Loneliness. *Psychiatry, 22*, 1-5.

Fromm-Reichman, F. (1960). *Principles of intensive psychotherapy.* Chicago, IL: The University of Chicago Press.

Fuchs, C. Z., & Rehn, L. P. (1977). A self-control behaviour therapy program for depression. *Journal of Consulting and Clinical Psychology, 45*, 206-215.

Gable, S.L., Gonzaga, G.C., & Strachman, A., (2006). Will you be there for me when things go right? Supportive responses to positive event disclosures. *Journal of personality and social psychology, 91*(5), 904-917.

Gable, S.L., & Reiss, H.T. (2001). Appetitive and aversive social interaction. In J. Harvey & A.Wenzel (Eds.) Close romantic relationships. Mahwa, New Jersey: Lawrence Erlbaum Associates, Publishers.

Gable, S.L. & Reis, H.T. (2006). Intimacy and the self: An interactive model of self and close relationships. In P. Noller & J.A. Feeney (Eds.), *Close relationships: Functions, forms and processes* (pp. 211-225). New York: Psychology Press.

Gable, S., Reis, H.T., Impett, E., & Asher, E.R. (2004). What do you do when things go right? The intrapersonal and interpersonal benefits of sharing positive events. *Journal of Personality and Society Psychology, 87*, 228-245.

Gagnon, M. D., Hersen, M., Kabacoff, R. I., & Van-Hasselt, V. B. (1999). Interpersonal and psychological correlates of marital dissatisfaction in late life: A review. *Clinical Psychology Review, 19*, 359–378.

Galanaki, E. (2004). Are children able to distinguish among the concepts of aloneness, loneliness, and solitude? *International Journal of Behavioral Development, 28*, 435-443.

Ganong, L. & Coleman, M. (1994*). Remarried family relationships.* Newbury Park, CA: Sage.

Gardner, K.A. & Cutrona, C.E. (2004). Social support communication in families. In A.L. Vangelisit (Ed.) *Handbook of Family Communication* (pp. 495-512). Mahwah, New Jersey: Lawrence Erlbaum.

Garfield, D. A. S. (1986). The use of primary process in psychotherapy: I. concrete thinking and the perception of syntax. *Psychotherapy: Theory, Research, Practice, Training, 23*(1), 75-80.

Gardner,W. L., Pickett, C. L., Jefferies, V., & Knowles, M. (2005). On the outside looking in: Loneliness and social monitoring. *Personality and Social Psychology Bulletin, 31*(11), 1549–1560.

Geary, D. C. (1998). *Male female: The evolution of human sex differences*. Washington, D.C.: American Psychological Association.

Geiss, S., & O'Leary, K. (1981) therapists ratings of frequency and severity of marital problems: Implications for research. *Journal of Marital and Family Therapy, 7*, 512-520.

Geller, J., Janson, P., McGovern, E., & Valdini, A. Gibran, K. (1951). Loneliness as a predictor of hospital emergency department use. *The Journal of Family Practice*, 48(10), 801-804. *The prophet.* NY: Knnopf.

Geller, J. Janson, P., McGovern, E.W., & Valdini, A. (1999). Loneliness as a predictor of hospital emergency department use. Family Practice, 48(10), 801-804.

Gerson, R. (1995). *The family life cycle: Phases, stages, and crises.* Washington, DC, US: American Psychological Association, Washington, DC. doi: http://dx.doi.org/10.1037/10172-005

Gilligan, C. (1982). In a different voice: Psychological theory and women's development. Cambridge, MA: Harvard University Press.

Ginn, J., & Fast, J. (2006). Employment and social integration in midlife: Preferred and actual time use across welfare regime types. *Research on Aging, 28*, 669–690.

Glaser, R., Kiecolt-Glaser, J. K., Bonneau, R. H., Malarky, W., Kennedy, S., & Hughes, J. (1992) Stress-induced modulation of the immune response to recombinant hepatitis B vaccine. *Psychosomatic Medicine, 54*, 22-29.

Glenn, N.D. & McLanahan, S. (1982). Children and marital happiness: A further specification of the relationship. *Journal of Marriage and the Family, 44*, (1), 63-72.

Glick, P. C. (1979). The future of the American family. *Current Population Reports* (Special Studies Series P-23, No.78). Washington, D. C.: US Government Printing Office.

Gold, D. T. (1999). Outcomes and the personal impact of osteoporosis. In E. S. Orwoll, (Ed.) *Osteoporosis in men: The effects of gender on skeletal health* (pp. 51-63). NY: Academic Press.

Goleman, D., Kaufman, P., & Ray, M. (1992). *The creative spirit*. New York: Penguin.

Gordon, L.H. (1993). Passage to intimacy. New York: Simon & Schuster.

Gordon, L.H. (2000) Passage to intimacy. Ami – incomplete ref.

Gordon, S. (1976*). Lonely in America*. NY: Simon & Schuster.

Gordon, J., & Mckinney, A. (2010). Love and lust: A phenomenological investigation. *Journal of the British Society for Phenomenology, 41*(1), 8-32.

Goossens, L., & Marcoen, A. (1999). Adolescent loneliness, self-reflection, and identity: from individual differences to developmental processes. In K. J. Rotenberg, & S. Hymel (Eds.), *Loneliness in Childhood and Adolescence* (pp. 225–243). Cambridge, UK: Cambridge University Press.

Goswick, R. A., & Jones, W. H. (1981). Loneliness, self-concept, and adjustment. Journal of Psychology, 107, 237−240.

Gottman, J.M., & Levenson, R. W. (1992). Marital processes predictive of later dissolution: Behavior, physiology, and health. *Journal of Personality and Social Psychology, 63*, 221-233.

Gottman, J.M. (1993). The role of conflict engagement, escalation, and avoidance in marital interaction: A longitudinal view of five types of couples. *Journal of Consulting and Clinical Psychology, 61*, 1, 6-15.

Gottman, J.M. (1994a). What predicts divorce? The relationship between marital processes and marital outcomes. Hillsdale, New Jersey: *Erlbaum.*

Gottman, J.M. (1994b). Why marriages succeed or fail. New York: *Fireside.*

Gottman, J.M. (1999a). The marriage clinic: A scientifically based marital therapy. New York: *W.W. Norton & Company.* ** Distinguish A or B in text.

Gottman, J.M. (1999b). The seven principles for making marriage work. New York: *The Rivers Press.* ** Distinguish A or B in text.

Gottman, J.M., Carrere, S., & Swanson, C. (1998). Predicting marital happiness and stability from newlywed interactions. *Journal of Marriage and the Family*, 60, 5-22.

Gottman, J.M., Driver, J., Yoshimoto, D., & Rushe R. (2002). Approaches to the study of power in violent and nonviolent marriages and in gay and lesbian cohabiting relationships. In P. Noller & J.A. Feeney (Eds.) Understanding marriage: Developments in the study of couple interaction (pp. 323-347). *Cambridge University Press.*

Gottman, J.M., & Gottman, J.S. (1999). The marriage survival kit. In R. Berger & M.T. Hannah (Eds.), Preventive approaches in couples therapy (pp. 304-330). Gottman, J.M., & Levinson, R.W. (1992). Marital princesses predictive of later dissolution: Behavior, physiology, and health. *Journal of Personality and Social Psychology,* 63, 221-233.

Gottman, J.M. & Notarius, C.I. (2002). Marital research in the 20th century and research agenda for the 21st century. *Family Processes,* 41, 2, 159-197.

Gottschall, J. & Nordlund, M. (2006). Romantic love: A literary universal? *Philosophy and Literature,* 30, 450-470.

Gove, W.R., & Shin, H.-C. (1989). The psychological well-being of divorced and widowed men and women: An empirical analysis. *Journal of Family Issues, 10,* 122-144.

Greene, J.M., Ennett, S.T.,& Ringwalt, C.L. (1999). Prevalence and correlates of survival sex among runaway and homeless youth. *American Journal of Public Health*, 89, 1406–1409.

Green, R. G., Harris, R. N., Forte, J. A., & Robinson, M. (1991). The wives data and FACES IV: Making things appear simple. *Family Process, 30*, 79-83.

Greenwood, D. N., & Long, C. R. (2009). Psychological predictors of media involvement: Solitude experiences and the need to belong. *Communication Research, 36*(5), 637-654.

Grossman, A. H. (1997). The virtual and actual identities of older lesbians and gay men. In M. Duberman (Ed.), *A queer world: The Center for Lesbian and Gay Studies reader* (pp. 615-626). New York: New York University Press.

Grossman, A.H., D'augelli, A.R., & O'connell, T.S. (2002). Being lesbian, gay, bisexual, and 60 or older in North America. *Journal of Gay & Lesbian Social Services,* (13) 4, 23 – 40.

Grote, N.K., & Frieze, I.H. (1998). Remembrance of things past: Perceptions of marital love from its beginning to the present. *Journal of Social and Personal Relationships,* 15, 91-109.

Guerney, B.G. (1977). Relationship enhancement. San Francisco: Jossey-Bass.

Guerrero, L. K., (1998). Attachment-style differences in the experience of expression of romantic jealousy. *Personal Relationships, 5*, 273-291.

Guerrero, L. K., Trost, M. R., & Yoshimura, S. M. (2005). Romantic jealousy: Emotions and communicative responses. *Personal Relationships, 12*, 233-252.

Guiaux, M., Van Tilburg, T., & Broese van Groenou, M. B. (2007). Changes in contact and social support exchange in personal networks after widowhood. *Personal Relationships,14*, 457-473.

Guyer, B., Lescocher, I., Gallagher, S. S., Hausman, A.,&Azzara, C. V. (1989). Intentional injuries among children and adolescents in Massachusetts. *New England Journal of Medicine, 321,* 1584-1589.

Hagan, J., McCarthy, B. (1997). *Mean streets: Youth crime and homelessness.* Cambridge University Press, Cambridge, UK

Hagerty, B.K., Lynch-Sauer, J., Patusky, K.L., Bouwsema, M. & Collier, P. (1992). Sense of belonging: A vital health concept. *Archives of Psychiatric Nursing, VI* (3), 172-177.

Hagerty, B.K., Patusky, K. (1995). Developing a measure of sense of belonging. *Nursing Research, 44(1),* 9-13.

Hagerty, B.M.,&Williams, R. A. (1999). The effects of sense of belonging, social support, conflict, and loneliness on depression. *Nursing Research, 48,* 215–219.

Hagerty B. M., Williams, R. A., Coyne, J. C., & Early, M. R. (1996). Sense of belonging and indicators of social and psychological functioning. *Archives of Psychiatric Nursing,* 10(4), 235-244. University Press, Cambridge, UK.

Halford, W.K. & Moor, E. N. (2002). Relationship education and the prevention of couple relationship problems. In A.S. Gurman & N.S. Jacobson (Eds.) *Clinical handbook of couple therapy* (3rd Edition) (pp. 400-419). New York: Guilford Press.

Halford, K. & Petch, J. (2010). Couple psycho education for new parents: Observed and potential effects on parenting. *Clinical Child Family Psychology Review,* 13, 164-180.

Halford, W.K., Wilson, K.L., Lizzio, A., & Moor, E. (2002). Does working at a relationship work? Relationship self-regulation and relationship outcomes. In P. Noller & J.A. Feeney (Eds.) Understanding marriage: Developments in the study of couple interaction (pp. 493-517). Cambridge, UK: *Cambridge University Press.*

Hall, G. S. (1904). Adolescence: Its psychology and its relation to physiology, anthropology, sociology, sex, crime, religion and education (Vols. I & II). Englewood Cliffs, N. J.: Prentice Hall.

Hall Gueldner, S. (2000). Introduction and overview. In S. Hall Gueldner, M. S. Burke, & H.Smiciklas-Wright (Eds.). *Preventing and managing osteoporosis.* (pp. 1-4). NY: Springer.

Halper, J. (2001). Advanced concepts in Multiple Sclerosis's nursing care. New York: Demos.

Halpern, L.F. & Mclean, W.A. Jr. (1997). Hey mom, look at me! Infant Behaviour and Development, 20,(5), 515-529.

Hallström, I. & Elander, G. (2007). Families' needs when a child is long-term ill: A literature review with reference to nursing research. *International Journal of Nursing Practice, 13,* 193–200.

Halvorsen, K. (2000). Social exclusion as a problem. *Journal of social research, 3,*(3), 157-171.

Hamilton, R. P. (2006). Love as a contested concept. *Journal for the Theory of Social Behaviour, 36*(3), 239-254. doi:10.1111/j.1468-5914.2006.00306.x

Hammen, C. (2005). Stress and depression. *Annual Review of Clinical Psychology,* 1, 293-319.

Hammen, C. (1991). The generation of stress in the course of unipolar depression. *Journal of Abnormal Psychology,* 100, 555-561.

Hanh, T. N. (1991). *Peace is every step.* New York: Bantam Books.

Hansen, D. G., Rosholm, J. U., Gichangi, A., & Vach,W. (2007, May 30). Increased use of antidepressants at the end of life: Population based study among people aged 65 years and above. Retrieved July 4, 2007, from htttp://ageing.oxfordjournals.org/cgi/content/abstract/afm056v1

Hansson, R. O., Jones, W. H., Carpenter, B. N., & Remondet, I. (1986) Loneliness adjustment to old age. *International Journal of Aging and Human Development, 24,* 41-53.

Harlow, H.F. (1958). The nature of love. *American Psychologist, 13,* 673-685.

Harlow, H.F. (1959). Love in infant monkeys. *Scientific American, 200,* 68-86.

Harris, H. (1995). Rethinking Polynesian heterosexual relationships: A case study on Mangaia, Cook Islands. In W. Jankowiak (Ed.), *Romantic Passion: A universal experience?* (pp. 95-127). NY: Columbia University Press.

Hart, S.D., Dutton, D.G., & Newlove, T. (1993). The prevalence of personality disorders among wife assaulters. *Journal of Personality Disorders, 7*(4), 329-341.

Hartog, J. (1980) The anatomization. In J. Hartog, R. J. Audy. & Y. A. Cohen (Eds.) *The Anatomy of loneliness.* New York: International Universities Press.(Pp.1-12).

Harvey, J.H. & Omarzu, J. (1997). Minding the close relationship. *Personality and Social Psychology Review, 1,* 224-240.

Harvey, J. H., & Omarzu, J. (2001). Are there superior options? commentary on spitzberg's "the status of attribution theory qua theory in personal relationships". New York, NY, US: Cambridge University Press, New York, NY.

Harvey, J. & Wenzel, A. (2001). Close romantic relationships: Maintenance and enhancement. Mahwah, New Jersey: *Lawrence Erlbaum Associates, Publishers.*

Haselton, M. G., Buss, D. M., Oubaid, V., & Angleitner, A. (2005). Sex, lies, and strategic interference: The psychology of deception between the sexes. *Personality and Social Psychology Bulletin, 31,* 3-23.

Hassebrauck, M. & Fehr, B. (2002). *Dimensions of relationship quality. Personal Relationships, 9,* 253-270.

Hatcher, R. A., Trussell, J., Stewart, F., & Stewart, G. (1994). *Contraceptive technology.* New York: Irvington.

Hatfield, E. & Walster, G.W. (1978). A new look at love. Lanham, MD: *University Press of America.*

Hatfield, E., & Rapson, R. L. (1993). *Love, sex, and intimacy: Their psychology, biology, and history.* New York: Harper Collins.

Hatfield, E., Pillemer, J. T., O'Brien, M. U., & Le, Y. L. (2008). The endurance of love: passionate and compassionate love in newlywed and long-term marriages. *Interpersona, 2*(1), 35-64.

Hatfield, E., Rapson, R. L., & Martel, L. D. (2007). "Passionate Love." In S. Kitayama & D. Cohen (Eds.), *Handbook of Cultural Psychology.* New York: Guilford Press.

Hatzenbuehler, M. L., Nolen-Hoeksema, S., & Erickson, S. J. (2008). Minority stress predictors of HIV risk behavior, substance use, and depressive symptoms: Results from a prospective study of bereaved gay men. *Health Psychology, 27,* 455–462.

Hawker, D.S. & Boulton, M.J. (2000). Twenty years' research on peer victimization and psychosocial maladjustment: A meta analytic review of cross sectional studies. *Journal of Child Psychology and Psychiatry, 41,* 411-455.

Hawkley, L.C., & Cacioppo, J.T. (2007). *Aging and loneliness: Downhill quickly?* Current Directions in Psychological Science, 16 (4), 187-191

Hawkley, L. C., & Cacioppo, J. P. (2003). Loneliness and pathways to disease. *Brain, Behavior, and Immunity, 17,* S98-S105.

Hawkley, L.C., & Cacioppo, J.T. (2009). Loneliness. Center for Cognitive and Social Neuroscience, the Department of Psychology, University of Chicago, pp. 1-29.

Hawkley, L.C., Browne, M.W., & Cacioppo, J.T. (2005). How can I connect with thee? *Psychological Science*, 16, 10, 798-804.

Hawkley, L.C. & Cacioppo, J.T. (2010). Loneliness matters: A theoretical and empirical review of consequences and mechanisms. *Annals of Behavioral Medicine*, 40, 218-227.

Hawkley, L.C., Hughes, M.E., Waite, L.J., Masi, C.M., Thisted, R.A., & Cacioppo, J.T. (2008). From social structure factors to perceptions of relationship quality and loneliness: The Chicago health, aging, and social relations study. *Journal of Gerontology: Social Sciences*, 63B, 6, S375-S384.

Hayden, D. (2000). Sexual addiction treatment therapy: A depth-psychology approach. Retrieved on February 10, 2005 from http://www.canadiancontent.net/en/jd/go?Url=http://www.sextreatment.com In Torress & Gore-Felton, 2007.

Hazan, C., Gur-Yaish, N., & Campa, M. (2004). What does it mean to be attached? In W.S. Rholes & J.A. Simpson (Eds.). *Adult attachment: Theory, research and clinical implications* (pp. 55-85). New York: Guilford.

Hazan, C. & Shaver, P.R. (1987). Romantic love conceptualized as an attachment process. *Journal of Personality and Social Psychology*, 52, 511-534.

Hazan, C., & Shaver, P.R. (1990). Love and work: An attachment-theoretical perspective. *Journal of Personality and Social Psychology*, 59, 270-280.

Hazan, C. & Shaver, P.R. (1994a). Attachment as an organizational framework for research on close relationships. *Psychological Inquiry*, 1994, 5(1), 1-22.

Hazan, C. & Shaver, P.R. (1994b). Deeper into attachment theory. *Psychological Inquiry*, 5, 68-79.

Hazan, C. & Zeifman, D. (1999). Pair bonds as attachments: Evaluating the evidence. In J. Cassidy & P.R. Shaver (Eds.) *Handbook of attachment: Theory, research, and clinical applications* (Pp. 336-354). NY: Guilford Press.

Heene, E., Buysse, L. D., & Van Oost A.P. (2005). Indirect pathways between depressive symptoms and marital distress: The role of conflict. *Family Process;* Dec 2005; 44 9(4), 413.

Heffner, K. L., Kiecolt-Glaser, J. K., Loving, T. J., Glaser, R., & Malarkey, W. B. (2004). Spousal support satisfaction as a modifier of physiological responses to marital conflict in younger and older couples. Journal of Behavioral Medicine, 27, 233–254.

Hegi, K. E., & Bergner, R. M. (2010). What is love? an empirically-based essentialist account. *Journal of Social and Personal Relationships, 27*(5), 620-636. doi:10.1177/0265407510369605

Heider, F. (1958). *The Psychology of Interpersonal Relations*. New York: Wiley

Heine, S.J., Lehman, D.R., Markus, H.R., & Kitayama, S. (1999). Is there a universal need for positive self-regard? *Psychological Review, 108*, 766-794.

Heinrich, L. M. & Gullone, E. (2006). The clinical significance of loneliness: A literature review. *Clinical Psychology Review*, 26, 695-718.

Helgeson, V. S., & Cohen, S. (1996). Social support and adjustment to cancer: Reconciling descriptive, and intervention research. *Health Psychology, 15*(2), 135-148.

Heikkinen, R. L. & Kauppinen, M. (2004). Depressive symptoms in late life: a 10-year follow-up. *Archives of Gerontology and Geriatrics, 38*, 239–250.

Heitland, W. (1986). An experimental communication program for premarital dating couples. *The School Counsellor*, 34, 57-61.

Heidegger, M. (1962). *Being and time* (J. Macquarrie & E. Robinson, Trans.). New York: Harper & Row.

Helms-Erickson, H. (2001). Marital quality 10 years after the transition to parenthood: Implications for the timing of parenthood and the division of housework. *Journal of Marriage and the Family,* 63, 1099-1110.

Hendrick, S.S. (2004). Understanding close relationships. New York: *Pearson.*

Hendrick, C. & Hendrick, S.S. (1986). A theory and method of love. *Journal of Personality and Social Psychology,* 50, 392-402.

Hendrick, S. S., & Hendrick, C. (1993). Lovers as friends. Journal of Personality and Social Relationships, 2, 55–65.

Hendrick, S.S. & Hendrick, C. (1995). Gender differences and similarities in sex and love. Personal Relationships, 2, 55-65.

Hendrick, S.S., & Hendrick,C. (1997). Love and satisfaction. In R.J. Sternberg & M. Hojjat (Eds.). *Satisfaction in close relationships* (pp. 56-78). New York: The Guilford Press.

Hendrick, C., & Hendrick, S.S. (2004). Sex and romantic love: Connectedness and disconnect. In J.H.Harvey, A. Wenzel, & S. Sprecher (Eds.). *The handbook of sexuality in close relationships* (pp. 159-182). Mahwah, New Jersey: Lawrence Erlbaum Associates.

Hendrick, C. & Hendrick, S.S. (2006). Styles of romantic love. In R.J. Sternberg & K. Weis (Eds.). *The new psychology of love* (pp. 149-170). New Haven, CT: Yale University Press.

Herek, G. M., Gillis, J. R.,&Cogan, J. C. (1999). Psychological sequelae of hate-crime victimization among lesbian, gay, and bisexual adults. *Journal of Consulting and Clinical Psychology, 67,* 945-951.

Hess, T. M. (2005). Memory and aging in context. *Psychological Bulletin,* 131, 383–406.

Hess, T. M., & Auman, C. (2001). Aging and social expertise: The impact of trait- diagnostic information on impressions of others. *Psychology and Aging,* 16, 497–510.

Hess, T.M.,Bolstad, C. A.,Woodburn, S. M.,&Auman,C. (1999). Trait diagnosticity versus behaviour consistency as determinants of impression change in adulthood. *Psychology and Aging,* 14, 77–89.

Higgins, E. T. (1997). Beyond pleasure and pain. *American Psychologist, 52,* 1280-1300.

Hill B., Rotegard L. & Bruininks R. (1984) The quality of life of mentally retarded people in residential care. Social Work 29, 275–281.

Hill, M.S. (1988). Marital stability and spouses shared time: A multidisciplinary hypothesis. *Journal of Family Issues,* 9, 427-451.

Hill, L. (2001). Finding refugee in writing, The Globe and Mail, December 28, p. A15.

Hodges, E. V. E., & Perry, D. G. (1996). Victims of peer abuse: An overview. *Journal of Emotional and Behavioural Problems,* 5, 23⁻28.

Hoff, S. & Bucholz, E.S. (1996).School psychologist know thyself: creativity and alone time for adaptive professional coping. Psychology in Schools, 33(4), 309-317.

Hoff, L. & Miller, W.R. (1981). Marriage enrichment. *Marriage and Family Review,* 3, (1-2), 1-27.

Holahan, C. J., Moos, R. H., Moerkbak, M. L., Cronkite, R. C., Holahan, C. K., & Kenney, B. A. (2007). Spousal similarity in coping and depressive symptoms over 10 years. *Journal of Family Psychology,* 21, 551-559.

Holman, T.B. (2001) Premarital prediction of marital quality or breakup: Research, theory and practice. New York: *Kluwer Academic- Plenum publishers.*

Holman, T.B., Larson, J.H., & Harmer, S.L. (1994). The development and predictive validity of a new premarital assessment instrument: The PREParation for marriage questionnaire. *Family Relations,* 43, 46-52.

Holman,T.B.& Linford, S.T. (2001). Assumptions and methods. In T.B. Holman (Ed.) *Premarital prediction of marital quality or breakup: Research, theory, and practice* (pp.29-45).New-York: Plenum publishers.

Holmes, J.G. & Rempel, J.K. (1989). Trust in close relationships. In C. Henrick (Ed.) *Review of personality and social psychology,* (Vol. 10, pp. 187-220). London: Sage.

Hombs, M. E. (1994). *American Homelessness.* Santa Barbara, CA: Abc-Cilo.

Hogan, B. E., Linden, W., & Najarian, B. (2002). Social support interventions: Do they work? *Clinical Psychology Review, 22*(3), 381-440.

Hojat, M. (1982). Psychometric characteristics of the UCLA loneliness scale: A study with Iranian college students. *Educational and Psychological Measurement,* 42, 917-925.

Hojat, M. (1983).Comparison of transitory and chronic loners on selected personality variables. *British Journal of Psychology,* 74, 199-202.

Hojat, M. (1987) A psychodynamic view of loneliness and mother-child relationships: A review of theoretical perspectives and empirical findings. In M. Hojat & R. Crandall (Eds.), Loneliness: theory, research, and applications [special issue]. *Journal of Sonul Behavior and Personality, 2,* 89-104.

Hojat, M. (1998). Satisfaction with early relationship with parents and psychosocial attributes in adulthood: which parent contributes more. *Journal of Genetic Psychology,* 159, 203-220.

Hojjat, M. (1997). Philosophy of life as a model of relationship satisfaction. In R.J. Sternberg & H. Mahzad (Eds.). *Satisfaction in close relationship.* New York: Guilford.

Holland, J. (1977) Psychological aspects of oncology. *Medical Clinics of North America, 61,* 737-748.

Holman, T.B. (2001) Premarital prediction of marital quality or breakup: Research, theory and practice. New York: *Kluwer Academic- Plenum publishers.*

Holmberg, D., Blair, K.L., & Phillips, M. (2010). Women's sexual satisfaction as predictor of well-being in same-sex versus mixed.

Holmen, K., Ericsson, K., Anderson, L., & Winblad, B. (1992). Loneliness among elderly people living in Stockholm: A population study. *Journal of Advanced Nursing, 17*(1), 43-51.

Holmen K., Ericsson K. & Winblad B. (2000) Social and emotional loneliness among non-demented and demented elderly people. Archives of Gerontology and Geriatrics 31, 17–7192.

Holmes T. H., & Rahe, T. H. (1967). The social readjustment rating scale. *Journal of Psychosomatic Research, 11*(2), 213-228.

Holmes, J.G. & Rempel, J.K. (1989). Trust in close relationships. In C. Henrick (Ed.) *Review of personality and social psychology,* (Vol. 10, pp. 187-220). London: Sage

Hook, M. Gerstein, L., Detterich, L. & Gridley, B. (2003). How close are we? Measuring intimacy and examining gender differences. *Journal of Counselling and Development, 81,* 462-472.

Horner, P. (1989). *Osteoporosis: The long road back*. Ottawa Canada: University of Ottawa Press.

Horney, K. (1937). The neurotic personality of our time. NY: W.W. Norton.

Horowitz, L.M., French, R.S., & Anderson, C.A. (1982). The prototype of a lonely person. In L.A. Peplau & D. Perlman (Eds.), *Loneliness: A sourcebook of current theory, research and therapy* (p. 183-205). NY: Wiley.

Horton, D., & Wohl, R. R. (1956). Mass communication and para-social interaction: Observations of intimacy at a distance. *Psychiatry, 19*, 215-229.

House, J.A. (1981). *Work stress and social support*. Reading, MA: Addison-Wesley.

House, J. S., Kahn, R. L, McLeod, J. D., & Williams, D. (1985). Measures and concepts of social support. In S. Cohen & S. L. Syme (Eds.), *Social support and health* (pp. 83-108). New York: Academic Press.

House, J. S., Landis, K. R., & Umberson, D.(1988) Social relationship and health. *Science, 241*, 540-545.

Hughes A. (1999) Befriending: a note of caution. British Journal of Learning Disabilities 27, 88–92.

Hughes, B. (2001). Psychology, hospitalization, and some thoughts on medical training. European Journal of psychotherapy and counselling, 4(1), 7-26.

Huston, T.L., Caughlin, J.P., Houts, R.M., Smith, S.E., & George, L.J. (2001). The connubial crucible: Newlywed years as predictors of marital delight, distress, and divorce. *Journal of Personality and Social Psychology, 80*, 237-252.

Huston, T. L. & Chorost, A. F. (1994). Behavioral buffers on the effect of negativity on marital satisfaction: A longitudinal study. *Personal Relationships, 1*, 223-239.

Huston, T.L., & Vangelisti, A.L. (1991). Socioemotional behavior and satisfaction in marital relationship: A longitudinal study, *Journal of Personality and Social Psychology*, 61, 721-733.

Hymel, S. & Franke, S (1985). Children's peer relations: Assessing self-perceptions. In B.H. Schneider, K.H. Rubin & J.E. Ledingham (Eds.), *Children's peer relations: Issues in assessment and intervention* (Pp. 75-91). New York: Springer-Verlag.

Hymel, S., Tarulli, D., Hayden Thompson, L., & Terrell-Deutch, B. (1999). Loneliness through the eyes of children. In K.J. Rotenberg, & S. Hymel (Eds.), *Loneliness in childhood and adolescence* (pp. 80-106). Cambridge, England: Cambridge University Press.

Ickes, W., Winson, L., Bissonmette, V., & Garcia, S. (1990). Naturalistic social cognition: Empathic accuracy in mixed-sex dyads. *Journal of Personality and Social Psychology, 39*, 730-742.

Impett, E.A., Gable, S.L., & Peplau, L.A. (2005). Giving up and giving in: The costs and benefits of daily sacrifice in intimate relationships. *Journal of Personality and Social Psychology, 89*, (3), 327-344.

Impett, E.A. & Gordon, A.M. (2008). For the good of others: Toward a positive psychology of sacrifice. In S.J. Lopez (Ed.) *Exploring the best in people* (pp. 79-100). Westport, CT: Greenwood.

Incalzi, R.A., Gema, A., Capparella, O., & Muzzolon, R. (1991). Effects of hospitalization on affective status of elderly patients. *International Psychogeriatrics, 3*(1), 67-74.

Inderbitzen-Pisaruk, H. Clark, M.L., & Solano, C.H. (1992).Correlates of loneliness in midadolescence. *Journal of Youth and Adolescence*, 21, 151-167.

International Association of Marriage and Family Counselors. (2001). Board approved draft of the code of ethics of the International Association of Marriage and Family Counselors. Retrieved January 3, 2002, from http:// www.iamfc.org/ethicalcodes.htm

Iida, M., Seidman, G., Shrout, P.E., Fujita, K., & Bolger, N. (2008). Modeling support provision in intimate relationships. *Journal of Personality and Social Psychology,* 4 (3), 460-478.

Irons, W. (1979). Cultural and biological success. In N. A. Chagnon & W. Irons (Eds.), *Natural selection and social behaviour* (pp. 257-272). North Scituate, MA: Duxbury Press.

Jackson, T., Soderlind, A., & Weiss, K. E. (2000). Personality traits and quality of relationships as predictors of future loneliness among American college students. *Social Behavior and Personality,* 28, 463—470.

Jackson, T., Chen, H., Guo, C., & Gao, X. (2006). Stories we love by: Conceptions of love among couples from the People's Republic of China and the United States. *Journal of Cross-Cultural Psychology, 37*, 446-464.

Jacobson, N.S. (1991). Behavioural versus insight-oriented marital therapy: Labels can be misleading. *Journal of Consulting and Clinical Psychology,* 59, 142-145.

Johnston, M. (1980). Anxiety in surgical patients. *Psychological Medicine*, 10(1), 145-152.

Johnson, M.P. (1991). Commitment t personal relationships. In W.H. Jones & D. Perlman (Eds.) *Advances in personal relationships* (Vol. 3, pp. 117-143). London: J. Kingsly.

Johnson, M.P. (1999). Personal, moral, and structural commitment to relationships: Experiences of choice and constraint. In J.M. Adams & W.H. Jones (Eds.). *Handbook of interpersonal commitment and relationship stability.* New York: Kluwer Academic/ Plenum Publishers (pp. 73-90).

Johnson, M.P., Caughlin, J.P., & Huston, T.L. (1999). The tripartite nature of marital commitment: Personal, moral, and structural, reasons to stay married. *Journal of Marriage and the Family,* 61, 160-177.

Johnson, S.M. & Greenberg, I.S. (1995). The emotionally focused approach to problems in adult attachment. In N.S. Jacobson & A.S. Gurman (Eds.) *Clinical Handbook of couple therapy* (pp. 121-141). New York: Guilford.

Johnson, H.D., LaVoie, J.C., Spenceri, M.C., & -Wernil, M.A. (2001). Poor conflict avoidance: Associations with loneliness, social anxiety and social avoidance. *Psychological Reports*, 88, 227-235.

Johnston, L. D., O'Malley, P. M., & Bachman, J. G. (1994). *National survey results on drug use from the Monitoring the Future study,* 1975-1993 (NIH Publication No. 94-3810). Washington, DC: U.S. Government Printing Office.

Joiner, T. E. (1997). Shyness and low social support as interactive diatheses, with loneliness as mediator: Testing an interpersonal-personality view of vulnerability to depressive symptoms. *Journal of Abnormal Psychology*, 106, 386–394.

Joiner, T.E. (2000). Depression vicious scree: self-propagating and erosive processes in depression chronicity. *Clinical Psychology: Science and Practice,* 7, 2, 203-218.

Jones, W.H. (1982). Loneliness and Social Behaviour. In L.A. Peplau & D. Perlman (Eds.), *Loneliness: A sourcebook of current theory, research and therapy*, (p. 238-252). NY: Wiley.

Jones, W. H., & Carver, M.D. (1991). Adjustment and coping implications of loneliness. In C. R. Snyder & D. R. Forsyth (Eds.), Handbook of social and clinical psychology: The healthy perspective (pp. 395-415). New York: Pergamon Press.

Jones, W.H., Cavert, C.W., Snider, R.L., & Bruce T. (1985). Relational stress: An analysis of situations and events associated with loneliness. In S. Duck & D. Perlman (Eds.), *Understanding personal relationships* (p. 221-242). London: Sage.

Jones, J., Doss, B.D., & Christensen, A. (2001). Integrative Behavioural Couple Therapy. In J. Harvey & A. Wenzel (Eds.). Close romantic relationships: Maintenance and enhancement. (pp. 321-344). Mahwah, New Jersey. Lawrence Erlbaum Pub. Fincham, F.D., Beach, S.R.H., & Davila, J. (2007). Longitudinal relations between forgiveness and conflict resolution in marriage. *Journal of Family Psychology, 21,* 2, 542-545.

Jones, W. H., Freemon, J. R., & Goswick, R. A. (1981). The persistence of loneliness: Self and other determinants. *Journal of Personality, 49,* 27-48.

Jose, A., O'Leary, K. D., & Moyer, A. (2010). Does premarital cohabitation predict subsequent marital stability and marital quality? A meta-analysis. *Journal of Marriage and Family, 72,* 105-116.

Jones, T.L. & Prinz, R.J. (2005). Potential roles of parental self-efficacy in parent and child adjustment: A review. *Psychology Review, 25,* (3), 341-363.

Josselson, R. (1996). The space between us: exploring the dimension of human relationships. Newbury Park,CA: Sage.

Joung, I. M. A., Stronks, K., van, d. M., van Poppel, F. W. A., van, d.M., & Mackenbach, J. P. (1997). The contribution of intermediary factors to marital status differences in self-reported health. *Journal of Marriage and the Family, 59*(2), 476-490.

Jung, C. G. (1960). *The collected works of C. G. Jung. Volume 8. Bollingen Series XX. Synchronicity: An causal connecting principle* (R.F.C. Hull, Trans.). Princeton, NJ: Princeton University Press.

Junttila, N., Vauras, M., & Laakkonen, E. (2007). The role of parenting self-efficacy in children's social and academic behaviour. *European Journal of Psychology of Education – EJPE, 22*(1), 41-46.

Jylhä, M. (2004). Old age and loneliness: Cross-sectional and longitudinal analyses in the Tampere longitudinal study on aging. *Canadian Journal on Aging/ La Revue Canadienne du Vieillissement, 23,* 157-168.

Kaasa, K.R.N. (1998). Loneliness in old age: psychosocial and health predictors. *Nor J Epidemiol,* (8), 195–201.

Kahn, R. L.,&Antonucci, T. C. (1980). Convoys over the life course: Attachment, roles, and social support. In P. B. Baltes, & O. Brim (Eds.), *Life-span development and behavior* (Vol. 3). New York: Academic Press.

Kalb, R. C. & Scheinberg, L. C. (Eds.) (1992) *Multiple Sclerosis and the family.* New York: Demos.

Kanner, A.D. & Gomes, M.E. (1995). The all-consuming self. In T.Roszak, M.E. Gomes & A.D. Kanner (Eds.), Ecopsychology (pp. 77-91) San Francisco, CA: Sierra Club Books.

Kashdan, T. B., & Rottenberg, J. (2010). Psychological flexibility as fundamental aspect of health. *Clinical Psychology Review, 30*(7), 865-878.

Kasser, T. & Kanner, A.D. (Eds.) (2003). *Psychology and consumer culture: The struggle for good life in a materialistic world.* Washington, DC: American Psychological Association.

Karney, B. R., & Bradbury, T. N. (1995). The longitudinal course of marital quality and stability: A review theory, methods, and research. *Psychological Bulletin, 118*, 3-34.

Karney, B.R. & Bradbury, T. (1997) Neuroticism, marital interaction, and the trajectory of marital satisfaction. *Journal of Personality and Social Psychology, 72*, 1057-1092.

Karney, B.R., Bradbury, T.N., Fincham, F.D., & Sullivan, K.T. (1994). The role of negative affectivity in the association between attributions and marital satisfaction. *Journal of personality and social psychology, 66*, (2), 413-424.

Karney, B.R., McNulty, J.K., & Frye, N.E. (2001). A social-cognitive perspective on the maintenance and deterioration of relationship satisfaction. In J. Harvey & A. Wenzel (Eds.) *Close romantic relationships: Maintenance and enhancement* (pp. 195-214). Mahwah New Jersey: Lawrence Erlbaum.

Karoly, P. 1993. "Mechanisms of self-regulation: a systems view." *Annual a Review of Psychology*, 44:23-52

Katz, J., Beach, S.R.H., &Anderson, P. (1996). Self-enhancement versus self-verification: Does spousal support always help. *Cognitive Therapy and Research*, 20, 345-360.

Katz, B (1988). *How to market professional services*. New York: Nichols.

Kaufman, G., & Uhlenberg, P. (1998). Effects of life course transitions on the quality of relationships between adults children and their parents. *Journal of Marriage and the Family, 60*, 924-938.

Kawachi, I., Berkman, L. (2001). Social ties and mental health. *Journal of Urban Health, 78*, 458-467.

Kayser, K. & Rao, S.S. (2006). Process of disaffection in relationship breakdown. (pp. 201-221). In M.A. Fine & J.H. Harvey (Eds.) *Handbook of divorce and relationship dissolution*. New York: Routledge.

Keene, J. R. & Quadagno, J. (2004). Predictors of perceived work-family balance: Gender difference or gender similarity? *Sociological Perspectives, 47*(1), 1-23.

Keller, S. (2000). How do I love thee? Let me count the properties. *American Philosophical Quarterly, 37*(2), 163-173.

Kelling, K. (1991). Older Homeless People in London (Age Concerns, London, UK).

Kelly, H. H. (1973). The process of causal attribution. American psychologist, 28(2), 107-128.Kelley, A., Fincham, F.D., & Beach, S.R. (2003). Emerging perspectives on couple communication. In J.O. Greene & B.R. Burleson (Eds.) *The handbook of communication and social interaction skills* (pp. 723-752). Mahwah, New Jersey: Erlbaum.

Kelly, H.H. (1983). Love and commitment. In H.H. Kelley, E. Berscheid, A. Christensen, J. Harvey, T. Huston, G. Levinger, I. McClintock, L.A. Peplau, & D. Peterson (Eds.) *Close relationships* (pp. 265-314). New York: W.H. Freemen.

Kelly, A., Fincham, F.D., Beach, S.R.H. (2003). Emerging perspectives on couple communication. In J.O. Greene & B.R. Burleson (Eds.) *The handbook of communication and social interaction skills* (pp.723-252). Mahwah New Jersey: Lawrence Erlbaum Associates.

Kelly, M. P., Strassberg, D. S., & Kircher, J. R. (1990). Attitudinal and experimental correlates of anorgasmia. *Archives of Sexual Behavior, 19*, 165–177.

Kelly, M.P., Strassberg, D.S., & Turner, C.M. (2004). Communication and associated relationship issues in female anorgasmia. *Journal of Sex and Marital Therapy*, 30, 263-276.

Kendig, S. & Bianchi, S.M. (2008). The battered child syndrome. *Journal of the American Medical Association.* 181, 17-24.

Kenna, K. (1999). New teen rampage rocks U.S. The Toronto Star, May 21, 1999. P. A3.

Kennedy, P. (1999). Working with physically disabled people. In. J. Marzillier & J. Hall (Eds.) *What is clinical psychology?* (Pp. 134-156). NY: Oxford University Press.

Kennedy C. & Itkonen T. (1996) Social relationships, influential variables and chance across the lifespan. In: *Positive Behavioural Support: Including People with Difficult Behaviour in the Community* (eds L. Koegel, R. Koegel & G. Dunlap),Section iii. Paul H. Brookes, Baltimore, MD.

Kennedy, S., Kiecolt-Glaser, J. K., & Glaser, R. (1988) Immunological consequences of acute and chronic stressors: mediating role of interpersonal relationships. *British Journal of Medical Psychology,* 61, 77-85.

Kenny, D.A., & Acitelli, L.K. (1994). Measuring similarity in couples. *Journal of Family Psychology,* 8 417-431.

Keuzenkamp, S.,&Bos, D. (2007). *Out in the Netherlands: Acceptance of homosexuality in the Netherlands.* Den Haag: SCP.

Kidd, S.A. (2004). The walls were closing in and we were trapped: A qualitative analysis of street youth suicide. *Youth and Society,* 36, 30–55.

Kidd, S.A. (2006). Factors precipitating suicidality among homeless youth: A quantitative follow-up. *Youth and Society,* 37, 393–422.

Kidd, S.A. (2007). Youth homelessness and social stigma. *Journal of Youth and Adolescence,* 36, 291–299.

Kiecolt-Glaser, J. K., McGuire, L., Robles, T. F. & Glaser, R. (2002) Psychoneuroimmunology: psychological influences on immune function and health. *Journal of Consulting and Clinical Psychology,* 70(3), 537-547.

Kilpatrick, S.H., Bissonnett, V.L., & Rusbult, C. E. (2002). Empathic accuracy and accommodative behaviour among newlywed married couples. *Personal Relationships,* 9, 369-396.

Kitson, G.C. (2006). Divorce and relationship dissolution research: Then and now. In M.A. Fine & J.H. Harvey (Eds.) *Handbook of divorce and relationship dissolution.* New York: Routledge (pp. 15-40).

Kitto, P. (1988) The patient as healer: how we can take part in our own recovery. In M.Kidel & S. Rowe-Leete (Eds.) *The meaning of illness* New York: Routledge. Pp. 109-119.

Kline, D. W., & Scialfa, C. T. (1996). Visual and auditory aging. In J. E. Birren & K. W. Schaie (Eds.), *Handbook of psychology and aging* (4th ed., pp. 181–204). San Diego, CA: Academic

Press. Knafl, K. A., & Deatrick, J. A. (2002). The challenge of normalization for families of children with chronic conditions. *Pediatric Nursing,* 28, 49-54.

Knoke, J., Burau, J., & Roehrle, B. (2010). Attachment styles, loneliness quality and stability of marital relationships. *Journal of Divorce and Remarriage,* 51,310-325.

Knox, M., Funk, J., Elliott, R., & Bush, E.G. (2000). Gender differences in adolescents' possible selves. *Youth & Society, 31(3),* 287-309.

Knox, D., & Schacht, C. (2010). Choices in relationships: An introduction to marriage and the family (10th ed.). Belmont, CA: Wadsworth.

Kobak, R.R., & Hazan, C. (1991). Attachment in marriage: Effects of security and accuracy of working models. *Journal of Personality and Social Psychology,* 60, 861-869.

Koball, H.l., Moiduddin, E., Henderson, J., Goesling, B., & Besculides, M. (2010). What do we know about the link between marriage and health? *Journal of Family Issues, 31,* 1019-1040.

Kochenderfer-Ladd, B. & Skinner, K. (2002). Children's coping strategies: Moderators of the effects of peer victimization? *Developmental Psychology*, 38, 267-278.

Kock, K., Morley, S. D., Mullins, J. J., &Schmale, H. (1994). Denatonium bitter tasting among transgenic mice expressing rat von ebner's gland protein.*Physiology & Behavior, 56*(6), 1173-1177.

Koenig, L. J., & Abrams, R. F. (1999). Adolescent loneliness and adjustment: A focus on gender differences. In K. J. Rotenberg & S. Hymel (Eds.), *Loneliness in childhood and adolescence* (pp. 296–322). Cambridge, UK: Cambridge University Press.

Kohut, H. (1977) *The restoration of the self.* New York: International Universities Press.

Koopman, C., Hermanson, K., Diamond, S., Angell, K., & Spiegel, D. (1998) Social support, life stress, pain and emotional adjustment to advanced breast cancer. *Psycho-Oncology, 7,* 101-111.

Korporaal, M., Broese van Groenou, M. I., & van Tilburg, T. G. (2008). Effects of own and spousal disability on loneliness among older adults. *Journal of Aging and Health, 20*(3), 306-325.

Koski, L.R., & Shaver, P.R. (1997). Attachment and relationship satisfaction across the lifespan. In R.J. Sternberg, & M. Hojjat (Eds.). *Satisfaction in close relationships.* New York: The Guilford Press (pp. 26-55).

Kouneski, E. & Olson, D.H. (2004). A practical look at intimacy: ENRICH couple typology. In D.J. Mashek & A. Aron (Eds.) *Handbook of closeness and intimacy.* (pp. 117-133). Mahwah, New Jersey: Lawrence Erlbaum Associates, Publishers.

Kramer, B.J. & Barker, J.C. (1996). Homelessness among older American Indians, Los Angeles, 1987-1989. *Human Organization, 55 (4)*, 396-408.

Kraus, A.S. & Lillienfeld, A. (1959). Some epidemiologic aspects of the high mortality rate in young widowed group. *Journal of Chronic Diseases*, 10, 207-217.

Krauss M., Seltzer M. & Goodman S. (1992) Social support networks of adults with mental retardation who live at home. American Journal on Mental Retardation 96, 432–441.

Krauss Whitbourne, S. (2001). *Adult development & Aging: Biopsychosocial perspectives.* New York: John Wiley & Sons.

Kraut, R. Patterson, M., Lundmark, V., Kiesler, S., Mukopadhyay, T., & Scher lis, W. (1998). Internet paradox: A social technology that reduces social involvement and psychological well-being? *American Psychologist, 53*(9), 1017-1031.

Krishnakumar, A. & Buehler, C. (2000). Interparental conflict and parenting behaviours: A meta-analytic review. *Family Review.* 49, 25-44.

Krueger, D.W. (1984). Emotional rehabilitation: An overview. In D.W. Krueger (Ed.). *Emotional rehabilitation of physical trauma and disability* (Pp. 3-12). NY: SP Medical & Scientific Books.

Kuebler, K.K., Berry, P.H. & Heidrich, E.E. (2002). *End of life care: Clinical practice guidelines.* NY: W.B. Saunders.

Kulik, J. A., & Mahler, H. I. (2006). Marital quality predicts hospital stay following coronary artery bypass surgery for women but not men. Social Science & Medicine, 63, 2031–2040.

Kumashiro, M. Rusbult, C.E., Finkenauer, C., & Stoker, S. (2007). *Journal of Social and Personal Relationships*, 24, (4), 591-611.

Kupersmidt, J. B., Sigda, K. B., Sedikides, C., & Voegler, M. E. (1999). In K. J. Rotenberg, & S. Hymel (Eds.), *Loneliness in childhood and adolescence* (pp. 263–279). Cambridge, UK: Cambridge University Press.

Kurdek, I.A. (1993). Predicting marital dissolution: A 5 year prospective longitudinal study of newlywed couples. *Journal of Personality and Social Psychology*, 64, 221-242.

Kurdek, L.A. (2000). The nature and predictors of the trajectory of change in marital quality for husbands and wives over the first 10 years of marriage. *Developmental Psychology*, 35, 1283-1296.

Kurdek, L.A. (2005). Gender and marital satisfaction early in marriage: A growth curve approach. *Journal of Marriage and the Family*, 67, 68-74.

Kurdek, L. A. (2006). Differences between partners from heterosexual, gay, and lesbian cohabiting couples. *Journal of Marriage and Family*, 68, 509-528.

Kuypers, J. A. & Bengston, V. L. (1973). Social breakdown and competence: A model of normal aging. *Human Development*, 16, 181-201.

Kuyper, L. & Fokkema, T. (2010). Loneliness Among Older Lesbian, Gay, and Bisexual Adults: The Role of Minority Stress. *Archives of Sexual Behaviours*, 39, 1171–1180. DOI 10.1007/s10508-009-9513-7

La Cour, P.: Religion og attachment: en kritisk oversight over teorier og empiriske fund. *Psyke & Logos*. 2003, 24, 769-777.

Ladd, G.W. (1996). Shifting ecologies during the 5 to 7 period: Predicting children's adjustment during the transition to grade school. In A.J. Sameroff & M.M. Haith (Eds.), *The five to seven shift: The age of reason and responsibility* (Pp. 363-386). Chicago, Ill: The University of Chicago Press.

Ladd, G.W., Buhs, E.S. & Seid, M. (2000). Children's initial sentiments about kindergarten: Is school linking an antecedent of early classroom participation and achievement? *Merrill-Palmer Quarterly*, 46, 255-279.

Lai, Y.M Hong, C. P. H., & Chee, C. Y. I. (2000). Stigma of Mental Illness Singapore Med Journal, 42(3), 111-114

Lamptey, P.R. (2002). Reducing heterosexual transmition of HIV in poor countries. *British Medical Journal*, 324, 207-211.

Langston, C.A. (1994). Capitalizing on and coping with daily-life events: Expressive responses to positive events. *Journal of Personality and Social Psychology*, 67, 1112-1125.

Lansford, J. E., Sherman, A. M., & Antonucci, T. C. (1998). Satisfaction with social networks: An examination of socioemotional selectivity theory across cohorts. *Psychology and Aging*, 3, 544–552.

Langston, C.A. (1994). Capitalizing on and coping with daily life events: Expressive responses to positive events. *Journal of Personality and Social Psychology*, 67, 1112-1125.

Larson, R., Csikszentmihalyi, M., & and Graef R. (1982). Time alone in daily experience: Loneliness or renewal? In L. A. Peplau & D. Perlman (Eds.) *Loneliness: A sourcebook of current theory, research and therapy* (Pp. 40–53). New York: John Wiley & Sons.

Larsen, A.S. & Olson, D.H. (1989). Predicting marital satisfaction using PREPARE: A replication study. *Journal of Marital and Family Therapy*, 15,(3), 311-322.

Larson, J.H. (2003). The great marriage tune-up book. San Francisco. CA: *Jossey Bass.*

Larson, H., & Holman, T.B. (1994) Premarital predictors of marital quality and stability. *Family Relations, 43,* 228-237.

Larzeler, R.E. & Huston, T.L. (1980). The dyadic trust scale: Toward understanding interpersonal trust in close relationships. *Journal of marriage and the family,* 42, 595-604.

Lasch, C. (1977). Haven in a Heartless World: The family besieged. New York: Basic Books.

Lau, S. (1989). Sex role orientation and domains of self-esteem. *Sex Roles, 21,* 415-422.

Lau, S. & Gruen, G.E. (1992). The social stigma of loneliness: Effect of target person's and perceiver's sex. *Personality and Social Psychology Bulletin*, 18(2), 182-189.

Laurenceau, J.P., Feldman Barrett, L., & Rovine, M.J. (2005). The interpersonal process model of intimacy in marriage: A daily-diary and multilevel modeling approach. *Journal of Family Psychology,* 19, (2), 314-323.

Laurenceau, J.P, Kleinman, B. M., Kaczynski, K. J., & Carver, C. S. (2010). Assessment of relationship-specific incentive and threat sensitivities: Predicting satisfaction and affect in adult intimate relationships. *Psychological Assessment, 22*(2), 407-419.

Laurenceau, J.P., Rivera, L.M., Schaffer, A.R., & Pietromonaco, P.R. (2004). Intimacy as an interpersonal process: current status and future directions. In D.J. Mashek & A. Aron (Eds.) *Handbook of closeness and intimacy* (pp. 62-80). Mahwah, New Jersey: Lawrence Erlbaum Pub.

Laurenceau, J.-P., Stanley, S., Olmos-Gallo, A., Baucom, B., & Markman, H. (2004). Community-based prevention of marital dysfunction: Multilevel modeling of a randomized effectiveness study. *Journal of Consulting and Clinical Psychology,* 72(6), 933.

Laursen, B., Coy, K. C., & Collins, W. A. (1998). Reconsidering changes in parent-child conflicts across adolescence: A meta-analysis. *Child Development, 69,* 817-832.

Lawrance, K., & Byers, E. (1992). Development of the interpersonal exchange model of sexual satisfaction in long-term relationships. *The Canadian Journal of Human Sexuality,* 1, 123-128.

Layton, J. (2000). Homelessness: The Making and Unmaking of a Crisis. (Penguin Books, Toronto, Canada).

Leary, M. R., & Springer, C. A. (2001). Hurt feelings: The neglected emotion. In R. Kowalski (Ed.), *Aversive behaviors and interpersonal transgression* (pp. 151–175). Washington, DC: American Psychological Association.

Ledermann, T., Bodenmann, G., Rudaz, M., & Bradbury, T. N. (2010). Stress, communication, and marital quality in couples. *Family Relations, 59,* 195-206.

Lee, J.A. (1973). He colors of love: An exploration of the ways of loving. Don Mills ON: *New Press.*

Leibowitz, M.R. (1983). The chemistry of love. Boston: *Little, Brown.*

Lester, A. & Lester, J. (1998). It takes two: The joy of intimate marriage. Louisville, KY: *Westminster John Knox Press.*

Leventhal, H., Leventhal, E.A., & Cameron, L. (2001). Representations, procedures, and affect in illness self-regulation. A perceptual-cognitive model. In A. Baum, T.A. Revenson, & J. E. Singer (Eds.), *Handbook of health psychology* (Pp. 19-47), Mawah, NJ:Earlbaum.

Levine, I. & Stokes, J. P. (1986). An examination of the relation between individual difference variables to loneliness. *Journal of Personality,* 54, 717-733.

Levinger, G. (1999). Duty toward whom? Reconsidering attractions and barriers as determinants of commitment in a relationship. In J.M. Adams & W. H. Jones (Eds.). *Handbook of interpersonal commitment and relationship stability.* New York: Kluwer Academic/ Plenum Publishers (pp. 37-52).

Levy-Shiff, R. (1999). Fathers' cognitive appraisals, coping strategies and support resources as correlates of adjustment to parenthood. Journal of Family Psychology, 13, 554-567

Lewinsohn, P. M. (1974). *A behavioral approach to depression.* (pp.318-xvii, 318). Oxford, England: John Wiley & Sons, Oxford.

Lewinsohn, P. M., Biglan, A., & Zeiss, A. M. (1976). Behavioural treatment of depression. In. P. O. Davidson (Ed.), *The behavioural management of anxiety, depression and pain* (pp. 91-145). New York: Brunner/Mazel.

Lewis, T., Amini, F. & Lannon, R. (2000). *A general theory of love.* New York: Random House.

Liao, S. (2001, March,21). Pub night stabbing in residence. *Excalibur,* 35(30), 1.

Liao, M., Chen, M., Chen, S., Chen, P. (2008). Uncertainty and anxiety during the diagnostic period for Women with suspected breast cancer. *Cancer Nursing*, 31(4), 274-283.

Liang, M. H., & Daltory, L. H. (1985). The impact of inflammatory arthritis on society and the individual: Options for public health programs. In N. M. Hadler & D. B. Gillings (Eds.). *Arthritis and society: The impact of musculoskeletal diseases* (pp. 5-16). London. UK: Butterworths.

Link, B. G., & Phelan, J. C. (2001). Conceptualizing Stigma. *Annual Review of Sociology*, 27, 363-385.

Litzinger, S., & Gordon, C.K. (2005). Exploring relationships among communication, sexual satisfaction and marital satisfaction. *Journal of sex and Marital Therapy,* 31, 409-424.

Lloyd-Cobb, P. and Dixon, D. R. (1995). A preliminary evaluation of the effects of a veterans' hospital domiciliary program of the homeless persons. Research on Social Work Practice 5(3), 309–316.

Lobdell, J., & Perlman, D. (1986). The intergenerational transmission of loneliness: A study of college females and their parents. Journal of Marriage and the Family, 48, 589-595.

Long, C.R. & Averill, J.R. (2003). Solitude: An exploration of benefits of being alone. *Journal for the Theory of Social Behaviour, 33*, 21-44.

Long, E.C., Cate, R.M., Fehsenfeld, D.A., & Williams, K.M. (1996). A longitudinal assessment of a measure of premarital sexual conflict. *Family Relations*, 45, 302-308.

Long, M.V. & Martin, P. (2000). Personality, relationship closeness, and loneliness of oldest old adults and their children. *Journal of Gerontology*, 55(B), 311–P319.

Long, C.R., Seburn, M. Averill, L.R. & More, T.A. (2003). Solitude experiences; varieties, settings, and individual differences. *Personality and Social Psychology Bulletin, 29* (5), 578-583.

Locker, D. (1983). *Disability and disadvantage: The consequences of chronic illness.* NY: Tavistock.

Löfvenmark, C., Mattiasson, A-C, Billing, E., & Edner, M. (2009). Perceived loneliness and social support in patients with chronic heart failure. *European Journal of Cardiovascular Nursing, 8*, 251-258.

Lucas, G. M., Knowles, M. L., Gardner, W.L., Molden, D.C., & Jefferis, V.E. (2010). Increasing social engagement among lonely individuals: The role of acceptance cues and promotion motivations. *Personality and Social Psychology Bulletin*, 36(10) 1346–1359.

Lund, M. (1985). The development of an investment and commitment scales for predicting continuity of personal relationships. *Journal of Social and Personal Relationships, 2*, 3-23.

Luong, G., Charles, S. T., & Fingerman, K. L. (2011). Better with age: Social relationships across adulthood. *Journal of Social and Personal Relationships, 28(1)*, 9–23

Lupton, D., & Seymour, W. (2000). Technology, selfhood and physical disability. *Social Science and Medicine, 50,* 1851-1862.

Lynch (1977) The Broken Heart: Medical Consequences of Loneliness. Basic Books, New York.

Lynch, J. J. (1979) The broken heart: the medical consequences of loneliness. New York: Basic Books.

Lynch. J.J. (2000). A cry unheard: New insights into the medical consequences of loneliness. Baltimore, MD: Bancroft Press.

Lyons, R. F., Sullivan, M. J. L., Ritvo, P. G., & Coyne, J. C. (1995). *Relationships in chronic illness and disability*. Thousand Oaks, CA: Sage.

Lyyra, T.M., Heikkinen, R.L., 2006. Perceived social support and mortality in older people. Journal of Gerontology Part B: *Psychological Sciences and Social Sciences* 61 (3), S147–S152.

MacDermid, S.M., Huston, T, L., & McHale, S.M. (1990). Changes in marriage associated with the transition to parenthood: Individual differences as a function of sex-role attitudes and changes in the decision of household labour. *Journal of Marriage and the Family,* 52 (2), 475-486.

MacDonald, G., & Leary, M.R. (2005). Why does social exclusion hurt? The relationship between social and physical pain. *Psychological Bulletin*, 131, 202-223.

Mace, D.R. (1979) Marriage and family enrichment. A new field? *Family Coordinator,* 28 (3), 409-419.

Mace, D.R. & Mace, V.C. (1975). Marriage enrichment: Wave of the future? *The Family Coordinator,* 24, 131-135.

Machen, A. (1923/2001). *The hill of dreams.* CA: Wildside Press.

Mackay, S.K. (1996). Nurturance: A neglected dimension in family therapy with adolescents. *Journal of Marital and Family Therapy*, 22, 489-508.

Maclean, M.G., Embry, L.E., Cauce, A.M. (1999). Homeless adolescents' paths to separation from family: Comparison of family characteristics, psychological adjustment, and victimization. *Journal of Community Psychology,* 27, 179–187.

MacNeil, S., & Byers, E.S. (1997). The relationship between sexual problems, communication, and sexual satisfaction: *The Canadian Journal of Human Sexuality*, 6, 277-287.

MacNeil, S., & Byers, E.S. (2005). Dyadic assessment of sexual self-disclosure and sexual satisfaction in heterosexual dating couples. *Journal of Social and Personal Relationships,* 22, 169-181.

Madsen, L.B. (2000). *Cognitive processes and attachment: The structure and function of working models.* Unpublished Masters thesis, University of Queensland, Brisbane, Australia.

Mages, N. L., & Mendelson, G. A. (1979) Effects of cancer patients' lives: A personological approach. In G. C. Stone, F. Cohen, & N. E. Adler (Eds.). *Health Psychology: a handbook.* San Francisco: Jossey-Bass. Pp.103-122.

Mah, K., & Binik, Y.M. (2004). Female orgasmic disorders: A clinical approach. *Urodinamica,* 14, 99-104.

Mahler, R. (2003). *Stillness: Daily gifts of solitude.* York Beach, ME: RedWheel/Weiser, LLC.

Mahon, N. E., & Yarcheski, A. (1992). Alternate explanations of loneliness in adolescents: A replication an extension study. *Nursing Research,* 41, 151−156.

Mahon, N. E., Yarcheski, A., Yarcheski, T. J., Cannella, B. L., & Hanks, M. M. (2006). A Meta-analytic

Mahoney, A., Pargament, K. I., Murray-Swank, A., & Murray-Swank, N. (2003). Religion and the sanctification of family relationships. *Review of Religious Research, 44,* 220-236. Study of Predictors for Loneliness During Adolescence. *Nursing Research, 55*(5), 308-315.

Malakoff, L. Z. (1991). Housing options for the elderly: The innovative process in community settings. New York: Garland.

Manusov, V. (2002). Thought and action: Connecting attributions to behaviours in married couple's interactions. In N. Noller & J.A. Feeney (Eds.) *Understanding marriage: Developments in the study of couple interaction* (pp.14-31). Cambridge, UK: Cambridge University Press.

Marcus, G. & Gross, S. (1991). Black and white students' perceptions of teacher treatment. *Journal of Educational Research,* 84, 363-367.

Margalit, M. (2010). *Lonely children and adolescents: self-perceptions, social exclusions, and hope.* NY: Springer.

Margolin, G. & Wampold, B.E. (1981). Sequential analysis of conflict and accord in distressed and nondistressed marital partners. *Journal of counselling and clinical psychology,* 49, 554-567.

Markman, H.J. (1979). Application of behavioural model of marriage in predicting relationship satisfaction of couples planning marriage. *Journal of Consulting and Clinical Psychology,* 47, 743-849.

Markman, H. J. (1981). Prediction of marital distress: A 5-year follow-up. *Journal of Consulting and Clinical Psychology, 49*(5), 760-762. doi: http://dx.doi.org/10.1037/0022-006X.49.5.760

Markman, H. J. (1984). The longitudinal study of couples interactions: Implications for understanding and predicting the development of marital distress. In K. Hahlweg & N.S. Jacobson (Eds.), *Marital Interaction: An Analysis and Modificiation,* (pp. 253-281). New York: Guilford Press.

Markman, H.J., Floyd, F.J., Stanley, S.M. & Storaasli, R.D. (1988). The prevention of marital distress: A longitudinal investigation. *Journal of Consulting and Clinical Psychology, Vol. 56,* No. 2, pp. 210-217.

Markman, H.J. (1991). Constructive marital conflict is NOT an oxymoron. *Behavioral Assessment,* 13, 83-96.

Markman, H.J., Renick, M.J., Floyd, F.J. Stanley, S.M., & Clements, M. (1993). Preventing marital distress through communication and conflict management training: A 4 – and – 5 year follow up. *Journal of Consulting and Clinical Psychology,* 61,(1), 70-77.

Markman, H.J. Stanley, S.M., Blumberg, S.L. (1994). Fighting for your marriage. San Francisco, CA: *Jossey-Bass.*

Markman HJ, Stanley SM, Blumberg SL.(2001) Fighting for your marriage. San Francisco: Jossey–Bass.

Markus, H. R., & Kitayama, S. (1991). Culture and the self: Implications for cognition, emotion, and motivation. *Psychological Review, 98,* 224–253.

Margulis ST, Derlega VJ, Winstead BA. (1984). Implications of social psychological concepts for a theory of loneliness. In: V. Derlega (Ed), *Communication, intimacy, and close relationships.* pp. 133–60) London: Academic Press.

Martin, J.I. & D'augelli, A. R. (2003). How lonely are gay and lesbian youth? *Psychological Reports,* 2003, 93, 486.

Martin, R., Davis, G. M., Baron, R. S., Suls, J. & Blanchard, E. B. (1994) Specificity in social support: Perceptions of helpful and unhelpful provider behaviors among irritable bowel syndrome, headache, and cancer patients. *Health Psychology, 13,* 432-439.

Martin, A. D., & Hetrick, E. S. (1988). The stigmatization of the gay and lesbian adolescent. *Journal of Homosexuality, 15*(1–2), 163–183.

Martin, P., Hagberg, B., & Poon, L. (1997). Predictors of loneliness in centenarians: A parallel study. *Journal of Cross-Cultural Gerontology,* 12, 203-224.

Martin, J.I. & Knox, J. (1997). Land sexual risk behaviour in gay men. *Psychological Reports,* 1997, 81, 815-825.

Martens, W.H. J. & Palermo G. B. (2005). Loneliness and Associated Violent Antisocial Behavior: Analysis of the Case Reports of Jeffrey Dahmer and Dennis Nilsen. *International Journal of Offender Therapy and Comparative Criminology,* 49(3), 298-307.

Masi, C.M., Chen, H.Y., Hawkley, L.C. & Cacioppo, J.T. (2011). *Personality and Social Psychology Review,* 15, 3, 219-266.

Maslow, A.H. (1968). Toward a psychology of being. New York: *Van Nostrand.*

Maslow, A. (1970). *Motivation and Personality.* New York: Harper & Row.

Masters, W.H., Johnson, V., & Kolodny, R. (1986). Sex and human loving. Boston, MA: *Little, Brown and Company.*

Masuda, M. & Duck, S. (2002). Issues in ebb and flow: Management and maintenance of relationships as a skilled activity. In J.H. Harvey & A. Wenzel (Eds.) *A clinical guide to maintaining and enhancing close relationships* (pp. 13-14). Mahwah, New Jersey: Lawrence Erlbaum Publishers.

Matthews, B., & Rice-Oxley, M. (2001). *Multiple Sclerosis: The Facts.* Oxford, UK: Oxford University Press.

Mate, G. (2003). When the body says no: The cost of hidden stress. Toronto, Canada: Vintage.

Matras, J. (1990). Dependency obligations, and entitlements: A new sociology of aging, the life course and the elderly. Englewood Cliffs, N. J.: Prentice Hall.

Mather, M. & Lavery, D. (2010)/. In US proportion married at lowest recorded levels. Population Reference Bureau, Retrieved from http://www.prb.org/Articles/2010 usmarriagedecline.aspx

Matthew, B. & Rice-Oxley, M. (2001). *Multiple sclerosis: the facts.* Oxford, UK: Oxford University Press.

Matthews, S. H. & Sun, R. (2006). Incidence of four-generation family linkages: Is timing of fertility or morality a better explanation? *Journal of Gerontology: Social Sciences, 61B (2)*, S99-106.

Matsushima, R., & Shiomi, K. (2001). The effect of hesitancy toward and the motivation for self disclosure on loneliness among Japanese high school students. *Social Behaviour and Personality*, 29 (7), 661-670.

Mayer Gaev, D. (1976). *The psychology of loneliness.* Chicago, IL: Adams.

Mayou, R. A., & Smith, K. A. (1997). Post traumatic symptoms following medical illness and treatment. *Journal of Psychosomatic Research, 43*, 121–3.

McAdoo, H.P. (1996). *Black Families.* (3rd Ed.) Thousand Oaks, CA: Sage.

McCarthy, B., Ginsberg, R.L., & Cintron, J.A. (2008). Primary prevention the first two years of marriage. *Journal of Family Psychotherapy, 19*(2), 143-156.

McGraw, J. G. (2000). The first of all evils. In S. A. Wawrytko (Ed.), *The problem of evil. An intercultural exploration* (pp. 145-158). Atlanta, GA: Editions Rodopi BV.

McManus, M. (1993). Marriage savers. Grand Rapids, MI: Zondervan.

McManus, M., & McManus, J. (2001, May 22). Statement before the Subcommittee on Human Resources of the House Committee on Ways and Means.WL 21756459.

McPherson, M., Smith-Lovin, L., & Brashears, M. E. (2006). Social Isolation in America: Changes in Core Discussion Networks over Two Decades. *American Sociological Review, 71*(3), 353-375.

McWhirter, B. (1990). Loneliness: A review of current literature with implications for counselling and research. *Journal of Counselling and Development, 68*(4), 417-422.

McWhirter, B. T., Besett-Alesch, T. M., Horibata, J., & Gat, I. (2002). Loneliness in high risk adolescents: The role of coping, self-esteem, and empathy. *Journal of Youth Studies*, 5, 69–84.

Medalie, J., & Goldbourt, U. (1976). Angina pectoris among 10,000 men: Psychosocial and other risk factors as evidenced by a multivariate analysis of a five year incidence study. *American Journal of Medicine, 60*, 910-921.

Meer, J. (1985). Loneliness: Whether being lonely is a sometime thing or a sad way of life, understanding its causes can help. *Psychology Today, 20,* 29-33.

Mellor, D., Stokes, M., Firth, L., Hayashi, Y., & Cummins, R. (2008). Need for belonging, relationship satisfaction, loneliness, and life satisfaction. *Personality and Individual Differences, 45*, 213-218.

Melton, L. J. (1999). Epidemiology of fractures. In E. S. Orwoll, (Ed.). Osteoporosis in men: The effects of gender on skeletal health (pp. 1-13). NY: Academic Press.

Metts, S. (1994). Relational transgressions. In W. R. Cupach & B. H. Spitzberg (Eds.), *The dark side of interpersonal communication* (pp. 217-239). Hillside, NJ: Erlbaum.

Metz, M.E., & Epstein, N. (2002). Assessing the role of relationship conflict in sexual dysfunction. *Journal of Sex and Marital Therapy, 28*, 139-164.

Merton, T. (1953). *Bread in the wilderness.* New York: New Directions.

Merton, T. (2000). *Thomas Merton: Essential writings.* New York: Orbis Books.

Meyer, I. H. (1995). Minority stress and mental health in gay men. *Journal of Health and Social Behavior, 36*, 38-56. *Meyer, I. H. (2003). Prejudice, social stress, and mental health in lesbian, gay, and bisexual populations: Conceptual issues and research evidence. Psychological Bulletin, 129, 674–697.*

Mijuskovic, B.(1979). *Loneliness in philosophy, psychology and literature.* The Netherlands:Van Gorcum

Mijuskovic, B. (1992). Organic communities, atomistic societies and loneliness. *Journal of Sociology and Social Welfare, 19(*2), 147-164.

Mikulincer, M. (1997). Adult attachment style and information processing: Individual differences in curiosity and cognitive closure. *Journal of Personality and Social Psychology, 72,* 1217-1230.

Mikulincer, M., Florian, V., Cowan, P.A., & Cowan, C.P. (2001). Attachment security in couple relationships: A systemic model and its implications for family dynamics. *Family Processes,* 41, 405-434.

Mikulincer, M., & Segal, J. (1999). A multidimensional analysis of the experience of loneliness. *Journal of Social and Personal Relationships,* 7, 209-230.

Mikulincer, M., & Shaver, P.R. (2007a). *Attachment patterns in adulthood: Structure, dynamics, and change.* New York: Guilford Press.

Mikulincer, M., & Shaver, P.R. (2007b). Boosting attachment security to promote mental health, prosocial values, and intergroup tolerance. *Psychological Inquiry,* 18, 139-156.

Millar, A.L. (2003). *Action plan for arthritis.* Champaign, Ill: Human Kinetics.

Milardo, R.M. (1988). Families and social networks. An overview of theory and methodology. In R.M. Milardo (Ed.) *Families and social networks* (pp. 13-47). Newbury Park, CA: Sage.

Miller, R. S. (2012). *Intimate relationships* (6th International ed.). New York, NY: McGraw Hill.

Miller, I. C. & Berg, J. (1984). Selectivity and urgency in interpersonal exchange. In V.J. Derelgal (Ed.), *Communication, intimacy, and close relationships.* Orland, FL: Academic Press.

Miller, S.A., & Byers, E.S. (2004). Actual and desired duration of foreplay and intercourse: Discordance and misperceptions within heterosexual couples. *The Journal of Sex Research,* 41, 301-309.

Mills, J. & Clark, M.S. (1986). Communications that should lead to perceived exploitation in communal and exchange relationships. *Journal of Social and Clinical Psychology,* 4, 225-234.

Mills, J. & Clark, M.S. (2001) Viewing close romantic relationships as communal relationships: Implications for maintenance and enhancement. In J. Harvey & A. Wenszel (Eds.). *Close romantic relationships* (pp.13-26). Mahwah, New Jersey: Lawrence Erlbaum Pub..

Mills, S. D., & Sprenkle, D. H. (1995). Family therapy in the postmodern era. *Family Relations, 44(4),* 368-376.

Minardi, H. A., & Blanchard, M. (2004). Older people with depression: pilot study. *Journal of Advanced Nursing, 46*(1), 23-32.

Mintz, S. (2004). *Huck's raft: A history of American Childhood.* Cambridge, MA: Belknap Press of Harvard University.

Minuchin, S. (1974). *Families & family therapy.* Cambridge: Harvard University Press.

Mitnick, D.M., Heyman, R.E., & Smith Slep, A.M. (2009). Changes in relationship satisfaction across the transition to parenthood: A meta analysis. *Journal of Family Psychology,* 23, (6), 848-852.

Mishel, M. H. (1997). Uncertainty in Acute Illness. *Annual Review of Nursing Research.* the hospital environment. *Journal of Clinical Nursing,* Mishel, M. (1984). Perceived uncertainty and stress in Illness. *Research in Nursing & Health, 7(3), 163-171.*

Mishel, M. (1988). Uncertainty in illness. *Journal of Nursing Scholarship*, 20,4, 225-232.

Modell, A. H. (1993). *The private self.* Cambridge, MA, US: Harvard University Press, Cambridge, MA.

Mohr, J., Cook-Lyon, R., & Kolchakian, M. R. (2010). Love imagined: Working models of future romantic attachment in emerging adults. *Personal Relationships, 17*, 457-473.

Molden, D.C., Lucas, G.M., Finkel, E.J., Kumashiro, M., & Rusbult, C. (2009) Perceived support for promotion focused and prevention focused goals: Association with well-being in unmarried and married couples. *Psychological Science,* 20(7), 787-793.

Monarch, N.D. Hartman, S.G., Whitton, S.W. Markman, H.J. (2002). The role of clinicians in the prevention of marital distress and divorce. In J.H. Harvey & A. Wenzel (Eds.) *A clinical guide to maintaining and enhancing close relationships* (pp. 233-259). Mahwah, New Jersey: Lawrence Erlbaum Pub.

Montesi, J.L., Fauber, R.L., Gordon, E.A., & Heimberg, R.G. (2010). The specific importance of communicating about sex to couples' sexual and overall relationship satisfaction. *Journal of Social and Personal Relationships, 28,* 591-609. Montagu, M. F. A. (1962).*Prenatal influences.* Oxford, England: Charles C Thomas, Oxford.

Moore, D. & Schultz, N.R. (1983). Loneliness at adolescence: Correlates, attributions and coping. *Journal of Youth and Adolescence*, 12, 95-100.

Morgan, H.J. & Shaver, P.R. (1999). Attachment processes and commitment to romantic relationships. In J.M. Adams & W.H. Jones (Eds.) *Handbook of interpersonal commitment and relationship stability* (pp. 109-124). New York: Kluwer Academic/Plenum.

Morris, L.M. & Carter, S.A. (1999). Transition to marriage: A literature review. *Journal of Family and Consumer Sciences Education, 17,* (1), 1-21.

Moskowitz, J.T. (2003). Positive affect predicts lower risk of AIDS mortality. *Psychosomatic Medicine,* 65, 520-626.

Moustakas, C.E. (1961). *Loneliness.* Engelwood Cliffs, NJ: Prentice Hall.

Moustakas, C.E. (1972). *Loneliness and love.* Englewood Cliffs, NJ: Prentice- Hall.

Moustakas, C. E. (1989). *Loneliness.* Upper Saddle River, NJ: Prentice Hall.

Muehlenhard, C. L., & Shippee, S. K. (2009). Men's and women's reports of pretending orgasm. *Journal of Sex Research, 46,* 1-16.

Mueller, P., Biswal, S., Halpern, E., Kaufman, J., & Lee, M. (2000). Interventional Radiologic procedures: Patient anxiety, perception of pain, understanding of procedure, and satisfaction with medication – a prospective study. *Radiology*, 215, 684-688.

Mueser, K.T., Bellack, A.S., Douglas, M.S, & Morrison, R.L. (1991). Prevalence and stability of social skill deficits in schizophrenia. Schizophrenia Research, 5, 167-176.

Murphy, P. M., & Kupshik, G. A. (1992). Loneliness, stress and well-being: A helper's guide. London: Routledge.

Murray, C.E. (2005). Prevention work: A professional responsibility for marriage and family counsellors. *The Family Journal: Counselling and Therapy for Couples and Families,* 13, (1), 27-34.

Murray, S. L., Holmes, J. G., & Collins, N. L. (2006). Optimizing assurance: The risk regulation system in relationships. *Psychological Bulletin, 132,* 641-666.

Murstein, B. I. (1988). A taxonomy of love. In R.J. Sternberg & M.L. Barnes (Eds.), *The psychology of love* (pp. 13-37). New Haven: Yale University Press.

Myers, S. M. (2006). Religious homogamy and marital quality: Historical and generational patterns, 1980-1997. *Journal of Marriage and Family, 68*, 292-304.

Neto, F., & Barros, J. (2000). Psychosocial concomitants of loneliness among students of Cape Verde and Portugal. *The Journal of Psychology, 134*, 503-514.

Newall, N.E., Chipperfield, J.G., Clifton, R.A., Perry, R.P., Swift, A.U. (2009). Causal beliefs, social participation, and loneliness among older adults: A longitudinal study. *Journal of Social and personal Relationships*, 26, 273–290.

Newman, B. S., & Muzzonigro, P. G. (1993). The effects of traditional family values on the coming out process of gay male adolescents. *Adolescence, 28*(109), 213–26.

Nexhipi, G. (1983). *Loneliness in childhood and adolescence.* A paper presented at the 36th annual convention of the Ontario Psychological Association, Toronto, Canada.

Nichols, W.C. (1988). Marital therapy: An integrative approach. New York: *The Guilford Press.*

Nichols, W.C. & Pace-Nichols, M.A. (2000). Family development and family therapy. In W.C. Nichols (Ed.) *Handbook of family development and intervention* (pp. 3-22) New York: John Wiley and Sons.

Nokes, K.M., & Kendrew, J. (1990). Loneliness in veterans with AIDS and its relationship to the development of infections. *Archive of Psychiatric Nursing, 4,* 272-277

Noller, P. & Feeney, J.A. (1998). Communication in early marriage: Responses to conflict, nonverbal accuracy, and conversational patterns. In T.N. Bradbury (Ed.) *The developmental course of marital dysfunction* (pp.11-43). Cambridge University Press.

Noller, P. & Ruzzene, M. (1991). Communication in marriage: The influence of affect and cognition. In G.J.O. Fletcher & F.D. Fincham (Eds.) *Cognitions in close relationships* (pp.203-233). Hillsdale, NJ: Erlbaum.

North, J.R., Holahan, C.J., Moos, R.H., & Cronkite, R.C. (2008). Family support, family income, and happiness: A 10-year perspective. *Journal of Family Psychology,* 22, 475-483.

Nurmi, J. E., & Salmela-Aro, K. (1997). Social strategies and loneliness: A prospective study. *Personality and Individual Differences, 23*, 205-215.

Olds, J., & Schwartz, R. S. (2009). *The lonely American: Drifting apart in the twenty-first century.* Boston, MA: Beacon Press.

O'Leary, K. D. & Cascardi, M. (1998). Physical aggression in marriage: A developmental analysis. In T. N. Bradbury (Ed.), *The Developmental Course of Marital Dysfunction* (pp. 433-374) Cambridge University Press.

Olson, D. H. (1986). Circumplex model VII: Validation studies and FACES III. *Family Process, 26*, 337-351.

Olson, D.H., & Fowers, B.J. (1993). Five types of marriage: An empirical typology based on ENRICH. *The Family Journal: Counseling and Therapy for Couples and Families,* 1, 3, 196-207.

Olson, H. & Olson, A.K. (1999). PREPARE/ENRICH program: version 2000. In R. Berger & M.T. Hannah (Eds.). *Preventive approaches in couple therapy.* (pp. 196-216). Philadelphia, PA: Brunner/Mazel.

Olson, D.H. & Olson, A.K. (2000). *Empowering Couples: Building on your strengths.* Minneapolis: MN: Life Innovations, Inc.

Olson, K.L., & Wong, E.H. (2001). Loneliness in marriage. *Family therapy, 28, 2,* 105-111.

Oltmanns, T., & Emery, E. (1998). Abnormal Psychology. 2nd ed. Upper: Prentic Hall.

Omarzo, J., Whalen, J., & Harvey, J.H. (2001). How well do you mind your relationship? A preliminary scale to test the minding theory. In J. Harvey & A. Wenzel (Eds.) *Close romantic relationships: Maintenance and enhancement* (pp. 345-357). Mahwah, New Jersey: Lawrence Erlbaum Publishers.

Ooms, T (1998). Toward more perfect unions: Putting marriage on the public agenda: A report from the Family Impact seminar. Washington, DC. Family Impact Seminar.

O'Reilly-Fleming, T. (1993). *Down and out in Canada: Homeless Canadians.* Toronto: Canadian Scholars Press.

Ornish, D. (1998) Love and survival: the scientific basis for the healing power of intimacy. New York: HarperCollins.

Ornish, D. (2007). *The spectrum.* NY: Balantine Books.

Ostrov, E. & Offer, D. (1978). Loneliness and the adolescent. In: S. Feinstein (Ed.) *Adolescent psychology.* Chicago: University of Chicago Press.

Ottati, V., Bodenhausen, G. V., & Newman, L. S. (2005).Social psychological models of mental illness stigma. In P.W. Corrigan, *On the stigma of mental illness: Practical strategies for research and social change.* Washington, DC: American Psychological Association.

Palkovitz, R. (1997). Reconstructing involvement: Expanding conceptualizations of men's caring in contemporary families. In: A. Hawkins & A. Dollahite (Eds.) *Generative fathering: Beyond deficit perspectives,* Vol.3 *Current Issues in the family* (pp. 200-216).

Palmer, S.E., Canzona, L. & Wai, L. (1984). Helping families respond effectively to chronic illness: Home dialysis as a case example. In R.H. Moos (Ed.), *Coping with physical illness 2: New perspectives* (Pp. 283-294). NY: Plenum Press.

Paloutzian, R. F., & Ellison, C. W. (1982). Loneliness, spiritual well-being, and the quality of life. In L. A. Peplau & D. Perlman (Eds.), *Loneliness: Current theory, research, and therapy* (pp. 224-237). New York: Wiley.

Pappano, L. (2001) *The connection gap: Why Americans feel so alone.* New Brunswick, N.J: Rutgers University Press.

Pargament, K.J. (2007). Spirituality integrated therapy: Understanding and addressing the sacred. New York, NY: Guilford Press.

Pargament, K.J., Murray-Swank, N., Magyar, G & Ano, G. (2005). Spiritual struggle: A phenomenon of interest to psychology and religion. In W.R. Miller & H. Delaney (Eds.), *Judeo-Christian perspectives in psychology: Human nature, motivation, and change* (pp. 245-268). Washington, DC: American Psychological Association.

Pargament, K.J. & Sweeney, P.J. (2011). Building spiritual fitness in the army: An innovative approach to a vital aspect of human development. *American Psychologist,* 66(1), 58-64.

Parker, J. G., Saxon, J. L., Asher, S. R., & Kovacs, D. M. (1999). Dimensions of children's friendship adjustment: Implications for understanding loneliness. In K. J. Rotenberg, & S. Hymel (Eds.), Loneliness in childhood and adolescence (pp. 201–221). Cambridge, England: Cambridge University Press.

Parkes, C.M. (1973). Separation anxiety: An aspect of the search for a lost object. In R.S. Weiss (Ed.) *Loneliness: the experience of social and emotional loneliness* (Pp.53-67). Cambridge Mass: The MIT Press.

Parkhurst, J. T., & Asher, S. R. (1992). Peer rejection in middle school: Subgroup differences in behavior, loneliness, and interpersonal concerns. *Developmental Psychology, 28,* 231-241.

Parkhurst, J. T.,&Hopmeyer, A. (1999). Developmental change in the sources of loneliness in childhood and adolescence: Constructing a theoretical model. In K. J. Rotenberg & S.Hymel (Eds.), *Loneliness in childhood and adolescence* (pp. 56–79). Cambridge, UK:Cambridge University Press.

Parkinson, J. (2006).Experiences of selves in isolation: A psychodynamic approach to the care of patients being treated in a specialized medical hospital unit. *Psychodynamic Practice, 12*(2), 149 -163.

Parse, R. R. (2007). The human becoming school of thought in2050. *Nursing Science Quarterly*, 20, 308-311.

Parsons, J. T., Halkitis, P. N., Wolitski, R. J., Gomez, C. A., & the Seropositive Urban Men's Study Team. (2003). Correlates of sexual risk behavior among HIV-positive men who have sex with men. *AIDS Education and Prevention, 15*(5), 383–400

Pasch, L.A., Bradbury, & Bradbury, T.N.(1998). Social support, conflict and the development of marital dysfunction. *Journal of Consulting and Clinical Psychology,* 66, 219-230.

Paterson, J., Blashko, C. & Janzen, H. (1991). *When You Stand Alone. Canadian Journal of Counselling and Psychotherapy,* 29 (1), Patrick, S., Sells, J.M., Giordano, F.G., & Tollerud, T.N. (2007). Intimacy differentiation and personality variables as predictors of marital satisfaction. *The Family Journal: Counselling and Therapy for Couples and Families,* 15(4), 359-367.

Patrick, H., Knee, C. R., Canevello, A., & Lonsbary, C. (2007). The role of need fulfillment in relationship functioning and well-being: A self-determination theory perspective. *Journal of Personality and Social Psychology*, 92, 434–457.

Patterson, G.R. & Hope, H. (1972). Coercion, a game for two: Intervention techniques for marital conflict. In R. Ulrich & P. Mouutjoy (Eds.) *The experimental analysis of social behaviours* (pp. 424-440). New York: Appleton Century Crofts.

Paul, C., Ayis, S., & Ebrahim, S. (2006). Psychological distress, loneliness and disability in old age. *Psychology, Health & Medicine, 11*(2), 221-232.

Paul, F. & Rattray, J.(2008). Short- and long-term impact of critical illness relatives: literature review. *Journal of Advanced Nursing, 62*(3), 276–292.

Pearlin, L. I., & Skaff, M. M. (1995). Stressors and adaptation in late life. In M. Gatz (Ed.), *Emerging issues in mental health and aging.* (pp. 97-123). Washington, DC: American Psychological Association.

Pietromonaco, P.R., Greenwood, D., & Feldman-Barrett, L. (2004). Conflict in adult close relationships: An attachment perspective. In W.S. Rholes & J.A. Simpson (Eds.) *Adult attachment: theory, research, and clinical implications* (pp.267-299). New York: The Guilford Press.

Peplau, L.A. (2002). Roles and Gender. In H.H. Kelley, E. Berscheid, A. Christensen, J.H. Harvey, T.L. Huston, G. Levinger, E. McClintock, L.A. Peplau & D.R. Peterson (Eds.), *Close relationships* (pp. 20-260). NY: Percheron Press.

Peplau, L.A. & Goldston, S.E. (1984). *Preventing the harmful consequences of severe and persistent loneliness.* Rockville, MD: Dept. of Health and Human Services.

Peplau, L. A., Miceli, M., & Morasch, B. (1982). Loneliness and self evaluation. In L. A. Peplau & Perlman, D. (Eds.) *Loneliness: A sourcebook of current theory, research and therapy.* (pp. 135-151). New York: Wiley & Sons.

Peplau, L. A. & Perlman, D. (1982). Perspectives on loneliness. In L. A. Peplau & D. Perlman (Eds.), *Loneliness: A sourcebook of current theory, research and therapy* (pp. 1-20). New York: Wiley & Sons.

Perlman, D. & Duck, S. (1987). Intimate relationships: Development, dynamics and deterioration. Beverly Hills CA: Sage.

Perlman, D., & Joshi, P. (1987). The revelation of loneliness. In M. Hojat & R. Crandall (Eds.), *Loneliness: Theory, research and applications* (Pp.63-76). London: Sage.

Perlman, D., & Peplau, L.A. (1998). Loneliness. In H. Friedman (Ed.). encyclopedia of mental health, vol. 2 (pp. 571-581). San Diego, CA: Academic Press.

Perlman, D., & Landolt, M. A. (1999). Examination of loneliness in children–adolescents and in adults: Two solitudes or a unified enterprise? In K. J.

Pernice-Duca, F. (2010). Family network support and mental health recovery. *Journal of marital and family therapy, 36* (1), 13-27.

Penn, D.I., Guyan, K., Daily, T., Spaulding, W.D., Carbin, C.P., & Sullivan, M. (1994). Dispelling the stigma of Schizophrenia: What sort of information is best? *Schizophrenia Bulletin,* 20, 567-577.

Penn, D.L., Mueser, K.T., & Doonan, R. (1997). Physical attractiveness in schizophrenia: The mediating role of social skill. Behavior Modification, 21, 78-85.

Pescosolido B. (2001) The role of social networks in the lives of persons with disabilities. In: Handbook of Disability Studies (eds G. Albrecht, K. Seelman & M. Bury) pp. 468–489. Sage Publications, Thousand Oaks, CA.

Petersen, M. (2007). Menopause and sexuality. In A. Fuglsang Owens & M. S. Tepper (Eds.), *Sexual Health: Physical Foundations (Vol. 2)* (pp. 197-222). New York: Praeger.

Peterson, L.T. (2010). Perceived partners generosity as a predictor of marital quality during the transition to parenthood for black and white couples. *A Doctoral Dissertation submitted to Case Western Reserve University* (Mandel School of Applied Social Science).

Phillips, M.J.(1990). Damaged goods: oral narratives of the experience of disability in American culture. Social Science & Medicine, (30), 849-57.

Phillips, D. (1996). Medical professional dominance and client dissatisfaction: a study of doctor–patient interaction and reported dissatisfaction with medical care among female patients at four hospitals in Trinidad and Tobago. *Social Science & Medicine, 42,* 1419-1425.

Phillips, M.J. (1990). Damaged goods: Oral narratives of disability on American culture. *Social Science & Medicine*, 30, 849-957.

Pick, J.R. & Sillar, A.L. (1985). Reciprocity of marital communication. *Journal of Social and Personal Relationships, 2,* 303-324.

Pierce, A.P. (2000). The coital alignment technique (CAT): An overview of studies. *Journal of Sex and Marriage, 26,* 257-268.

Pilisuk, M. & Hillier Parks, S. (1986). *The healing web: Social networks and human survival.* Hanover, NH: University Press of New England.

Pilkonis, P. A. (1977). The behavioral consequences of anxiety. *Journal of Personality, 45,* 596-611.

Pinel, E.C., Long, A.E., Landau, M.J., Alexander, K., & Pyszczynski, T. (2006). Seeing I to I: A pathway to interpersonal connectedness. *Journal of personality and social psychology,* 90, (2), 243-257.

Pines, A. M., & Aronson, E. (1988). *Career burnout.* New York: The Free Press.

Pinquart, M. (2003). Loneliness in married, widowed, divorced, and never-married older adults. *Journal of Social and Personal Relationships, 20*(1), 31-53.

Pinquart, M., & Sörensen, S. (2001). Influences on loneliness in older adults: A meta-analysis. *Basic and Applied Social Psychology, 23,* 245-266.

Pinquart, m., & Sorensen, S. (2003). Risk factors for loneliness in adulthood and old age: A eta-analysis. In S.P. Shohov (Ed.). *Advances in psychology research,* vol. 19. (pp. 111-143). Hauppauge, N.Y.: Nova Science.

Pinsof, W. M. (2002). The death of 'til death us do part': The transformation of pair-bonding in the 20th Century. *Family Process, 41,* 135-157.

Pistol, M.C., Clark, E.M., & Tubbs, A.L. (1995). Love relationships: Attachment style and the investment model. *Journal of Mental Health Counselling,* 17, 199-209.

Polimeni, A. & Moore, S. (2002). Insight into women's experiences of hospital stays: perceived control, powerlessness and satisfaction. *Behaviour Change, 19*(1), 52-64.

Pond, R.S., Brey, J., & DeWall, C.N. (2011). Denying the need to belong: How social exclusion impairs human functioning and how people can protect against it. In: Bevinn, S.J. (Ed.). *Psychology of loneliness* (Pp. 107-122). NY: Nova Science Pub.

Potthoff, H. H. (1976). *Loneliness: Understanding and dealing with it.* Nashville, Tennessee: Dimension Books.

Powers, W.C. & Hutchinson, K. (1979). The measurement of communication apprehension in the marriage relationship. *Journal of Marriage and Family,* 41(1), 89-95.

Prager, K. J., & Roberts, L. J. (2004). *Deep intimate connection: Self and intimacy in couple relationships.* Mahwah, NJ, US: Lawrence Erlbaum Associates Publishers, Mahwah, NJ.

Prager, K.J. (1995). The psychology of intimacy. New York: *The Guildford Press.*

Prager, K.J. & Roberts, L.J. (2004). Deep intimate connection: self and intimacy in couple relationships. In D.J. Mashek & A. Aron (Eds.) *Handbook of closeness and intimacy* (pp. 43-60). Mahwah, New Jersey: Lawrence Erlbaum Associates, Publishers.

Pressman, S. D., Cohen, S., Miller, G. E., Barkin, A., Rabin, B. S., & Treanor, J. J. (2005). Loneliness, social network size, and immune response to influenza vaccination in college freshmen. *Health Psychology, 24*(3), 297-306.

Pressman, M. R., Meyer, T. J., Peterson, D. D., Greenspon, L. W., & Figueroa, W. G. (1997). *Effects of hospitalization, surgery, and anesthesia on sleep and biological rhythms.* Washington, DC: American Psychological Association.

Price, M. (2011). Alone in a crowd. *Monitor on Psychology,* 42(6), 26-28.

Price, M.A, Tennant, C.C., Butow, P.N., Smith, R.C., Kennedy, S.J., Kossoff, M.B., & Dunn, S.M. (2001). The role of psychosocial factors in the development of breast carcinoma. Part II: Life event stressor, social support, defence style, and emotional control and their interactions. *Cancer, 91*(4), 686-697.

Prince, M., Harwood, R., Blizard, R., Thomas, A., & Mann, A. (1997). Impairment, disability and handicap as risk factors for depression in old age. The Gospel Oak Project V. Psychological Medicine, 27, 311 – 321.

Purnine, D.M., & Carey, M.P. (1997). Interpersonal communication and sexual adjustment: The role of understanding and agreement. *Journal of Consulting and Clinical Psychology,* 65, 1017-1025.

Putnam, R. D. (2000). Bowling Alone: The collapse and revival of American community. New York: Simon & Schuster.

Putney, N. M. & Bengtson, V. L. (2001). Families, intergenerational relationships, and kinkeeping in midlife. In M. E. Lachman (Ed.), *Handbook of midlife development* (pp. 528- 570). Hoboken, NJ: John Wiley & Sons.

Qualter, P., Brown, S., Munn, P., & Rotenberg, K. (2010). Childhood loneliness as a predictor of adolescent depressive symptoms: An 8-year longitudinal study. *European Child & Adolescent Psychiatry, 19*(6)m 493-501.

Qualter, P. & Munn, P. (2002). The separateness of social and emotional loneliness in children. *Journal of Child Psychology and Psychiatry*, 43, 233-244.

Rabasca, L. (1999). Happiness may increase with age. *American Psychological Association Monitor,* p. 11.

Radnitz, C. L. & Tirch, D.D. (1997). Physical disability. In R. L. Leahy (Ed.). *Practicing cognitive therapy: A guide to intervention.* (Pp. 373-389). Northvale, N.J.: Jason Aronson.

Raikes, H. A., & Thompson, R. A. (2008). Attachment security and parenting quality predict children's problem-solving, attributions, and loneliness with peers. Attachment & Human Development, 10(3), 1-26.Rando, T. (1984). *Grief, dying and death.* Champaign, Ill: Research Press.

Rank, O. (1929). *The trauma of birth.* Oxford, England: Harcourt, Brace, Oxford.

Rankin Williams, L. & Hickle, K.E. (2010). "I know what love means": Qualitative descriptions from Mexican American and white adolescents. *Journal of Human Behavior in the Social Environment,* 20, 581-600.

Rapley M. & Beyer S. (1996) Daily activity, community participation and quality of life in an ordinary housing network. Journal of Applied Research in Intellectual Disabilities 9, 31–39.

Raps, C. S., Peterson, C., Jonas, M., & Seligman, M. E. P. (1982). Patient behavior in hospitals: Helplessness, reactance, or both? *Journal of Personality and Social Psychology, 42,* 1036–1041.

Rathus, S.S. & Etaugh, C. (1995). The world of children. New York: Harcourt Brace College Pub.

Rattray, M., Johnston, J. A., & Wildsmith, W. (2005). Predictors of emotional outcomes of intensive care. *Anesthesia, 60,* 1085-1092.

Reher, D. S. (1998). Family ties in Western Europe: Persistent contrasts. *Population and Development Review, 24,* 203–234.

Reinhardt, J. P. & Fisher, C. B. (1988). Kinship versus friendship: Social adaptation in married and widowed elderly women. *Women and Health, 14,* 191-211.

Reis, H.T. (2007). Steps toward the ripening of relationship science. *Personal Relationships,* 14, 1-23.

Reis, H. T., Clark, M. S., & Holmes, J. G. (2004). Perceived partner responsiveness as an organizing construct in the study of intimacy and closeness. In D. J. Mashek & A. Aron (Eds.), *Handbook of closeness and intimacy* (pp. 201-225). Mahwah, NJ: Erlbaum.

Reis, H.T., Shaver, P.R. (1988). Intimacy as an interpersonal process. In S. Duck & D.F. Hay (Eds.) *Handbook of personal relationships: Theory, research, and interventions* (pp. 367-389). New York: Wiley.

Reis, H.T. & Gable, S.L. (2003). Toward a positive psychology of relationships. In C.L. Keys & J. Haidt (Eds.), *Flourishing: The positive person and the good life* (pp. 129-159). Washington, D.C.: American Psychological Association.

Reis, H.T. & Patrick, B.C. (1996). Attachment and intimacy: Component processes. In A. Kruglanski & E.T. Higgins (Eds.) *Social Psychology: Handbook of basic principles* (pp. 523-563). New York: Guilford Press.

Reis, H.T., Smith, S.M., Tsai, F.F., Carmichael, C.L., Caprarielle, P.A., Rodrigues, A., & Maniaci, M.R. (2010). Are you happy for me? How sharing positive events with others provide personal and interpersonal benefits. *Journal of Personality and Social Psychology*, 99, (2), 311-329.

Reissman, C. Aron, A., & Bergen, M.R. (1993). Shared activities and marital satisfaction: Causal direction and self-expression verses boredom. *Journal of Social and Personal Relationships*, 10, 243-254.

Rempel, J.K., Holmes, J.G., & Zanna, M.P. (1985). Trust in close relationships. *Journal of personality and social psychology*, 49, (1), 95-112.

Renick, M.j., Blumberg, S.L., & Markman, H.J. (1992). The Prevention and relationship enhancement program (PREP). An empirically based preventive intervention program for couples. *Family Relations*, 41, 141-147.

Renshaw, P.D. & Brown, P.J. (2000). Loneliness in middle childhood. *Journal of Social Psychology*, 132, 545-548.

Resnick, S. G., Rosenheck, R. A., & Lehman, A. F. (2004). An exploratory analysis of correlates of recovery. *Psychiatric Services*, 55(5), 540-547.

Revenson, T. A., Wollman, A., & Felton, B. J. (1983) Social supports as stress buffers for adult cancer patients. *Psychosomatic Medicine*, 45, 321-331.

Rholes, W.S., Simpson, J.A., Campbell, L., & Grinch, J. (2001). Adult attachment and the transition to parenthood. *Journal of Personality and Social Psychology*, 8, (3), 421-435.

Ridley, C.A., Jorgensen, S.R., Morgan, A.G., & Avery, A.W. (1982). Relationship enhancement with premarital couples: An assessment of effects on marital quality. *The American Journal of Family Therapy*, 10, 41-48.

Ridley, C., Wilhelm, M.S., & Surra, C.A. (2001). Married couples' conflict responses and marital quality. *Journal of Social and Personal Relationships*, 18, 517-534.

Riela, S., Rodriguez, G., Aron, A., Xu, X., & Acevedo, B. P. (2010). Experiences of falling in love: Investigating cultural, ethnicity, gender, and speed. *Journal of Social and Personal Relationships*, 27, 473-493.

Rime, B. (2007) Interpersonal emotion regulation. In J.J. Gross (Ed.) *Handbook of emotion regulation.* (pp. 466-485). New York: Guilford Press.

Rishel, C.W. (2007). Evidence-based prevention practice in mental health: What is it and how do we get there? *Journal of Orthopsychiatry*, 77, 153-164.

Rishter, J. B. & Phelan, J. C. (2004). Internalized stigma predicts erosion of morale among psychiatric outpatients. *Psychiatry Research*, 129, 257-265.

Roberts, P. (2005). A brief comparison of the marriage-related provisions in welfare reauthorization bills (No. 05-29). Washington, D.C.: Center for Law & Social Policy.

Roberts, L.J. & Greenberg, D.R. (2002). Observational "windows" to intimacy process in marriage. In P. Noller & J.A. Feeney (Eds.) *Understanding marriage: Developments in the study of couple interaction* (pp. 118-149). Cambridge University Press.

Roberts, L.J. & Krokoff, L.J. (1990). A time series analysis of withdraw, hostility and displeasure. *Journal of Marriage and the Family, 52,* 229-236.

Robinson, F. M., West, D. & Woodworth, D. (1995). Coping + plus: Dimensions of disability. Westport, Connecticut: Praeger.

Rodrigues, A.E., Hall, J.H., & Fincham, F.D. (2006). What predicts divorce and relationship dissolution. In M.A. Fine & J.H. Harvey (Eds.) *Handbook of divorce and relationship dissolution.* New York: Routledge (pp. 85-112).

Rogers, C. R. (1959). A theory of therapy, personality, and interpersonal relationships, as developed in the client-centered framework. In S. Koch (Ed.), *Psychology: A study of a science* (Vol. 3, pp. 184-256). New York: McGraw-Hill.

Rogers, C. R. (1961). The loneliness of contemporary man as seen in the "Case of Ellen West." *Annals of Psychotherapy*, 1, 22-27.

Rogers, C.R. (1983). *Freedom to Learn.* Ohio: Charles E. Merrill.

Rokach, A. (1986). Psychotherapy: Close encounters of the intimate kind. *Journal of Contemporary Psychotherapy, 16(2),* 161-182.

Rokach, A. (1988a). The experience of loneliness: A tri-level model. *Journal of Psychology, 122,* 531-544.

Rokach, A. (1988b). Theoretical approaches to loneliness: from a univariate to a multidimensional experience. *Review of Existential Psychology and Psychiatry, 19(2&3),* 225-254.

Rokach, A. (1989). Antecedents of loneliness: A factorial analysis. *Journal of Psychology,* 123(4), 369-384.

Rokach, A. (1990). Surviving and coping with loneliness. *The Journal of Psychology, 124(1),* 39-54.

Rokach, A. (1998). Loneliness in singlehood and marriage. *Psychology: A Journal of Human Behaviour, 35(2),* 2-17.

Rokach, A. (2000). Loneliness and the life cycle. *Psychological Reports, 86,* 629-642.

Rokach, A. (2003). Loneliness among loved ones: Alienation in the family. *Psychology and Education: An interdisciplinary Journal,* 40, (3/4), 1-18.

Rokach, A. (2007). Loneliness and intimate partner violence: Antecedents of alienation of abused women. *Social Work in Health Care*, 45(1), 19-31.

Rokach, A. & Brock, H. (1995) The effects of gender, marital status, and the chronicity and immediacy of loneliness. *Journal of Social Behaviour and Personality, 10(4),* 833-848.

Rokach, A. & Brock, H. (1996). The causes of loneliness. *Psychology: Journal of Human Behavior, 33,* 1-11.

Rokach, A. & Brock, H. (1997a). Loneliness and the effects of life changes. *Journal of Psychology,* 131(3), 284-298.

Rokach, A. & Brock, H. (1997b). Loneliness: A Multidimensional Experience. *Psychology: A Journal of Human Behaviour, 34*(1), 1-9.

Rokach, A., Matalon, R., Safarov, A. & Bercovitch, M. (2007). The dying, those who care for them, and how they cope with loneliness. *American Journal of Hospice & Palliative Medicine, 24*(5), 399-407.

Rokach, A. & Neto, F. (2000) Causes of loneliness in adolescence: a cross-cultural study. *International Journal of Adolescence and Youth. 8,* 65-80.

Rokach, A. & Rokach, B. (2005*). The dying and the living: Caring for the patient and for the professional who treats him/her.* A keynote address delivered at the eighth annual Conference of Palliative Medicine, Tzfat, Israel, May 19.

Rokach, A. & Sharma, M. (1996). The loneliness experience in a cultural context. *Journal of Social Behaviour and Personality, 11*(4), 827-839.

Rolheiser, R. (1979). The loneliness factor: Its religious and spiritual meaning. Denville, NJ: Dimension Books.

Rollins, J. A. (2004). Evidence-based hospital design improves health care outcomes for patients, families and staff. *Pediatric Nursing, 30*(4), 338-339.

Rook, K. S. (1984a). Research on social support, loneliness, and social isolation: Toward an integration. In P. Shaver (Ed.), *Review of Personality and Social Psychology: Emotions, Relationships, and Health* (Vol. 5, pp. 239-264). Beverly Hills, CA: Sage.

Rook, K. S. (1984b). The negative side of social interaction: Impact on psychological well-being. *Journal of Personality and Social Psychology, 46,* 1097-1108.

Rook, K. S. (1987). Reciprocity and social exchange and social satisfaction among older women. *Journal of Personality and Social Psychology, 52 (1),* 145-154.

Rook, K.S. (1988). Toward a more differentiated view of loneliness. In S. Duck (Ed.) *Handbook of personal relationships: Theory, research and intervention* (pp. 571-589). Toronto: John Wiley & Sons.

Rook, K.S. (2001). Emotional health and Positive versus negative social exchange: a daily diary analysis. Applied Developmental Science, 5, 2, 86-97.

Rook KS. Investigating the positive and negative sides of personal relationships: Through a glass darkly? In: Spitzberg BH, Cupach WR, editors. The dark side of close relationships. Erlbaum; Mahwah, NJ: 1998. pp. 369–393.

Rook, K. S., & Peplau, L. A. (1982). Perspectives on helping the lonely. In L. A. Peplau & D. Perlman (Eds.), *Loneliness: A sourcebook of current theory, research and therapy* (pp. 351−378). New York: Wiley.

Rosedale, M. (2007). Loneliness: An exploration of meaning. *Journal of American Psychiatric Nurses Association, 13*(4), 201-209.

Rosenkoetter, M. M., Garris, J. M., & Engdahl, R. A. (2001). Postretirement use of time: Implications for preretirement planning and postretirement management *Activities, Adaptation & Aging,* 25, 1–18.

Rosenthal, R. (2000) Imaging homelessness and homeless people: Visions and strategies within the movement(s)'. *Journal of Social Distress and the Homeless,* 9(2), 111–126.

Rotenberg, & S. Hymel (Eds.), Loneliness in childhood and adolescence (pp. 325−347). Cambridge, England: Cambridge University Press.

Routasalo, P., & Pitkala, K.H. (2003). Loneliness among older people. Reviews in Clinical Gerontology, 13, 303–311.

Rowe, M. A. (1996). The impact of internal and external resources on functional outcome in chronic illness. *Research and Nursing in Health, 19(6),* 485-97.

Rubenstein, C.M., & Shaver, P. (1982). The experience of loneliness. In L.A. Peplau & D. Perlman (Eds.), *Loneliness: A sourcebook of current theory, research and therapy* (p. 206-223). NY: Wiley.

Rubin, Z. (1970). Measurement of romantic love. *Journal of Personality and Social Psychology,* 16, 265-273.

Rubin, Z. (1973). Liking and loving. NY: *Holt, Reinhart & Winston.*

Rubin, K. H., & Mills, R. S. (1988). The many faces of social isolation in childhood. Journal of Consulting and Clinical Psychology, 56, 916–924.

Rusbult, C.E. (1983). A longitudinal test of the investment model: The development (and deterioration) of satisfaction and commitment in heterosexual involvement. *Journal of Personality and Social Psychology,* 45, 101-117.

Rusbult, C.E. (1980). Commitment and satisfaction in romantic associations: A test of the investment model. *Journal of Experimental Social Psychology.* 16, 172-186.

Rusbult, C. E. (1991). Commentary on Johnson's "Commitment to personal relationships": What's interesting, and what's new? In W. H. Jones & D. W. Perlman (Eds.), *Advances in personal relationships* (Vol. 3, pp. 151-169). London: Kingsley.

Rusbult, C.E., Zembrodt, I.M., & Gunn, L.K. (1982). Exit, voice, loyalty, and neglect: Responses to dissatisfaction in romantic involvements. *Journal of Personality and Social Psychology, 43, 1230-1242.*

Rusbult, C.E. (1993). Understanding Reponses to dissatisfaction in close relationship: The exit-voice-loyalty-neglect model. In S. Worchel & J.A. Simpson (Eds.) *Conflict between people and groups* (pp. 30-59). Chicago: Nelson-Hall.

Rusbult, C.E., Bissonnette, V.L., Arriage, X.B., & Cox, C.L. (1998). Accommodation process during the early years of marriage. In T.N. Bradbury (Ed.) *The developmental course of marital dysfunction.* Cambridge University Press (pp. 74-113).

Rusbult, C.E. & Buunk, B.P. (1993). Committed process in close relationships: An interdependence analysis. *Journal of Social and Personal Relationships,* 10, 175-204.

Rusbult, C.E., Kumashiro, M., Finkel, E.J., & Wildschut, T. (2002). The war of the roses: an interdependence analysis of betrayal and forgiveness. In P. Noller & J.A. Feeney (Eds.) *Understanding marriage: Developments in the study of couple interaction* (pp. 251-281). Cambridge, UK: Cambridge University Press.

Rusbult, C.E., Kumashiro, M., Kuback, K.E., & Finkel, E. (2009). The part of me that you bring out? Ideal similarity and the Michelangelo Phenomenon. *Journal of Personality and Social Psychology,* 96, (1), 61-82.

Rusbult, C.E., Kumashiro, M., Stoker, S.L., Kirchner, J.L., Finkel, E.J., & Coolsen, M.K. (2005). Self process in interdependence relationships: Partner affirmation a Michelangelo Phenomenon. *Interaction Studies,* 6, (3), 375-391.

Rusbult, C.E., Olsen, N., Davis, J.L., Hannon, P.E. (2001). Commitment and relationship maintenance mechanisms. In J.H. & A. Wenzel (Eds.). *Close romantic relationships: Maintenance and enhancement* (pp. 87-113). Mahwah, New Jersey: Lawrence Erlbaum.

Rusbult, C.E., Wieselquist, J., Foster, C.A., & Witcher, B.S. (1999). Commitment and trust in close relationships. In J.M. Adams & Jones, W.H. (Eds.) *Handbook of interpersonal commitment and relationship stability* (pp. 427-450). New York: Kluwer Academic-Plenum.

Russek, L. & Schawrtz, G. (1997). Feelings of parental caring predict health status in midlife: A 35 year follow up of the Harvard mastery of stress study. *Journal of Behavioural Medicine,* 1, 1-13.

Russell, D. W. (1996) UCLA Loneliness Scale (Version 3): reliability, validity, and factor structure. *Journal* of *Personality Assessment,* 66, 20-40.

Russell, D., Cutrona, C. E., Rose, J., & Yurko, K. (1984) Social and emotional loneliness: An examination of Weiss's typology of loneliness. *Journal of Personality and Social Psychology, 46,* 1313-1321.

Russell, D., Peplau, L. A., & Cutrona, C. E. (1980). The Revised UCLA Loneliness Scale: Concurrent and discriminant validity evidence. *Journal of Personality and Social Psychology, 39,* 472-480.

Rychlak, J.F. (1981). Introduction to personality and psychotherapy: A theory-construction approach. Boston: Houghton-Mifflin.

Sacher, J.A. & Fine, M.A. (1996). Predicting relationship status and satisfaction after six months among dating couples. *Journal of Marriage and the Family, 58,* 21-32.

Sadler, W. A. & Johnson, T. B. (1980). From loneliness to anomia. In J. Hartog, R. J. Audy &Y. A. Cohen (Eds.), *The anatomy of loneliness.* New York: International Universities Press.

Safilios-Rothschild, C. (1977). *Love, sex, and sex roles.* NJ: Prentice Hall, Spectrum Books.

Sanderson, C.A. (2004). The link between the pursuit of intimacy goals and satisfaction in close relationships: An examination of the underlying process. In D.J. Mashek & A, Aron (Eds.). *Handbook of closeness and intimacy.* Mahwa, New Jersey: Laurence Erlbaum Associates, Publishers (pp. 247-266).

Sanderson, C.A. & Cantor, N. (1995). Social dating goals in the late adolescence: Implications for safer sexual activity. *Journal of Personality and Social Psychology.*

Sanders, MR, Nicholson, JM & Floyd, F 1997, *'Couples' relationships and children',* in WK Halford & HJ Markman(eds), Clinical handbook of couple relationships and couples intervention, John Wiley, New York

Sanderson, C.A. & Evans, S.M. (2001). Seeing one's partner through intimacy-colored glasses: An examination of the processes underlying the intimacy goals-relationship satisfaction link. *Personality and Social Psychology Bulletin, 27,* 4, 463-473.

Sartre, J. P. (1957). *Existentialism and human emotions.* New York: Philosophical Library.

Sarason, S.B. (1974). The psychological sense of community: Prospects for a community psychology. San Francisco: Jossey-Bass.

Savikko, N., Routasalo, P.,Tilvis, R.S., Strandberg, T.E, & Pitkälä, K.H. (2005). Predictors and subjective causes of loneliness in an aged population. *Archives of Gerontology and Geriatrics 41,* 223-233.

Sayers, S.L., Kohn, C.S., & Heavey, C. (1998). Prevention of marital dysfunction: Behavioural approaches and beyond. *Clinical Psychology Review, 18,* 713-744.

Schachner, D. A., Shaver, P. R. & Mikulincer, M. (2003). Adult attachment theory, psychodynamics, and couple relationships: An overview. In S. M. Johnson & V. E. Whiffen (Eds.) *Attachment processes in couple and family therapy* (Pp. 18-42).NY: The Guilford Press.

Schachter, S. (1959). The psychology of affiliation: Experimental studies of the sources of gregariousness. Palo Alto, CA, US: Stanford Univer. Press, Palo Alto, CA.

Scharfe, E., & Bartholomew, K. (1995). Accommodation and attachment representation in couples. *Journal of Social and Personal Relationships, 12,* 389-401.

Schilling, D. L., Washington, K., Billingsley, F., & Deitz, J. (2003). Classroom seating for children with attention deficit hyperactivity: Balls versus chairs. American Journal of Occupational Therapy, 57, 534–541

Schmidt Bunkers, S. (2008). The gifts of silence and solitude. *Nursing Science Quarterly, 21* (1), 22-25.

Schnittker, J. (2007). Look (closely) at all the lonely people: Age and the social psychology of social support. *Journal of Aging and Health*, 19, 659–682.

Schoen, R., & Weinick, R.M. (1993). The slowing metabolism of marriage. *Demography, 30*, 737-746.

Schultz, T. (1976). Bittersweet: Surviving and growing from loneliness. NY: T. Crowell.

Schuyf, J. (1996). Oud roze: De positie van lesbische en homoseksuele ouderen in Nederland [*Old rose: The position of aging lesbians and gays in the Netherlands*]. Utrecht: Homostudies/ISOR, Universiteit Utrecht.

Schwartz, M. D. (1977) An information and discussion program for women after mastectomy. *Archives of Surgery, 12*, 276-281.

Seeman, T. E., & McEwen, B. S. (1996). Impact of social environment characteristics on neuroendocrine regulation. *Psychosomatic Medicine, 58*(5), 459-471.

Scragg, P., Jones, A. & Fauvel, N. (2001). Psychological problems following ICU treatment. *Anaesthesia, 56* (1), 9–14.

Seeman, T. (2000). Health promoting effects of friends and family on health outcomes in older adults. *American Journal of Health Promotion, 14*(6), 362-370.

Seeman, T. E., Dubin, L. F., & Seeman, M. (2003). Religiosity/Spirituality and health: A critical review of the evidence for biological pathways. *American Psychologist, 58*(1), 53-63.

Seeman, M., & Seeman, T. E. (1983). Health behavior and personal autonomy: a longitudinal study of the sense of control in illness. *Journal of Health and Social* Behavior, 24 (2), 144-160.

Segrin, C. (1998). Disrupted interpersonal relationships and mental health problems. In B. H. Spitzberg & W. R. Cupach (Eds.), *The dark side of close relationships* (pp. 327-365). Mahwah, NJ: Erlbaum.

Segrin, C. & Passalacqu, S.A. (2010). Functions of loneliness & social support, health behaviours and stress, in association with poor health. *Health Communication, 25*, 312-122.

Seligman, M.E. (1988, October). Boomer blues. *Psychology Today,* 51-55.

Sellick, S. M., & Edwardson, A. D. (2007). Screening new cancer patients for psychological distress using the hospital anxiety and depression scale. *Psycho-Oncology, 16*(6), 534-542.

Semple, C. J., & McCance, T. (2010). Parents' experience of cancer who have young children. *Cancer Nursing, 33*(2), 110-118.

Semple, S. J., Patterson, T. L., & Grant, I. (2000). Psychosocial predictors of unprotected anal intercourse in a sample of HIV positive gay men who volunteer for a sexual risk reduction intervention. *AIDS Education and Prevention, 12*, 416–430.

Shackelford, T.K., & Buss, D.M. (1997). Marital satisfaction in evolutionary psychological perspective. In R.J. Sternberg & M. Hojjat. *Satisfaction in close relationships.* New York: Te Guilford Press (pp. 7-25).

Shafer, C. S., & Hammitt, W. E. (1995). Congruency among experience dimensions, condition indicators, and coping behaviors in wilderness. *Leisure Sciences, 17*, 263-279.

Shapiro, A.F. & Gottman, J.M. (2005). Effects on marriage of psycho-communicative-education intervention with couples undergoing the transition to parenthood, evaluation a 1-year post intervention. *The Journal of Family Communication,* 5,1,1-24.

Shapiro, A.F., Gottman, J.M., & Sybil, C. (2000). The baby and the marriage: Identifying factors that buffer against decline in marital satisfaction after the first baby arrive. *Journal of Family Psychology,* 14, 1, 59-70.

Shaver, P.R. & Brennan, K.A. (1992). Attachment styles and the "big five" personality traits: Their connections with each other and with romantic relationship outcomes. *Personality and Social Psychology Bulletin,* 18, 536-545.

Shaver, P. & Buhrmeister, D. (1983). Loneliness, sex role orientation and group life: Social needs perspective. IN: P.B. Baulus (Ed.), *Basic group processes* (Pp. 259-288). New York: Springer-Verlag.

Shaver, P., Furman, W., & Buhrmester, D. (1985). Transition to college: Network changes, social skills, and loneliness. In S. Duck & D. Perlman (Eds.), Understanding personal relationships: An interdisciplinary approach (pp. 193-219). London: Sage.

Shaver, P., & Rubenstein, C. (1980). Childhood attachment experience and adult loneliness. In L. Wheeler (Ed.), *Review of personality and social psychology* (Vol. 1, pp. 42-73)., Beverly Hills, CA: Sage Publications.

Shaver, P. & Hazan C. (1985). Incompatibility, loneliness, and "limerence". In W. Ickes (Ed.). Compatibility and incompatibility in relationships (pp. 163-184). NY: Springer-Verlag

Shaver, P. & Hazan, C. (1987). Being lonely, falling in love: Perspectives from attachment theory. *Journal of Social Behavior and Personality*, 2(2), 105-124.

Shaver, P.R. & Mikulincer, M. (2002). Attachment related psychodynamics. Attachment and Human Development, 4, 133-161.

Shaver, P.R. & Mikulincer, M. (2005). Attachment theory and research: Resurrection of the psychodynamic approach to personality. *Journal of Research in Personality,* 39, 22-45.

Shaver, P.R., Hazan, C., & Bradshaw, D. (1988). Love as attachment: The integration of three Behavioral systems. In R.J. Sternberg & M. Barnes (Eds.), *The psychology of lo*ve (pp. 68-99). New Haven, CT: Yale University Press.

Shaver, P.R., Murdaya, U., & Farley, R.C. (2001). Stru8cture of the Indonesian emotion lexicon. *Asian Journal of Social Psychology,* 4, 201-224.

Shaver, P. & Rubenstein, C. (1980). Childhood attachment experience and adult loneliness. In L. Wheeler (Ed.), Review of personality and social psychology (Vol. 1, pp. 42-73), Beverly Hills, CA: Sage.

Shillito, D. J., Kellas, S. L., & Kirkpatrick, L. A. (1999) Loneliness, social support, and perceived relationships with God. *Journal of Social and Personal Relationships*, 16, 513-522.

Silberfarb, P. M. & Greer, S. (1982) Psychological concomitants of cancer: Clinical suspects. *American Journal of Psychotherapy, 36,* 470-479.

Sillars, A., Leonard, K.E., Roberts, L.J., & Dun, T. (2002). Cognition and communication during marital conflict: How alcohol affects subjective coding of interaction in aggressive and nonaggressive couples. In P. Noller & J.A. Feeney (Eds.) *Understanding marriage: developments in the study of couple interaction* (pp. 85-112). Cambridge, UK: Cambridge University Press.

Simpson, J.A. (1990). Influence of attachment styles on romantic relationships. *Journal of Personality and Social Psychology,* 59, 971-980.

Simpson, J.A., Ickes, W., & Blackston, T. (1995). When the head protects the heart: Empathic accuracy in dating relationships. *Journal of Personality and Social Psychology,* 69, 4, 629-641

Simpson, J.A. Ickes, W. & Orina, M. (2001). Empathic accuracy and pre-emptive relationship maintenance. In J. Harvey & A. Wenzel (Eds.) *Close romantic relationships: Maintenance and enhancement,* (pp. 27-46). Mahwah, New Jersey: Lawrence Erlbaum Pub.

Simpson, J.A., Campbell, L., & Weisberg, Y.J. (2006). Daily perceptions of conflict and support in romantic relationships: The ups and downs of anxiously attached individuals. In M.Mikulincer, & G.S. Goodman (Eds.). *Dynamics of romantic love.* New York: The Guilford Press (pp. 216-239).

Simpson, J.A., Ickes, W., & Grich, J. (1999). When accuracy hurts: Reactions of anxious-ambivalent dating partners to a relationship-threatening situation. *Journal of Personality and Social Psychology,* 76, 754-769.

Simpson, J.A., Ickes, W., & Orina, M. (2001). Empathic accuracy and preemptive relationships maintenance. In J. Harvey & A. Wenzel (Eds.). *Close romantic relationships: Maintenance and enhancement.* Mahwah, New Jersey: Lawrence Erlbaum Associates, Publishers. (pp.27-46).

Singer, B. A. (1983) Psychosocial trauma, defence strategies, and treatment considerations in cancer patients and their families. *The American Journal of Family,11,* 15-21.

Singer, I. (1984).The nature of love, Vol. 1: From Plato to Luther (2nd Ed.). Chicago, Ill: University of Chicago Press.

Sippola, L. K., & Bukowski, W. M. (1999). Self, other, and loneliness from a developmental perspective. In K. J. Rotenberg, & S. Hymel (Eds.), Loneliness in childhood and adolescence (pp. 280–295). Cambridge, England: Cambridge University Press.

Slatcher, R. B. (2010a). Marital functioning and physical health: Implications for social and personality psychology. *Social and Personality Psychology Compass 4/7,* 455-469.

Slatcher, R. B. (2010b). When Harry and Sally met Dick and Jane: Creating closeness between couples. *Personal Relationships, 17*

Sleek, S. (1998). Isolation increases with Internet use. *APA Monitor, 29*(9), 1, 30, & 31.

Smetana, J. G. (1988). Concepts of self and social convention: Adolescents' and parents' reasoning about hypothetical and actual family conflicts. In M. Gunnar & W. A. Collins (Eds.), *Minnesota Symposium on Child Psychology* (Vol. 21, pp. 79-122). Hillsdale, N. J.: Eribaum.

Smith, J., & Baltes, P. B. (1993). Differential psychological aging: Profiles of the oldest old. *Ageing and Society, 13,* 551-587l

Smith, B.L. (2011). Are Internet affairs different? *Monitor on Psychology,* 42(3), 48-50.

Snow, D. L. and L. Anderson: 1993, Down on their Luck: A Study of Homeless Street People. (University of California Press, Berkeley, CA).

Snyder, M. (1992). Motivational foundations of behavioral confirmation. In M.P. Zanna (Ed.). *Advances in experimental social psychology* (vol. 25, pp. 67-114). San Diego, CA: Academic Press.

Snyder, M., & Stakas, A.A., Jr. (1999). Interpersonal processes: The interplay of cognitive motivational and behavioral activities in social interaction. *Annual Review of Psychology,* 50, 273-303.

Sokolski, D.M. (1995). A study of marital satisfaction in graduate student marriages. *Unpublished doctoral dissertation,* Texan Tech University.

Soderberg, J. (2001) MS and the family system. In R. C. Kalb & L. C. Scheinberg (Eds.), *Multiple sclerosis and the family.* New York: Demos. Pp. 1-8.

Solano, C.H. (1980). Two measures of loneliness: A comparison. *Psychological Reports, 46,* 23-28.

Solano, C. H. (1987). Loneliness and perceptions of control: General traits versus specific attributions. *Journal of Social Behavior and Personality,* 2(2, Pt 2), 201−214.

Solano, C.H., Battan, P.G., & Parish, E.A. (1982). *Journal of Personality and Social Psychology,* 43, 3, 524-5

Solarz, A. & Bogat G. A. (1990). When social support fails: The homeless. *Journal of Community Psychology,* 18, 79–96.

Sommer, K. L., Williams, K. D., Ciarocco, N. J., & Baumeister, R. F. (2001). When silence speaks louder than words: Explorations into the intrapsychic and interpersonal consequences of social ostracism. *Basic and Applied Social Psychology, 23,* 225-243.

Sontag, S. (1988). *AIDS and its metaphors.* New York: Farrar, Straus, & Giroux.

Sperling, M.B., Burman, W.H. & Fagen, G. (1994). Classification of adult attachment: An integrative taxonomy from attachment and psychoanalytic theories. Journal of Personality Assessment, 59, 239-247.

Sprecher, S. (1999). I love you more than yesterday: Perceptions of changes in love and related affect over time. *Journal of Personality and Social Psychology, 76,* 46-53.

Sprecher, S. (2002). Sexual satisfaction in premarital relationships: Associations with satisfaction, love, commitment, and stability. *The Journal of Sex Research,* 39, 190-196.

Sprecher, S. (2006). Sexuality in close relationships. In P. Noller & J.A. Feeney (Eds.). *Close relationships: Functions, forms, and processes* (pp. 267-284). Hove, VK: Psychology Press/ Taylor & Francis.

Sprecher, S., & Cate, R.M. (2004). Sexual satisfaction and sexual expression as predictors of relationships satisfaction and stability. In J.H. Harvey, A. Wenzel, & S. Sprecher (eds.), *Handbook of sexuality in close relationships* (pp.235-256). Mahawah, N.J.: Erlbaum.

Sprecher, S., & Regan, P. C. (1998). Passionate and compassionate love in courting and young married couples. *Sociological Inquiry, 68,* 163-185.

Stack, St. (1990). New micro level data on the impact of divorce on suicide, 1959- 1980. *Journal of Marriage and the Family, 52,*119-127.

Stack, S. (1998). Marriage, family and loneliness: Across-national study. Sociological Perspectives, 41, 415-432.

Stanfeld S. (1999) Social support and social cohesion. In: *Social Determinants of Health* (eds M. Marmot & R. Wilkinson),pp. 155−178. Oxford University Press, Oxford.

Stangier, U., Heidenreich, T., & Schermelleh-Engel, K. (2006). Safety behaviors and social performance in patients with generalized social phobia. *Journal of Cognitive Psychotherapy, 20,* 17-31.

Stanley, S. M., Lobitz, W. C., & Dickson, F. C. (1999). Using what we know: Commitment and cognitions in marital therapy. In J. M. Adams & W. H. Jones (Eds.), Handbook of interpersonal commitment and relationship stability (pp. 379-392). Dordrecht, Netherlands: Kluwer Academic Publishers.

Stanley, S.M., & Markman, H.J. (1992). Assessing commitment in personal relationships. *Journal of Marriage and the Family, 54, 595-608.*

Stanley, S.M. & Markman, H.J. (1998). Acting on what we know: The hope of prevention in strategies to strengthen marriage: What we know, what we need to know. Washington, D.C.: *Family Impact Seminar.*

Stanley, S.M. Markman, H.J., St. Peters, M., & Leber, D. (1995). Strengthening marriage and preventing divorce: New directions in prevention research. *Family Relations, 44, 392-401*

Stanley, S.M., Markman, H.J., Prado, L.M., Olmos-Gallo, P.A., Tonelli, L., St. Peters, M., Leber, B.D., Bobulinski, M., Cordorva, A., & Witton, S.W. (2001). Community-based premarital prevention: Clergy and lay leaders on the front line. *Family Relations*, 50, 67-76.

Stanley, S.M., Whitton, S.W., Sadberry, S.L., Clements, M.L., & Markman, H.J. (2006). Sacrifice as a predictor of marital outcomes. *Family Process,* 45, (3), 289-303

Stearns, N., Lauria, M., Hermann, F., & Fogelberg, P. (1993) *Oncology social work: a Clinician's guide.* New York: American Cancer Society.

Steck, R., Levitan, D., McLane, D., & Kelley, H.H. (1982). Care, need and conceptions of love. *Journal of Personality and Social Psychology, 43, 481-491.*

Steinberg, L., & Levine, A. (1997). *You and your adolescent: A parents' guide for ages 10 to 20.* New York: Harper Perennial.

Stephenson, K.R., & Meston, C.M. (2011). The association between sexual costs and sexual satisfaction in women: An exploration of the Interpersonal Exchange Model of Sexual Satisfaction. *The Canadian Journal of Human Sexuality,* 20, 1, 31-40.

Sternberg, R. J. (1986). A triangular theory of love. *Psychological Review, 93,* 119-135.

Sternberg, R.J. (1998). Cupid's arrow: The course of love through time. Cambridge, England: Cambridge Press.

Stevens, N.I. (1989). *Well-being in widowhood: A question of balance.* Unpublished dissertation, Katholieke Universiteit Nijmegen.

Stevens, N. & Westerhof, G. J. (2006a). Marriage, social integration, and loneliness in the second half of life: A comparison of Dutch and German men and women. *Research on Aging, 28*(6), 713-729.

Stevens, N & Westerhof, G.J. (2006b). Partners and others: Social provisions and loneliness among married Dutch men and women in the second half of life. *Journal of Social and Personal Relationships. 23*(6), 921-941.

Stillman, T.F., Baumiester, R.F., Lambert, N.M., Crescioni, A.W., Dweall, C.N., & Fincham, F.D. (2009). Alone and without purpose: Life losses meaning following social exclusion. *Journal of Experimental Social Psychology, 45*(3), 686-694.

Stivers, R. (2004). Shades of loneliness: Pathologies of a technological society. N.Y.: Rowman & Littlefield.

Stoeckli, G. (2009). The roles of individual and social factors in classroom loneliness. *The Journal of Educational Research,* 103, 28-39.

Storr, A. (1988). *Solitude.* Uk; London: Harper and Row.

Story, L.B., Rothman, A.D., & Bradbury, T.M. (2002). Risk factors, risk processes and the longitudinal course of newlywed marriage. In P. Noller, & J.A. Freeney (Eds.).

Understanding marriage: Developments in the study of couple interaction. Cambridge University Press (pp/ 468-492).

Strong, B., DeValut, C., & Cohen, T.F. (2011). *The marriage and family experience: intimate relationships in a changing society* (11th ed.) Belmont, CA: Wadsworth.

Subrahmanyam K., & Lin, G. (2007). Adolescents on the net: Internet use and well being. Adolescence, 42, 659-677.

Suedfeld, P. (1982). Aloneness as a healing experience. In L.A. Peplau & D. Perlman (Eds.) *Loneliness: A sourcebook of current theory, research and therapy* (pp. 54-67). New York: John Wiley & Sons.

Sullivan H.S. (1953) The interpersonal theory of psychiatry. NY: Norton.

Sullivan KT, Bradbury TN. (1997). Are premarital prevention programs reaching couples at risk for marital discord? *J. Consult. Clin.Psychol*. 65:24.30

Sullivan, M. (2003). The new subjective medicine: Taking the patient's point of view on health care and health. *Social Science & Medicine*, 56, 1595-1604.

Sumerlin, J.R. (1995). Adaptation to homelessness: Self-actualization, loneliness, and Depression in street homeless men. *Psychological Reports*, 77, 295–314.

Sumerlin, J. R. (1996). Discriminant analyses of willingness to talk with a counsellor and most difficult issues in the experience of unsheltered homeless men; self-actualization, loneliness, and depression. *Psychological Reports*, 78, 659–672.

Surra, C.A. (1990). Research and theory on mate selection and premarital relationships in the 1980's. *Journal of Marriage and the Family,* 52, 844-865.

Taku, K., Cann, A., Calhoun, L.G., & Tedeschi, R.G. (2008). The factor structure of the Posttraumatic Growth Inventory: A comparison of five models using confirmatory factor analysis. *Journal of Traumatic Stress*, 21, 158-164.

Talbot, M. (1997). Love American style. *New Republic,* 216 (15), 30-47.

Tattersall, A.J., Bennett, P. and Pugh, S. (1999). Stress and coping in hospitals. *Stress Medicine*, 15, 109–13.

Taylor, P. (Ed.). (2010). The decline of marriage and the rise of new families. *Pew Research Bureau*. Retrieved from http://pewsocialtrends.org/files/2010/11/pew-social-trends-2010-families.pdf

Tedeschi, R.G. & Calhoun, L.G. (2004). Posttraumatic growth: Conceptual foundations and empirical evidence. *Psychological inquiry*, 15(1), 1-18.

Tedeschi, R.G. & McNally, R.J. (2011). Can we facilitate posttraumatic growth in combat veterans? *American Psychologist*, 66(1), 19-24.

Tennov, D. (1979). Love and limerence: The experience of being in love. NY: Stein & Day.

Terman, L.M., Butterweiser, P., Ferguson, L.W., Johnson, W.B., Wilson, D.P. (1938). *Psychological factors in marital happiness*. Stanford CA: Stanford University Press.

Teti, D.M. & Gelfand, D.M. (1991). Behavioural competence among mothers of infants in the first year: The meditational role of maternal self-efficacy. *Child Development*, 62, 918-929.

Theeke, L. A. (2009). Predictors of loneliness in U.S. adults over age sixty-five. *Archives of Psychiatric Nursing,* 23(5), 387-396.

Thibault, J. W. & Kelley, H. H. (1959). *The Social Psychology of Groups.* New York: Wiley.

Thomas, L. H., & Bond, S. (1996). Measuring patients' satisfaction with nursing: 1990-1994. *Journal of Advanced Nursing*, 23, 747-756.

Thompson-Hayes, M. & Webb, L.M. (2004). Commitment under construction: A dyadic and communicative model of marital commitment. *The Journal of Family Communication*, 4 (3&4), 249-260.

Thoreau, H.D. (1981). Walden. In J.W. Krutch (Ed.), *Walden and other writings by Henry David Thoreau* (Pp. 105–341). New York: Bantam (Original work published 1854).

Thorne, S., Harris, S., Hislop, G., & Vestrup, J. (1999). The Experience of waiting for diagnosis after an abnormal mammogram. *The Breast Journal*, 5(1), 42-51.

Thornicroft, G. (2006). Shunned: Discrimination against people with mental illness. Oxford, UK: Oxford University Press.

Thornton, A. & Young-DeMarco, L. (2001). Four decades of trends in attitude toward family issues in the United States: the 1960's through the 1990's. *Journal of Marriage and Family*. 63, 1009-1037.

Thurer, S.L. (1991). Women and rehabilitation. In R.P. Marinelli & A. E. Dell Orto (Eds.). *The psychological and social impact of disability*. (Pp. 32-38). New York: Springer.

Tick, E. (1988). Creativity and Loneliness, The Psychotherapy Patient, 4: 1, 131 — 137.

Tillich, P. (1963). *The eternal now*. New York: Charles Scribner's Sons.

Tilvis, R. S., Kähönen-Vare, M. H., Jolkkonen, J., Valvanne, J., Pitkala, K. H., & Strandberg, T. E. (2004). Predictors of cognitive decline and mortality of aged people over a 10-year period. *The Journals of Gerontology: Series A, 59*(3), M268-M274.

Tornstam, L. (1992). Loneliness in marriage. *Journal of Social and Personal Relationships,* 9, 197-217.

Tomassini, C., Glaser, K., & Askham, J. (2003). Getting by without a spouse: Living arrangements and support of older people in Italy and Britain. In: S. Arber, K. Davison & J. Ginn (Eds.) *Gender and ageing: Changing roles and relationships* (Pp. 111-126). Maidenhead, PA: Open University Press.

Topf, M. (1992). Effects of personal control over hospital noise on sleep. *Research* in Nursing & Health, 15, 19-28.

Topf, M. (2000). Hospital noise: an environmental stress model to guide research and clinical interventions. *Journal of Advanced Nursing, 31*(3), 520-528.

Trachman, M., & Bluestone, C. (2005). What's love got to do with it? *College Teaching, 53*, 131-136.

Traue, H. C., & Deighton, R. (1990). Inhibition, disclosure, and health: Don't simply slash the Gordian knot. Advances in Mind-Body Medicine, 15, 184–193.

Tucker, P. & Aron, A. (1993). Passionate love and marital satisfaction at key transition points in the family life cycle. *Journal of Social and Clinical Psychology, 12,* 2, 135-147.

Twenge, J. M., Zhang, L., Catanese, K. R., Dolan-Pasco, B., Lyche, L. F., & Baumeister, R. F. (2007). Replenishing connectedness: Reminders of social activity reduce aggression after social exclusion. *British Journal of Social Psychology, 46*, 205-224.

Twenge, J. M., & Campbell, W. K. (2010). Birth cohort differences in the Monitoring the Future dataset and elsewhere: Further evidence for Generation Me-commentary on Trzesniewski & Donnellan. *Perspective on Psychological Science, 5*, 81-88.

Twycross, R. (2003). *Introducing palliative care* (4th edition). Oxon, UK: Radcliffe Medical Press. Uchino, B.N., Cacioppo, J.T., & Kiecolt-Glaser, J.K. (1996).The relationship between social support and physiological processes: A review with emphasis on underlying mechanisms and implications for health. *Psychological Bulletin*, 119, 488-531.

Umberson, D., Williams, K., Powers, D. A., Hui, L., & Needham, B. (2005). Stress in childhood and adulthood: Effects on marital quality over time. *Journal of Marriage and Family, 67*, 1332-1347.

United State Bureau of Census. (2000). Statistics abstract of the United State: 2000. Washington, D.C.: U.S. Government Printing Office.

U.S. Census Bureau (2008a). Current population survey reports, America's families and living arrangements.

U.S. Census Bureau. (2008b). *American Community Survey data on marriage and divorce.* Retrieved from http://www.census.gov/hhes/socdemo/marriage/data/acs/index.html

Vachon, M. L. S. (1998) *How to successfully live with cancer.* Unpublished manuscript.

Valeski, T.N. & Stipek, D.J. (2001). Young children's feelings about school. *Child Development, 72*,1198-1213.

Van Buskirk, A. M., & Duke, M. P. (1991). The relationship between coping style and loneliness in adolescents: Can "sad passivity" be adaptive? *The Journal of Genetic Psychology*, 152, 144–157.

Van de Meerendonk, B., Adriaensen, R., & Vanwesenbeeck, I. (2003). Op weg naar een Vrolijke Herfst? Zorgbehoeften van en zorgverlening aan lesbische en homoseksuele ouderen in Nederland [*On their way to a Gay Autumn? The caring needs of and care facilities for gay and lesbian elderly*]. Utrecht: Rutgers Nisso Groep/Schorerstichting.

Van Den Berg, J.H. (1972). A different existence. Pittsburgh: Duquesne University Press.

Van Lang, P.A.M., Rusbult, C.E., Drigotas, S.M., Arriaga, X.B., Witcher, B.S., & Cox, C.L. (1997). Willingness to sacrifice in close relationships. *Journal of personality and Social Psychology, 72*, (6), 1373-1395.

Van Tilburg, T. (1995). Delineation of the social network and differences in network size. In C. P. M. Knipscheer, J. de Jong Gierveld, T. G. van Tilberg, & P. A. Dykstra (Eds.), *Living Arrangements and social networks for older adults* (pp. 83–96). Amsterdam: VU University Press.

Van Tilburg, T. G., & Broese van Groenou, M. I. (2002). Network and health changes among older Dutch adults. *Journal of Social Issues, 58*, 697-713.

Vandeleur, C. L., Perrez, M., & Schoebi, D. (2007). Associations between measures of emotion and familial dynamics in normative families with adolescents. *Swiss Journal of Psychology, 66*(1), 5-16.

VanderVoort, D. (1999). Quality of social support in mental and physical health. *Current Psychology, 18* (2), 205–222.

Vangelisti, A. L. (Ed.). (2009). *Feeling hurt in close relationships.* New York: Cambridge University Press.

Vangelisti, A.L., Alexander, A.L. (2002). Coping with disappointment in marriage: when partner's standards are unmet. In P. Noller & J.A. Feeney. *Understanding marriage development in the study of couple interaction* (pp. 201-227). Cambridge: Cambridge University Press.

Van Willigen, M. (2000). Differential benefits of volunteering across the life course. *Journal of Gerontology: Social Sciences, 55B (5)*, S308-318.

Veith, J. (1980). Hermits and recluses: Healing aspects of voluntary withdrawal from society. In J. Hartog, J.R. Audy, & Y.A. Cohen (Eds.). The anatomy of loneliness (pp. 537-546) International Universities Press.

Victor, C., Scambler, S., Bond, J., & Bowling, A. (2000). Being alone in later life: Loneliness, social isolation and living alone. *Reviews in Clinical Gerontology, 10*, 407-417.

Viegas, L., Turrini, R., & da Silva Bastos Cerullo, J. (2010). An analysis of nursing diagnoses for patients undergoing procedures in a Brazilian interventional radiology suite. *AORN Journal*, 91(5), 544-547.

Vrij, A., Granhag, P. A., & Porter, S. (2010). Pitfalls and opportunities in nonverbal and verbal lie detection. *Psychological Science in the Public Interest, 11*, 89-121.

Waite, L. J., & Gallagher, M. (2000). The case for marriage: Why married people are happier, healthier, and better off financially. New York, NY: Doubleday.

Waldinger, R.J., Diguer, L., Guastella, F., Lefebre, J.P.A., Luborsky, L., & Hauser, S.T. (2002). The same old song?- Stability and change in relationship schemas from adolescence to young adulthood. *Journal of Youth and Adolescence*, 13,1, 17-29.

Walker, C., Curry, L. C., & Hogstel, M. O. (2007). Relocation stress syndrome in older adults transitioning from home to long term care facility: Myth or reality? *Journal of Psychosocial Nursing and Mental Health Services, 45*(1), 38-47.

Walster, E., & Walster, G. W. (1978). *A new look at love*. Reading, MA: Addison-Wesley.

Wang, J. J., Snyder, M., & Kaas, M. (2001). Stress, loneliness, and depression in Taiwanese rural community-dwelling elders. *International Journal of Nursing Studies, 38*(3), 339-347.

Ward, D.B. & McCollum, E.E. (2005). Treatment effectiveness and its correlates in a marriage and family therapy training clinic. *American Journal of Family Therapy*, 33,(3), 207-223.

Waugh, C.E. & Fredrickson, B.L. (2006). Nice to know you: Positive emotional, self-other overlap, and complex understanding in the formation of a new relationship. *The Journal of Positive Psychology,* 1, (2), 93-106.

Weil, A. (1997). Eight weeks to optimum health: A proven program for taking full advantage of your body's natural healing power. New York: Knopf.

Weinrich, N. K. (1999). *Hand-on social marketing*. Thousand Oaks, CA: Sage Publications Inc.

Weiss, R. (1973). Loneliness: The experience of emotional and social isolation. Cambridge: MIT Press.

Weiss, R.S. (1974). The provisions of social relationships. In Z. Rubin (Ed.). Doing onto others. Englewood Cliffs, N.J.: Prentice-Hall.

Weiss, R. (1982). Issues in the study of loneliness. In L. A. Peplau & D. Perlman (Eds.), *Loneliness: A sourcebook of current theory, research and therapy* (pp. 71-80). New York: Wiley.

Weiss, R.S. (2006). Trying to understand close relationships. In M.A. Fine & J.H. Harvey (Eds.). *Handbook of divorce and relationship dissolution.* (pp. 605-618). New York: Routledge.

Weiss, R.L. & Heyman, R.E. (1990). Observation of marital interaction. In F.D. Finchman & T.N. Bradbury (Eds.), *The psychology of marriage: Basic issues and applications* (pp. 87-117). New York: Guilford Press.

Wenger, G.C., Davies, R., Shahtahmasebi, S., & Scott, A. (1996). Social isolation and loneliness in old age: review and model refinement. *Ageing Society*, (16), 333–358.

West, D. A., Kellner, R. & Moore-West, M. (1986). The effects of loneliness: A review of the literature. *Comprehensive Psychiatry, 27(4),* 351-363.

Westefeld, J.S., Maples, M. R., Buford, B., Taylor, S. (2001). Gay, Lesbian, and Bisexual College Students: The Relationship Between Sexual Orientation and Depression, Loneliness, and Suicide. *Journal of College Student Psychotherapy*, 15(3), 71- 82.

Wethington, E., Kessler, R. C., & Pixley, J. E. (2004). Turning points in adulthood. In O. G. Brim, C. D. Ryff, & R. C. Kessler (Eds). *How healthy are we? A national study of well-being at midlife* (pp. 586-613). Chicago, IL: University of Chicago Press.

Wheaton, B. (1991). Chronic stress: Models and measurement. *Paper presented at the Society for Social Problems meetings in Cincinnati,* Ohio, August 19-21, 1991.

Whisman, M. A. (1997). Satisfaction in close relationships: Challenges for the 21st century. In R. J. Sternberg & M. Hojjat (Eds.), *Satisfaction in close relationships* (pp. 385-410). New York: Guilford Press.

Whisman, M.A., Uebelacker, L.A., & Weinstock, M.L. (2004). Psychopathology and marital satisfaction: The importance of evaluating both partners. *Journal of Consulting and Clinical Psychology, 72,* 5, 830-838.

Whitbeck, L.B., Hoyt, D.R., Bao, W. (2000). Depressive symptoms and co-occurring depressive symptoms, substance abuse, and conduct problems among runaway and homeless adolescents. *Child Development,*71,721–732.

Whitbeck, L.B. and R.L. Simons. (1990). Life on the streets; The victimization of runaway and homeless adolescents, Youth & Society 22, pp. 108–125.

Whitton, S.W., Stanley, S.M., & Markman, H.J. (2007). If I help my partner, will I hurt me? Perceptions of sacrifice in romantic relationships. *Journal of Social and Clinical Psychology, 26,* 64-92.

Wickrama, K. A. A., Lorenz, F. O., & Conger, R. D. (1997). Marital quality and physical illness: A latent growth curve analysis. *Journal of Marriage and the Family, 59,* 143-155.

Wieselquist, J., Rusbult, C.E., Agnew, C.R., & Foster, C.A. (1999). *Journal of Personality and Social Psychology,* 77, (5), 942-966.

William, G. A., & Asher, S. R. (1992). Assessment of loneliness at school among children with mild mental retardation. *American Journal on Mental Retardation, 96,* 373-385.

Williams, K. D. (2007). Ostracism. *Annual Review of Psychology, 58,* 425-452.

Williams, L. (2003). Communication training, marriage enrichment, and premarital counselling. In L.L. Hecker & J.L. Wetchler (Eds.), An introduction to marriage and family therapy (pp. 337-368). Binghampton, NY: Haworth Clinical Practice Press.

William, A. M., Dawson, S., & Kristjanson, L. J. (2008). Exploring the relationship between personal control and the hospital environment. *Journal of Clinical Nursing, 17*(12), 1601-1609.

Williams, G. A.,&Asher, S. R. (1992). Assessment of loneliness in children with mild mental retardation. *American Journal on Mental Retardation, 96,* 373–385.

Williams, A. M., & Irurita, V. F. (2005). Enhancing the therapeutic potential of hospital environment by increasing the personal control and emotional comfort of hospitalized patients. *Applied Nursing Research, 18,* 22-28.

Williams, T.M., Joy, L.A., Travis, L., Gotowiec, A., Bloom-Steel, M., Aiken, L.S., Painter, S.L., & Davidson, S.M. (1987). Transition to motherhood: A longitudinal study. Infant Mental Health Journal, 8, 251-265.

Willis, R. J. (1985). "The life of therapy": An exploration of therapeutic method. *Psychotherapy in Private Practice, 3*(1), 63-70.

Wills, T. A., & Cleary, S. D. (1996). How are social support effects mediated? A test with parental support and adolescent substance use. *Journal of Personality and Social Psychology, 71*(5), 937-952.

Willis, S. L., & Reid, J. D. (1999). *Life in the middle: Psychological and social development in middle age.* In. San Diego, CA, US: Academic Press.

Willis, A.G., Willis, G. G., Manderscheid, R. W., Male, A., & Henderson, M. (1998). Mental illness and disability in the U.S adult household population. In R.W Manderscheid & M.J. Henderson (Eds.), *Mental health, United States, 1998* (pp. 113-123) (DHHS Publication No. SMA 99-3285). Centre for Mental Health Services. Substance Abuse and Mental Health Services Administration. Washington, DC: U.S Government Printing Office.

Wilson, J., Calsyn, R., & Orlofsky, J. L. (1994). Impact of sibling relationships on social support and morale in the elderly. *Journal of Gerontological Social Network, 22*, 157-170.

Wilson, R.S., Krueger, K.R., Arnold, S.E., Schneider, J.A., Kelley, J.F., Barnes, L.L. et al. (2007). Loneliness and risk of Alzheimer disease. Archives of General Psychiatry, 64(2), 234-240.

Winnicott, D. (1958). The capacity to be alone. International Journalof Psychoanalysis, 39, 416–420.

Winnicott, D.W. (1964). *The child, the family and the outside world.* Reading, MA: Addison Wesley.

Whitbeck, L.B., & Simons, R.L. (1990). *Life on the streets: The victimization of runaway and homeless adolescents. Youth & Society, 22, 108-125.*

Wolfinger, Nicholas H. 1999. Trends in the intergenerational transmission of divorce, Demography 36(3): 415-20.

Wolfinger, N. H., & Wilcox, W. B. (2008). Happily ever after? Religion, marital status, gender, and relationship quality in urban families. *Social Forces, 86*, 1311 – 1337.

Wood, L. A. (1986). Loneliness. In R. Harré (Ed.), The social construction of emotions (pp. 184–208). Oxford: Blackwell.

Woollett, A. & Parr, M. (1997). Psychological tasks for women and men in the post partum. *Journal of Reproductive and Infant Psychology,* 15, (2), 159-174.

Wortman, C. B. & Dunkel- Schetter, C. (1979) Interpersonal relationships and cancer: a theoretical analysis. *Journal of Social Issues, 35*, 120-155.

Xu, X., Aron, A., Brown, L., Cao, G., Feng, T., & Weng, X. (2011). Reward and motivation systems: A brain mapping study of early-stage intense romantic love in Chinese participants. *Human Brain Mapping, 32*, 249-257.

Yabiku, S.T., & Gager, C.T. (2009). Sexual frequency and the stability of marital and cohabiting unions. *Journal of Marriage and the Family,* 71, 4, 983-1000.

Yang., K. & Victor C. (2011) The prevalence of loneliness in 25 European Countries. *Ageing & Society, 31,* 1-2

Yarnold, P.R., Michelson, E.A., Thompson, D.A., & Adams, S.L., (1998). Predicting patient satisfaction: A study of two emergency departments. *Journal of Behavioral Medicine, 21*, 545-563.

Yeh, S-C.J. & LO, S.K. (2004). Living alone, social support, and feeling lonely among the elderly. *Social Behaviour and Personality, 32* (2), 129-138.

Yeh, H., Lorenz, F. O., Wickrama, K. A. S., Conger, R. D., & Elder, G. H. (2006). Relationships among sexual satisfaction, marital quality, and marital instability at midlife. *Journal of Family Psychology,* 20(2), 339-343. doi: http://dx.doi.org/10.1037/08933200.20.2.339

Young. L.D. (1993). Rheumatoid arthritis. In R.J. Gatchel & E.B. Blanchard (Eds.), *Psychophysiological disorders: Research and clinical applications* (Pp. 269-298). Washington, DC: American Psychological Association.

Young, J.E. (1982). Loneliness, depression and cognitive therapy: Theory and applications. In L.A. Peplau & D. Perlman (Eds.). *Loneliness: A sourcebook of current theory, research and therapy* (pp. 379-405). New York: Wiley.

Young, J.E. (1994). Cognitive therapy for personality disorders: A schema-focused approach. Sarasota, Fl: *Professional Resource Press.*

Young, J.E., Kloska, J.S., & Weishaar, M. (2003). Schema therapy: A practitioner's guide. New York: *Guilford Press.*

Young, J., & Gluhoski, V. (1997). A schema-focused perspective on satisfaction in close relationships. In R.J. Sternberg & M. Hojjat (Eds.). *Satisfaction in close relationships.* (pp.356-381). New York: The Guilford Press.

Young, M., Denny, G., Young, T., & Luquis, R. (2000). Sexual satisfaction among married women. *American Journal of Health Studies,* 16, 73-84.

Yovetich, N.A. & Rusbult, C.E. (1994). Accommodative behaviour in close relationships: Exploring transformation of motivation. *Journal of Experimental Social Psychology*, 30, 138-164.

Zamboni, B. D., & Crawford, I. (2007). Minority stress and sexual problems among African-American gay and bisexual men. *Archives of Sexual Behavior*, 36, 569–578.

Zhang, S., & Kline, S. L. (2009). Can I make my own decision? A cross-cultural study of perceived social network influence in mate selection. *Journal of Cross-Cultural Psychology, 40*, 3-23.

Zilboorg, C. (1938). Loneliness. *Atlantic Monthly*, 161, 45-54.

ABOUT THE AUTHORS

Ami Rokach holds a Ph.D. in psychology from Purdue University. He is the Executive Editor of the *Journal of Psychology: Interdisciplinary and Applied, and* is a clinical psychologist who combines offering individual, couple and sex therapy with teaching and research. Ami is an associate professor and is teaching psychology at The Center for Academic Studies in Israel, and is also a member of the psychology departments at York University in Canada, and Walden University in the USA. His therapeutic and research interests include loneliness, sexuality, couple & sex therapy, anxiety and phobias, traumatic experiences and personal growth, stress management, and palliative care. After 35 years of 'doing' psychology he is still intrigued by human nature, people's suffering, and the real opportunity that we all have to grow, flourish, and reinvent ourselves despite obstacles and painful experiences.

Ami Sha'ked holds a Ph.D. in psychology from the University of Wisconsin in Madison where he also taught graduate courses at the Rehabilitation Psychology Graduate Program. He also held a teaching position in the School of Psychology at Indiana Purdue University. Currently Dr. Sha'ked is a senior lecturer and Chair of the Psychology program at the Center for Academic Studies and he is the co-founder and Director for Academic Affairs of the Israeli Institute for Marriage and Family Studies both in Israel. Having trained in couple's therapy and sex therapy at the Masters and Johnson Institute in St. Louis Missouri, Dr Sha'ked founded and directed for 20 years a Marriage and Sex and Clinic at Sheba Medical Center in Israel. Dr. Sha'ked is the Founding Editor of Sexuality and Disability, a Journal published by Springer and devoted to the psychological and medical aspects of sexuality in rehabilitation and community settings, and the Editor of Human Sexuality in Rehabilitation Medicine, part of the Rehabilitation Medicine Library, published by Williams and Wilkins. For almost four decades Dr. Sha'ked conducts a private practice in marriage and sex therapy.

INDEX

B

C

F

I

S

V

W

Y

Z